standard catalog of®
American Flyer Trains

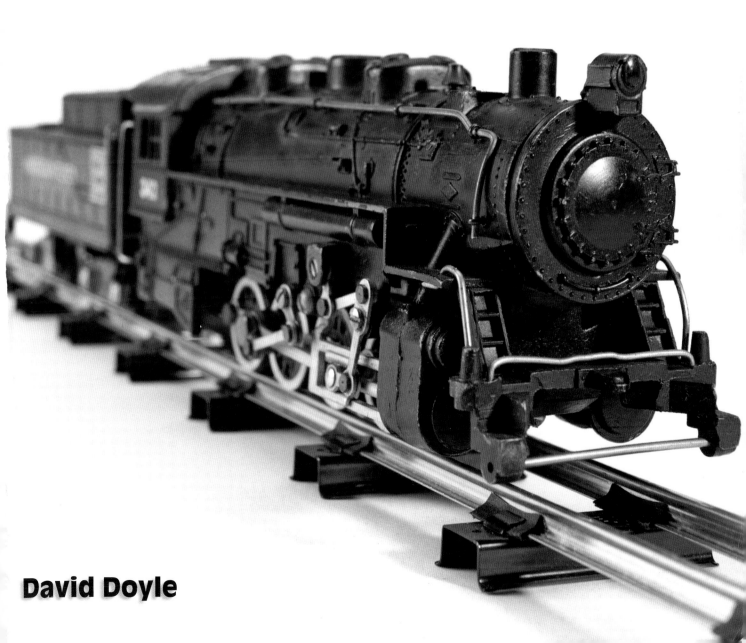

David Doyle

©2007 David Doyle
Published by

kp **krause publications**
An Imprint of F+W Publications

700 East State Street • Iola, WI 54990-0001
715-445-2214 • 888-457-2873
www.krausebooks.com

Our toll-free number to place an order or obtain
a free catalog is (800) 258-0929.

Library of Congress Control Number: 2006935769

ISBN-13: 978-0-89689-515-7
ISBN-10: 0-89689-515-7

Designed by Kay Sanders
Edited by Justin Moen

Printed in China

ACKNOWLEDGMENTS

I will confess that I am a life-long collector of trains made by the "other" guys—the ones from Irvington. I have friends who collect trains made by A.C. Gilbert and his predecessors, when I had a hobby store I handled many of these products. I always found the attention to detail, as well as the variety of animation offered, interesting and entertaining.

But such a passing interest in not enough to author a book of this scope. So I turned to my aforementioned friends, and they in turn put me in touch with their friends. Soon, I had many new friends as well—friends whose lifelong passion was American Flyer—and who were eager to share their enthusiasm, collections and knowledge with me. With this book, I am passing this information to you.

As the work progressed, this widespread group of collectors offered correction, criticism and commentary on subjects ranging from value and scarcity to fraudulent pieces. It seemed daily I submitted some new correction or detail to my diligent editor, Justin Moen, who somehow kept all of this straight. Every effort has been made to present complete and factual information—and any errors herein are purely my own.

The items included in this volume are by and large "normal production" items—trains likely to be encountered by the typical collector. Omitted were the occasional factory error, prototype and paint sample which even the most advanced collector is likely to encounter, and even fewer are interested in. The exceptions to this are prototype pieces, which have been widely reproduced.

Jack Sommerfeld of www.sommerfelds.com graciously allowed me to photograph part of his extensive inventory of fine S-Gauge pieces—and even allowed me to bring select pieces to the publisher's photo studio. There, Krause's skilled photographers Bob Best and Kris Candler shot the covers, as well as the chapter opening photos.

The contribution of Greg Stout to this volume cannot be overstated. Greg's firm, Stout Auctions, is one of the nation's premier sellers of collectable Lionel trains. Not only did Greg provide open access to the prices realized at these auctions through the years—which were taken into account in this volume, along with other factors—Greg also graciously allowed us to reproduce many photos from his color auction catalogs.

Father and son Bill and Mike Farner opened their wonderfully comprehensive collection for me to photograph, and spent countless hours teaching, reviewing and correcting my knowledge of S-Gauge trains.

Dave Martiny invited the KP Books crew and myself into his home for two days to photograph a portion of his outstanding collection. Clem Clement and Jim Nicholson allowed us similar multi-day access to their collections of prewar O- and Wide-Gauge collections. Without their help those portions of this book would be slim indeed.

The catalogs shown, and the information relating to them, come from the collections of the National Toy Train Museum, and American Flyer dean L. Andrew Jugle's archive, and train catalog guru Bob Osterhoff's www.trainpaper.com. Additional catalog images were provided by Joel Fugazzotto. Don Heimburger, publisher of "S Gaugian" magazine, provided much needed information. "Greg Nicholas at www.NicksTrains.com" also supplied photos of some of the desirable Flyer items from his inventory. Ron Williams kindly allowed me to photograph his American Flyer pieces as well. Special thanks to Orville Appelbaum for his contribution to this volume. Thanks are also due to Bob Bubeck, Jeff Symanski, George Martin, Charles Nolen, and Ed Lyon for their help in creating this volume, without their help this volume would not have been complete.

I want to especially thank my son Andrew, and my special lady Denise who waited patiently too many hours—and gave up much of their time—to bring this project to completion, spending a considerable amount of time retrieving items to be photographed, then patiently cleaning them before the photo sessions.

While some contributing to this volume choose to remain anonymous, there are two whose obscurity is not deliberate: Paul Kennedy, who persuaded the publisher to make this edition a reality; and Kay Sanders, the skilled designer who not only put it all together, but also endured countless phone calls and emails to incorporate last minute changes. Thank you all.

CONTENTS

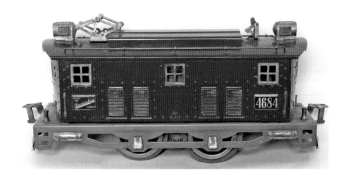

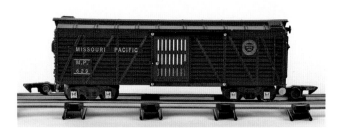

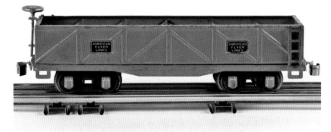

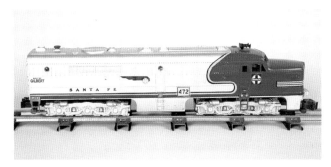

INTRODUCTION

The company that is best remembered today as American Flyer was founded in Chicago around 1907. William Hafner, an experienced toymaker, developed a clockwork-powered train. His friend, William O. Coleman, had gained control of a struggling hardware manufacturer, the Edmonds-Metzel Manufacturing Co., and that firm's excess capacity was turned to toy production. Hafner, also a superb salesman, secured orders totaling $15,000 from Montgomery Ward and G. Sommers & Co., and the company was firmly in the toy business. Beginning in 1908, Edmonds-Metzel trains were marketed as "American Flyer," and in 1910 the firm's name was changed as well. Edmonds-Metzel was gone, as was hardware production, but American Flyer trains were in full swing. Brothers Herman and Roy Mack were now involved in the firm, and it was their contributions that made this project line notable.

By 1913, the collaboration between Hafner and Coleman, which had created the successful line, began to fail, resulting in Hafner leaving American Flyer. Hafner went on to form his own company, Hafner Manufacturing Co.

American Flyer introduced other types of toys to its product line, but the 1918 introduction of electric trains (the line previously had consisted of clockwork O-Gauge trains) set the company on its course for the next five decades. But the joy of a new product was dampened by the death of William O. Coleman. With the passing of his father, W.O. Coleman Jr. took the helm of the company. Junior was gregarious, but neither a leader nor an innovator. The Mack brothers remained the foundation of American Flyer.

In 1925, Flyer augmented its production of O-Gauge trains with the introduction of larger Wide-Gauge trains. American Flyer's Wide-Gauge trains operated on the same size track as Standard-Gauge, but the latter term was a proprietary trade name of Lionel.

Three years later, one of Flyer's chief competitors, Ives, filed bankruptcy, setting the stage for the latter firm's takeover by a partnership of Lionel and American Flyer. This partnership lasted until 1930, when Lionel became sole owner of Ives. However, even with one competitor eliminated, Flyer still faced stiff competition. In the economy market, Flyer had to face Louis Marx, whose economy of scale in both manufacturing and distribution dwarfed Flyer. Lionel, who had superb marketing, challenged American Flyer for the premium train marketplace. The deteriorating national economy as well as their stiff competition forced American Flyer to withdraw from the declining Wide-Gauge market after 1936.

A needed infusion of money and talent came in 1938 when Coleman sold out to famous Olympic athlete, and Erector Set proprietor, A.C. Gilbert. Gilbert moved production to Connecticut, and redesigned the line to 1/64 scale proportions the following year. At the same time, the much smaller HO-Gauge line was introduced. HO literally stands for "Half Oh," and was considerably more realistic than even the redesigned O-Gauge line. HO remained part of the American Flyer line through 1963, even though in later years subcontractors such as Tru-Scale, Mantua or Varney produced much of the line.

Like other U.S. train manufacturers, Gilbert suspended production during WWII, its facilities used instead for war production. At the conclusion of hostilities, American Flyer retooled its trains for the new S-Gauge. Advertising of the period touted the realism of the two-rail track the new trains ran on, much to the chagrin of both Lionel and Marx, who continued to rely on three-rail track.

Despite the scale-like appearance of the new product line and Gilbert's marketing talent, American Flyer never achieved more than the number two market position in the toy train market. The declining market for electric trains and A.C. Gilbert's passing in 1961 led to the sale of the venerable firm to oil tycoon cum entertainment magnate Jack Wrather. Wrather was flush with cash from his successful "Lassie" and "Lone Ranger" television series, but sorely lacked experience in the toy market. Production of American Flyer trains ceased in 1966, and in 1967 Lionel gained ownership of the tooling and brand in exchange for liquidating the remaining inventory of American Flyer trains.

Since 1979, Lionel has offered a few American Flyer items almost every year, recently expanding these offerings to include magnificent steam locomotives. But still, collectors yearn for the glory days of Chicago or New Haven.

Perhaps it is memories of a small child remembering expectations of Christmases long ago, or sneaking the new catalog to school, hidden in a tablet, hoping to one day own that special item that fuels today's interest in yesterday's toys. Now that the baby boomers have reached adulthood, many of childhood's financial constraints are lifted—the toys of youthful dreams are at last within grasp.

Toy train collectors are their own fraternity, eagerly welcoming new buffs with a sincere interest in toy trains. Avail yourself of this knowledge base and friendship, whether you are an experienced collector or a rookie, and something can always be learned. There is no substitute for experience in this hobby, as in any other. No book, no matter how complete, contains all the answers. Thousands of words and the best illustrations cannot equal the experience gained by holding a piece in your own hands. There is no finer place for an enthusiast than in the home of a friend and fellow collector. The piece that is not for sale can be examined unhurried and questions answered honestly. It is excellent preparation for seeking an item in the marketplace.

The advent of Internet auctions has been a boon for collectors in remote areas. But for those in more populous areas, there is no substitute for shopping in the company of fellow collectors in hobby shops and train shows. Examining an item personally, with the counsel of more experienced collectors, is especially important when purchasing expensive, often repaired, or forged items.

Enthusiasts have been collecting toy trains perhaps as long as the trains have been produced. In the United States, the largest and oldest collectors group is the Train Collectors Association, or TCA. Founded in 1954 in Yardley Pa., the group has grown to more than 31,000 members. An annual convention is held at various locations around the country each summer. Smaller, regional divisions and chapters dot the nation. Twice each year, one such group, the Eastern Division, hosts the largest toy train show in the world. The York Fairgrounds in York, Pa. becomes a veritable Mecca for the toy train buff; with several buildings encompassing tens of thousands of square feet are full of toy trains for sale or trade. Members of the TCA agree to abide by a code of conduct, assuring fair and honest dealings between members. The nationally recognized grading standards were developed by the TCA.

The TCA headquarters is located in its Toy Train Museum and can be reached at:

The Train Collectors Association
P.O. Box 248
300 Paradise Lane
Strasburg, PA 17579
(717) 687-8623

The second-oldest organization is the Toy Train Operating Society, formed on the West Coast in 1966. It is similar in style and purpose to the TCA. Traditionally, the bulk of the TTOS members and events have been in the West, but the group has been gradually spreading eastward. The TTOS can be contacted at:

Toy Train Operating Society
25 W. Walnut Street, Suite 308
Pasadena, CA 91103
Phone (626) 578-0673

HOW TO USE THIS STANDARD CATALOG

This book is intended to aid both the novice and the experienced collector of American Flyer trains. American Flyer produced trains in a number of gauges for many years. To catalog this production, these items have been broken down into groups and subgroups, beginning with the most obvious classification, size and type.

We begin with S-Gauge, which, though introduced by the A.C. Gilbert Co. last (beginning in 1946), is probably the most collected of American Flyer's production. This category is further broken down into subgroups: Steam locomotives, diesel locomotives, flatcars, tank cars, passenger cars, accessories, etc. Within these subcategories the items are arranged numerically by stock number. The stock number on the vast majority of Gilbert's trains was stamped either on the side or the underside of the item.

Thus, if you pick up a flatcar that is numbered "928," you can turn to the flatcar section and move through the listings until you reach the number "928." You will then find that this car was produced in 1956 and 1957, and was lettered "New Haven." Near most listings you will find a photo of the item described.

The items are listed in numeric order in each chapter. The variations of each item are presented in chronological order, if known.

For items produced over a period of years, several details must be studied to accurately date each piece. Most of these dating clues involve the trucks and couplers on the cars, or boxes they were packaged in. These changes are detailed in this chapter.

Near the end of the S-Gauge section the contents of each S-Gauge set CATALOGED by Gilbert during the postwar era are listed. Be advised that Gilbert also produced a number of uncataloged sets for retailers and as premiums during this time, and these uncataloged sets are too numerous to list.

Next we have listed HO. American Flyer introduced this gauge of train immediately after A.C. Gilbert's takeover of the firm, which was previously an independent Chicago-based manufacturer. Gilbert moved the operations to Connecticut, and strove to increase the realism of all the products. Production of HO-Gauge trains began in 1938, and although interrupted by WWII, continued until 1963.

The next list of collectibles consists of the consumer catalogs produced by American Flyer. In most instances we have shown the covers of these catalogs, and their size and page count have been listed.

After catalogs we move into the area of American Flyer trains that were made prior to World War II— O- and Wide-Gauges.

We begin with accessories, because oftentimes a single accessory was intended for use with both of these sizes of trains—some were even carried over into the postwar era and sold for use with S-Gauge trains! Because many of the prewar accessories do not have visible model numbers for identification, rather than the numeric listing that is the norm for this book, this chapter is arranged by type (building, tunnel, etc.) first, then by number to speed identification.

We follow the accessory listing with a chapter about American Flyer's Wide-Gauge trains. Though a short-lived product line, this area has great collector interest, and is arranged in the same manner as the S-Gauge listings.

The final chapter concerns American Flyer's O-Gauge production. Though spanning the greatest number of years, this category has the least collector interest. Hence these items are arranged on a strictly numeric basis and with a minimum of description.

To the collector, condition is everything, and the Train Collectors Association, the world's oldest and largest train collector group has established very precise language for describing the condition of collectable trains in order to protect both the buyer and the seller. All reputable dealers and collectors use this terminology, and failure to properly use these terms in transactions between members can result in expulsion from the organization.

These grading standards are as follows:

Fair: Well-scratched, chipped, dented, rusted, warped.

Good, or C2: Small dents, scratches, dirty.

Very Good, or C6: Few scratches, exceptionally clean, no major dents or rust.

Excellent, or C7: Minute scratches or nicks, no dents or rust, all original, less than average wear.

Like New, or C8: Only the slightest signs of handling and wheel wear, brilliant colors and crisp markings; literally like new. As a rule, trains must have their original boxes in comparable condition to realize the prices listed in the grade.

Mint, or C10: Brand new, absolutely unmarred, all original and unused. Items dusty or faded from display, or with fingerprints from handling, cannot be considered mint. Items "test run" by consumers cannot be considered mint. Most collectors expect mint items to come with all associated packaging with which they were originally supplied. As one can imagine, Mint pieces command premium prices. The supply is extremely limited, and the demand among collectors is great. Often it is the billfold of the buyer, rather than a more natural supply and demand situation, that dictates the price of such pieces.

Demand is one of the key factors influencing values. The Santa Fe PA diesel was one of the most-produced locomotives in the Gilbert line, yet clean examples still command premium prices due to demand. Its classic beauty endures, and essentially every enthusiast or collector wants one.

Rarity, or scarcity, is also a factor influencing the value of trains. Low production quantities or extreme fragility make some items substantially more difficult to find than others. When scarcity is coupled with demand the result is a premium price, while other items, though extremely scarce, command only moderate prices due to lack of demand, or appreciation, on the part of collectors. In this guide we have rated each item on a scale of 1 to 8 for rarity. One represents the most common items, such as the 638 caboose, while eight is assigned to those items hardest to find, such as the gray 633F G.Fox & Co. boxcar. It is hoped that this rarity rating will help the collector when they are faced with the proverbial "How likely am I to get this chance again?" question.

Supply is related to rarity and also affects price. If only one sought-after item is at a given show, the seller is unlikely to negotiate or reduce his price. If, however, multiple sellers at a given event have identical items, no matter how rare, the temporary market glut can bring about temporarily reduced prices.

Lastly, the **buyer's intent** will effect what they are willing to pay. A collector who intends to add a piece to their permanent collection will normally be willing to pay more for an item than a dealer who is intending to resell the item.

Prices are given in this guide for trains in Very Good, Excellent and Like New condition. Trains in less than Very Good condition are not generally considered collectable, and as mentioned earlier, Mint condition trains are too uncommon to establish pricing on.

The prices listed are what a group of collectors would consider a reasonable market value—a price they would be willing to pay to add that piece to their collection. When contemplating a sale to a dealer, you should expect to receive 30 to 50 percent less, with the poorer condition of the trains, the greater the amount of discount, due to the greater difficulty the dealer will have selling them. Remember that these prices are only a guideline. When you are spending your money, what an item is worth to you is of greater importance than what it is worth to the author. Conversely, the publisher of this book does not sell trains, this is not a mail-order catalog, and you should not expect a dealer or collector to "price match."

Unlike certain other collectibles, the age of a train is not a factor in its value. That is, an older train is not inherently more valuable than a newer train. It is rather the variations in construction throughout an item's production run that effect its scarcity, and thus its collector value. Many American Flyer trains are marked on the sides with "New" or "Built" dates. These dates are totally irrelevant to when a piece was actually produced, and are decorative only.

Although a few collectors specialize in a specific year or two of American Flyer production, they are the exception as opposed to the rule. Most instead collect trains based on gauge. Establishing the production dates of these trains is usually done more out of curiosity for most collectors, or when they are trying to properly and precisely recreate a given train set.

Among the key aids to dating trains are the construction techniques used in the manufacture of the trucks and couplers, and the type of original packaging used, if it's still present.

Aids To Dating S-Gauge Trains

American Flyer trains were produced as toys, not as collectibles. Thus, there were manufacturing variations induced by supply shortages and the company's continuing efforts to reduce costs. These variations, having been carefully studied, can today be used as an aid in dating given pieces. No components are more universally used than trucks and couplers. In railroading terms, a truck is the assembly of wheels, axles, and suspension components. In most instances each truck has two axles and four wheels, though in some cases there were three axles and six wheels. In real railroad practice, occasionally trucks were found with four axles and eight wheels.

Gilbert used the interruption of toy production during WWII to convert from a 3/16 scale, O-Gauge three-rail track to a 3/16 scale, S-Gauge track with two rails. It is the changes to the latter with which this segment is concerned.

Values for each condition are in U.S. dollars. | **Scarcity** = Scale from 1-8 with 8 being the hardest to find.

9

Couplers

At left is the classic American Flyer operating knuckle coupler, to the right, its predecessor, the link coupler.

Link couplers without weights were used during the 1946 production. The shanks of these couplers were only 1/8-inch thick, making them somewhat fragile. In 1947, the shank thickness was increased to 1/4 inch. To combat a tendency of the early link couplers to uncouple unexpectedly, in 1948, a brass weight was added to the coupler shank. This weight was changed to blackened steel in 1949.

In 1952, Gilbert introduced a realistic operating knuckle coupler, and by 1954 this was being used throughout the product line. Oftentimes collectors find cars predating this that are equipped with knuckle couplers. The explanation is simple— Gilbert sold two types of conversion kits for this purpose. One type of kit included the entire truck with coupler, making it easy to merely replace the trucks on older rolling stock. The other kit included a special knuckle coupler with split mounting shank. These were used to replace the link coupler of older cars with the new knuckle type coupler cleanly, and with minimal labor.

In 1958, Gilbert introduced a new knuckle coupler, which was non-operating. Completely compatible with the operating version, this coupler was used on certain lower-end items.

Because trucks and couplers are produced in such vast numbers, any cost reduction per unit to these items is magnified many-fold. As the fortunes of the A.C. Gilbert Co. dwindled, cost savings took some degree of urgency. Trucks and couplers were an obvious area of great potential savings. These efforts resulted in the Pike Master truck and coupler introduced in 1961. This design featured truck side frames, bolster and knuckle coupler molded from a single piece of plastic. Unfortunately, the flexibility of the plastic, which allowed it to move enough to couple, also allows it to become permanently distorted, or break, without much abuse.

Freight Car Trucks

The trucks themselves had sheet metal bolsters and side frames from 1946 until the knuckle couplers were introduced in 1952. When the new coupler was introduced, it was mounted on a new truck, with a stamped sheet metal bolster and sintered-iron side frames. Sintering is a metallurgy process whereby powdered metal is poured into a mold and subjected to heat and pressure, thus forming a single part. The earlier all sheet metal truck was phased out along with the link couplers, but the sintered-iron truck was used through the end of production. As previously mentioned, the Pike Master combined truck and coupler was introduced in 1961 and remained in the line through 1966.

Boxes

Gilbert, like other manufacturers, boxed its products to ease handling and protect the trains. For much of the prewar era, they were strictly utilitarian, with no thought was given to their visual appeal.

Late in the prewar era, some thought was given to using the boxes for promotional purposes, with this illustrated box. Still, during the 1940s and '50s, it was intended that the trains be sold by attentive, trained salespeople. Self-service and consumer-oriented packaging was not part of American Flyer's marketing plan.

The **classic blue** box with yellow lettering was introduced in 1940. The box was again used after World War II, but supplies finally became exhausted around 1955.

In 1960, Gilbert introduced this innovative, but short-lived packaging. Known as **Kleer-Pak**, these boxes allowed consumers to see up close the rolling stock contained inside. The ends were removable, allowing access to the contents. Both HO- and S-Gauge cars were packed in these, but they were not used throughout the line. Kleer-Pak boxes were discontinued after 1961.

A yellow box with blue "another GILBERT HALL OF SCIENCE product" lettering was introduced in 1947. This box was used intermittently as late as 1957.

A variation of this box was introduced around 1950. On this box the tag line was changed to read "DEVELOPED AT THE GILBERT HALL OF SCIENCE." Like the previous version, this box remained in use through 1957. In addition to trains, the firm produced many scientifically minded toys: Erector sets, chemistry sets, etc., of which Mr. Gilbert was especially proud—labeling each of his showrooms which dotted the globe "Hall of Science," and emblazoning the name on the boxes. In addition to the sleeve-type box shown here, other blue and yellow boxes were produced which had a top-opening "hinged" lid. It is these yellow and blue boxes that to many collectors represent the classic era of American Flyer production—and that provided the inspiration for the color tabs of this book."

Red and white became the standard colors for Gilbert packaging in 1955-56. The slogan stamped on the first of these boxes read "3/16" SCALE TRAIN-REAL TWO RAIL TRACK." This box was used until 1960.

In 1960, Gilbert's marketing people changed the tag line to "THE SCALE MODEL LINE," and of course the red and white boxes were changed to reflect this. These boxes were used through 1964. The box shown here is from their HO line, but the S-Gauge box was identical.

Values for each condition are in U.S. dollars. | **Scarcity** = Scale from 1-8 with 8 being the hardest to find.

11

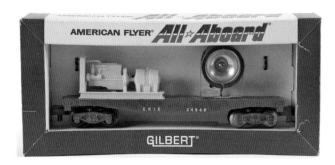

All Aboard

In 1965 and 1966, Gilbert packed their trains in these red, white and blue cardboard boxes. Across the top of the box was the legend "American Flyer ALL ABOARD." The front of the box was open. Once the car was placed in the box, the combination was shrink-wrapped. While at the time this allowed good display of the product, it offered poor protection for the trains, and made the box somewhat more "disposable" than its predecessors.

Gilbert's HO line came in these gray boxes with clear fronts. Some of the HO items came in Kleer-Pak boxes during 1960-61.

The information provided above concerning truck, coupler and box variations, along with the information in the detailed listings, will allow you to accurately date Gilbert's American Flyer S-Gauge trains.

HOW TO USE THIS STANDARD CATALOG

REFERENCE EXAMPLE

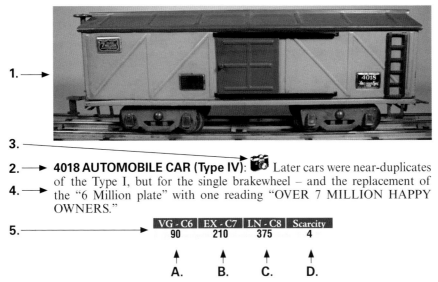

1. →

3. →

2. → **4018 AUTOMOBILE CAR (Type IV):** Later cars were near-duplicates of the Type I, but for the single brakewheel – and the replacement of

4. → the "6 Million plate" with one reading "OVER 7 MILLION HAPPY OWNERS."

5. →

VG - C6	EX - C7	LN - C8	Scarcity
90	210	375	4

↑ A.   ↑ B.   ↑ C.   ↑ D.

1.) Photo: In some listings, photos are supplied to better help identify and verify what Model and Type you possess.

2.) Listing Name/Type: Items will be listed by Model number and Variation number (Type).

3.) Photo Indicator: Items with a 📷 icon indicates that this listing is accompanied by a photo. If the image is not directly above its given listing, it will more times than not be in an enlarged two-column format or on the following page.

4.) Listing Description: Located directly after the Listing Name/Type is a brief description of the listing, giving vital information to better help identification.

5.) Values Table: Below the Listing Description is the Values Table. Values for each condition are in U.S. Dollars.

Note: To better assist you, located on the bottom of every right hand page is a quick reference on how to use the Values Table.

   A.) VG=*Very Good*: Few scratches, exceptionally clean, no major dents or rust, also known as C6.

   B.) EX=*Excellent*: Minute scratches or nicks, no dents or rust, all original, less than average wear, now known as C7.

   C.) LN=*Like New*: Only the slightest signs of handling and wheel wear, brilliant colors and crisp markings; literally like new, or C8. As a rule, Like New trains must have their original boxes in comparable condition to realize the prices listed in this guide.

   D.) Rarity: On a scale of 1-8, this system will assess the accessibility and rarity of the particular listing. On occasion, an item may be so rare that there is not enough reference to place a price or rarity.

Values for each condition are in U.S. dollars. | **Scarcity** = Scale from 1-8 with 8 being the hardest to find.

13

S-Gauge

STEAM LOCOMOTIVES

While the flashy diesel streamliners had a certain appeal, the smoke-billowing steam locomotive powered children's imaginations during the heyday of Gilbert—and probably even today.

The A.C. Gilbert Co. produced a variety of die-cast—and later plastic steam locomotives during the postwar era. Those initially produced were based on the 3/16-scale O-Gauge locomotives produced prior to World War II. Later new designs were added as well.

Like the rest of the American Flyer product line, the quality and detail of the mighty steam engines deteriorated through the years. With the bodies changing from die-cast to plastic, two-position reverse units replaced the four-position units initially used, and operating headlights, smoke, choo-choo and even operating couplers were phased out.

263: See 21004.

282: This 4-6-2 Pacific steam locomotive was produced from 1952-53. The tender was decorated with white "CHICAGO NORTHWESTERN LINE" logos, as well as the American Flyer markings. The locomotive body, as well as that of the tender, was painted black, and beneath the cab window the catalog number was stamped in white. The locomotive had an operating headlight, and the boiler housed both a smoke unit and a choo-choo mechanism.

282 (Type I): When first produced, the locomotive was furnished with a sheet metal tender lettered "AMERICAN FLYER," riding on sheet metal trucks. At the rear of the tender was a link coupler, although the example shown above has been converted to knuckle coupler.

VG - C6	EX - C7	LN - C8	Scarcity
35	50	90	3

282 (Type II): Tenders with plastic bodies accompanied later locomotives; still riding on sheet metal trucks was a link coupler to the rear.

VG - C6	EX - C7	LN - C8	Scarcity
35	50	90	3

282 (Type III): Some of the tenders were equipped with simulated stoker screws and marker lights. The trucks had sintered-iron side frames.

VG - C6	EX - C7	LN - C8	Scarcity
45	70	100	4

282 (Type IV): Some of the tenders with stoker screws were lettered "AMERICAN FLYER LINES."

VG - C6	EX - C7	LN - C8	Scarcity
45	70	100	4

283: 📷 From 1953 through 1957, Gilbert produced this 4-6-2 Pacific. The accompanying tender bore "CHICAGO NORTHWESTERN LINE" as well as "AMERICAN FLYER LINES" markings. Both the locomotive and the tender were painted black. The tender rode on trucks with sintered-iron side frames and had an operating knuckle coupler at the rear. Inside the tender was a four-position reverse unit. The locomotive boiler housed an operating headlight, smoke unit and choo-choo sound assembly, as well as the motor.

VG - C6	EX - C7	LN - C8	Scarcity
30	45	80	2

285: This 4-6-2 Pacific was produced in 1952. The plastic boiler and sheet metal tender were both painted black. The locomotive was numbered in white, and the same color was used for the "CHICAGO NORTH-WESTERN LINE" logo and "AMERICAN FLYER" lettering on the tender. In addition to the motor, the boiler housed an operating headlight, smoke and choo-choo units. The tender housed not only the four-position reverse unit, but also an air-chime whistle. Sheet metal trucks were installed on the tender with a link coupler, although the example above has been converted to knuckle coupler.

VG - C6	EX - C7	LN - C8	Scarcity
35	65	135	5

287: Cataloged only in 1954, but included in some 1955 uncataloged sets, this 4-6-2 Pacific had a black-painted body and a matching black-painted plastic tender. Both the locomotive and tender were marked in white, the locomotive had the number stamped below the cab window, and the tender baring the "CHICAGO NORTH-WESTERN LINE" logo and "AMERICAN FLYER LINES" lettering. The locomotive featured an operating headlight, but did not have smoke or choo-choo. The four-position reverse unit was housed in the tender, which rode on trucks with sintered-iron side frames and had an operating knuckle coupler.

283

287 (Type I): The "AMERICAN FLYER LINES" lettering on some of the tenders were of a sans-serif style. This tender is wired directly to the locomotive.

VG - C6	EX - C7	LN - C8	Scarcity
20	40	80	3

287 (Type II): Other tenders had "AMERICAN FLYER LINES" printed in serif lettering. The tender wiring plugs into the locomotive.

VG - C6	EX - C7	LN - C8	Scarcity
20	40	80	3

289: Produced in 1956, but uncataloged, this 4-6-2 Pacific had an operating headlight, but no smoke or choo-choo. The tender, which like the locomotive had a black-painted plastic body, housed a four-position reverse unit and an air-chime whistle and was lettered "CHICAGO NORTHWESTERN LINE." The tender trucks had sintered-iron side frames and an operating knuckle coupler at the rear.

VG - C6	EX - C7	LN - C8	Scarcity
80	175	325	7

290: This die-cast 4-6-2 Pacific was offered from 1949 through 1951. The lettering—the number "290" below the cab windows and a sans-serif "AMERICAN FLYER" on each side of the tender—was done in white. The tender body was sheet metal, and sheet metal trucks were used with a link coupler on the rear. The black-painted boiler of the locomotive housed not only a motor, but also smoke and choo-choo units. The four-position reverse unit was mounted inside the tender.

290 (Type I): Locomotive and tender as described above.

VG - C6	EX - C7	LN - C8	Scarcity
25	40	80	3

290 (Type II): In addition to "American Flyer," some tenders were marked with the diamond-shaped "Reading Lines" logo.

VG - C6	EX - C7	LN - C8	Scarcity
25	40	80	3

293: Produced from 1953 through 1958, this black die-cast 4-6-2 Pacific was trimmed with a white running board stripe and white drivers. In most instances, the tender housed a four-position reverse unit, and the black plastic body was always lettered "The New York New Haven and Hartford Railroad Co." in white. The locomotive number was also stamped in white beneath the cab window. The tender molding included a simulated stoker and marker lights, and the tender was equipped with trucks with sintered-iron side frames and a rear-mounted knuckle coupler.

293 (Type I): 📷 In 1953, units had four wires plugged in and the fifth separately connected.

VG - C6	EX - C7	LN - C8	Scarcity
50	75	150	4

293 (Type II): From 1954 through 1957, these locomotives were permanently connected to the tender through five wires, a group of four and a separate fifth.

VG - C6	EX - C7	LN - C8	Scarcity
50	75	150	4

293 (Type III): An uncataloged, whistle-equipped, version of the locomotive was produced in 1958. The reverse unit in this instance was mounted in the cab.

VG - C6	EX - C7	LN - C8	Scarcity
100	175	450	7

293 (Type I)

Values for each condition are in U.S. dollars. | **Scarcity** = Scale from 1-8 with 8 being the hardest to find.

17

300 (Type II)

295: Gilbert offered this 4-6-2 Pacific only in 1951. The locomotive die-cast boiler and sheet metal tender were both painted black. The locomotive was equipped with an internal smoke unit and choo-choo. The tender housed a four-position reverse unit and air-chime whistle. Both locomotive and tender markings were rendered in white, with the number "295" appearing beneath the cab window, and a sans-serif "AMERICAN FLYER" on the flanks of the tender.

VG - C6	EX - C7	LN - C8	Scarcity
75	150	250	5

296: This 4-6-2 Pacific, made in 1955, was not cataloged. Construction was the standard single-piece die-cast boiler of the era, painted black. The tender was lettered "New York, New Haven & Hartford." It featured a simulated stoker and marker lights, and housed a four-position reverse unit and air-chime whistle. It was equipped with sintered-iron side frame trucks and a knuckle coupler.

VG - C6	EX - C7	LN - C8	Scarcity
100	200	400	7

299: Another of the uncataloged steamers produced by Gilbert was this 1954-built 4-4-2 Atlantic. Both the

locomotive and tender were painted black. The locomotive had an operating headlight, and a four-position reverse unit was housed in the tender, which rode on sheet metal trucks and a link coupler. The numbers beneath the cab windows, as well as the tender markings, were stamped in white. Tender decoration included not only the "AMERICAN FLYER LINES" name, but also a "Reading Lines" herald. This locomotive is notable as being the only link coupler equipped with the Pull-Mor traction device.

VG - C6	EX - C7	LN - C8	Scarcity
50	100	250	7

300: This humble 4-4-2 was sold in 1946-47, and then returned in 1952. During this time the Atlantic was produced in three major construction styles, and numerous minor variations. The locomotive had an operating headlight, and was decorated with both "Reading" and "American Flyer" markings.

300 (Type I): When first produced the boiler was comprised of four die-cast pieces. Three sets of separately applied wire handrails decorated the locomotive. "READING" was stamped in silver within an indentation in the tender side. Because the locomotive did not have smoke or choo-choo, there was plenty of room for the four-position reverse unit in the boiler.

VG - C6	EX - C7	LN - C8	Scarcity
20	45	75	4

300 (Type II): 📷 Other 1946 tenders lacked the indentation, but were still stamped "READING" in silver. This type of tender marking continued to be used into 1947.

VG - C6	EX - C7	LN - C8	Scarcity
20	45	75	4

300 (Type III): The "READING" lettering was stamped in white on other tenders.

VG - C6	EX - C7	LN - C8	Scarcity
20	45	75	4

300 (Type IV): In 1947, the stamping on the flat-sided tender was changed. Replacing the "Reading" lettering was a white-stamped "AMERICAN FLYER." Ahead and above that a diamond-shaped "Reading Lines" herald was also stamped.

VG - C6	EX - C7	LN - C8	Scarcity
15	30	45	2

300 (Type V): When the 300 returned in 1952, it had been extensively revised. The boiler, while still die-cast, was now a single piece rather than the four pieces used previously. At the same time, the separately installed handrails were eliminated, replaced with cast-in simulated rails, which turned down beneath the smokestack. The white stamping on the tender continued to include both the "AMERICAN FLYER" name and the Reading Lines logo. A link coupler was mounted at the rear of the tender.

VG - C6	EX - C7	LN - C8	Scarcity
15	30	45	2

300 (Type VI): Later in 1952, the boiler was molded of plastic rather than die-cast. Even though black plastic was used, the boiler was painted black as well. The molded-in handrails on these locomotives extended all the way to the front of the boiler. The tender markings and couplings were unchanged from the Type V.

VG - C6	EX - C7	LN - C8	Scarcity
15	30	45	2

300AC: In 1949 and 1950, the white number stamped beneath the windows of the 4-4-2 Atlantic was 300AC. The locomotive lacked smoke and choo-choo, but did have an operating headlight and a four-position reverse unit mounted in the boiler. The sheet metal tender was equipped with sheet metal trucks and had a link coupler at the rear. The tender stamping included both the "AMERICAN FLYER" name and the Reading Lines logo.

300AC (Type I): As first produced, the locomotive used a four-piece boiler casting with wire handrails.

VG - C6	EX - C7	LN - C8	Scarcity
20	40	60	3

300AC (Type II): In 1950, a single-piece die-cast boiler was used. The handrails on these locomotives were not separately installed pieces of wire, but rather were represented in the boiler casting itself.

VG - C6	EX - C7	LN - C8	Scarcity
15	25	45	1

300AC (Type III): Some of the 1950 tenders were assembled with frames that were too long, and these frames extend slightly beyond the body. The balance of the locomotive and tender were the same as Type II.

VG - C6	EX - C7	LN - C8	Scarcity
20	40	60	5

301: This 4-4-2 Atlantic was produced in 1953. The plastic boiler was painted black. The locomotive was equipped with an operating headlight and a choo-choo unit. The four-position reverse unit was mounted in the tender, which rode on sheet metal trucks and had a link coupler at the rear.

301 (Type I): Some of the tenders were marked with a "Reading Lines" herald and "AMERICAN FLYER" lettering.

VG - C6	EX - C7	LN - C8	Scarcity
15	25	45	1

301 (Type II): Other tenders were lettered "AMERICAN FLYER LINES" in addition to baring the Reading's diamond-shaped herald.

VG - C6	EX - C7	LN - C8	Scarcity
15	25	45	1

302: A 4-4-2 Atlantic with this catalog number first appeared in 1948, then the number was dropped, returning again in 1951, staying in the line through 1953. This range of production resulted in multiple significant variations of the locomotive. All versions featured an operating headlight and a tender with sheet metal trucks and a link coupler. The tender bore the diamond-shaped logo of Reading Lines, in addition to other markings described below.

302 (Type I): As introduced in 1948, the locomotive was built with a four-piece die-cast boiler. Inside that boiler was smoke and choo-choo. The sheet metal tender, which was marked with "AMERICAN FLYER," housed a four-position reverse unit.

VG - C6	EX - C7	LN - C8	Scarcity
15	30	60	3

302 (Type II): When the 302 returned to the line in 1952, it sported a one-piece plastic boiler. The sheet metal tender was lettered "AMERICAN FLYER" in white, and contained a four-position reverse unit. The smoke and choo-choo was located in the locomotive boiler.

VG - C6	EX - C7	LN - C8	Scarcity
15	25	50	1

Values for each condition are in U.S. dollars. | **Scarcity** = Scale from 1-8 with 8 being the hardest to find.

302 (Type II)

302 (Type III): Other plastic locomotives came with sheet metal tenders, which were marked "AMERICAN FLYER" in white. The remainder of the locomotive-tender combination was identical to the Type II.

VG - C6	EX - C7	LN - C8	Scarcity
15	25	50	1

302 (Type IV): In 1953, the plastic boiler equipped 4-4-2 was coupled to a tender with a plastic body. On the flanks of the tender was printed "AMERICAN FLYER" in white. The smoke and choo-choo unit continued to be installed in the locomotive, and the reverse unit in the tender.

VG - C6	EX - C7	LN - C8	Scarcity
15	25	50	1

302 (Type V): The white lettering on some tenders read "AMERICAN FLYER LINES," though it continued to house the four-position reverse unit. The smoke and choo-choo remained in the locomotive.

VG - C6	EX - C7	LN - C8	Scarcity
15	25	50	1

302AC: Like the 302, the AC version of the Atlantic debuted in 1948, was dropped, then returned in 1950. The locomotive was discontinued again after 1952. The boiler of the locomotive housed an operating headlight as well as a smoke and choo-choo unit. The four-position reverse unit was housed in the tender, which was decorated with a "Reading Lines" herald and "AMERICAN FLYER" lettering.

302AC (Type I): The 1948 edition of the locomotive had a four-piece die-cast boiler and sheet metal tender.

VG - C6	EX - C7	LN - C8	Scarcity
15	25	55	2

302AC (Type II): When the locomotive returned in 1950, it featured a one-piece die-cast boiler and a sheet metal tender.

VG - C6	EX - C7	LN - C8	Scarcity
20	35	60	3

302AC (Type III): In 1952, the locomotive was assembled with a plastic boiler. The cast-in handrails of this boiler extend all the way to the boiler front, whereas the cast-in handrails of the one-piece die-cast boiler end below the smoke stack.

VG - C6	EX - C7	LN - C8	Scarcity
20	35	60	3

303: From 1954 through 1957, Gilbert produced this 4-4-2 Atlantic with one-piece black-painted plastic boiler. White lettering was used for the "303" catalog number stamped beneath the cab window, as well as the diamond-shaped "Reading Lines" logo and sans-serif "AMERICAN FLYER LINES" lettering on the tender. Inside the boiler was an operating headlight and smoke and choo-choo unit. The plastic bodied tender, which had trucks with sintered-iron side frames and an operating knuckle coupler, housed a four-position reverse unit.

VG - C6	EX - C7	LN - C8	Scarcity
20	35	60	2

305: This Reading 4-4-2 Atlantic was cataloged in 1951, but not produced.

307: From 1954 through 1957, this 4-4-2 Atlantic graced the pages of the American Flyer catalog. The locomotive had an operating headlight, but lacked smoke and choo-choo. Both the tender and locomotive bodies were molded plastic. The tender had trucks with sintered-iron side frames, and the rear truck was fitted with a knuckle coupler. The tender was marked with a white "Reading Lines" logo and sans-serif "AMERICAN FLYER LINES" lettering.

310 (Type I)

307 (Type I): Initially, the four wires from the tender-mounted four-position reverse unit plugged into the rear of the locomotive.

VG - C6	EX - C7	LN - C8	Scarcity
10	20	40	1

307 (Type II): In later production the tender-mounted reverse unit was hard wired directly to the locomotive.

VG - C6	EX - C7	LN - C8	Scarcity
10	20	40	1

307 (Type III): Near the end of production a two-position reverse unit was mounted in the back of the locomotive.

VG - C6	EX - C7	LN - C8	Scarcity
10	20	40	1

308: This 1956-only 4-4-2 Atlantic had a black plastic one-piece boiler. Inside this boiler, which was numbered in white, were an operating headlight and a choo-choo unit. A four-position reverse unit was mounted inside the plastic tender body, which was decorated with the diamond-shaped "Reading Lines" logo and sans-serif "AMERICAN FLYER LINES" lettering. The tender was equipped with trucks with sintered-iron side frames, and a knuckle coupler was mounted at the rear.

VG - C6	EX - C7	LN - C8	Scarcity
25	55	90	5

310: The S-Gauge 4-6-2 Pacific was introduced in 1946 with this unit, which was also produced in 1947. The body of the locomotive was comprised of four die-castings, and beneath the cab window the number "310"

was stamped in silver. The locomotive was equipped with an operating headlight, and a four-position reverse unit was mounted inside the boiler.

310 (Type I): In 1946, "PENNSYLVANIA" was stamped in silver on both sides of the tender.

VG - C6	EX - C7	LN - C8	Scarcity
40	75	150	5

310 (Type II): In 1947, the tender decoration was changed. The words "AMERICAN FLYER LINES" appeared each side of the tender, while slightly above and ahead of the lettering was stamped the keystone "PRR" herald of the Pennsylvania railroad.

VG - C6	EX - C7	LN - C8	Scarcity
30	60	125	6

312: Gilbert first cataloged a locomotive with this number in 1946. This 4-6-2 Pacific remained in the catalog through 1948. The 1951 and 1952 catalogs also list a 312, but in all likelihood the 312AC locomotives were the ones actually shipped during this time period. The 1946-48 locomotive had a four-piece die-cast boiler with wire handrails. It featured an operating headlight, smoke and choo-choo, and a four-position reverse unit.

312 (Type I): When introduced in 1946, the smoke and choo-choo unit of the 312 was mounted inside the tender,

Values for each condition are in U.S. dollars. | **Scarcity** = Scale from 1-8 with 8 being the hardest to find.

21

312 (Type IV)

which was lettered "PENNSYLVANIA" in silver. The reverse unit was mounted in the boiler. Sheet metal trucks and a link coupler were installed on the tender.

VG - C6	EX - C7	LN - C8	Scarcity
60	90	175	5

312 (Type II): Perhaps as early as late 1946—and certainly in 1947—white "AMERICAN FLYER LINES" lettering appeared on the tender sides in lieu of "Pennsylvania." The keystone-shaped logo of the Pennsy, complete with "PRR" initials, was printed slightly ahead and above the new road name on the tender.

VG - C6	EX - C7	LN - C8	Scarcity
60	90	175	5

This 312 has been retrofitted with a knuckle coupler.

312 (Type III): Other units were stamped in white rather than silver, but were otherwise identical to the Type II.

VG - C6	EX - C7	LN - C8	Scarcity
60	90	175	5

312 (Type IV): 📷 Eventually the smoke and choo-choo unit was moved from the tender to the boiler. At the same time the reverse unit was moved into the white-lettered "AMERICAN FLYER LINES" tender. The Pennsylvania keystone continued to appear on the tender.

VG - C6	EX - C7	LN - C8	Scarcity
30	60	125	3

312AC: For 1949 through 1951—and perhaps 1952 as well—the 312 4-6-2 Pacific was known as the 312AC. The boiler continued to be comprised of four die-castings, and white "312 AC" markings appeared below the cab windows. The die-cast tender body was stamped with both the "PRR" keystone herald and serif "AMERICAN FLYER LINES" lettering. The smoke and choo-choo unit was housed in the boiler, while the four-position reverse unit was installed in the tender. Sheet metal trucks were used on the tender, and a link coupler was installed at the rear.

312AC (Type I): The early locomotives used a sheet metal trailing truck without side frames with integral drawbar.

VG - C6	EX - C7	LN - C8	Scarcity
50	80	130	4

312AC (Type II): Later locomotives used a nicely detailed die-cast trailing truck.

VG - C6	EX - C7	LN - C8	Scarcity
50	80	130	4

313: This die-cast 4-6-2 Pacific was available from 1955 through 1957. Smoke and choo-choo was mounted in the boiler, while the die-cast tender housed the four-position reverse unit. The tender was marked with the P.R.R. keystone logo, and also had "AMERICAN FLYER LINES" markings. Trucks with sintered-iron side frames were used, with a knuckle coupler installed at the rear. The motors in the 1956 and 1957 versions were larger than those found in the 1955 edition.

VG - C6	EX - C7	LN - C8	Scarcity
60	150	275	5

314AW: This die-cast 1949-50 4-6-2 Pacific and tender combination included a whistle. The locomotive featured an operating headlight, and the die-cast tender housed a four-position reverse unit as well as the whistle. The locomotive was stamped "314AW" in white below the cab window, while the tender markings included a "PRR" keystone herald and sans-serif "AMERICAN FLYER" lettering. These locomotives were furnished with a whistle control box, and it's assumed to be present in the values listed below.

314AW (Type I): The early locomotives used a sheet metal trailing truck without side frames with integral drawbar.

VG - C6	EX - C7	LN - C8	Scarcity
100	200	350	6

314AW (Type II): Later locomotives used a nicely detailed die-cast trailing truck.

VG - C6	EX - C7	LN - C8	Scarcity
90	180	300	5

315: Produced only in 1952—even though it was cataloged in 1951—this version of the die-cast 4-6-2 Pacific featured an operating headlight, as well as smoke and choo-choo mounted in the boiler. The die-cast tender accompanying the locomotive housed a four-position reverse unit. The white markings included the catalog number beneath the cab window, and on the tender sides a "PRR" keystone herald and sans-serif "AMERICAN FLYER" lettering.

VG - C6	EX - C7	LN - C8	Scarcity
75	150	300	5

316: A 4-6-2 Pacific was again cataloged in 1953 and 1954. This version of the locomotive featured smoke and choo-choo, as well as an operating headlight mounted in the boiler. The die-cast tender was marked with a "PRR" keystone and "AMERICAN FLYER LINES" in white. It housed the four-position reverse unit and air-chime whistle. The tender trucks had sintered-iron side frames, and a knuckle coupler was found at the rear.

VG - C6	EX - C7	LN - C8	Scarcity
75	150	275	5

320: The famed New York Central 4-6-4 Hudson arrived on Gilbert's S-Gauge rails in 1946. The locomotive, which had an operating headlight and four-position reverse unit housed in the cab, remained in the product line through 1947. No smoke or choo-choo units were incorporated in the locomotive or tender. The tender had not only a die-cast body, but rode on six-wheel trucks with die-cast side frames. A link coupler was installed at the rear of the tender.

320 (Type I): The 1946 production of the Hudson was combined with a tender lettered "NEW YORK CENTRAL."

VG - C6	EX - C7	LN - C8	Scarcity
60	100	200	5

320 (Type II): In 1947, the tender lettering was changed to "AMERICAN FLYER LINES," and the oval "New York Central System" logo was printed high and near the front of each side of the tender's coal bunker.

VG - C6	EX - C7	LN - C8	Scarcity
60	100	200	5

321: Also available in 1946-47 was a second 4-6-4 Hudson, the 321, which included smoke and choo-choo. The locomotive, which had an operating headlight and four-position reverse unit housed in the boiler, remained in the product line through 1947. The tender had not only a die-cast body, but rode on six-wheel trucks with die-cast side frames. A link coupler was installed at the rear of the tender.

321 (Type I): Most of the 1946 edition of the 321 sported a tender lettered "NEW YORK CENTRAL," and housed a smoke and choo-choo unit.

VG - C6	EX - C7	LN - C8	Scarcity
50	125	225	5

321 (Type II): In 1947, the tender lettering was changed to "AMERICAN FLYER LINES," and the oval "New York Central System" logo was printed high and near the front of each side of the tender's coal bunker.

VG - C6	EX - C7	LN - C8	Scarcity
60	135	250	6

322: Also available from 1946 through 1948, this version of the 4-6-4 Hudson featured an operating headlight, four-position reverse unit, smoke and choo-choo.

Values for each condition are in U.S. dollars. | **Scarcity** = Scale from 1-8 with 8 being the hardest to find.

23

322 (Type I): Most of the 1946 edition of the 322 sported a tender lettered "NEW YORK CENTRAL," and housed a smoke and choo-choo unit. The reverse unit was housed in the locomotive boiler, and shiny handrails were used.

VG - C6	EX - C7	LN - C8	Scarcity
60	100	200	5

322 (Type II): In 1947, the tender lettering was changed to "AMERICAN FLYER LINES," and the oval "New York Central System" logo was printed high and near the front of each side of the tender's coal bunker. The reverse unit was located in the locomotive boiler. Blackened handrails were installed on the locomotive.

VG - C6	EX - C7	LN - C8	Scarcity
35	75	150	4

322 (Type III): In 1948, the smoke and choo-choo unit was moved into the boiler, where it was driven by the same motor that powered the locomotive. This design change obviously reduced Gilbert's cost substantially. To accommodate these units in the boiler, the reverse unit was moved to the die-cast tender. The tender was lettered "AMERICAN FLYER LINES" in white, and also bore the oval logo of the "New York Central System."

VG - C6	EX - C7	LN - C8	Scarcity
35	75	150	4

322AC: The 1949-51 edition of the 4-6-4 Hudson was numbered "322AC" in white. Trailing the locomotive was a tender with a die-cast body, which housed the four-position reverse unit. Its trucks were die-cast six-wheel units, and a link coupler was installed at the rear. Inside the locomotive boiler was a smoke and choo-choo unit.

322AC (Type I): In 1949, in addition to the small oval "New York Central System" logo, the tenders were lettered "AMERICAN FLYER LINES" in white. Shiny handrails were installed on the locomotive. A single rivet was used to create a friction fit to hold the boiler front in place.

VG - C6	EX - C7	LN - C8	Scarcity
40	80	160	4

322AC (Type II): In 1950 and 1951, the tender lettering changed to "AMERICAN FLYER," although the "New York Central System" oval logo continued to be printed on the tender as well. The boiler front was held in place by a flat spring made by a single piece of brass strip.

VG - C6	EX - C7	LN - C8	Scarcity
40	80	160	4

324AC: This version of the New York Central 4-6-4 Hudson was produced only in 1950. An electronic whistle was installed in the tender. Also housed in the tender, which rode on six-wheel trucks with die-cast side frames, was the four-position reverse unit. The die-cast tender that had a link coupler at its rear was decorated with white "AMERICAN FLYER" lettering as well as the oval "New York Central System" herald. A smoke and choo-choo unit was mounted in the locomotive boiler.

324AC (Type I): Some of the tenders were marked with serif lettering.

VG - C6	EX - C7	LN - C8	Scarcity
75	150	250	7

324AC (Type II): Sans-serif lettering was used on other tenders.

VG - C6	EX - C7	LN - C8	Scarcity
75	150	250	7

322 (Type IV)

325AC: This 1951-built 4-6-4 Hudson came with a die-cast tender which was lettered "AMERICAN FLYER" in white, and was further decorated with the oval herald of the "New York Central System." The center axle of the tender trucks—trucks, which were designed to have six wheels—was removed and replaced with a sliding shoe contact. This contact allowed better functioning of the air-chime whistle, which along with the reverse unit, was housed in the tender. Smoke, choo-choo and an operating headlight were all located in the locomotive boiler. A link coupler was mounted at the rear of the tender.

325AC (Type I): Some of the tenders were marked with serif lettering.

VG - C6	EX - C7	LN - C8	Scarcity
50	100	190	5

325AC (Type II): Sans-serif lettering was used on other tenders.

VG - C6	EX - C7	LN - C8	Scarcity
50	100	190	5

K325: Knuckle couplers were used on the 325 4-6-4 Hudson in 1952, and the number was changed to reflect this. The smoke and choo-choo unit was mounted in the boiler, and an air-chime whistle unit was installed in the tender, along with the reverse unit.

K325 (Type I): In addition to the small oval "New York Central System" logo, some tenders were lettered "AMERICAN FLYER LINES" in white.

VG - C6	EX - C7	LN - C8	Scarcity
50	125	225	5

K325 (Type II): Other tenders were printed "AMERICAN FLYER" in addition to being marked with the New York Central herald.

VG - C6	EX - C7	LN - C8	Scarcity
50	125	225	5

326: From 1953 through 1957, the die-cast 4-6-4 Hudson was cataloged with this number. The locomotive had a smoke and choo-choo unit, as well as an operating headlight installed in the boiler. The die-cast tender housed the four-position reverse unit and air-chime whistle. The tender rode on six-wheel trucks with die-cast side frames, and a knuckle coupler was mounted at the rear. In addition to the small oval "New York Central System" logo, the tenders were lettered "AMERICAN FLYER LINES" in white.

326 (Type I): In 1953 and early 1954, the steamer was powered by a small motor and cloth-covered wires joined the locomotive and tender.

VG - C6	EX - C7	LN - C8	Scarcity
50	110	225	4

326 (Type II): From late 1954 through 1957, a larger motor was used, and plastic-covered wires connected the locomotive and tender.

VG - C6	EX - C7	LN - C8	Scarcity
100	175	300	5

326 (Type III): Some large-motor locomotives have been reported with motor-mounted two-position reverse units and plastic tenders. This dates from 1958.

VG - C6	EX - C7	LN - C8	Scarcity
100	175	300	5

332: The biggest of the Gilbert steamers was the 4-8-4 Northern, modeled after steamers used by the Union Pacific railroad. This locomotive is often referred to as the "Challenger"—not after the Union Pacific locomotives of that name, which were 4-6-6-4 steamers, but rather after the Union Pacific "Challenger" passenger train. The 332 was sold from 1946 through 1949. Its tender was fitted with a link coupler at the rear, and after 1946 the Union Pacific shield emblem was printed on the tender.

332 (Type I): A handful of these locomotives were assembled in 1946. These featured silver "UNION PACIFIC" lettering on the tender. The tender also housed a smoke and choo-choo unit, while the reverse unit was in the boiler.

VG - C6	EX - C7	LN - C8	Scarcity
Too rarely traded to accurately establish pricing.			

332 (Type II): In early 1947, the tender was lettered "AMERICAN FLYER LINES" in white. The tender continued to house the smoke and choo-choo unit, as the reverse unit was mounted in the boiler.

VG - C6	EX - C7	LN - C8	Scarcity
1,200	1,800	2,400	8

Values for each condition are in U.S. dollars. | **Scarcity** = Scale from 1-8 with 8 being the hardest to find.

25

332 (Type III): In 1948, a DC motor was installed, and no reverse unit was required. The smoke and choo-choo were mounted in the boiler. The white lettering on the tender read "AMERICAN FLYER LINES."

VG - C6	EX - C7	LN - C8	Scarcity
175	275	450	6

332 (Type IV): In 1949, white "AMERICAN FLYER" lettering was used on the tenders, and white stripes now lined the running board of the locomotive. Most of these locomotives were DC, but some AC examples have been reported

VG - C6	EX - C7	LN - C8	Scarcity
150	250	400	5

332AC: In 1951, the AC-powered 4-8-4 Northern locomotives were distinguished by the "AC" suffix added to the catalog number, and stamped together beneath the cab window. The white markings on the die-cast tender included the Union Pacific shield herald and sans-serif "AMERICAN FLYER" lettering. The link coupler-equipped tender housed the reverse unit. Inside the locomotive boiler was a smoke and choo-choo unit, as well as an operating headlight. A white stripe was applied to the edge of the locomotive running board.

VG - C6	EX - C7	LN - C8	Scarcity
150	250	425	6

332DC: A DC-powered version of the big die-cast Northern was offered. The "332DC" catalog number was stamped in white beneath each cab window, and the edge of the running board was trimmed in white. No reverse unit was required, and the smoke and choo-choo unit, as well as the operating headlight, were housed in the boiler. The white markings on the link coupler-equipped die-cast tender included the Union Pacific shield herald and sans-serif "AMERICAN FLYER" lettering.

VG - C6	EX - C7	LN - C8	Scarcity
150	275	500	7

334DC: The 4-8-4 was cataloged with this number only in 1950. The white markings on the link coupler-equipped die-cast tender housed an electronic whistle, and its markings included the Union Pacific shield herald and a sans-serif "AMERICAN FLYER." No reverse unit was required, and the smoke and choo-choo unit, as well as the operating headlight, were housed in the boiler. A white stripe ran along the edge of the locomotive's running boards.

VG - C6	EX - C7	LN - C8	Scarcity
150	275	500	7

K335: A knuckle coupler was installed in the Northern's tender in 1952, resulting in a number change to K335. The locomotive's smoke and choo-choo mechanism was housed in the boiler. The die-cast tender housed an air-chime whistle and rode on six-wheel trucks with the center axle replaced with a sliding shoe. The tender was printed with the Union Pacific shield herald and sans-serif "AMERICAN FLYER" lettering. White stripes ran along the locomotive running boards.

VG - C6	EX - C7	LN - C8	Scarcity
150	250	450	5

336: The Northern bore this number from 1953 through 1957. During this time the reverse unit and air-chime whistle were mounted in the die-cast tender. Inside the

342 (Type II)

locomotive boiler was an operating headlight and a smoke and choo-choo unit. The tender was decorated with a white Union Pacific shield herald and sans-serif "AMERICAN FLYER LINES" lettering. A white stripe was painted on the edge of the running board. The tender had a knuckle coupler at the rear, and was equipped with die-cast side frame six-wheel trucks, however the center axle of each truck was replaced with an electrical contact.

336 (Type I): The early 1953 locomotives had smaller motors than did later models.

VG - C6	EX - C7	LN - C8	Scarcity
150	275	500	8

336 (Type II): A large motor was used from late 1953 through 1957.

VG - C6	EX - C7	LN - C8	Scarcity
175	300	550	7

342: This very nicely detailed die-cast 0-8-0 switcher was sold from 1946 through 1948, then again in 1952. The die-cast tender rode on sheet metal trucks and was lettered with the words "NICKEL PLATE ROAD," and after 1946 with the words "AMERICAN FLYER LINES" as well. A link coupler was installed at the rear of the tender. Across the front of the locomotive was a bar which link couplers could engage. Both the locomotive and tender featured operating headlights.

342 (Type I): A handful of locomotives were produced in 1946. The tenders accompanying these units were lettered only "NICKEL PLATE ROAD," and housed the smoke and choo-choo unit. The reverse unit was located in the boiler along with the AC motor.

VG-C6	EX-C7	LN-C8	Scarcity
Too rarely traded to accurately establish pricing.			

342 (Type II): 📷 "AMERICAN FLYER LINES" lettering was added to the tender in 1947. The AC motor was still used. The smoke and choo-choo unit was mounted in the tender, and the reverse unit was mounted in the locomotive boiler.

VG - C6	EX - C7	LN - C8	Scarcity
125	300	500	7

342 (Type III): In 1948, a brass coupler weight was added to the coupler on the rear tender truck, as it was to link couplers throughout the Gilbert line. The balance of the AC-powered locomotive and tender was unchanged from the Type II.

VG - C6	EX - C7	LN - C8	Scarcity
100	200	325	5

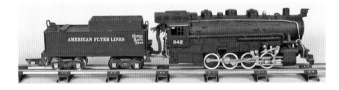

342 (Type IV): In 1948, AC-powered units were produced with the smoke and choo-choo units mounted in the boiler, rather than the tender. The tender was lettered "AMERICAN

Values for each condition are in U.S. dollars. | **Scarcity** = Scale from 1-8 with 8 being the hardest to find.

27

FLYER LINES," in addition to the "NICKEL PLATE ROAD" markings, and housed the reverse unit.

VG - C6	EX - C7	LN - C8	Scarcity
100	175	350	6

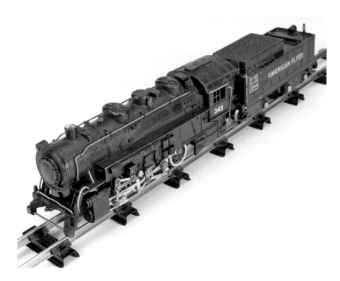

342 (Type V): When the 342 returned in 1952, an AC motor, which was controlled by a tender-mounted reverse unit, powered it. The markings on the tender differed from that used earlier. Now the "NICKEL PLATE ROAD" lettering was in the form of the road's herald, and the "LINES" was removed from the sans-serif "AMERICAN FLYER" printing.

VG - C6	EX - C7	LN - C8	Scarcity
100	200	400	7

342AC: From 1949 through 1951, this AC powered—and labeled—die-cast 0-8-0 switcher was sold. Operating headlamps were mounted in both the locomotive and die-cast tender. The tender also housed the reverse unit, and was equipped with a link coupler. The smoke and choo-choo unit was located in the boiler, along with the motor. Across the front of the locomotive was a bar which link couplers could engage. The "NICKEL PLATE ROAD" lettering was now inside the road's herald, and the tender also had sans-serif "AMERICAN FLYER LINES" or "AMERICAN FLYER" lettering.

342AC (Type I): In 1949, the locomotive was numbered with large "342AC" characters and the tender was lettered "AMERICAN FLYER LINES."

VG - C6	EX - C7	LN - C8	Scarcity
100	175	325	5

342AC (Type II): In 1950 and 1951, the "342AC" was printed in smaller type.

VG - C6	EX - C7	LN - C8	Scarcity
100	175	325	5

342AC (Type III): Some of the 1951 locomotives were marked with the large "342AC" characters.

VG - C6	EX - C7	LN - C8	Scarcity
100	175	325	5

342DC: A DC-powered version of the die-cast 0-8-0 was made from 1949 through 1950. Operating headlamps were mounted in both the locomotive and die-cast tender. The tender was equipped with a link coupler. The smoke and choo-choo unit was located in the boiler, along with the motor. Across the front of the locomotive was a bar which link couplers could engage. "NICKEL PLATE ROAD" lettering was printed on the tender sides, along with "American Flyer" markings.

342DC (Type I): Some of the locomotives in 1949 had a large "342DC" stamped in thin white letters below the cab windows. In addition to the "Nickel Plate Road" lettering the tender was marked "AMERICAN FLYER LINES." A rivet was used to create a force fit holding the boiler front in place.

VG - C6	EX - C7	LN - C8	Scarcity
100	175	325	5

342DC (Type II): Other 1948 locomotives had very large "342DC" lettering printed with thick white characters. The tender was lettered "AMERICAN FLYER LINES."

VG - C6	EX - C7	LN - C8	Scarcity
100	175	325	5

342DC (Type III): In 1949, the very large thick white "342DC" lettering was used again. The tender was lettered "AMERICAN FLYER LINES."

VG - C6	EX - C7	LN - C8	Scarcity
100	175	325	5

342DC (Type IV): Small 342DC lettering returned in 1950. The thicker typeface was used for the locomotive number. The tender was lettered "AMERICAN FLYER" in addition to "NICKEL PLATE ROAD." A flat brass spring secured the boiler front.

VG - C6	EX - C7	LN - C8	Scarcity
100	160	300	4

343: The die-cast 0-8-0 locomotive had a new number from 1953 through 1958—343. As with the late 342, the "Nickel Plate Road" lettering on this locomotive's tender was inside the road's logo. The tender was also lettered "AMERICAN FLYER LINES," and like the NKP logo and number, it was printed in white. A knuckle coupler was mounted on the locomotive pilot and at the rear of the tender. Both the locomotive and tender also had operating lights. The smoke and choo-choo unit was installed in the boiler.

343 (Type I): The 1953 and 1954 production had serif "AMERICAN FLYER LINES" lettering on the tender, which also housed the reverse unit.

VG - C6	EX - C7	LN - C8	Scarcity
110	175	350	5

343 (Type II): In 1955-56, a four-position reverse unit was mounted on the rear of the motor. The tender was marked with serif "AMERICAN FLYER LINES" lettering. The 343 was available, but not cataloged, in 1955.

VG - C6	EX - C7	LN - C8	Scarcity
125	250	450	6

343 (Type III): In 1957, the reverse unit was still mounted on the rear of the motor, but now it was a two-position unit, which worked better than the 1955-56 unit.

"AMERICAN FLYER LINES" was printed in white serif lettering on the tender.

VG - C6	EX - C7	LN - C8	Scarcity
125	250	450	6

346 NICKEL PLATE ROAD: Cataloged only in 1955, this version of the die-cast 0-8-0 switcher had an air-chime whistle mounted in the tender. This was accomplished by mounting the reverse unit on the back of a motor. Both the locomotive and tender were painted black and had operating headlights. A smoke and choo-choo unit was mounted in the boiler. The tender was marked with the square "NICKEL PLATE ROAD" herald and white serif "AMERICAN FLYER LINES" lettering.

VG - C6	EX - C7	LN - C8	Scarcity
225	375	625	7

350 THE ROYAL BLUE: This streamlined 4-6-2 Pacific was sold in 1948 and 1950. The die-cast steamer and its sheet metal tender were painted blue and lettered in white. The reverse unit, as well as the operating headlight, was housed in the boiler. No smoke or choo-choo unit was fitted. The number "350" appeared below the cab window, and the words "THE ROYAL BLUE" were printed above the drivers. The tender coal pile and the deck were painted black, and sheet metal trucks were used on the tender. A link coupler was installed at the rear.

350 (Type I): Locomotives produced in 1948 were equipped with separately applied wire handrails. "AMERICAN FLYER LINES" with serif were printed in an indented area on each tender side. The Capital dome herald of the B & O railroad could be found printed either before or after the "American Flyer Lines" lettering. These early locomotives also had separate trailing trucks and drawbars.

VG - C6	EX - C7	LN - C8	Scarcity
75	150	300	7

350 (Type II): Some later tenders only had the B & O herald behind the lettering. The trailing truck and drawbar became an assembly fairly early in the locos production run, and remained so for the rest of 350's manufacture.

VG - C6	EX - C7	LN - C8	Scarcity
50	100	200	4

Values for each condition are in U.S. dollars. | **Scarcity** = Scale from 1-8 with 8 being the hardest to find.

29

350 (Type III):  The indentations were eliminated from the tender sides on some units. The B & O herald was printed forward of the serif "AMERICAN FLYER LINES" lettering.

VG - C6	EX - C7	LN - C8	Scarcity
50	100	200	4

350 (Type IV): Other locomotives and tenders were identical to the Type III, however sans-serif lettering was used.

VG - C6	EX - C7	LN - C8	Scarcity
50	100	200	4

350 (Type V): Heavy block sans-serif lettering was used on some of the 1948 locomotives and tenders. The tender lettering read only "AMERICAN FLYER," and no B & O herald was applied.

VG - C6	EX - C7	LN - C8	Scarcity
60	175	275	6

350 (Type VI): Other locomotives have been reported that were duplicates of the Type V, except for the omission of the pilot handrails.

VG - C6	EX - C7	LN - C8	Scarcity
60	175	275	6

350 (Type VII): When the Royal Blue returned in 1950, the separately applied wire handrails had been replaced by cast-in representations. The tender was not marked with a B & O herald, but was printed with heavy block lettering reading "AMERICAN FLYER."

VG - C6	EX - C7	LN - C8	Scarcity
45	85	165	4

350 (Type VIII): In 1950, a few units were produced with both the locomotive and tender lettered "THE ROYAL BLUE." No "American Flyer" or "B & O" markings were used.

VG-6	EX-C7	LN-C8	Scarcity
Too rarely traded to accurately establish pricing.			

353 AMERICAN FLYER CIRCUS: Introduced in 1950—and carried over into 1951—was a second streamlined 4-6-2 Pacific. This one was painted red and the sans-serif yellow lettering above the drive wheels revealed its special purpose "AMERICAN FLYER CIRCUS." The reverse unit, as well as the operating headlight, was housed in the boiler. No smoke or choo-choo unit was fitted. The coal pile and deck of the tender were painted black. A link coupler was mounted on the rearmost of the tender's two sheet metal trucks.

353 (Type I):  A few—only two are known at this time—examples of the 353 exist with separately applied wire handrails.

VG-6	EX-C7	LN-C8	Scarcity
Too rarely traded to accurately establish pricing.			

353 (Type II): The standard circus locomotive had cast-in simulated handrails.

VG - C6	EX - C7	LN - C8	Scarcity
125	275	550	7

354 SILVER BULLET: In 1954, the streamlined 4-6-2 Pacific was painted silver and molded of plastic. The decoration was applied using decals—a blue and gold "SILVER BULLET" decal above the drive wheels and a red, white and blue "AMERICAN FLYER LINES" shield on the pilot. Beneath the cab windows were blue-outlined yellow decals with the number "354." The sheet metal tender was painted silver as well, and was decorated with the same style decal that was used above the locomotive drivers. The tender rode on trucks with sintered-iron side frames, and had a knuckle coupler at the rear.

VG - C6	EX - C7	LN - C8	Scarcity
100	200	300	6

350 (Type III)

356 SILVER BULLET: For 1953, the streamlined 4-6-2 Pacific got a bright new color scheme. The decoration was applied using decals—a blue and gold "SILVER BULLET" decal above the drive wheels and a red, white and blue "AMERICAN FLYER LINES" shield on the pilot. Beneath the cab windows were blue-outlined yellow decals with the number "356." The sheet metal tender was decorated with the same style decal that was used above the locomotive drivers. The tender rode on sheet metal trucks and had a link coupler at the rear.

356 (Type I): As first produced, the locomotive and tender were chrome plated. The plating did not adhere well, and was discontinued. Units with bright intact plating are particularly sought after and bring premium prices.

VG - C6	EX - C7	LN - C8	Scarcity
75	125	350	5

356 (Type II): Because the problems with the chrome plating, the locomotives and tenders were painted silver instead.

VG - C6	EX - C7	LN - C8	Scarcity
100	150	200	4

L2001: Created to power the 1963 20800 Game Train Set, Gilbert provided this unpainted plastic 4-4-0 American type locomotive. The tender was lettered "CASEY JONES" and a "GAME TRAIN" herald was applied.

The locomotive did not have a reverse unit, nor an operating headlight, smoke or choo-choo. Pike Master trucks were installed on the tender, the rearward of which was equipped with a Pike Master coupler.

VG - C6	EX - C7	LN - C8	Scarcity
15	25	40	1

L2002: This uncataloged 4-4-0 was produced in 1963. Both the locomotive and tender were made of unpainted black plastic. The tender was lettered "AMERICAN FLYER LINES" and a "BURLINGTON ROUTE" herald was applied. The locomotive did not have a reverse unit, nor an operating headlight, smoke or choo-choo. Pike Master trucks were installed on the tender, the rearward of which was equipped with a Pike Master coupler. The locomotive shown above is equipped with an Erie tender, although it has not been confirmed that this combination is factory original.

VG - C6	EX - C7	LN - C8	Scarcity
60	150	275	7

21004: This uncataloged black-painted plastic 0-6-0 switcher was produced in 1957. The catalog of that year illustrated this locomotive with the number "263," but it was not produced in that form. The product

353 (Type I)

Values for each condition are in U.S. dollars. | **Scarcity** = Scale from 1-8 with 8 being the hardest to find.

31

number was stamped in white below the cab window, while the tender was decorated with the PRR keystone herald and sans-serif "AMERICAN FLYER LINES" lettering on each side. Both the locomotive and tender had operating headlights. Smoke and choo-choo were mounted in the boiler, and the two-position reverse unit was attached to the rear of the motor. The rear drivers were equipped with Pull-Mor traction tires. Knuckle couplers were located on the front of the steamer and rear of the tender. The tender was equipped with trucks with sintered-iron side frames. The reversing unit of these locomotives was hidden by a housing.

VG - C6	EX - C7	LN - C8	Scarcity
125	225	400	6

21005: This 0-6-0 switcher was offered. The catalog number was stamped in white below the cab window, while the tender was decorated with the PRR keystone herald and sans-serif "AMERICAN FLYER LINES" lettering on each side. The operating headlight, as well as the smoke and choo-choo were mounted in the boiler, and the two-position reverse unit was attached to the rear of the motor. The edges of the running boards were painted white. The rear drivers were equipped with Pull-Mor traction tires. Knuckle couplers were located on the front of the steamer and rear of the tender. The tender was equipped with trucks with sintered-iron side frames, but it did not have an operating light.

VG - C6	EX - C7	LN - C8	Scarcity
150	325	525	7

21030: In 1957, the 307 Reading locomotive was sold and packaged as the 21030.

21034: In 1957, the 303 Reading locomotive was sold and packaged as the 21034.

21044: In 1957, the 313 Pennsylvania locomotive was sold and packaged as the 21044.

21058: In 1957, the 326 New York Central locomotive was sold and packaged as the 21058.

21084: 📷 Although uncataloged, this black-painted plastic 4-6-2 Pacific was produced in 1957. White lettering on the locomotive read "21084," while the tender was decorated with the "CHICAGO NORTHWESTERN LINE" herald and sans-serif "AMERICAN FLYER LINES" lettering. The tender, which rode on trucks with sintered-iron side frames, housed a four-position reverse unit, and had a knuckle coupler at the rear. In addition to an operating headlight, the locomotive boiler housed a smoke and choo-choo unit.

VG - C6	EX - C7	LN - C8	Scarcity
40	75	150	4

21085: Locomotives with this number were cataloged from 1958 through 1965. The 4-6-2 Pacifics featured black-painted plastic boilers and tender bodies. The loco was equipped with an operating headlight, smoke and choo-choo, all mounted in the boiler. A two-position reverse unit was installed on the rear of the motor. The rear drive wheels were fitted with Pull-Mor tires.

21085 (TYPE I): From 1958 through 1962, the tender bore the logo of the "CHICAGO NORTHWESTERN LINE" in addition to "American Flyer Lines" lettering. It was equipped with trucks with sintered-iron side frames and had an operating knuckle coupler. The locomotive rode on die-cast drive wheels with white tires.

VG - C6	EX - C7	LN - C8	Scarcity
35	55	100	3

21085 (TYPE II): In 1961, the "CHICAGO NORTHWESTERN LINE" tender was equipped with Pike Master trucks and a Pike Master coupler. Black plastic drivers with white tires were used on the locomotive.

VG - C6	EX - C7	LN - C8	Scarcity
35	55	100	3

21085 (TYPE III): Other locomotives were identical to the Type III, but the driver tires were not painted white.

VG - C6	EX - C7	LN - C8	Scarcity
35	55	100	3

21085 (TYPE IV): In 1963, the logo on the tender switched to that of the "CHICAGO MILWAUKEE ST. PAUL AND PACIFIC," although the lettering splashed across the side continued to read "AMERICAN FLYER LINES." The tender was equipped with a Pike Master coupler and Pike Master trucks. The tires on the locomotive drive wheels were painted white.

VG-6	EX-C7	LN-C8	Scarcity
35	55	100	3

21085 (TYPE V): Other locomotives were identical to the Type V, but the driver tires were not painted white.

VG-6	EX-C7	LN-C8	Scarcity
35	55	100	3

21085 (TYPE VI): Probably near the end of production, a version of the "CHICAGO MILWAUKEE ST. PAUL AND PACIFIC" 4-6-2 was made with the center drive wheels all-black, while the front and rear drive wheels had white tires. The Pull-Mor tires were on the front axle of these units. The tender continued to be equipped with Pike Master trucks and a Pike Master coupler.

VG-6	EX-C7	LN-C8	Scarcity
35	55	100	3

21088 F. Y. & P.: Introduced in 1959 and also sold in 1960, the styling of this 4-4-0 was that of a 19th century steam locomotive. Plastic was the primary construction material for the colorful steamer. All the markings were applied using paper stickers. The headlight did not operate, although the locomotive did have working smoke and choo-choo. A two-position reverse unit was located in the tender, which rode on trucks with sintered-iron side frames and had a knuckle coupler.

21088 (Type I): The first 50 of these "Franklin" locomotives came with tenders lettered "ONE OF THE FIRST FIFTY."

VG-C6	EX-C7	LN-C8	Scarcity
Too rarely traded to accurately establish pricing.			

21088 (Type II): Some of the locomotives were built with red-painted pilots.

VG - C6	EX - C7	LN - C8	Scarcity
50	75	125	2

21088 (Type III): Others were built with unpainted red plastic pilots.

VG - C6	EX - C7	LN - C8	Scarcity
50	75	125	2

21088 (Type IV): Some of these units were assembled at the factory as presentation models. Lacking motor and smoke unit, the locomotive and tender were mounted on a 15-inch long section of track with a black rubber roadbed. The track and roadbed were affixed to a wooden base, and a brass plate was attached that read "THE FRANKLIN THE A.C. GILBERT CO. NEW HAVEN, CONN."

VG-C6	EX-C7	LN-C8	Scarcity
Too rarely traded to accurately establish pricing.			

21089 F. Y. & P. R. R.: Sold in 1960 and 1961, the styling of this colorful plastic 4-4-0 American followed that of 19th century steam locomotives. All the lettering was applied using gold paper stickers. The headlight did not operate, but the locomotive did have smoke and choo-choo. The two-position reverse unit was mounted in the tender, which was equipped with trucks with sintered-iron side frames and an operating knuckle coupler.

VG - C6	EX - C7	LN - C8	Scarcity
75	150	300	6

21095: This die-cast New York, New Haven and Hartford railroad Pacific was listed in the 1957 catalog, but did not enter regular production. A few locomotives do exist with this number, and collectors are divided as to whether these are pieces created by A.C. Gilbert for promotional purposes, or that these shells were obtained separately through the Gilbert service department.

VG-C6	EX-C7	LN-C8	Scarcity
Too rarely traded to accurately establish pricing.			

21084

Values for each condition are in U.S. dollars. | Scarcity = Scale from 1-8 with 8 being the hardest to find.

21099: This die-cast 4-6-2 Pacific steamer was produced only in 1958. The boiler, with its white-edged running boards, housed an operating headlight, smoke and choo-choo, and a motor with two-position reverse unit mounted on its rear. The accompanying black-painted plastic tender was lettered not only with white serif "AMERICAN FLYER LINES" markings, but also the herald of "The New York New Haven and Hartford Railroad Co." Its body housed an air-chime whistle, and it rode on trucks with sintered-iron side frames and had a knuckle coupler on the rear. A simulated stoker adorned the tender.

VG - C6	EX - C7	LN - C8	Scarcity
125	200	475	5

21100: This 4-4-2 Atlantic was produced in 1957, but it did not appear in the catalog. Its black-painted boiler

was made of plastic, as was the tender body, which was also painted black. The product number was stamped under the cab window in white, and the same color printing was used for both the "Reading Lines" herald and the sans-serif "AMERICAN FLYER LINES" tender markings. The locomotive had an operating headlight, a two-position reverse unit, and Pull-Mor traction tires; the latter were mounted on the front drive wheels.

VG - C6	EX - C7	LN - C8	Scarcity
15	25	40	1

21105: This black-painted plastic 4-4-2 Atlantic was first cataloged in 1957, but was available from 1958 through 1960. The tender body was also painted black. The product number was stamped under the cab window in white, and the same color printing was used for both the "Reading Lines" herald and the sans-serif "AMERICAN FLYER LINES" tender markings. Inside the locomotive was an operating headlight, smoke and choo-choo, a two-position reverse unit; the latter was mounted on the rear of the motor. Pull-Mor traction tires were also found on the locomotive. The tender rode on trucks with sintered-iron side frames and had a knuckle coupler on the rear.

21105 (Type I): Some of these locomotives had a separately installed metal bell and whistle. Even more notable, the drive wheels had unpainted aluminum tires.

VG-C6	EX-C7	LN-C8	Scarcity
Too rarely traded to accurately establish pricing.			

21105 (Type II): Later locomotives had black die-cast drive wheels with white-painted tires, but were otherwise identical to the Type I locos.

VG - C6	EX - C7	LN - C8	Scarcity
25	50	100	3

21089 F. Y. & P. R. R.

21105 (Type III): Later the bell and whistle became plastic, and were molded integral with the boiler. The black plastic drive wheels featured white-painted tires.

VG - C6	EX - C7	LN - C8	Scarcity
15	25	50	1

21106: This 4-4-2 Atlantic was produced in 1959, but it did not appear in the catalog. Its black-painted boiler was made of plastic, as was the tender body, which was also painted black. The product number was stamped under the cab window in white, and the same color printing was used for both the "Reading Lines" herald and the sans-serif "AMERICAN FLYER LINES" tender markings. The locomotive had an operating headlight, a two-position reverse unit and Pull-Mor traction tires. These locomotives were built with smoke and choo-choo mounted in the boiler. These units had a separately installed metal bell and whistle, and white-painted tires on the drivers.

VG - C6	EX - C7	LN - C8	Scarcity
75	150	250	6

21107: From 1964 through 1966, Gilbert produced this black-painted plastic 4-4-2 Atlantic. The locomotive featured an operating headlight, smoke and choo-choo, and the two-position reverse unit was attached to the rear of the motor. The black-painted plastic tender was equipped with Pike Master trucks and had a Pike Master coupler at the rear.

21107 (Type I): In 1964, the tender was marked with the "PRR" keystone herald in addition to the white sans-serif "AMERICAN FLYER LINES" lettering. The locomotive drive wheels had white tires.

VG - C6	EX - C7	LN - C8	Scarcity
10	20	40	1

21107 (Type II): Otherwise identical locomotives were produced in 1965, however, rather than the PRR keystone, the "Burlington Route" logo was printed on the tender side.

VG - C6	EX - C7	LN - C8	Scarcity
10	20	40	1

21107 (Type III): The PRR keystone returned in 1966, but the drive wheels lost their white trim.

VG - C6	EX - C7	LN - C8	Scarcity
10	20	40	1

21115: This 1958-produced die-cast K-5 4-6-2 Pacific was equipped with an operating headlight, smoke and choo-choo, two-position reverse unit, Pull-Mor traction tires on the rear drivers, and a black-painted plastic tender. The white markings printed on the tender body included the keystone-shaped "PRR" herald of the Pennsylvania Railroad and serif "AMERICAN FLYER LINES" lettering. The tender had trucks with sintered-iron side frames and an operating knuckle coupler.

VG - C6	EX - C7	LN - C8	Scarcity
250	500	1,000	7

21105 (Type I)

21129: The 1958 edition of the New York Central 4-6-4 Hudson had an operating headlight, smoke and choo-choo all mounted in the boiler, while an air-chime whistle was installed in the six-wheel truck-equipped tender. The two-position reverse unit was mounted on the back of the motor, and on the back of the tender was an operating knuckle coupler. The black-painted plastic tender was decorated with an oval "NEW YORK CENTRAL SYSTEM" herald, and serif "AMERICAN FLYER LINES" lettering, both printed in white.

21129 (Type I): Some of the locomotives had white tires and were built with a one-piece chassis.

VG - C6	EX - C7	LN - C8	Scarcity
250	600	1,400	8

21129 (Type II): Other locomotives had unpainted aluminum tires and were built with a two-piece chassis.

VG - C6	EX - C7	LN - C8	Scarcity
250	600	1,400	8

21130: The 1959-64 revision of the New York Central 4-6-4 Hudson lacked the air-chime whistle of its predecessor. However, the operating headlight, smoke and choo-choo and motor-mounted two-position reverse unit were all retained. The locomotives had black plastic drive wheels with unpainted aluminum tires. The black-painted plastic tender was decorated with an oval "NEW YORK CENTRAL SYSTEM" herald, and serif "AMERICAN FLYER LINES" lettering, both printed in white. An operating knuckle coupler was installed on the tender rear. Note: the steps on this tender are frequently damaged or missing.

21130 (Type I): The 1959-60 locomotive tender wiring connection was made by a plug.

VG - C6	EX - C7	LN - C8	Scarcity
150	250	500	7

21130 (Type II): The tender was direct-wired to the locomotive.

VG - C6	EX - C7	LN - C8	Scarcity
150	250	500	7

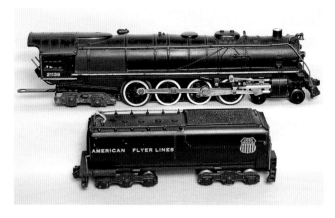

21139: The 1958-59 version of the big Union Pacific 4-8-4 Northern had an operating headlight, smoke and choo-choo all mounted in the boiler, while an air-chime whistle was installed in the six-wheel truck-equipped die-cast tender. The two-position reverse unit was mounted on the back of the motor, and on the back of the tender was an operating knuckle coupler. The black-painted plastic tender was decorated with an "UNION PACIFIC" shield herald, and sans-serif "AMERICAN FLYER LINES" lettering, both printed in white.

VG - C6	EX - C7	LN - C8	Scarcity
250	450	900	7

21106

21140 UNION PACIFIC: In 1960, the die-cast Union Pacific 4-8-4 Northern was equipped with an operating headlight, smoke and choo-choo all mounted in the boiler. A six-wheel truck-equipped die-cast tender accompanied the locomotive. The two-position reverse unit was mounted on the back of the motor, and on the back of the tender was an operating knuckle coupler. The black-painted plastic tender was decorated with a "UNION PACIFIC" shield herald, and sans-serif "AMERICAN FLYER LINES" lettering, both printed in white.

VG - C6	EX - C7	LN - C8	Scarcity
475	1,000	1,800	8

21155: The tank-type 0-6-0T Docksider switcher was introduced in 1958, the only year this particular model number was available. The locomotive did not have an operating headlight, but it did have smoke and choo-choo. A two position reverse unit controlled the motor, and an operating knuckle coupler was mounted on each end of the steamer.

VG - C6	EX - C7	LN - C8	Scarcity
100	225	475	5

21156: The 0-6-0T Docksider returned in 1959. This version of the diminutive switcher not only did not have an operating headlight, it had no smoke or choo-choo either. It did have a two-position reverse unit and an operating knuckle coupler at both front and rear.

VG - C6	EX - C7	LN - C8	Scarcity
75	150	300	5

21145: The die-cast 0-8-0 locomotive had a new number in 1958—21145. As with its predecessor, the "Nickel Plate Road" lettering on this locomotive's tender was inside the road's logo. The tender was also lettered "AMERICAN FLYER LINES," like the NKP logo and number, printed in white. A knuckle coupler was mounted on the locomotive pilot and at the rear of the tender. Both the locomotive and tender also had operating headlights. The smoke and choo-choo unit were installed in the boiler, and a two-position reverse unit was mounted on the rear of the motor.

VG - C6	EX - C7	LN - C8	Scarcity
175	350	700	7

21158: An uncataloged edition of the 0-6-0T Docksider switcher was produced in 1960. It was notable for being blue unpainted plastic. This locomotive had no smoke, choo-choo, headlight nor in most cases a reverse unit.

21158 (Type I): Most locomotives did not have a reverse unit.

VG - C6	EX - C7	LN - C8	Scarcity
40	75	150	4

Values for each condition are in U.S. dollars. | **Scarcity** = Scale from 1-8 with 8 being the hardest to find.

37

21158 (Type II): Several examples of this locomotive have been reported with a two-position reverse unit.

VG - C6	EX - C7	LN - C8	Scarcity
40	75	150	4

21160: This uncataloged 4-4-2 Atlantic is believed to date from 1960. The black-painted plastic boiler was numbered "21160" in white. The locomotive did not have an operating headlight, nor smoke or choo-choo, and had only a manual reverse. The black-painted tender body was decorated with the "Reading Lines" herald and sans-serif "AMERICAN FLYER LINES" lettering. Its trucks had sintered-iron side frames and an operating knuckle coupler at the rear.

21160 (Type I): Some of the locomotives included a metal bell and whistle.

VG - C6	EX - C7	LN - C8	Scarcity
10	20	30	1

21160 (Type II): On others, the bell and whistle were molded integral to the boiler.

VG - C6	EX - C7	LN - C8	Scarcity
10	20	30	1

21161: This 4-4-2 Atlantic, though uncataloged, was produced in 1960. This was a bare-bones loco, having no headlight, smoke, choo-choo or reverse unit. The locomotive was numbered in white "21161," and the same color was used for the tender's "Reading Lines" herald and sans-serif "AMERICAN FLYER LINES" lettering.

21161 (Type I): Some of the locomotives were painted black and the tenders were equipped with an operating knuckle coupler.

VG - C6	EX - C7	LN - C8	Scarcity
10	15	25	1

21161 (Type II):  Otherwise identical locomotives had unpainted black plastic cabs.

VG - C6	EX - C7	LN - C8	Scarcity
10	15	25	1

21161 (Type III): A few of the black-painted locomotives were labeled "PRESTONE CAR CARE EXPRESS" in white. The tenders with this locomotive were equipped with a solid non-operating knuckle coupler.

VG - C6	EX - C7	LN - C8	Scarcity
75	125	275	7

21165: This 4-4-0 American was sold in 1961 and 1962, discontinued, then returned in 1966. The locomotive did not have an operating headlight, smoke or choo-choo, but it did have a two-position reverse unit. The tender had an unpainted plastic body that was decorated with a diamond-shaped "ERIE" logo and "AMERICAN FLYER LINES" lettering, both in white.

21165 (Type I): The tender of the 1961 version had trucks with sintered-iron side frames and an operating knuckle coupler at the rear.

VG - C6	EX - C7	LN - C8	Scarcity
10	15	25	1

21161 (Type II)

21165 (Type II): The 1962 and 1966 versions had Pike Master trucks and coupler.

VG - C6	EX - C7	LN - C8	Scarcity
10	15	25	1

21166: From 1963 through 1965, this unpainted black plastic 4-4-0 American was available. The locomotive did not have an operating headlight, smoke or choo-choo, but it did have a two-position reverse unit. The tender had an unpainted plastic body that was decorated with a "Burlington Route" herald and "AMERICAN FLYER LINES" lettering, both in white. Pike Master trucks and couplers were used on the tender.

21166 (Type I): Most of the tenders were marked with "Burlington Route" in white letters.

VG - C6	EX - C7	LN - C8	Scarcity
10	15	25	1

21166 (Type II): Relatively few tenders were made with the "Burlington Route" herald reverse printed, with a white field contrasting against the unpainted black letters.

VG - C6	EX - C7	LN - C8	Scarcity
85	150	300	6

21168: The only "Casey Jones" style 4-4-0 American to be equipped with smoke and choo-choo is this Southern Railway loco produced from 1961 through 1963. The loco also had an operating headlight. The tender had an unpainted plastic body that was decorated with an "SR - THE SOUTHERN SERVES THE SOUTH" circular herald and "AMERICAN FLYER LINES" lettering, both in white.

21168 (Type I): The tender accompanying the 1961 edition of the locomotive had sintered-iron side frame trucks and an operating knuckle coupler.

VG - C6	EX - C7	LN - C8	Scarcity
30	60	90	4

21168 (Type II): In 1962 and 1963, Pike Master trucks and coupler were installed on the tender.

VG - C6	EX - C7	LN - C8	Scarcity
30	60	90	4

21168 (Type II)

Values for each condition are in U.S. dollars. | **Scarcity** = Scale from 1-8 with 8 being the hardest to find.

39

DIESEL LOCOMOTIVES

American Flyer began producing diesel locomotives in 1950. Mimicking the rivalry that existed in real railroading at that time, Gilbert introduced two styles—one was a replica of the General Motors' Electro-Motive Division GP-7. The other, destined to be a classic both in miniature as well as full size, was American Locomotive Co.'s PA.

These styles were joined in 1956 by a miniature replica of a Baldwin S-12—a unit that did not meet with great success with full-sized railroads. In 1961, the final new S-Gauge Diesel design produced by A.C. Gilbert Co. was introduced. This was a replica of the famed EMD F-9. Unfortunately, the miniature train business was no longer profitable and many corners were cut in the design and production, and the resulting unit never approached the quality of the earlier models.

Sound was included in the diesel units from the inception. Dubbed the Electronic Air-Chime Horn

in 1950, the unit was first installed in PB units. The AMERICAN FLYER ELECTRONIC WHISTLE CONTROL, the heart of which is the RCA 117P7 GT vacuum tube, activated the unit, which was redesigned—and renamed the Nathan Air Chime Whistle in 1951.

In 1955, the sound system changed again, and renamed a horn. Also at this time, Diesel Roar was introduced. This unit consisted of a spring-mounted weight that vibrated due to the magnetic field generated by a coil. This vibration replicated the sound of a diesel engine.

Both the Diesel Roar and the horns were discontinued in 1959, and replaced by a mechanical bell. The limber spring supporting the clapper deflected enough that the bell did not ring at high speeds, but did ring when the train moved slowly. Even this simple noisemaker was dropped after 1961 as Gilbert struggled to cut costs.

362 SANTA FE 360/361 PA/PB (Type III)

234: See 21234.

355 CHICAGO NORTHWESTERN SYSTEM: In 1956 and 1957, American Flyer offered this Baldwin switcher finished in an attractive yellow and green CNW scheme.

355 CHICAGO NORTHWESTERN SYSTEM (Type I): The earliest locomotives, which were painted green, utilized a paper herald.

VG - C6	EX - C7	LN - C8	Scarcity
180	250	400	7

355 CHICAGO NORTHWESTERN SYSTEM (Type II): Later locomotives had an unpainted green plastic body.

VG - C6	EX - C7	LN - C8	Scarcity
70	100	150	3

360: See 362 or 365.

362 SANTA FE 360/361: Modeled on the classic lines of the famed Alco PA and PB passenger units, these locomotives were introduced in 1950. Gilbert's Electronic Air-Chime Horn was housed in the B-unit, which like the A-unit rode on die-cast simulated six-wheel trucks.

362 SANTA FE 360/361 PA/PB (Type I): Strangely, some chrome-plated locomotives with wire handrails were produced without the famed "warbonnet."

VG - C6	EX - C7	LN - C8	Scarcity
Too rarely traded to accurately establish pricing.			

362 SANTA FE 360/361 PA/PB (Type II): The wire handrails were eliminated, but this version still lacked the warbonnet paint scheme.

VG - C6	EX - C7	LN - C8	Scarcity
225	325	450	5

362 SANTA FE 360/361 PA/PB (Type III): Near the end of chrome-plated locomotive production, some of the tarnished chrome bodies were painted with the ATSF warbonnet scheme.

VG - C6	EX - C7	LN - C8	Scarcity
Too rarely traded to accurately establish pricing.			

362 SANTA FE 360/361 PA/PB (Type IV): Ultimately American Flyer abandoned their attempt at chrome-plating these units, and began producing them with bodies painted silver and featuring the warbonnet paint scheme.

VG - C6	EX - C7	LN - C8	Scarcity
150	225	300	4

365 SANTA FE 360/364 PA/PB: The paired A and B Alco units returned in 1951 with a new number, "365," and a new number for the B-unit, "364," which now included an Air-Chime whistle. These numbers were retained through 1952.

365 SANTA FE 360/364 PA/PB (Type I): 📷 Most of the new units were painted in the silver and red warbonnet scheme.

VG - C6	EX - C7	LN - C8	Scarcity
150	200	250	4

365 SANTA FE 360/364 PA/PB (Type II): Some of the B-units were stamped "364" on the doorway.

VG - C6	EX - C7	LN - C8	Scarcity
175	225	275	5

365 SANTA FE 360/364 PA/PB (Type I)

370 GM/AMERICAN FLYER: Diesel road switchers entered the American Flyer line in 1950 with this GP-7 switcher, which were painted in a reasonable facsimile of General Motors' Electro Motive Division's demonstrator paint scheme. Despite the overall realistic appearance of the locomotive, an unusual coupling system was devised in order to be compatible with the link couplers then in use. Rather than a coupler, each end of this locomotive had a wire running between the steps. The link coupler of cars would engage this bar, allowing the locomotive to tow them. The double-worm drive motor powered the two die-cast four-wheel trucks beneath the locomotive, and was controlled by a four-position reverse unit. The catalog number appeared on the illuminated white plastic number boards, which had square corners. The unit remained in the product line through 1953.

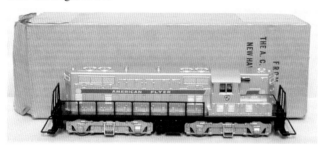

370 GM/AMERICAN FLYER (Type I): Initially the coupler bars were secured to thick tabs on sides of the steps and even the non-powered truck had a die-cast frame.

VG - C6	EX - C7	LN - C8	Scarcity
60	110	170	3

370 GM/AMERICAN FLYER (Type II): Later locomotives featured the coupler bars inserted directly into the vertical members of the steps, and the thick mounting tabs used on previous models were omitted. These locomotives also had dummy trucks with sheet metal frames.

VG - C6	EX - C7	LN - C8	Scarcity
60	110	170	3

370 GM/AMERICAN FLYER (Type III): Because they are so abundant, it is believed that many locomotives were retrofitted with knuckle couplers by the factory in 1953.

VG - C6	EX - C7	LN - C8	Scarcity
60	110	170	3

371 GM/AMERICAN FLYER: The GM demonstrator was updated in 1954. The paint job remained the same, but now the locomotive was equipped with link couplers on each end.

VG - C6	EX - C7	LN - C8	Scarcity
160	220	300	5

372 UNION PACIFIC: A new paint scheme appeared on the GP-7 in 1955, and was used through 1957. The new colors were the classic Union Pacific Armour yellow and harbor mist gray paint scheme. The Union Pacific name and "372" catalog number were stamped in red on the sides of the long hood, while "SERVES ALL THE WEST," the UP slogan at that time, appeared below the cab window. Both the die-cast frame and the die-cast truck side frames were painted harbor mist gray. Knuckle couplers were installed on each end, and the unit had a four-position reverse. Various shades of gray have been reported, with no effect on value or scarcity.

372 UNION PACIFIC (Type I): When first produced, the sides of the short hood were stamped "MADE BY AMERICAN FLYER" in red.

VG - C6	EX - C7	LN - C8	Scarcity
225	300	400	5

372 UNION PACIFIC (Type I)

372 UNION PACIFIC (Type II): Later, and continuing through 1957, the short hood stamping was changed to "BUILT BY GILBERT."

VG - C6	EX - C7	LN - C8	Scarcity
150	225	300	4

374/375 T & P: See 3745.

375 GM/AMERICAN FLYER: This 1953 version of the silver GM demonstrator GP-7 locomotive was equipped with knuckle couplers. This is the scarcest of the three locos to wear the scheme, and is often fraudulently reproduced. The locomotive had a sheet metal frame with die-cast details riveted to it, and die-cast steps screwed to it. The 375 was equipped with an air-chime horn.

VG - C6	EX - C7	LN - C8	Scarcity
500	1,000	1,500	8

377/378 T & P: See 3778.

377 T & P: In 1957, a single powered unit from the 3778 combo was offered as an uncataloged item.

VG - C6	EX - C7	LN - C8	Scarcity
150	125	325	6

405 SILVER STREAK: This chrome-plated Alco PA was sold in 1952. With its solid pilot there was no provision for a front coupler, but at the rear was a link coupler. The locomotive sides and nose were decorated with decals, but the catalog number was nowhere on the unit. Inside was a four-position reversing unit and an air-chime horn. A double worm-drive motor powered one of the silver-painted simulated six-wheel trucks. Much of the value of top-condition locomotives is predicated on having untarnished chrome.

405 SILVER STREAK (Type I): Yellow decals with black lettering.

VG - C6	EX - C7	LN - C8	Scarcity
Too rarely traded to accurately establish pricing.			

Values for each condition are in U.S. dollars. | **Scarcity** = Scale from 1-8 with 8 being the hardest to find.

43

405 SILVER STREAK (Type II): Red decals with white lettering.

VG - C6	EX - C7	LN - C8	Scarcity
100	200	300	6

466 COMET: This 1953-55 Alco PA had blue decorations and thin yellow stripes. One of the simulated six-wheel trucks was powered by a double-worm drive motor, and both trucks had die-cast side frames painted silver. The unit had a four-position reverse and operating headlight.

466 COMET (Type I): The earliest locomotives had a chrome-plated body decorated with decal lettering.

VG - C6	EX - C7	LN - C8	Scarcity
75	150	250	4

466 COMET (Type II): In 1954-55, units had silver-painted bodies, but continued to be decorated with decal lettering.

VG - C6	EX - C7	LN - C8	Scarcity
70	125	225	4

466 COMET (Type III): The final production of these engines had silver-painted bodies with stamped lettering.

VG - C6	EX - C7	LN - C8	Scarcity
100	200	325	7

467 COMET: In 1955, American Flyer cataloged this separate sale Alco PB unit. However, very few were actually produced—perhaps fewer than six. Far more reproduced 467 B-units exist than originals. Hence, extreme caution should be utilized when considering the purchase of such an item.

VG - C6	EX - C7	LN - C8	Scarcity
7,000	8,500	10,000	8

470/471/473 SANTA FE: See 4713.

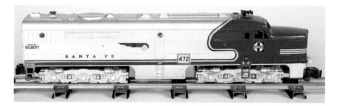

472 SANTA FE: This Santa Fe PA was produced only in 1956, and was included in set 5640TBH. The locomotive was painted in the familiar silver, red, yellow and black warbonnet scheme. It was equipped with knuckle couplers, operating headlight, four-position reverse unit, Pull-Mor traction tires, and a double-worm drive motor powering one truck.

VG - C6	EX - C7	LN - C8	Scarcity
100	200	300	5

474/475 ROCKET: See 4745.

476 ROCKET: Another PB unit cataloged in 1955, but not mass-produced, was this silver and green unit. Like the 467, it is believed that fewer than six of these units were actually produced by American Flyer—but far more have been reproduced. Hence, extreme caution is urged when considering purchasing one of these units. The unit was equipped with Diesel Roar.

VG - C6	EX - C7	LN - C8	Scarcity
Too rarely traded to accurately establish pricing.			

477/478 SILVER FLASH: See 4778.

479 SILVER FLASH: Sold in 1955 only, this silver-painted PA was decorated with brown and orange markings, and sheet metal steps mounted with two drive pins each. One truck was powered by a double-worm drive motor and equipped with Pull-Mor traction tires. Knuckle couplers were installed at both ends.

VG - C6	EX - C7	LN - C8	Scarcity
110	225	350	6

480 SILVER FLASH: 📷 The third PB unit cataloged in 1955 is also the only one produced in any significant quantity, the 480. Its silver-painted body was decorated with wide dark brown and thin orange stripes, and sheet metal steps mounted with two drive pins each. Internally, there was Diesel Roar and a diesel horn. The silver-painted simulated six-wheel trucks were equipped with knuckle couplers. Beware, far more reproductions than originals exist.

VG - C6	EX - C7	LN - C8	Scarcity
1,500	2,200	2,700	8

480 SILVER FLASH

481 SILVER FLASH: In 1956, the Silver Flash PA was revised, and the Diesel Roar and horn were moved from the ill-fated B-unit into the A-unit. The unit continued to be painted silver and decorated with brown and orange markings, and riveted-on sheet metal steps. One truck was powered by a double-worm drive motor and equipped with Pull-Mor traction tires. Knuckle couplers were installed at both ends, and sheet metal steps mounted with two drive pins each.

VG - C6	EX - C7	LN - C8	Scarcity
125	250	375	6

484/485/486 SANTA FE: See 4856.

490/491/493 NORTHERN PACIFIC: See 4913.

490/492 NORTHERN PACIFIC: See 21916.

494/495 NEW HAVEN: See 4945.

497 NEW HAVEN: In 1957, American Flyer produced this primarily black Alco PA, which was decorated in "NEW HAVEN" markings. The number "497" appeared on the sides, and a decaled "NH" on the nose. One of the silver-painted trucks was powered by a double-worm drive motor and equipped with Pull-Mor traction tires. Knuckle couplers were installed at both ends. Two metal steps were installed on each side of the locomotive, but their mounting method varied during the production run.

497 NEW HAVEN (Type I): Each of the steps on the earliest locomotives was mounted with two drive pins each.

VG - C6	EX - C7	LN - C8	Scarcity
115	225	375	5

497 NEW HAVEN (Type II): Later units had only one rivet securing each step.

VG - C6	EX - C7	LN - C8	Scarcity
115	225	375	5

499 NEW HAVEN: See Electric Locomotives section.
812: See 21812.

L-2004 RIO GRANDE: Sold in 1962, this F-9 locomotive had an unpainted red plastic body, which strangely bore the white markings of Rio Grande—a road not noted for using red in their paint schemes. The unit was propelled by a single-worm drive motor, which was controlled by a two-position reverse unit. It rode on four-wheel trucks with black plastic side frames, and the powered truck had Pull-Mor traction tires.

VG - C6	EX - C7	LN - C8	Scarcity
75	150	225	5

Values for each condition are in U.S. dollars. | **Scarcity** = Scale from 1-8 with 8 being the hardest to find.

45

3745 T & P: In 1954-55, this pair of orange and black GP-7 locos was sold. Although the lettering on the long hood read "AMERICAN FLYER LINES," beneath the cab window was a yellow "T & P" diamond-shaped decal. One unit, the 375, was a non-powered dummy, while the 374 had a single-powered truck with a Pull-Mor wheel on each side. Both units were illuminated and equipped with knuckle couplers, and a four-position reverse unit was installed in the power unit.

3745 T & P (Type I): In 1954, the units were built with sheet metal frames.

VG - C6	EX - C7	LN - C8	Scarcity
175	325	475	6

3745 T & P (Type II): Die-cast frames were used in 1955.

VG - C6	EX - C7	LN - C8	Scarcity
150	275	425	6

3778 T & P: In 1956, the numbers of the T & P twin GP-7 units changed. The combo was sold as 3778, and the individual

numbers were now 377 and 378—numbers that were used through 1957. The powered unit was equipped with a four-position reverse unit and a double-worm drive power truck. The dummy unit housed Diesel Roar and a horn. Both units were illuminated and equipped with knuckle couplers.

VG - C6	EX - C7	LN - C8	Scarcity
175	375	575	6

4713 SANTA FE: From 1953 through 1957, the big Alco diesels, wearing the Santa Fe's warbonnet scheme, were offered as a three-unit A-B-A combination. The powered PA unit, the 470, housed a motor for each truck and an operating headlight. The PB unit, the 471, housed an air-chime whistle. While the dummy PA had an operating headlight. Each unit was equipped with operating knuckle couplers. All units rode on simulated trucks with die-cast side frames.

4713 SANTA FE (Type I): The bodies of the units were chrome-plated in 1953. On the nose were "CHIEF" decals. The sides were lettered "AMERICAN FLYER LINES," and no Santa Fe circled cross logos were applied. The locomotive was equipped with a four-position reverse unit, but did not have Diesel Roar. Two drive pins each attached the sheet metal steps.

VG - C6	EX - C7	LN - C8	Scarcity
150	325	500	5

4713 SANTA FE (Type II): The bodies were painted silver in 1954, but the markings and mechanical features remained the same as those of the Type I.

VG - C6	EX - C7	LN - C8	Scarcity
125	300	475	5

4713 SANTA FE (Type III): In 1955, the body continued to be painted silver, but the decoration changed substantially.

The nose decals now read a prototypical "SANTA FE," while "SANTA FE" and "BUILT BY GILBERT" now appeared on the sides of the units. The steps were mounted with two drive pins each, and the Diesel Roar unit was added to the PB unit. This configuration remained the norm into 1957.

VG - C6	EX - C7	LN - C8	Scarcity
125	300	475	5

4713 SANTA FE (Type IV): In 1956, paper stickers with Santa Fe's circled cross logo were applied below the cab windows. The remainder of the markings remained the same as those on the Type III units. At first the metal steps were mounted with two drive pins each.

VG - C6	EX - C7	LN - C8	Scarcity
125	300	475	5

4713 SANTA FE (Type V): In 1957, only a single rivet was used to secure each step. The remainder of the unit was unchanged from Type IV.

VG - C6	EX - C7	LN - C8	Scarcity
125	300	475	5

4745 ROCKET: This double A pair of Alco PA units was sold from 1953 through 1955. The green and yellow trim applied to these units was highlighted with "ROCKET" lettering and a rocket logo, as well as the catalog number and "AMERICAN FLYER LINES" lettering. The powered unit, the 474 housed two motors, each with a Pull-Mor traction tire, and a four-position reverse unit. The dummy unit housed the sound generator, and both units were illuminated and equipped with knuckle couplers.

4745 ROCKET (Type I): In 1953, the locomotive bodies were chrome-plated.

VG - C6	EX - C7	LN - C8	Scarcity
125	225	375	5

4745 ROCKET (Type II): The 1954 and 1955 units were painted silver, and included a diesel horn.

VG - C6	EX - C7	LN - C8	Scarcity
125	225	375	5

4778 SILVER FLASH: This knuckle coupler-equipped PA-PB combination was sold in 1953 and 1954. They were decorated with wide dark brown and thin orange stripes, and sheet metal steps retained by two drive pins each. The silver-painted simulated six-wheel trucks of the powered unit each had their own motor. An air-chime horn or whistle is housed in the 478 PB unit. Knuckle couplers were mounted on each end of both units.

4778 SILVER FLASH (Type I): Units produced in 1953 were chrome-plated.

VG - C6	EX - C7	LN - C8	Scarcity
200	400	675	7

4778 SILVER FLASH (Type II): In 1954, silver paint replaced the chrome plating.

VG - C6	EX - C7	LN - C8	Scarcity
150	300	600	7

4856 SANTA FE: In 1956, American Flyer began offering the PA-PB-PA combination in the blue and yellow freight scheme of the Santa Fe railway. The same units were offered again in 1957, at which time they were often shipped in boxes numbered "21910." The illuminated 484 powered unit had a motor installed for each simulated six-wheel truck. The 485 PB housed an electronic horn and Diesel Roar system. The dummy A—the 486, was illuminated, and like the other two units was equipped with operating knuckle couplers.

Values for each condition are in U.S. dollars. | Scarcity = Scale from 1-8 with 8 being the hardest to find.

47

4856 SANTA FE (Type I): In 1956, two drive pins were used to mount each sheet metal step.

VG - C6	EX - C7	LN - C8	Scarcity
200	475	800	6

4856 SANTA FE (Type II): Sometime in 1957, the steps were reatined by one rivet each.

VG - C6	EX - C7	LN - C8	Scarcity
200	475	800	6

4913 NORTHERN PACIFIC: Sold in 1956, this three-unit PA/PB/PA combination was painted in the attractive two-tone green and white livery of the Northern Pacific. The 490 was equipped with two powered silver-painted simulated six-wheel trucks, with one rubber Pull-Mor wheel on each truck. The locomotive was illuminated and equipped with a four-position reversing unit. The dummy PA, the 493, had an operating headlight as well. The PB unit, numbered "491," had an electronic horn and Diesel Roar. Each unit was equipped with knuckle couplers.

VG-C6	EX-C7	LN-C8	Scarcity
500	950	1,500	7

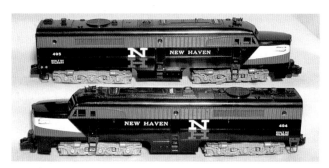

4945 NEW HAVEN: Twin black-painted New Haven PA units were sold in 1956. An orange-painted stripe ran

through the ventilator screens on each side of the unit, as were the catalog numbers and "NEW HAVEN" and "BUILT BY GILBERT" in white. The powered unit, numbered "494," had two power trucks with double-worm drive motors and one Pull-Mor rubber wheel on each. The dummy unit, the 495, had an operating headlight, electronic horn and Diesel Roar. Both units were equipped with knuckle couplers.

VG-C6	EX-C7	LN-C8	Scarcity
200	500	800	7

21205 BOSTON AND MAINE: Debuting in 1961, this unpainted blue F-9 diesel was a new design from Gilbert. The locomotive did not have a conventional frame, rather the truck assemblies snapped into the bodies. A two-position reverse unit controlled the single-worm drive motor. The white lettering on the side of the locomotive included a large "BOSTON AND MAINE" and a small "AMERICAN FLYER LINES." The locomotive did not have a headlight or a front coupler, nor was the pilot open to accept a coupler.

21205 BOSTON AND MAINE (Type I): As initially produced, the molded-in steps underneath the doors had squared lower corners, like actual F-9 units.

VG-C6	EX-C7	LN-C8	Scarcity
75	150	225	5

21205 BOSTON AND MAINE (Type II): Later in the year the steps were reinforced with a tapered filet on the leading edge. Some collectors refer to these as "streamlined" steps.

VG-C6	EX-C7	LN-C8	Scarcity
75	125	200	4

4856 SANTA FE (Type II)

21205/21205-1 BOSTON AND MAINE

21205/21205-1 BOSTON AND MAINE: 📷 A matching dummy unit was produced, which was then paired with the powered F-9A, and the combination included uncataloged Firestone and Jordon Marsh sets in 1961. Both units of the AA combination featured the "streamlined" steps.

VG-C6	EX-C7	LN-C8	Scarcity
100	200	300	6

21206/21206-1 SANTA FE: 📷 This pair of unpainted red F-9 units was included in uncataloged outfits in 1961 and is believed to have been shipped in 1962 as well. The Santa Fe logo, like the rest of the markings, was stamped in white. A single-worm drive power truck with Pull-Mor traction tires was installed in the 21206 unit, and a two-position reverse unit controlled it.

21206/21206-1 SANTA FE (Type I): These units had the reverse unit mounted on the front power truck.

VG-C6	EX-C7	LN-C8	Scarcity
125	200	300	4

21206/21206-1 SANTA FE (Type II): A few locomotives have been reported with both front and rear couplers on the powered as well as the dummy units.

VG-C6	EX-C7	LN-C8	Scarcity
150	225	350	6

21207/21207-1 GREAT NORTHERN: In 1963-64, twin orange F-9s were available. The roofs of the units were painted dark green, and the same color was used for the markings. As with all the F-9 locomotives, the units did not have a conventional frame, rather the truck assemblies snapped into the bodies. A two-position reverse unit controlled the single-worm drive motor.

21207/21207-1 GREAT NORTHERN (Type I): Most of units were produced with unpainted orange bodies and did not have an operating headlight.

VG-C6	EX-C7	LN-C8	Scarcity
100	200	300	3

21207/21207-1 GREAT NORTHERN (Type II): A few of the unpainted orange units were produced with an operating headlight in the powered unit.

VG-C6	EX-C7	LN-C8	Scarcity
150	250	375	7

21207/21207-1 GREAT NORTHERN (Type III): Another scarce variation did not include an operating headlight, but was painted orange, rather than molded orange.

VG-C6	EX-C7	LN-C8	Scarcity
200	300	400	7

21210 BURLINGTON: In 1961, Flyer produced this unpainted red F-9 lettered "BURLINGTON" in white. A silver stripe ran along each side. The interior of the nose of most locomotives was painted black to prevent the headlight from causing it to "glow." A truck powered it with a single-worm drive motor and Pull-Mor traction tires.

21206/21206-1 SANTA FE

Values for each condition are in U.S. dollars. | **Scarcity** = Scale from 1-8 with 8 being the hardest to find.

49

21210 BURLINGTON (Type I): A few examples with squared-off steps have been reported—these were likely sales or engineering samples.

VG-C6	EX-C7	LN-C8	Scarcity
Too rarely traded to accurately establish pricing.			

21210 BURLINGTON (Type II): Production locomotives had "streamlined" steps. All of these had a silver stripe.

VG-C6	EX-C7	LN-C8	Scarcity
75	150	225	4

21215/21215-1 UNION PACIFIC: Shipped in 1961 and 1962, these yellow twin F-9 units bore the red markings of Union Pacific. Red was also used for trim on the locomotives, and the roof was painted gray. On the nose was pasted a red, white and blue Union Pacific logo. A truck provided power with a single-worm drive motor and Pull-Mor traction tires. The steps molded into the body were the "streamlined" type, and operating knuckle couplers were installed at front and rear.

21215/21215-1 UNION PACIFIC (Type I): Yellow-painted gray plastic bodies were used on some units.

VG-C6	EX-C7	LN-C8	Scarcity
100	200	300	5

21215/21215-1 UNION PACIFIC (Type II): Other units were built with unpainted yellow plastic bodies.

VG-C6	EX-C7	LN-C8	Scarcity
100	200	300	5

21215/21215-1 UNION PACIFIC (Type III): Some units have been observed with unpainted gray plastic trucks.

VG-C6	EX-C7	LN-C8	Scarcity
Too rarely traded to accurately establish pricing.			

21215/21216 UNION PACIFIC: An extremely scarce version of the dual Union Pacific F-9 was produced early in 1961. These units, which may be painted yellow, or left as unpainted molded yellow, are numbered "21215" and "21216," rather then the conventional "21215" and "21215-1." The bodies of these units have the square-type steps.

VG-C6	EX-C7	LN-C8	Scarcity
Too rarely traded to accurately establish pricing.			

21234 CHESAPEAKE & OHIO: The GP-7 was sold with a large yellow "CHESAPEAKE & OHIO" name and C & O logo on its blue side from 1959 through 1961. The die-cast frame of the locomotive was painted yellow, and is prone to chipping, leading to many of these components being repainted. Below the cab window only the number "234" appeared. The locomotive was illuminated and equipped with a two-position reverse unit, and a mechanical ringing bell. A double-worm drive motor powered it, and two Pull-Mor traction tires were installed on the truck. Knuckle couplers were installed on both ends of the unit.

21234 CHESAPEAKE & OHIO (Type I): Long steps hung from the ends of the frames in 1959 and 1960.

VG-C6	EX-C7	LN-C8	Scarcity
150	325	550	5

21234 CHESAPEAKE & OHIO (Type II): The steps were shortened in 1961 to better allow the operation of the locomotive on Pike Master track.

VG-C6	EX-C7	LN-C8	Scarcity
175	375	650	7

21551 NORTHERN PACIFIC: This two-tone green and white Northern Pacific Alco PA was produced in 1958. White script lettering with the NP's slogan "Main Street of the Northwest" appeared on each side, along with a printed in "BUILT BY GILBERT" and "21551." The locomotive had one powered truck with a double-worm drive motor, controlled by a two-position reverse unit. An operating headlight and two operating knuckle couplers were installed.

21551 NORTHERN PACIFIC (Type I): The initial production of these locomotives had sheet metal steps held in place by a single rivet. The portholes along the sides of the body were molded open.

VG-C6	EX-C7	LN-C8	Scarcity
175	300	425	5

21551 NORTHERN PACIFIC (Type II): Early in the production run, the body molding was changed. The steps were now molded integral with the body and portholes were molded solid.

VG-C6	EX-C7	LN-C8	Scarcity
150	250	375	5

21552/21556 NORTHERN PACIFIC: In 1957, the twin 490 and 492 twin PA Diesels were sold in boxes stamped "21552" and "21556."

21560 NEW HAVEN: In 1957, the 497 New Haven PAs came in a box marked "21560."

21561 NEW HAVEN: This 1957-58 black-painted PA was decorated in the orange and white markings of the New Haven. The locomotive had a single power truck with a double-worm drive motor. Operating knuckle couplers were installed on both ends of the diesel.

21561 NEW HAVEN (Type I): A few glossy black painted units were produced that had the sheet metal steps held in place with two drive pins each.

VG-C6	EX-C7	LN-C8	Scarcity
Too rarely traded to accurately establish pricing.			

21561 NEW HAVEN (Type II): Sometime in 1957, a single rivet was used to mount the sheet metal steps.

VG-C6	EX-C7	LN-C8	Scarcity
125	225	350	6

21561 NEW HAVEN (Type III): Ultimately, the body molding was changed so that the steps became integral. At the same time the portholes were molded shut.

VG-C6	EX-C7	LN-C8	Scarcity
150	250	400	6

21720 SANTA FE: This uncataloged blue and yellow Santa Fe PB unit was sold in 1958. The metal steps on the unit were held in place with one rivet each, and the locomotive rode on silver-painted simulated six-wheel trucks with knuckle couplers. Inside the dummy unit was filled with electric gear—the electronic horn and Diesel Roar.

VG-C6	EX-C7	LN-C8	Scarcity
500	1,000	1,500	8

21800 CHICAGO NORTHWESTERN SYSTEM: The 355 Baldwin switchers sold in 1957 came in boxes marked "21800."

21801 CHICAGO NORTHWESTERN SYSTEM: The green and yellow Chicago North Western Baldwin switcher returned in 1957 and 1958 with a new number. The CNW logo was paper. A two-position reverse unit controlled the sole power truck. Operating knuckle couplers were installed on both ends of the unit.

21801 CHICAGO NORTHWESTERN SYSTEM (Type I): Some of these units had bodies made of unpainted green plastic.

VG-C6	EX-C7	LN-C8	Scarcity
50	100	175	3

Values for each condition are in U.S. dollars. | Scarcity = Scale from 1-8 with 8 being the hardest to find.

51

21801-1 CHICAGO NORTHWESTERN SYSTEM

21801 CHICAGO NORTHWESTERN SYSTEM (Type II): The bodies of other units were painted green.

VG-C6	EX-C7	LN-C8	Scarcity
75	120	250	5

21801-1 CHICAGO NORTHWESTERN SYSTEM: 📷

In 1958, an uncataloged, unpowered companion to the CNW Baldwin switcher was produced. It was decorated in the same manner as the powered unit.

21801-1 CHICAGO NORTHWESTERN SYSTEM (Type I): Some of these units had bodies made of unpainted green plastic.

VG-C6	EX-C7	LN-C8	Scarcity
75	150	250	3

21801-1 CHICAGO NORTHWESTERN SYSTEM (Type II): The bodies of other units were painted green.

VG-C6	EX-C7	LN-C8	Scarcity
100	200	300	5

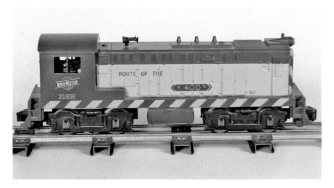

21808 CHICAGO NORTHWESTERN SYSTEM: Green and yellow CNW markings were also used on this uncataloged 1958 Baldwin switcher. The body of this unit was painted, and one power truck with two Pull-Mor wheels was installed. Operating knuckle couplers were mounted on both ends of the locomotive.

VG-C6	EX-C7	LN-C8	Scarcity
50	100	150	4

21812 TEXAS & PACIFIC: This black and orange Baldwin switcher, with black "TEXAS & PACIFIC" lettering was sold in 1959 and 1960. Beneath the cab window was the number "812." The locomotive featured an operating headlight, operating knuckle couplers, a two-position reverse unit and one power truck with two Pull-Mor traction wheels.

21812 TEXAS & PACIFIC (Type I): The earliest versions of the locomotive were painted black and had extended step boards.

VG-C6	EX-C7	LN-C8	Scarcity
75	150	225	4

21812 TEXAS & PACIFIC (Type II): Some of the locomotives with extended step boards were molded in black with only the orange painted on.

VG-C6	EX-C7	LN-C8	Scarcity
75	150	225	4

21812 TEXAS & PACIFIC (Type III): Sometime in 1959, the step boards were shortened.

VG-C6	EX-C7	LN-C8	Scarcity
75	125	200	4

21813 M. St. L.: This uncataloged, unpainted red plastic Baldwin switcher, decorated with white "M. St. L." and "PEORIA GATEWAY" markings, was sold in 1958 and again in 1960. The unit did not have an operating headlight, but it did have operating knuckle couplers on each end.

21813 M. St. L. (Type I): The 1958 version of the locomotive can be distinguished by its unpainted aluminum frame and extended step boards of the body.

VG-C6	EX-C7	LN-C8	Scarcity
200	325	600	7

21813 M. St. L. (Type II): The frames of the 1960 editions were painted black, and the body molding did not have extended step boards.

VG-C6	EX-C7	LN-C8	Scarcity
200	325	600	7

21820 UNION PACIFIC: In 1957, some of the "BUILT BY GILBERT" version of the 372 UP GP-7 came packaged in a box numbered "21820."

21821 UNION PACIFIC: In 1957, some of the "BUILT BY GILBERT" versions of the 372 UP GP-7 came packaged in a box numbered "21821."

21831 TEXAS & PACIFIC: In 1958, Flyer offered the GP-7 road switcher in a distinctive black and orange scheme. The unit had a black-painted die-cast frame, operating headlight, and a two-position reverse unit controlling its double-worm drive motor. Operating couplers were on each end of the locomotive.

21831 TEXAS & PACIFIC (Type I): The long hood of most units was lettered "AMERICAN FLYER LINES."

VG-C6	EX-C7	LN-C8	Scarcity
150	275	450	6

21831 TEXAS & PACIFIC (Type II): Some of the units were "TEXAS & PACIFIC" along the long hood in thin sans serif characters.

VG-C6	EX-C7	LN-C8	Scarcity
200	400	750	7

21831 TEXAS & PACIFIC (Type III): Thick sans serif "TEXAS & PACIFIC" lettering was used on other units.

VG-C6	EX-C7	LN-C8	Scarcity
200	400	750	4

21910/21910-1/21910-2 SANTA FE: American Flyer painted their big three-unit Alco PA-PB-PA combination in blue and yellow Santa Fe freight colors in 1957 and 1958. The non-powered PB unit, 21910-1, was equipped with electronic horn and Diesel Roar. The 21910 powered PA featured two double-worm drive motors and operating headlight, while the 21910-2 dummy unit had an operating headlight only. All three units were equipped with operating knuckle couplers.

VG-C6	EX-C7	LN-C8	Scarcity
500	950	1,200	7

The 21916 was made with single and double rivet steps.

21916 NORTHERN PACIFIC: Numbered 490 and 492, this two-unit Northern Pacific PA set was produced in 1957. It was painted in two-tone green with a white stripe, and the units carried the "Main Street of the Northwest" slogan on their sides in script. The 490 was powered by double-worm drive motors driving each simulated six-wheel truck, and featured an operating headlight. The 492 housed an operating headlight, electronic horn and Diesel Roar. Both units were equipped with knuckle couplers.

21916 NORTHERN PACIFIC (Type I): When initially produced, each sheet metal step was held in place by two rivets.

VG-C6	EX-C7	LN-C8	Scarcity
225	450	775	7

21916 NORTHERN PACIFIC (Type II): Later production units secured the steps with a single rivet in each.

VG-C6	EX-C7	LN-C8	Scarcity
225	450	775	7

Values for each condition are in U.S. dollars. | Scarcity = Scale from 1-8 with 8 being the hardest to find.

21918/21918-1 SEABOARD: These twin black and red Baldwin switchers were produced in 1958. Extensive decoration was a hallmark of these locos, with the black and red color scheme being highlighted by yellow safety stripes, white lettering and Seaboard logo. Both units had operating headlights and knuckle couplers.

VG-C6	EX-C7	LN-C8	Scarcity
325	500	850	7

21920/21920-1 MISSOURI PACIFIC: The blue, silver and yellow colors of Missouri Pacific decorated these 1958 Alco PA units. The powered unit featured two powered trucks, each with double-worm drive and Pull-Mor tires. The non-powered unit had an electronic horn, but no Diesel Roar. Both units had operating headlights and knuckle couplers. Black sheet metal steps, each held in place with a single rivet, trimmed the units.

VG-C6	EX-C7	LN-C8	Scarcity
350	800	1,200	8

21920 MISSOURI PACIFIC: The 21920 number was revived as a single PA unit in 1963-64. However, the returning number had only one power truck with double-worm drive, and rather than sheet metal steps, molded integral steps were part of the body.

VG-C6	EX-C7	LN-C8	Scarcity
200	450	750	8

21922/21922-1 MISSOURI PACIFIC: In 1959 and 1960, the twin MoPac PA units were numbered "21922" and "21922-1." The powered unit had two power trucks with double-worm drive motors with Pull-Mor traction tires and an operating headlight. The dummy unit had an operating headlight and automatic ringing bell. Both units had operating knuckle couplers.

21922/21922-1 MISSOURI PACIFIC (Type I): A few examples have been reported with sheet metal steps secured by one rivet each on the powered units.

VG-C6	EX-C7	LN-C8	Scarcity
Too rarely traded to accurately establish pricing.			

21922/21922-1 MISSOURI PACIFIC (Type II): Most units have their steps molded integral to the body.

VG-C6	EX-C7	LN-C8	Scarcity
300	600	1,000	7

21925/21925-1 UNION PACIFIC: These Armour Yellow and harbor mist gray twin PA units were sold in 1959 and 1960. The markings were applied in red, and the die-cast side frames of the simulated six-wheel trucks were painted gray. The powered unit had two power trucks with double-worm drive motors with Pull-Mor traction tires and an operating headlight. The dummy unit had an operating headlight and automatic ringing bell. Both units had operating knuckle couplers.

VG-C6	EX-C7	LN-C8	Scarcity
400	700	1,100	7

21927 SANTA FE: The familiar red and silver warbonnet paint scheme of the Santa Fe was splashed across this 1960-62 PA unit. Only one truck was powered by a double-worm drive motor and equipped with two Pull-Mor rubber tires. A two-position reverse unit controlled the motor.

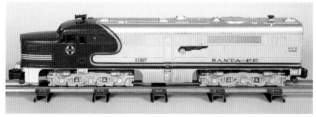

21927 SANTA FE (Type I): The units produced in 1960 had knuckle couplers mounted at the front and rear.

VG-C6	EX-C7	LN-C8	Scarcity
125	200	325	6

21927 SANTA FE (Type II): In 1961 and 1962, the front coupler was eliminated to aid in tracking.

VG-C6	EX-C7	LN-C8	Scarcity
125	200	325	6

ELECTRIC LOCOMOTIVES

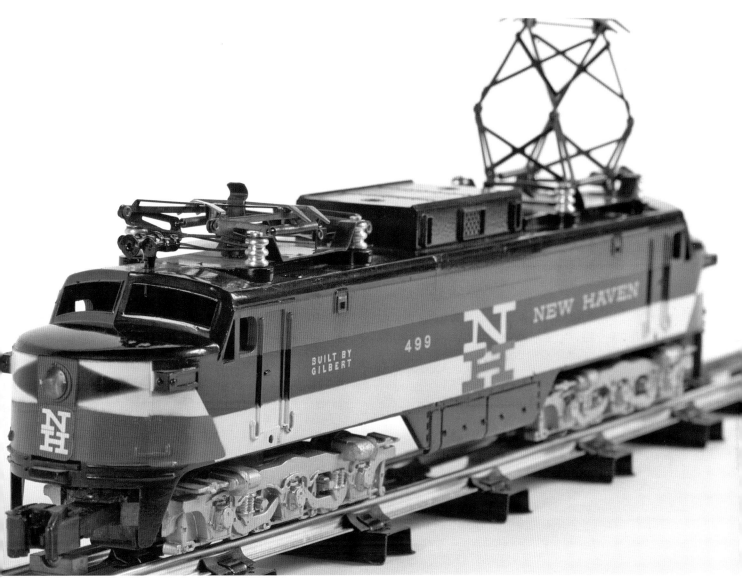

In contrast to American Flyer rival Lionel, or even Flyer's own prewar offerings, the selection of S-Gauge electric locomotives can be described as "limited." While cataloged with two different model numbers, in fact the sole electric locomotive Flyer chose to replicate was the New Haven's General Electric EP-5 rectifier.

Some enthusiasts refer to the EP-5 as a "rectifier" because the actual locomotive had DC motors that were fed current from an AC overhead wire. In order for the motors to use this current, it had to be converted to DC by huge rectifiers inside the locomotive. However, to New Haven buffs, the EP-5 was known as the "Jet"—so named

because of the sound made by the huge blowers on each end that cooled the electrical apparatus of the locomotive. Rated at 4,000 horsepower, the jets could quickly accelerate heavy passenger trains to 105 mph.

American Flyer chose to use the same six-wheel trucks with knuckle couplers on its EP-5 that had been placed at the front of the firm's Alco PA diesel models. These trucks were similar to the trucks used by the big GEs. An operating headlight was placed in each end of the locomotive. Like the real locomotive, Flyer's EP-5 was painted in the distinctive black, white and orange block scheme favored by NH President Patrick McGinnis.

Values for each condition are in U.S. dollars. | **Scarcity** = Scale from 1-8 with 8 being the hardest to find.

55

499 NEW HAVEN: American Flyer introduced its replica of the EP-5 in 1956, one year after the actual locomotive debuted. It was initially assigned catalog number "499," the number it retained into 1957. The cab of the locomotive was molded of black plastic, which was then painted with the distinctive black, orange and white "McGinnis" paint scheme, including the stacked "NH" logo. The sides of the locomotive were also marked with white "BUILT BY GILBERT" and "499" markings, as well as the full "NEW HAVEN" name. At the top of the model were two operating pantographs, and a black plastic horn was installed above both cabs. An electronic whistle was mounted inside, as was a four-position reverse unit and a single motor.

Prototype locomotives are operated with only one pantograph—the rear one—raised. In the event that the pantograph is damaged, it is lowered, and the front one raised. This prevents any debris from a damaged pantograph from being dragged backwards and fouling the second pantograph.

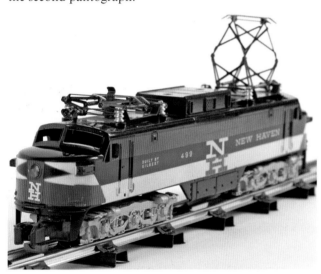

499 NEW HAVEN (Type I): Some of the EP-5 locomotives were built with silver-painted trucks, and empty step rivet-sized holes were below the cab doors on one side of the body.

VG-C6	EX-C7	LN-C8	Scarcity
150	250	500	6

499 NEW HAVEN (Type II): Other models continued to have silver-painted trucks, but no rivet holes were found in the body.

VG-C6	EX-C7	LN-C8	Scarcity
140	225	450	5

21570 NEW HAVEN: In 1957, some of the 499 locomotives came in a box marked "21570."

21571 NEW HAVEN: Other 499 locomotives packed in 1957 were placed in boxes marked "21571."

21573 NEW HAVEN: In 1958, the New Haven EP-5 returned with a new five-digit number, brought about by Gilbert's use of IBM machines for inventory control and sales. The locomotive, with its new number, remained in the catalog through 1959.

While the 21573 looked essentially identical to the 499, internally there were some changes. The new model lacked the operating whistle, and some locomotives have been reported with only two-position reversing units.

21573 NEW HAVEN (Type I): In 1958, the 21573 was included in a freight outfit and its black was glossy.

VG-C6	EX-C7	LN-C8	Scarcity
150	325	475	5

21573 NEW HAVEN (Type II): In 1959, the EP-5 headed a passenger train, and strangely matte black paint was used.

VG-C6	EX-C7	LN-C8	Scarcity
150	350	500	6

MOTORIZED UNITS

740 AMERICAN FLYER LINES (Type III)

Unlike archrival Lionel, who produced a wide variety of small-motorized gang cars, diminutive locomotives and handcars, American Flyer produced a relatively narrow range of such units.

740 AMERICAN FLYER LINES: Sold from 1952 through 1954, this orange-painted handcar was crewed by two rubber men, who pumped furiously on a black sheet metal bar. Painted details enhanced the realism of the crewmen. Despite their efforts, the car was actually propelled by a worm-drive motor driving one axle. The chassis of the car was die-cast. The catalog number did not appear on the car.

However, those items that did leave New Haven were top quality and continue to amuse collectors and operators alike.

740 AMERICAN FLYER LINES (Type I): The earliest of the handcars were marked with black "AMERICAN FLYER LINES" lettering, but had no decals or motor vent holes.

VG-C6	EX-C7	LN-C8	Scarcity
50	80	125	6

740 AMERICAN FLYER LINES (Type II): Later in 1952, a multicolor decal was used on the handcar, which enhanced the appearance of the car substantially. A pair of translucent red lanterns was added to the car, one on each end platform. There were not yet vent holes in the motor housing.

VG-C6	EX-C7	LN-C8	Scarcity
30	50	80	4

740 AMERICAN FLYER LINES (Type III): 📷 Vent holes were provided for the motor. They were located in the raised portion of the housing that supported the pump bar. These cars utilized the multicolor decal and translucent lanterns.

VG-C6	EX-C7	LN-C8	Scarcity
30	50	80	4

740 AMERICAN FLYER LINES (Type IV): 📷 Some of the cars, known as the 740A, were equipped with a drawbar. These handcars were supplied as components of outfit 5300T, the mine train. Price here for handcar only.

VG-C6	EX-C7	LN-C8	Scarcity
50	80	125	6

The earliest of the cars, with or without the decals, did not have vent holes in the bar support.

Values for each condition are in U.S. dollars. | **Scarcity** = Scale from 1-8 with 8 being the hardest to find.

741 HANDCAR AND SHED: In 1953-54, the ventilated 740 handcar was combined with a tool shed. The tool shed had a gray sheet metal base, white metal sides and red plastic roof.

VG-C6	EX-C7	LN-C8	Scarcity
100	150	225	6

742 AMERICAN FLYER LINES: A reversing mechanism was added to the handcar in 1955 and the feature continued to be used in 1956 as well. Though the orange car still was not marked with the catalog number, the 742 can be distinguished from the 740 by the movable black metal rod extending under the end of the platform. When the rod strikes an object, the car reverses direction.

742 AMERICAN FLYER LINES (Type I): The early cars utilized the same multicolor decal with "wings" as was used on the 740.

VG-C6	EX-C7	LN-C8	Scarcity
60	100	150	6

742 AMERICAN FLYER LINES (Type II): The decals on later cars lacked the red, white and blue striped "wings."

VG-C6	EX-C7	LN-C8	Scarcity
60	100	150	6

742 AMERICAN FLYER LINES (Type III): Examples of the reversing handcar have been reported that have the die-cast chassis with the drawbar cutout.

VG-C6	EX-C7	LN-C8	Scarcity
60	100	150	6

743 TRACK MAINTENANCE CAR: Rare examples of the 23743 have been found which are marked only "743." These were packed in Kleer-Pak boxes numbered "23743."

VG-C6	EX-C7	LN-C8	Scarcity
Too rarely traded to accurately establish pricing.			

23743 TRACK MAINTENANCE CAR: Handcars became obsolete on real railroads and were replaced by motorcars. Perhaps it was images of such motor cars that American Flyer hoped to evoke with the 1960 introduction of this item. The 23743, which remained in the line through 1964, had an unpainted yellow plastic body with black markings. A small Japanese-made motor rated at a maximum of nine volts powered the car, which came in a Kleer-Pak box.

VG-C6	EX-C7	LN-C8	Scarcity
60	100	150	6

25516 ROCKET SLED: Evidence suggests that a few examples of the rocket sled, which was developed as a component of the 25515 U.S.A.F. flatcar, were sold separately. The mechanism of the sled was similar to that of the 23743 as well as the Gilbert slot cars.

VG-C6	EX-C7	LN-C8	Scarcity
Too rarely traded to accurately establish pricing.			

740 AMERICAN FLYER LINES (Type IV)

CABOOSES

Naturally every freight set produced by American Flyer included a caboose—and additional cabooses were produced for separate sale. Hence, it is not surprising that while cabooses exist in many numbers, styles and variations, only a handful of these can be considered collectable.

The most desirable of these cars' styles as a whole are the ones introduced in 1957, which featured the bizarre combination of bay windows and offset cupola. These cars were produced in both operating (with moving brakemen) and non-operating versions. Flyer had introduced the operating mechanism in 1955 as part of the 977 center-cupola caboose.

With thousands of cabooses being produced annually, they were a natural for cost savings as the toy train market lost profitability. Various details—brakewheels, window glazing and smokejacks were phased out in later years.

Values for each condition are in U.S. dollars. | **Scarcity** = Scale from 1-8 with 8 being the hardest to find.

59

FREIGHT AHEAD: This unpainted red caboose had a snap-in sheet metal frame and was equipped with Pike Master trucks and couplers. It was not lighted, nor did it have a smokejack or brakewheels. The white markings on its side read "FREIGHT AHEAD" and included the "GAME TRAIN" logo. It was produced in 1963.

VG-C6	EX-C7	LN-C8	Scarcity
4	8	12	2

607 AMERICAN FLYER LINES: Based on a flatcar, this 1953 car was equipped as a boom tender or work caboose, with a small cabin on one end. The car was equipped with link couplers.

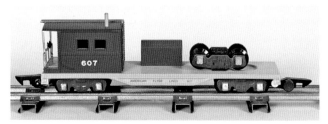

607 AMERICAN FLYER LINES (Type I): Some of the cars were painted gray and had a sheet metal truck mounted on its deck.

VG-C6	EX-C7	LN-C8	Scarcity
20	40	60	4

607 AMERICAN FLYER LINES (Type II): Painted gray, but had a truck with sintered-iron side frames riveted to the deck.

VG-C6	EX-C7	LN-C8	Scarcity
20	40	60	4

607 AMERICAN FLYER LINES (Type III): Some of the cars had a black-painted sheet metal base.

VG-C6	EX-C7	LN-C8	Scarcity
Too rarely traded to accurately establish pricing.			

630 READING: In production from 1946 through 1952, the 630 Reading caboose exists in many variations. The car was equipped with sheet metal trucks and link couplers, and had a solid metal smokejack.

630 READING (Type I): In 1946, cabooses were built with red plastic frames and bodies, which were decorated with silver lettering. The car had link couplers and was not illuminated.

VG-C6	EX-C7	LN-C8	Scarcity
8	15	25	4

630 READING (Type II): Other cars featured white lettering and were illuminated, but retained the unpainted red plastic frame and body.

VG-C6	EX-C7	LN-C8	Scarcity
8	15	25	4

630 READING (Type III): More common were black plastic frames beneath unpainted red caboose bodies stamped with silver lettering.

VG-C6	EX-C7	LN-C8	Scarcity
8	15	25	4

630 READING (Type IV): White lettering was found on some of the cars with black plastic frames.

VG-C6	EX-C7	LN-C8	Scarcity
8	15	25	4

630 READING (Type V): No doubt to combat the warpage problems prevalent in Flyer's early use of plastics, the caboose frame was changed to die-cast in late 1946 or early 1947. This version was available through 1948 and again in 1950. Like the plastic frame, the die-cast frame included molded toolboxes. The unpainted red body was stamped with white lettering. The caboose continued to use link couplers and sheet metal trucks, but was not illuminated.

VG-C6	EX-C7	LN-C8	Scarcity
5	10	15	1

630 READING (Type VI): This car essentially duplicated the Type V, but for the addition of interior illumination.

VG-C6	EX-C7	LN-C8	Scarcity
5	10	15	1

630 READING (Type VII): A sheet metal frame was used in 1950. Some of these cars continued to have unpainted red plastic bodies with white lettering. The stamped frame did not include simulated toolboxes.

VG-C6	EX-C7	LN-C8	Scarcity
5	10	15	1

630 READING (Type VIII): Some cars, which were otherwise identical to the Type VII, had bodies painted red.

VG-C6	EX-C7	LN-C8	Scarcity
5	10	15	1

630 AMERICAN FLYER: In 1952, the number "630" returned. However rather than Reading, the red-painted caboose was marked "AMERICAN FLYER" in white. The car was illuminated, and was equipped with link couplers.

VG-C6	EX-C7	LN-C8	Scarcity
30	60	90	6

630 AMERICAN FLYER LINES: In 1953, the white-lettered name on the side of the caboose was appended to include "LINES." The car body was painted red and mounted on a sheet metal frame. The car was equipped with link couplers and interior illumination.

VG-C6	EX-C7	LN-C8	Scarcity
15	30	50	5

630 AMERICAN FLYER LINES (Type I): The markings on some of these cars included reporting marks in the lower left corner. Among those markings was a built date.

VG-C6	EX-C7	LN-C8	Scarcity
15	30	50	5

630 AMERICAN FLYER LINES (Type II): The markings of other cabooses omitted these reporting marks.

VG-C6	EX-C7	LN-C8	Scarcity
15	30	50	5

638 AMERICAN FLYER: First offered in 1949, this red caboose remained in the product line through 1952. The car lacked interior illumination, and rode on sheet metal trucks with link couplers. Both painted and unpainted versions were produced, with no difference in value or desirability in today's market.

VG-C6	EX-C7	LN-C8	Scarcity
3	5	10	1

638 AMERICAN FLYER LINES: Like the 630, the name printed on the side of the 1953 638 included the word "LINES." The car lacked interior illumination and rode on sheet metal trucks with link couplers.

638 AMERICAN FLYER LINES (Type I): Some of these cars were produced with painted-red bodies and white lettering.

VG-C6	EX-C7	LN-C8	Scarcity
5	10	15	2

638 AMERICAN FLYER LINES (Type II): Other painted red cars had silver lettering.

VG-C6	EX-C7	LN-C8	Scarcity
5	10	15	2

638 AMERICAN FLYER LINES (Type III): Silver lettering was also used on cars with unpainted red bodies.

VG-C6	EX-C7	LN-C8	Scarcity
5	10	15	2

638 AMERICAN FLYER LINES (Type IV): Other cars with unpainted red plastic bodies had white lettering.

VG-C6	EX-C7	LN-C8	Scarcity
5	10	15	2

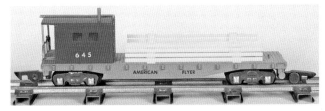

645 AMERICAN FLYER: This gray-painted die-cast-based work car was produced in 1950. The car had black

Values for each condition are in U.S. dollars. | **Scarcity** = Scale from 1-8 with 8 being the hardest to find.

61

"AMERICAN FLYER" lettering and an unpainted red plastic shed, and was equipped with link couplers. The car had yellow fences but no toolbox. Note: reproduction fence sections are available.

VG-C6	EX-C7	LN-C8	Scarcity
25	50	75	5

645A AMERICAN FLYER or AMERICAN FLYER LINES: In 1951, this car was introduced as a successor to the 645. It remained in the product line through 1953. Like the 645 it was based on a die-cast flatcar chassis painted gray. The car had link couplers, and a toolbox was added to the non-cabin end. Note: reproduction fence sections are available.

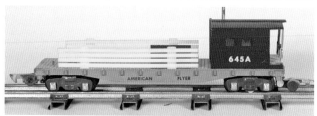

645A AMERICAN FLYER (Type I): Some of the cars had cabins painted red and the gray chassis stamped "AMERICAN FLYER." Yellow fences were used.

VG-C6	EX-C7	LN-C8	Scarcity
25	50	75	4

645A AMERICAN FLYER (Type II): Other cars were identical to the Type I cars, but the structure and fences were painted Tuscan.

VG-C6	EX-C7	LN-C8	Scarcity
20	40	60	3

645A AMERICAN FLYER LINES (Type III): The chassis of later cars were lettered "AMERICAN FLYER LINES." Some of these cars had Tuscan-painted cabins and yellow fences.

VG-C6	EX-C7	LN-C8	Scarcity
20	40	60	3

645A AMERICAN FLYER LINES (Type IV): Other cars were identical to the Type III, but utilized Tuscan fences.

VG-C6	EX-C7	LN-C8	Scarcity
20	40	60	3

645A AMERICAN FLYER LINES (Type V): Another variation had a Tuscan cabin and fences, but was based on a chassis painted blue gray.

VG-C6	EX-C7	LN-C8	Scarcity
30	60	90	5

806 AMERICAN FLYER LINES: From 1956 and into 1957, this unpainted red plastic caboose was part of the American Flyer product line. The caboose, which had neither illumination nor smokejack, rode on trucks with sintered-iron side frames and knuckle couplers.

VG-C6	EX-C7	LN-C8	Scarcity
5	10	15	2

904 AMERICAN FLYER LINES: Cataloged in 1956, this non-illuminated bore white "AMERICAN FLYER LINES" lettering on its painted-red body. The car had a sheet metal frame and trucks with sintered-iron side frames. A metal smokejack was mounted on the roof.

904 AMERICAN FLYER LINES (Type I): Some of the cars had solid knuckle couplers.

VG-C6	EX-C7	LN-C8	Scarcity
10	20	35	5

904 AMERICAN FLYER LINES (Type II): Other cars were equipped with operating knuckle couplers.

VG-C6	EX-C7	LN-C8	Scarcity
10	20	35	5

907 AMERICAN FLYER LINES: This 1954 car had a gray-painted sheet metal chassis lettered "AMERICAN

FLYER LINES 907." The cabin mounted on the car was painted Tuscan, and a red toolbox was mounted on the deck along with a truck with sintered-iron side frames.

VG-C6	EX-C7	LN-C8	Scarcity
20	40	60	3

930 AMERICAN FLYER: Produced in 1952, this illuminated caboose rode on trucks with sintered-iron side frames and operating knuckle couplers.

930 AMERICAN FLYER (Type I): Some of the cars were painted Tuscan.

VG-C6	EX-C7	LN-C8	Scarcity
50	100	150	6

930 AMERICAN FLYER (Type II): Other cars had red-painted bodies.

VG-C6	EX-C7	LN-C8	Scarcity
20	40	60	5

930 AMERICAN FLYER LINES: From 1953 through 1957, this Tuscan-painted caboose with white "AMERICAN FLYER LINES" lettering was available. The illuminated caboose was equipped with operating knuckle couplers and trucks with sintered-iron side frames.

930 AMERICAN FLYER LINES (Type I): As described above.

VG-C6	EX-C7	LN-C8	Scarcity
10	15	30	3

930 AMERICAN FLYER LINES (Type II): Some cars came with a label on the underside, which read "TO

CHANGE LAMP REMOVE SCREW FROM END OF BODY." The box for this car was numbered "24608."

VG-C6	EX-C7	LN-C8	Scarcity
75	150	250	7

934 AMERICAN FLYER LINES: Though not shown in the catalog, this red caboose was manufactured in 1955. The white lettering on the side of this non-illuminated caboose read "AMERICAN FLYER LINES." The car had a sheet metal frame, sintered-iron side frames on trucks and knuckle couplers.

934 AMERICAN FLYER LINES (Type I): Some of these cabooses had steps that were noticeably narrower than those of others.

VG-C6	EX-C7	LN-C8	Scarcity
20	40	60	5

934 AMERICAN FLYER LINES (Type II): Some of these cabooses had steps that were noticeably wider than others.

VG-C6	EX-C7	LN-C8	Scarcity
20	40	60	5

935 AMERICAN FLYER LINES: In 1957, this Tuscan-painted illuminated bay window caboose with yellow lettering was produced. The car had a plastic smokejack, sheet metal handrails and frame. Trucks with sintered-iron side frames and knuckle couplers.

VG-C6	EX-C7	LN-C8	Scarcity
30	60	90	5

CABOOSES

Values for each condition are in U.S. dollars. | **Scarcity** = Scale from 1-8 with 8 being the hardest to find.

63

938 AMERICAN FLYER LINES: This 1954-55 caboose was painted red and equipped with knuckle couplers and trucks with sintered-iron side frames. Its frame was sheet metal and a solid-metal smokejack was mounted on the roof.

VG-C6	EX-C7	LN-C8	Scarcity
5	10	15	1

945 AMERICAN FLYER LINES: This knuckle coupler-equipped work caboose was sold from 1952 through 1957. The chassis of the car was painted gray and lettered "AMERICAN FLYER LINES." The number "945" was stamped in white on the sides of the cabin, which was painted Tuscan.

945 AMERICAN FLYER (Type I): In 1952, the gray-painted die-cast chassis was lettered "AMERICAN FLYER" and the red toolbox was made of wood.

VG-C6	EX-C7	LN-C8	Scarcity
35	70	110	6

945 AMERICAN FLYER LINES (Type II): Very soon the lettering on the cars began to read "AMERICAN FLYER LINES." On some of these cars, the steps were removed from before assembly.

VG-C6	EX-C7	LN-C8	Scarcity
15	30	50	4

945 AMERICAN FLYER LINES (Type III): Plastic toolboxes—painted Tuscan—ultimately replaced the wooden ones.

VG-C6	EX-C7	LN-C8	Scarcity
15	30	50	4

945 AMERICAN FLYER LINES (Type IV): Unpainted red plastic toolboxes were used on some cars.

VG-C6	EX-C7	LN-C8	Scarcity
15	30	50	4

945 AMERICAN FLYER LINES (Type V): The die-cast chassis of some cars was painted blue-gray rather than simple gray on some of the cars sold in 1953-54.

VG-C6	EX-C7	LN-C8	Scarcity
25	45	65	5

945 AMERICAN FLYER LINES (Type VI): In 1957, the chassis of the cars were made of injection-molded plastic, which was painted gray. Some of these cars had red-painted plastic toolboxes.

VG-C6	EX-C7	LN-C8	Scarcity
15	30	50	4

945 AMERICAN FLYER LINES (Type VII): Other cars built with gray-painted plastic chassis had yellow-painted toolboxes.

VG-C6	EX-C7	LN-C8	Scarcity
15	30	50	4

977 AMERICAN FLYER LINES: Introduced in 1955, this operating caboose was part of the product line through 1957. The body was painted Tuscan and was lettered in white. The car had a sheet metal frame and sintered-iron truck side frames. Illumination and operating knuckle couplers were provided. A figure on the rear platform moved.

977 AMERICAN FLYER LINES (Type I): In 1955, the brakeman figure was a painted metal silhouette.

VG-C6	EX-C7	LN-C8	Scarcity
20	40	60	4

977 AMERICAN FLYER LINES (Type II): Some of these figures had painted-on facial details.

VG-C6	EX-C7	LN-C8	Scarcity
20	40	60	4

977 AMERICAN FLYER LINES (Type III): Beginning in 1956, the brakeman figure was molded rubber.

VG-C6	EX-C7	LN-C8	Scarcity
25	50	75	5

979 AMERICAN FLYER LINES: 📷 This Tuscan-painted bay window-equipped operating caboose was sold in 1957. On the rear platform was a moveable rubber man on a moving label.

VG-C6	EX-C7	LN-C8	Scarcity
50	100	150	6

979 AMERICAN FLYER LINES

24546 AMERICAN FLYER LINES: Introduced in 1958, this flatcar-based work caboose remained in the product line through 1964. On the gray plastic chassis was mounted a Tuscan-painted cabin and a Tuscan-painted plastic toolbox. The fences on this car were striped yellow and Tuscan. On the cabin the number "24546" was stamped in white, while the chassis was stamped "AMERICAN FLYER LINES" in black.

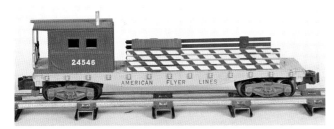

24546 AMERICAN FLYER LINES (Type I): Some of the cars were fitted with trucks with sintered-iron side frames and knuckle couplers.

VG-C6	EX-C7	LN-C8	Scarcity
15	30	45	3

24546 AMERICAN FLYER LINES (Type II): Otherwise identical cars were produced with Pike Master trucks and couplers.

VG-C6	EX-C7	LN-C8	Scarcity
15	30	45	3

24603 AMERICAN FLYER LINES: This red plastic caboose was shipped in 1957 and 1958. It was not illuminated, and had no smokejack or window coverings.

24603 AMERICAN FLYER LINES (Type I): Unpainted red plastic formed the body of this car, which had non-operating couplers.

VG-C6	EX-C7	LN-C8	Scarcity
5	10	15	1

24603 AMERICAN FLYER LINES (Type II): Some of the cars with unpainted red bodies had operating couplers.

VG-C6	EX-C7	LN-C8	Scarcity
5	10	15	1

24603 AMERICAN FLYER LINES (Type III): A few cars were produced with red-painted bodies.

VG-C6	EX-C7	LN-C8	Scarcity
200	350	500	8

24608 AMERICAN FLYER LINES: In 1957, the 930 with the "TO CHANGE LAMP REMOVE SCREW FROM END OF BODY" label came packed in a box numbered "24608."

Values for each condition are in U.S. dollars. | Scarcity = Scale from 1-8 with 8 being the hardest to find.

65

24610 AMERICAN FLYER LINES: Though uncataloged, this unpainted red plastic caboose was shipped from 1958 through 1960. The cars came with sheet metal frames and trucks with sintered-iron side frames, but were not illuminated and did not have smokejacks.

24610 AMERICAN FLYER LINES (Type I): Some of these cars were produced with non-operating knuckle couplers.

VG-C6	EX-C7	LN-C8	Scarcity
3	6	10	1

24610 AMERICAN FLYER LINES (Type II): Another version of the 24610 came with operating knuckle couplers.

VG-C6	EX-C7	LN-C8	Scarcity
3	6	10	1

24618 AMERICAN FLYER LINES: In 1957, the 935 was shipped in a box numbered "24618."

24619 AMERICAN FLYER LINES: In 1958, this Tuscan-painted bay window caboose was available. The car had a sheet metal frame, knuckle couplers and trucks with a sintered-iron side frames. It was decorated with a black plastic smokejack, three red lanterns, brakewheels and roof top ladders.

VG-C6	EX-C7	LN-C8	Scarcity
50	100	150	6

24626 AMERICAN FLYER LINES: In 1958, this yellow-painted caboose left the factory. The roof of the car was painted silver, as were the cupola ends and roof. The car was not illuminated, and rode on trucks with sintered-iron side frames and knuckle couplers.

VG-C6	EX-C7	LN-C8	Scarcity
15	30	45	4

24627 AMERICAN FLYER LINES: This red caboose was made in 1959 and 1960. It was marked with white "AMERICAN FLYER LINES" lettering. The car was not illuminated and had only one coupler, which was an operating knuckle-type. The trucks had sintered-iron side frames.

24627 AMERICAN FLYER LINES (Type I): Some of the cars had unpainted red plastic bodies.

VG-C6	EX-C7	LN-C8	Scarcity
3	5	10	1

24627 AMERICAN FLYER LINES (Type II): The bodies of other cars were painted red.

VG-C6	EX-C7	LN-C8	Scarcity
3	5	10	1

24630 AMERICAN FLYER LINES: Although not cataloged, this unpainted red center cupola caboose was shipped from 1959 through 1961. The car had no lighting, no smokejack, no brakewheels, no window glazing, and a coupler on only one end.

24630 AMERICAN FLYER LINES (Type I): Some of the cars had trucks with sintered-iron side frames and a single operating knuckle coupler.

VG-C6	EX-C7	LN-C8	Scarcity
3	5	10	1

24630 AMERICAN FLYER LINES (Type II): Other cars had a non-operating knuckle coupler, although they continued to have trucks with sintered-iron side frames.

VG-C6	EX-C7	LN-C8	Scarcity
3	5	10	1

24631 AMERICAN FLYER LINES: This yellow caboose was produced in a variety of years and in a number of variations. First available from 1959 through 1961, the car returned to the line from 1963 through 1965. While it had a metal smokejack, it did not have brakewheels or internal lighting.

24631 AMERICAN FLYER LINES (Type I): Some of the cars in 1959-60 were painted glossy yellow with a red-orange stripe and grab irons. This car was equipped with operating knuckle couplers.

VG-C6	EX-C7	LN-C8	Scarcity
10	20	30	3

24631 AMERICAN FLYER LINES (Type II): Other 1959-60 cars were almost identical to the Type I, except it was painted matte yellow rather than glossy.

VG-C6	EX-C7	LN-C8	Scarcity
10	20	30	3

24631 AMERICAN FLYER LINES (Type III): When the car was reintroduced in 1963 it was equipped with Pike Master trucks and couplers. Some of the cars were painted glossy yellow and had maroon stripes and grab irons. Cars were available in this configuration through 1965.

VG-C6	EX-C7	LN-C8	Scarcity
10	20	30	3

24631 AMERICAN FLYER LINES (Type IV): The painted-on stripe and grab irons were omitted from some of the 1965 cars.

VG-C6	EX-C7	LN-C8	Scarcity
100	200	300	7

24632 AMERICAN FLYER LINES: In 1959, another glossy yellow caboose was made—the 24632. This car had a silver roof, which like the sides, was painted. It had a red-orange stripe and grab irons. It did not have illumination or brakewheels, but it did have a metal smokejack and trucks with sintered-iron side frames. Only one coupler was installed, which was the knuckle type.

VG-C6	EX-C7	LN-C8	Scarcity
100	200	300	7

24633 AMERICAN FLYER LINES: This silver painted caboose with bay windows was sold from 1959 through 1962. The car had a sheet metal frame, black plastic smokejack, three red lanterns, brakewheels and rooftop ladders.

24633 AMERICAN FLYER LINES (Type I): Some of the cars were equipped with sintered-iron side frame trucks and knuckle couplers.

VG-C6	EX-C7	LN-C8	Scarcity
30	55	80	6

24633 AMERICAN FLYER LINES (Type II): Other cars were fitted with Pike Master trucks and couplers.

VG-C6	EX-C7	LN-C8	Scarcity
30	55	80	6

24634 AMERICAN FLYER LINES: This red bay window-equipped caboose was offered from 1963 through 1966. The car rode on Pike Master trucks with Pike Master couplers and pickups.

Values for each condition are in U.S. dollars. | **Scarcity** = Scale from 1-8 with 8 being the hardest to find.

67

24634 AMERICAN FLYER LINES (Type I): Some of these cars were painted red and the white markings included both "AMERICAN FLYER LINES" and "RADIO EQUIPPED."

VG-C6	EX-C7	LN-C8	Scarcity
20	40	60	4

24634 AMERICAN FLYER LINES (Type II): Other red-painted cars were marked only with "AMERICAN FLYER LINES" lettering.

VG-C6	EX-C7	LN-C8	Scarcity
20	40	60	4

24634 AMERICAN FLYER LINES (Type III): "AMERICAN FLYER LINES" were the only markings applied to cars that were unpainted molded red plastic.

VG-C6	EX-C7	LN-C8	Scarcity
20	40	60	4

24636 AMERICAN FLYER LINES: This caboose was available from 1961 through 1966. The car did not have illumination, brakewheels, smokejack or window glazing. It was equipped with Pike Master trucks and couplers.

24636 AMERICAN FLYER LINES (Type I): Some of the cars had unpainted red plastic bodies. The lettering on the car did not include "RADIO EQUIPPED."

24636 AMERICAN FLYER LINES (Type II): Other cars, while still unpainted red plastic, included white "RADIO EQUIPPED" lettering.

VG-C6	EX-C7	LN-C8	Scarcity
5	10	15	1

24636 AMERICAN FLYER LINES (Type III): Other cars retained the "RADIO EQUIPPED" lettering, but the bodies were painted red.

VG-C6	EX-C7	LN-C8	Scarcity
	Too rarely traded to accurately establish pricing.		

24636 AMERICAN FLYER LINES (Type IV): Other cars were also painted, but yellow rather than red, and the roof was painted silver.

VG-C6	EX-C7	LN-C8	Scarcity
200	400	600	8

24638 AMERICAN FLYER LINES: This uncataloged silver-painted illuminated but non-operating bay window-equipped caboose was sold in 1962. It was equipped with Pike Master trucks and couplers.

VG-C6	EX-C7	LN-C8	Scarcity
75	125	200	6

25031 AMERICAN FLYER LINES: This operating center-cupola caboose was shown in the 1958 catalog.

VG-C6	EX-C7	LN-C8	Scarcity
	Too rarely traded to accurately establish pricing.		

25035 AMERICAN FLYER LINES: In 1957, some of the 979 Deluxe Action Cabooses were sold in boxes marked "25035."

25036 AMERICAN FLYER LINES: Also in 1957, 979 Deluxe Action Cabooses reportedly came in boxes numbered "25036."

25052 AMERICAN FLYER LINES: This 1958 operating bay window-equipped caboose was painted silver and had red lettering. On one platform was a rubber brakeman figure mounted on a lever. The car rode on trucks with sintered-iron side frames and operating knuckle couplers.

VG-C6	EX-C7	LN-C8	Scarcity
60	120	180	6

CRANE CARS

Wrecking cranes—known to railroaders as the "Big Hook"—have largely disappeared from the real railroad scene. During their heyday, railroad operating and maintenance departments hoped these specialized cars would remain idle in the yards. However, for young miniature railroaders this was not the case. Wrecking cranes often circled the track endlessly, and American Flyer thoughtfully provided controls allowing the cranes to hoist various light loads.

606 AMERICAN FLYER LINES: In marked contrast to American Flyer's more elaborate cranes, this 1953 car consisted of essentially a gray sheet metal flatcar with a yellow crane cab mounted on top. The cab roof was red and the crane boom green.

606 AMERICAN FLYER LINES (Type I): Some of these cars had a one-piece brakewheel.

VG-C6	EX-C7	LN-C8	Scarcity
20	40	65	4

606 AMERICAN FLYER LINES (Type II): Other cars were equipped with a two-piece brakewheel.

VG-C6	EX-C7	LN-C8	Scarcity
20	40	65	4

635 C & N W R Y: The crane was introduced in 1946 and remained in the product line through 1949.

635 C & N W R Y (Type I): The earliest cars, those dating from 1946, were based on gray plastic flatcars. However, it was found that these flatcars often warped; hence the following year die-cast bodies were used. The 1946 cars were lettered with decals and their cabs were yellow and were lettered "AMERICAN FLYER LINES" and "635." Top value requires minimal warping.

VG-C6	EX-C7	LN-C8	Scarcity
30	60	125	6

635 C & N W R Y (Type II): In 1947, the gray-painted flatcar crane was die-cast and the lettering on it was rubber stamped. The silver lettering on the cab continued with the decals and was arranged with "635" on the right side and "AMERICAN FLYER LINES" to the left.

VG-C6	EX-C7	LN-C8	Scarcity
20	40	70	4

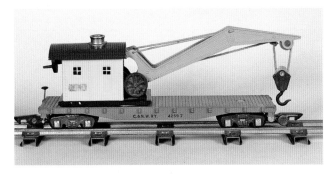

635 C & N W R Y (Type III): In 1948, the placement of the decals on some of the crane cabs were reversed, with "635" on the left side and "AMERICAN FLYER LINES" on the right.

VG-C6	EX-C7	LN-C8	Scarcity
20	40	70	4

635 C & N W R Y (Type IV): Sometime in 1948, the crane got a minor overhaul. The number "635" was omitted completely from the car, and the roof of some cars were unpainted blued steel with chrome stack.

VG-C6	EX-C7	LN-C8	Scarcity
Too rarely traded to accurately establish pricing.			

635 C & N W R Y (Type V): Other 1948 cranes had red cabs with red roofs and chrome stacks. Once again, the number "635" did not appear anywhere on the car.

VG-C6	EX-C7	LN-C8	Scarcity
300	425	550	7

635 C & N W R Y (Type VI): Yellow cabs with red roofs were found on several cars lacking the "635" numberings. Both chrome and black stacks have been found on this variation.

VG-C6	EX-C7	LN-C8	Scarcity
15	35	60	3

644 AMERICAN FLYER: This well-detailed realistic crane was introduced in 1950 and remained in the product line through 1953. The boom was marked "INDUSTRIAL BROWNHOIST," while the cab was stamped "AMERICAN FLYER 644." The chassis was gray. It rode on simulated six-wheel trucks, created by omitting the center axle from six-wheel tender trucks. The crane included a jack beam, which stabilized it during lifting operations. While the crank knobs came with and without handles, these parts are so easily changed that no deviation of values should be attributed to this variation. Though most of these cars have link couplers, it has been reported that some were fitted with knuckle couplers at the factory.

644 AMERICAN FLYER (Type I): In 1950, some of the cranes came with Tuscan cabs and were equipped with green booms.

VG-C6	EX-C7	LN-C8	Scarcity
60	110	150	6

644 AMERICAN FLYER (Type III)

644 AMERICAN FLYER (Type II): Other 1950 cranes, while retaining the green boom, had unpainted red plastic cabs.

VG-C6	EX-C7	LN-C8	Scarcity
30	60	100	4

644 AMERICAN FLYER (Type III): 📷 Some of the 1950 cranes had unpainted red cabs and unpainted black plastic booms.

VG-C6	EX-C7	LN-C8	Scarcity
70	140	200	6

644 AMERICAN FLYER (Type IV): Most of the cranes had black cabs and booms.

VG-C6	EX-C7	LN-C8	Scarcity
30	60	100	4

906 AMERICAN FLYER LINES: This 1954 car was essentially a knuckle coupler-equipped version of the 606. Its cab was yellow with a red roof with a black smokestack. The die-cast boom was green. The cab was stamped "AMERICAN FLYER LINES," while the flatcar base was lettered "AMERICAN FLYER LINES 906."

906 AMERICAN FLYER LINES (Type I): The chassis of some of these cars were painted gray.

VG-C6	EX-C7	LN-C8	Scarcity
25	50	75	4

906 AMERICAN FLYER LINES (Type II): Other cars had blue-gray chassis.

VG-C6	EX-C7	LN-C8	Scarcity
30	60	100	5

944 AMERICAN FLYER: This knuckle coupler equipped version of the 644 was introduced in 1952 and remained in the product line through 1957. The cab and boom were black, with the boom stamped with sans-serif white "INDUSTRIAL BROWNHOIST" markings. Like the 644, this crane rode on six-wheel tender trucks with the center axle omitted.

944 AMERICAN FLYER (Type I): The chassis of some cars was painted gray.

VG-C6	EX-C7	LN-C8	Scarcity
30	50	80	3

944 AMERICAN FLYER (Type II): Other cars had a metallic blue-gray chassis.

VG-C6	EX-C7	LN-C8	Scarcity
40	85	130	6

944 AMERICAN FLYER (Type III): Some cars had the "AMERICAN FLYER 944" markings stamped on the right end of the chassis, which was opposite of the norm.

VG-C6	EX-C7	LN-C8	Scarcity
Too rarely traded to accurately establish pricing.			

Values for each condition are in U.S. dollars. | **Scarcity** = Scale from 1-8 with 8 being the hardest to find.

71

24523 AMERICAN FLYER: In 1957, some 944 cranes were packed in boxes marked "24523."

24543 AMERICAN FLYER LINES: This 1958 crane was based on a gray-painted plastic flatcar body. The cab of the crane was black, as was the boom, which was lettered "INDUSTRIAL BROWNHOIST." The car was lettered with "AMERICAN FLYER LINES" in black and "AMERICAN FLYER 24543" in white. The car was equipped with knuckle couplers.

VG-C6	EX-C7	LN-C8	Scarcity
10	25	40	3

24561 AMERICAN FLYER LINES: This car was shipped from 1959 through 1961, and again in 1965-66. It combined a modified version of the nicely detailed cab of the 644/944 with a gray flatcar and the chassis. The cab as used on this car had a closed top panel.

24561 AMERICAN FLYER LINES (Type I): In 1959, the car had a cab painted black and the chassis with a boom was painted gray. It rode on sintered-iron trucks and had knuckle couplers.

VG-C6	EX-C7	LN-C8	Scarcity
10	20	30	1

24561 AMERICAN FLYER LINES (Type II): Other cars had identical trucks and similar color scheme—but this time achieved through plastic colors rather than painting.

VG-C6	EX-C7	LN-C8	Scarcity
10	20	30	1

24561 AMERICAN FLYER LINES (Type III): By 1961, the car rode on Pike Master trucks. Though the chassis was unpainted gray plastic, the cab and boom were painted black.

VG-C6	EX-C7	LN-C8	Scarcity
10	20	30	1

24569 AMERICAN FLYER LINES: This crane was available from 1961-66. An unpainted gray plastic flatcar lettered "AMERICAN FLYER LINES" formed the chassis. The cab was lettered "AMERICAN FLYER 24569" in white, while the gray plastic boom was stamped "INDUSTRIAL BROWNHOIST" in black. The car was equipped with Pike Master trucks and couplers.

24569 AMERICAN FLYER LINES (Type I): Cranes numbered "24561" were packaged in both traditional red and white and All Aboard boxes numbered "24569."

VG-C6	EX-C7	LN-C8	Scarcity
10	15	25	1

24569 AMERICAN FLYER LINES (Type II): The cabs of some cranes were unpainted black plastic.

VG-C6	EX-C7	LN-C8	Scarcity
10	15	25	1

24569 AMERICAN FLYER LINES (Type III): The cabs of other cranes were painted black.

VG-C6	EX-C7	LN-C8	Scarcity
10	15	25	1

42597: See 635.

24543 AMERICAN FLYER LINES

FLATCARS

For real railroads, the means of transporting bulky cargo not prone to weather damage is the flatcar. The wide-open construction makes placing the cargo easy, and minimizes construction and maintenance expenses. The same held true for the A.C. Gilbert Co. Most of the car bodies could be formed from a single piece of steel, plastic or pressed wood. The cars were then painted, and a range of cargoes added, including lumber, logs, girders and automobiles. Flatcars even served as the basis for the firm's work cabooses. Today, the cargo items constitute much of the value of cars so equipped, and many of them have been reproduced.

The flatcars also provided a basis for various operating cars, including searchlight cars, log dump cars, self-unloading automobile cars and track cleaning cars. The variety of colors, cargoes and construction techniques can make a collection of flatcars quite interesting—and large.

Values for each condition are in U.S. dollars. | **Scarcity** = Scale from 1-8 with 8 being the hardest to find.

73

AMERICAN FLYER CIRCUS: See 643.
BORDENS: See 24575.
NEW HAVEN: See 24564.
ROCKET LAUNCHER and USM: See 25056.
65 F. Y. & P. R. R.: See 24565.

605 AMERICAN FLYER LINES: This 1953 flatcar came with a load of six stained logs, which were held in place by two black-formed steel straps. The car was equipped with sheet metal trucks with link couplers.

605 AMERICAN FLYER LINES (Type I): The bodies of some cars were painted gray.

VG-C6	EX-C7	LN-C8	Scarcity
10	25	45	5

605 AMERICAN FLYER LINES (Type II): Other car bodies were painted silver.

VG-C6	EX-C7	LN-C8	Scarcity
10	25	45	5

607 AMERICAN FLYER LINES: Based on a flatcar, this 1953 car was equipped as a boom tender or work caboose, with a small cabin on one end. The car was equipped with link couplers.

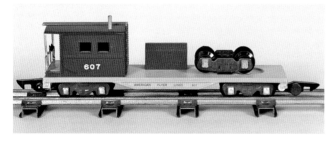

607 AMERICAN FLYER LINES (Type I): Some of the cars were painted gray and had a sheet metal truck mounted on its deck.

VG-C6	EX-C7	LN-C8	Scarcity
20	40	60	4

607 AMERICAN FLYER LINES (Type II): Also painted gray. But had a truck with sintered-iron side frames riveted to the deck.

VG-C6	EX-C7	LN-C8	Scarcity
20	40	60	4

607 AMERICAN FLYER LINES (Type III): Some of the cars had a black-painted sheet metal base.

VG-C6	EX-C7	LN-C8	Scarcity
Too rarely traded to accurately establish pricing.			

609 AMERICAN FLYER LINES: Offered in 1953 was this gray sheet metal flatcar with an orange die-cast girder load. Two metal bands held the load in place on the car, which was lettered and numbered in black. The car had sheet metal trucks and link couplers.

VG-C6	EX-C7	LN-C8	Scarcity
15	25	50	5

627 C. & N. W. RY.: This black-lettered flatcar was sold from 1946 through 1950. It was furnished with an orange die-cast girder cargo, which was held in place by two metal bands. One side of the girder was lettered "AMERICAN FLYER LINES" and the other bore the number "627." The car itself was numbered "42597," and was equipped with sheet metal trucks and link couplers.

627 C. & N. W. RY. (Type I): Cars produced in 1946 had unpainted plastic bodies. Some of these were white.

VG-C6	EX-C7	LN-C8	Scarcity
40	80	150	6

627 C. & N. W. RY. (Type II): Other 1946 cars had unpainted light gray plastic bodies.

VG-C6	EX-C7	LN-C8	Scarcity
40	80	150	6

627 C. & N. W. RY. (Type III): Perhaps in 1947, flatcars with unpainted dark gray plastic bodies were produced.

VG-C6	EX-C7	LN-C8	Scarcity
40	80	150	6

627 C. & N. W. RY. (Type IV): To combat a widespread problem with warping of the car bodies, Gilbert began making the flatcar itself from die-cast metal, probably in late 1946. These cars were painted gray, and remained in the catalog through 1950, with the annual changes to coupler weights.

VG-C6	EX-C7	LN-C8	Scarcity
10	20	30	2

627 AMERICAN FLYER: In 1950, a version of the gray die-cast flatcar with girder load was produced which was lettered "AMERICAN FLYER" in black, rather than "C. &. N. W. RY." The car had sheet metal trucks and link couplers.

VG-C6	EX-C7	LN-C8	Scarcity
20	40	60	5

628 C. & N. W. RY.: Introduced in 1946, and remaining in the product line through 1953, this flatcar was laden with six logs. Two formed steel straps held the logs in place. The car rode on sheet metal trucks with link couplers.

628 C. & N. W. RY. (Type I): Cars produced in 1946 had unpainted plastic bodies. Some of these were white.

VG-C6	EX-C7	LN-C8	Scarcity
10	20	30	3

628 C. W. RY. (Type II): Other 1946 cars had unpainted light gray plastic bodies.

VG-C6	EX-C7	LN-C8	Scarcity
10	20	30	3

628 C. & N. W. RY. (Type III): Perhaps in 1947, flatcars with unpainted dark gray plastic bodies were produced.

VG-C6	EX-C7	LN-C8	Scarcity
10	20	30	3

628 C. & N. W. RY. (Type IV): To combat a widespread problem with warping of the car bodies, Gilbert began making the flatcar itself from die-cast metal, probably in late 1946. These cars were painted gray, and remained in the catalog through 1950, with the annual changes to coupler weights.

VG-C6	EX-C7	LN-C8	Scarcity
8	15	25	2

628 C. & N. W. RY. (Type V): Materials shortages, perhaps due to the Korean War, led Gilbert to begin constructing these cars from pressed wood in 1951. This remained the norm through 1952.

VG-C6	EX-C7	LN-C8	Scarcity
30	50	80	6

628 C. & N. W. RY. (Type VI): In 1953, the bodies reverted to die-cast and were painted blue-gray.

VG-C6	EX-C7	LN-C8	Scarcity
8	15	25	2

634 C. & N. W. RY.: The ever-popular searchlight car was cataloged as a number 534 from 1946 through 1949, and then returned for a final year in 1953. The side of the car was lettered "C. & N.W.RY. 42597," but the sheet metal superstructure was lettered "AMERICAN FLYER LINES" and "634." The die-cast lamp housings were painted silver, black or yellow. The car rode on sheet metal trucks with link couplers.

634 C. & N. W. RY. (Type I): The 1946 version of the car had a plastic body. Some of these cars were unpainted medium gray plastic with black lamp housings. Tall handrails are found on this version.

VG-C6	EX-C7	LN-C8	Scarcity
25	50	75	4

634 C. & N. W. RY. (Type II): Other cars were identical to the Type I, except their bodies were unpainted white plastic.

VG-C6	EX-C7	LN-C8	Scarcity
25	50	75	4

Values for each condition are in U.S. dollars. | **Scarcity** = Scale from 1-8 with 8 being the hardest to find.

75

634 C. & N. W. RY. (Type III): Still, other 1946 cars differed from the Type I only by having a yellow lamp housing.

VG-C6	EX-C7	LN-C8	Scarcity
10	20	40	3

634 C. & N. W. RY. (Type IV): Some cars were near-duplicates of the Type I, except the handrails were short.

VG-C6	EX-C7	LN-C8	Scarcity
10	20	40	3

634 C. & N. W. RY. (Type V): This car was a short-handrail version of the Type II searchlight car.

VG-C6	EX-C7	LN-C8	Scarcity
10	20	40	3

634 C. & N. W. RY. (Type VI): Short handrails are also found on some of the gray cars with yellow lamp housings.

VG-C6	EX-C7	LN-C8	Scarcity
10	20	40	3

634 C. & N. W. RY. (Type VII): Yellow lamp housings are also found on some of the white plastic cars with short handrails.

VG-C6	EX-C7	LN-C8	Scarcity
10	20	40	3

634 C. & N. W. RY. (Type VIII): In 1947, Gilbert produced the car with a gray-painted die-cast body rather than plastic. The short handrails were retained, as was a yellow lamp housing. This car was produced into 1948.

VG-C6	EX-C7	LN-C8	Scarcity
10	20	40	3

634 C. & N. W. RY. (Type IX): In 1949, the color of the lamp housing was changed to silver.

VG-C6	EX-C7	LN-C8	Scarcity
10	20	40	3

636 ERIE: This impressive looking 12-wheel depressed center car was available from 1948 through 1953. The car was laden with a cable reel, and the catalog number appeared on the yellow metal sides of the reel. The car itself bore the markings "ERIE 7210." The reel was screwed to the car, but simulated retaining wires appeared to hold it in place. The car was equipped with link couplers.

636 ERIE (Type I): When introduced in 1948, the die-cast body of the car was painted gray and lettered "NEW 5-28." The sides of the reel were painted dark yellow, and lettered "AMERICAN FLYER" around the top, and "MFD BY THE A.C. GILBERT CO. NEW HAVEN,

CONN. U.S.A." horizontally near the bottom—all in black. This version was produced through 1950.

VG-C6	EX-C7	LN-C8	Scarcity
15	25	45	3

636 ERIE (Type II): Other 1948-50 cars were identical, but for the "built date," which in this instance was stamped "NEW 5-29."

VG-C6	EX-C7	LN-C8	Scarcity
15	25	45	3

636 ERIE (Type III): In 1951-52, the car body was made from pressed wood.

VG-C6	EX-C7	LN-C8	Scarcity
75	175	350	7

636 ERIE (Type IV): Die-cast bodies returned in 1953. Some of these cars were marked "NEW 5-28."

VG-C6	EX-C7	LN-C8	Scarcity
15	25	45	3

636 ERIE (Type V): Other cars were identical to the Type IV, but for the date, which in this case read "NEW 5-29."

VG-C6	EX-C7	LN-C8	Scarcity
15	25	45	3

636 ERIE (Type VI): Some of the cars produced in 1953 came with cable reels that were lettered "AMERICAN FLYER LINES" instead of "American Flyer."

VG-C6	EX-C7	LN-C8	Scarcity
100	200	400	7

643 AMERICAN FLYER CIRCUS: This car was offered from 1950 through 1953. The car had sheet metal trucks and link couplers. The lettering on the car read "AMERICAN FLYER CIRCUS"; but the number was omitted. The cargo of the flatcar consisted of a truck-tractor and two wheeled cages with animals. The truck-tractor is most commonly found in green, although red as well as yellow examples are sometimes found. Cages were produced in blue, green, red and yellow versions. The cage designed varied slightly during the production run, but these details are of little consequence to most collectors. Reproductions have been made of all the load items, both of die-cast metal and, like the originals, of plastic.

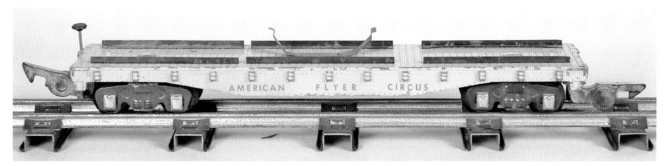

643 AMERICAN FLYER CIRCUS (Type I)

643 AMERICAN FLYER CIRCUS (Type I): 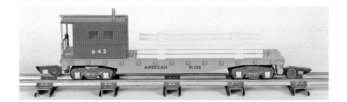 The earliest cars, which were die-cast, had their loads retained by six metal boxcar door guides which were riveted to the deck of the car. Some of these cars were yellow.

VG-C6	EX-C7	LN-C8	Scarcity
225	425	850	8

643 AMERICAN FLYER CIRCUS (Type II): Fairly early, a wooden strip was used to hold the loads in place on the die-cast car, rather than using door guides.

VG-C6	EX-C7	LN-C8	Scarcity
100	200	300	6

643 AMERICAN FLYER CIRCUS (Type III): Another version of the car also used the wooden strip as a cargo retainer, but the body was painted red rather than yellow.

VG-C6	EX-C7	LN-C8	Scarcity
200	400	700	7

643 AMERICAN FLYER CIRCUS (Type IV): The Circus Flatcar was also available from 1951 through 1953, but during this time frame the body of the car was made from a pressed wood.

VG-C6	EX-C7	LN-C8	Scarcity
125	250	400	6

645 AMERICAN FLYER: This gray-painted die-cast-based work car was produced in 1950. The car had black "AMERICAN FLYER" lettering and an unpainted red plastic shed, and was equipped with link couplers. The car had yellow fences but no toolbox. Note: reproduction fence sections are available.

VG-C6	EX-C7	LN-C8	Scarcity
25	50	75	5

645A AMERICAN FLYER or AMERICAN FLYER LINES: In 1951, this car was introduced as a successor to the 645. It remained in the product line through 1953. Like the 645, it was based on a die-cast flatcar chassis painted gray. The car had link couplers, and a toolbox was added to the non-cabin end. Note: reproduction fence sections are available.

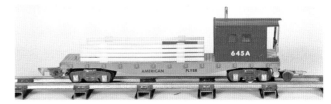

645A AMERICAN FLYER (Type I): Some of the cars had cabins painted red and the gray chassis were stamped "AMERICAN FLYER." Yellow fences were used.

VG-C6	EX-C7	LN-C8	Scarcity
25	50	75	4

645A AMERICAN FLYER (Type II): Other cars were identical to the Type I cars, but the structure was painted Tuscan.

VG-C6	EX-C7	LN-C8	Scarcity
20	40	60	3

FLATCARS

Values for each condition are in U.S. dollars. | **Scarcity** = Scale from 1-8 with 8 being the hardest to find.

77

645A AMERICAN FLYER LINES (Type III): The chassis of later cars were lettered "AMERICAN FLYER LINES." Some of these cars had Tuscan-painted cabins and yellow fences.

VG-C6	EX-C7	LN-C8	Scarcity
20	40	60	3

645A AMERICAN FLYER LINES (Type IV): Other cars were identical to the Type III, but utilized Tuscan fences.

VG-C6	EX-C7	LN-C8	Scarcity
20	40	60	3

645A AMERICAN FLYER LINES (Type V): Another variation had a Tuscan cabin and fences, but was based on a chassis painted blue-gray.

VG-C6	EX-C7	LN-C8	Scarcity
30	60	90	5

646 ERIE: The 12-wheel die-cast depressed center flatcar was the basis of this 1950-53 operating searchlight car. The number "646" did not appear on the car, rather the gray car was stamped "ERIE 7210" in black. The car was fitted with link couplers. The generator, located in the center of the car, was at first die-cast—later plastic. The two screws to mount the latter were located on either side, while in the case of the die-cast units the mounting screws were near the ends.

646 ERIE (Type I): The first year of production, 1950, included a light green-painted die-cast motor-generator. The light housing was chrome-plated, and the reporting marks on the flatcar included "NEW 5-29."

VG-C6	EX-C7	LN-C8	Scarcity
50	100	250	6

646 ERIE (Type II): 📷 The generators mounted on some later cars were made of plastic. Some of these were molded of white plastic, then painted light green. The lamp housing of these units were painted silver. Markings on these cars include "NEW 5-29."

VG-C6	EX-C7	LN-C8	Scarcity
Too rarely traded to accurately establish pricing.			

646 ERIE (Type III): Silver-painted lamp housings were also used on some cars with plastic generators that were painted red. The cars were marked "NEW 5-29."

VG-C6	EX-C7	LN-C8	Scarcity
15	30	45	4

646 ERIE (Type IV): Painted red generators were also found on some cars with chrome-plated lamp housings. These cars were also marked "NEW 5-29."

VG-C6	EX-C7	LN-C8	Scarcity
15	30	45	4

646 ERIE (Type V): Some of the cars with red-painted generators and silver-painted lamp housings were marked "NEW 5-28."

VG-C6	EX-C7	LN-C8	Scarcity
15	30	45	4

646 ERIE (Type VI): Other cars had unpainted dark green plastic generators and chrome-plated lamp housings. These cars were also marked "NEW 5-29."

VG-C6	EX-C7	LN-C8	Scarcity
15	30	45	4

646 ERIE (Type VII): During the 1951-52 production, the cars had unpainted dark green plastic motor-generator assemblies. The lamp housings on these units were painted silver. The cars were marked "NEW 5-29."

VG-C6	EX-C7	LN-C8	Scarcity
15	30	45	4

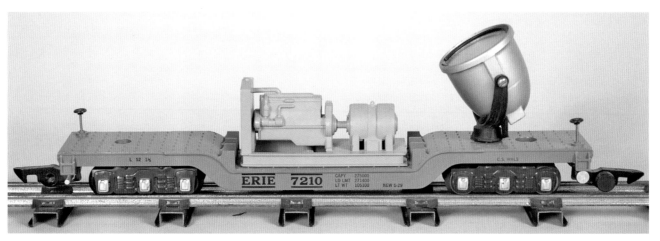

646 ERIE (Type II)

646 ERIE (Type VIII): Unpainted red plastic motor-generator units were installed on some of the 1951-52 cars. These cars had silver-painted lamp housings and were marked "NEW 5-29."

VG-C6	EX-C7	LN-C8	Scarcity
15	30	45	4

648 AMERICAN FLYER: This 1952-54 flatcar was outfitted for track cleaning. It rode on four-wheel sheet metal trucks with link couplers. A spring-loaded replaceable felt-cleaning pad was mounted between the truck and the depression of the car body.

648 AMERICAN FLYER (Type I): The body of some of the cars was red.

VG-C6	EX-C7	LN-C8	Scarcity
15	25	40	4

648 AMERICAN FLYER (Type II): Other cars had a Tuscan body.

VG-C6	EX-C7	LN-C8	Scarcity
10	20	30	3

714 LOG UNLOADING CAR: Though basic in appearance, this 1951-54 operating log dump car added considerable enjoyment for operators. The car had a die-cast chassis and a sheet metal tilting platform. The chassis was painted black, and the tilting platform gray. The car had sheet metal trucks and link couplers. It came with three logs.

714 LOG UNLOADING CAR (Type I): The tilting platform of some of the cars was stamped "714" and "AMERICAN FLYER."

VG-C6	EX-C7	LN-C8	Scarcity
15	30	60	4

714 LOG UNLOADING CAR (Type II): Other cars were stamped only "714" on the tilting platform.

VG-C6	EX-C7	LN-C8	Scarcity
15	30	60	4

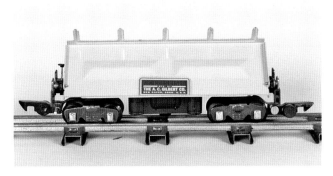

714 LOG UNLOADING CAR (Type III): Rather than being stamped as above, other cars were marked with a decal on the platform. The decal was blue, with red and yellow lettering and yellow border.

VG-C6	EX-C7	LN-C8	Scarcity
15	30	60	4

715 AMERICAN FLYER LINES: Sold from 1946 through 1954, this vehicle-transporting railcar is a classic among the Flyer line. The car had a sheet metal body, topped by a sheet metal housing supporting a tilting ramp, also made of sheet metal. The solenoid operating mechanism caused the ramp to swing out, then tilt down and the vehicle to roll off.

715 AMERICAN FLYER LINES (Type I): When introduced in 1946, the car had a black body and yellow ramp. Its cargo was a military armored car. Cars produced in 1946 were equipped with an inside electrical pickup shoe.

VG-C6	EX-C7	LN-C8	Scarcity
50	100	150	6

715 AMERICAN FLYER LINES (Type II): In 1947, the pickup shoe was moved to an outside position.

VG-C6	EX-C7	LN-C8	Scarcity
50	100	150	6

715 AMERICAN FLYER LINES (Type III): In 1948, the cargo changed to a die-cast Manoil coupe. Various colors of automobiles were used.

VG-C6	EX-C7	LN-C8	Scarcity
25	50	75	4

Values for each condition are in U.S. dollars. | Scarcity = Scale from 1-8 with 8 being the hardest to find.

79

715 AMERICAN FLYER LINES (Type IV): In 1949, the lettering of the car, which had previously been decals, was rubber stamped.

VG-C6	EX-C7	LN-C8	Scarcity
25	50	75	4

715 AMERICAN FLYER LINES (Type V): In 1951, some cars were produced with gray bodies and yellow ramps. These cars carried the Manoil die-cast coupe.

VG-C6	EX-C7	LN-C8	Scarcity
30	55	85	5

715 AMERICAN FLYER LINES (Type VI): In 1952, cars were made with a blue ramp mounted on the black body. The cargo of this car was the Manoil coupe.

VG-C6	EX-C7	LN-C8	Scarcity
25	50	75	4

715 AMERICAN FLYER LINES (Type VII): Identical to the Type VI was this car, which carried a Tootsietoy racecar.

VG-C6	EX-C7	LN-C8	Scarcity
30	55	85	5

715 AMERICAN FLYER LINES (Type VIII): For 1953 and 1954, the yellow ramp returned. The body was still black, and the cargo was a Tootsietoy racecar.

VG-C6	EX-C7	LN-C8	Scarcity
30	55	85	5

717 AMERICAN FLYER LINES: Though basic in appearance, this 1946-52 operating log dump car added considerable enjoyment for operators. The car had a sheet metal chassis and tilting platform. The chassis was painted black, and the tilting platform yellow. The car had sheet metal trucks and link couplers. It came with three logs.

717 AMERICAN FLYER LINES (Type I): In 1946, the car had an inside truck power pickup. One end of the car deck was a "717" decal, and on the other "AMERICAN FLYER LINES."

VG-C6	EX-C7	LN-C8	Scarcity
15	30	60	4

717 AMERICAN FLYER LINES (Type II): The 1947 cars had "AMERICAN FLYER LINES" decals on both ends of the deck.

VG-C6	EX-C7	LN-C8	Scarcity
15	30	60	4

717 AMERICAN FLYER LINES (Type III): In 1948, the car was redesigned to incorporate outside power pickup.

VG-C6	EX-C7	LN-C8	Scarcity
15	30	60	4

717 AMERICAN FLYER LINES (Type IV): In 1949, the size of the logs was reduced from 6-1/4 inches long to 5-1/2 inches. The car remained available in this form through 1952.

VG-C6	EX-C7	LN-C8	Scarcity
15	30	60	4

905 AMERICAN FLYER LINES: This 1954 sheet metal flatcar was loaded with six brown-stained logs. Two metal bands held the logs in place. The car rode on trucks with sintered-iron side frames and knuckle couplers. The lettering on the cars, "AMERICAN FLYER LINES" and "905," was stamped in black.

905 AMERICAN FLYER LINES (Type I): Some of the cars were painted blue-gray.

VG-C6	EX-C7	LN-C8	Scarcity
15	30	60	4

905 AMERICAN FLYER LINES (Type II): Other cars were painted gray.

VG-C6	EX-C7	LN-C8	Scarcity
15	30	60	4

907 AMERICAN FLYER LINES: This 1954 car had a gray-painted sheet metal chassis lettered "AMERICAN FLYER LINES 907." The cabin mounted on the car was painted Tuscan, and a red toolbox was mounted on the deck along with a truck with sintered-iron side frames.

VG-C6	EX-C7	LN-C8	Scarcity
20	40	60	3

909 AMERICAN FLYER LINES: This 1954 sheet metal flatcar was loaded with an unlettered orange die-cast girder. Two metal bands held the girder in place. The car rode on trucks with sintered-iron side frames and knuckle couplers. The lettering on the cars, "AMERICAN FLYER LINES" and "909," was stamped in black.

909 AMERICAN FLYER LINES (Type I): Some of the cars were painted blue-gray.

VG-C6	EX-C7	LN-C8	Scarcity
30	50	100	6

909 AMERICAN FLYER LINES (Type II): Other cars were painted gray.

VG-C6	EX-C7	LN-C8	Scarcity
15	30	60	4

914 AMERICAN FLYER LINES: Though basic in appearance, this 1953-57 operating log dump car added considerable enjoyment for operators. The car had a die-cast chassis and a sheet metal tilting platform. The chassis was painted black, and the tilting platform was either unpainted aluminum or gray-painted sheet metal. The car had sheet metal trucks and link couplers. It came with three logs.

914 AMERICAN FLYER LINES (Type I): Initially the dump platform of the cars was sheet metal and painted gray. In 1953 and 1954, the car carried three 7/8-inch or 13/16-inch diameter logs.

VG-C6	EX-C7	LN-C8	Scarcity
20	35	60	4

914 AMERICAN FLYER LINES (Type II): In 1955, the cargo was changed to 4-1/2 x 5-1/4-inch logs.

VG-C6	EX-C7	LN-C8	Scarcity
20	35	60	4

914 AMERICAN FLYER LINES (Type III): In 1956, the diameter of the logs reverted to the earlier large sizes.

VG-C6	EX-C7	LN-C8	Scarcity
20	35	60	4

914 AMERICAN FLYER LINES (Type IV): The 1957 production of the car included unpainted aluminum dump platforms.

VG-C6	EX-C7	LN-C8	Scarcity
20	35	60	4

915 AMERICAN FLYER LINES: The vehicle-unloading car was equipped with knuckle couplers in 1953, and given a new number—915—accordingly. The car remained in the product line through 1957, but some variation was created. In all cases, a solenoid causes a ramp to swing out from the car, whereupon the weight of the toy vehicle causes the ramp to tilt and the vehicle to roll away.

915 AMERICAN FLYER LINES (Type I): Cars produced in 1953-54 had black bodies, red base and yellow tilting ramps. They were laden with a blue, gray, orange, red, silver, or yellow Tootsietoy racer.

VG-C6	EX-C7	LN-C8	Scarcity
25	40	80	5

915 AMERICAN FLYER LINES (Type II): Cars produced from 1955 through 1957 were painted gray with brown unloading ramps. The cargo now was a Renwal gasoline tanker.

VG-C6	EX-C7	LN-C8	Scarcity
25	40	80	5

928 C. & N. W. RY.: Offered from 1952 through 1954, this gray flatcar transported six brown logs. The logs were held in place by two formed-steel straps, and the car rode on trucks with sintered-iron side frames and knuckle couplers.

928 C. & N. W. RY. (Type I): When introduced, the bodies of these cars were made of pressed wood. The lettering on some of these cars was larger than that found on most C. & N. W. RY. flatcars.

VG-C6	EX-C7	LN-C8	Scarcity
30	60	90	6

928 C. & N. W. RY. (Type II): Other cars, also with pressed wood bodies, had lettering of the conventional size.

VG-C6	EX-C7	LN-C8	Scarcity
30	60	90	6

928 C. & N. W. RY. (Type III): In 1953, the cars were made with die-cast bodies. This continued to be the case in 1954.

VG-C6	EX-C7	LN-C8	Scarcity
10	20	30	1

928 NEW HAVEN: This black flatcar was produced in 1956 and 1957. The white lettering on the car included "NH 928," "NEW HAVEN" and "CAPY 100000."

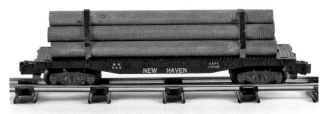

928 NEW HAVEN (Type I): Some of the cars assembled in 1956 had die-cast bodies painted black. Equipped with knuckle couplers and trucks with sintered-iron side frames, the car transported six stained logs bound to the car with two black metal bands.

VG-C6	EX-C7	LN-C8	Scarcity
10	20	35	4

Values for each condition are in U.S. dollars. | **Scarcity** = Scale from 1-8 with 8 being the hardest to find.

81

FLATCARS

928 NEW HAVEN (Type II): Other cars, produced in 1956-57, had plastic bodies. Eight black sheet metal stakes held a cargo of four blocks of wood in place on these cars. The cars, which came both unpainted black and painted black, had trucks with sintered-iron side frames and knuckle couplers.

VG-C6	EX-C7	LN-C8	Scarcity
15	25	40	4

934 C. & N. W. RY.: This die-cast searchlight car was cataloged in 1953 and 1954. The lamp housing was painted silver, and its die-cast support black. The trucks had sintered-iron side frames and knuckle couplers.

934 C. & N. W. RY. (Type I): Some of the cars had gray-painted bodies.

VG-C6	EX-C7	LN-C8	Scarcity
10	20	30	1

934 C. & N. W. RY. (Type II): Other cars had bodies painted blue-gray.

VG-C6	EX-C7	LN-C8	Scarcity
15	25	40	4

934 SOUTHERN PACIFIC: This uncataloged Tuscan-painted die-cast searchlight car was produced in 1954. The lamp housing was painted silver, and its die-cast support black. The trucks had sintered-iron side frames and knuckle couplers.

VG-C6	EX-C7	LN-C8	Scarcity
20	40	60	4

936 ERIE: The gray die-cast 12-wheel cable reel car was offered with knuckle couplers during 1953-54. Naturally, the car was also equipped with trucks with sintered-iron side frames at this time. The catalog number was stamped on the yellow metal cable reel sides. On the car itself were the black markings "ERIE 7210."

936 ERIE (Type I): The reporting marks of some cars included the line "NEW 5-28."

VG-C6	EX-C7	LN-C8	Scarcity
15	25	45	4

936 ERIE (Type II): Other cars were marked "NEW 5-29."

VG-C6	EX-C7	LN-C8	Scarcity
15	25	45	4

936 PENNSYLVANIA: From 1955 through 1957, the 12-wheel die-cast depressed-center reel carrier was painted Tuscan and bore the white markings of the "PENNSYLVANIA" railroad. The cable reel was notably different from that used on earlier cars, with simulated spokes, gray paint and "WESTERN ELECTRIC" lettering.

VG-C6	EX-C7	LN-C8	Scarcity
50	100	160	6

945 AMERICAN FLYER LINES: This knuckle coupler-equipped work caboose was sold from 1952 through 1957. The chassis of the car was painted gray and lettered "AMERICAN FLYER LINES." The number "945" was stamped in white on the sides of the cabin, which was painted Tuscan.

945 AMERICAN FLYER (Type I): In 1952, the gray-painted die-cast chassis was lettered "AMERICAN FLYER" and the red toolbox was made of wood.

VG-C6	EX-C7	LN-C8	Scarcity
35	70	110	6

945 AMERICAN FLYER LINES (Type II): Very soon the lettering on the cars began to read "AMERICAN FLYER LINES." On some of these cars, the steps were removed from before assembly.

VG-C6	EX-C7	LN-C8	Scarcity
15	30	50	4

945 AMERICAN FLYER LINES (Type III): Plastic toolboxes, painted Tuscan, ultimately replaced the wooden ones.

VG-C6	EX-C7	LN-C8	Scarcity
15	30	50	4

945 AMERICAN FLYER LINES (Type IV): Unpainted red plastic tool boxes were used on some cars.

VG-C6	EX-C7	LN-C8	Scarcity
15	30	50	4

945 AMERICAN FLYER LINES (Type V): The die-cast chassis of some cars was painted blue-gray rather than simple gray on some of the cars sold in 1953-54.

VG-C6	EX-C7	LN-C8	Scarcity
25	45	65	5

945 AMERICAN FLYER LINES (Type VI): In 1957, the chassis of the cars were made of injection-molded plastic, which was painted gray. Some of these cars had red-painted plastic toolboxes.

VG-C6	EX-C7	LN-C8	Scarcity
15	30	50	4

945 AMERICAN FLYER LINES (Type VII): Other cars built with gray-painted plastic chassis had yellow-painted toolboxes.

VG-C6	EX-C7	LN-C8	Scarcity
15	30	50	4

946 ERIE: The 12-wheel die-cast depressed center flatcar was the basis of this 1953-57 operating searchlight car. The number "646" did not appear on the car, rather the gray car was stamped "ERIE 7210" in black. The car was fitted with six-wheel trucks with sintered-iron side frames and knuckle couplers. The generator, located in the center of the car, was plastic.

946 ERIE (Type I): Some of the cars had plastic generators painted green and reporting marks with the date "NEW 5-29."

VG-C6	EX-C7	LN-C8	Scarcity
15	30	45	2

946 ERIE (Type II): Unpainted green plastic generators are found on some cars that are stamped with the date "NEW 5-28."

VG-C6	EX-C7	LN-C8	Scarcity
15	30	45	2

946 ERIE (Type III): Other cars had plastic generators painted red. The date on some of these cars read "NEW 5-28."

VG-C6	EX-C7	LN-C8	Scarcity
15	30	45	2

946 ERIE (Type IV): Other cars were identical to the Type III, but bore the date "NEW 5-29."

VG-C6	EX-C7	LN-C8	Scarcity
15	30	45	2

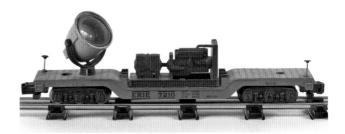

946 ERIE (Type V): Unpainted red plastic generators were mounted on some cars with the date "NEW 5-29."

VG-C6	EX-C7	LN-C8	Scarcity
20	40	60	5

948 AMERICAN FLYER LINES: This Tuscan 1953-57 flatcar was outfitted for track cleaning. The die-cast car rode on four-wheel trucks with sintered-iron side frames and knuckle couplers. A spring-loaded replaceable felt-cleaning pad was mounted between the truck and the depression of the car body.

VG-C6	EX-C7	LN-C8	Scarcity
10	20	30	1

956 MONON: This 1956-57 gray flatcar came with two piggyback vans. The colorful markings on the vans promoted American Flyer trains and other Gilbert products. The red markings of the flatcar were those of the Monon railroad. Note: this car is not compatible with the unloader.

VG-C6	EX-C7	LN-C8	Scarcity
30	60	90	5

Values for each condition are in U.S. dollars. | Scarcity = Scale from 1-8 with 8 being the hardest to find.

FLATCARS

83

969 ROCKET LAUNCHER: Though not cataloged, this unpainted black car was produced in 1957. The white lettering on the side "ROCKET LAUNCHER," describes exactly what this action car does. The solenoid mechanism, wrapped in red tape, was plainly visible adjacent to the gray launch base on the deck of the car. A Tuscan-painted toolbox was also mounted on the deck. Various color combinations of the rockets have been found with this car. Beware: the rockets have been reproduced.

969 ROCKET LAUNCHER (Type I): Some cars came with a red, white and blue rocket.

VG-C6	EX-C7	LN-C8	Scarcity
20	40	70	4

969 ROCKET LAUNCHER (Type II): A red, yellow and blue rocket was supplied with other cars.

VG-C6	EX-C7	LN-C8	Scarcity
20	40	70	4

969 ROCKET LAUNCHER (Type III): Red, green and blue were the colors of the rocket supplied with this car.

VG-C6	EX-C7	LN-C8	Scarcity
20	40	70	4

971 SOUTHERN PACIFIC: Popularly known as "Moe" and "Joe," the two blue figures on this Tuscan-colored operating lumber car unloaded the eight pieces of lumber furnished with the car. The car was sold in 1956-57, and naturally had sintered-iron side frame equipped trucks and knuckle couplers.

971 SOUTHERN PACIFIC (Type I): Some of the cars were molded of Tuscan-colored plastic, and the painted Tuscan as well.

VG-C6	EX-C7	LN-C8	Scarcity
40	80	140	6

971 SOUTHERN PACIFIC (Type II): Other cars were unpainted Tuscan-colored plastic.

VG-C6	EX-C7	LN-C8	Scarcity
40	80	140	6

7210 ERIE: See 636, 646, 936, 946, or 24529.

24515 NEW HAVEN: In 1957, the 928 lumber car came in a box marked "24515."

24516 NEW HAVEN: This unpainted black plastic flatcar with lumber load was sold from 1957 through 1959. Eight sheet metal stakes retained the cargo of four blocks of wood. The car bore white "NEW HAVEN" markings and rode on trucks with sintered-iron side frames and knuckle couplers.

VG-C6	EX-C7	LN-C8	Scarcity
10	15	30	4

24518 PENNSYLVANIA: In 1957, the 936 Pennsylvania depressed-center flatcar came in a box marked "24518."

24519 PENNSYLVANIA: The Tuscan Pennsy reel-carrying depressed center flatcar was available with this number in 1957 and 1958. The cargo of this car was a single gray "WESTERN ELECTRIC" cable reel. The car had knuckle couplers, and its six-wheel trucks had sintered-iron side frames.

VG-C6	EX-C7	LN-C8	Scarcity
250	600	1,200	8

24525 AMERICAN FLYER LINES: In 1957, the 945 came packaged in a box marked "24525."

24529 ERIE: The catalog number of this 1957-58 searchlight car appeared nowhere on it. Instead, the lettering on its gray die-cast depressed center read "ERIE 7210." The generator was unpainted yellow plastic, and the lamp housing was painted silver. The car had knuckle couplers, and its six-wheel trucks had sintered-iron side frames.

VG-C6	EX-C7	LN-C8	Scarcity
15	30	75	6

24533 AMERICAN FLYER LINES: Sold from 1957 through 1966, this Tuscan depressed center track-cleaning car had one of the longest life spans of any Gilbert flatcar. Not surprisingly, for a car in production so long, numerous versions were made.

24533 AMERICAN FLYER LINES (Type I): From 1957 through 1960, the car had a horizontal silver-painted tank. The car had trucks with sintered-iron side frames and knuckle couplers. In 1960, the car was packed in a Kleer-Pak box.

VG-C6	EX-C7	LN-C8	Scarcity
10	20	35	2

24533 AMERICAN FLYER LINES (Type II): Beginning in 1961, the car rode on Pike Master trucks. This continued to be the case through 1964.

VG-C6	EX-C7	LN-C8	Scarcity
10	20	35	2

24533 AMERICAN FLYER LINES (Type III): Some cars made in 1965-66 had two vertical silver-painted tanks, rather than the single horizontal tank used previously. The car rode on Pike Master trucks.

VG-C6	EX-C7	LN-C8	Scarcity
10	20	30	1

24533 AMERICAN FLYER LINES (Type IV): Other 1965-66 cars had two vertical white-painted plastic tanks. Like the Type III, this car was equipped with Pike Master trucks.

VG-C6	EX-C7	LN-C8	Scarcity
10	20	30	1

24535 MONON:  In 1957, the 956 came packaged in boxes marked "956 PIGGYBACK 24535."

24536 MONON: This 1958 gray flatcar came with two piggyback vans. The colorful markings on the vans promoted American Flyer trains and other Gilbert products. The red markings of the flatcar were those of the Monon railroad. Note: this car is not compatible with the unloader.

24536 MONON (Type I): Some of these cars came with two brackets to hold the trailers in position.

VG-C6	EX-C7	LN-C8	Scarcity
400	750	1,500	8

24536 MONON (Type II): Other cars had only one bracket to secure the trailer to the car.

VG-C6	EX-C7	LN-C8	Scarcity
400	750	1,500	8

24537 NEW HAVEN: Although not cataloged, this black-painted car was made in 1958. The car was lettered in white, and came with eight black sheet metal stakes, which retained three silver-colored plastic pipes. The trucks had sintered-iron side frames and operating knuckle couplers.

VG-C6	EX-C7	LN-C8	Scarcity
10	20	45	6

24539 NEW HAVEN: First offered in 1958-59, this black car returned to the line in 1963 and 1964. Eight sheet metal stakes retained the three pipes that were the cargo of this white-lettered car.

24535 MONON

Values for each condition are in U.S. dollars. | Scarcity = Scale from 1-8 with 8 being the hardest to find.

85

FLATCARS

24539 NEW HAVEN (Type I): Some of the cars produced in 1958 and 1959 were painted black. Its cargo consisted of three silver plastic pipes, and its trucks had sintered-iron side frames and knuckle couplers. A two-piece brakewheel was installed.

VG-C6	EX-C7	LN-C8	Scarcity
10	20	30	3

24539 NEW HAVEN (Type II): Other cars of the 1958-59 era had unpainted black plastic bodies. The cargo, trucks and brakewheel were identical to those of the Type I.

VG-C6	EX-C7	LN-C8	Scarcity
10	20	30	3

24539 NEW HAVEN (Type III): Some cars otherwise identical to the Type II were furnished with a one-piece plastic brakestand.

VG-C6	EX-C7	LN-C8	Scarcity
10	20	30	3

24539 NEW HAVEN (Type IV): 1958-59, unpainted black plastic body, three silver-colored cardboard pipes were furnished with some of the unpainted 1958-59 cars. These cars had trucks with sintered-iron side frames.

VG-C6	EX-C7	LN-C8	Scarcity
10	20	30	3

24539 NEW HAVEN (Type V): Some of the unpainted 1958-59 cars were equipped with solid non-operating knuckle couplers.

VG-C6	EX-C7	LN-C8	Scarcity
10	20	30	3

24539 NEW HAVEN (Type VI): When the car returned in 1963-64, the body was unpainted black plastic. At this time, the cargo consisted of three orange cardboard pipes. The car had Pike Master trucks and couplers, and a one-piece plastic brakestand.

VG-C6	EX-C7	LN-C8	Scarcity
20	40	80	5

24540 NEW HAVEN: This unpainted black flatcar, carrying three silver cardboard pipes, was produced in 1960—but was not cataloged. The lettering of the car was white, and eight black sheet metal stakes retained the load.

VG-C6	EX-C7	LN-C8	Scarcity
60	125	200	6

24546 AMERICAN FLYER LINES: Introduced in 1958, this flatcar-based work caboose remained in the product line through 1964. On the gray plastic chassis was mounted a Tuscan-painted cabin and a Tuscan-painted plastic toolbox. The fences on this car were striped yellow and Tuscan. On the cabin the number "24546" was stamped in white, while the chassis was stamped "AMERICAN FLYER LINES" in black.

24546 AMERICAN FLYER LINES (Type I): Some of the cars were fitted with trucks with sintered-iron side frames and knuckle couplers.

VG-C6	EX-C7	LN-C8	Scarcity
15	30	45	3

24546 AMERICAN FLYER LINES (Type II): Otherwise, identical cars were produced with Pike Master trucks and couplers.

VG-C6	EX-C7	LN-C8	Scarcity
15	30	45	3

24547 ERIE: 📷 The Tuscan-painted plastic base of this car supported an unpainted yellow plastic generator and

24547 ERIE

a silver-painted lamp housing. Though not cataloged, this car was produced in 1958. The "ERIE" lettering, as well as the product number "24547," were stamped in white. The car had knuckle couplers and trucks with sintered-iron side frames.

VG-C6	EX-C7	LN-C8	Scarcity
225	500	800	8

24549 ERIE: Sold from 1958 through 1966, this Tuscan-painted flatcar supported an unpainted generator as well as a lamp housing. Many variations of the car exist.

24549 ERIE (Type I): Early cars had black die-cast lamp brackets, a silver-painted die-cast lamp housing and a yellow generator. The trucks used with this car had sintered-iron side frames and operating knuckle couplers.

VG-C6	EX-C7	LN-C8	Scarcity
15	30	50	4

24549 ERIE (Type II): Other cars, otherwise identical to the Type I, had unpainted red generators installed.

VG-C6	EX-C7	LN-C8	Scarcity
15	30	50	4

24549 ERIE (Type III): Also similar to the Type I was this car, which was equipped with Pike Master trucks and couplers.

VG-C6	EX-C7	LN-C8	Scarcity
15	30	50	4

24549 ERIE (Type IV): Later cars continued to use die-cast lamp housings, but the lamp supports became stamped steel rather than die-cast. The car had a yellow generator and Pike Master trucks and couplers.

VG-C6	EX-C7	LN-C8	Scarcity
10	20	30	4

24549 ERIE (Type V): This car was almost identical to the Type IV, except it featured an unpainted molded black plastic lamp housing.

VG-C6	EX-C7	LN-C8	Scarcity
10	20	30	4

24549 ERIE (Type VI): Other cars had unpainted white plastic lamp housings. They were otherwise duplicates of the Type V.

VG-C6	EX-C7	LN-C8	Scarcity
10	20	30	4

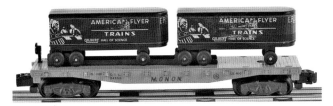

24550 MONON: Sold from 1959 through 1964, this gray flatcar came with two piggyback vans. The colorful markings on the vans promoted American Flyer trains and other Gilbert products. The red markings of the flatcar were those of the Monon railroad. Note: this car IS compatible with the 23830 unloader.

VG-C6	EX-C7	LN-C8	Scarcity
30	60	90	4

24553 ROCKET TRANSPORT: This 1958-1960 rocket transporting flatcar was painted olive drab, and lettered in white. The two spring-steel brackets on the car each held a rocket. Beware: reproduction rockets have been made.

24553 ROCKET TRANSPORT (Type I): In 1958 and 1959, the cars came with a red, white and blue rocket.

VG-C6	EX-C7	LN-C8	Scarcity
30	60	90	5

24553 ROCKET TRANSPORT (Type II): In 1960, the rockets were red and white single-piece units.

VG-C6	EX-C7	LN-C8	Scarcity
30	60	90	5

24556 ROCK ISLAND: Offered in 1959, this unpainted black plastic flatcar was laden with four-wheel and axle assemblies, held in place by a sheet metal bracket. The car rode on trucks with sintered-iron side frames and knuckle couplers.

24556 ROCK ISLAND (Type I): Some of the cars had a two-piece brakewheel installed.

VG-C6	EX-C7	LN-C8	Scarcity
30	60	90	5

FLATCARS

Values for each condition are in U.S. dollars. | **Scarcity** = Scale from 1-8 with 8 being the hardest to find.

87

24556 ROCK ISLAND (Type II): Other cars used a one-piece plastic brakestand.

VG-C6	EX-C7	LN-C8	Scarcity
30	60	90	5

24557 U. S. NAVY: From 1959 through 1961, this gray-painted flatcar loaded with two Tootsietoy Jeeps was offered. The sheet metal cargo retainer was the same as the one used on the 24556.

24557 U. S. NAVY (Type I): The earliest cars came with a two-piece brakewheel.

VG-C6	EX-C7	LN-C8	Scarcity
30	75	125	3

24557 U. S. NAVY (Type II): Later cars were equipped with a one-piece plastic brakestand.

VG-C6	EX-C7	LN-C8	Scarcity
30	75	125	3

24558 CANADIAN PACIFIC: Cataloged in 1959 and 1960, this Tuscan-painted car carried four Christmas trees. The trees were originally packed in a bag, and eight sheet metal stakes came with the car. The trucks had sintered-iron side frames and knuckle couplers.

24558 CANADIAN PACIFIC (Type I): The early cars had fiber-type trees and two-piece brakewheel.

VG-C6	EX-C7	LN-C8	Scarcity
75	175	375	7

24558 CANADIAN PACIFIC (Type II): Later cars came with rubber-type trees and were equipped with a one-piece plastic brakewheel stand.

VG-C6	EX-C7	LN-C8	Scarcity
75	175	375	7

24559 NEW HAVEN: Although not cataloged, this car was produced in 1959. The unladen car was lettered in white. The trucks had sintered-iron side frames and knuckle couplers. This car was included in Sears outfit 20059.

24559 NEW HAVEN (Type I): Some of the cars were painted black.

VG-C6	EX-C7	LN-C8	Scarcity
75	175	375	7

24559 NEW HAVEN (Type II): Other cars were made of unpainted black plastic.

VG-C6	EX-C7	LN-C8	Scarcity
75	175	375	7

24562 NEW YORK CENTRAL: This unladen, unpainted black car was built in 1960. Its lettering was white, and the car came with four blackened sheet metal stakes. The trucks had sintered-iron side frames and knuckle couplers. The car was included in the 20610 outfit—but not sold separately.

VG-C6	EX-C7	LN-C8	Scarcity
15	25	45	4

24564 NEW HAVEN: Though uncataloged, this unpainted black car was produced in 1960. The car was lettered in white, and was furnished with blackened sheet metal stakes and three pipes. The car rode on Pike Master trucks, and used Pike Master couplers.

24564 NEW HAVEN (Type I): Some of the cars came with plastic pipes.

VG-C6	EX-C7	LN-C8	Scarcity
15	25	45	4

24564 NEW HAVEN (Type II): Other cars came with orange cardboard pipes.

VG-C6	EX-C7	LN-C8	Scarcity
25	45	75	6

24565 F. Y. & P. R. R.: Sold in 1960 and 1961, this unpainted tan flatcar, decorated with brown camouflage, was loaded with a metal replica of a black powder cannon. Rather than the entire catalog number, only the "65" was stamped on the removable sides of the car. The cannon was brown with a black barrel.

24565 F. Y. & P. R. R. (Type I): Some of the cars were equipped with sintered-iron side frame trucks and knuckle couplers.

VG-C6	EX-C7	LN-C8	Scarcity
40	80	165	6

24565 F. Y. & P. R. R. (Type II): Other cars had Pike Master trucks and couplers.

VG-C6	EX-C7	LN-C8	Scarcity
40	80	165	6

24566 NEW HAVEN: Sold from 1961 through 1964, this car was loaded with a truck pulling an auto transport trailer. A sheet metal bracket was used to secure the tractor to the flatcar, and the trailer in turn was secured to the tractor. The tractor, which could be blue or red, pulled a silver trailer, which hauled five plastic automobiles—one each blue, green, orange, red and yellow. The railcar had Pike Master trucks and couplers, but no brakewheel was installed.

24566 NEW HAVEN (Type I): Some of the flatcars produced in 1961 had unpainted gray plastic bodies with black "NEW HAVEN" lettering.

VG-C6	EX-C7	LN-C8	Scarcity
300	600	1,000	8

24566 NEW HAVEN (Type II): The vast majority of the flatcars were unpainted black plastic bodies with white "NEW HAVEN" lettering.

VG-C6	EX-C7	LN-C8	Scarcity
30	60	100	5

24572 U. S. NAVY: Sold in 1961, this gray flatcar transported two olive drab or red Jeeps. "24572 U.S. NAVY 24572" was stamped in black on the sides of the flatcar body.
24572 U. S. NAVY (Type I): Some of the car bodies were painted gray.

VG-C6	EX-C7	LN-C8	Scarcity
50	100	200	7

24572 U. S. NAVY (Type II): Other cars were unpainted light gray plastic.

VG-C6	EX-C7	LN-C8	Scarcity
40	85	160	5

24574 U. S. AIR FORCE: This blue-painted flatcar was sold in 1960 and 1961. The yellow lettering on the car sides read "24574," "U S AIR FORCE" and "UNIT II." Two vertical silver tanks were the cargo and were held in place by a pair of red bulkheads.

24574 U. S. AIR FORCE (Type I): Some of the cars came with sintered-iron side frame trucks with knuckle couplers. Some cars of this type are known to have come in Kleer-Pak boxes.

VG-C6	EX-C7	LN-C8	Scarcity
50	100	200	5

24574 U. S. AIR FORCE (Type II): Other cars were equipped with Pike Master trucks and couplers.

VG-C6	EX-C7	LN-C8	Scarcity
40	90	175	5

24575 NATIONAL CAR CO.: Sold from 1960 through 1966, this unpainted black flatcar carried to white "Bordens" milk containers.

24575 NATIONAL CAR CO. (Type I): Cars made in 1960 and 1961 had knuckle couplers and trucks with sintered-iron side frames, as well as a one-piece brakewheel. The flatcar was lettered "24575," "NATIONAL CAR CO." and "BLT. 10-30" in white.

VG-C6	EX-C7	LN-C8	Scarcity
25	50	100	5

Values for each condition are in U.S. dollars. | **Scarcity** = Scale from 1-8 with 8 being the hardest to find.

24575 NATIONAL CAR CO. (Type II): In 1962, Pike Master trucks and couplers were used, as was the case through 1966. The car still had a one-piece brakewheel and was lettered "24575," "NATIONAL CAR CO." and "BLT. 10-30" in white.

VG-C6	EX-C7	LN-C8	Scarcity
20	40	80	4

24575 UNLETTERED (Type III): Though not illustrated in the catalog in this configuration, some of the 1966 cars did not have any lettering stamped on the unpainted black flatcar. The two white milk containers however continued to be stamped "Bordens" in black. This version of the car did not have brakewheels, and featured Pike Master trucks and couplers. It is suspected that these cars were assembled outside of the Gilbert factory by dealers using surplus parts.

VG-C6	EX-C7	LN-C8	Scarcity
15	30	60	3

24577 ILLINOIS CENTRAL: This black flatcar with white "24577," "ILLINOIS CENTRAL" and "BLT 57" lettering was first sold in 1960-61. Then it was dropped in 1962, and then returned again in 1963-64. Its cargo was two accurately modeled jet engine transport containers. Lettering on these containers, stamped in black, read "TURBO JET J-75 ENGINE," "RELEASE AIR BEFORE OPENING" and "DO NOT DESTROY CONTAINER."

24577 ILLINOIS CENTRAL (Type I): Some of the early cars had sintered-iron side frame trucks and knuckle couplers. These cars also had a one-piece plastic brakewheel, and sometimes came in a Kleer-Pak box.

VG-C6	EX-C7	LN-C8	Scarcity
50	100	200	5

24577 ILLINOIS CENTRAL (Type II): Later cars had no brakewheel and were equipped with Pike Master trucks and couplers.

VG-C6	EX-C7	LN-C8	Scarcity
40	75	150	5

24578 NEW HAVEN: The cargo of this unpainted black plastic 1962-63 flatcar was a Chevrolet Corvette. The railcar was lettered for the New Haven in white, and the plastic automobile could be blue, green, red, yellow, or white. A gray figure was at the wheel of the car—even though a train was transporting the car! Pike Master trucks and couplers were used, and no brakewheel was installed.

VG-C6	EX-C7	LN-C8	Scarcity
90	175	325	6

24579 ILLINOIS CENTRAL: This Tuscan-painted 1960-61 flatcar is known as a multiple-purpose car. Lettered "24579," "ILLINOIS CENTRAL" and "BLT. 9-59," the car came with: eight sheet metal stakes, two red-painted sheet metal bulkheads, two silver-painted black plastic containers with black "DELAWARE AND HUDSON" lettering, three pieces of lumber, and four pipes.

24579 ILLINOIS CENTRAL (Type I): Some of the cars came with sintered-iron side frame trucks and knuckle couplers. The pipe with these cars could be either silver plastic or silver cardboard.

VG-C6	EX-C7	LN-C8	Scarcity
50	100	200	5

24579 ILLINOIS CENTRAL (Type II): Other cars retained the metal trucks, but carried four orange cardboard pipes. This version had been found in Kleer-Pak boxes.

VG-C6	EX-C7	LN-C8	Scarcity
60	110	225	6

24579 ILLINOIS CENTRAL (Type III): Other cars transporting four orange cardboard pipes had Pike Master trucks and couplers.

VG-C6	EX-C7	LN-C8	Scarcity
50	100	200	6

25003 AMERICAN FLYER: Though basic in appearance, this 1957-60 operating log dump car added considerable enjoyment for operators. The car had a die-cast chassis and a sheet metal tilting platform. The chassis was painted black, and the tilting platform was either unpainted aluminum, or gray-painted sheet metal. The car had sheet metal trucks and link couplers. It came with four logs.

25003 AMERICAN FLYER (Type I): Some cars had unpainted aluminum tilt platforms. The upper surface of the platform was lettered "25003" and "AMERICAN FLYER."

VG-C6	EX-C7	LN-C8	Scarcity
100	200	450	7

25003 AMERICAN FLYER (Type II): The tilt platform of other cars was painted gray. The upper surface of the platform was lettered "25003" and "AMERICAN FLYER."

VG-C6	EX-C7	LN-C8	Scarcity
100	200	450	7

25003 AMERICAN FLYER (Type III): Some cars were produced with unpainted aluminum tilt platforms with no lettering.

VG-C6	EX-C7	LN-C8	Scarcity
15	30	55	4

25015 SOUTHERN PACIFIC: In 1957, the 971 was packaged in a box marked "25015."

25016 SOUTHERN PACIFIC: The 1957-60 version of the "SOUTHERN PACIFIC" "Moe" and "Joe" lumber unloading car was unpainted Tuscan plastic. The car came with eight planks, two figures and sintered-iron side frame trucks with knuckle couplers.

VG-C6	EX-C7	LN-C8	Scarcity
50	100	150	5

25032 AMERICAN FLYER LINES: In 1957, the gray 915 with a brown ramp hauling a Renwal gasoline truck came in a box numbered "25032."

25033 AMERICAN FLYER LINES: In 1957, the 915 came in a box numbered "25033."

25044 ROCKET LAUNCHER: In 1957, the 969 came in a box numbered "25044."

25045 ROCKET LAUNCHER: This unpainted black flatcar was offered from 1957 through 1960. The white lettering on the side "ROCKET LAUNCHER," describes exactly what this action car does. The solenoid mechanism, wrapped in red tape, was plainly visible adjacent to the gray die-cast vertical launch base on the deck of the car. A Tuscan-painted toolbox was also mounted on the deck. Various color combinations of rockets have been found with this car. Beware: the rockets have been reproduced.

VG-C6	EX-C7	LN-C8	Scarcity
25	50	75	4

25046 ROCKET LAUNCHER: In 1960, this 45-degree rocket launch flatcar was sold. Although shown here with the red and white rocket for the 25056, this car actually came with a red, white and blue rocket, as seen in the photo of the 25056.

25046 ROCKET LAUNCHER (Type I): Some of the cars had unpainted black plastic bodies.

VG-C6	EX-C7	LN-C8	Scarcity
25	60	90	5

25046 ROCKET LAUNCHER (Type II): Other cars were painted black.

VG-C6	EX-C7	LN-C8	Scarcity
25	60	90	5

25056 ROCKET LAUNCHER and U. S. M.: This two-car set appeared in the 1959 20525 "Defender" train set.

FLATCARS

Values for each condition are in U.S. dollars. | **Scarcity** = Scale from 1-8 with 8 being the hardest to find.

91

The 25056 was comprised of a painted yellow boxcar and rocket-launching flatcar. A tether connected the three-door boxcar to the flatcar. Although the rocket shown above is red, white and blue, the correct rocket for this car has a red nose and all-white body.

25056 ROCKET LAUNCHER and U. S. M. (Type I): The door guides of the cars believed to be the first produced was secured with rivets.

VG-C6	EX-C7	LN-C8	Scarcity
125	225	500	7

25056 ROCKET LAUNCHER and U. S. M. (Type II): The door guides on other boxcars were secured with tabs.

VG-C6	EX-C7	LN-C8	Scarcity
125	225	500	7

25058 SOUTHERN PACIFIC: The Tuscan "Moe" and "Joe" unloading flatcar was re-equipped with Pike Master trucks and couplers in 1961, necessitating the number change to "25058." The car was sold in this configuration through 1964.

VG-C6	EX-C7	LN-C8	Scarcity
45	80	175	5

25059 ROCKET LAUNCHER: This 45-degree rocket launcher was sold from 1960 through 1964. The black-painted flatcar was lettered in white, and carried a blue plastic launch unit. The car had Pike Master trucks and couplers.

25059 ROCKET LAUNCHER (Type I): Most cars were lettered "ROCKET LAUNCHER."

VG-C6	EX-C7	LN-C8	Scarcity
20	40	75	4

25059 ROCKET LAUNCHER (Type II): In 1962-64, cars were produced with no name on the sides.

VG-C6	EX-C7	LN-C8	Scarcity
20	40	75	4

25071 AMERICAN FLYER TIE CAR: This orange, gray and brown car was sold from 1961 through 1964. When activated by the trackside trip—two versions of which were furnished with the car, one for Pike Master track and another for standard track—the car ejected four crossties. The car was equipped with Pike Master trucks and couplers.

25071 AMERICAN FLYER TIE CAR (Type I): Some of the cars were lettered "AMERICAN FLYER TIE CAR 25071" in black.

VG-C6	EX-C7	LN-C8	Scarcity
10	20	35	4

25071 AMERICAN FLYER TIE CAR (Type II): Other cars had no lettering.

VG-C6	EX-C7	LN-C8	Scarcity
10	20	35	4

25515 U. S. A. F.: This black 1960-63 flatcar was laden with an unpainted yellow rocket sled replica—which made the car top heavy and caused it to track poorly. The rocket sled could run on the track under its own power, being motorized with a Gilbert slot car motor. A mechanism in the sled would eject the pilot.

25515 U. S. A. F. (Type I): Some of these cars had trucks with sintered-iron side frames and knuckle couplers. The carried a yellow plastic rocket sled, and came in Kleer-Pak boxes.

VG-C6	EX-C7	LN-C8	Scarcity
60	125	250	7

25515 U. S. A. F. (Type II): Other cars had Pike Master trucks and couplers.

VG-C6	EX-C7	LN-C8	Scarcity
60	125	250	7

42597 C. & N. W. RY.: See 627, 628, 634, 928, or 934.

GONDOLA AND DUMP CARS

No matter the era, gauge or maker, gondola cars are among the most commonly produced type of toy train car. Their simple design makes them inexpensive to produce; yet their walled sides lend them to transporting an array of toys for young enthusiasts. Countless Lincoln Logs, Erector beams and American Bricks have ridden in the ubiquitous gondolas.

Despite the widespread appearance of this type of car, there are nevertheless some rare cars and variations.

Basic dating of the various cars follows the following pattern: The steps on the car corners were reinforced in 1949. Cars with a rectangular gap above the couplers were made prior to 1953. In 1952, Flyer began to phase in a body with this opening having beveled sides, which was then used through 1966.

Values for each condition are in U.S. dollars. | **Scarcity** = Scale from 1-8 with 8 being the hardest to find.

93

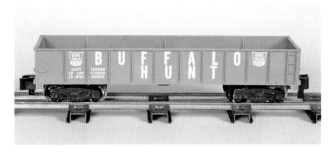

NO NUMBER BUFFALO HUNT: This unpainted green car was offered in 1963. The large white sans serif lettering on the car side read "BUFFALO HUNT." As indicated by the "GAME TRAIN," the car was included in outfits by the same name. It was equipped with Pike Master trucks and couplers.

VG-C6	EX-C7	LN-C8	Scarcity
5	10	15	2

620 SOUTHERN: Sold in 1953, this car was either unpainted black plastic or painted black. The white "SOUTHERN" lettering along the sides of the cars also came in two styles—evenly spaced or unevenly spaced.

VG-C6	EX-C7	LN-C8	Scarcity
30	60	100	7

631 TEXAS & PACIFIC: One of the longest-lived of all pieces of American Flyer rolling stock is this link coupler equipped 1946-53 gondola. Typically found in green, the car also exists in red and gray.

631 TEXAS & PACIFIC (Type I): In 1946-47, the gondola had an unpainted dark green plastic body and couplers without weights.

VG-C6	EX-C7	LN-C8	Scarcity
20	40	60	6

631 TEXAS & PACIFIC (Type II): In 1948, weighted couplers were used, although the car continued to be unpainted green plastic. This version of the car was produced through 1951.

VG-C6	EX-C7	LN-C8	Scarcity
5	10	20	1

631 TEXAS & PACIFIC (Type III): In 1948, a few cars were produced with unpainted gray plastic bodies. This version was not shown in the Flyer catalog.

VG-C6	EX-C7	LN-C8	Scarcity
125	250	450	7

631 TEXAS & PACIFIC (Type IV): Painted green bodies have been found on some cars produced between 1951 and 1953.

VG-C6	EX-C7	LN-C8	Scarcity
5	10	20	1

631 TEXAS & PACIFIC (Type V): Another uncataloged color variation was created around 1951, when the red-painted car rolled off the assembly line.

VG-C6	EX-C7	LN-C8	Scarcity
70	125	200	6

641 AMERICAN FLYER: This 1949-52 gondola is known to have come with either link or knuckle couplers. Regardless of the body color, the sides were lettered "AMERICAN FLYER" and "641" in two lines with white printing. The spacing of the letters was adjusted to accommodate the ribs molded in the car sides.

641 AMERICAN FLYER (Type I): Body painted red.

VG-C6	EX-C7	LN-C8	Scarcity
10	15	25	4

641 AMERICAN FLYER (Type II): Unpainted red plastic bodies were used in 1949-50.

VG-C6	EX-C7	LN-C8	Scarcity
5	10	15	1

641 AMERICAN FLYER (Type III): Unpainted gray plastic bodies were used on some uncataloged cars produced in 1951.

VG-C6	EX-C7	LN-C8	Scarcity
125	250	450	7

641 FRISCO: The body of this 1953 was painted Tuscan and lettered "FRISCO LINES" in white. It was equipped with link couplers.

VG-C6	EX-C7	LN-C8	Scarcity
10	15	30	3

719 C. B. & Q.: This 1950-54 dump car was equipped with link couplers and came packaged with a 712 control rail, bag of coal, receiving bin and a control button.

719 C. B. & Q. (Type I): Red unpainted cars was produced in 1950.

VG-C6	EX-C7	LN-C8	Scarcity
30	60	100	6

719 C. B. & Q. (Type II): Beginning in 1951, the car bodies were molded of black plastic, which were then painted Tuscan.

VG-C6	EX-C7	LN-C8	Scarcity
20	40	80	4

804 NORFOLK AND WESTERN: Also produced in 1956-57 was another unpainted black gondola with knuckle couplers—this time lettered "NORFOLK AND WESTERN N & W."

VG-C6	EX-C7	LN-C8	Scarcity
10	15	20	2

805 PENNSYLVANIA: Equipped with knuckle couplers, this 1956-57 gondola carried the name and logo of the famed Pennsylvania railroad.

805 PENNSYLVANIA (Type I): Most cars were unpainted Tuscan plastic.

VG-C6	EX-C7	LN-C8	Scarcity
5	10	15	1

805 PENNSYLVANIA (Type II): However, some cars were molded in black plastic, which was then painted Tuscan.

VG-C6	EX-C7	LN-C8	Scarcity
15	25	35	5

911 CHESAPEAKE & OHIO: Another of the 1955-57 gondolas bore the "C & O" markings of the Chesapeake and Ohio. In most instances the black car was laden with silver pipes that were held in place by yellow plastic brackets. The cars featured knuckle couplers.

911 CHESAPEAKE & OHIO (Type I): Some cars had unpainted black bodies with large "PROGRESS" in logo.

VG-C6	EX-C7	LN-C8	Scarcity
10	20	35	3

911 CHESAPEAKE & OHIO (Type II): Painted black body with large "PROGRESS" in logo.

VG-C6	EX-C7	LN-C8	Scarcity
10	25	40	4

911 CHESAPEAKE & OHIO (Type III): Also painted black was this car with smaller "PROGRESS" markings.

VG-C6	EX-C7	LN-C8	Scarcity
10	25	40	4

911 CHESAPEAKE & OHIO (Type IV): Some of the painted black 1955 cars bore a brown plastic pipe.

VG-C6	EX-C7	LN-C8	Scarcity
75	200	300	7

916 DELAWARE & HUDSON: The body of this 1955-56 gondola was painted Tuscan and carried the white markings of "The D & H." The car was furnished with five silver LCL canisters, which were marked "DELAWARE AND HUDSON" in black. The car was equipped with knuckle couplers.

916 DELAWARE & HUDSON (Type I): Markings include "LT.WT. 52300" and "CU FT 4318."

VG-C6	EX-C7	LN-C8	Scarcity
10	20	35	2

916 DELAWARE & HUDSON (Type II): The reporting marks on other cars read "LT.WT. 52900" and "CU FT 4316."

VG-C6	EX-C7	LN-C8	Scarcity
10	20	35	2

919 C. B. & Q.: This Tuscan-painted side dump car was sold from 1953 through 1956 and came with control rail,

Values for each condition are in U.S. dollars. | **Scarcity** = Scale from 1-8 with 8 being the hardest to find.

95

control button, receiving bin and bag of coal. It was equipped with knuckle couplers.

919 C. B. & Q. (Type I): The white markings of some of the cars included "CAPY. 38 CU. YD. LD. LMT. 106000 LB. LT. WT. 58100 LB."

VG-C6	EX-C7	LN-C8	Scarcity
20	45	85	4

919 C. B. & Q. (Type II): Other cars were marked "CAPY. 30 CU. YD. LD. LMT. 108100 LB. LT. WT. 60100 LB."

VG-C6	EX-C7	LN-C8	Scarcity
20	45	85	4

920 SOUTHERN: From 1953 through 1956, black gondolas with knuckle couplers and "SOUTHERN" markings were sold.

920 SOUTHERN (Type I): Some of the cars were painted black.

VG-C6	EX-C7	LN-C8	Scarcity
10	18	25	2

920 SOUTHERN (Type II): Other cars had unpainted black plastic bodies.

VG-C6	EX-C7	LN-C8	Scarcity
10	18	25	2

931 TEXAS & PACIFIC: This green gondola was sold from 1952 through 1955. It bore white "T & P TEXAS & PACIFIC 931" markings and was equipped with knuckle couplers.

931 TEXAS & PACIFIC (Type I): Body painted dark green.

VG-C6	EX-C7	LN-C8	Scarcity
10	15	20	1

931 TEXAS & PACIFIC (Type II): The body of some cars was unpainted dark green plastic.

VG-C6	EX-C7	LN-C8	Scarcity
10	15	20	1

941 FRISCO LINES: This Tuscan-painted "FRISCO LINES" gondola was offered from 1953 through 1956. This car, which was available for separate sale only, came with knuckle couplers.

VG-C6	EX-C7	LN-C8	Scarcity
10	15	20	3

C-2009 TEXAS & PACIFIC: Offered from 1962 through 1964, this car, equipped with Pike Master trucks and couplers, was stamped with white "TEXAS & PACIFIC," "T & P" and "C-2009" markings.

C-2009 TEXAS & PACIFIC (Type I): What is believed to be the earliest of these cars were painted dark green.

VG-C6	EX-C7	LN-C8	Scarcity
Too rarely traded to accurately establish pricing.			

C-2009 TEXAS & PACIFIC (Type II): Most of the cars had unpainted light green plastic bodies.

VG-C6	EX-C7	LN-C8	Scarcity
4	7	15	1

24103 NORFOLK AND WESTERN: Black gondola cars with this number were sold during two widely separate time periods.

24103 NORFOLK AND WESTERN (Type I): The earliest cars were produced in 1958 and had knuckle couplers and trucks with sintered-iron side frames.

VG-C6	EX-C7	LN-C8	Scarcity
5	10	15	2

24103 NORFOLK AND WESTERN (Type II): The 1963-64 production cars were equipped with Pike Master trucks and couplers.

VG-C6	EX-C7	LN-C8	Scarcity
5	10	15	1

24106 PENNSYLVANIA: This uncataloged Tuscan gondola was produced in 1960.

24106 PENNSYLVANIA (Type I): Some of these cars were painted Tuscan.

VG-C6	EX-C7	LN-C8	Scarcity
100	175	250	7

24106 PENNSYLVANIA (Type II): Most cars, however, were unpainted Tuscan plastic.

VG-C6	EX-C7	LN-C8	Scarcity
5	10	15	1

24108 CHESAPEAKE & OHIO: This 1957 car was merely a serif-lettered 911 in a 24108 box.

24109 CHESAPEAKE & OHIO: Offered from 1958 through 1960, this black car had C & O markings and yellow pipe retainers.

24109 CHESAPEAKE & OHIO (Type I): Cars sold in 1958 were furnished with silver plastic pipes.

VG-C6	EX-C7	LN-C8	Scarcity
20	35	60	4

24109 CHESAPEAKE & OHIO (Type II): Beginning in 1959, cardboard pipes were used. The cardboard pipes with this version were silver.

VG-C6	EX-C7	LN-C8	Scarcity
20	35	60	4

24109 CHESAPEAKE & OHIO (Type III): A few cars were shipped with orange cardboard pipes.

VG-C6	EX-C7	LN-C8	Scarcity
40	80	120	7

24110 PENNSYLVANIA: This uncataloged, unpainted Tuscan gondola was produced in 1959.

VG-C6	EX-C7	LN-C8	Scarcity
5	10	15	1

24112 DELAWARE AND HUDSON: In 1957, Flyer sold 916 gondolas in boxes numbered "24112."

24113 DELAWARE AND HUDSON: This 1957-59 Tuscan-painted gondola was decorated with white "The D & H" markings. The car was laden with canisters painted silver and marked "DELAWARE AND HUDSON" in black. The car had knuckle couplers.

24113 DELAWARE AND HUDSON (Type I): Some of the cars came with five canisters and the sides of the car were marked "LT. WT. 52300" and "CU FT 4318."

VG-C6	EX-C7	LN-C8	Scarcity
10	20	40	4

24113 DELAWARE AND HUDSON (Type II): Other cars were printed with "LT. WT. 52900" and "CU FT 4316"; but continued to come with five canisters.

VG-C6	EX-C7	LN-C8	Scarcity
10	20	40	4

24113 DELAWARE AND HUDSON (Type III): The cars furnished in the 1959 set 20515 were "LT. WT. 52900" and "CU FT 4316." These cars came with only three canisters.

VG-C6	EX-C7	LN-C8	Scarcity
10	20	40	4

24115 SOUTHERN: In 1957, some 920 gondolas were packaged in 24115 boxes.

24116 SOUTHERN: From 1957 through 1960, this black gondola with white lettering and knuckle couplers was sold.

VG-C6	EX-C7	LN-C8	Scarcity
40	80	125	6

Values for each condition are in U.S. dollars. | **Scarcity** = Scale from 1-8 with 8 being the hardest to find.

24120 T & P: In 1960, this unpainted dark green gondola with Pike Master trucks and couplers was produced, but not cataloged.

VG-C6	EX-C7	LN-C8	Scarcity
25	50	80	5

24122 FRISCO: In 1957, 941 gondola cars were packaged in boxes numbered "24122."

24124 BOSTON AND MAINE: The bright blue of these cars was a sharp contrast to the dull Tuscan and black used on most gondolas. These 1963-64 cars had white lettering and came with Pike Master trucks and couplers.

24124 BOSTON AND MAINE (Type I): Unpainted blue plastic was used for most of the cars.

VG-C6	EX-C7	LN-C8	Scarcity
5	10	20	1

24124 BOSTON AND MAINE (Type II): Some cars were made of unpainted blue-green plastic.

VG-C6	EX-C7	LN-C8	Scarcity
5	10	20	1

24124 BOSTON AND MAINE (Type III): A few cars were painted blue.

VG-C6	EX-C7	LN-C8	Scarcity
100	200	400	7

24125 BETHLEHEM STEEL: From 1960 through 1964, American Flyer produced these gray gondola cars lettered "BETHLEHEM STEEL."

24125 BETHLEHEM STEEL (Type I): Some cars were painted gray and were decorated with red lettering. The trucks on these cars had operating knuckle couplers. It was loaded with four 7-5/8-inch long rails for S-Gauge track, which were held in place by two metal holders. These holders have been reproduced.

VG-C6	EX-C7	LN-C8	Scarcity
50	100	150	7

24125 BETHLEHEM STEEL (Type II): Other cars, still painted gray and lettered in red, were equipped with Pike Master trucks and couplers. The same load and brackets were used.

VG-C6	EX-C7	LN-C8	Scarcity
40	80	120	6

24125 BETHLEHEM STEEL (Type III): In 1965 and 1966, the car was made of unpainted light gray plastic. These cars, which did not have loads, rode on Pike Master trucks and couplers. These cars were lettered with maroon, orange or red printing.

VG-C6	EX-C7	LN-C8	Scarcity
5	10	15	1

24124 BOSTON AND MAINE (Type III)

24126 FRISCO: An unpainted Tuscan Frisco gondola returned in 1961 with a new number—24126—for this year only. The car came with Pike Master trucks and couplers.

VG-C6	EX-C7	LN-C8	Scarcity
45	90	140	6

24127 MONON: Sold between 1961 and 1965, this unpainted light gray gondola was lettered in dark red and was equipped with Pike Master trucks and couplers.

VG-C6	EX-C7	LN-C8	Scarcity
5	10	15	1

24130 PENNSYLVANIA: The markings on this brown plastic car did NOT include the product number, but did include white "PENNSYLVANIA" lettering and keystone logo. Though uncataloged, the car was made in 1960 and came with Pike Master trucks and couplers.

24130 PENNSYLVANIA (Type I): Most of these cars were made with unpainted bodies.

VG-C6	EX-C7	LN-C8	Scarcity
8	16	24	2

24130 PENNSYLVANIA (Type II): A handful of these cars were produced with painted bodies.

VG-C6	EX-C7	LN-C8	Scarcity
Too rarely traded to accurately establish pricing.			

25008 C. B. & Q.: In 1957, the 919 dump car, along with its bag of coal, receiving tray, control rail and control button, were packaged in a box numbered "25008."

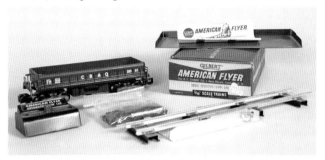

25025 C. B. & Q.: The body of this 1958-60 tilting dump car was painted Tuscan and lettered in white. The car came with a small bag of coal, 712 special rail section and a control box lettered "AMERICAN FLYER AUTOMATIC DUMP CAR."

VG-C6	EX-C7	LN-C8	Scarcity
85	150	250	7

25060 C. B. & Q.: 📷 In 1961-64, the white-lettered Tuscan dump car continued to be decorated in white. This car was packaged with a 26700 straight track, 712 contact rail, a small bag of coal, sheet metal receiving bin, four Pike Master/Standard S adapter pins and control box, lettered "AMERICAN FLYER AUTOMATIC DUMP CAR".

VG-C6	EX-C7	LN-C8	Scarcity
100	200	300	8

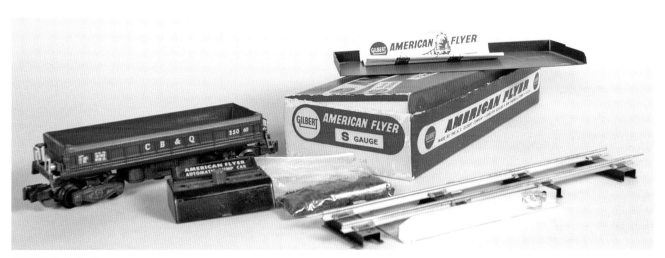

25060 C.B.& Q.

GONDOLA AND DUMP CARS

HOPPER CARS

Hopper cars were a staple of many outfits offered by American Flyer during the Gilbert era. No doubt one factor is the simple one-piece body used by many of these cars, which equated to lower manufacturing costs.

Various styles of hoppers were produced however, including die-cast and plastic two-bay hoppers, with the latter including covered variations. Molded plastic simulated loads were created for use in some of the two-bay hoppers. The prewar operating hopper car was adapted to S-Gauge and carried over briefly into the postwar era. A plastic three-bay hopper was added to the line in 1958. Many versions of the hopper were offered for separate sale, but as the Gilbert era came to a close hoppers were relegated to set components only with the 24225 Santa Fe—the last of the hoppers.

632 VIRGINIAN: The first S-Gauge hopper, the 1946 Virginian, utilized the die-cast body that had been developed prior to WWII for use in the 3/16-inch scale O-Gauge line. The catalog number was not printed on the car, which was marked only with black sans serif "VIRGINIAN" lettering. Four operating sheet metal doors closed the bottom.

632 VIRGINIAN (Type I): Some cars were painted blue-gray.

VG-C6	EX-C7	LN-C8	Scarcity
50	80	125	6

632 VIRGINIAN (Type II): Other cars were painted gray.

VG-C6	EX-C7	LN-C8	Scarcity
50	80	125	6

632 L N E: This hopper car was first produced in 1946 with a die-cast body, but before that year was out the body material changed to plastic, which remained through 1953. Regardless of body material, the car was decorated with the circular "LEHIGH NEW ENGLAND" logo and used sheet metal trucks and link couplers.

632 L N E (Type I): Cars produced in early 1946 had gray-painted die-cast bodies with black opening bottom hatches.

VG-C6	EX-C7	LN-C8	Scarcity
100	200	300	7

632 L N E (Type II): Cars produced in mid-1946 had unpainted black plastic bodies.

VG-C6	EX-C7	LN-C8	Scarcity
20	45	75	5

632 L N E (Type III): By late 1946, the body was unpainted light gray plastic.

VG-C6	EX-C7	LN-C8	Scarcity
5	10	20	1

632 L N E (Type IV): Dark gray unpainted bodies appeared in 1947.

VG-C6	EX-C7	LN-C8	Scarcity
5	10	20	1

632 L N E (Type V): In 1950, a few cars were produced with unpainted white bodies.

VG-C6	EX-C7	LN-C8	Scarcity
45	100	140	6

632 L N E (Type VI): It is believed that some cars were painted gray in 1953.

VG-C6	EX-C7	LN-C8	Scarcity
20	45	75	5

640 AMERICAN FLYER: From 1949 through 1953, hopper cars were also produced with "AMERICAN FLYER 640" markings. These cars were made exclusively for use as components of inexpensive sets.

640 AMERICAN FLYER (Type I): The cars were typically molded of gray plastic—which came in various shades—and left unpainted. They were stamped with white lettering.

VG-C6	EX-C7	LN-C8	Scarcity
5	10	15	1

640 AMERICAN FLYER (Type II): Some cars had unpainted gray plastic bodies, but the lettering was stamped in black.

VG-C6	EX-C7	LN-C8	Scarcity
15	35	60	5

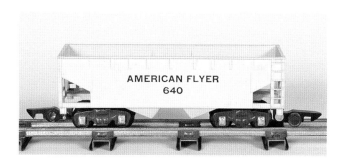

640 AMERICAN FLYER (Type III): Some cars had unpainted white bodies with black lettering.

VG-C6	EX-C7	LN-C8	Scarcity
30	60	100	6

640 AMERICAN FLYER (Type IV): A handful of cars were produced with black bodies and white lettering.

VG-C6	EX-C7	LN-C8	Scarcity
Too rarely traded to accurately establish pricing.			

640 AMERICAN FLYER (Type V): Some cars had painted gray bodies, with the lettering stamped in white.

VG-C6	EX-C7	LN-C8	Scarcity
Too rarely traded to accurately establish pricing.			

Values for each condition are in U.S. dollars. | **Scarcity** = Scale from 1-8 with 8 being the hardest to find.

101

HOPPER CARS

640 WABASH: In 1953, this black-painted hopper car with white "WABASH" lettering was sold. The cars came with link couplers and with or without truck weights.

VG-C6	EX-C7	LN-C8	Scarcity
10	20	30	3

716 AMERICAN FLYER LINES: Sold from 1946 through 1951, this red operating side dump car was equipped with link couplers. The car was constructed of sheet metal and was ultimately replaced in the Flyer product line by the plastic-bodied side dump cars, which are described in the gondola portion of this book.

716 AMERICAN FLYER LINES (Type I): In 1946 and into 1947, the car was equipped with an inside truck-mounted pickup shoe for use with 710 contact rails.

VG-C6	EX-C7	LN-C8	Scarcity
25	50	75	5

716 AMERICAN FLYER LINES (Type II): Beginning in 1947 and continuing through 1951, the car was fitted outside third rail pickups for use with the 712 contact rails.

VG-C6	EX-C7	LN-C8	Scarcity
20	30	50	4

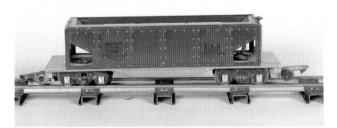

716 AMERICAN FLYER LINES (Type III): In 1951, the frames of some cars were painted gray rather than black.

VG-C6	EX-C7	LN-C8	Scarcity
20	40	60	5

801 B & O: This unpainted black 1956-57 hopper bore B & O markings and was equipped with knuckle couplers.

VG-C6	EX-C7	LN-C8	Scarcity
10	15	20	1

921 C. B. & Q.: From 1953 through 1956, this Tuscan "BURLINGTON ROUTE" hopper with simulated coal load was sold. The car came with knuckle couplers.

VG-C6	EX-C7	LN-C8	Scarcity
10	20	35	4

924 C R P: From 1953 through 1957, this covered hopper with black "FOR BULK CEMENT ONLY" "JERSEY CENTRAL LINES" lettering was available.

924 C R P (Type I): Some cars were painted gray.

VG-C6	EX-C7	LN-C8	Scarcity
10	15	25	4

924 C R P (Type II): Other cars had a distinct blue tint to the gray.

VG-C6	EX-C7	LN-C8	Scarcity
10	15	25	4

940 WABASH: This black hopper car was sold from 1953 through 1957. It was equipped with knuckle couplers.

VG-C6	EX-C7	LN-C8	Scarcity
10	15	20	1

24203 B & O: This black B & O hopper was available for three years over a six-year period, 1958 and 1963-64.

24203 B & O (Type I): In 1958, some of the cars were unpainted black plastic and came with knuckle couplers.

VG-C6	EX-C7	LN-C8	Scarcity
10	15	25	1

24203 B & O (Type II): In 1963, some of the cars were painted black and came with Pike Master trucks and couplers.

VG-C6	EX-C7	LN-C8	Scarcity
Too rarely traded to accurately establish pricing.			

24203 B & O (Type III): Most of the 1963-64 Pike Master-equipped cars had unpainted glossy black plastic bodies.

VG-C6	EX-C7	LN-C8	Scarcity
20	40	60	4

24205 C. B. & Q.: In 1957, some 921 hopper cars were sold in boxes numbered "24205-921."

24206 C. B. & Q.: This coal-laden Tuscan "BURLING-TON ROUTE" hopper was sold in 1958. It was equipped with knuckle couplers.

VG-C6	EX-C7	LN-C8	Scarcity
40	80	120	6

24208 C R P: In 1957, some 924 hopper cars were sold in boxes numbered "24208."

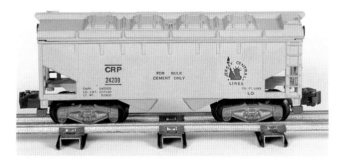

24209 C R P: This gray-painted covered hopper was sold from 1958 through 1960. The black markings on the sides of the car include the Jersey Central's famed Liberty with torch logo and the words "FOR BULK CEMENT ONLY." The car was equipped with knuckle couplers.

VG-C6	EX-C7	LN-C8	Scarcity
30	60	100	5

24213 WABASH: Beginning in 1958 and continuing through 1960, this black open-top un-laden hopper car with white "WABASH" lettering was sold. The car featured knuckle couplers.

24213 WABASH (Type I): Some of the cars had un-painted black plastic bodies.

VG-C6	EX-C7	LN-C8	Scarcity
15	30	50	3

24213 WABASH (Type II): A seemingly equal number of cars were painted black.

VG-C6	EX-C7	LN-C8	Scarcity
15	30	50	3

24216 UNION PACIFIC: This three-bay Tuscan-painted car was introduced in 1958. The yellow-lettered, knuckle coupler-equipped car remained in the product line through 1960.

VG-C6	EX-C7	LN-C8	Scarcity
25	50	75	4

24219 WESTERN MARYLAND: This brown car with white lettering and knuckle couplers was available in 1958 and 1959 only.

VG-C6	EX-C7	LN-C8	Scarcity
40	75	125	6

24221 C & E I: This painted gray car had a large red "C & E I" on its sides throughout its 1959-60 production. The car always came with knuckle couplers and sometimes was packed in a Kleer-Pak box.

VG-C6	EX-C7	LN-C8	Scarcity
100	150	200	7

Values for each condition are in U.S. dollars. | Scarcity = Scale from 1-8 with 8 being the hardest to find.

HOPPER CARS

103

24222 DOMINO SUGARS: One of the most desirable of all American Flyer rolling stock is this attractive yellow-painted two-bay covered hopper cataloged in 1963-64. The car, which rode on Pike Master trucks, had dark blue lettering and no brakewheel.

VG-C6	EX-C7	LN-C8	Scarcity
150	250	425	7

24225 SANTA FE: From 1960 through 1965, American Flyer offered this red two-bay hopper with gray molded gravel load. A large white "Santa Fe" was splashed across the side. In 1960, the cars were packed in Kleer-Pak boxes.

24225 SANTA FE (Type I): Some of the cars had knuckle couplers and painted red bodies.

VG-C6	EX-C7	LN-C8	Scarcity
15	25	45	3

24225 SANTA FE (Type II): Other cars continued to be painted red, but were equipped with Pike Master trucks and couplers.

VG-C6	EX-C7	LN-C8	Scarcity
15	25	45	3

24225 SANTA FE (Type III): A few cars were made with unpainted red plastic bodies and Pike Master trucks and couplers.

VG-C6	EX-C7	LN-C8	Scarcity
15	25	45	3

24230 PEABODY: The three-bay hopper bearing the green markings of the Peabody Coal Co. was sold from 1961 through 1964.

24230 PEABODY (Type I): It has been reported that some of these cars were produced with knuckle couplers and trucks with sintered-iron side frames. This variation could be easily faked, so caution is advised.

VG-C6	EX-C7	LN-C8	Scarcity
Too rarely traded to accurately establish pricing.			

24230 PEABODY (Type II): 📷 Most cars were equipped with Pike Master trucks and couplers, and had painted bodies like this one.

VG-C6	EX-C7	LN-C8	Scarcity
20	40	60	6

24230 PEABODY (Type III): Other Pike Master-equipped cars had unpainted cream-colored plastic bodies.

VG-C6	EX-C7	LN-C8	Scarcity
20	40	60	6

24230 PEABODY (Type II)

HOUSE CARS

The term used by railcar builders and the publication Association of American Railroads that broadly captures boxcars, refrigerator and stock cars, as well as other rolling stock of this general shape and construction is "house cars."

To American Flyer collectors, this category includes some of the most colorful and collectible S-Gauge items. Many of these cars were produced for a number of years and in many variations. The listings below describe the variations that most collectors consider significant.

Values for each condition are in U.S. dollars. | **Scarcity** = Scale from 1-8 with 8 being the hardest to find.

105

G. FOX & CO.: See 633F.
KEYSTONE: See 24067.
SIMMONS: See 24420.
55: See 24055.

These two boxcars were offered in 1953, notice the colorful markings of the 622 GAEX contrasting with the drab colors of the 613.

613 GREAT NORTHERN: This Tuscan-painted 1953 boxcar was built with a sheet metal frame. The markings were applied in white, and the black metal door guides were riveted on.

613 GREAT NORTHERN (Type I): The cars believed to be the earliest had link couplers, sheet metal trucks, nickel door latches and a two-piece metal brakewheel.

VG-C6	EX-C7	LN-C8	Scarcity
30	60	100	6

613 GREAT NORTHERN (Type II): Later cars had black door guides and one-piece plastic brakewheels. The car continued to use sheet metal trucks and link couplers.

VG-C6	EX-C7	LN-C8	Scarcity
30	60	100	6

622 GAEX: Also available in 1953 was this green-painted boxcar with stamped yellow markings. The car had a sheet metal frame, black metal door guides and sheet metal trucks with link couplers. A large yellow decal with green "DF" damage-free logo appeared to the right of the door on each side.

622 GAEX (Type I): Some cars had two-piece metal brakewheels.

VG-C6	EX-C7	LN-C8	Scarcity
30	60	90	5

622 GAEX (Type II): Other cars had plastic brakewheels.

VG-C6	EX-C7	LN-C8	Scarcity
30	60	90	5

623 ILLINOIS CENTRAL: Also sold only in 1953 was this orange-painted refrigerator car with green lettering and IC logo. These cars had sheet metal frames and trucks, and link couplers. Note: ALL factory-produced 623 cars are marked in green—those marked in blue are fraudulent.

VG-C6	EX-C7	LN-C8	Scarcity
10	20	30	4

629 MISSOURI PACIFIC: This Missouri Pacific stock car was one of the cars S-Gauge first introduced in 1946, and it remained in the product line through 1953. It had a two-piece brakewheel, and riveted-on sheet metal door guides. The car rode on sheet metal trucks and had link couplers.

629 MISSOURI PACIFIC (Type I): In its first year of production the car had silver lettering applied to an unpainted red plastic body, which was molded with prototypically open slats. A plastic frame was used on this car.

VG-C6	EX-C7	LN-C8	Scarcity
10	20	35	1

629 MISSOURI PACIFIC (Type II): Some of the cars were painted Tuscan, but continued to use silver lettering and plastic frames.

VG-C6	EX-C7	LN-C8	Scarcity
10	20	35	1

629 MISSOURI PACIFIC (Type III): Solid bodies, the slats only simulated, were used on some of the silver-lettered red cars with plastic frames.

VG-C6	EX-C7	LN-C8	Scarcity
10	20	35	1

629 MISSOURI PACIFIC (Type IV): White lettering has been reported on some cars otherwise identical to the Type III.

VG-C6	EX-C7	LN-C8	Scarcity
10	20	35	1

629 MISSOURI PACIFIC (Type V): Die-cast frames were used on these cars beginning in 1947. Some of these cars had unpainted red plastic open-slat bodies with white lettering.

VG-C6	EX-C7	LN-C8	Scarcity
10	20	35	1

629 MISSOURI PACIFIC (Type VI): The white-lettered solid-molded bodies were also mounted on die-cast frames.

VG-C6	EX-C7	LN-C8	Scarcity
10	20	35	1

629 MISSOURI PACIFIC (Type VII): Silver lettering has also been found on some of the cars with solid-molded bodies and die-cast frames.

VG-C6	EX-C7	LN-C8	Scarcity
10	20	35	1

629 MISSOURI PACIFIC (Type VIII): Sheet metal frames were used in 1949, and continued through 1953. Some of these cars utilize the unpainted bodies without open slats.

VG-C6	EX-C7	LN-C8	Scarcity
10	20	35	1

629 MISSOURI PACIFIC (Type IX): This car was identical to the Type VIII, but was painted red.

VG-C6	EX-C7	LN-C8	Scarcity
10	20	35	1

633 BALTIMORE & OHIO BOXCAR: With a production run spanning 1946 through 1953, it is not surprising that this boxcar exists in many variations. All of the cars featured "BALTIMORE & OHIO" lettering and B & O Capitol Dome herald. Link couplers were used on the car, as were black door latches.

633: White sides, Tuscan ends and roof.

633 BALTIMORE & OHIO (Type I): In 1946, this boxcar with unpainted white sides and Tuscan-painted roof and ends was produced. The car had a plastic frame, which was prone to warping. The markings on the car were black.

VG-C6	EX-C7	LN-C8	Scarcity
10	20	30	4

633 BALTIMORE & OHIO (Type II): To avoid the warping problem of the early plastic frames, die-cast frames were used later in 1946, and continued into 1948.

VG-C6	EX-C7	LN-C8	Scarcity
10	20	30	4

633 BALTIMORE & OHIO (Type III): Sometime in 1948, sheet metal frames were used and continued to be the norm through 1950.

VG-C6	EX-C7	LN-C8	Scarcity
10	20	30	4

633 BALTIMORE & OHIO (Type IV): In 1953, Gilbert revived the white-sided boxcar with Tuscan ends and a roof. The sides and roof, as well as the doors, were painted their respective colors. The car had a sheet metal frame and link couplers.

VG-C6	EX-C7	LN-C8	Scarcity
10	20	30	4

633 TUSCAN BOXCAR:

633 BALTIMORE & OHIO (Type V): Also introduced in 1946 was this Tuscan-painted version of the boxcar, lettered in silver. These cars were equipped with a plastic frame and link couplers.

VG-C6	EX-C7	LN-C8	Scarcity
100	200	300	7

633 BALTIMORE & OHIO (Type VI): The Tuscan-painted, plastic-framed version was also produced with white lettering. Link couplers continued to be fitted.

VG-C6	EX-C7	LN-C8	Scarcity
15	30	50	5

633 BALTIMORE & OHIO (Type VII): Like the white car, the white-lettered Tuscan boxcar eventually was based on a die-cast frame. These cars were equipped with link couplers.

VG-C6	EX-C7	LN-C8	Scarcity
15	30	50	5

633 BALTIMORE & OHIO (Type VIII): From 1949 through 1952, the Tuscan-painted boxcar came with a sheet metal frame. The lettering remained white and the couplers were the link-type.

VG-C6	EX-C7	LN-C8	Scarcity
15	30	50	5

633 RED UNPAINTED BOXCARS:

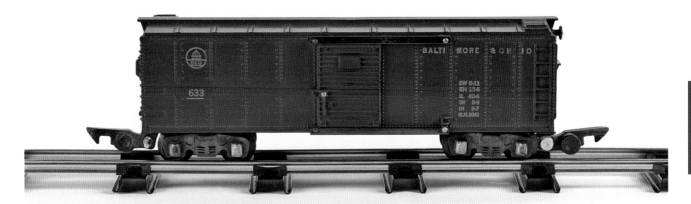

633 BALTIMORE & OHIO (Type VIII)

Values for each condition are in U.S. dollars. | **Scarcity** = Scale from 1-8 with 8 being the hardest to find.

107

HOUSE CARS

633 BALTIMORE & OHIO (Type IX): The 633 boxcar was also produced with an unpainted red plastic body and die-cast frame. Link couplers were used.

VG-C6	EX-C7	LN-C8	Scarcity
10	15	25	3

633 BALTIMORE & OHIO (Type X): Sheet metal frames were used in the unpainted red plastic boxcars produced from 1949 through 1952.

VG-C6	EX-C7	LN-C8	Scarcity
10	15	25	3

633 RED-PAINTED BOXCARS:

633 BALTIMORE & OHIO (Type XI): Beginning in 1948 and continuing through 1952, some of the red boxcars were painted. Sheet metal frames were used and the lettering was white.

VG-C6	EX-C7	LN-C8	Scarcity
15	25	40	5

633 BALTIMORE & OHIO REFRIGERATOR: In 1952, the 633 number and white B & O markings were applied to a refrigerator car. The car had opening doors held in place by black metal door guides, which in turn were riveted to the body. The car had sheet metal trucks and link couplers.

633 BALTIMORE & OHIO REFRIGERATOR (Type I): Some of these cars were painted red.

VG-C6	EX-C7	LN-C8	Scarcity
100	150	250	6

633 BALTIMORE & OHIO REFRIGERATOR (Type II): Other cars were painted Tuscan.

VG-C6	EX-C7	LN-C8	Scarcity
125	175	275	7

633F G. FOX & CO.: This uncataloged Tuscan-painted boxcar was produced in 1947 for Connecticut-based G. Fox & Co. department stores. Lettering to the right of the door read "The New York, New Haven and Hartford RAILROAD CO." in white. To the left of the door was the distinctive white markings "G. FOX & CO.," "SERVES CONNECTICUT."

VG-C6	EX-C7	LN-C8	Scarcity
2,000	3,500	5,000	8

637 M-K-T: This yellow link coupler-equipped boxcar was offered from 1949 through 1953. The car was lettered in black and the black metal door guides were riveted in place. Several shades of yellow cars have been found—other colors are fraudulent.

637 M-K-T (Type I): Some of these cars were painted yellow and mounted on a die-cast frame. A two-piece brakewheel was used.

VG-C6	EX-C7	LN-C8	Scarcity
15	25	35	2

637 M-K-T (Type II): Other painted yellow boxcars had sheet metal frames. Two-piece brakewheels were used on these cars.

VG-C6	EX-C7	LN-C8	Scarcity
15	25	35	2

637 M-K-T (Type III): The painted yellow boxcars with sheet metal frames sometimes came with one-piece brakewheels.

VG-C6	EX-C7	LN-C8	Scarcity
15	25	35	2

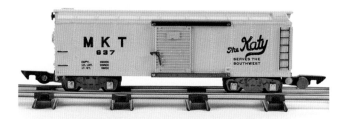

637 M-K-T (Type IV): The unpainted bright yellow boxcar had a sheet metal frame and a two-piece brakewheel.

VG-C6	EX-C7	LN-C8	Scarcity
15	25	35	2

639 AMERICAN FLYER BOXCAR: This 1949 through 1952 boxcar was produced in three colors—commonly yellow and Tuscan, and rarely red. The car had link couplers, sheet metal frames and no brakewheels. The doors of the car did not open.

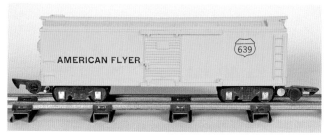

639 AMERICAN FLYER (Type I): The most common version, and the boxcar produced through the years 1949-52, was the unpainted yellow plastic variation.

VG-C6	EX-C7	LN-C8	Scarcity
5	10	15	1

639 AMERICAN FLYER (Type II)

639 AMERICAN FLYER (Type II): 📷 In 1950 or 1951, a few of the boxcars were painted red.

VG-C6	EX-C7	LN-C8	Scarcity
Too rarely traded to accurately establish pricing.			

639 AMERICAN FLYER (Type III): Also produced in 1950 or 1951, but in greater numbers, was this Tuscan-painted version.

VG-C6	EX-C7	LN-C8	Scarcity
35	60	100	6

639 AMERICAN FLYER (Type IV): The yellow boxcar was also produced in a painted version.

VG-C6	EX-C7	LN-C8	Scarcity
15	25	35	2

639 AMERICAN FLYER REFRIGERATOR: This uncataloged 1951-52 refrigerator car had non-opening doors. The "AMERICAN FLYER" shield, numbered "639," was stamped in black. The car had a sheet metal frame and link couplers.

639 AMERICAN FLYER REFRIGERATOR (Type I): In 1951 and 1952, some of these cars were made with unpainted yellow plastic bodies.

VG-C6	EX-C7	LN-C8	Scarcity
5	10	15	1

639 AMERICAN FLYER REFRIGERATOR (Type II): Other cars assembled in 1951 had bodies painted yellow.

VG-C6	EX-C7	LN-C8	Scarcity
10	15	20	5

639 AMERICAN FLYER REFRIGERATOR (Type III): A few cars were produced with unpainted cream-colored plastic bodies.

VG-C6	EX-C7	LN-C8	Scarcity
75	150	250	6

642 AMERICAN FLYER BOXCAR: This boxcar was offered from 1951 through 1952. The white-lettered car, which did not have brakewheels or opening doors, was equipped with link couplers.

642 AMERICAN FLYER (Type I): Some of these cars had unpainted red plastic bodies.

VG-C6	EX-C7	LN-C8	Scarcity
10	20	30	2

642 AMERICAN FLYER (Type II): Other cars were painted Tuscan.

VG-C6	EX-C7	LN-C8	Scarcity
15	30	40	4

Values for each condition are in U.S. dollars. | Scarcity = Scale from 1-8 with 8 being the hardest to find.

109

642 SEABOARD (Type I)

642 AMERICAN FLYER (Type III): Probably the last boxcar of the 642 series produced was this painted red version.

VG-C6	EX-C7	LN-C8	Scarcity
15	25	35	3

642 AMERICAN FLYER REFRIGERATOR: This uncataloged refrigerator car was produced in both red and Tuscan in 1952. The doors were molded in place, and the white-stamped body was mounted on a sheet metal frame. The car had link couplers and sheet metal trucks.

642 AMERICAN FLYER REFRIGERATOR (Type I): Some of the cars had unpainted red bodies.

VG-C6	EX-C7	LN-C8	Scarcity
10	15	25	1

642 AMERICAN FLYER REFRIGERATOR (Type II): The red bodies of other cars were painted red.

VG-C6	EX-C7	LN-C8	Scarcity
10	15	25	1

642 AMERICAN FLYER REFRIGERATOR (Type III): Other cars were painted Tuscan.

VG-C6	EX-C7	LN-C8	Scarcity
8	15	25	1

642 SEABOARD BOXCAR: This Tuscan-painted boxcar was produced in 1953. The white lettering of this car included the distinctive "ROUTE OF THE Silver Meteor" markings. The doors of the boxcar did not open, and the car had a sheet metal frame. Link couplers were installed.

642 SEABOARD (Type I): Some cars were not fitted with brakewheels.

VG-C6	EX-C7	LN-C8	Scarcity
15	30	50	4

642 SEABOARD (Type II): Other cars were equipped with one-piece brakewheels.

VG-C6	EX-C7	LN-C8	Scarcity
15	30	50	4

647 NORTHERN PACIFIC: This attractive orange and Tuscan refrigerator was produced in 1952 and 1953. Among the stamped-black lettering applied to the car was a "CLOSE AND LOCK DOOR BEFORE MOVING CAR" stamped on the sliding refrigerator doors. A multi-color NP decal was applied to the side of the car. The ladders and grab irons were painted black. The car had a sheet metal frame.

647 NORTHERN PACIFIC (Type I): The 1952 edition of the car was equipped with a two-piece brakewheel.

VG-C6	EX-C7	LN-C8	Scarcity
15	30	45	4

647 NORTHERN PACIFIC (Type II): In 1953, a one-piece brakewheel was used.

VG-C6	EX-C7	LN-C8	Scarcity
15	30	45	4

734 AMERICAN FLYER: This operating boxcar was sold from 1950 through 1954. One non-operating door was found on one side, but the other side had two operating doors. The operating doors were mounted using metal door guides, which in turn were mounted with rivets. The cars had sheet metal frames and trucks, link couplers and two-piece brakewheels.

734 AMERICAN FLYER (Type I): Some cars had unpainted red plastic bodies.

VG-C6	EX-C7	LN-C8	Scarcity
20	40	60	4

734 AMERICAN FLYER (Type II): Other cars were painted red.

VG-C6	EX-C7	LN-C8	Scarcity
35	70	100	6

734 AMERICAN FLYER (Type III): The color of some of the painted cars was Tuscan.

VG-C6	EX-C7	LN-C8	Scarcity
25	50	75	5

734 AMERICAN FLYER (Type IV): Some of the Tuscan-painted cars were lettered "AMERICAN FLYER LINES" rather than merely "American Flyer."

VG-C6	EX-C7	LN-C8	Scarcity
60	120	180	7

734 AMERICAN FLYER (Type V): Some examples have been reported which were painted silver.

VG-C6	EX-C7	LN-C8	Scarcity
Too rarely traded to accurately establish pricing.			

736 MISSOURI PACIFIC: This red operating Missouri Pacific stock car was sold, along with its accompanying 771 stockyard, from 1950 through 1954. The markings on the car were stamped in white. The car rode on sheet metal trucks, and was equipped with link couplers. Although this car was only available with its corral when new, it is valued here as the car alone. For values of the combination with the stockyard, please see the accessories chapter.

736 MISSOURI PACIFIC (Type I): Some of the cars had bodies that were painted red, and all three doors slid open on metal door guides, which in turn were riveted in place.

VG-C6	EX-C7	LN-C8	Scarcity
15	20	35	3

736 MISSOURI PACIFIC (Type II): Otherwise identical cars had unpainted red plastic bodies, stamped with white Missouri Pacific markings.

VG-C6	EX-C7	LN-C8	Scarcity
15	20	35	3

802 ILLINOIS CENTRAL: In 1956 and 1957, this orange refrigerator car with green markings was available. The car, which was imprinted with the diamond-shaped Illinois Central herald, did not have opening doors. The car had a sheet metal frame and trucks with sintered-iron side frames and operating knuckle couplers. Cars with lettering in colors other than green have been altered after leaving the Gilbert factory.

802 ILLINOIS CENTRAL (Type I): Most of the cars had unpainted orange plastic bodies, and came with or without a one-piece brakewheel.

VG-C6	EX-C7	LN-C8	Scarcity
10	15	20	1

802 ILLINOIS CENTRAL (Type II): A handful of cars were painted orange.

VG-C6	EX-C7	LN-C8	Scarcity
100	225	350	7

803 SANTA FE: In 1956 and 1957, Gilbert manufactured this unpainted Tuscan boxcar with non-opening doors. Markings on the car include "The Chief FAMOUS DAILY STREAMLINER West" stamped in white, and the Santa Fe's circled cross logo printed on paper. The car had knuckle couplers.

VG-C6	EX-C7	LN-C8	Scarcity
15	30	50	4

807 RIO GRANDE: In 1957, Gilbert began producing this white boxcar wearing the famed "Cookie Box" markings of the Rio Grande. The "Cookie Box" designation was stamped in red, while the remaining markings were done in black. The car had a sheet metal frame and knuckle couplers.

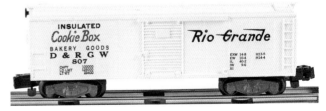

807 RIO GRANDE (Type I): The bulk of these cars were produced with unpainted white bodies with non-operating doors.

VG-C6	EX-C7	LN-C8	Scarcity
20	30	40	3

Values for each condition are in U.S. dollars. | Scarcity = Scale from 1-8 with 8 being the hardest to find.

111

HOUSE CARS

807 RIO GRANDE (Type II): A few of the cars with molded-in place doors were painted white.

VG-C6	EX-C7	LN-C8	Scarcity
250	500	800	7

807 RIO GRANDE (Type III): Even harder to find is a car with opening doors and black sheet metal door guides.

VG-C6	EX-C7	LN-C8	Scarcity
Too rarely traded to accurately establish pricing.			

913 GREAT NORTHERN BOXCAR: From 1953 through 1958, this Tuscan-painted boxcar was produced. The car had black sheet metal frame and door guides, knuckle couplers and trucks with sintered-iron side frames.

913 GREAT NORTHERN (Type I): When first produced in 1953, the GN's goat logo was stamped on the car, and a two-piece brakewheel was installed.

VG-C6	EX-C7	LN-C8	Scarcity
15	30	50	4

913 GREAT NORTHERN (Type II): Very quickly the two-piece brakewheel gave way to a one-piece brakewheel.

VG-C6	EX-C7	LN-C8	Scarcity
15	30	50	5

913 GREAT NORTHERN (Type III): Because of problems with the process, the stamped goat herald gave way to a self-adhesive logo in 1954, and this was used for the remainder of the car's production.

VG-C6	EX-C7	LN-C8	Scarcity
15	25	40	4

922 GAEX: This 1953-57 green boxcar was essentially a knuckle coupler-equipped 622. Like the 622, the car body was painted green and decorated in yellow, with a broad yellow diagonal stripe. The car rode on trucks with sintered-iron side frames.

922 GAEX (Type I): As first produced, the broad diagonal yellow stripe on the car was applied using a water-slide decal. Two-piece brakewheels were used on the car as well.

VG-C6	EX-C7	LN-C8	Scarcity
20	30	45	4

922 GAEX (Type II): Later, the broad yellow stripe was printed on the car, and a two-piece brakewheel was installed.

VG-C6	EX-C7	LN-C8	Scarcity
15	25	40	4

923 ILLINOIS CENTRAL: The orange IC refrigerator was equipped with knuckle couplers in 1954, and naturally the number changed to 923 at that time. The green-lettered car was also produced in 1955. The car did not have brakewheels, but did have trucks with sintered-iron side frames and knuckle couplers.

923 ILLINOIS CENTRAL (Type I): The bodies of some of these cars were painted orange.

VG-C6	EX-C7	LN-C8	Scarcity
10	15	25	1

923 ILLINOIS CENTRAL (Type II): Other cars had an unpainted orange body.

VG-C6	EX-C7	LN-C8	Scarcity
10	15	25	1

929 MISSOURI PACIFIC: Lettered in white, this Missouri Pacific stock car was available from 1953 through 1957. Until 1957, only the doors actually had the open construction of a real stock car, the body was merely molded to represent the slats. The car was equipped with riveted-on sheet metal door guides, trucks with sintered-iron side frames and knuckle couplers.

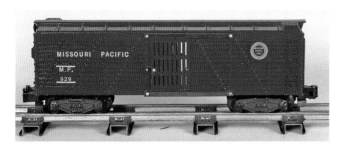

929 MISSOURI PACIFIC (Type I): The early cars were painted red, and had a two-piece brakewheel.

VG-C6	EX-C7	LN-C8	Scarcity
10	20	35	1

929 MISSOURI PACIFIC (Type II): Later cars were produced with painted Tuscan and continued to use the two-piece brakewheel.

VG-C6	EX-C7	LN-C8	Scarcity
10	20	35	1

929 MISSOURI PACIFIC (Type III): Some cars were painted Tuscan, but equipped with a one-piece brakewheel.

VG-C6	EX-C7	LN-C8	Scarcity
10	20	35	1

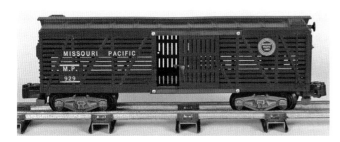

929 MISSOURI PACIFIC (Type IV): In 1957, an uncataloged Tuscan 929 was produced, which is easily distinguished by its prototypical open slat sides.

VG-C6	EX-C7	LN-C8	Scarcity
100	225	350	8

933 BALTIMORE & OHIO: Knuckle couplers were also installed on the brown-roofed, white-sided Baltimore and Ohio boxcar, with the 1953-54 car numbered "933." The frame of the car was sheet metal, and sintered-iron side frames were found on the trucks.

VG-C6	EX-C7	LN-C8	Scarcity
20	35	50	4

937 M-K-T: From 1953 through 1958, the M-K-T boxcar was offered with knuckle couplers and riding on trucks with sintered-iron side frames. The car had sheet metal door guides and a frame. The cast-in ladders and grab irons of this car were painted black.

937 M-K-T (Type I): From 1953 through 1954, most of the boxcars were painted yellow and were equipped with two-piece brakewheels.

VG-C6	EX-C7	LN-C8	Scarcity
20	35	50	5

937 M-K-T (Type II): From 1955 through 1958, the sides of the cars were painted yellow, while the roof and ends were painted Tuscan. One-piece brakewheels were used on these cars.

VG-C6	EX-C7	LN-C8	Scarcity
15	25	40	4

942 SEABOARD: First produced in 1953 as a set component, and cataloged in 1954 for separate sale only, this car was a knuckle coupler-equipped version of the 642. The car was painted Tuscan and lettered in white.

VG-C6	EX-C7	LN-C8	Scarcity
10	20	30	3

Values for each condition are in U.S. dollars. | **Scarcity** = Scale from 1-8 with 8 being the hardest to find.

113

947 NORTHERN PACIFIC: Introduced in 1953, this orange and Tuscan-painted car remained in the product line through 1958. The car had a sheet metal frame and trucks with sintered-iron side frames and operating knuckle couplers.

947 NORTHERN PACIFIC (Type I): Initially, a two-piece brakewheel was used on the car.

VG-C6	EX-C7	LN-C8	Scarcity
15	25	50	4

947 NORTHERN PACIFIC (Type II): Later, one-piece brakewheels were used on the 947.

VG-C6	EX-C7	LN-C8	Scarcity
15	25	50	4

947 NORTHERN PACIFIC (Type III): The markings on the doors in 1957 and 1958 differed from earlier years, with an ampersand replacing the "AND" in the legend.

VG-C6	EX-C7	LN-C8	Scarcity
15	25	50	4

957 ERIE: 📷 This uncataloged Tuscan-painted boxcar was produced only in 1957. The car had two operating doors on one side and one non-operating door on the other. Its markings included a diamond-shaped paper "ERIE" herald. The car had trucks with sintered-iron side frames and knuckle couplers. It was furnished with four aluminum barrels and a control box lettered "957 ACTION BOX CAR." This car is found in boxes numbered "25041" or "25042."

VG-C6	EX-C7	LN-C8	Scarcity
75	150	225	5

970 SEABOARD: Smitty the Walking Brakeman spent 1956 and 1957 walking the roof of this Tuscan-painted Seaboard boxcar. The car was lettered in white, and the brakeman on the roof had blue pants, shirt, hat and a red bandana. The hands and face of the brakeman, who has been reproduced, were painted a flesh color.

VG-C6	EX-C7	LN-C8	Scarcity
25	50	75	4

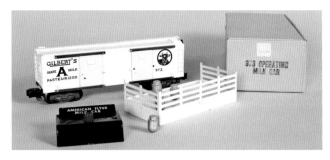

973 GILBERT'S: This boxcar, which was painted white and lettered in black "GILBERT'S GRADE A MILK PASTEURIZED" was sold in 1956 and 1957. The door on one side of the car did not open, but the other side of the car had two opening doors installed with riveted-on metal door guides. The black man inside with a white uniform placed four milk cans on a white-painted metal stand, which came with the car—along with a control rail. The car was furnished with a control box lettered "AMERICAN FLYER MILK CAR."

VG-C6	EX-C7	LN-C8	Scarcity
50	100	150	5

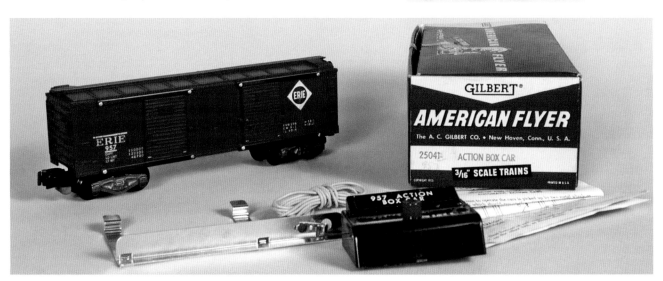

957 ERIE

974 AMERICAN FLYER LINES: In 1953 and 1954, Gilbert sold this Tuscan-painted operating boxcar designed with the K775 baggage loader. The car was lettered in white and rode on trucks with sintered-iron side frames and operating knuckle couplers. The value below is for the car alone.

VG-C6	EX-C7	LN-C8	Scarcity
25	50	75	4

974 ERIE: In 1955, the Tuscan operating boxcar began to bear a paper diamond logo of the "ERIE" railroad, although the number did not change. The car was lettered in white, and continued to use a steel frame and have trucks with sintered-iron side frames and operating knuckle couplers.

VG-C6	EX-C7	LN-C8	Scarcity
150	300	450	7

976 MISSOURI PACIFIC: This three-door Tuscan-painted operating cattle car was available continually from 1953 through 1962. Originally this car was not sold individually, but rather was a component of the K771 and 23771 stockyard. The car was marked with white "MISSOURI PACIFIC" lettering and the MoPac buzz saw herald. Today however, these cars frequently are sold without the stockyard, and the folowing values are for the car alone.

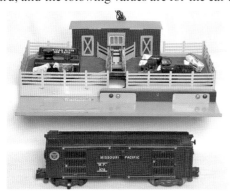

The 976 stock car was originally supplied with a stockyard as seen above. This combination is described in detail in the accessories portion of this book. However, today the stock car is often offered for sale by itself, and is so described here.

976 MISSOURI PACIFIC (Type I): Some of the cars had two-piece brakewheels, and the door on the single-door side was glued in place without door guides. Riveted-on door guides secured the operating doors.

VG-C6	EX-C7	LN-C8	Scarcity
25	50	75	5

976 MISSOURI PACIFIC (Type II): Other cars had an opening door on the single door side, and were trimmed with a one-piece brakewheel. Riveted-on door guides were used on this car.

VG-C6	EX-C7	LN-C8	Scarcity
25	50	75	5

976 MISSOURI PACIFIC (Type III): Glued-on single doors were used on some of the cars with one-piece brakewheels. The guides for the opening doors were secured with rivets.

VG-C6	EX-C7	LN-C8	Scarcity
25	50	75	5

976 MISSOURI PACIFIC (Type IV): Later production cars had door guides that were tabbed on rather than riveted on. One-piece brakewheels were used on these cars.

VG-C6	EX-C7	LN-C8	Scarcity
25	50	75	5

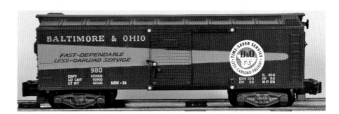

980 BALTIMORE & OHIO: This 1956-57 boxcar wore the blue and orange colors of the B & O "Time-Saver" paint scheme. The logo of this special freight service, a circular emblem reading "T-S" and "B & O TIME-SAVER SERVICE LESS-CARLOAD FREIGHT" was a paper emblem.

VG-C6	EX-C7	LN-C8	Scarcity
100	125	150	5

981 CENTRAL OF GEORGIA: This attractive black and silver boxcar was sold in 1956 and 1957. The large silver oval and silver roof were painted on the black-painted car body. The yellow "CENTRAL OF GEORGIA" emblem was a paper label. The car had trucks with sintered-iron side frames and operating knuckle couplers.

981 CENTRAL OF GEORGIA (Type I): It is believed that the initial production of these cars was painted with matte black.

VG-C6	EX-C7	LN-C8	Scarcity
75	175	300	6

Values for each condition are in U.S. dollars. | **Scarcity** = Scale from 1-8 with 8 being the hardest to find.

115

981 CENTRAL OF GEORGIA (Type II): Probably sometime in the first year of the production run the black paint was changed to gloss.

VG-C6	EX-C7	LN-C8	Scarcity
50	100	150	5

982 BANGOR AND AROOSTOOK: This 1956-57 boxcar was painted in the red, white and blue colors of the famed "State of Maine" color scheme. This paint scheme was subsidized to the real railroads by Maine in order to promote their potato and paper industries. Gilbert equipped their cars with sheet metal frames and door guides, and trucks with sintered-iron side frames and knuckle couplers.

VG-C6	EX-C7	LN-C8	Scarcity
50	75	125	5

983 MISSOURI PACIFIC: Also produced in 1956-57 was this boxcar finished in the blue, gray and yellow colors of the Missouri Pacific "Eagle Merchandise Service." The real railroad introduced this "LCL" (Less than Car Load) service in 1950. Initially this service and these cars were only between points on the Missouri Pacific and its subsidiary the Texas and Pacific—though this provision changed in 1960. Gilbert's version of this car included in its decoration a pressure-sensitive version of the MP "buzz saw" herald.

VG-C6	EX-C7	LN-C8	Scarcity
50	100	150	5

984 NEW HAVEN: Another of the colorful freight cars sold in 1956-57 was this orange boxcar with the black and white logo of the New Haven railroad. Sheet metal door guides held the orange-painted doors in place. Like the other cars of the era, this car had knuckle couplers and trucks with sintered-iron side frames.

VG-C6	EX-C7	LN-C8	Scarcity
35	65	100	5

985 B & M: This blue-painted boxcar with black doors was produced in 1957. The car was stamped with the large black and white "BM" logo. The car had a sheet metal frame, sheet metal door guides held in place with rivets, knuckle couplers, and trucks with sintered-iron side frames.

VG-C6	EX-C7	LN-C8	Scarcity
75	125	175	5

988 AMERICAN REFRIGERATOR TRANSIT CO.: Sold in 1956 and 1957, this car was painted with orange sides and silver roof and ends. It was decorated with color paper ART, Wabash and Missouri Pacific emblems. The car had operating knuckle couplers and trucks with sintered-iron side frames.

VG-C6	EX-C7	LN-C8	Scarcity
40	75	125	6

989 NORTHWESTERN: Finished in green and yellow, this 1956-58 refrigerator car bore the markings and logo of the "NORTH-WESTERN REFRIGERATOR LINE COMPANY." The car had a metal frame and door guides, single-piece brakewheel, operating knuckle couplers, and trucks with sintered-iron side frames.

989 NORTHWESTERN (Type I): The background of the paper "NORTH-WESTERN" logo on some cars was yellow.

VG-C6	EX-C7	LN-C8	Scarcity
50	100	200	6

989 NORTHWESTERN (Type II): The logo of the background on other cars was printed in orange.

VG-C6	EX-C7	LN-C8	Scarcity
50	100	200	6

994 UNION PACIFIC: Produced only in 1957, this stock car had sides painted yellow and its roof and ends were painted silver. The car had sintered-iron side frame trucks and knuckle couplers. The sheet metal door guides were riveted on.

VG-C6	EX-C7	LN-C8	Scarcity
125	225	350	7

C1001 WSX: This yellow boxcar was produced in 1962, although it was not shown in the consumer catalog. Instead this car was produced for inclusion in special sets sold to White's Discount Centers. The car had a sheet metal frame and was equipped with Pike Master trucks and couplers. Beware; reproductions of this car have been made.

VG-C6	EX-C7	LN-C8	Scarcity
450	950	1,350	8

C2001 POST: In 1962, this operating ventilated boxcar was produced in two versions—but neither was cataloged. The car had an unpainted white plastic body lettered in orange for Post Cereals. The car was equipped with Pike Master trucks and couplers.

C2001 POST (Type I): This car held a "Hayjector" mechanism which when triggered caused the car to discharge plastic hay bales.

VG-C6	EX-C7	LN-C8	Scarcity
15	30	45	3

C1001 WSX

C2001 POST (Type II): Some cars did not have the operating mechanism.

VG-C6	EX-C7	LN-C8	Scarcity
10	20	30	1

24003 SANTA FE: Compared to the other cars offered in 1958, this Tuscan-painted Santa Fe boxcar was rather drab, although prototypical. White lettering was stamped on the car sides, and a black and white Santa Fe encircled cross paper logo was applied as well.

24003 SANTA FE (Type I): Most of the cars had unpainted Tuscan plastic bodies.

VG-C6	EX-C7	LN-C8	Scarcity
15	25	45	4

24003 SANTA FE (Type II): A few cars were produced with bodies that were painted Tuscan.

VG-C6	EX-C7	LN-C8	Scarcity
Too rarely traded to accurately establish pricing.			

24006 GREAT NORTHERN: Gilbert adopted a five-digit number system in 1957. At that time all items, which previously had three-digit catalog numbers, were assigned five-digit numbers—including those with a substantial inventory remaining in stock, such as the 913 Great Northern. However, for exhibition and promotional purposes, the company wanted to show cars that were actually imprinted with the five-digit numbers. Thus, a handful of 24006 Great Northern cars were produced for this purpose. Consumers continued to be supplied with cars stamped 913.

VG-C6	EX-C7	LN-C8	Scarcity
Too rarely traded to accurately establish pricing.			

24016 M-K-T: Evidently fewer 937 boxcars were on hand than 913s, or the demand for them was greater, because

in 1958 Gilbert actually had to produce a handful of the five-digit version of this car for the consumer market. These cars had yellow-painted sides and Tuscan-painted ends and roof. The molded-in grab irons and ladders were painted black. The sheet metal door guides were mounted using rivets, and the trucks had sintered-iron side frames and knuckle couplers.

VG-C6	EX-C7	LN-C8	Scarcity
400	850	1,300	8

24019 SEABOARD: This uncataloged Tuscan-painted boxcar bore the white markings of the Seaboard Air Line railroad, including their "ROUTE OF THE Silver Meteor" slogan.

24019 SEABOARD (Type I): When produced in 1958, the car had operating knuckle couplers and trucks with sintered-iron side frames.

VG-C6	EX-C7	LN-C8	Scarcity
15	30	45	4

24019 SEABOARD (Type II): When reprised in 1961, Pike Master trucks and couplers were used.

VG-C6	EX-C7	LN-C8	Scarcity
15	30	45	4

24022 BALTIMORE & OHIO: In 1957, the 980 was packed in boxes stamped "24022."

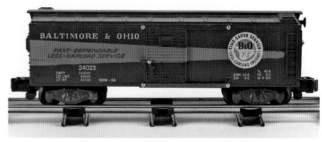

24023 BALTIMORE & OHIO: The blue and orange 981 B & O "Time-Saver" continued in 1958-59 with a new number—24023. A paper logo, a circular emblem reading "T-S" and "B & O TIME-SAVER SERVICE LESS-CARLOAD FREIGHT" was applied on each side of the car. The car came with knuckle couplers and trucks with sintered-iron side frames.

VG-C6	EX-C7	LN-C8	Scarcity
50	115	175	5

24025 CENTRAL OF GEORGIA: In 1957, the 981 was packed in boxes stamped "24025."

24026 CENTRAL OF GEORGIA: The black and silver Central of Georgia boxcar returned in 1958 with a five-digit number. The yellow herald continued to be a paper label. Naturally, the car had operating knuckle couplers and trucks with sintered-iron side frames. The car had a sheet metal frame, riveted-on sheet metal door guides and black metal door latches.

VG-C6	EX-C7	LN-C8	Scarcity
60	125	175	5

24029 BANGOR AND AROOSTOOK: The red, white and blue "State of Maine" boxcar returned with a five-digit number from 1957 through 1961. The cars had sheet metal frames, black door latches and one-piece brakewheels.

24029 BANGOR AND AROOSTOOK (Type I): The bulk of the cars had trucks with sintered-iron side frames, and the door guides were held in place with rivets.

VG-C6	EX-C7	LN-C8	Scarcity
75	150	225	5

24029 BANGOR AND AROOSTOOK (Type II): A few cars produced in 1961 had Pike Master trucks and couplers. The door guides on these cars were mounted by bending over the tabs.

VG-C6	EX-C7	LN-C8	Scarcity
75	150	225	7

24030 M-K-T: In 1960, Gilbert produced this uncataloged yellow boxcar. The black lettering on the car was that of the Missouri-Kansas-Texas railroad, otherwise known as the "Katy." The ladders and the grab irons on the car were painted black, and it was equipped with Pike Master trucks and couplers.

24030 M-K-T (Type I): Most of the cars had bodies made of unpainted yellow plastic.

VG-C6	EX-C7	LN-C8	Scarcity
5	10	20	1

24030 M-K-T (Type II): A handful of cars—today very sought after—had bodies that were painted yellow.

VG-C6	EX-C7	LN-C8	Scarcity
150	300	500	8

24033 MISSOURI PACIFIC: The Missouri Pacific "Eagle" boxcar got a new five-digit number in 1958. The car bore the new number for only 1958. The red pressure-sensitive MoPac buzz saw logo was still attached to sides of the cars. Operating knuckle couplers and trucks with sintered-iron side frames.

VG-C6	EX-C7	LN-C8	Scarcity
50	100	150	5

24035 NEW HAVEN: In 1957, the 984 boxcars were sold in packages marked "24035 — N.H. Box Car."

24036 NEW HAVEN: In 1958, the orange New Haven boxcar was renumbered with a five-digit number as well. The car continued to be produced through 1960. The cars had a sheet metal frame, knuckle couplers and trucks with sintered-iron side frames.

24036 NEW HAVEN (Type I): Initially the door guides were mounted with rivets.

VG-C6	EX-C7	LN-C8	Scarcity
30	50	100	5

HOUSE CARS

24036 NEW HAVEN (Type II): Later cars had door guides that were inserted into the car sides, and tabs then bent to hold them in place.

VG-C6	EX-C7	LN-C8	Scarcity
30	50	100	5

24039 RIO GRANDE: In 1959, the white "Cookie Box" box markings of the Rio Grande were used with this new number. The "Cookie Box" designation was stamped in red, while the remaining markings were done in black. The doors of the car were molded in place. The car had a sheet metal frame and knuckle couplers.

24039 RIO GRANDE (Type I): The bulk of these cars were produced with unpainted white bodies.

VG-C6	EX-C7	LN-C8	Scarcity
20	30	40	3

24039 RIO GRANDE (Type II): A few of the cars were painted white.

VG-C6	EX-C7	LN-C8	Scarcity
250	500	800	7

24042 B & M: In 1957, the 985 was packed in boxes stamped "24042."

24043 B & M: This blue boxcar with black doors returned in 1958 with a new number. The car, which had trucks with sintered-iron truck side frames and knuckle couplers, remained part of the line through 1960.

24043 B & M (Type I): Initially the door guides were mounted to the car with rivets.

VG-C6	EX-C7	LN-C8	Scarcity
40	75	125	5

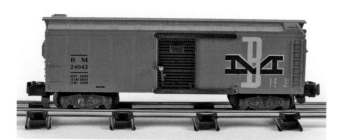

24043 B & M (Type II): The door guides of later cars were secured by bending integral tabs through holes in the car.

VG-C6	EX-C7	LN-C8	Scarcity
40	75	125	5

24045 MAINE CENTRAL: Only a few examples of this uncataloged, green-painted boxcar were produced. The cars had opening doors, and the yellow lettering on the car includes "NEW 3-56" and the Maine Central tree

herald. The green doors were held in place with riveted-on door guides. The trucks have sintered-iron side frames and operating knuckle couplers.

VG-C6	EX-C7	LN-C8	Scarcity
Too rarely traded to accurately establish pricing.			

24047 GREAT NORTHERN: This red boxcar with white lettering and non-operating doors was produced in 1959.

VG-C6	EX-C7	LN-C8	Scarcity
75	150	250	6

24048 M St. L: From 1959 through 1962, A.C. Gilbert offered this red boxcar with white stamped-on lettering and a black "The Peoria Gateway" paper label. The red opening doors were held in place by black door guides, that themselves were held in place with bent tabs. The car had a one-piece brakewheel.

24048 M St. L (Type I): Some of these cars were equipped with trucks with sintered-iron side frames.

VG-C6	EX-C7	LN-C8	Scarcity
50	100	150	5

24048 M St. L (Type II): Other versions of the car had Pike Master trucks and couplers.

VG-C6	EX-C7	LN-C8	Scarcity
50	100	150	5

24052 UNITED FRUIT GROWERS EXPRESS: This car, which some wrongly describe as a Civil War-era car, is in fact a replica of a ventilated boxcar. During the early 1900s, prior to the advent of refrigeration, many fruits were imported into this country in a partially ripened state. The ripening process, which gives off heat, was expected to continue during transit. Thus, the ventilated boxcar was developed to transport such perishables. Gilbert's rendering of this car was fairly accurate, including its "24052 UNITED FRUIT GROWERS EXPRESS" lettering.

The car had no brakewheel, but it did have a sheet metal frame and was equipped with Pike Master trucks and couplers.

24052 UNITED FRUIT GROWERS EXPRESS (Type I): Some of the cars had unpainted light yellow plastic bodies.

VG-C6	EX-C7	LN-C8	Scarcity
5	10	20	1

24052 UNITED FRUIT GROWERS EXPRESS (Type II): Other cars had bodies made of unpainted dark yellow plastic.

VG-C6	EX-C7	LN-C8	Scarcity
5	10	20	1

24052 UNITED FRUIT GROWERS EXPRESS (Type III): The bodies of other cars were painted yellow.

VG-C6	EX-C7	LN-C8	Scarcity
Too rarely traded to accurately establish pricing.			

24054 SANTA FE: This red boxcar with white Santa Fe "Super SHOCK CONTROL" markings was offered from 1962 through 1966. The metal door guides were mounted by means of tabs instead of rivets. One-piece brakewheels were used on these cars, as were sheet metal frames and Pike Master trucks and couplers.

24054 SANTA FE (Type I):  From 1962 through 1964, the car body was painted red. Most of the cars had their ladders and grab irons painted black.

VG-C6	EX-C7	LN-C8	Scarcity
30	65	100	6

24054 SANTA FE (Type II): Some of the cars shipped from 1962 through 1964 did not have their ladders and grab irons painted black. Instead, they were left red.

VG-C6	EX-C7	LN-C8	Scarcity
30	65	100	6

24054 SANTA FE (Type III): Beginning in 1965 and continuing through 1966, the car was built with an unpainted red plastic body.

VG-C6	EX-C7	LN-C8	Scarcity
10	30	50	2

24055 THE GOLD BELT LINE: In 1960, Gilbert introduced a new style of boxcar, the ventilated boxcar. Actual railroads used this type of car to move certain perishable foods prior to the introduction of refrigerator cars. Several variations of the 24055 car exist, but all have unpainted yellow plastic bodies with hazy red stripes painted on. The full catalog number does not appear on the car. Instead, the number "55" was stamped on the car in black and a foil sticker with "THE GOLD BELT LINE" was applied to the car.

24055 THE GOLD BELT LINE (Type I): The body of some of these cars was formed with the door on one side molded shut, and the door on the other side completely omitted. The car rode on trucks with sintered-iron side frames and was equipped with knuckle couplers.

VG-C6	EX-C7	LN-C8	Scarcity
15	30	45	4

24054 SANTA FE (Type I)

24055 THE GOLD BELT LINE (Type II): Other car bodies were molded with one door closed and the other door "open"—the door being present but formed into the body to the left of the opening. Trucks with sintered-iron side frames and operating knuckle couplers were used on these cars.

VG-C6	EX-C7	LN-C8	Scarcity
20	35	50	4

24055 THE GOLD BELT LINE (Type III): Some of the same style bodies used on the Type II cars were equipped with Pike Master trucks and couplers.

VG-C6	EX-C7	LN-C8	Scarcity
20	35	50	4

24056 B & M: The blue Boston and Maine boxcar with black doors returned in 1961 with a new number—24056. This number was used for only one year. The metal door guides were now tabbed, rather than riveted, to the car body. A one-piece brakewheel was used, as were Pike Master trucks and couplers.

24056 B & M (Type I): Most of these cars had unpainted blue plastic bodies.

VG-C6	EX-C7	LN-C8	Scarcity
30	80	125	5

24056 B & M (Type II): The bodies of other cars were painted blue.

VG-C6	EX-C7	LN-C8	Scarcity
100	200	350	7

24057 MOUNDS: The ventilated boxcar was decorated with maroon lettering promoting "PETER PAUL INDESCRIBABLY DELICIOUS MOUNDS" candy bars for this 1961-only item. The body molding chosen for this use had one door molded open, the other molded shut. The car rode on Pike Master trucks, with Pike Master couplers.

24057 MOUNDS (Type I): 📷 Some of the car bodies were molded from ivory-colored plastic, which was left unpainted.

VG-C6	EX-C7	LN-C8	Scarcity
10	20	30	2

24057 MOUNDS (Type II): Other cars had pure white plastic bodies.

VG-C6	EX-C7	LN-C8	Scarcity
5	10	20	1

24058 POST: This car, shipped in 1963 and 1964, was marked with the logo of Post breakfast cereals. It did not have opening doors, but it did have a one-piece brakewheel and Pike Master trucks and couplers. As a rule, the bodies were unpainted white or ivory plastic.

24058 POST (Type I): Some of the cars were stamped "Breakfast Cereal."

VG-C6	EX-C7	LN-C8	Scarcity
5	10	20	1

24058 POST (Type II): Other cars were stamped "Breakfast Cereals."

VG-C6	EX-C7	LN-C8	Scarcity
10	20	30	2

24058 POST (Type III): Some of the cars stamped "Breakfast Cereal" had bodies made of plastic with "marble" swirl coloring.

VG-C6	EX-C7	LN-C8	Scarcity
5	10	20	1

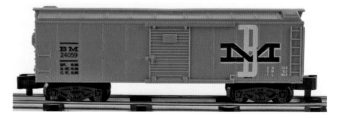

24059 B & M: Blue Boston and Maine boxcars were revived again in 1963 with a new number—24059, which was used one year only. This version of the car did not have opening doors, nor did it have a brakewheel. It was equipped with Pike Master trucks and couplers.

VG-C6	EX-C7	LN-C8	Scarcity
75	150	225	5

24060 M St. L: An unpainted red body molding with non-opening doors was used for this 1963-64 M St. L boxcar, which was lettered in white. The car had no brakewheel, but did have Pike Master trucks and couplers.

24060 M St. L (Type I): Some of the cars were decorated with circular black self-adhesive "The Peoria Gateway" logos.

VG-C6	EX-C7	LN-C8	Scarcity
40	90	150	5

24060 M St. L (Type II): "The Peoria Gateway" heralds of other cars were painted on in white with red lettering.

VG-C6	EX-C7	LN-C8	Scarcity
40	90	150	5

24065 N Y C: Gilbert sold this jade-green painted boxcar from 1960 through 1964. Metal door guides tabbed into place held the car's opening doors in place. The black and white New York Central System logo was paper. A one-piece brakewheel was installed and the car utilized a sheet metal frame.

24065 N Y C (Type I): In 1960, the car had sintered-iron side frame trucks.

VG-C6	EX-C7	LN-C8	Scarcity
40	80	120	6

24065 N Y C (Type II): From 1961 through 1964, Pike Master trucks and couplers were used.

VG-C6	EX-C7	LN-C8	Scarcity
30	60	90	4

24066 LOUISVILLE & NASHVILLE: The boxcar was produced in 1960. The doors of the painted blue car did not open, but it did have a one-piece brakewheel. The car bore the yellow "Dixie Line" markings of the L & N and rode on trucks with sintered-iron side frames and equipped with operating knuckle couplers.

VG-C6	EX-C7	LN-C8	Scarcity
125	275	375	5

24067 KEYSTONE LINE: This uncataloged orange boxcar was produced in 1960 as a promotion for Keystone camera. On its side was printed "The KEYSTONE LINE" and "Fastest Route to Top Profits" in black. The car had opening doors, held in place with black metal door guides, themselves retained by rivets. Excellent, and sometimes unmarked, reproductions of this car have been made.

VG-C6	EX-C7	LN-C8	Scarcity
1,250	1,800	2,500	8

24068 PLANTERS PEANUTS: This uncataloged 1961 ventilated boxcar is quite possibly the scarcest of all Flyer S-Gauge freight cars. The car had an unpainted white plastic body with two molded-in doors, one in the open position. The car was decorated with blue "Planters Peanuts" lettering in a red surround and a blue Mr. Peanut logo. The car was equipped with Pike Master trucks and couplers. Beware; reproductions have been made.

VG-C6	EX-C7	LN-C8	Scarcity
Too rarely traded to accurately establish pricing.			

Values for each condition are in U.S. dollars. | Scarcity = Scale from 1-8 with 8 being the hardest to find.

123

24072 MISSOURI PACIFIC: In 1956, the 929 stock car was packaged in boxes marked "24072."

24075 UNION PACIFIC: In 1957, the 994 was packed in a box stamped "24075."

24076 UNION PACIFIC: This attractive stock car with yellow sides and silver roof and ends was available from 1957 through 1960. The car had a sheet metal frame and sheet metal door guides.

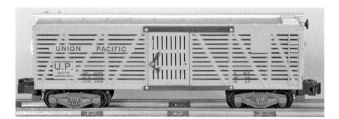

24076 UNION PACIFIC (Type I): Some of the cars had riveted-on door guides and red lettering. The car rode on trucks with sintered-iron side frames and knuckle couplers.

VG-C6	EX-C7	LN-C8	Scarcity
30	45	85	4

24076 UNION PACIFIC (Type II): Other cars had red lettering, Pike Master trucks and couplers, and the door guides of these cars were tabbed on.

VG-C6	EX-C7	LN-C8	Scarcity
20	35	60	4

24076 UNION PACIFIC (Type III): Cars also exist that are identical to the Type II, except they are lettered in maroon.

VG-C6	EX-C7	LN-C8	Scarcity
20	35	60	4

24077 NORTHERN PACIFIC: Known as the "PIG PALACE"—and so marked on an aluminum plate, this red 1959-62 car is the most desirable of Gilbert's stock cars. Lettering on the car was stamped in white, and its roof and ends were painted silver.

24077 NORTHERN PACIFIC (Type I): The early cars had trucks with sintered-iron side frames.

VG-C6	EX-C7	LN-C8	Scarcity
150	250	375	7

24077 NORTHERN PACIFIC (Type II): Later, some cars were produced with Pike Master trucks and couplers.

VG-C6	EX-C7	LN-C8	Scarcity
150	250	375	7

24403 ILLINOIS CENTRAL: The orange Illinois Central refrigerator car returned in 1958, and remained in the line through 1959. The car continued to be stamped in green, and continued to have non-operating doors. The car had a sheet metal frame, and knuckle couplers, along with trucks with sintered-iron side frames.

24403 ILLINOIS CENTRAL (Type I): Most of the cars had unpainted orange plastic bodies.

VG-C6	EX-C7	LN-C8	Scarcity
10	15	25	1

24403 ILLINOIS CENTRAL (Type II): A few cars were made with orange painted bodies.

VG-C6	EX-C7	LN-C8	Scarcity
Too rarely traded to accurately establish pricing.			

24409 NORTHERN PACIFIC: This car, with orange-painted sides and Tuscan-painted roof and ends, was available in 1958. It was decorated with black lettering and a multicolor decal of the NP logo. The car had a one-piece brakewheel, sheet metal frame, operating knuckle couplers and sintered-iron side frames.

VG-C6	EX-C7	LN-C8	Scarcity
450	800	1,300	8

24413 AMERICAN REFRIGERATOR TRANSIT CO.: This orange refrigerator car with silver sides was sold from 1957 through 1960. It had black stamping and was further decorated with three paper insignias, showing in color the logos of ART, Wabash and Missouri Pacific. The door guides were held in place by tabs—and the trucks featured sintered-iron side frames and operating knuckle couplers.

24413 AMERICAN REFRIGERATOR TRANSIT CO. (Type I): The door stenciling on some cars read "CLOSE AND LOCK DOOR."

VG-C6	EX-C7	LN-C8	Scarcity
50	75	135	5

24413 AMERICAN REFRIGERATOR TRANSIT CO. (Type II): Other doors were marked "CLOSE & LOCK DOOR."

VG-C6	EX-C7	LN-C8	Scarcity
50	75	135	5

24416 NORTHWESTERN: Painted in green and yellow, this 1958 refrigerator car bore the markings and paper logo of the "NORTH-WESTERN REFRIGERATOR LINE COMPANY." The car had a metal frame and door guides, single-piece brakewheel, operating knuckle couplers and trucks with sintered-iron side frames.

VG-C6	EX-C7	LN-C8	Scarcity
650	1,200	2,200	8

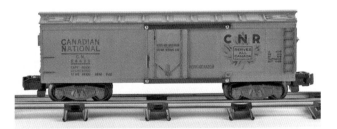

24419 CANADIAN NATIONAL: Sold in 1958-59, this gray-painted refrigerator car bore the red markings of "CANADIAN NATIONAL." A paper label with the green and red maple leaf "CNR" logo was attached to each side. The car had riveted-on metal door guides, one-piece brakewheel, operating knuckle couplers, and trucks with sintered-iron side frames.

VG-C6	EX-C7	LN-C8	Scarcity
200	375	525	7

24420 SIMMONS CARLOAD BARGAINS SALE: This uncataloged, unpainted orange 1958 refrigerator car, was lettered "SIMMONS CARLOAD BARGAINS SALE." This car had a sheet metal frame, but no brakewheel. It had trucks with sintered-iron side frames and solid, non-operating knuckle couplers. Beware; this car is very desirable and has been reproduced.

VG-C6	EX-C7	LN-C8	Scarcity
300	600	1,000	8

24422 GREAT NORTHERN BOXCAR: Though shown in the catalog only from 1963 through 1965, this car was also available in 1966. The car had a light green body with doors molded in place. The stamped white markings included the "GREAT NORTHERN" name and logo. Pike Master trucks with couplers were secured to the car's sheet metal frame.

24422 GREAT NORTHERN (Type I): The body of some cars was painted green.

VG-C6	EX-C7	LN-C8	Scarcity
60	125	175	7

24422 GREAT NORTHERN (Type II): Other cars were made with unpainted green plastic bodies.

VG-C6	EX-C7	LN-C8	Scarcity
50	100	150	5

24422 GREAT NORTHERN REFRIGERATOR: In addition to a boxcar with this number, Gilbert produced this green refrigerator car. This car was shown in the catalog from 1963 through 1965, but was also available—though uncataloged, in 1966. It was decorated with white Great Northern stamping.

24422 GREAT NORTHERN (Type I): Some of the cars had non-operating doors and no brakewheels, and were made with unpainted green plastic bodies.

VG-C6	EX-C7	LN-C8	Scarcity
10	15	25	1

Values for each condition are in U.S. dollars. | Scarcity = Scale from 1-8 with 8 being the hardest to find.

125

24422 GREAT NORTHERN (Type II): Other cars had one-piece brakewheels, but were otherwise identical to the Type I.

VG-C6	EX-C7	LN-C8	Scarcity
10	15	25	1

24422 GREAT NORTHERN (Type III): Some cars were painted green, but continued to have non-opening doors.

VG-C6	EX-C7	LN-C8	Scarcity
60	110	200	6

24422 GREAT NORTHERN (Type IV): Some cars were also produced with doors that slid open. These cars had green-painted bodies.

VG-C6	EX-C7	LN-C8	Scarcity
75	110	220	7

24425 BANGOR & AROOSTOOK: This 1960 refrigerator car was painted red and bore a paper label with the logo of the "BANGOR & AROOSTOOK RAILROAD." The sheet metal door guides were tabbed onto the body. A one-piece brakewheel was installed.

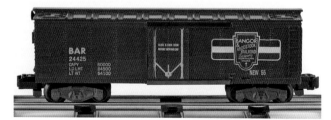

24425 BANGOR & AROOSTOOK (Type I): Some cars came with sintered-iron side frame trucks.

VG-C6	EX-C7	LN-C8	Scarcity
325	525	725	7

24425 BANGOR & AROOSTOOK (Type II): Other cars had Pike Master trucks.

VG-C6	EX-C7	LN-C8	Scarcity
325	525	725	7

24426 RATH PACKING CO.: This car, with its orange-painted sides and Tuscan-painted roof, was sold in 1960 and 1961. The car was lettered in black, and further decorated with a paper label featuring Rath's red, white and blue Indian head logo. The metal door guides were tabbed onto the body of these cars, which had sheet metal frames.

24426 RATH PACKING CO. (Type I): Some of these cars had trucks with sintered-iron side frames.

VG-C6	EX-C7	LN-C8	Scarcity
350	550	750	7

24426 RATH PACKING CO. (Type II): Other cars had Pike Master trucks.

VG-C6	EX-C7	LN-C8	Scarcity
325	500	700	7

25012 SEABOARD: In 1957, the 970 was packed in boxes numbered "25012."

25018 GILBERT'S: In 1957, the 973 came in a box numbered "25018."

25019 GILBERT'S: The Gilbert's milk car was re-equipped with knuckle couplers in 1957, and renumbered to 25019—the number it wore through 1960. The remainder of the three-door car, platform and cans was essentially unchanged from the 973. It was packaged with a control labeled "American Flyer Milk Car." All these ancillary items are included in the values listed below.

25019 GILBERT'S (Type I): Door guides attached with rivets.

VG-C6	EX-C7	LN-C8	Scarcity
75	150	225	5

25019 GILBERT'S (Type II): Door guides attached with tabs.

VG-C6	EX-C7	LN-C8	Scarcity
75	150	225	5

25019 GILBERT'S (Type I)

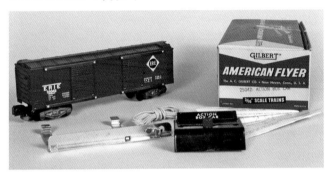

25042 ERIE: This Tuscan operating boxcar was produced in 1958. One side had a single fixed door, while the other side had two opening doors sliding on riveted-on door guides. The car was decorated with a black and white "ERIE" decal and featured a one-piece brakewheel. It rode on sintered-iron side frame trucks and had knuckle couplers. It was shipped with four barrels and a control box, both of which are included in the values listed below.

VG-C6	EX-C7	LN-C8	Scarcity
75	150	225	5

25049 RIO GRANDE: Smitty the Walking Brakeman began traversing the roof walk of the famed D & R G W "Cookie Box" in 1958. He continued to walk this path through 1960. The car had a sheet metal frame and a one-piece brakewheel and trucks with sintered-iron side frames and knuckle couplers.

VG-C6	EX-C7	LN-C8	Scarcity
125	225	350	7

25056 ROCKET LAUNCHER and U S M: This two-car set appeared in the 1959 20525 "Defender" train set. The 25056 was comprised of a painted yellow boxcar and rocket-launching flatcar. A tether connected the three-door boxcar to the flatcar. Although the rocket shown above is red, white and blue, the correct rocket for this car has a red nose and all-white body.

25056 ROCKET LAUNCHER and U S M (Type I): The door guides of the cars believed to be the first produced was secured with rivets.

VG-C6	EX-C7	LN-C8	Scarcity
125	225	500	7

25056 ROCKET LAUNCHER and U S M (Type II): The door guides on other boxcars were secured with tabs.

VG-C6	EX-C7	LN-C8	Scarcity
125	225	500	7

25057 TNT: This exploding boxcar was made in 1960. The five-piece plastic body was mounted on a sheet metal frame that was equipped with operating knuckle couplers and trucks with sintered-iron side frames. The solenoid-triggered operating mechanism housed in the car force the pieces apart violently when actuated, simulating the inadvertent detonation of the cargo.

VG-C6	EX-C7	LN-C8	Scarcity
75	175	275	6

HOUSE CARS

Values for each condition are in U.S. dollars. | **Scarcity =** Scale from 1-8 with 8 being the hardest to find.

127

25061 TNT: The exploding TNT car was renumbered in 1961, becoming the 25061. The number change was due to the addition of a second contact trip, which was designed for installation on the new Pike Master track.

VG-C6	EX-C7	LN-C8	Scarcity
125	225	350	6

25062 MINE CARRIER: The exploding TNT car became even more ominous in 1962, when its markings were changed to read "25062 MINE CARRIER." It bore these markings through 1964. The car was always equipped with operating knuckle couplers and trucks with sintered-iron side frames.

25062 MINE CARRIER (Type I): The roof and ends of some cars were painted silver.

VG-C6	EX-C7	LN-C8	Scarcity
150	300	500	7

25062 MINE CARRIER (Type II): Other cars had a Tuscan roof, and ends of the car were painted yellow.

VG-C6	EX-C7	LN-C8	Scarcity
175	350	550	7

25062 MINE CARRIER (Type III): The yellow ends of some cars were unpainted plastic, though the roof continued to be Tuscan.

VG-C6	EX-C7	LN-C8	Scarcity
150	300	500	7

25081 NYC: Introduced in 1961, this unpainted green ventilated boxcar remained in the product line through 1964. The car featured white New York Central markings, and more importantly housed a mechanism that discharged yellow plastic "hay bales." The car was equipped with Pike Master trucks and couplers.

VG-C6	EX-C7	LN-C8	Scarcity
15	30	50	4

25082 NEW HAVEN: 📷 This orange operating boxcar was available from 1961 through 1964. Inside the orange sliding doors was a mechanism which when triggered hurled plastic simulated "hay bales" out the door. The cars came in assorted shades of orange.

VG-C6	EX-C7	LN-C8	Scarcity
15	25	50	4

25082 NEW HAVEN

TANK CARS

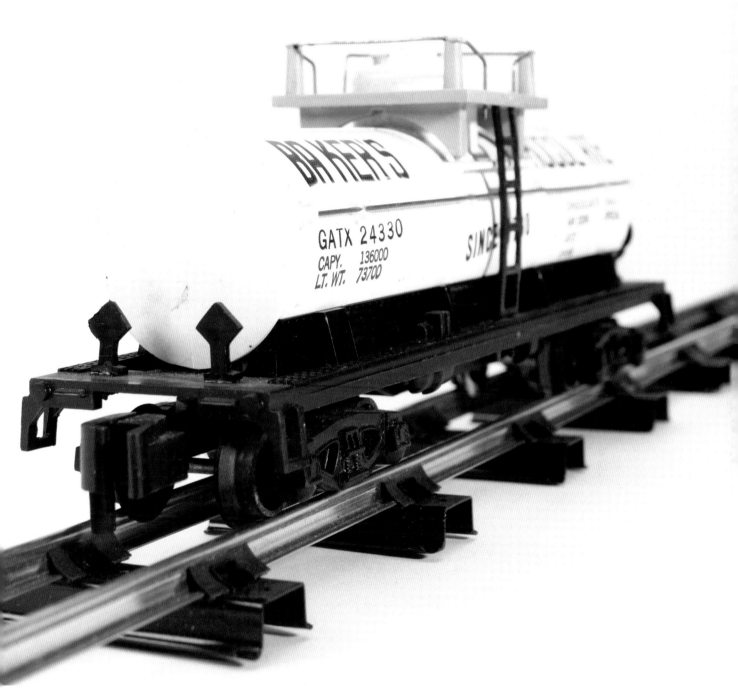

American Flyer produced tank cars in both single and three-dome styles during the postwar era. Considerably more complex than many other styles of rolling stock, through the years many minor design changes were made in order to simplify and economize the production of the cars. Chemical and oil companies of the time had colorful and distinctive markings, allowing many attractive, and today collectable, cars to be produced.

Values for each condition are in U.S. dollars. | **Scarcity =** Scale from 1-8 with 8 being the hardest to find.

129

625 SHELL: American Flyer's first plastic tank car was the 625 Shell, produced from 1946 through 1950. There are numerous variations in color, as well as material and markings of these cars. All the versions of this car used link couplers.

625 SHELL (Type I): The earliest of the 1946 cars were painted semi-gloss orange and had black ends and a dome top. The cars were stamped "CAPACITY 8000 LBS." Original cars invariably display signs of warping—unmarked reproductions of this car are not typically warped. The lettering on these cars is not as heavy as that on later cars.

VG-C6	EX-C7	LN-C8	Scarcity
500	750	1,000	8

625 SHELL (Type II): Other 1946 tank cars had flat orange painted plastic tanks with black ends and a dome top. The capacity of this car is listed as "80000 lbs.," but no other dimensional data is stamped on the car.

VG-C6	EX-C7	LN-C8	Scarcity
350	550	800	8

625 SHELL (Type III): Most of the 1946 tankers were unpainted orange plastic and marked "CAPACITY 80000 LBS." These cars also had black ends and dome tops, and black ladders.

VG-C6	EX-C7	LN-C8	Scarcity
350	525	775	7

625 SHELL (Type IV): Nickel-plated ladders were used on some of the 1946 unpainted orange "CAPACITY 80000 LBS." cars. The tank ends and dome top continued to be black.

VG-C6	EX-C7	LN-C8	Scarcity
350	525	775	7

625 SHELL (Type V): Sometime in 1946, cars with unpainted black plastic tanks were produced. These cars were stamped with silver lettering, including the absurd "CAPACITY 8000 LBS." reporting marks.

VG-C6	EX-C7	LN-C8	Scarcity
15	30	45	4

625 SHELL (Type VI): 📷 The more reasonable "CAPACITY 80000 LBS." was stamped in silver on some black 1946 cars.

VG-C6	EX-C7	LN-C8	Scarcity
15	30	45	4

625 SHELL (Type VII): To combat the body warping, a die-cast frame were used in late 1946 or early 1947. On this frame was mounted an unpainted black plastic tank with silver "CAPACITY 80000 LBS." lettering.

VG-C6	EX-C7	LN-C8	Scarcity
15	30	45	4

625 SHELL (Type VI)

625 Gulf

625 SHELL (Type VIII): Die-cast frame-equipped cars produced in 1947, and perhaps in late 1946, were stamped with white lettering on their unpainted black plastic tanks. The markings include "CAPACITY 80000 LBS."

VG-C6	EX-C7	LN-C8	Scarcity
15	30	45	4

625 SHELL (Type IX): In 1947, the body of some of the cars were painted silver. This would remain the color of the car through 1950, its final year of production. The black lettering on the car sides included "CAPACITY 80000 LBS."

VG-C6	EX-C7	LN-C8	Scarcity
10	15	25	2

625 SHELL (Type X): Near the end of production, the black lettering on the sides of the cars included an incredible "CAPACITY 800000 LBS."

VG-C6	EX-C7	LN-C8	Scarcity
10	15	25	2

625 GULF: In 1951, Gilbert entered into a licensing agreement with Gulf Oil Co., which resulted in a change in the decoration of the 625 tank car. The car continued to be painted silver, and the number remained 625, and a die-cast frame was used. This car, with its link couplers, remained in the product line through 1953.

625 GULF (Type I): When the car was initially produced, American Flyer erroneously continued to stamp the cars with the Shell reporting marks "S.E.P.X. 8681."

VG-C6	EX-C7	LN-C8	Scarcity
15	30	45	5

625 GULF (Type II): This mistake was caught, and the reporting marks changed to the correct "GRCX 5016."

VG-C6	EX-C7	LN-C8	Scarcity
15	30	45	5

625G GULF: In 1952 and 1953, this silver uncataloged tank car was produced. The car was produced with link couplers and silver-colored ladders.

VG-C6	EX-C7	LN-C8	Scarcity
10	18	25	2

910 GILBERT CHEMICALS: This attractive 1954 tank car wore the colors of Celanese Chemicals, but due to licensing issues, was lettered instead "GILBERT CHEMICALS." It was equipped with black platform, ladders and handrails. It was equipped with a die-cast frame, sintered-iron side frame trucks and knuckle couplers. Both light and medium green examples exist, with no difference in value or desirability.

VG-C6	EX-C7	LN-C8	Scarcity
150	250	375	6

TANK CARS

Values for each condition are in U.S. dollars. | **Scarcity** = Scale from 1-8 with 8 being the hardest to find.

131

912 KOPPERS: From 1955 through 1957, this black-painted single-dome tanker with yellow "KOPPERS CHEMICALS-PLASTICS" markings was offered. The car had a platform and black handrails. The car also had a "KOPPERS" label pasted on the sides, and rode on sintered-iron side frame trucks with knuckle couplers.

912 KOPPERS (Type I): Some of the cars had die-cast frames.

VG-C6	EX-C7	LN-C8	Scarcity
25	50	75	3

912 KOPPERS (Type II): Less than half of these cars seem to have been assembled with plastic frames.

VG-C6	EX-C7	LN-C8	Scarcity
40	65	100	6

925 GULF: This 1952-57 single-dome tanker was painted silver with black lettering. It rode on trucks with sintered-iron side frames and knuckle couplers.

925 GULF (Type I): Initially the cars were built with die-cast frames.

VG-C6	EX-C7	LN-C8	Scarcity
10	16	25	1

925 GULF (Type II): Some cars have been found with plastic frames.

VG-C6	EX-C7	LN-C8	Scarcity
10	16	25	1

926 GULF: Introduced in 1955, this new three-dome tank car remained in the line through 1957. The cars all were equipped with trucks with sintered-iron side frames and knuckle couplers.

926 GULF (Type I): Cars have been reported with die-cast frames.

VG-C6	EX-C7	LN-C8	Scarcity
20	40	60	4

926 GULF (Type II): Plastic frames have been reported on other cars.

VG-C6	EX-C7	LN-C8	Scarcity
20	40	60	4

958 MOBILGAS: This white-lettered red single-dome tank car was produced in 1957.

958 MOBILGAS (Type I): Some cars had a metal frame and were stamped "NEW 4-51."

VG-C6	EX-C7	LN-C8	Scarcity
80	120	175	6

958 MOBILGAS (Type I):

958 MOBILGAS (Type II): Other cars came with plastic frames, and continued to be stamped "NEW 4-51."

VG-C6	EX-C7	LN-C8	Scarcity
80	120	175	6

958 MOBILGAS (Type III): The markings on other cars read "NEW 6-51."

VG-C6	EX-C7	LN-C8	Scarcity
80	120	175	6

24305 KOPPERS: In 1957, the 912 came packed in a box marked "24305."

VG-C6	EX-C7	LN-C8	Scarcity
See 912 (Type II) for value.			

24309 GULF: This 1958 silver-painted single-dome tank car featured black "G.R.C.X. 5016" lettering.

24309 GULF (Type I): Some of these cars were equipped with inexpensive non-operating knuckle couplers.

VG-C6	EX-C7	LN-C8	Scarcity
5	10	25	1

24309 GULF (Type II): Other cars had the standard operating knuckle couplers and shiny handrails.

VG-C6	EX-C7	LN-C8	Scarcity
5	10	25	1

24309 GULF (Type III): Black handrails are found on other cars with operating knuckle couplers.

VG-C6	EX-C7	LN-C8	Scarcity
5	10	25	1

24310 GULF: This silver-painted single-dome tank car appeared in the American Flyer line from 1958 through 1960.

24310 GULF (Type I): Some of these cars were equipped with inexpensive non-operating knuckle couplers.

VG-C6	EX-C7	LN-C8	Scarcity
5	10	25	1

24310 GULF (Type II): Other cars had the standard operating knuckle couplers.

VG-C6	EX-C7	LN-C8	Scarcity
5	10	25	1

24312 GULF: In 1957, the 926 three-dome tank car came packaged in boxes marked "24312."

24313 GULF: Also sold from 1958-60 was a silver-painted three-dome tank car with black "G.A.T.X. 33648" markings and the Gulf logo. The car had a plastic frame, and trucks with sintered-iron side frames and knuckle couplers.

24313 GULF (Type I): 📷 As described above.

VG-C6	EX-C7	LN-C8	Scarcity
30	60	90	5

24313 GULF (Type II): In 1960, the manufacturing process changed, and the lower portion of the tank were molded integral with the plastic frame.

VG-C6	EX-C7	LN-C8	Scarcity
Too rarely traded to accurately establish pricing.			

24315 MOBILGAS: In 1957, the 958 tank car was sold in boxes marked "24315."

24313 GULF (Type I)

TANK CARS

24316 MOBILGAS: This red single-dome tank car was offered from 1958 through 1961 and again in 1965-66. It bore white Mobilgas markings.

24316 MOBILGAS (Type I): Some of the cars were marked "NEW 4-57" and utilized plastic frames and separate tanks. The tank was mounted with a screw, and the trucks had sintered-iron side frames and knuckle couplers.

VG-C6	EX-C7	LN-C8	Scarcity
15	25	45	3

24316 MOBILGAS (Type II): Other cars were assembled using snap-together construction rather than screwing the tank and frame together.

VG-C6	EX-C7	LN-C8	Scarcity
15	25	45	3

24316 MOBILGAS (Type III): A variation in marking occurred when some of the screwed together cars were marked "NEW 4-51."

VG-C6	EX-C7	LN-C8	Scarcity
15	25	45	3

24316 MOBILGAS (Type IV): The "NEW 4-51" markings were also used on some of the snapped together cars.

VG-C6	EX-C7	LN-C8	Scarcity
15	25	45	3

24316 MOBILGAS (Type V): Pike Master trucks and couplers were used on some of the cars marked "NEW 4-57."

VG-C6	EX-C7	LN-C8	Scarcity
5	10	25	1

24316 MOBILGAS (Type VI): The 1960-introduced frame with integral tank bottom was used on some of the cars marked "NEW 4-57." Knuckle couplers and trucks with sintered-iron side frames are found on some of these cars.

VG-C6	EX-C7	LN-C8	Scarcity
Too rarely traded to accurately establish pricing.			

24316 MOBILGAS (Type VII): Other cars with the 1960-introduced frame with integral tank bottom came with Pike Master trucks and couplers. The cars were marked with "NEW 4-51."

VG-C6	EX-C7	LN-C8	Scarcity
5	10	25	1

24319 PENNSYLVANIA SALT: This spectacular blue-painted tank car was offered only in 1958. One of the most desirable of all American Flyer rolling stock, this car has also been reproduced, hence caution should be observed when contemplating a purchase. One indicator of authenticity is the keystone herald, which is crisp on reproductions, yet originals have fuzzy edges.

VG-C6	EX-C7	LN-C8	Scarcity
250	400	750	7

24320 DEEP ROCK: 1960; This black plastic single-dome tank car was produced in 1960. The car's "DEEP ROCK" and "DPX 24320" markings were stamped in yellow. All cars had plastic frames and trucks with sintered-iron side frame trucks as well as solid knuckle couplers.

24319 PENNSYLVANIA SALT

24320 DEEP ROCK (Type I): Some of the cars lacked handrails and ladders.

VG-C6	EX-C7	LN-C8	Scarcity
200	400	600	7

24320 DEEP ROCK (Type II): Other cars included a separately installed handrail and ladder detailing.

VG-C6	EX-C7	LN-C8	Scarcity
200	400	600	7

24320 DEEP ROCK (Type III): Some of the sans handrail cars were built on frames with integral tank bottoms.

VG-C6	EX-C7	LN-C8	Scarcity
200	400	600	7

24321 DEEP ROCK: The 1959 edition of the Deep Rock tank car had yellow lettering reading "DEEP ROCK" and "DRX/24321." Like the later 24320, the 24321 came with or without handrails.

24321 DEEP ROCK (Type I): Some of the tank cars were equipped with handrails and ladders.

VG-C6	EX-C7	LN-C8	Scarcity
15	35	75	5

24321 DEEP ROCK (Type II): Other cars had neither handrails nor ladders.

VG-C6	EX-C7	LN-C8	Scarcity
15	35	75	5

24321 DEEP ROCK (Type III): Some cars had shiny handrails but no ladders.

VG-C6	EX-C7	LN-C8	Scarcity
15	35	75	5

24322 GULF: This silver tank car was sold in 1959. In addition to the orange paper "GULF" logo, this car was stamped with black reporting marks reading "GRCX 5016" and "CAPACITY 100000 LBS. LT. WT. 48900."

24322 GULF (Type I): Some of the cars were built with separate tanks and frames, and handrails were installed on the tank.

VG-C6	EX-C7	LN-C8	Scarcity
25	50	75	4

24322 GULF (Type II): Other cars continued to use the separate frame and tank, but lacked handrails.

VG-C6	EX-C7	LN-C8	Scarcity
25	50	75	4

24322 GULF (Type III): Other cars were built using the frame with integral tank bottom.

VG-C6	EX-C7	LN-C8	Scarcity
40	80	120	6

24323 BAKER'S CHOCOLATE: In 1959 and 1960, American Flyer sold this attractive car. Its decoration included an adhesive logo depicting a lady in a brown and white dress, and a red "SINCE 1780" label. The car rode on trucks with sintered-iron side frames. In 1960, the cars were packed in Kleer-Pak boxes.

24321 DEEP ROCK (Type II)

TANK CARS

24323 BAKER'S CHOCOLATE (Type I): Initially, the car had an unpainted white tank with painted gray ends and dome top. The tank on this car was a completely separate part held to the frame with tabs. A gray platform surrounded the dome.

VG-C6	EX-C7	LN-C8	Scarcity
150	300	400	6

24323 BAKER'S CHOCOLATE (Type II): Other cars had separate tanks painted white, while the tank's ends and dome top were painted gray, and a gray platform surrounded the dome.

VG-C6	EX-C7	LN-C8	Scarcity
150	300	400	6

24323 BAKER'S CHOCOLATE (Type III): Some of the cars featured a white tank with white ends and gray dome top mounted on a plastic frame. The bottom of the tank was integral with the frame. A gray platform surrounded the dome.

VG-C6	EX-C7	LN-C8	Scarcity
500	1,000	2,000	8

24324 HOOKER: The distinctive orange and black color scheme of the Hooker Chemical Co. adorned this 1959-60 offering. The black center band was unpainted plastic, while the orange was painted on. The car was equipped with trucks featuring sintered-iron side frames and operating knuckle couplers.

VG-C6	EX-C7	LN-C8	Scarcity
45	90	135	6

24325 GULF: This painted silver version of the Gulf single-dome tank car was produced in 1960, and appeared in numerous variations.

24325 GULF (Type I): Some of these cars were equipped with handrails and trucks with sintered-iron side frames and operating knuckle couplers. The tank was a separate subassembly.

VG-C6	EX-C7	LN-C8	Scarcity
5	10	20	1

24325 GULF (Type II): Other cars were essentially identical to the Type I, but were equipped with solid knuckle couplers.

VG-C6	EX-C7	LN-C8	Scarcity
5	10	20	1

24325 GULF (Type III): This car duplicated the Type II, but did not have handrails.

VG-C6	EX-C7	LN-C8	Scarcity
5	10	20	1

24324 HOOKER

24325 GULF (Type IV): Some cars had the bottom portion of the tank molded as part of the frame. In this instance, trucks with sintered-iron side frames and solid knuckle couplers were fitted.

VG-C6	EX-C7	LN-C8	Scarcity
15	35	60	3

24325 GULF (Type V): Other cars used Pike Master trucks and couplers in conjunction with the frame that was molded to include the bottom of the tank.

VG-C6	EX-C7	LN-C8	Scarcity
15	35	60	3

24328 SHELL: This 1962-66 tanker had a yellow tank decorated with Shell markings, including a red and yellow adhesive decal. The bottom of the tank was integral with the frame molding.

24328 SHELL (Type I): 📷 A few cars were built with tanks that were painted yellow.

VG-C6	EX-C7	LN-C8	Scarcity
Too rarely traded to accurately establish pricing.			

24328 SHELL (Type II): Much more common are cars with unpainted yellow-molded tanks.

VG-C6	EX-C7	LN-C8	Scarcity
5	10	20	1

24329 HOOKER: The Hooker logo returned for this car which was produced in numerous variations and over several years as described below. The car rode on Pike Master trucks.

24329 HOOKER (Type I): From 1961 through 1965, the car was produced with an unpainted orange tank. Though the car had the familiar "HOOKER CHEMICALS PLASTICS" logo, but the catalog number "24329" appeared nowhere on the car.

VG-C6	EX-C7	LN-C8	Scarcity
10	25	40	4

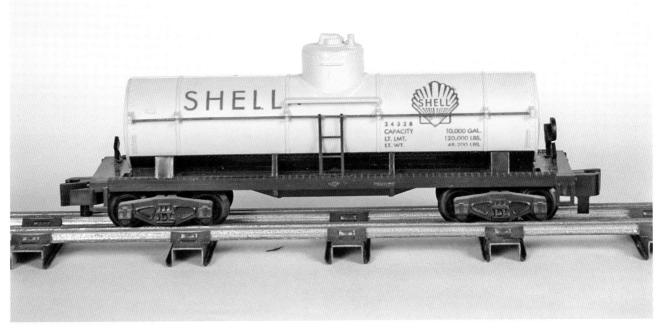

24328 SHELL (Type I)

TANK CARS

24330 BAKER'S CHOCOLATE (Type I)

24329 HOOKER (Type II): Some cars, believed to be produced in 1965 and 1966, had unpainted orange plastic tanks with the black center band painted on. The markings on this car included "HOOKER" and "NIAGARA FALLS N.Y. GATX 24329."

VG-C6	EX-C7	LN-C8	Scarcity
10	20	30	3

24330 BAKER'S CHOCOLATE: Baker's chocolate markings returned in 1961 and 1962 with a different number. This car had an unpainted white plastic tank with white dome top. Brown lettering on the car read "BAKER'S CHOCOLATE" while black lettering was

used for the remaining markings, including "SINCE 1780." It was fitted with Pike Master trucks and couplers.

24330 BAKER'S CHOCOLATE (Type I): Some of the cars had gray platforms.

VG-C6	EX-C7	LN-C8	Scarcity
30	60	100	6

24330 BAKER'S CHOCOLATE (Type II): The platforms of other cars were painted black.

VG-C6	EX-C7	LN-C8	Scarcity
30	60	100	6

PASSENGER CARS

For real railroads, passenger service was rarely directly profitable. Rather, at a time when most freight moved from town to town by train, passenger service was excellent exposure. For the A.C. Gilbert Co., passenger sets offered limited expansion capabilities—unlike freight sets that could have individual cars added to it over a period of time. A myriad of operating lineside accessories were also produced to work in conjunction with freight trains.

Modeled on that, Gilbert produced a few passenger-train oriented accessories. Further, most of the passenger cars were also sold separately, allowing enthusiasts to add passenger trains to the existing freight empires.

Six body styles of cars were produced during this time: The small "New Haven" style cars; heavyweight cars in early or late styles, streamlined cars, in both extruded aluminum and molded plastic, and 19th century style cars. From these six basic types Gilbert created numerous styles by varying details, installing operating mechanisms and changing decorations.

Values for each condition are in U.S. dollars. | **Scarcity** = Scale from 1-8 with 8 being the hardest to find.

139

AMERICAN FLYER CIRCUS: See 649.

20: See 24720.

30: See 24730.

40: See 24740.

50: See 24750.

500 AMERICAN FLYER LINES: Cataloged in 1952—but also available in 1953, the streamlined combination car—or combine, was produced in both chrome-plated and satin-silver finishes. The windows of this car were printed with passenger silhouettes. The car had die-cast four-wheel trucks and was illuminated. The lettering was stamped on nickel plates, which were then riveted to the car side.

500 AMERICAN FLYER LINES (Type I): Some of these cars had bodies with a chrome finish.

VG-C6	EX-C7	LN-C8	Scarcity
100	225	375	7

500 AMERICAN FLYER LINES (Type II): 📷 In 1953, these cars had a satin-silver finish.

VG-C6	EX-C7	LN-C8	Scarcity
150	300	550	8

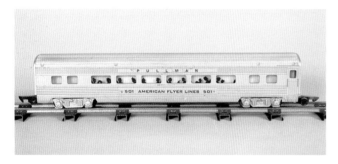

501 AMERICAN FLYER LINES: Introduced in 1953, this satin-silver-painted streamlined coach matched the 500 combination car. Like the combine, it had windows and silhouettes. It also rode on die-cast four-wheel trucks and had link couplers. A chrome-plated version of this car was not produced

502 AMERICAN FLYER LINES: This Vista Dome was made in 1952 and was the companion to the 500 and 501, sharing their construction features.

502 AMERICAN FLYER LINES (Type I): Some of these cars had bodies with a chrome finish.

VG-C6	EX-C7	LN-C8	Scarcity
100	225	375	7

502 AMERICAN FLYER LINES (Type II): Other cars had a satin-silver finish and produced in 1953.

VG-C6	EX-C7	LN-C8	Scarcity
150	300	550	8

503 AMERICAN FLYER LINES: This streamlined observation car, though uncataloged, has been dated to 1952 or 1953. Its plastic body was painted satin-silver. The car, which was illuminated, had silhouettes of passengers appearing in the windows. The car was equipped with die-cast trucks and link couplers.

VG-C6	EX-C7	LN-C8	Scarcity
175	350	600	8

649 AMERICAN FLYER CIRCUS: A unique car was this yellow New Haven-style coach sold from 1950 through 1952. The red lettering on the car read "AMERICAN FLYER CIRCUS" above the windows, and below the windows was the legend "WORLDS GREATEST SHOW!!" The cars, which were illuminated, were equipped with sheet metal trucks and link couplers.

500 AMERICAN FLYER LINES (Type II)

649 AMERICAN FLYER CIRCUS (Type I): Some of the cars, believed to be produced in 1950, had yellow-painted bodies.

VG-C6	EX-C7	LN-C8	Scarcity
60	120	200	7

649 AMERICAN FLYER CIRCUS (Type II):  Die-cast frames and unpainted yellow plastic bodies are characteristics of most of the circus coaches.

VG-C6	EX-C7	LN-C8	Scarcity
40	80	120	6

649 AMERICAN FLYER CIRCUS (Type III): Unpainted yellow bodies were also mounted on sheet metal frames in 1952.

VG-C6	EX-C7	LN-C8	Scarcity
40	80	120	6

650 NEW HAVEN: Offered from 1946 through 1953, these plastic cars were the mainstay of the Gilbert passenger fleet during the early years of S-Gauge. Known to many collectors as the New Haven, the cars were equipped with sheet metal trucks and link couplers.

Red

650 NEW HAVEN (Type I): Initially the cars were illuminated and had unpainted red plastic bodies and plastic frames.

VG-C6	EX-C7	LN-C8	Scarcity
20	50	90	6

650 NEW HAVEN (Type II): In 1947, the frame became die-cast, and the body were painted red. The car was illuminated.

VG-C6	EX-C7	LN-C8	Scarcity
20	40	60	4

650 NEW HAVEN (Type III): In 1948, the body reverted to unpainted plastic, but the frame remained die-cast, and lighting was retained. Unpainted red plastic cars with die-cast frames were shipped through 1951.

VG-C6	EX-C7	LN-C8	Scarcity
20	40	60	4

650 NEW HAVEN (Type IV): Once again in 1949, and occasionally through 1951, the bodies of some of these cars were painted red. Die-cast frames were used, and the cars were illuminated.

VG-C6	EX-C7	LN-C8	Scarcity
20	40	60	4

650 NEW HAVEN (Type V): In 1952, sheet metal frames were used in the unpainted red plastic illuminated cars. Sheet metal frames were used through 1953.

VG-C6	EX-C7	LN-C8	Scarcity
20	40	60	4

650 NEW HAVEN (Type VI): Sheet metal frames were also used in red-painted cars in 1952-53. The cars were illuminated.

VG-C6	EX-C7	LN-C8	Scarcity
20	40	60	4

Green

650 NEW HAVEN (Type VII): Other 1946 cars were illuminated and had unpainted green plastic bodies and plastic frames.

VG-C6	EX-C7	LN-C8	Scarcity
20	50	90	6

650 NEW HAVEN (Type VIII): Some of the green 1946 cars with plastic frames lacked illumination.

VG-C6	EX-C7	LN-C8	Scarcity
20	50	90	6

650 NEW HAVEN (Type IX): In 1947-48, the green illuminated cars were built on die-cast frames. This remained the norm through 1951.

VG-C6	EX-C7	LN-C8	Scarcity
20	40	60	4

650 NEW HAVEN (Type X): In 1952, sheet metal frames were used in the unpainted green plastic illuminated cars. Sheet metal frames were used through 1953.

VG-C6	EX-C7	LN-C8	Scarcity
20	40	60	4

649 AMERICAN FLYER CIRCUS (Type II)

Values for each condition are in U.S. dollars. | Scarcity = Scale from 1-8 with 8 being the hardest to find.

141

650 NEW HAVEN (Type XI): Sheet metal frames were also used in green-painted cars in 1952-53. These cars also were illuminated.

VG-C6	EX-C7	LN-C8	Scarcity
20	40	60	4

651 NEW HAVEN: Produced from 1946 through 1953, this baggage car was the companion to the 650 New Haven-style coach listed above. Unlike the coach, however, the baggage car was not illuminated.

Red

651 NEW HAVEN (Type I): Initially the cars had unpainted red plastic bodies and plastic frames.

VG-C6	EX-C7	LN-C8	Scarcity
20	50	90	6

651 NEW HAVEN (Type II): In 1947, the frame became die-cast, and the body was painted red.

VG-C6	EX-C7	LN-C8	Scarcity
20	40	60	4

651 NEW HAVEN (Type III): In 1948, the body reverted to unpainted plastic, but the frame remained die-cast. Unpainted red plastic cars with die-cast frames were shipped through 1951.

VG-C6	EX-C7	LN-C8	Scarcity
20	40	60	4

651 NEW HAVEN (Type IV): Once again in 1949, and occasionally through 1951, the bodies of some of these cars were painted red. Die-cast frames were used.

VG-C6	EX-C7	LN-C8	Scarcity
20	40	60	4

651 NEW HAVEN (Type V): In 1952, sheet metal frames were used in the unpainted red plastic cars. Sheet-metal frames were used through 1953.

VG-C6	EX-C7	LN-C8	Scarcity
20	40	60	4

651 NEW HAVEN (Type VI): Sheet metal frames were also used in red-painted cars in 1952-53.

VG-C6	EX-C7	LN-C8	Scarcity
20	40	60	4

Green

651 NEW HAVEN (Type VII): Other 1946 cars had unpainted green plastic bodies and plastic frames.

VG-C6	EX-C7	LN-C8	Scarcity
20	50	90	6

651 NEW HAVEN (Type VIII): In 1947-48, the green cars were built on die-cast frames. This remained the norm through 1951.

VG-C6	EX-C7	LN-C8	Scarcity
20	40	60	4

651 NEW HAVEN (Type IX): In 1952, sheet metal frames were used in the unpainted green plastic cars. Sheet metal frames were used through 1953.

VG-C6	EX-C7	LN-C8	Scarcity
20	40	60	4

651 NEW HAVEN (Type X): Sheet metal frames were also used in green-painted cars in 1952-53.

VG-C6	EX-C7	LN-C8	Scarcity
20	40	60	4

651 NEW HAVEN (Type XI): In 1953, some of the green-painted cars were stamped "AMERICAN FLYER LINES" rather than "New Haven" and "RAILWAY EXPRESS AGENCY" beneath the number.

VG-C6	EX-C7	LN-C8	Scarcity
20	40	60	4

Tuscan

651 NEW HAVEN (Type XII): A few 1953 cars stamped "AMERICAN FLYER LINES" and "RAILWAY EXPRESS AGENCY" were painted Tuscan.

VG-C6	EX-C7	LN-C8	Scarcity
Too rarely traded to accurately establish pricing.			

652 PULLMAN: These heavyweight cars were based on Flyer's prewar die-cast cars. Offered in a variety of colors between 1946 and 1953, these illuminated cars rode on sheet metal six-wheel trucks, which were equipped with link couplers.

Red

652 PULLMAN (Type I): In 1947, the trucks of these cars were just over 2-1/2 inches long. The number "652" is stamped twice on each side of the red cars, once near either end.

VG-C6	EX-C7	LN-C8	Scarcity
75	150	250	7

652 PULLMAN (Type II): In 1948, the trucks beneath the red-painted car were changed, becoming about 2-1/8 inches long. The car number continued to be stamped near each end of the car.

VG-C6	EX-C7	LN-C8	Scarcity
50	125	175	5

652 PULLMAN (Type III): Unpainted red cars were also built with the centered "652" stamping.

VG-C6	EX-C7	LN-C8	Scarcity
45	100	160	4

652 PULLMAN (Type IV): In 1953, a red 652 returned to the lineup. The body used was identical to the 900-series passenger cars with non-operating doors. Also, stamped below the windows in white was "PIKES PEAK," the number "652" was stamped near each door on both sides. Also stamped near each door was the small word "PULLMAN," and a large "AMERICAN FLYER LINES" was centered above the windows.

VG-C6	EX-C7	LN-C8	Scarcity
75	150	250	7

Green

652 PULLMAN (Type V): Green-painted plastic bodies were used on some of the 1947 cars with 2-1/2-inch long trucks. The number "652" is stamped twice on each side of these cars, once near either end.

VG-C6	EX-C7	LN-C8	Scarcity
75	150	250	7

652 PULLMAN (Type VI): In 1948, the green-painted cars were fitted with trucks that were about 2-1/8 inches long. These trucks were used through the remaining balance of production. The car number continued to be stamped near each end of the car.

VG-C6	EX-C7	LN-C8	Scarcity
50	125	175	5

652 PULLMAN (Type VII): Some of these cars, probably those made late in 1948, were unpainted olive green plastic. The trucks and stamping on these cars were identical to those in the Type V.

VG-C6	EX-C7	LN-C8	Scarcity
45	100	160	4

652 PULLMAN (Type VIII): In 1949, the stamping of the cars was changed, such that the number "652" was only stamped once—centered—on each side.

VG-C6	EX-C7	LN-C8	Scarcity
45	100	160	4

652 PULLMAN (Type IX): From 1949 through 1952, unpainted olive green plastic versions of these cars were made. The number "652" was only stamped once—centered—on each side.

VG-C6	EX-C7	LN-C8	Scarcity
45	100	160	4

652 PULLMAN (Type X): In 1953, the body and the markings of the green-painted cars were changed. The body was identical to the 900-series passenger cars with non-operating doors. Also, stamped below the windows in white was "PIKES PEAK," the number "652" was stamped near each door on both sides. Also stamped near each door was the small word "PULLMAN," and a large "AMERICAN FLYER LINES" was centered above the windows.

VG-C6	EX-C7	LN-C8	Scarcity
75	150	250	7

Tuscan

652 PULLMAN (Type XI): Late in 1948, the big Pullman was produced with an unpainted Tuscan plastic body. The first of these cars had the number "652" near each end of the car. Trucks 2-1/2 inches long were used on these cars.

VG-C6	EX-C7	LN-C8	Scarcity
45	100	160	4

653 COMBINE: This illuminated heavyweight combine was sold from 1946 through 1953 as a companion to the 652 Pullman. On one end of the car sides were the passenger windows and on the other a large sliding baggage car.

Values for each condition are in U.S. dollars. | **Scarcity =** Scale from 1-8 with 8 being the hardest to find.

143

Red

653 COMBINE (Type I): In 1947, the trucks of these cars were just over 2-1/2 inches long. The number "653" is stamped twice on each side of the red cars, once near either end.

VG-C6	EX-C7	LN-C8	Scarcity
75	150	250	7

653 COMBINE (Type II): In 1948, the trucks beneath the red-painted car were changed, becoming about 2-1/8 inches long. The car number continued to be stamped near each end of the car.

VG-C6	EX-C7	LN-C8	Scarcity
50	125	175	5

Green

653 COMBINE (Type III): Green-painted plastic bodies were used on some of the 1947 cars with 2-1/2-inch long trucks. The number "653" is stamped twice on each side of these cars, once near either end.

VG-C6	EX-C7	LN-C8	Scarcity
75	150	250	7

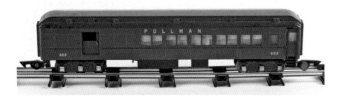

653 COMBINE (Type IV): In 1948, the green-painted cars were fitted with trucks that were about 2-1/8 inches long. These trucks were used through the balance of production. The car number continued to be stamped near each end of the car.

VG-C6	EX-C7	LN-C8	Scarcity
50	125	175	5

653 COMBINE (Type V): Some of these cars, probably those made late in 1948, were unpainted green plastic. The trucks and stamping on these cars were identical to those in the Type IV.

VG-C6	EX-C7	LN-C8	Scarcity
45	100	160	4

653 COMBINE (Type VI): In 1949, the stamping of the cars were changed, such that the number "653" was only stamped once—centered—on each side. Some of these cars were painted green.

VG-C6	EX-C7	LN-C8	Scarcity
45	100	160	4

653 COMBINE (Type VII): From 1949 through 1952, unpainted olive green plastic versions of these cars were made. The number "653" was only stamped once—centered—on each side.

VG-C6	EX-C7	LN-C8	Scarcity
45	100	160	4

Tuscan

653 COMBINE (Type VIII): Late in 1948, the combine was produced with an unpainted Tuscan plastic body. The first of these cars had the number "653" near each end of the car. Trucks 2-1/8 inches long were used on these cars.

VG-C6	EX-C7	LN-C8	Scarcity
45	100	160	4

653 COMBINE (Type IX): From 1949 through 1952, unpainted Tuscan plastic versions of these cars were made. The number "653" was only stamped once—centered—on each side.

VG-C6	EX-C7	LN-C8	Scarcity
45	100	160	4

654 PULLMAN OBSERVATION: This 1946-53 heavyweight observation car was the mate to the 652 and 653, and was offered in variations accordingly.

Red

654 PULLMAN OBSERVATION (Type I): In 1947, the trucks of these cars were just over 2-1/2 inches long. The number "654" is stamped twice on each side of the red cars, once near either end.

VG-C6	EX-C7	LN-C8	Scarcity
75	150	250	7

654 PULLMAN OBSERVATION (Type II): In 1948, the trucks beneath the red-painted car were changed, becoming about 2-1/8 inches long. The car number continued to be stamped near each end of the car.

VG-C6	EX-C7	LN-C8	Scarcity
50	125	175	5

Green

654 PULLMAN OBSERVATION (Type III): Green-painted plastic bodies were used on some of the 1947 cars with 2-1/2-inch long trucks. The number "653" is stamped twice on each side of these cars, once near either end.

VG-C6	EX-C7	LN-C8	Scarcity
75	150	250	7

654 PULLMAN OBSERVATION (Type IV): In 1948, the green-painted cars were fitted with trucks that were about 2-1/8 inches long. These trucks were used through the balance of production. The car number continued to be stamped near each end of the car.

VG-C6	EX-C7	LN-C8	Scarcity
50	125	175	5

654 PULLMAN OBSERVATION (Type V): Some of these cars, probably those made late in 1948, were unpainted green plastic. The trucks and stamping on these cars were identical to those in the Type IV.

VG-C6	EX-C7	LN-C8	Scarcity
45	100	160	4

654 PULLMAN OBSERVATION (Type VI): In 1949, the stamping of the cars was changed, such that the number "654" was only stamped once—centered—on each side. Some of these cars were painted green.

VG-C6	EX-C7	LN-C8	Scarcity
45	100	160	4

654 PULLMAN OBSERVATION (Type VII): From 1949 through 1952, unpainted olive green plastic versions of these cars were made. The number "654" was only stamped once—centered—on each side. The platform windows of the early versions of these later cars were molded shut.

VG-C6	EX-C7	LN-C8	Scarcity
45	100	160	4

654 PULLMAN OBSERVATION (Type VIII): On later cars the rear windows were molded open.

VG-C6	EX-C7	LN-C8	Scarcity
45	100	160	4

Tuscan

654 PULLMAN OBSERVATION (Type IX): Late in 1948, the observation was produced with an unpainted Tuscan plastic body. The first of these cars had the number "654" near each end of the car. Trucks 2-1/8 inches long were used on these cars.

VG-C6	EX-C7	LN-C8	Scarcity
60	150	225	6

654 PULLMAN OBSERVATION (Type X): From 1949 through 1952, unpainted Tuscan plastic versions of these cars were made. The number "654" was only stamped once—centered—on each side. The platform windows of the early versions of these later cars were molded shut.

VG-C6	EX-C7	LN-C8	Scarcity
45	100	160	4

654 PULLMAN OBSERVATION (Type XI): On later cars the rear windows were molded open.

VG-C6	EX-C7	LN-C8	Scarcity
45	100	160	4

655 SILVER BULLET: This gleaming coach was produced in 1953. The car was lettered "AMERICAN FLYER LINES" in black above the windows, and numbered "655" near the doors on each end. A blue and yellow decal reading "SILVER BULLET," complete with a projectile logo, was applied beneath the windows on both sides of the car. The cars, which had sheet metal trucks and link couplers, lacked illumination.

655 SILVER BULLET (Type I): Some of the cars had chrome-plated bodies.

VG-C6	EX-C7	LN-C8	Scarcity
25	75	125	5

655 SILVER BULLET (Type II): Other cars were painted in a satin-silver color.

VG-C6	EX-C7	LN-C8	Scarcity
20	50	100	4

655 AMERICAN FLYER LINES: Also produced in 1953 was this American Flyer Lines New Haven-style coach. The lettering centered above the windows read "AMERICAN FLYER LINES," while centered below the windows was the catalog number "655." The car, which was not illuminated, had sheet metal trucks and link couplers.

655 AMERICAN FLYER LINES (Type I): Some of these cars were painted red.

VG-C6	EX-C7	LN-C8	Scarcity
25	50	75	4

Values for each condition are in U.S. dollars. | **Scarcity** = Scale from 1-8 with 8 being the hardest to find.

655 AMERICAN FLYER LINES (Type II): Other cars were painted green.

VG-C6	EX-C7	LN-C8	Scarcity
25	50	75	4

660 AMERICAN FLYER LINES COMBINATION: In 1950, Gilbert introduced a series of streamlined passenger cars. These cars were built in two large categories. Some of the cars were made with extruded aluminum bodies. But in 1952, the cars' final year, this process was replaced by an injection molding process. Though this meant a complete redesign of the car, American Flyer retained the same catalog numbers.

The lowest number of this series was the 660, a combination car.

660 AMERICAN FLYER LINES COMBINATION (Type I): In 1950 and 1951, the car was made with an extruded aluminum body.

VG-C6	EX-C7	LN-C8	Scarcity
25	50	75	4

660 AMERICAN FLYER LINES COMBINATION (Type II): In 1952, the car was made with a chrome-plated plastic body.

VG-C6	EX-C7	LN-C8	Scarcity
35	65	110	6

661 AMERICAN FLYER LINES COACH: Also produced from 1950 through 1952 was this streamlined coach. Like the 660, the car was first built with an aluminum body, and then was manufactured with a molded plastic body in 1952.

661 AMERICAN FLYER LINES COACH (Type I): In 1950 and 1951, the car was made with an extruded aluminum body.

VG-C6	EX-C7	LN-C8	Scarcity
25	50	75	4

661 AMERICAN FLYER LINES COACH (Type II): In 1952, the car was made with a chrome-plated plastic body.

VG-C6	EX-C7	LN-C8	Scarcity
35	65	110	6

662 AMERICAN FLYER LINES: A streamlined Vista Dome car was made in this series as well. Like the other cars, in 1950 and 1951 the car was aluminum, and in 1952 it was injection-molded plastic.

662 AMERICAN FLYER LINES VISTA DOME (Type I): In 1950 and 1951, the car was made with an extruded aluminum body.

VG-C6	EX-C7	LN-C8	Scarcity
25	50	75	4

662 AMERICAN FLYER LINES VISTA DOME (Type II): In 1952, the car was made with a chrome-plated plastic body.

VG-C6	EX-C7	LN-C8	Scarcity
35	65	110	6

663 AMERICAN FLYER LINES OBSERVATION: To bring up the rear of the train, a streamlined observation car was produced. Like the other cars in this series, in 1950 and 1951 the car was aluminum, and in 1952 it was injection molded plastic.

VG-C6	EX-C7	LN-C8	Scarcity
25	50	75	4

663 AMERICAN FLYER LINES OBSERVATION (Type I): In 1950 and 1951, the car was made with an extruded aluminum body.

VG-C6	EX-C7	LN-C8	Scarcity
25	50	75	4

663 AMERICAN FLYER LINES OBSERVATION (Type II): In 1952, an extremely scarce version of the car was made with a chrome-plated plastic body.

VG-C6	EX-C7	LN-C8	Scarcity
Too rarely traded to accurately establish pricing.			

718 NEW HAVEN or AMERICAN FLYER LINES: This operating mail pickup car was sold between 1946 and 1954, inclusive. The car duplicated the action of a railway post office picking up mail while the train was in motion, achieving this replication by the use of a solenoid-actuated stamped metal mail pick arm. The car had two opening baggage doors on one side, and a non-operating door on the other side. The car was packaged with a 711 mail pickup pole, two mailbags and a control button.

718 NEW HAVEN (Type I): The earliest of these cars had an unpainted red body with a red painted mail pickup arm and plastic frame.

VG-C6	EX-C7	LN-C8	Scarcity
175	250	450	7

718 NEW HAVEN (Type II): A near duplicate of the 1946 car was made in 1947, differing only by having a die-cast frame.

VG-C6	EX-C7	LN-C8	Scarcity
175	250	450	7

718 NEW HAVEN (Type III): Beginning in 1948, the mail pick up arm was no longer painted red. It continued in this manner until 1954.

718 AMERICAN FLYER LINES (Type IV): In 1952, the 718 was stamped with the road name "AMERICAN FLYER LINES" rather than New Haven. Also, the car was painted red, rather than unpainted red plastic.

VG-C6	EX-C7	LN-C8	Scarcity
125	200	350	7

Green

718 NEW HAVEN (Type V): From 1952 to 1954, the operating mail car was also available with an unpainted green plastic body and die-cast frame.

VG-C6	EX-C7	LN-C8	Scarcity
35	65	110	6

718 AMERICAN FLYER LINES (Type VI): In 1952, the 718 was stamped with the road name "AMERICAN FLYER LINES" rather than New Haven. Also, the car was painted green, rather than unpainted green plastic.

VG-C6	EX-C7	LN-C8	Scarcity
125	200	350	8

Tuscan

718 AMERICAN FLYER LINES (Type VII): Also manufactured in 1952 was a Tuscan-painted version of the 718. The car was stamped with the road name "AMERICAN FLYER LINES" rather than New Haven.

VG-C6	EX-C7	LN-C8	Scarcity
125	200	350	8

732 AMERICAN FLYER: From 1950 through 1954, Gilbert offered this operating baggage car. Built on a die-cast frame, this car housed a mechanism, which, by means of a blue figure, ejects a tiny simulated packing crate.

732 AMERICAN FLYER (Type I): In 1950, this car was produced with an unpainted red plastic body and red-painted metal operating door.

VG-C6	EX-C7	LN-C8	Scarcity
50	85	125	5

732 AMERICAN FLYER (Type II): Unpainted green plastic cars were also produced in 1950—however these cars remained in the catalog through 1952.

VG-C6	EX-C7	LN-C8	Scarcity
25	50	75	4

Values for each condition are in U.S. dollars. | **Scarcity** = Scale from 1-8 with 8 being the hardest to find.

147

732 AMERICAN FLYER (Type III): In 1953 and 1954, a green-painted version of the car was produced.

VG-C6	EX-C7	LN-C8	Scarcity
35	70	110	4

732 AMERICAN FLYER LINES (Type IV): A handful of the green cars made in 1954 were stamped "AMERICAN FLYER LINES" rather than "American Flyer."

VG-C6	EX-C7	LN-C8	Scarcity
Too rarely traded to accurately establish pricing.			

735 NEW HAVEN: This animated coach was produced for use with the 766 animated station from 1952 through 1954. The car and station worked in conjunction for an effect much like that of the animated cattle corral—with the passenger figures moving from station to car and then back to station. The values listed below are for the car alone.

735 NEW HAVEN (Type I): Some of the cars were stamped "NEW HAVEN" above the windows.

VG-C6	EX-C7	LN-C8	Scarcity
35	60	100	5

735 NEW HAVEN (Type II): The "NEW HAVEN" stamping was below the windows of other cars.

VG-C6	EX-C7	LN-C8	Scarcity
35	60	100	5

900 NORTHERN PACIFIC COMBINE: Introduced in 1956, and also available in 1957, was this series of passenger cars in the striking two-tone green livery of the Northern Pacific. The illuminated cars had silhouettes of passengers visible through the windows. The car bodies were molded plastic, while the frame was sheet metal. The four-wheel die-cast passenger car trucks were finished in silver, and equipped with knuckle couplers. The lowest number of the series, 900, was assigned to this combine car.

VG-C6	EX-C7	LN-C8	Scarcity
100	200	300	7

901 NORTHERN PACIFIC COACH: This coach was sold in 1956 and 1957—and matched the 900 combine car described above.

VG-C6	EX-C7	LN-C8	Scarcity
100	200	300	7

902 NORTHERN PACIFIC VISTA DOME: This Vista Dome was sold in 1956 and 1957—and matched the 900 combine car described above.

VG-C6	EX-C7	LN-C8	Scarcity
100	200	300	7

903 NORTHERN PACIFIC OBSERVATION: The Northern Pacific set of 1956 and 1957 was completed by this observation car, which matched the 900 combine car described above.

VG-C6	EX-C7	LN-C8	Scarcity
100	200	300	7

918 AMERICAN FLYER LINES: Essentially a knuckle-coupler equipped version of the 718, this operating mail pickup car was sold between 1953 and 1958, inclusive. The car duplicated the action of a railway post office picking up mail while the train was in motion, achieving this replication by the use of a solenoid-actuated stamped metal mail pick arm. The car had two opening baggage doors on one side, and a non-operating door on the other. The car was packaged with a 711 mail pickup pole, two mailbags and a control button. This maroon car was lettered "AMERICAN FLYER LINES" above the windows.

VG-C6	EX-C7	LN-C8	Scarcity
30	50	100	4

951 AMERICAN FLYER LINES BAGGAGE: This New Haven-style baggage car was sold from 1953 and 1957. It came in an assortment of colors. The non-illuminated cars had sheet metal frames and rode on trucks with sintered-iron side frames and knuckle couplers.

Red

951 AMERICAN FLYER LINES BAGGAGE (Type I): The car was produced with a red-painted plastic body and white lettering.

VG-C6	EX-C7	LN-C8	Scarcity
15	30	50	4

951 AMERICAN FLYER LINES BAGGAGE (Type II): Unpainted red plastic bodies with white lettering were used on other cars.

VG-C6	EX-C7	LN-C8	Scarcity
15	30	50	4

Green

951 AMERICAN FLYER LINES BAGGAGE (Type III): Unpainted green plastic cars with white lettering were also made.

VG-C6	EX-C7	LN-C8	Scarcity
20	40	65	5

951 AMERICAN FLYER LINES BAGGAGE (Type IV): Green cars were also made with painted bodies and white stamping.

VG-C6	EX-C7	LN-C8	Scarcity
20	40	65	5

951: Tuscan.
951 AMERICAN FLYER LINES BAGGAGE (Type V): The car was also produced in a Tuscan-painted version with white lettering.

VG-C6	EX-C7	LN-C8	Scarcity
20	40	65	5

952 AMERICAN FLYER LINES PULLMAN: From 1953 through 1958, these well-proportioned, accurately detailed cars rode the rails of American Flyer catalogs. The tooling to produce these cars was completely new, and replaced the previously used "heavyweight" car tooling, which had origins dating to before WWII. The

illuminated cars had well-detailed unpainted black plastic frames. The cars were fitted with new six-wheel trucks with die-cast side frames.

952 AMERICAN FLYER LINES PULLMAN (Type I): In 1953 and 1954, Gilbert produced this green-painted car. No passenger silhouettes were visible in the windows.

VG-C6	EX-C7	LN-C8	Scarcity
50	100	175	5

952 AMERICAN FLYER LINES PULLMAN (Type II): Also available in 1953 and 1954 was this Tuscan-painted car. No passenger silhouettes were visible in the windows.

VG-C6	EX-C7	LN-C8	Scarcity
50	100	175	5

952 AMERICAN FLYER LINES PULLMAN (Type III): Beginning in 1955, the silhouettes of passengers were visible in the windows of the Tuscan-painted cars. These cars remained in the line through 1958.

VG-C6	EX-C7	LN-C8	Scarcity
75	175	300	7

953 AMERICAN FLYER LINES COMBINE: Also available from 1953 through 1958 was this heavyweight combine, which was produced in several variations to match the Pullman listed above.

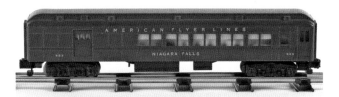

953 AMERICAN FLYER LINES COMBINE (Type I): In 1953 and 1954, Gilbert produced this green-painted car. No passenger silhouettes were visible in the windows.

VG-C6	EX-C7	LN-C8	Scarcity
50	100	175	5

Values for each condition are in U.S. dollars. | **Scarcity** = Scale from 1-8 with 8 being the hardest to find.

149

953 AMERICAN FLYER LINES COMBINE (Type II): Also available in 1953 and 1954 was this Tuscan-painted car. No passenger silhouettes were visible in the windows.

VG-C6	EX-C7	LN-C8	Scarcity
50	100	175	5

953 AMERICAN FLYER LINES COMBINE (Type III): Beginning in 1955, the silhouettes of passengers were visible in the windows of the Tuscan-painted cars. These cars remained in the line through 1958.

VG-C6	EX-C7	LN-C8	Scarcity
75	175	300	7

954 AMERICAN FLYER LINES OBSERVATION: Completing the 1953 through 1958 heavyweight passenger train was this observation car, which was produced in several variations to match the Pullman and combine listed above.

954 AMERICAN FLYER LINES OBSERVATION (Type I): In 1953 and 1954, Gilbert produced this green-painted car. No passenger silhouettes were visible in the windows.

VG-C6	EX-C7	LN-C8	Scarcity
50	100	175	5

954 AMERICAN FLYER LINES OBSERVATION (Type II): Also available in 1953 and 1954 was this Tuscan-painted car. No passenger silhouettes were visible in the windows.

VG-C6	EX-C7	LN-C8	Scarcity
50	100	175	5

954 AMERICAN FLYER LINES OBSERVATION (Type III): Beginning in 1955, the silhouettes of passengers were visible in the windows of the Tuscan-painted cars. These cars remained in the line through 1958.

VG-C6	EX-C7	LN-C8	Scarcity
75	175	300	7

955 AMERICAN FLYER LINES: This New Haven style coach was cataloged in 1954 and 1955 in a variety of colors and decorations.

955 AMERICAN FLYER LINES (Type I): A gleaming satin-silver version of this coach was produced in 1954 and 1955. The car was lettered "AMERICAN FLYER LINES" in black above the windows and numbered "955" near the doors on each end. A blue and yellow decal reading "SILVER BULLET," complete with a projectile logo, was applied beneath the windows on both sides of the car. The cars, which had trucks with sintered-iron side frames and knuckle couplers, lacked illumination.

VG-C6	EX-C7	LN-C8	Scarcity
40	75	125	5

955 AMERICAN FLYER LINES (Type II): Other versions of the car were painted green and lettered in white.

VG-C6	EX-C7	LN-C8	Scarcity
40	75	125	5

955 AMERICAN FLYER LINES (Type III): A Tuscan-painted version of the car was also produced.

VG-C6	EX-C7	LN-C8	Scarcity
30	60	90	5

955 AMERICAN FLYER LINES (Type IV): Some of the Tuscan-painted cars had passenger silhouettes visible in the windows.

VG-C6	EX-C7	LN-C8	Scarcity
50	100	150	6

955 AMERICAN FLYER LINES (Type V): In addition to the silhouettes, some cars also had white borders trimming the windows.

VG-C6	EX-C7	LN-C8	Scarcity
50	100	150	6

960 AMERICAN FLYER LINES COMBINE: Between 1953 and 1956, Gilbert produced these molded plastic streamlined cars. Though the various cars were decorated with stripes of assorted colors, all were decorated with stripes above the window nameplates reading "AMERICAN FLYER LINES," and below the window plates with the car names and numbers. Silhouettes of passengers were visible in the car windows. The car had a sheet metal frame and rode on four-wheel passenger car trucks with knuckle couplers.

The lower name and number plate on this combine car read "960 COLUMBUS 960."

960 AMERICAN FLYER LINES COMBINE (Type I): Some of the 1953 cars were finished in chrome, without a colored stripe.

VG-C6	EX-C7	LN-C8	Scarcity
30	75	125	4

960 AMERICAN FLYER LINES COMBINE (Type II): Other cars assembled in 1953 had bodies that were merely painted silver.

VG-C6	EX-C7	LN-C8	Scarcity
35	85	135	4

960 AMERICAN FLYER LINES COMBINE (Type III): In 1954 and 1955, the silver-painted cars were trimmed with a broad blue stripe painted through the window area.

VG-C6	EX-C7	LN-C8	Scarcity
40	90	150	4

960 AMERICAN FLYER LINES COMBINE (Type IV): In 1954, some cars were built with a broad chestnut-colored stripe painted through the window area.

VG-C6	EX-C7	LN-C8	Scarcity
75	175	300	7

960 AMERICAN FLYER LINES COMBINE (Type V): Cars with a green window stripe were produced in 1955.

VG-C6	EX-C7	LN-C8	Scarcity
40	90	150	4

960 AMERICAN FLYER LINES COMBINE (Type VI): From 1954 through 1956, a red band was painted through the window line of some cars.

VG-C6	EX-C7	LN-C8	Scarcity
40	90	150	4

960 AMERICAN FLYER LINES COMBINE (Type VII): In 1956, cars were produced with an orange stripe painted through the window area. Some of these cars had the car name stamped on a separately applied nameplate.

VG-C6	EX-C7	LN-C8	Scarcity
50	100	200	5

Values for each condition are in U.S. dollars. | **Scarcity** = Scale from 1-8 with 8 being the hardest to find.

151

960 AMERICAN FLYER LINES COMBINE (Type VIII): Other orange-striped cars did not have the lower nameplate. Instead the car name and number were stamped directly on the car body.

VG-C6	EX-C7	LN-C8	Scarcity
50	100	200	5

961 AMERICAN FLYER LINES COACH: From 1953 through 1958, this streamlined coach was produced—and in most cases—painted to match the 960 combine listed above. The lower nameplate on this car was stamped "961 JEFFERSON 961."

961 AMERICAN FLYER LINES COACH (Type I): Some of the 1953 cars were finished in chrome, without a colored stripe.

VG-C6	EX-C7	LN-C8	Scarcity
30	75	125	4

961 AMERICAN FLYER LINES COACH (Type II): 📷
In 1954, some cars were built with a broad chestnut-colored stripe painted through the window area.

VG-C6	EX-C7	LN-C8	Scarcity
75	175	300	7

961 AMERICAN FLYER LINES COACH (Type III): Cars with a green window stripe were produced in 1955.

VG-C6	EX-C7	LN-C8	Scarcity
40	90	150	4

961 AMERICAN FLYER LINES COACH (Type IV): From 1954 through 1956, a red band was painted through the window line of some cars.

VG-C6	EX-C7	LN-C8	Scarcity
40	90	150	4

961 AMERICAN FLYER LINES COACH (Type V): In 1956, cars were produced with an orange stripe painted through the window area. Some of these cars had the car name stamped on a separately applied nameplate.

VG-C6	EX-C7	LN-C8	Scarcity
50	100	200	5

961 AMERICAN FLYER LINES COACH (Type VI): Other orange-striped cars did not have the lower nameplate. Instead the car name and number were stamped directly on the car body.

VG-C6	EX-C7	LN-C8	Scarcity
50	100	200	5

962 AMERICAN FLYER LINES VISTA DOME: From 1953 through 1958, this Vista Dome car was produced—and in most cases—painted to match the 960 combine listed above. The lower nameplate on this car was stamped "962 HAMILTON 962."

962 AMERICAN FLYER LINES VISTA DOME (Type I): Some of the 1953 cars were finished in chrome, without a colored stripe.

VG-C6	EX-C7	LN-C8	Scarcity
30	75	125	4

961 AMERICAN FLYER LINES COACH (Type II)

962 AMERICAN FLYER LINES VISTA DOME (Type II):
Other cars assembled in 1953 had bodies that were merely painted silver.

VG-C6	EX-C7	LN-C8	Scarcity
35	85	135	4

962 AMERICAN FLYER LINES VISTA DOME (Type III):
In 1954 and 1955, the silver-painted cars were trimmed with a broad blue stripe painted through the window area.

VG-C6	EX-C7	LN-C8	Scarcity
40	90	150	4

962 AMERICAN FLYER LINES VISTA DOME (Type IV):
In 1954, some cars were built with a broad chestnut-colored stripe painted through the window area.

VG-C6	EX-C7	LN-C8	Scarcity
75	175	300	7

962 AMERICAN FLYER LINES VISTA DOME (Type V):
Cars with a green window stripe were produced in 1955.

VG-C6	EX-C7	LN-C8	Scarcity
40	90	150	4

962 AMERICAN FLYER LINES VISTA DOME (Type VI):
From 1954 through 1956, a red band was painted through the window line of some cars.

VG-C6	EX-C7	LN-C8	Scarcity
40	90	150	4

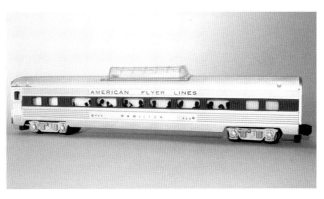

962 AMERICAN FLYER LINES VISTA DOME (Type VII):
In 1956, cars were produced with an orange stripe painted through the window area. Some of these cars had the car name stamped on a separately applied nameplate.

VG-C6	EX-C7	LN-C8	Scarcity
50	100	200	5

963 AMERICAN FLYER LINES OBSERVATION:
From 1953 through 1958, this observation car was produced—and in most cases—painted to match the 960 combine listed above. The lower nameplate on this car was stamped "963 WASHINGTON 963."

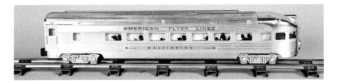

963 AMERICAN FLYER LINES OBSERVATION (Type I):
Some of the 1953 cars were finished in chrome, without a colored stripe.

VG-C6	EX-C7	LN-C8	Scarcity
30	75	125	4

963 AMERICAN FLYER LINES OBSERVATION (Type II):
Other cars assembled in 1953 had bodies that were merely painted silver.

VG-C6	EX-C7	LN-C8	Scarcity
35	85	135	4

963 AMERICAN FLYER LINES OBSERVATION (Type III):
In 1954 and 1955, the silver-painted cars were trimmed with a broad blue stripe painted through the window area.

VG-C6	EX-C7	LN-C8	Scarcity
40	90	150	4

Values for each condition are in U.S. dollars. | Scarcity = Scale from 1-8 with 8 being the hardest to find.

153

963 AMERICAN FLYER LINES OBSERVATION (Type IV)

963 AMERICAN FLYER LINES OBSERVATION (Type IV):
In 1954, some cars were built with a broad chestnut-colored stripe painted through the window area.

VG-C6	EX-C7	LN-C8	Scarcity
75	175	300	7

963 AMERICAN FLYER LINES OBSERVATION (Type V):
Cars with a green window stripe were produced in 1955.

VG-C6	EX-C7	LN-C8	Scarcity
40	90	150	4

963 AMERICAN FLYER LINES OBSERVATION (Type VI):
From 1954 through 1956, a red band was painted through the window line of some cars.

VG-C6	EX-C7	LN-C8	Scarcity
40	90	150	4

963 AMERICAN FLYER LINES OBSERVATION (Type VII):
In 1956, cars were produced with an orange stripe painted through the window area. Some of these cars had the car name stamped on a separately applied nameplate.

VG-C6	EX-C7	LN-C8	Scarcity
50	100	200	5

963 AMERICAN FLYER LINES OBSERVATION (Type VII!):
Other orange-striped cars did not have the lower nameplate. Instead the car name and number were stamped directly on the car body.

VG-C6	EX-C7	LN-C8	Scarcity
50	100	200	5

975 AMERICAN FLYER LINES:
This 1954-55 animated coach was essentially a knuckle coupler-equipped version of the 735. Much like its predecessor, this car was produced for use with the K766 animated station in 1955. The car and station worked in conjunction for an effect much like that of the animated cattle corral—with the passenger figures moving from station to car and then back to station. The values listed below are for the car alone.

VG-C6	EX-C7	LN-C8	Scarcity
35	65	110	5

978 AMERICAN FLYER LINES OBSERVATION:
Between 1956 and 1958, Gilbert offered this Tuscan-painted animated heavyweight observation car. A blue figure representing a brakeman was installed on the brass-railed observation platform. When the train stopped, the figure moves out as if inspecting the cars, returning to his normal position when the train moves out.

978 AMERICAN FLYER LINES OBSERVATION (Type I):
Some of the cars have three steps.

VG-C6	EX-C7	LN-C8	Scarcity
150	300	500	7

978 AMERICAN FLYER LINES OBSERVATION (Type II): Other cars have four steps.

VG-C6	EX-C7	LN-C8	Scarcity
150	300	500	7

24702 NORTHERN PACIFIC: In 1957, the 901 streamlined coach came in a box marked "24702."

24705 NORTHERN PACIFIC: In 1957, the 900 streamlined combine came in a box marked "24705."

24708 NORTHERN PACIFIC: In 1957, the 902 streamlined Vista Dome came in a box marked "24708."

24712 NORTHERN PACIFIC: In 1957, the 903 streamlined observation came in a box marked "24712."

24720 F. Y. & P. R. R. COACH: This replica of a 19th century coach was produced from 1959 through 1961. Though not illuminated, the car was well detailed, even on the undercarriage. The somewhat whimsical reporting marks "F. Y. & P. R. R." abbreviate "Fifty Years of Progress in Railroading." Only the last two digits of the catalog number actually were stamped on the body.

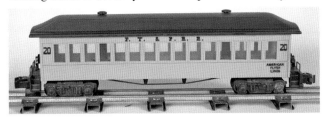

24720 F. Y. & P. R. R. COACH (Type I): The sides and ends of some of the cars, probably those made first, were painted yellow.

VG-C6	EX-C7	LN-C8	Scarcity
30	60	90	5

24720 F. Y. & P. R. R. COACH (Type II): Other painted yellow cars were lettered "AMERICAN FLYER LINES" below the windows.

VG-C6	EX-C7	LN-C8	Scarcity
25	50	80	5

24720 F. Y. & P. R. R. COACH (Type III): Later cars were still lettered "AMERICAN FLYER LINES" below the windows, but had unpainted yellow sides and ends.

VG-C6	EX-C7	LN-C8	Scarcity
20	40	60	4

24730 F. Y. & P. R. R. BAGGAGE: To match the 24720 coach, Gilbert created this 19th century baggage car. Like this coach, this car was available in 1959 and 1960, and only the last two digits of its catalog number were stamped on the car. This car was offered as a free premium with purchase of the Frontiersman set in 1959. In addition to the "F. Y. & P. R. R." lettering above the windows, "OVERLAND EXPRESS" was stamped below the windows, and "AMERICAN FLYER LINES" was stamped on each side in the lower right. A paper label with a red and green "OVERLAND EXPRESS" logo was in the lower left corner of both sides.

24730 F. Y. & P. R. R. BAGGAGE (Type I): The sides and ends of some of the cars, probably those made first, were painted yellow.

VG-C6	EX-C7	LN-C8	Scarcity
30	60	90	5

24730 F. Y. & P. R. R. BAGGAGE (Type II): Later cars had unpainted yellow sides and ends.

VG-C6	EX-C7	LN-C8	Scarcity
20	40	60	4

24733 AMERICAN FLYER LINES: In 1957, the heavyweight passenger car "PIKES PEAK" was assigned a new five-digit number, but only a few were made with this number, most instead being stamped with the older "952" number.

VG-C6	EX-C7	LN-C8	Scarcity
150	350	600	8

24739 AMERICAN FLYER LINES: Similarly in 1957, the heavyweight combine "NIAGARA FALLS" was assigned a new five-digit number, but only a handful were made with this number, most instead being stamped with the older "953" number.

VG-C6	EX-C7	LN-C8	Scarcity
Too rarely traded to accurately establish pricing.			

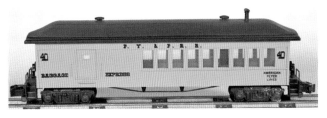

24740 BAGGAGE EXPRESS: In 1960, Gilbert introduced this yellow 19th century combination baggage-express car. Though not illuminated, the car was well detailed, even on the undercarriage. The somewhat whimsical reporting marks "F. Y. & P. R. R." abbreviate "Fifty Years of Progress in Railroading." Only the last two digits of the catalog number actually were stamped on the body.

VG-C6	EX-C7	LN-C8	Scarcity
20	40	60	4

Values for each condition are in U.S. dollars. | Scarcity = Scale from 1-8 with 8 being the hardest to find.

155

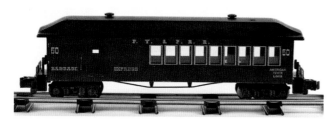

24750 F. Y. & P. R. R: The body color of this 1960-61 19th century combination baggage-express car was red. Though not illuminated, the car was well detailed, even on the undercarriage. The somewhat whimsical yellow reporting marks "F. Y. & P. R. R." abbreviate "Fifty Years of Progress in Railroading." Only the last two digits of the catalog number actually were stamped on the body.

VG-C6	EX-C7	LN-C8	Scarcity
50	100	175	5

24772 AMERICAN FLYER LINES: In 1957, some of the red-striped streamlined 960 combine cars came in boxes marked "24772."

24773 AMERICAN FLYER LINES: Cataloged in 1957 and 1958—but probably only produced from 1960 through 1962—was this molded plastic streamlined combine. The car had a broad red stripe through the window line. Above the windows the car was lettered "AMERICAN FLYER LINES" in black, and below the windows was stamped "24773 COLUMBUS 24773." The car was illuminated and equipped with knuckle couplers.

VG-C6	EX-C7	LN-C8	Scarcity
60	100	180	5

24775 AMERICAN FLYER LINES: In 1957, some of the orange-striped streamlined 960 combine cars came in boxes marked "24775."

24776 AMERICAN FLYER LINES: Available in 1959, this molded plastic streamlined combine was painted silver with a broad orange stripe through the window area. The car was illuminated and passenger silhouettes were visible through the windows. The black lettering, "AMERICAN FLYER LINES" above the windows, and "24776 COLUMBUS 24776" below the windows, was stamped directly on the car bodies. The car had knuckle couplers.

VG-C6	EX-C7	LN-C8	Scarcity
60	100	185	5

24792 AMERICAN FLYER LINES: In 1957, some of the red-striped streamlined 961 Pullman cars came in boxes marked "24792."

24793 AMERICAN FLYER LINES: Cataloged in 1957 and 1958—but probably only produced from 1960 through 1962—this molded plastic streamlined combine was available. The car had a broad red stripe through the window line. Above the windows the car was lettered "AMERICAN FLYER LINES" in black, and below the windows was stamped "24793 JEFFERSON 24793"—both stamped directly on the car body. The car was illuminated and equipped with knuckle couplers.

VG-C6	EX-C7	LN-C8	Scarcity
100	175	250	5

24794 AMERICAN FLYER LINES: Among the most difficult to find Gilbert passenger cars is this streamlined Pullman. The silver-painted car had a broad orange band painted through the window line. The black sans-serif lettering, stamped directly on the car read "AMERICAN FLYER LINES" above the windows and "24794 JEFFERSON 24794" below the windows.

VG-C6	EX-C7	LN-C8	Scarcity
500	1,500	3,000	8

24795 AMERICAN FLYER LINES: In 1957, some of the red-striped streamlined 961 Pullman cars came in boxes marked "24795."

24796 AMERICAN FLYER LINES: Not produced.

24812 AMERICAN FLYER LINES: In 1957, some of the red-striped streamlined 962 Vista Dome cars came in boxes marked "24812."

24813 AMERICAN FLYER LINES: Cataloged in 1957 and 1958—but probably only produced from 1960 through 1962—was this molded plastic streamlined Vista Dome. The car had a broad red stripe through the window line. Above the windows the car was lettered "AMERICAN FLYER LINES" in black, and below the windows was stamped "24813 HAMILTON 24813." The car was illuminated and equipped with knuckle couplers.

VG-C6	EX-C7	LN-C8	Scarcity
60	100	180	5

24816 AMERICAN FLYER LINES: Available in 1959, this molded plastic streamlined Vista Dome was painted silver with a broad orange stripe through the window area. The car was illuminated, and passenger silhouettes were visible through the windows. The black lettering, "AMERICAN FLYER LINES" above the windows, and "24816 HAMILTON 24816" below the windows, was stamped directly on the car bodies. The car had knuckle couplers.

VG-C6	EX-C7	LN-C8	Scarcity
60	100	185	5

24832 AMERICAN FLYER LINES: In 1957, some of the red-striped streamlined 963 observation cars came in boxes marked "24832."

24833 AMERICAN FLYER LINES: Cataloged in 1957 and 1958—but probably only produced from 1960 through 1962—was this molded plastic streamlined observation car. The car had a broad red stripe through the window line. Above the windows the car was lettered "AMERICAN FLYER LINES" in black, and below the windows was stamped "24833 WASHINGTON 24833."

The car was illuminated and equipped with knuckle couplers.

VG-C6	EX-C7	LN-C8	Scarcity
60	100	180	5

24835 AMERICAN FLYER LINES: In 1957, some of the orange-striped streamlined 963 observation cars came in boxes marked "24835."

24836 AMERICAN FLYER LINES: Available in 1959, this molded plastic streamlined observation car was painted silver with a broad orange stripe through the window area. The car was illuminated, and passenger silhouettes were visible through the windows. The black lettering "AMERICAN FLYER LINES" above the windows, and "24836 WASHINGTON 24836" below the windows, was stamped directly on the car bodies. The car had knuckle couplers.

VG-C6	EX-C7	LN-C8	Scarcity
60	100	185	5

24837 UNION PACIFIC COMBINE: 📷 Introduced in 1959, and carrying over into the following year, this Armour yellow and harbor mist gray combine is part of one of the most desirable Flyer sets ever produced. The molded plastic streamliner was illuminated, and passenger's silhouettes were visible in the windows. The markings of the car were stamped in red, and included in addition to the road name "UNION PACIFIC," the stock number "24837" and the car name "STAR DUST." The number showing in the window however was that of the earlier Northern Pacific combine "24843." The car had knuckle couplers, and the die-cast side frames of the passenger trucks were painted harbor mist gray to match the roof and skirts of the car.

VG-C6	EX-C7	LN-C8	Scarcity
100	190	325	7

24837 UNION PACIFIC COMBINE

Values for each condition are in U.S. dollars. | **Scarcity** = Scale from 1-8 with 8 being the hardest to find.

157

24838 UNION PACIFIC COACH: 1959-60, this yellow and gray streamlined passenger car, named "DREAM CLOUD," was constructed, painted and decorated to match the 24837 combine listed above.

VG-C6	EX-C7	LN-C8	Scarcity
125	250	375	7

24839 UNION PACIFIC VISTA DOME: The gray and Armour yellow Vista Dome of the 1959-60 Union Pacific set was the red-lettered "COLUMBIA RIVER." The construction, painting and decoration of this car mimicked that of the 24837 combine.

VG-C6	EX-C7	LN-C8	Scarcity
125	250	375	7

24840 UNION PACIFIC OBSERVATION: Bringing up the rear of the 1959-60 Union Pacific streamliner was the "MOON GLOW" observation. Although the number boards on the side of the car read "24840," the number legible in the window was "24853," the number of the Northern Pacific observation, which used the same windows.

VG-C6	EX-C7	LN-C8	Scarcity
125	250	375	7

24843 NORTHERN PACIFIC COMBINE: This 1958 streamlined combine car was finished in the two-tone green paint scheme and white markings of the Northern Pacific North Coast streamliner. Though the car was not illuminated, it did have operating knuckle couplers and silver four-wheel passenger car trucks.

VG-C6	EX-C7	LN-C8	Scarcity
75	175	275	6

24846 NORTHERN PACIFIC COACH: Also produced in 1958, this streamlined coach matched the 24843 combine in construction, paint and markings.

VG-C6	EX-C7	LN-C8	Scarcity
100	200	300	6

24849 NORTHERN PACIFIC VISTA DOME: This was the dome car for the 1958 Northern Pacific North Coast Limited. The paint, markings and construction of this car matched those of the 24843 combine.

VG-C6	EX-C7	LN-C8	Scarcity
100	200	300	6

24853 NORTHERN PACIFIC OBSERVATION: Bringing up the rear of Gilbert's 1958 rendition of the North Coast Limited was this observation car.

VG-C6	EX-C7	LN-C8	Scarcity
75	175	275	6

24856 MISSOURI PACIFIC EAGLE HILL COMBINE: Vying with the Union Pacific set for the honor of "most desirable Gilbert passenger train" was this silver and blue Missouri Pacific "Eagle." This attractive car was first produced in 1958, then dropped, only to return to the product line in 1963 and 1964. Though the real cars were painted in blue, cream and gray, American Flyer opted for a simpler blue and silver scheme.

24856 MISSOURI PACIFIC EAGLE HILL COMBINE (Type I): Cars produced in 1958 were painted such that the blue stripes extended through the vestibule doors.

VG-C6	EX-C7	LN-C8	Scarcity
125	275	450	8

24856 MISSOURI PACIFIC EAGLE HILL COMBINE (Type II): When the cars were reissued in 1963-64, the blue stripe stopped at the edge of the passenger doors.

VG-C6	EX-C7	LN-C8	Scarcity
100	250	425	8

24859 MISSOURI PACIFIC EAGLE LAKE COACH: Like the 24856, this attractive car was first produced in 1958, then dropped, only to return to the product line in 1963 and 1964. Though the real cars were painted in blue, cream and gray, American Flyer opted for a simpler blue and silver scheme. Above the window were the words "THE EAGLE" and below the windows "24859 EAGLE LAKE 24859."

24859 MISSOURI PACIFIC EAGLE HILL COACH (Type I): Cars produced in 1958 were painted such that the blue stripes extended through the vestibule doors.

VG-C6	EX-C7	LN-C8	Scarcity
150	300	500	8

24859 MISSOURI PACIFIC EAGLE HILL COACH (Type II): When the cars were reissued in 1963-64, the blue stripe stopped at the edge of the passenger doors.

VG-C6	EX-C7	LN-C8	Scarcity
125	275	475	8

24863 MISSOURI PACIFIC EAGLE CREEK VISTA DOME: Like the rest of this series, this attractive car was first produced in 1958, then dropped, only to return to the product line in 1963 and 1964. Though the real cars were painted in blue, cream and gray, American Flyer opted for a simpler blue and silver scheme. Above the window were the words "THE EAGLE" and below the windows "24863 EAGLE CREEK 24863."

24863 MISSOURI PACIFIC EAGLE CREEK VISTA DOME (Type I): Cars produced in 1958 were painted such that the blue stripes extended through the vestibule doors.

VG-C6	EX-C7	LN-C8	Scarcity
150	300	500	8

24863 MISSOURI PACIFIC EAGLE CREEK VISTA DOME (Type II): When the cars were reissued in 1963-64, the blue stripe stopped at the edge of the passenger doors.

VG-C6	EX-C7	LN-C8	Scarcity
25	275	475	8

24866 MISSOURI PACIFIC EAGLE VALLEY OBSERVATION: Bringing up the rear of the Eagle, this observation car was first produced in 1958, then dropped, only to return to the product line in 1963 and 1964. Though the real cars were painted in blue, cream and gray, American Flyer opted for a simpler blue and silver scheme. Above the window were the words "THE EAGLE" and below the windows "24866 EAGLE VALLEY 24866."

24866 MISSOURI PACIFIC EAGLE VALLEY OBSERVATION (Type I): 📷 Cars produced in 1958 were painted such that the blue stripes extended through the vestibule doors.

VG-C6	EX-C7	LN-C8	Scarcity
125	275	450	8

24866 MISSOURI PACIFIC EAGLE VALLEY OBSERVATION (Type II): When the cars were reissued in 1963-64, the blue stripe stopped at the edge of the passenger doors.

VG-C6	EX-C7	LN-C8	Scarcity
100	250	425	8

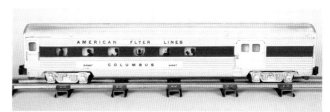

24867 AMERICAN FLYER LINES COMBINE: First available in 1958, then returning in 1960, this molded plastic streamlined combine was painted silver with a broad red stripe through the window area. The car was not illuminated, but passenger silhouettes were visible through the windows. The black lettering "AMERICAN FLYER LINES" above the windows, and "24867 COLUMBUS 24867" below the windows, was stamped directly on the car bodies. The car had knuckle couplers. The bodies of the 1958 production were mounted with screws, while in 1960 six-metal pins were used.

VG-C6	EX-C7	LN-C8	Scarcity
60	100	185	5

24866 MISSOURI PACIFIC EAGLE VALLEY OBSERVATION (Type I)

Values for each condition are in U.S. dollars. | **Scarcity** = Scale from 1-8 with 8 being the hardest to find.

159

24868 AMERICAN FLYER LINES OBSERVATION: First available in 1958, then returning in 1960, this molded plastic streamlined observation car was painted silver with a broad red stripe through the window area. The car was not illuminated, but passenger silhouettes were visible through the windows. The black lettering "AMERICAN FLYER LINES" above the windows, and "24868 WASHINGTON 24868" below the windows, was stamped directly on the car bodies. The car had knuckle couplers. The bodies of the 1958 production were mounted with screws, while in 1960 six-metal pins were used.

VG-C6	EX-C7	LN-C8	Scarcity
60	100	185	5

24869 AMERICAN FLYER LINES COACH: First available in 1958, then returning in 1960, this molded plastic streamlined coach car was painted silver with a broad red stripe through the window area. The car was not illuminated, but passenger silhouettes were visible through the windows. The black lettering "AMERICAN FLYER LINES" above the windows, and "24869 JEFFERSON 24869" below the windows, was stamped directly on the car bodies. The car had knuckle couplers. The bodies of the 1958 production were mounted with screws, while in 1960 six-metal pins were used.

VG-C6	EX-C7	LN-C8	Scarcity
60	100	185	5

24963 CAR ASSORTMENT: In 1958, Gilbert offered this bulk-pack assortment of four Tuscan-painted passenger cars. Included were three heavyweight passenger cars and an operating baggage mail car.

VG-C6	EX-C7	LN-C8	Scarcity
Too rarely traded to accurately establish pricing.			

25005 AMERICAN FLYER LINES: This mail car was offered in 1957 . The Tuscan-painted car was essentially a five-digit version of the 918. Only a handful of these cars were actually produced—consumers instead receiving the 918.

VG-C6	EX-C7	LN-C8	Scarcity
Too rarely traded to accurately establish pricing.			

25006 AMERICAN FLYER LINES: In 1957, the 918 operating mail pickup car was shipped in a box marked "25006."

24869 AMERICAN FLYER LINES COACH

ACCESSORIES

Accessories fulfilled two roles in the world of miniature railroads. For the consumer, they added life to their small empires. For children, it provided a means to enter the world of their toy trains—manipulating the cranes, logs, coal and other cargoes established a connection between the trains and the imagination. Enthusiasts now *operated* the trains rather than merely watching them circle endlessly.

For A.C. Gilbert and other manufacturers, accessories represented a huge profit center. Many of the entry level sets were sold at cost, the company literally banking on add-on sales for profits, and many of those add-on sales were in the form of accessories. Gilbert's range of accessories was broad—but not as broad as it may seem from these listings. Gilbert improved and revised their accessories, adding an "A" suffix to the catalog number to reflect this, and then in 1957 converted to a five-digit number system. As a result, the same basic item could exist with three different catalog numbers! All these numbers and various lesser variations of these items are listed below—resulting in this being the longest chapter in this volume. Please note, accessories were—but for track and similar items, despite Gilbert's best efforts—built in smaller quantities than trains, and the scarcity listings below are relative to each other rather than to the other items in this book.

1 TRANSFORMER: This black-painted oval sheet metal 25-Watt transformer was made from 1950 through 1952.

VG-C6	EX-C7	LN-C8	Scarcity
5	10	15	3

1 TRANSFORMER: This 35-Watt black-painted rectangular metal transformer was shipped in 1956.

VG-C6	EX-C7	LN-C8	Scarcity
3	6	10	1

1A TRANSFORMER: This uncataloged 1957 40-Watt transformer had a black Bakelite plastic case and built-in circuit breaker. It was shown in the 1957 catalog, but listed with the number "22020."

VG-C6	EX-C7	LN-C8	Scarcity
3	6	10	1

1-1/2 TRANSFORMER: This 45-Watt sheet metal transformer was made in 1953.

Values for each condition are in U.S. dollars. | **Scarcity** = Scale from 1-8 with 8 being the hardest to find.

161

2 (Type II)

1-1/2 (Type I): Some units had painted letters on the case.

VG-C6	EX-C7	LN-C8	Scarcity
2	5	8	1

1-1/2 (Type II): Other units had embossed letters on the case.

VG-C6	EX-C7	LN-C8	Scarcity
2	5	8	1

1-1/2 TRANSFORMER: The 50-Watt black Bakelite transformer was sold in 1954-55.

VG-C6	EX-C7	LN-C8	Scarcity
2	5	8	1

1-1/2B TRANSFORMER: This circuit breaker-equipped 50-Watt transformer was produced in 1956.

1-1/2B (Type I): Some units had painted letters on the case.

VG-C6	EX-C7	LN-C8	Scarcity
2	5	8	1

1-1/2B (Type II): Other units had raised letters on the case.

VG-C6	EX-C7	LN-C8	Scarcity
2	5	8	1

2 TRANSFORMER: This 75-Watt transformer was available from 1947 through 1952.

2 (Type I): Some of the transformers had dark red throttle levers.

VG-C6	EX-C7	LN-C8	Scarcity
3	6	10	1

2 (Type II): Other transformers had black throttle levers.

VG-C6	EX-C7	LN-C8	Scarcity
3	6	10	1

2 (Type III): Some of these transformers had 230-250 volt primary windings.

VG-C6	EX-C7	LN-C8	Scarcity
3	6	10	1

2B TRANSFORMER: This 75-Watt circuit breaker-equipped sheet metal transformer was made in 1948.

VG-C6	EX-C7	LN-C8	Scarcity
3	6	10	1

3 TRANSFORMER: Although uncataloged, this sheet metal 50-Watt transformer was produced in 1946.

VG-C6	EX-C7	LN-C8	Scarcity
2	5	8	1

4B TRANSFORMER: This 100-Watt circuit breaker-equipped transformer was part of the product line from 1949 through 1956, and came in several variations.

4B (Type I): A sheet metal case was used from 1949 through 1953. Some of these were painted black.

VG-C6	EX-C7	LN-C8	Scarcity
10	15	25	3

4B (Type II): Gray paint was used on some of the sheet metal cases.

VG-C6	EX-C7	LN-C8	Scarcity
10	15	25	3

4B (Type III): Beginning in 1954, a Bakelite case was used. This remained the norm through 1956.

VG-C6	EX-C7	LN-C8	Scarcity
10	15	25	3

5 TRANSFORMER: This 50-Watt sheet metal cased transformer was a 1946 product.

VG-C6	EX-C7	LN-C8	Scarcity
2	5	8	1

5A TRANSFORMER: A 25-cycle version of the 50-Watt transformer was also made in 1946.

VG-C6	EX-C7	LN-C8	Scarcity
10	15	25	3

5B TRANSFORMER: A built-in circuit breaker was included in this 50-Watt transformer dating from 1946.

VG-C6	EX-C7	LN-C8	Scarcity
2	5	8	1

6 TRANSFORMER: This oval-shaped 75-Watt transformer without circuit breaker was made in 1946.
6 (Type I): Some of these transformers have three binding posts.

VG-C6	EX-C7	LN-C8	Scarcity
2	5	8	1

6 (Type II): Others have four binding posts.

VG-C6	EX-C7	LN-C8	Scarcity
2	5	8	1

6A TRANSFORMER: This 25-cycle, 75-Watt oval transformer was made in 1946.

VG-C6	EX-C7	LN-C8	Scarcity
2	5	8	1

7 TRANSFORMER: This uncataloged 1946 75-Watt transformer was equipped with a circuit breaker and pilot light.

VG-C6	EX-C7	LN-C8	Scarcity
2	5	8	4

7B TRANSFORMER: 1946; 75 Watts, black-painted oval sheet metal case, nickel oval sheet metal plate on top, red pilot light, circuit breaker.

VG-C6	EX-C7	LN-C8	Scarcity
2	5	8	1

8B TRANSFORMER: From 1946 through 1952, Gilbert produced this dark-gray 100-Watt transformer. The transformer was equipped with a built-in circuit breaker and red and green pilot lights.
8B (Type I): Some of the throttle levers were die-cast.

VG-C6	EX-C7	LN-C8	Scarcity
10	15	25	3

8B (Type II): Others had a plastic throttle lever.

VG-C6	EX-C7	LN-C8	Scarcity
10	15	25	3

8B (Type III): The 1951-52 edition of the transformer had a plastic throttle and a reversing button.

VG-C6	EX-C7	LN-C8	Scarcity
10	15	25	3

9B TRANSFORMER: This 150-Watt dual control transformer was made in 1946. It featured a built-in circuit breaker, on-off switch, pilot lights and a reset button.

VG-C6	EX-C7	LN-C8	Scarcity
15	25	35	4

10 DC INVERTOR: This black sheet metal 1946 product was used to convert DC to AC.

VG-C6	EX-C7	LN-C8	Scarcity
15	25	35	7

11 CIRCUIT BREAKER: This separate circuit breaker was produced in 1946. It included a reset button and red pilot light.

VG-C6	EX-C7	LN-C8	Scarcity
3	5	10	5

12B TRANSFORMER: From 1946 through 1952, this 250-Watt gray unit was the top of the line transformer. It featured a built-in circuit breaker, on-off switch, red and green pilot lights and a reset button.

VG-C6	EX-C7	LN-C8	Scarcity
30	60	120	5

13 CIRCUIT BREAKER: This separate circuit breaker was sold from 1952 through 1955.

VG-C6	EX-C7	LN-C8	Scarcity
3	5	7	3

14 ELECTRONIC RECTIFORMER: Rated at 150 Watts, this combination rectifier and transformer was sold in 1947 and 1949. Included were two built-in circuit breakers.

VG-C6	EX-C7	LN-C8	Scarcity
10	20	35	5

15 DIRECTRONIC RECTIFIER: This device, sold from 1948 through 1952, was used to convert low voltage AC to DC. Rated at four amps, the unit included a reverse switch.
15 (Type I): Some units were built on a wooden base.

VG-C6	EX-C7	LN-C8	Scarcity
10	15	25	5

15 (Type II): Others had a metal base.

VG-C6	EX-C7	LN-C8	Scarcity
10	15	25	5

15B TRANSFORMER: This 1953 transformer was rated at 110 Watts. The throttle lever was a hinged "Dead Man's Control," and the unit had red and green pilot lights.

VG-C6	EX-C7	LN-C8	Scarcity
15	25	45	4

Values for each condition are in U.S. dollars. | **Scarcity** = Scale from 1-8 with 8 being the hardest to find.

163

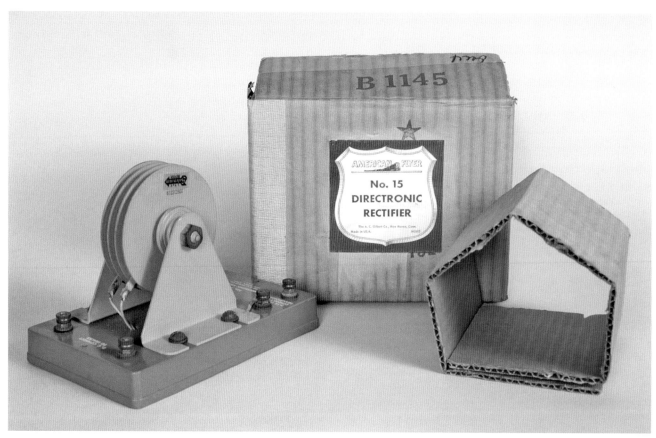

15 (Type I)

16 ELECTRONIC RECTIFORMER: This combination rectifier and transformer was sold in 1950. It included two built-in circuit breakers.

VG-C6	EX-C7	LN-C8	Scarcity
10	20	40	5

16B TRANSFORMER: The 1953 version of this transformer was rated at 190 Watts. The throttle lever was a hinged "Dead Man's Control," and the unit had red and green pilot lights and built-in circuit breaker.

VG-C6	EX-C7	LN-C8	Scarcity
30	50	75	5

16B TRANSFORMER: From 1954 through 1956, a 175-Watt version of this transformer was produced. The throttle lever was a hinged "Dead Man's Control," and the unit had red and green pilot lights and built-in circuit breaker.

VG-C6	EX-C7	LN-C8	Scarcity
30	50	75	5

16C TRANSFORMER: This sheet metal 1958 transformer was rated at 35 Watts.

VG-C6	EX-C7	LN-C8	Scarcity
6	10	15	1

17B TRANSFORMER: Rated at 190 Watts, this single-control transformer was built in 1952. The throttle lever was a "Dead Man's Control" type and the transformer had volt and amp meters, red and green pilot lights, as well as a built-in circuit breaker.

VG-C6	EX-C7	LN-C8	Scarcity
25	50	80	5

18 FILTER: Even though uncataloged, this device was built in 1950. It was used to eliminate the humming sounds caused by using a DC power supply to run sound-equipped AC locomotives.

VG-C6	EX-C7	LN-C8	Scarcity
Too rarely traded to accurately establish pricing.			

18B TRANSFORMER: This 190-Watt dual control transformer was sold in 1953. This transformer was equipped with two "Dead Man's Control" handles and circuit breakers.

VG-C6	EX-C7	LN-C8	Scarcity
30	50	90	4

18B TRANSFORMER: This 175-Watt dual control transformer was sold from 1954-56. This transformer was equipped with two "Dead Man's Control" handles, red and green pilot lights, and circuit breakers.

VG-C6	EX-C7	LN-C8	Scarcity
25	40	80	4

19B TRANSFORMER: Rated at 300 Watts, this single-control transformer was offered from 1952 through 1955. The throttle lever was a "Dead Man's Control" type and the transformer had volt and amp meters, red and green pilot lights, an on-off switch, as well as a built-in circuit breaker.

VG-C6	EX-C7	LN-C8	Scarcity
50	95	150	5

21 IMITATION GRASS: 1949-50, about one-half pound of green dyed sawdust was packaged for sale as artificial grass in 1949 and 1950.

21 (Type I): Some were packed in white paper bags with blue lettering.

VG-C6	EX-C7	LN-C8	Scarcity
15	20	30	4

21 (Type II): White-lettered clear cellophane bags were also used.

VG-C6	EX-C7	LN-C8	Scarcity
15	20	30	4

21A IMITATION GRASS: From 1951 through 1956, the half-pound bag of artificial grass came in a clear cellophane bag.

21A (Type I): Some bags were lettered in white.

VG-C6	EX-C7	LN-C8	Scarcity
15	20	30	4

21A (Type II): Other bags were lettered in red.

VG-C6	EX-C7	LN-C8	Scarcity
15	20	30	4

22 SCENERY GRAVEL: From 1949 through 1956, Gilbert sold 22-ounce paper bags of artificial gravel.

22 (Type I): Some were packed in white paper bags with blue lettering.

VG-C6	EX-C7	LN-C8	Scarcity
12	18	25	3

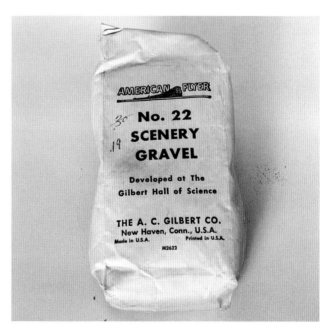

22 (Type II): Other bags were lettered in black.

VG-C6	EX-C7	LN-C8	Scarcity
12	18	25	3

Values for each condition are in U.S. dollars. | **Scarcity** = Scale from 1-8 with 8 being the hardest to find.

23 ARTIFICIAL COAL: Gilbert sold these bags of artificial coal from 1949 through 1956. Each bag contained approximately one-half pound of product.

23 (Type I): Some were packed in white cloth bags.

VG-C6	EX-C7	LN-C8	Scarcity
12	18	25	3

23 (Type II): Clear plastic bags were also used.

VG-C6	EX-C7	LN-C8	Scarcity
12	18	25	3

24 RAINBOW WIRE: Gilbert sold this 25-foot roll of four-conductor multi-strand green, black, yellow and red ribbon wire from 1949 through 1956.

VG-C6	EX-C7	LN-C8	Scarcity
3	5	10	4

25 SMOKE CARTRIDGE: These boxes of 12 small red plastic capsules with funnel and pipe cleaner were sold from 1947 through 1956.

25 (Type I): The earliest version of the 25 came in a blue box with yellow label numbered "M2426."

VG-C6	EX-C7	LN-C8	Scarcity
5	10	15	1

25 (Type II): 📷 Later versions came in yellow boxes numbered "B-1082" with blue lettering.

VG-C6	EX-C7	LN-C8	Scarcity
5	10	15	1

25 (Type III): The final version, numbered "M2660," consisted of a single smoke capsule, funnel and pipe cleaner in a white envelope.

VG-C6	EX-C7	LN-C8	Scarcity
5	10	15	1

26 SERVICE KIT: This 1952-56 kit contained the basics for maintaining your Gilbert empire: oil, grease, track cleaning fluid, brush, sanding sticks, commutator cleaning stick, tube cleaners, cloth, and a 12-page service manual.

VG-C6	EX-C7	LN-C8	Scarcity
10	20	30	3

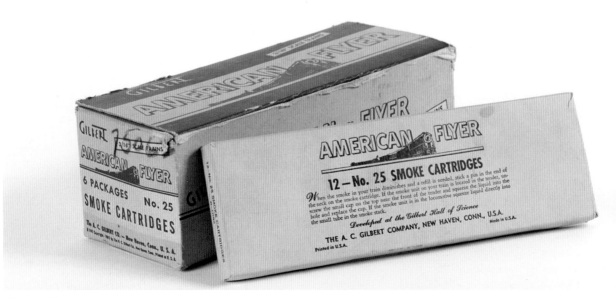

25 (Type II)

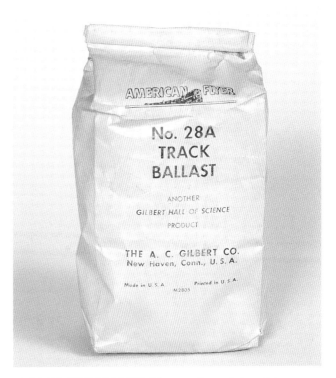

27 TRACK CLEANING FLUID: This eight-ounce bottle of blue track cleaning fluid was sold from 1952 through 1956.

VG-C6	EX-C7	LN-C8	Scarcity
2	5	10	2

28A TRACK BALLAST: The number of the white paper one-half pound bag of artificial ballast changed to 28A from 1951 through 1953.

VG-C6	EX-C7	LN-C8	Scarcity
5	10	15	4

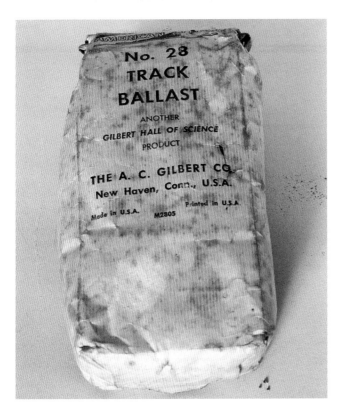

28 TRACK BALLAST: This white paper one-half pound bag of artificial ballast was sold in 1950.

VG-C6	EX-C7	LN-C8	Scarcity
3	5	10	3

29 IMITATION SNOW: This scarce cellophane bag with yellow label was sold only in 1950.

VG-C6	EX-C7	LN-C8	Scarcity
75	150	300	7

Values for each condition are in U.S. dollars. | **Scarcity** = Scale from 1-8 with 8 being the hardest to find.

167

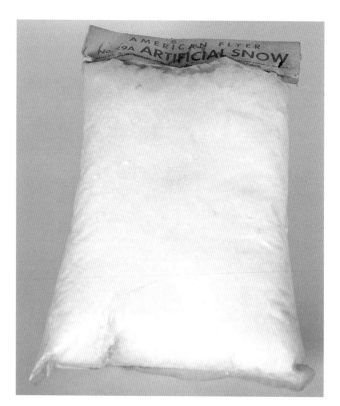

29A IMITATION SNOW: This white paper bag of snow was sold from 1951 through 1953.

VG-C6	EX-C7	LN-C8	Scarcity
75	150	300	7

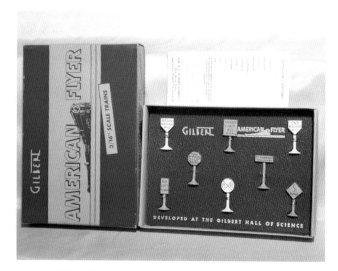

30 HIGHWAY SIGNS: This assortment of signs was sold from 1949 through 1952. Various combinations and colors were offered during this time, all of equal value. The original packaging is critical for the values below.

30 (Type I): In 1949 and 1950, the signs were packed in a yellow box with blue insert.

VG-C6	EX-C7	LN-C8	Scarcity
50	100	175	5

30 (Type II): In 1951 and 1952, the box was designed to open and form a merchandising display.

VG-C6	EX-C7	LN-C8	Scarcity
50	100	175	5

30B TRANSFORMER: Rated at 300 Watts, this dual-control transformer was offered from 1952 through 1955. The throttle levers were of the "Dead Man's Control" type and the transformer had dual volt meters, red and green pilot light, as well as dual built-in circuit breakers.

VG-C6	EX-C7	LN-C8	Scarcity
75	125	200	4

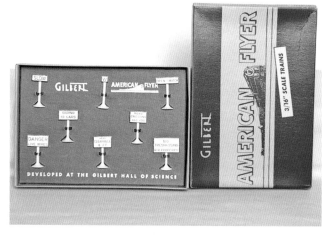

31 RAILROAD SIGNS: This 1949-50 assortment of eight white-painted die-cast line side signs with black lettering came packaged in a yellow box with blue insert. The box is critical to the values below.

VG-C6	EX-C7	LN-C8	Scarcity
75	150	250	6

31A RAILROAD SIGNS: This revised set of eight white-painted die-cast line side signs with black lettering came packaged in a yellow box with blue insert in 1951-52. The box is critical to the values below.

VG-C6	EX-C7	LN-C8	Scarcity
60	125	225	5

32 CITY STREET EQUIPMENT: Four green park benches, two fire hydrants and two mailboxes were attached to a blue cardboard insert inside of a yellow box. The combination was sold in 1949 and 1950. The box is critical to the values below.

VG-C6	EX-C7	LN-C8	Scarcity
50	100	200	5

32A PARK SET: The 1951 edition of the park set contained four figures and a trash can, in addition to four green park benches and one mailbox. The box is critical to the values below.

VG-C6	EX-C7	LN-C8	Scarcity
50	100	200	5

33 PASSENGER AND TRAIN FIGURE SET: This set of eight hand-painted die-cast figures was sold in 1951 and 1952. The original packaging is critical to the values below.

VG-C6	EX-C7	LN-C8	Scarcity
60	110	225	5

34 RAILWAY FIGURE SET: This 25-piece was sold in 1953. It contained an assortment of figures, signs and scenery details. This set is very difficult to find in its original packaging, which is critical to the values below.

VG-C6	EX-C7	LN-C8	Scarcity
150	400	800	7

35 BRAKEMAN WITH LANTERN: This 1950-52 yellow box with blue insert contained three brakemen figures with blue overalls and red lanterns. The original packaging is critical to the values below.

35 (Type I): As above.

VG-C6	EX-C7	LN-C8	Scarcity
50	100	175	5

Values for each condition are in U.S. dollars. | **Scarcity** = Scale from 1-8 with 8 being the hardest to find.

169

35 (Type II): Some of these sets were packed in pop-up display packaging.

VG-C6	EX-C7	LN-C8	Scarcity
50	100	175	5

40 SMOKE SET: This 1953-55 contained a capsule, brush and funnel.

VG-C6	EX-C7	LN-C8	Scarcity
2	3	4	1

50 DISTRICT SCHOOL: This proverbial one-room red schoolhouse, with illumination, was sold in 1953 and 1954.

VG-C6	EX-C7	LN-C8	Scarcity
75	150	250	6

100 UNIVERSAL LOCKON: This lockon had provisions for use with both S- and O-Gauge track.

VG-C6	EX-C7	LN-C8	Scarcity
1	2	3	2

160 STATION PLATFORM: The 1953 "Valley View" station platform was made of wood for Gilbert by Mini-craft.

VG-C6	EX-C7	LN-C8	Scarcity
175	350	550	8

161 BUNGALOW: Another of the 1953 structures made by Mini-craft and sold by Gilbert was this illuminated one-and-one-half-story house with blue roof.

VG-C6	EX-C7	LN-C8	Scarcity
100	175	225	6

162 FACTORY: This illuminated two-and-one-half-story illuminated building, painted tan, was made for Gilbert by Mini-craft in 1953. In a nod to A.C. Gilbert's background, the factory's sign read "MYSTO-MAGIC COMPANY."

VG-C6	EX-C7	LN-C8	Scarcity
100	175	250	6

163 FLYERVILLE STATION: Mini-craft also produced this station for Gilbert in 1953.

163 (Type I): Some of the stations were decorated with a Chiclets advertisement, vending machine and a Masonite roof.

VG-C6	EX-C7	LN-C8	Scarcity
125	200	300	5

163 (Type II): Other stations had "KENT, RKO THEATERS" and "OLD GOLD KING CIGARETTES" advertisements, and a simulated scale on the platform. The building had a plastic roof.

VG-C6	EX-C7	LN-C8	Scarcity
125	200	300	5

164 RED BARN: Gilbert also represented the classic red barn in one of the 1953 buildings built by Mini-craft.

VG-C6	EX-C7	LN-C8	Scarcity
100	250	400	7

165 GRAIN ELEVATOR: This illuminated tan structure was cataloged by Gilbert in 1953 but made by Mini-craft.

VG-C6	EX-C7	LN-C8	Scarcity
50	150	250	6

166 CHURCH: Complete with simulated stained-glass windows, this white church was made for Gilbert by Mini-craft in 1953.

VG-C6	EX-C7	LN-C8	Scarcity
100	200	325	7

167 TOWN HALL: This large red illuminated structure was billed as a town hall in 1953 when Mini-craft produced it for Gilbert.

VG-C6	EX-C7	LN-C8	Scarcity
100	200	325	7

Values for each condition are in U.S. dollars. | **Scarcity** = Scale from 1-8 with 8 being the hardest to find.

171

168 HOTEL: This porch-surrounded illuminated building was produced for Gilbert by Mini-craft in 1953. It was advertised as a hotel.

VG-C6	EX-C7	LN-C8	Scarcity
110	225	350	7

247 TUNNEL: This 11-inch long tunnel was sold from 1946 through 1948.

VG-C6	EX-C7	LN-C8	Scarcity
20	30	50	7

248 TUNNEL: This 14-inch long tunnel was sold from 1946 through 1948.

VG-C6	EX-C7	LN-C8	Scarcity
20	30	50	7

249 TUNNEL: This 11-1/2-inch long tunnel was offered from 1947 through 1956.

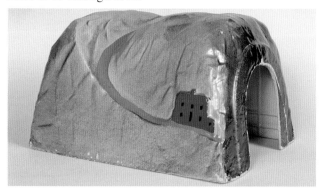

249 (Type I): Fiber construction was used for the earliest version of this tunnel, which was decorated with a house and winding road.

VG-C6	EX-C7	LN-C8	Scarcity
15	30	45	4

249 (Type II): Later tunnels were made of Styrofoam, but had identical decoration.

VG-C6	EX-C7	LN-C8	Scarcity
30	40	50	5

270 NEWS AND FRANK STAND: This paper-covered structure was made for Gilbert by Mini-craft in 1952 and 1953. Two figures were among the decorations of the structure.

270 (Type I): One version had a blue-shirted figure and a red-shirted figure.

VG-C6	EX-C7	LN-C8	Scarcity
50	75	125	5

270 (Type II): Others had two figures clad in cream-colored shirts.

VG-C6	EX-C7	LN-C8	Scarcity
50	75	125	5

270 (Type III): Merchants in red shirts staffed other buildings.

VG-C6	EX-C7	LN-C8	Scarcity
50	75	125	5

270 (Type IV): Some stands came with one cream-shirted figure and one blue-shirted figure.

VG-C6	EX-C7	LN-C8	Scarcity
50	75	125	5

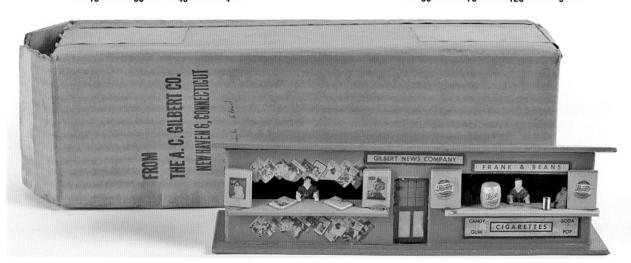

270 (Type I)

271 THREE-PIECE "WHISTLE STOP" SET: This is a set of three station-scene buildings made in 1952-53 by Mini-craft for Gilbert. Note: Mini-craft also sold these buildings independently of Gilbert.

VG-C6	EX-C7	LN-C8	Scarcity
50	125	225	6

272 GLENDALE STATION AND NEWSSTAND: Another of the 1952-53 Mini-craft manufactured Gilbert structures was this combination newsstand and station.

VG-C6	EX-C7	LN-C8	Scarcity
50	125	200	5

273 SUBURBAN RAILROAD STATION: This Masonite structure was made by Mini-craft for Gilbert in 1952 and 1953. Like most of the Mini-craft produced line side structures, many small details give the building character.

273 (Type I): Some of the buildings had blue roofs and trim. Their signs read "FOREST PARK."

VG-C6	EX-C7	LN-C8	Scarcity
60	125	225	5

273 (Type II): Others had black roofs and trim. The sign continued to read "FOREST PARK."

VG-C6	EX-C7	LN-C8	Scarcity
60	125	225	5

273 (Type III): Chocolate brown roofs, along with green doors and windows were used on other "FOREST PARK" stations.

VG-C6	EX-C7	LN-C8	Scarcity
60	125	225	5

273 (Type IV): A green roof and trim was used on the "LAKE PARK" station.

VG-C6	EX-C7	LN-C8	Scarcity
60	125	225	5

Values for each condition are in U.S. dollars. | **Scarcity** = Scale from 1-8 with 8 being the hardest to find.

173

273 (Type V): Red was the color for the roof and trim of the "OAK PARK" station.

VG-C6	EX-C7	LN-C8	Scarcity
60	125	225	5

274 HARBOR JUNCTION FREIGHT STATION: Produced by Mini-craft in 1952-53, this illuminated wooden station was sold under both the Gilbert and Mini-craft label.

274 (Type I): Some of the stations had red trim.

VG-C6	EX-C7	LN-C8	Scarcity
50	125	225	5

274 (Type II): Others had green trim.

VG-C6	EX-C7	LN-C8	Scarcity
100	225	400	7

275 EUREKA DINER: This illuminated diner was produced by Mini-craft for Gilbert in 1952 and 1953. Mini-craft also sold the diner under their own label, although as with the other Mini-craft/Gilbert buildings, the decoration varied slightly from what is listed here.

275 (Type I): Some of the diners had a dark blue roof and windows.

VG-C6	EX-C7	LN-C8	Scarcity
50	125	200	5

275 (Type II): Others had a dark green roof and windows.

VG-C6	EX-C7	LN-C8	Scarcity
50	125	200	5

275 (Type III): Some of the buildings had green roofs and orange windows.

VG-C6	EX-C7	LN-C8	Scarcity
50	125	200	5

275 (Type IV): A red roof and trim was used on other diners.

VG-C6	EX-C7	LN-C8	Scarcity
50	125	200	5

440 LAMP: Three clear 14-volt lamps.

VG-C6	EX-C7	LN-C8	Scarcity
3	5	10	4

441 LAMP: Three red 18-volt lamps.

VG-C6	EX-C7	LN-C8	Scarcity
3	5	10	4

442 LAMP: Three clear six- to eight-volt lamps.

VG-C6	EX-C7	LN-C8	Scarcity
3	5	10	4

443 LAMP: Three green 18-volt lamps.

VG-C6	EX-C7	LN-C8	Scarcity
3	5	10	4

444 LAMP: Three clear 18-volt lamps.

VG-C6	EX-C7	LN-C8	Scarcity
3	5	10	4

450 TRACK TERMINAL: This track terminal, originally sold prior to World War II, was again offered from 1946 through 1948. It was designed for use with O-Gauge track.

VG-C6	EX-C7	LN-C8	Scarcity
2	3	5	1

451 LAMP: One boxed frosted 18-volt lamp.

VG-C6	EX-C7	LN-C8	Scarcity
3	5	10	4

452 LAMP: One boxed clear 14-volt lamp.

VG-C6	EX-C7	LN-C8	Scarcity
3	5	10	4

453 LAMP (Type I): The 1946-48 version was a boxed clear 18-volt lamp.

VG-C6	EX-C7	LN-C8	Scarcity
3	5	10	4

453 LAMP (Type II): Later, three clear 18-volt lamps were in the box.

VG-C6	EX-C7	LN-C8	Scarcity
3	5	10	4

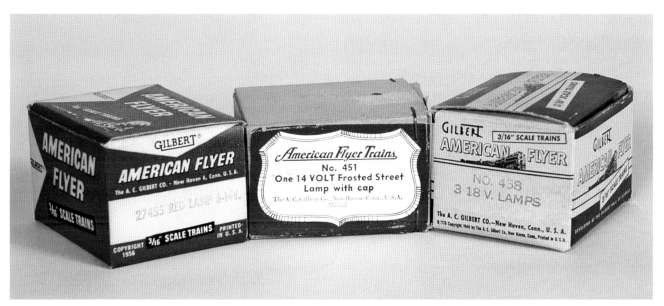

Gilbert sold boxed replacement lamps for their trains and accessories. Different styles of packaging, as seen here, were used through the years.

Values for each condition are in U.S. dollars. | **Scarcity** = Scale from 1-8 with 8 being the hardest to find.

175

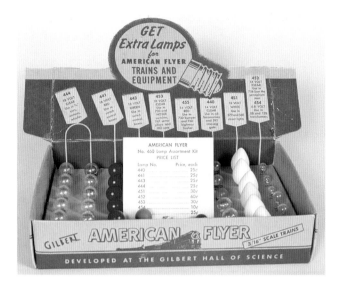

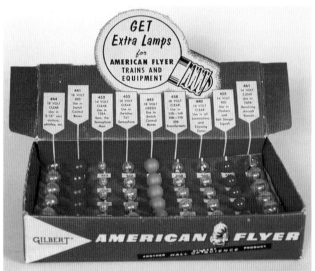

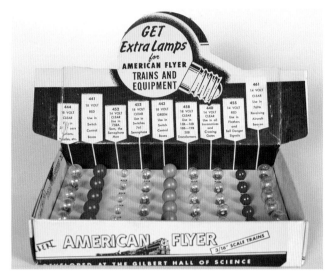

460 AMERICAN FLYER BULBS: This assortment of 54 replacement light bulbs, in a dealer counter display was available in 1951, then again in 1953-54. A variety of packaging was used, and the assortment of bulbs varied slightly through the years.

VG-C6	EX-C7	LN-C8	Scarcity
35	75	125	7

461 LAMP: Three clear 14-volt lamps for 769A revolving beacon.

VG-C6	EX-C7	LN-C8	Scarcity
3	5	10	4

520 KNUCKLE COUPLER KIT: From 1954 through 1956, Gilbert sold this envelope containing one pair of knuckle couplers with split shank, two rivets and a rivet-removing tool.

VG-C6	EX-C7	LN-C8	Scarcity
2	3	5	2

521 KNUCKLE COUPLER KIT: This 1953 envelope contains 12 knuckle couplers and rivets.

VG-C6	EX-C7	LN-C8	Scarcity
10	20	30	7

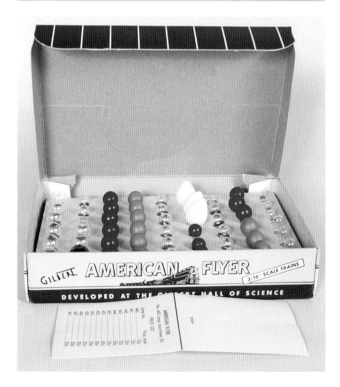

525 KNUCKLE COUPLER TRUCKS: From 1953 through 1956, a boxed pair of sintered-iron trucks with plastic wheels with rivets and instructions was sold. They were designed for non-illuminated cars. The values below include all original packaging.

VG-C6	EX-C7	LN-C8	Scarcity
15	25	35	7

526 KNUCKLE COUPLER TRUCKS: A boxed pair of four-wheel sintered-iron trucks for illuminated cars, with mounting rivets and instructions, was also available from 1953 through 1956. The values below include all original packaging.

VG-C6	EX-C7	LN-C8	Scarcity
15	25	35	7

527 KNUCKLE COUPLER TRUCKS: This pair of trucks, with rivets and instructions, was designed for use on action cars. It was available from 1953 through 1956. The values below include all original packaging.

VG-C6	EX-C7	LN-C8	Scarcity
15	25	35	7

528 KNUCKLE COUPLER TRUCKS: Also sold from 1953 through 1956 was this pair of trucks for streamlined passenger cars, which came with rivets and instructions. The values below include all original packaging.

VG-C6	EX-C7	LN-C8	Scarcity
15	25	35	7

529 KNUCKLE COUPLER TRUCKS: One pair of six-wheel trucks for illuminated heavyweight passenger cars, with instructions and rivets, were in this 1953-56 separate sale box. The values below include all original packaging.

VG-C6	EX-C7	LN-C8	Scarcity
15	25	35	7

530 KNUCKLE COUPLER TRUCKS: Also available from 1953-56, this box contained one pair of six-wheel trucks for the 644-944 crane, with instructions and rivets. The values below include all original packaging.

VG-C6	EX-C7	LN-C8	Scarcity
15	25	35	7

531 KNUCKLE COUPLER TRUCK: Contains rear truck for 12-wheel tender, available from 1953 through 1956. The values below include all original packaging.

VG-C6	EX-C7	LN-C8	Scarcity
15	25	35	7

532 KNUCKLE COUPLER TRUCKS: A boxed pair of six-wheel trucks for freight cars, with rivets and instructions, was sold from 1953 through 1956. The values below include all original packaging.

VG-C6	EX-C7	LN-C8	Scarcity
15	25	35	7

561 BILLBOARD HORN: This popular accessory was cataloged in 1955 and 1956. The non-illuminated billboard housed a diesel horn sound generator.

561 (Type I): The scene on other billboards showed a Santa Fe PA with a steam locomotive passing over it on a bridge. Some of these units had a light green steel base.

VG-C6	EX-C7	LN-C8	Scarcity
20	30	50	2

Values for each condition are in U.S. dollars. | **Scarcity** = Scale from 1-8 with 8 being the hardest to find.

177

561 (Type II): Otherwise identical to the Type I, some billboards had a dark green base.

VG-C6	EX-C7	LN-C8	Scarcity
20	30	50	2

561 (Type III): Some had a billboard scene depicting an A/B/A trio of Santa Fe Alco passenger diesels pulling a freight train through the desert.

VG-C6	EX-C7	LN-C8	Scarcity
20	30	50	2

566 WHISTLING BILLBOARD: From 1951 through 1955, Gilbert sold this whistling billboard with a paper advertisement featuring a Santa Fe PA with a steam locomotive passing over it on a bridge.

566 (Type I): From 1951 through 1953, the billboard base was light green.

VG-C6	EX-C7	LN-C8	Scarcity
15	30	45	2

566 (Type II): Units produced in 1954 had a dark green base.

VG-C6	EX-C7	LN-C8	Scarcity
15	30	45	2

568 WHISTLING BILLBOARD: 📷 The whistling billboard was sold with a new number, and new scene, in 1956. Now depicted on the paper billboard was a freight train powered by a 4-8-4 steam locomotive.

VG-C6	EX-C7	LN-C8	Scarcity
20	30	45	2

571 TRUSS BRIDGE: This bridge with stamped steel base and plastic trusses was sold in 1955-56. Orange, black and red trusses have been found without effect to value.

VG-C6	EX-C7	LN-C8	Scarcity
15	25	40	2

Shown here are three of the records that were used in Gilbert's sound-generating accessories.

568 WHISTLING BILLBOARD

577 WHISTLING BILLBOARD

573 A. F. TALKING STATION RECORD: This replacement record, sold in a plain envelope, had no number on the label.

VG-C6	EX-C7	LN-C8	Scarcity
Too rarely traded to accurately establish pricing.			

577 WHISTLING BILLBOARD: 📷 Originally produced prior to World War II, this illuminated billboard was again offered from 1946 through 1950. The sign usually depicted a clown and normally promoted the "RINGLING BROS. AND BARNUM & BAILEY" circus – The GREATEST SHOW ON EARTH."

577 (Type I): A die-cast billboard frame was used on some billboards in 1946-47.

VG-C6	EX-C7	LN-C8	Scarcity
25	60	100	4

577 (Type II): Beginning in 1947, and continuing through 1950, white-painted pressed-steel frames were used for the billboard.

VG-C6	EX-C7	LN-C8	Scarcity
25	60	100	4

577 (Type III): A limited number of billboards were produced in 1947 to promote Foxmart department stores. Shown on the light blue sign was a building and the dark blue legend read "VISIT THE FOXMART" "A DIVISION OF 'G. FOX & CO.,' SERVING RURAL CONNECTICUT, ROUTE 5 BETWEEN EAST HARTFORD AND EAST WINDSOR HILLS." This billboard was included in set 4605F, fitting available from the G. Fox Co. Department Store, Hartford, Conn.

VG-C6	EX-C7	LN-C8	Scarcity
500	1,000	2,000	8

577 (Type IV): The 1950 edition of the billboard advertised American Flyer trains.

VG-C6	EX-C7	LN-C8	Scarcity
25	35	45	1

577NL BILLBOARD: A non-illuminated version of the billboard was produced in 1950.

VG-C6	EX-C7	LN-C8	Scarcity
15	25	50	4

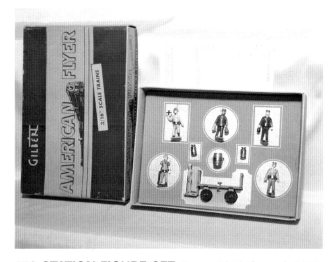

578 STATION FIGURE SET: From 1946 through 1952, Gilbert offered this six-figure set of railroad terminal workers. The original packaging of a yellow box with blue cardboard insert is critical to the values here.

VG-C6	EX-C7	LN-C8	Scarcity
50	100	175	5

579 SINGLE STREET LAMP: The value of this die-cast streetlight, originally sold from 1946 through 1949, is heavily dependent on the original box with insert.

Values for each condition are in U.S. dollars. | **Scarcity** = Scale from 1-8 with 8 being the hardest to find.

179

579 (Type I): Some lamps were light green.

VG-C6	EX-C7	LN-C8	Scarcity
15	30	50	4

579 (Type II): Others were painted silver.

VG-C6	EX-C7	LN-C8	Scarcity
15	30	50	4

580 DOUBLE STREETLIGHT: 1946-49, this die-cast two-bulb streetlight was offered from 1946 through 1949. The values below are predicated on the presence of the original box, insert and tin holding the bulbs.

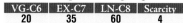

580 (Type I): Some lamps were light green.

VG-C6	EX-C7	LN-C8	Scarcity
20	35	60	4

580 (Type II): Others were painted silver.

VG-C6	EX-C7	LN-C8	Scarcity
20	35	60	4

581 GIRDER BRIDGE: This 10-inch long bridge with sheet metal base and die-cast sides was sold from 1946 through 1956.

581 (Type I): From 1946 through 1949, the bridge was black and lettered "LACKAWANNA" in white.

VG-C6	EX-C7	LN-C8	Scarcity
10	20	30	4

581 (Type II): In 1950, as well as 1952, 1954 and 1956, the sides were painted silver and the bridge was lettered "AMERICAN FLYER" in black.

VG-C6	EX-C7	LN-C8	Scarcity
10	20	30	4

581 (Type III): A least some of the bridges produced in 1951 were painted silver and lettered "LACKAWANNA" in black.

VG-C6	EX-C7	LN-C8	Scarcity
10	20	30	4

581 (Type IV): Some bridges were painted black and lettered "AMERICAN FLYER" in white.

VG-C6	EX-C7	LN-C8	Scarcity
10	20	30	4

581 (Type V): Other black-painted bridges had white "AMERICAN FLYER LINES" lettering, and the number "581" was stamped in white near both ends.

VG-C6	EX-C7	LN-C8	Scarcity
10	20	30	4

582 AUTOMATIC BLINKER SIGNAL: Activated by a track trip, this accessory sold from 1946 through 1948 flashed its lights as the train passed.

VG-C6	EX-C7	LN-C8	Scarcity
60	200	375	7

583 ELECTROMATIC CRANE: Available from 1946 through 1949, this remote control operating crane came with a gray metal receiving bin. The boom could be green or gray, and the electromagnet was red. The motor was equipped with a sequence reverse unit, and the controller had one button.

VG-C6	EX-C7	LN-C8	Scarcity
75	150	225	6

583A ELECTROMAGNETIC CRANE: This improved crane was sold from 1950 through 1953. No sequence reverse unit was installed, so the controller now had two buttons. The die-cast boom was green, and the electromagnet red.

583A (Type I): Some of these cranes had an all-gray supporting structure.

VG-C6	EX-C7	LN-C8	Scarcity
85	160	250	6

583A (Type II): Others had a silver-painted supporting structure.

VG-C6	EX-C7	LN-C8	Scarcity
85	160	250	6

583A (Type III): A third version had a gray base and silver-painted legs.

VG-C6	EX-C7	LN-C8	Scarcity
85	160	250	6

Values for each condition are in U.S. dollars. | **Scarcity** = Scale from 1-8 with 8 being the hardest to find.

584 BELL DANGER SIGNAL: This 1946-47 accessory included flashing grade crossing lights and a ringing bell—mounted—along with a watchman on a simulated roadway.

VG-C6	EX-C7	LN-C8	Scarcity
225	600	1,000	8

585 TOOL SHED: This white sheet metal building on gray base was sold from 1946 through 1952.
585 (Type I): Some had a dark red roof.

VG-C6	EX-C7	LN-C8	Scarcity
25	50	75	4

585 (Type II): Others had a light red roof.

VG-C6	EX-C7	LN-C8	Scarcity
25	50	75	4

586F WAYSIDE STATION: This sheet metal and die-cast station was sold for a decade from 1946 through 1956. It was decorated with two figures and a green cart.

586F (Type I): In 1946-49, gray posts supported the roof.

VG-C6	EX-C7	LN-C8	Scarcity
40	80	120	3

586F (Type II): 📷 From 1950 through 1956, green posts were used.

VG-C6	EX-C7	LN-C8	Scarcity
40	80	120	3

587 BLOCK SIGNAL: This block signal, with trips and control, was sold in 1946-47.

587 (Type I): Some signals had a metal mast supporting a green die-cast signal head.

VG-C6	EX-C7	LN-C8	Scarcity
60	150	275	7

587 (Type II): Others had a cardboard mast and black die-cast signal head.

VG-C6	EX-C7	LN-C8	Scarcity
60	150	275	7

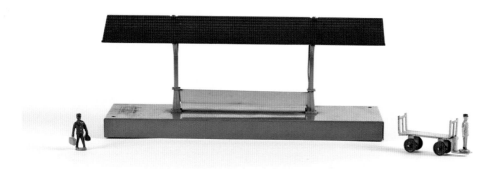

586F (Type II)

588 SEMAPHORE BLOCK SIGNAL: Cataloged from 1946 through 1948, this scarce semaphore had a gray base and black die-cast signal head. It came with two automatic track trips and a remote-control box.

VG-C6	EX-C7	LN-C8	Scarcity
600	1,200	2,000	8

589 PASSENGER AND FREIGHT STATION: This gray sheet metal illuminated "MYSTIC" station was offered from 1946 through 1956.

589 (Type I): Some of the stations had green roofs.

VG-C6	EX-C7	LN-C8	Scarcity
15	35	60	4

589 (Type II):  Others had black roofs.

VG-C6	EX-C7	LN-C8	Scarcity
20	40	70	5

589 (Type III): The roof on some stations was painted dark green.

VG-C6	EX-C7	LN-C8	Scarcity
15	35	60	4

590 CONTROL TOWER: Bachmann Bros. of Philadelphia produced this tan plastic control tower for Gilbert in 1955-56. "CEDAR HILL JUNCTION" signs were on the roof. Bachmann also sold the same tower in their "Plasticville" line.

VG-C6	EX-C7	LN-C8	Scarcity
25	60	100	4

591 CROSSING GATE: This illuminated die-cast crossing gate with shanty and walkway gate mounted on a roadway was sold from 1946 through 1948. It was packaged with a 707 track trip.

591 (Type I): In 1946, the accessory had a plastic gate and the shanty roof did not include a smokestack.

VG-C6	EX-C7	LN-C8	Scarcity
25	60	100	5

591 (Type II): Later, an aluminum gate was introduced, and the black crackle-finished shanty roof sported a smokestack.

VG-C6	EX-C7	LN-C8	Scarcity
25	60	100	5

589 (Type II)

Values for each condition are in U.S. dollars. | **Scarcity** = Scale from 1-8 with 8 being the hardest to find.

183

591 (Type III): The aluminum gate was also used in conjunction with light green shanty roofs with smokestacks.

VG-C6	EX-C7	LN-C8	Scarcity
25	60	100	5

592 CROSSING GATE: In 1949-50, Gilbert offered this crossing gate with shanty installed on a die-cast base. It was supplied with a 697 track trip.

592 (Type I): The 1949 edition had four binding post terminals.

VG-C6	EX-C7	LN-C8	Scarcity
25	60	100	4

592 (Type II): In 1950, only two binding posts were used.

VG-C6	EX-C7	LN-C8	Scarcity
25	60	100	4

592A CROSSING GATE: This version of the illuminated crossing gate with shanty was sold from 1951 through 1953.

592A (Type I): As initially introduced this accessory had a Bakelite base.

VG-C6	EX-C7	LN-C8	Scarcity
25	60	100	4

592A (Type II): Later, a die-cast base was used.

VG-C6	EX-C7	LN-C8	Scarcity
25	60	100	4

593 SIGNAL TOWER: This illuminated sheet metal tower was cataloged from 1946 through 1954.

593 (Type I): The earliest of these towers were yellow and brown, probably indicating they were assembled from left over pre-WWII components.

VG-C6	EX-C7	LN-C8	Scarcity
30	60	100	6

593 (Type II): The standard postwar colors for the tower were red and white.

VG-C6	EX-C7	LN-C8	Scarcity
30	60	100	5

594 ANIMATED TRACK GANG SET: One of the most desirable of all Flyer accessories is this animated accessory cataloged first in 1941-42, then again in 1946-47. On the green base was mounted a simulated yellow air compressor, a workman, a flagman and two workmen with air compressor. As a train neared the flagman approached the track, and the jack-hammer-wielding workman moved away from the track. Once the train passed, the workers all returned to their original positions. The prewar version used fabric-covered wires, while the postwar version used plastic insulation. Beware: reproductions exist.

VG-C6	EX-C7	LN-C8	Scarcity
500	1,500	2,500	8

596 OPERATING WATER TANK: First offered from 1940-1942, this water tank was cataloged for an additional decade in the postwar era. Like its predecessor the spout of the 1946-56 version could be lowered by remote control, using the included "AMERICAN FLYER WATER TANK" on operating button. A yellow arrow decal was installed on the roof.

596 (Type I): Some of the 1946-47 towers had dark gray leg supports and wooden downspouts.

VG-C6	EX-C7	LN-C8	Scarcity
25	50	75	4

596 (Type III): Gray support legs and roof were used on some towers.

VG-C6	EX-C7	LN-C8	Scarcity
25	50	75	4

596 (Type II): A black roof was used in conjunction with gray legs on other towers.

VG-C6	EX-C7	LN-C8	Scarcity
25	50	75	4

596 (Type IV): Black legs and a black roof were used on some of the water tanks.

VG-C6	EX-C7	LN-C8	Scarcity
25	50	75	4

598 TALKING STATION RECORD: The record was available from 1946 through 1956. Intended for use in the 755 or 799 talking station accessories, one side had diesel locomotive sounds; the other side had steam locomotive sounds.

VG-C6	EX-C7	LN-C8	Scarcity
10	15	20	5

Values for each condition are in U.S. dollars. | **Scarcity** = Scale from 1-8 with 8 being the hardest to find.

185

599 TALKING STATION FREIGHT RECORD: This 1956 double-sided record includes dispatcher and conductor conversations and railroad sounds. Intended for use in the 799 station, this is a scarce record.

VG-C6	EX-C7	LN-C8	Scarcity
15	30	50	7

600 CROSSING GATE WITH BELL: Gilbert offered this operating illuminated crossing gate with bell from 1954 through 1956. The shanty held the ringing bell mechanism.

VG-C6	EX-C7	LN-C8	Scarcity
30	60	100	5

612 FREIGHT PASSENGER STATION WITH CRANE: This 1946 through 1954 accessory included an illuminated sheet metal building and manually operated rotating crane.

612 (Type I): Some of these accessories had a gray base, green roof and black rotating crane platform.

VG-C6	EX-C7	LN-C8	Scarcity
60	110	175	5

612 (Type II): Others were identical to the Type I, but for the color or the rotating crane platform, which was now gray.

VG-C6	EX-C7	LN-C8	Scarcity
60	110	175	5

612 (Type III): A green base distinguished this version, which had a tan station roof and gray rotating crane platform.

VG-C6	EX-C7	LN-C8	Scarcity
60	110	175	5

612 (Type IV): Some of these accessories had a brown base, green station roof and black rotating crane platform.

VG-C6	EX-C7	LN-C8	Scarcity
60	110	175	5

621 THREE-RAIL STRAIGHT TRACK, HALF-SECTION: Sold for many years prior to WWII, this half-section of three-rail O-Gauge straight track was again offered from 1946 through 1948.

VG-C6	EX-C7	LN-C8	Scarcity
.20	.30	.50	1

622 THREE-RAIL CURVE TRACK, HALF-SECTION: Sold for many years prior to WWII, this half-section of three-rail O-Gauge curved track was again offered from 1946 through 1948.

VG-C6	EX-C7	LN-C8	Scarcity
.20	.30	.50	1

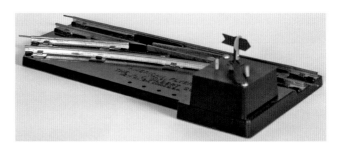

668 MANUAL LEFT-HAND SWITCH: From 1953 through 1955, Gilbert produced this left-hand S-Gauge turnout. Red and green flags, often damaged today, were mounted on the switch throw lever. An electrical switch mounted on the turnout allowed the selection of regular or two-train operation.

VG-C6	EX-C7	LN-C8	Scarcity
5	8	10	1

612 (Type I)

669 MANUAL RIGHT-HAND SWITCH: Also produced from 1953-55, this turnout was identical to the 668, except turned to the right rather than the left.

VG-C6	EX-C7	LN-C8	Scarcity
5	8	10	1

670 ELECTRIC TRACK TRIP: Offered in 1955 and 1956, the trip clipped to one rail and could be used to control block signals, turnouts, signals, etc.

670 (Type I): Some trips were adjustable.

VG-C6	EX-C7	LN-C8	Scarcity
4	8	20	5

670 (Type II): Others had no adjustment screw.

VG-C6	EX-C7	LN-C8	Scarcity
4	8	20	5

678 LEFT-HAND REMOTE-CONTROL SWITCH: This was the 1953-56 remote control version of the left-hand turnout. Four Fahnstock clips were used to connect the controller to the turnout.

VG-C6	EX-C7	LN-C8	Scarcity
10	15	20	1

679 RIGHT-HAND REMOTE-CONTROL SWITCH: Naturally, a right-hand remote control turnout was also available in 1953-56.

VG-C6	EX-C7	LN-C8	Scarcity
10	15	20	1

680 THREE-RAIL CURVE TRACK: Sold for many years prior to WWII, this section of three-rail O-Gauge curved track was again offered from 1946 through 1948.

VG-C6	EX-C7	LN-C8	Scarcity
.20	.30	.50	1

681 THREE-RAIL STRAIGHT TRACK: Sold for many years prior to WWII, this section of three-rail O-Gauge straight track was again offered from 1946 through 1948.

VG-C6	EX-C7	LN-C8	Scarcity
.20	.30	.50	1

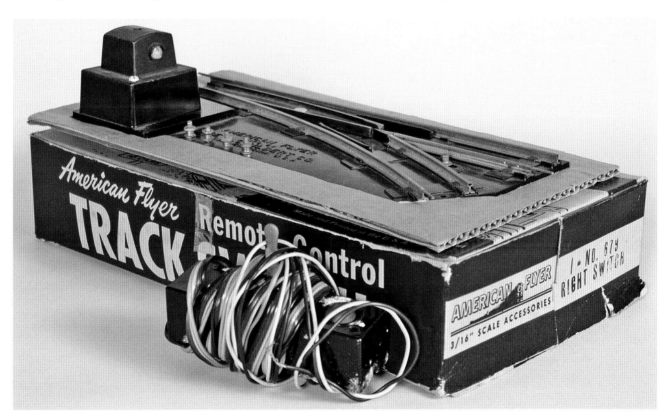

679 RIGHT-HAND REMOTE-CONTROL SWITCH

Values for each condition are in U.S. dollars. | Scarcity = Scale from 1-8 with 8 being the hardest to find.

688 THREE-RAIL REMOTE-CONTROL SWITCHES: Introduced prior to WWII, this O-Gauge turnout was also sold from 1946 through 1948.

VG-C6	EX-C7	LN-C8	Scarcity
.20	.30	.50	1

690 TRACK TERMINAL: This track terminal was designed for use with S-Gauge track, and was sold from 1946 through 1956. Most had a black fiberboard base.

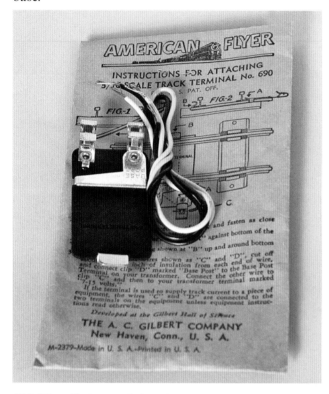

690 (Type I): Some of these lockons employed Fahnstock clips for wiring connections.

VG-C6	EX-C7	LN-C8	Scarcity
.25	.50	.75	1

690 (Type II): Some lockons were made with brown fiberboard bases.

VG-C6	EX-C7	LN-C8	Scarcity
.25	.50	.75	1

690 (Type III): Zip clips replaced Fahnstock clips on other lockons.

VG-C6	EX-C7	LN-C8	Scarcity
.25	.50	.75	1

691 STEEL TRACK PINS: This envelope containing one dozen steel pins was sold in 1946-48.

VG-C6	EX-C7	LN-C8	Scarcity
.50	.75	1	1

692 FIBER TRACK PINS: This envelope containing four fiber pins was sold in 1946-48.

VG-C6	EX-C7	LN-C8	Scarcity
.25	.50	.75	1

693 TRACK LOCKS: The spring steel clips were used to prevent track sections from pulling apart on floor layouts. These were offered from 1948 through 1956. Through the years varying quantities were included in the envelope.

VG-C6	EX-C7	LN-C8	Scarcity
.05	.07	.15	1

694 AUTOMATIC COUPLERS, TRUCKS, WHEELS AND AXLES: From 1946 through 1953, Gilbert sold the box containing a pair of trucks with link couplers. These were intended to be used to convert prewar 3/16 O-Gauge cars to S-Gauge.

VG-C6	EX-C7	LN-C8	Scarcity
3	5	10	4

695 AUTOMATIC TRACK TRIP: This 1946-only trip featured two metal sensing plates.

VG-C6	EX-C7	LN-C8	Scarcity
10	20	30	7

695 REVERSE LOOP RELAY: American Flyer's two-rail operating system, while realistic, had one integral operational problem. A reverse loop track layout inherently created a short circuit. To overcome this, Gilbert devised a relay, which reversed the polarity of part of the track layout. This was the least common of Gilbert's reverse loop relays, and it was cataloged in 1955 and 1956.

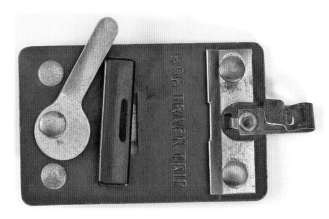

696 (Type III): Two rivets were used on other units.

VG-C6	EX-C7	LN-C8	Scarcity
5	10	15	3

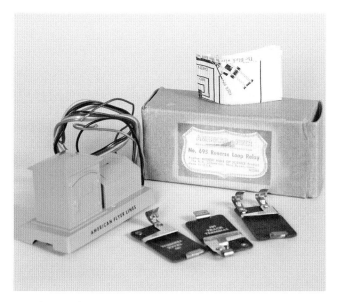

695 (Type I): Some relays came with two 707 and one 690 track terminals and two fiber pins.

VG-C6	EX-C7	LN-C8	Scarcity
25	50	80	5

695 (Type II): Others came with three 707 track terminals.

VG-C6	EX-C7	LN-C8	Scarcity
25	50	80	5

696 TRACK TRIP: Utilized to actuate various accessories, a trip with this number was first sold from 1946 through 1948, then again from 1955 through 1957.

696 (Type I): The earliest of these had a die-cast actuating shoe.

VG-C6	EX-C7	LN-C8	Scarcity
10	15	30	7

696 (Type II): The plastic actuating shoe of some of the trips was retained by a single screw.

VG-C6	EX-C7	LN-C8	Scarcity
5	10	15	3

697 TRACK TRIP: This Bakelite accessory trip was offered from 1950 through 1954. The weight of the passing train overcomes spring pressure to close the contacts on this trip, thereby actuating an accessory.

VG-C6	EX-C7	LN-C8	Scarcity
5	10	15	3

698 REVERSE LOOP KIT: Sold from 1949 through 1954—except for 1951—this set contained everything needed to wire a reverse loop in a two-rail track system.

The contents included a double-pole, double-throw switch (DPDT), three 690 track terminals, six fiber pins; two wood screws, instructions, and 10 feet of wire.

VG-C6	EX-C7	LN-C8	Scarcity
20	40	75	5

700 STRAIGHT TRACK: Standard 10-inch long section of T-rail S-Gauge track with four black ties; sold from 1946 through 1956.

700 (Type I): In 1946, the track had black rails.

VG-C6	EX-C7	LN-C8	Scarcity
.50	.75	1	1

700 (Type II): From 1947 through 1956, the rails were shiny.

VG-C6	EX-C7	LN-C8	Scarcity
.50	.75	1	1

Values for each condition are in U.S. dollars. | **Scarcity** = Scale from 1-8 with 8 being the hardest to find.

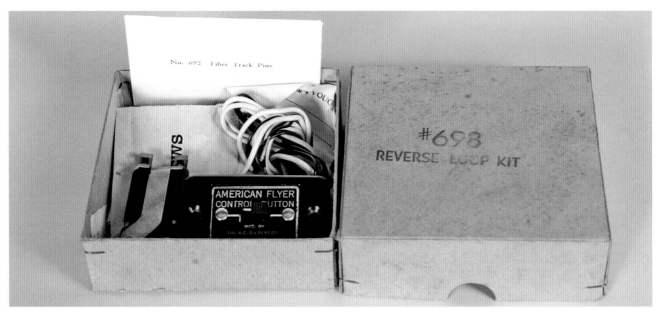

698 REVERSE LOOP KIT

701 STRAIGHT TRACK HALF SECTION: Standard five-inch long section of T-rail S-Gauge track, sold from 1946 through 1956.

701 (Type I): In 1946, the track had black rails.

VG-C6	EX-C7	LN-C8	Scarcity
.50	.75	1	1

701 (Type II): From 1947 through 1956, the rails were shiny.

VG-C6	EX-C7	LN-C8	Scarcity
.50	.75	1	1

702 CURVE TRACK: Standard curved section of T-rail S-Gauge track with four black ties; sold from 1946 through 1956. Twelve sections form a 40-inch circle.

702 (Type I): In 1946, the track had black rails.

VG-C6	EX-C7	LN-C8	Scarcity
.15	.25	.50	1

702 (Type II): From 1947 through 1956, the rails were shiny.

VG-C6	EX-C7	LN-C8	Scarcity
.15	.25	.50	1

703 CURVE TRACK HALF SECTION: Standard one-half curved section of T-rail S-Gauge track, sold from 1946 through 1956.

701 (Type I): In 1946, the track had black rails.

VG-C6	EX-C7	LN-C8	Scarcity
.15	.25	.50	1

701 (Type II): From 1947 through 1956, the rails were shiny.

VG-C6	EX-C7	LN-C8	Scarcity
.15	.25	.50	1

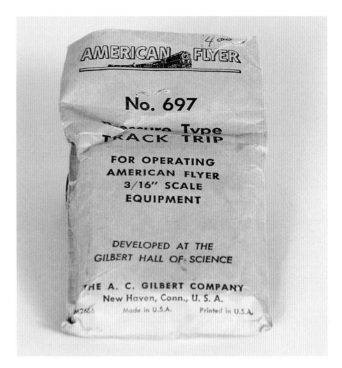

704 MANUAL UNCOUPLER: This common item was made from 1952 through 1956. There were numerous minor variations, none of any consequence.

VG-C6	EX-C7	LN-C8	Scarcity
.50	1	2	1

705 REMOTE-CONTROL ELECTRIC UNCOUPLER: In 1946 and 1947, this remote control uncoupler was part of the Gilbert line. Two binding posts protruded from the Bakelite housing, and the entire unit was permanently attached to a straight track section.

VG-C6	EX-C7	LN-C8	Scarcity
2	3	5	1

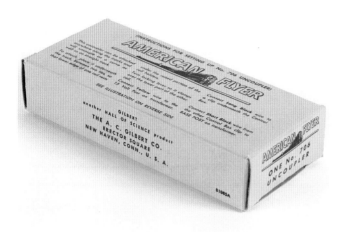

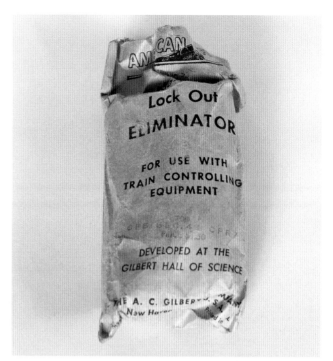

706 REMOTE UNCOUPLER: This was the remote control uncoupler sold by Gilbert from 1948 through 1956. It was produced in several minor variations, the most noticeable of which were the housing cover, which could be either yellow or green, but none of which affect value.

VG-C6	EX-C7	LN-C8	Scarcity
.50	1	3	1

707 TRACK TERMINAL: Used with accessories, this 1946-59 lockon had only one electrical terminal.

707 (Type I): Some of these wire junctions were Fahnstock clip.

VG-C6	EX-C7	LN-C8	Scarcity
.50	1	2	1

707 (Type II): Others had a zip clip.

VG-C6	EX-C7	LN-C8	Scarcity
.50	1	2	1

708 AIR-CHIME WHISTLE REMOTE-CONTROL UNIT: This control box, which could be black or gray plastic, was from 1951 through 1956. Permanently attached four-color rainbow wire was used to connect it to the track.

708 (Type I): In 1951 and 1952, the unit was known as the "AIR CHIME WHISTLE CONTROL."

VG-C6	EX-C7	LN-C8	Scarcity
5	10	15	1

708 (Type II): For 1953-54 "708 AIR CHIME WHISTLE REMOTE CONTROL UNIT."

VG-C6	EX-C7	LN-C8	Scarcity
5	10	15	1

708 (Type III): In 1955 and 1956, the label read "708 DIESEL HORN CONTROL."

VG-C6	EX-C7	LN-C8	Scarcity
5	10	15	1

709 LOCKOUT ELIMINATOR: This small device was sold from 1950 through 1955, it eliminated the need to lock out the reverse unit of locomotives when using train stop accessories.

VG-C6	EX-C7	LN-C8	Scarcity
2	5	10	3

710 AUTOMATIC TRACK SECTION: This 1946-47 track section was used in conjunction with operating cars of this era, whose electrical contacts were beneath the car.

VG-C6	EX-C7	LN-C8	Scarcity
2	3	5	4

710 STEAM WHISTLE CONTROL: This is the better style of Gilbert's whistle controls, and it was available in 1955 and 1956. A slide lever was at the front of the base.

VG-C6	EX-C7	LN-C8	Scarcity
10	20	40	6

Values for each condition are in U.S. dollars. | **Scarcity** = Scale from 1-8 with 8 being the hardest to find.

191

711 MAIL PICKUP TRACK SECTION: This 10-inch section of track came with 718 operating mail cars in 1946-47.

VG-C6	EX-C7	LN-C8	Scarcity
Too rarely traded to accurately establish pricing.			

712 SPECIAL RAIL SECTION: This operating car activation section was sold from 1947 through 1956. Many minor variations of the unit were made, but none are particularly valuable.

VG-C6	EX-C7	LN-C8	Scarcity
2	3	5	1

713 SPECIAL RAIL SECTION: This special 1947-56 track section includes an integral stand for a mail post. It was designed for use with the 718 and 918 mail pickup cars.

VG-C6	EX-C7	LN-C8	Scarcity
10	15	25	1

720 REMOTE-CONTROL SWITCHES: This pair of switches was sold from 1946 through 1949. Four-color ribbon wire is used to connect each switch with the single two-lever illuminated controller used by the pair.

VG-C6	EX-C7	LN-C8	Scarcity
20	35	50	1

720A REMOTE-CONTROL SWITCHES: An improved turnout pair was introduced in 1949 and remained in the product line through 1956. Four-color ribbon wire is used to connect each switch with the single two-lever illuminated controller used by the pair.
720A (Type I): The 1951 edition used binding posts to secure the controller leads to the turnouts.

VG-C6	EX-C7	LN-C8	Scarcity
20	35	50	1

720A (Type II): Later turnouts used Fahnstock clips for the controller connection.

VG-C6	EX-C7	LN-C8	Scarcity
20	35	50	1

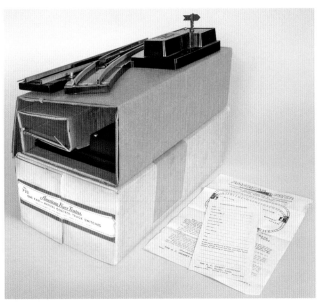

722 MANUAL SWITCHES: These pairs of manual turnouts were sold from 1946 through 1951. Fragile red and green flags indicated the turnout position. An electrical switch was provided to allow either regular or two-train operation.

VG-C6	EX-C7	LN-C8	Scarcity
10	15	20	1

722A MANUAL SWITCHES: The manual turnouts were revised in 1952, and the new switch remained in the product line through 1956. Fragile red and green flags indicated the turnout position. An electrical switch was provided to allow either regular or two-train operation.

VG-C6	EX-C7	LN-C8	Scarcity
10	15	20	1

725 CROSSING: This S-Gauge 90-degree crossing was sold from 1946 through 1956.

725 (Type I): The 1946 edition of the crossing had brass strips visible in the flangeways.

VG-C6	EX-C7	LN-C8	Scarcity
Too rarely traded to accurately establish pricing.			

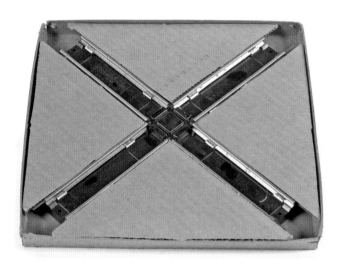

725 (Type II): The brass strips were omitted from later production.

VG-C6	EX-C7	LN-C8	Scarcity
3	5	10	1

726 STRAIGHT RUBBER ROADBED: Rubber roadbed was sold from 1950 through 1956. The roadbed was designed to secure a single piece of straight track.

726 (Type I): Initially the roadbed was gray, and six simulated crossties were molded in.

VG-C6	EX-C7	LN-C8	Scarcity
.50	1	2	2

726 (Type II): Later roadbed was identical to the Type I, but was black rubber.

VG-C6	EX-C7	LN-C8	Scarcity
.50	1	2	2

726 (Type III): For the final year of production, the black rubber roadbed was molded with 23 ties.

VG-C6	EX-C7	LN-C8	Scarcity
.50	1	2	2

727 CURVED RUBBER ROADBED: 1950-56; gray or black rubber, molded-on roadbed detail with six or 23 ties, provides snug fit for one 702 curved track section.

727 (Type I): Initially the roadbed was gray, and six simulated crossties were molded in.

VG-C6	EX-C7	LN-C8	Scarcity
.50	1	1.50	2

727 (Type II): Later roadbed was identical to the Type I, but was black rubber.

VG-C6	EX-C7	LN-C8	Scarcity
.50	1	1.50	2

727 (Type III): For the final year of production, the black rubber roadbed was molded with 23 ties.

VG-C6	EX-C7	LN-C8	Scarcity
.50	1	1.50	2

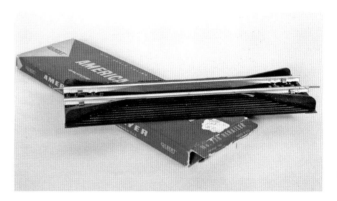

728 RERAILER: This 10-inch long rerailer was made only in 1956 and was designed to resemble a rural grade crossing.

VG-C6	EX-C7	LN-C8	Scarcity
5	10	20	1

730 BUMPER: Gilbert sold this illuminated bumper from 1946 through 1956 in either green or red plastic. It came attached to a section of straight track.

730 (Type I): Some of the bumpers were molded of bluish-green plastic.

VG-C6	EX-C7	LN-C8	Scarcity
10	15	20	1

Values for each condition are in U.S. dollars. | **Scarcity** = Scale from 1-8 with 8 being the hardest to find.

193

730 (Type II): Others are molded of medium green plastic.

VG-C6	EX-C7	LN-C8	Scarcity
10	15	20	1

730 (Type III): In 1951, some of the bumpers were molded in red.

VG-C6	EX-C7	LN-C8	Scarcity
30	75	125	6

731 PIKE PLANNING KIT: This 1952-56 tool set included a plastic template of Gilbert track components, sheets of Dietzgen graph paper and M3127 Instruction books.

VG-C6	EX-C7	LN-C8	Scarcity
10	20	35	1

741 HANDCAR AND SHED: In 1953-54, the ventilated 740 handcar was combined with a tool shed. The tool shed had a gray sheet metal base, white metal sides and a red plastic roof.

VG-C6	EX-C7	LN-C8	Scarcity
100	150	225	6

747 FIGURE 8 TRESTLE SET: This uncataloged trestle set was made of heavy cardboard. A total of 106 pieces are included. The values listed below are for unpunched sheets of parts in their original box.

VG-C6	EX-C7	LN-C8	Scarcity
10	20	30	4

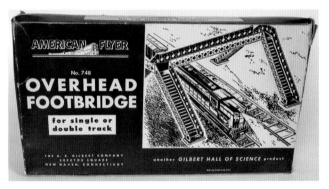

748 OVERHEAD FOOT BRIDGE: Gilbert sold this sheet metal structure, produced by Colber, in 1951-52.

748 (Type I): Some of the bridges were bluish-silver.

VG-C6	EX-C7	LN-C8	Scarcity
30	40	60	5

748 (Type II): Others were painted gray.

VG-C6	EX-C7	LN-C8	Scarcity
10	20	35	4

748 GIRDER, TRESTLE AND TOWER BRIDGE: This
uncataloged cardboard bridge was produced in 1958.

VG-C6	EX-C7	LN-C8	Scarcity
50	125	200	7

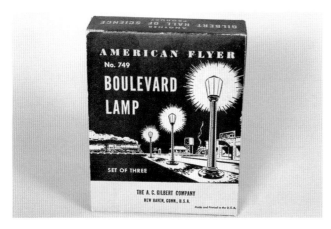

749 STREET LAMP SET: Three gold-colored plastic lamp
posts came in this set, which was sold from 1950 through
1952. A nylon globe covered the bulb on these lamps.

VG-C6	EX-C7	LN-C8	Scarcity
10	15	25	1

750 TRESTLE BRIDGE: This attractive bridge with
detailed steelwork was sold from 1946 through 1956. Atop
the bridge was the same steel structure that served as the cab
of the 635 crane, now acting as a bridge tender's shanty.

750 (Type I): Some of the bridges were painted black.

VG-C6	EX-C7	LN-C8	Scarcity
20	50	80	5

750 (Type II): Other bridges were painted silver.

VG-C6	EX-C7	LN-C8	Scarcity
20	50	80	5

750 (Type III): Less common are bridges painted metallic
blue-gray.

VG-C6	EX-C7	LN-C8	Scarcity
20	50	80	6

751 LOG LOADER: Fairly sophisticated, and interesting
to watch, this accessory was available from 1946 through
1950. It was designed to be used in conjunction with
American Flyer's various log dumping cars.

751 (Type I): The 1946-47 log loaders had yellow painted
Bakelite bases.

VG-C6	EX-C7	LN-C8	Scarcity
50	125	250	7

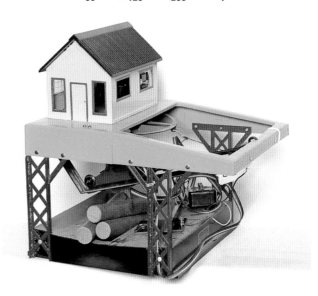

751 (Type II): Later editions of the accessories had
unpainted black Bakelite bases.

VG-C6	EX-C7	LN-C8	Scarcity
40	100	200	6

751A OPERATING LOG LOADER: The revised operating
log loader was first offered in 1951 and was available
through 1953.

VG-C6	EX-C7	LN-C8	Scarcity
50	125	225	6

752 SEABOARD COALER: This towering accessory was
sold from 1946 through 1950. The clamshell bucket of
this accessory was lowered into the car below, where it

Values for each condition are in U.S. dollars. | **Scarcity** = Scale from 1-8 with 8 being the hardest to find.

195

closed and lifted the material to the upper bin. Gravity caused the coal to flow into a car on the adjacent track.

VG-C6	EX-C7	LN-C8	Scarcity
100	200	325	7

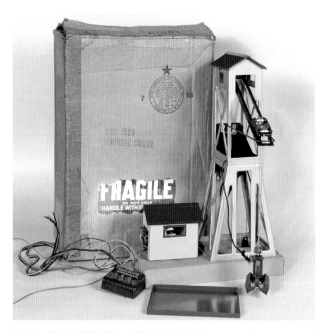

752A SEABOARD COALER: This revised version of the coal loader was available in 1951-52. The action was similar to that of the 752.

VG-C6	EX-C7	LN-C8	Scarcity
100	200	325	7

753 SINGLE TRESTLE BRIDGE: This 1952 gray-painted sheet metal bridge was well detailed and illuminated.

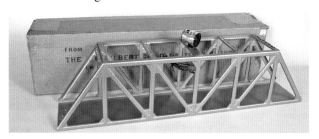

753 (Type I): The bridge was cataloged and produced with a rotating beacon at the center top of the span.

VG-C6	EX-C7	LN-C8	Scarcity
20	35	50	5

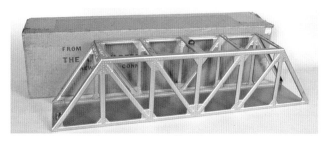

753 (Type II): An uncataloged version was also produced with a non-rotating red warning light.

VG-C6	EX-C7	LN-C8	Scarcity
20	35	50	5

753 MOUNTAIN, TUNNEL AND PASS SET: This uncataloged cardboard accessory dates from 1960. The four double-sided cutouts were decorated with photos of mountains.

VG-C6	EX-C7	LN-C8	Scarcity
20	35	50	5

754 DOUBLE TRESTLE BRIDGE: Sold from 1950 through 1952, this impressive illuminated bridge could accommodate to parallel tracks on its 24-inch long span.

754 (Type I): The 1950-1951 version was produced with a non-rotating red warning light.

VG-C6	EX-C7	LN-C8	Scarcity
60	125	250	6

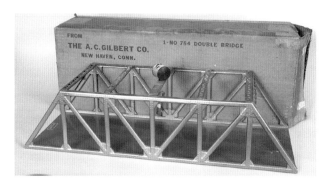

754 (Type II): The bridge was produced in 1952 with a rotating beacon at the center top of the span.

VG-C6	EX-C7	LN-C8	Scarcity
60	125	250	6

755 TALKING STATION: The Mystic talking station was cataloged from 1948 through 1950. It came with a 598 record, although the 599 could be used with it. A gray plastic controller marked "AMERICAN FLYER TALKING STATION" actuated the station's record player.

755 (Type I): Some of the stations had green roofs.

VG-C6	EX-C7	LN-C8	Scarcity
50	75	125	5

755 (Type II): A blue roof was used on other versions of the station.

VG-C6	EX-C7	LN-C8	Scarcity
75	125	200	6

758 SAM THE SEMAPHORE MAN: This accessory was produced in 1949. When control button is pressed, the figure "Sam" emerges from his shack and approaches the semaphore, which lowers, and the train stops. When the button is released the semaphore rises, "Sam" returns to his shack and the train resumes its journey.

758 (Type I): Some of the accessories have metal identification plates.

VG-C6	EX-C7	LN-C8	Scarcity
30	65	110	4

758 (Type II): Others are identified by decal.

VG-C6	EX-C7	LN-C8	Scarcity
30	65	110	4

758A SAM THE SEMAPHORE MAN: This accessory was revised for 1950 and remained in the line through 1956. The action remained the same, but now a two-button controller was used. The red button caused "Sam" to emerge, while the green restarted the train and made "Sam" retreat to his shack. A circuit is included to prevent the cycling of the reverse unit.

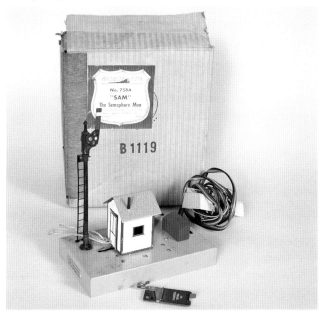

758A (Type I): Some of the accessories had green bases.

VG-C6	EX-C7	LN-C8	Scarcity
35	75	125	5

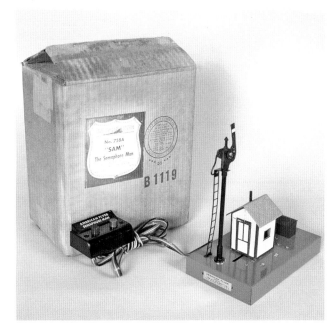

758A (Type II): Others used a gray base.

VG-C6	EX-C7	LN-C8	Scarcity
35	75	125	5

759 BELL DANGER SIGNAL: This flashing grade crossing signal included a warning bell which was housed in a shanty. The accessory was furnished with two 696 track trips.

759 (Type I): Some of the accessories had a green die-cast base and a black roof.

VG-C6	EX-C7	LN-C8	Scarcity
25	50	85	4

759 (Type II): Others reversed those covers, having a black die-cast base and a green roof.

VG-C6	EX-C7	LN-C8	Scarcity
25	50	85	4

759 (Type III): A dark green die-cast base and light green roof were features of other of the accessories.

VG-C6	EX-C7	LN-C8	Scarcity
25	50	85	4

Values for each condition are in U.S. dollars. | **Scarcity** = Scale from 1-8 with 8 being the hardest to find.

197

759 (Type IV): Others featured a black roof and dark green die-cast base.

VG-C6	EX-C7	LN-C8	Scarcity
25	50	85	4

759 (Type V): A later version of the accessory used a green sheet metal base and black roof.

VG-C6	EX-C7	LN-C8	Scarcity
25	50	85	4

759 (Type VI): Some were produced with both the sheet metal base and the roof painted green.

VG-C6	EX-C7	LN-C8	Scarcity
25	50	85	4

760 AUTOMATIC HIGHWAY FLASHER: 📷 This popular 1949-56 accessory was mounted on a gray-painted die-cast base. Furnished with a 696 track trip, a passing train activated the flashing lights mounted near the crossbuck.

VG-C6	EX-C7	LN-C8	Scarcity
10	20	45	4

761 AUTOMATIC SEMAPHORE: This die-cast base illuminated operating semaphore came with two 697 track trips and a warning tag reading "CAUTION—Do not allow train to stand on track trip at any time or coil may be-come overheated."

VG-C6	EX-C7	LN-C8	Scarcity
25	50	75	4

760 AUTOMATIC HIGHWAY FLASHER

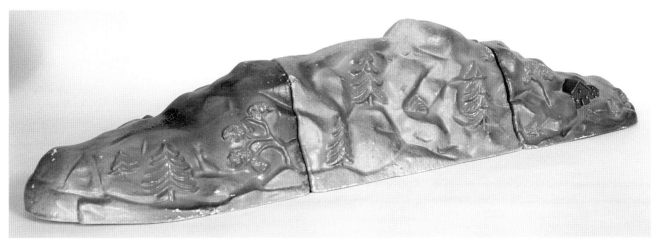

763 MOUNTAIN SET

762 TWO IN ONE WHISTLE: This 1949-50 billboard, which advertised American Flyer's sister company "ERECTOR," had a unique operating feature—it created two different whistle sounds. One was nearby, the other distant—the two button control allowed the operator to select the desired sound.

VG-C6	EX-C7	LN-C8	Scarcity
40	85	125	5

763 MOUNTAIN SET: 📷 This three-piece molded composition board mountain was sold in 1949-50. It was designed so it could be used as a continuous mountain range, or separated, allowing the track to pass through "cuts."

VG-C6	EX-C7	LN-C8	Scarcity
50	100	175	5

764 EXPRESS OFFICE: This illuminated gray sheet metal building was cataloged in 1950 and 1951.

764 (Type I): Some of the medium gray buildings were attached to green bases.

VG-C6	EX-C7	LN-C8	Scarcity
60	100	200	6

764 (Type II): A gray base was used with other medium gray Express Offices.

VG-C6	EX-C7	LN-C8	Scarcity
60	100	200	6

764 (Type III): A light gray building also came with a green base. Rather than the metal identification plate used with Type I and II, this version used a decal.

VG-C6	EX-C7	LN-C8	Scarcity
50	85	160	5

766 ANIMATED STATION: This 1952-54 station, with a sign reading "GUILFORD," was furnished with a 735 special passenger car. The two units worked in conjunction, allowing two male and two female passengers to shuttle to and from the coach. The special controller was labeled "AMERICAN FLYER ANIMATED STATION."

766 (Type I): As first offered, the station was cream and had a gray base and maroon roof. The figures were metal and their bases were painted gray to match the platform.

VG-C6	EX-C7	LN-C8	Scarcity
Too rarely traded to accurately establish pricing.			

766 (Type II): Painting the base of the metal figures was a process that was soon stopped. The station changed to white, but the roof remained maroon and the base gray.

VG-C6	EX-C7	LN-C8	Scarcity
65	125	250	5

Values for each condition are in U.S. dollars. | **Scarcity** = Scale from 1-8 with 8 being the hardest to find.

199

766 (Type III): Later in 1952, the stations were white and had a green base and red roof. These came with plastic passengers and remained the norm through 1954.

VG-C6	EX-C7	LN-C8	Scarcity
50	100	200	5

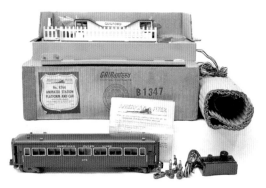

K766 ANIMATED STATION: In 1953, the animated station came with the knuckle-coupler equipped 975. It continued in this form through 1955. The station was white and had a green base and red roof. It came with plastic passengers.

VG-C6	EX-C7	LN-C8	Scarcity
50	100	200	5

767 ROADSIDE DINER: This 1950-54 accessory was based on a yellow heavyweight passenger car body. The red advertising on the diner sides promoted "Television every nite" and a wire TV antenna—often missing today—extended from the roof.

767 (Type I): Unpainted yellow plastic bodies were used in 1950 and 1951.

VG-C6	EX-C7	LN-C8	Scarcity
40	75	125	5

767 (Type II): The bodies were painted yellow from 1952 through 1954.

VG-C6	EX-C7	LN-C8	Scarcity
50	95	150	6

768 OIL SUPPLY DEPOT: This 1950 accessory mounted two Shell tank car bodies and a white sheet metal shack on a green sheet metal base, along with some simulated piping.

VG-C6	EX-C7	LN-C8	Scarcity
40	75	125	5

768G OIL SUPPLY DEPOT: From 1951 through 1953, Gulf logo decals were used on the tank car bodies of the oil supply depot. The accessory was otherwise identical to the 768.

VG-C6	EX-C7	LN-C8	Scarcity
55	100	175	6

769 REVOLVING AIRCRAFT BEACON: This red and gray plastic illuminated accessory was sold in 1950. Hot air rising from the special dimple-topped bulb at the top of the 12-inch tall accessory caused the beacon to slowly revolve. Produced by Colber for Gilbert.

769 (Type I): Some of these had black plastic lamp socket enclosures.

VG-C6	EX-C7	LN-C8	Scarcity
15	30	50	4

769 (Type II): Gray socket enclosures were used on others.

VG-C6	EX-C7	LN-C8	Scarcity
15	30	50	4

769A REVOLVING AIRCRAFT BEACON: In 1951, a revised beacon was issued with a green base. It remained in the product line through 1956. It too operated by the rising hot air of the bulb.

769A (Type I): The 1951-52 version of the accessory, also made by Colber, shared construction features with the 769.

VG-C6	EX-C7	LN-C8	Scarcity
20	40	65	4

769A (Type II): Some of the new Gilbert-produced beacons had dark gray towers. A metal shed was attached to the base, and a green light socket housing was used.

VG-C6	EX-C7	LN-C8	Scarcity
20	40	65	4

769A (Type III): A lighter gray tower and metal shed was used on some beacons with gray light socket housings.

VG-C6	EX-C7	LN-C8	Scarcity
20	40	65	4

769A (Type IV): Some beacons featured a combination of a dark gray tower and plastic sheds.

VG-C6	EX-C7	LN-C8	Scarcity
20	40	65	4

770 LOADING PLATFORM: This 1950-52 animated accessory had a green sheet metal base and yellow "conveyor." A red-shirted figure appeared to move the four boxes or milk cans supplied with the 770. This accessory could be used in conjunction with the 732 baggage or 734 boxcars, neither of which came with this item. The unit did come with a control button lettered "AMERICAN FLYER 770 PLATFORM."

VG-C6	EX-C7	LN-C8	Scarcity
30	60	90	4

770 GIRDER TRESTLE SET: This uncataloged 1960 accessory consisted of heavy cardboard with photographic overlays on each side the 30 trestle bents, 30 crossties and four bridge sides.

VG-C6	EX-C7	LN-C8	Scarcity
5	15	20	1

771 OPERATING STOCKYARD: Operating cattle corral, with 736 stock car, was sold from 1950 through 1954. It came with four brown and four black plastic cows with white-painted heads and a remote control lettered "AMERICAN FLYER STOCK YARD." The "brushes" on the bottom of the cars could be black, gray or red.

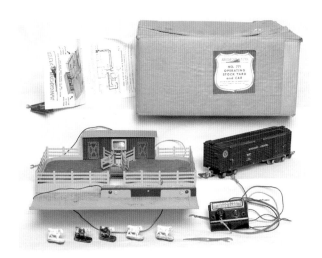

772 WATER TOWER: This bubbling tower was initially made by the Colber Corp. of Irvington, N.J., and sold by American Flyer. An improved version, produced by Gilbert was made later, resulting in two major—and several minor—variations during the accessories' 1950-57 production run.

771 (Type I): Most of the accessories had green bases. A black mat was used in the bottom of the corral. The yellow trim on the barn doors of this version was connected.

VG-C6	EX-C7	LN-C8	Scarcity
40	75	125	3

771 (Type II): Other versions were identical to the Type I, except a white mat was used in the bottom of the corral.

VG-C6	EX-C7	LN-C8	Scarcity
40	75	125	3

771 (Type III): Others differed from the Type I only in that the yellow trim lines on the barn doors was not connected.

VG-C6	EX-C7	LN-C8	Scarcity
40	75	125	3

771 (Type IV): Some of the operating stockyards were produced with a base painted blue.

VG-C6	EX-C7	LN-C8	Scarcity
50	100	150	5

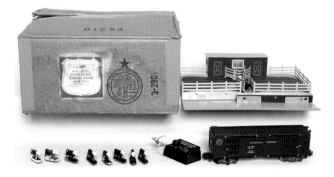

K771 OPERATING STOCKYARD AND CAR: In 1953, the operating stockyard accessory was revised to include a knuckle coupler-equipped 976 operating cattle car. The base of the accessory was painted green and it came with four brown and four black plastic cows with white-painted heads and a remote control lettered "AMERICAN FLYER STOCK YARD." The "brushes" on the bottom of the cars could be black, gray or red.

VG-C6	EX-C7	LN-C8	Scarcity
50	100	150	5

772 (Type I): Some of the 1950-52 production included a gray tank mounted on a red tower and base.

VG-C6	EX-C7	LN-C8	Scarcity
30	50	75	5

772 (Type II): Other towers of the 1950-52 period had a red tank and gray tower and base.

VG-C6	EX-C7	LN-C8	Scarcity
30	50	75	5

772 (Type III): The Gilbert-produced 1953-57 version had a notably larger water tank decorated in a checkerboard pattern. Its dark gray supporting structure, along with a metal shack, were attached to a green base.

VG-C6	EX-C7	LN-C8	Scarcity
40	75	125	6

772 (Type IV): Some of the Gilbert-produced large checkerboard tanks had gray bases and black towers.

VG-C6	EX-C7	LN-C8	Scarcity
40	75	125	6

772 (Type V): The final version of this tower had a checkerboard tank supported by a black tower. A white plastic shack was at the base.

VG-C6	EX-C7	LN-C8	Scarcity
50	100	175	6

773 OIL DERRICK: Another of the 1950-52 Colber-produced Gilbert sold accessories was this bubbling oil derrick. Heat from the lamp mounted in the base makes the liquid inside the tube bubble. This accessory is prone to warping.

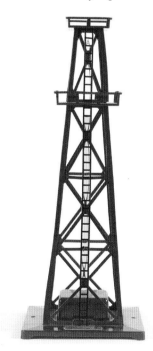

773 (Type I): Some of the derricks had both a red base and tower.

VG-C6	EX-C7	LN-C8	Scarcity
40	100	150	4

773 (Type II): Others had a gray base and tower.

VG-C6	EX-C7	LN-C8	Scarcity
40	100	150	4

773 (Type III): A red tower with an orange and blue "GULF" logo has been reported to exist.

VG-C6	EX-C7	LN-C8	Scarcity
Too rarely traded to accurately establish pricing.			

774 FLOODLIGHT TOWER: This illuminated floodlight tower was initially made by the Colber Corp. of Irvington, N.J., and sold by American Flyer. An improved version, produced by Gilbert was made later, resulting in two major—and several minor—variations during the accessories' 1951-57 production run.

774 (Type I): The first towers produced in 1951 had a red base and gray plastic tower and platform. Included was painted plastic workman with a wrench on the ladder.

VG-C6	EX-C7	LN-C8	Scarcity
Too rarely traded to accurately establish pricing.			

774 (Type II): The balance of the 1951-52 production omitted the workman, but continued to use a gray plastic tower and platform mounted on a red base.

VG-C6	EX-C7	LN-C8	Scarcity
20	50	100	5

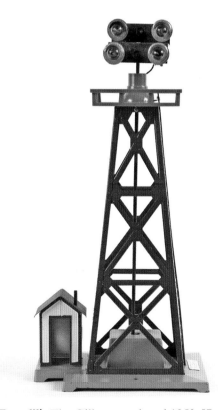

774 (Type III): The Gilbert-produced 1953-57 version had a metal supporting structure and irregularly shaped base with sheet metal shack. Some of these had a red supporting structure and a gray platform as well as a gray base.

VG-C6	EX-C7	LN-C8	Scarcity
20	50	100	5

Values for each condition are in U.S. dollars. | **Scarcity** = Scale from 1-8 with 8 being the hardest to find.

203

774 (Type IV): Other towers were identical to the Type III except the platform was painted silver.

VG-C6	EX-C7	LN-C8	Scarcity
20	50	100	5

774 (Type V): Still, others had a white platform, but otherwise duplicated the Type III.

VG-C6	EX-C7	LN-C8	Scarcity
20	50	100	5

774 (Type VI): A dark green platform was used on other red towers with gray bases.

VG-C6	EX-C7	LN-C8	Scarcity
20	50	100	5

774 (Type VII): A black platform was used in conjunction with a gray base and red tower on other towers.

VG-C6	EX-C7	LN-C8	Scarcity
20	50	100	5

775 BAGGAGE LOADING PLATFORM AND CAR:

This 1953-54 animated accessory came with a 734 boxcar and had a sheet metal base and yellow "conveyor." A red-shirted figure appeared to move the four boxes or milk cans supplied with the 775 into the waiting boxcar. The unit came with a control button lettered "AMERICAN FLYER LOADING PLATFORM."

775 (Type I): Some of these accessories had black sheet metal basis.

VG-C6	EX-C7	LN-C8	Scarcity
25	70	125	5

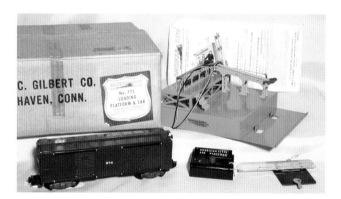

775 (Type II): A green base was used on other loaders.

VG-C6	EX-C7	LN-C8	Scarcity
25	70	125	5

K775 BAGGAGE LOADING PLATFORM AND CAR:
A knuckle coupler-equipped 974 boxcar was furnished with the loading platform from 1953 through 1955, resulting in a number change to K775. The platform had a green sheet metal base and yellow "conveyor." A red-shirted figure appeared to move the four boxes or milk cans supplied with the 775 into the waiting boxcar. The unit came with a control button lettered "AMERICAN FLYER LOADING PLATFORM."

VG-C6	EX-C7	LN-C8	Scarcity
35	80	125	5

778 STREET LAMP SET: This set of three street lamps was sold from 1953 through 1956. The sets included one plain lamp, and one each with mailbox and fire alarm box.

VG-C6	EX-C7	LN-C8	Scarcity
10	20	30	5

779 OIL DRUM LOADER: This largely plastic operating accessory was cataloged in 1955 and 1956. The metal barrels were tipped onto the forklift, which transports them to a rail car (not included). The accessory was activated by a controller lettered "AMERICAN FLYER OIL DRUM LOADER."

VG-C6	EX-C7	LN-C8	Scarcity
50	85	150	5

780 RAILROAD TRESTLE SET: From 1953 through 1956, Gilbert sold thousands of this 24- or 26-piece orange trestle set. Track locks were included with the set.

VG-C6	EX-C7	LN-C8	Scarcity
5	10	15	1

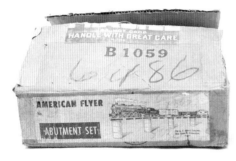

781 RAILROAD ABUTMENT SET: This 1953 accessory included 62 simulated concrete abutments in three sizes, as well as 26 track locks.

VG-C6	EX-C7	LN-C8	Scarcity
25	50	75	5

782 RAILROAD ABUTMENT SET: This set, also made in 1953, included 48 extra abutment sections to expand the 781.

VG-C6	EX-C7	LN-C8	Scarcity
50	100	150	7

783 HI-TRESTLE SECTIONS: Twelve orange plastic trestle piers were included in this 1952-56 accessory. Together with the included dozen track locks, this could extend the 780.

VG-C6	EX-C7	LN-C8	Scarcity
10	30	60	5

784 RAILROAD HUMP SET: This hard to find 1955 accessory is totally unremarkable without its original box. The item consisted of three sections of 700 straight track, two sections of 702 curve track, one 730 bumper, one 706 remote-control uncoupler, six 693 track locks, six plastic trestle piers, and one 678 left or 679 right remote-control switch. The original packaging and instruction sheet is key to the value.

VG-C6	EX-C7	LN-C8	Scarcity
75	150	300	7

785 COAL LOADER: This imposing structure was sold in 1955 and 1956. The operation, activated by a three-button controller lettered "AMERICAN FLYER COAL LOADER," began with the clamshell bucket lowering into a loaded car adjacent to the tower, where it opened. The second button would close the bucket and hoist it into the structure, where it automatically opened. Depressing the third button would open a door, allowing the coal to flow into a car waiting beneath the tower.

VG-C6	EX-C7	LN-C8	Scarcity
125	225	325	7

787 LOG LOADER: This largely plastic operating log loader was sold in 1955 and 1956. Logs were raised by a cam, where they were picked up by a hook, which then transported them to a position above a waiting car and dropped them.

VG-C6	EX-C7	LN-C8	Scarcity
75	175	275	7

Values for each condition are in U.S. dollars. | **Scarcity** = Scale from 1-8 with 8 being the hardest to find.

205

788 SUBURBAN STATION: This unpainted white 1956 non-illuminated station had an unpainted green plastic roof and red chimney. It was similar to the 789 animated station.

788 (Type I): Some had a medium gray base.

VG-C6	EX-C7	LN-C8	Scarcity
10	30	50	7

788 (Type II): Others used a dark gray base.

VG-C6	EX-C7	LN-C8	Scarcity
10	30	50	7

789 STATION AND BAGGAGE SMASHER: This whimsical 1956-57 animated station included a porter, "Billy The Baggage Smasher," moving a trunk on a hand truck along the gray station platform. The building, which was not illuminated, was white with a green roof.

VG-C6	EX-C7	LN-C8	Scarcity
60	150	275	6

790 TRAINORAMA: These cardboard scenic backdrop panels, though uncataloged, were produced in 1953. Values below assume original packaging.

VG-C6	EX-C7	LN-C8	Scarcity
50	145	200	5

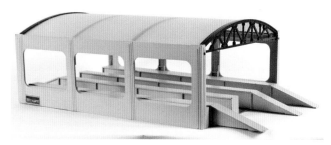

792 RAILROAD TERMINAL: This train shed was styled to serve as a companion to the 793, 794 or 799. The train shed, which could span up to three tracks, came with five matching tan platforms that could be positioned, as the operator desired. It was cataloged from 1954 through 1956.

VG-C6	EX-C7	LN-C8	Scarcity
50	150	220	6

793 UNION STATION: This large tan illuminated station with clock tower was cataloged in 1955 and 1956.

VG-C6	EX-C7	LN-C8	Scarcity
40	80	120	5

794 UNION STATION WITH TWO LAMPS: In 1954, this large illuminated station also included a clock tower and came with two gold-painted streetlights, one with a mailbox on the pole and the other with a fire alarm box.

VG-C6	EX-C7	LN-C8	Scarcity
50	150	250	5

795 UNION STATION AND TERMINAL: This 1954 item was a combination of the 792 and 793. Much of the value is in the original packaging.

VG-C6	EX-C7	LN-C8	Scarcity
100	300	525	7

799 AUTOMATIC TALKING STATION: This big illuminated station, sold in 1954 and 1956, included a record player and stop device. The mechanism stopped the train, the record played train sounds, and when it was finished playing, the train took off again.

VG-C6	EX-C7	LN-C8	Scarcity
40	150	225	5

1-1024A TRESTLE SET: This uncataloged 1952 combo pack consisted of a 747 figure eight trestle set, two sections of straight track and eight sections of curved track packed inside a single cardboard box.

VG-C6	EX-C7	LN-C8	Scarcity
10	20	45	3

22004 TRANSFORMER: This 40-Watt Bakelite transformer was available from 1959 through 1964.

22004 (Type I): As described previously.

VG-C6	EX-C7	LN-C8	Scarcity
2	5	10	1

22004 (Type II): Later transformers left the factory with paper labels highlighting that the transformers were circuit breaker equipped.

VG-C6	EX-C7	LN-C8	Scarcity
2	5	10	1

22006 TRANSFORMER: This 25-Watt transformer was produced in 1963.

VG-C6	EX-C7	LN-C8	Scarcity
2	5	10	1

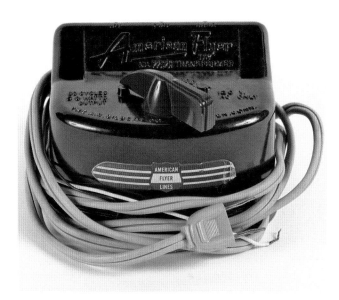

22020 TRANSFORMER: From 1957 through 1964, this 50-Watt Bakelite transformer with a built-in circuit breaker was available. The transformer was decorated with a paper red, white and blue American Flyer shield label.

VG-C6	EX-C7	LN-C8	Scarcity
2	3	5	1

22030 TRANSFORMER: From 1957 through 1964, this 100-Watt Bakelite transformer with built-in circuit breaker was available. The transformer was decorated with a paper red, white and blue American Flyer shield label.

VG-C6	EX-C7	LN-C8	Scarcity
5	10	20	2

22033 TRANSFORMER: This sheet metal 25-Watt transformer was produced in 1965.

VG-C6	EX-C7	LN-C8	Scarcity
2	3	5	1

22034 TRANSFORMER: This 110-Watt transformer was made in 1965.

22034 (Type I): Some of the transformers were labeled Gilbert-All Aboard.

VG-C6	EX-C7	LN-C8	Scarcity
5	10	15	3

Values for each condition are in U.S. dollars. | **Scarcity** = Scale from 1-8 with 8 being the hardest to find.

207

22034 (Type II): Others were labeled Gilbert-American Flyer.

VG-C6	EX-C7	LN-C8	Scarcity
5	10	15	3

22035 TRANSFORMER: From 1957 through 1964, this 175-Watt transformer graced the pages of the Flyer catalog. A circuit in the transformer prevented the cycling of locomotive reverse units unless the double pole center off switch on the transformer was used. The transformer was equipped with a manual-reset circuit breaker.

VG-C6	EX-C7	LN-C8	Scarcity
20	40	60	2

22040 TRANSFORMER: In 1957 and 1958, this 110-Watt transformer with red and green pilot lights was produced. The transformer was equipped with a "Dead Man's Control" throttle and built-in circuit breaker.

VG-C6	EX-C7	LN-C8	Scarcity
10	20	30	3

22050 TRANSFORMER: Sold in 1957 and 1958, this 175-Watt transformer was equipped with red and green pilot lights and an on/off toggle switch. The transformer was equipped with a "Dead Man's Control" throttle and built-in circuit breaker.

VG-C6	EX-C7	LN-C8	Scarcity
15	25	40	3

22060 TRANSFORMER: In 1957 and 1958, this dual throttle 175-Watt transformer with red and green pilot lights was produced. The transformer was equipped with two "Dead Man's Control" throttles and built-in circuit breakers.

VG-C6	EX-C7	LN-C8	Scarcity
15	25	40	3

22080 TRANSFORMER: The big power supply offered in 1957 and 1958 was this 300-Watt dual throttle unit. Both throttles were of the "Dead Man's Control" type and were protected by built-in circuit breakers. Meters monitored the power output, and the transformer was equipped with pilot lights and an on/off toggle switch.

VG-C6	EX-C7	LN-C8	Scarcity
40	100	165	5

22090 TRANSFORMER: The 1959-64 top transformer was this 350-Watt behemoth. Two throttles varied the power output, which was protected by a manual-reset circuit breaker. A special circuit prevented the automatic cycling of the reverse units unless the "ON OFF ON" switches were used.

VG-C6	EX-C7	LN-C8	Scarcity
50	100	175	6

23021 IMITATION GRASS: This plastic bag contained one and a half pounds of dyed sawdust simulating grass and was sold from 1957 through 1959.

VG-C6	EX-C7	LN-C8	Scarcity
5	15	25	3

23022 SCENERY GRAVEL: This blue-lettered white paper bag of gravel was sold from 1957 through 1959.

VG-C6	EX-C7	LN-C8	Scarcity
5	15	25	3

23023 IMITATION COAL: This eight-ounce bag of fine artificial coal was sold from 1957 through 1959.

VG-C6	EX-C7	LN-C8	Scarcity
5	10	15	4

23024 RAINBOW WIRE: Twenty-five feet of four-color (yellow, red, green and black) ribbon wire was sold under this number from 1957 through 1964.

VG-C6	EX-C7	LN-C8	Scarcity
4	7	10	4

23025 SMOKE CARTRIDGES: This package, sold from 1957 through 1959, contained 12 plastic capsules of smoke fluid and one small funnel.

VG-C6	EX-C7	LN-C8	Scarcity
5	10	15	1

23026 SERVICE KIT: This 1959-64 kit contained the basics for maintaining your Gilbert empire: oil, grease, track cleaning fluid, brush, sanding sticks, commutator cleaning stick, tube cleaners, and instruction manual.

VG-C6	EX-C7	LN-C8	Scarcity
5	15	25	4

23036 MONEY SAVER KIT: This counter display contained 12 bottles of track cleaner and smoke. It was available to dealers in 1960, 1962 and 1964. Much of the value is in the packaging of this item.

VG-C6	EX-C7	LN-C8	Scarcity
50	100	200	7

23027 TRACK CLEANING FLUID: 1957-59, bottle with red and white label, claimed to be "non-toxic, non-corrosive."

VG-C6	EX-C7	LN-C8	Scarcity
1	2	4	1

23040 MOUNTAIN, TUNNEL AND PASS SET: This Styrofoam accessory was cataloged in 1958.

VG-C6	EX-C7	LN-C8	Scarcity
Too rarely traded to accurately establish pricing.			

23028 SMOKE FLUID DISPENSER: This squeeze tube of smoke fluid for S and HO locomotives was sold from 1960 through 1964.

VG-C6	EX-C7	LN-C8	Scarcity
1	3	5	1

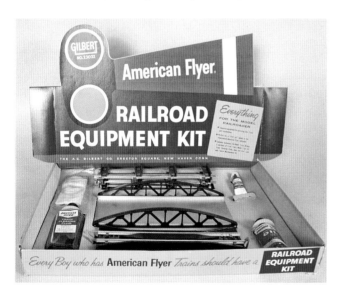

23249 TUNNEL: This 11-inch long fiber tunnel with house and winding road was cataloged from 1957 through 1967.

VG-C6	EX-C7	LN-C8	Scarcity
10	25	40	4

23561 BILLBOARD HORN: From 1957 through 1959, Gilbert sold this plastic billboard with horn. The billboard displayed an image of an Alco PA-PB-PA triple diesel with an "AMERICAN FLYER Made By Gilbert" legend.

VG-C6	EX-C7	LN-C8	Scarcity
10	30	50	4

23032 RAILROAD EQUIPMENT KIT: This 1960-61 assortment included a truss bridge, rerailer, five sections of straight track, re-railer, track cleaning fluid, grease, oil, and instruction manual. The box is the key to the values below.

VG-C6	EX-C7	LN-C8	Scarcity
30	50	100	7

23568 WHISTLING BILLBOARD: A whistling counterpart was offered from 1957 through 1964. Also plastic, the sign on this billboard showed the 4-8-4 Northern steam locomotive with an "AMERICAN FLYER Made By Gilbert" legend.

VG-C6	EX-C7	LN-C8	Scarcity
10	30	50	4

Values for each condition are in U.S. dollars. | **Scarcity** = Scale from 1-8 with 8 being the hardest to find.

209

23571 TRUSS BRIDGE: The base of this 1957-64 bridge was stamped steel. The arcing truss sides were black, orange or red plastic.

VG-C6	EX-C7	LN-C8	Scarcity
10	20	30	1

23581 GIRDER BRIDGE: This 10-inch long bridge with sheet metal base and die-cast sides was sold from 1957 through 1964.

23581 (Type I): The sides of some bridges were painted silver and the bridge was lettered "AMERICAN FLYER" in black.

VG-C6	EX-C7	LN-C8	Scarcity
10	20	30	4

23581 (Type II): Some bridges were painted black and lettered "AMERICAN FLYER" in white.

VG-C6	EX-C7	LN-C8	Scarcity
10	20	30	4

23581 (Type III): Other black-painted bridges had white "AMERICAN FLYER LINES" lettering.

VG-C6	EX-C7	LN-C8	Scarcity
10	20	30	4

23586 WAYSIDE STATION: This sheet metal and die-cast station was sold from 1957 through 1959. It was decorated with two figures and a green cart. Two green-painted die-cast posts supported a red roof above a yellow bench attached to a gray sheet metal base.

VG-C6	EX-C7	LN-C8	Scarcity
25	85	110	5

23589 PASSENGER AND FREIGHT STATION: This illuminated, uncataloged 1959 "MYSTIC" station had a white building with crackle-green finished roof and gray base.

VG-C6	EX-C7	LN-C8	Scarcity
15	35	60	4

23590 CONTROL TOWER: Bachmann Bros. of Philadelphia produced this tan plastic control tower for Gilbert from 1957 through 1959. "CEDAR HILL JUNCTION" signs were on the roof. Bachmann also sold the same tower in their "Plasticville" line.

VG-C6	EX-C7	LN-C8	Scarcity
25	75	125	5

23596 OPERATING WATER TANK: Like its predecessor the plastic spout of this 1957-58 version of the burnt orange water tank could be lowered by remote-control, using the included "AMERICAN FLYER WATER TANK" on operating button. A yellow arrow decal was installed on the roof. The base was green and the support legs were gray.

VG-C6	EX-C7	LN-C8	Scarcity
25	60	100	4

23598 TALKING STATION RECORD: This replacement record for 799 and 23786 talking stations was sold from 1957 through 1959.

VG-C6	EX-C7	LN-C8	Scarcity
5	10	20	4

23599 TALKING STATION RECORD: This 1957 double-sided record includes dispatcher and conductor conversations and railroad sounds. Intended for use in the 799 station, this is a scarce record.

VG-C6	EX-C7	LN-C8	Scarcity
10	25	40	5

23600 CROSSING GATE WITH BELL: Gilbert offered this operating illuminated crossing gate with bell in 1957 and 1958. The shanty held the ringing bell mechanism.

VG-C6	EX-C7	LN-C8	Scarcity
20	50	100	5

23601 CROSSING GATE: This 1959-62 crossing gate, with red and white watchman's shanty, came on a gray plastic base with roadway. This accessory was triggered by an operator-controlled push button.

VG-C6	EX-C7	LN-C8	Scarcity
25	50	75	5

23602 CROSSING GATE: This 1963-64 crossing gate, with red and white watchman's shanty, came on a gray plastic base without roadway. This accessory was triggered by an operator-controlled push button.

VG-C6	EX-C7	LN-C8	Scarcity
25	50	75	5

23750 TRESTLE BRIDGE: This attractive bridge with detailed steelwork was sold from 1957 through 1961.

Atop the bridge was the same steel structure that served as the cab of the 635 crane, now acting as a bridge tender's shanty.

VG-C6	EX-C7	LN-C8	Scarcity
25	50	75	4

23758 SAM THE SEMAPHORE MAN: This accessory was a 758A packaged for sale in 1957 with a five-digit number. The action remained the same, but now a two-button controller was used. The red button caused "Sam" to emerge, while the green restarted the train, and made "Sam" retreat to his shack. A circuit is included to prevent the cycling of the reverse unit.

VG-C6	EX-C7	LN-C8	Scarcity
30	60	100	5

23759 BELL DANGER SIGNAL: This 1957 through 1960 flashing grade crossing signal included a warning bell which was housed in a shanty. The accessory was furnished with a 696 track trip.

23759 (Type I): The 1956 version of this accessory had plastic paper identification.

VG-C6	EX-C7	LN-C8	Scarcity
15	35	60	4

23759 (Type II): From 1957 to 1960, the signal had a dark green base and a brown shack.

VG-C6	EX-C7	LN-C8	Scarcity
15	35	60	4

23760 AUTOMATIC HIGHWAY FLASHER: This popular 1957-60 accessory was mounted on a gray-

Values for each condition are in U.S. dollars. | **Scarcity** = Scale from 1-8 with 8 being the hardest to find.

211

painted die-cast base. It was furnished with a 696 track trip for conventional track and one XA16A593 flasher trip for Pike Master track, a passing train activated the flashing lights mounted near the crossbuck.

VG-C6	EX-C7	LN-C8	Scarcity
10	25	45	4

23761 AUTOMATIC SEMAPHORE: This die-cast base illuminated operating semaphore was a five-digit version of the 761. It came with a warning tag reading "CAUTION—Do not allow train to stand on track trip at any time or coil may be-come overheated."

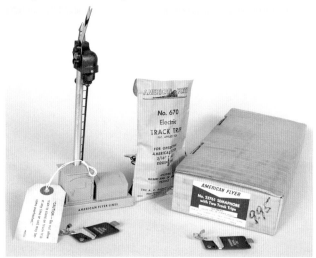

23761 (Type I): The early versions of the semaphore came with track trips.

VG-C6	EX-C7	LN-C8	Scarcity
25	50	75	4

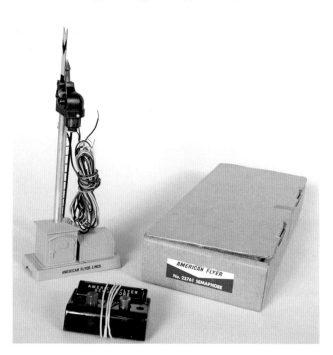

23761 (Type II): Later versions came with push-button controls.

VG-C6	EX-C7	LN-C8	Scarcity
25	50	75	4

23763 BELL DANGER SIGNAL: Sold from 1961 through 1964, this warning signal and brown sheet metal shanty was mounted on a light green plastic base. The approaching train, through either of the supplied trips (one 696 track trip and one XA16A593) activated the lights and bell.

VG-C6	EX-C7	LN-C8	Scarcity
15	35	60	4

23764 FLASHER SIGNAL: The gray die-cast base of this 1961-64 accessory supported a flashing grade crossing signal with crossbuck. It was furnished with one 696 track trip and one XA16A593 flasher trip for Pike Master track.

VG-C6	EX-C7	LN-C8	Scarcity
10	20	35	4

23769 REVOLVING AIRCRAFT BEACON: Between 1957 and 1964, this Gilbert-produced beacon had a dark gray tower. A metal shed was attached to the base and a gray light socket housing was used. Hot air rising from the dimple-topped bulb made the beacon housing revolve.

VG-C6	EX-C7	LN-C8	Scarcity
15	45	75	4

23771 OPERATING STOCKYARD AND CAR: The stockyard was given a five-digit number in 1957, which it used through 1961. The accessory included a knuckle coupler-equipped 976 operating cattle car. The base of the accessory was painted green, and it came with four brown and four black plastic cows with white-painted heads and a remote-control lettered "AMERICAN FLYER STOCK YARD." The "brushes" on the bottom of the cars could be black, gray or red.

VG-C6	EX-C7	LN-C8	Scarcity
30	60	125	5

23772 WATER TOWER: From 1957 through 1964, Gilbert-produced this large water tank decorated in a checkerboard pattern. Its black supporting structure, along with a metal shack, was attached to a gray plastic base. A bulb heated liquid in a tube at the center of the tower, causing it to bubble.

VG-C6	EX-C7	LN-C8	Scarcity
50	100	200	6

23774 FLOODLIGHT TOWER: Produced by Gilbert from 1957 through 1964, this illuminated floodlight tower had a gray plastic base and a white plastic shack. Its gray platform supported four stamped floodlights.

VG-C6	EX-C7	LN-C8	Scarcity
25	50	100	6

23778 STREET LAMP SET: This set of three street lamps was sold from 1957 through 1964. The sets included one plain lamp, and one each with mailbox and fire alarm box.

VG-C6	EX-C7	LN-C8	Scarcity
10	25	40	4

23779 OIL DRUM LOADER: This five-digit version of the 779 largely plastic operating accessory was cataloged from 1957 through 1961. The metal barrels were tipped onto the forklift, which transports them to a rail car (not included). The accessory was activated by a controller lettered "AMERICAN FLYER OIL DRUM LOADER."

VG-C6	EX-C7	LN-C8	Scarcity
50	100	175	5

23779 OIL DRUM LOADER

Values for each condition are in U.S. dollars. | **Scarcity** = Scale from 1-8 with 8 being the hardest to find.

213

23786 AUTOMATIC TALKING STATION: This non-illuminated talking station was sold from 1957 through 1959. It had an unpainted white plastic building, green roof and gray platform. Inside was a record player and record.

VG-C6	EX-C7	LN-C8	Scarcity
75	150	250	7

23787 REMOTE-CONTROL LOG LOADER: This largely plastic operating log loader was sold from 1957 through 1960. A cam with a hook that transported them to a position above a waiting car dropped them, picked them up and raised logs.

VG-C6	EX-C7	LN-C8	Scarcity
75	150	300	7

23788 SUBURBAN STATION: This unpainted white 1957-64 non-illuminated station had an unpainted green plastic roof, red chimney and gray base. It was similar to the 789 animated station.

VG-C6	EX-C7	LN-C8	Scarcity
10	30	50	4

23780 GABE THE LAMPLIGHTER: This very desirable accessory was offered in 1958 and 1959. The action of the accessory was as follows. "Gabe" climbs the tower one step at a time, he reaches the top, and the four floodlights flash on and off, and "Gabe" slides back down the ladder. Another switch allows the lights to stay on. The black plastic controller had green, copper and red buttons, and was lettered "AMERICAN FLYER LAMPLIGHTER" in white.

23780 (Type I): Most of these accessories had dark green bases and catwalks.

VG-C6	EX-C7	LN-C8	Scarcity
300	500	800	8

23780 (Type II): Some had emerald green bases and catwalks.

VG-C6	EX-C7	LN-C8	Scarcity
750	1,100	1,500	8

23785 OPERATING COAL LOADER: The five-digit version of this imposing structure was sold between 1957 and 1960. The operation, activated by a three-button controller lettered "AMERICAN FLYER COAL LOADER," began with the clamshell bucket lowering into a loaded car adjacent to the tower, where it opened. The second button would close the bucket and hoist it into the structure, where it automatically opened. Depressing the third button would open a door, allowing the coal to flow into a car waiting beneath the tower.

VG-C6	EX-C7	LN-C8	Scarcity
125	250	375	6

23789 STATION & BAGGAGE SMASHER: The five-digit version of this animated station was sold in 1958 and 1959. It included a porter, "Billy The Baggage Smasher," moving a trunk on a hand truck along the gray station platform. The building, which was not illuminated, was white with a green roof.

VG-C6	EX-C7	LN-C8	Scarcity
50	150	250	5

23791 COW-ON-TRACK: One of Gilbert's more amusing accessories was this 1957-59 item. The green plastic base housed the mechanism that made the cow move onto the track at the operator's whim. When the cow was on the track, the approaching train would stop, resuming its travel when the cow was safely out of the way.

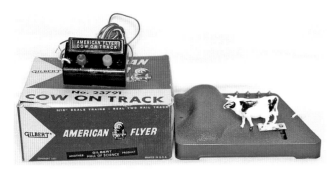

23791 (Type I): Some of the cows were black and white.

VG-C6	EX-C7	LN-C8	Scarcity
25	50	100	4

23791 (Type II): Other cows were brown and white.

VG-C6	EX-C7	LN-C8	Scarcity
25	50	100	4

23796 REMOTE-CONTROL SAWMILL: Cataloged first in 1957, this operating sawmill was available through 1964. A trolley moved a "log" past a simulated circular saw blade, and a hoist picks up the planks that have been "sawn," then drops them into the waiting rail car (not supplied with the sawmill).

VG-C6	EX-C7	LN-C8	Scarcity
100	200	300	6

23830 PIGGYBACK UNLOADER AND CAR: This beige, largely plastic, accessory was sold in 1959 and 1960. It came with a 24550 Monon flatcar with two trailers. Backing the car into the structure allows the manually operated mechanism to lift the trailer from the car and for it to roll to the ground. Reversing the action will reload the trailers onto the car.

VG-C6	EX-C7	LN-C8	Scarcity
15	30	60	5

25261 Snow scene curved panel

26101 SCENIC CURVE TRACK PANEL: In 1965-66, Gilbert sold hand-decorated green 17 x 17-inch plastic panels with attached Pike Master track sections. This particular panel included two sections of curved track, pre-painted gray roads, a plastic hill, three trees, various signs, a street lamp, and a telephone pole.

VG-C6	EX-C7	LN-C8	Scarcity
5	10	15	4

26121 SCENIC STRAIGHT TRACK PANEL: Scenic panels with straight track were also offered in 1965-66. It was decorated in a similar manner to 26261. During the production run, there were some variations in houses and decorations.

26121 (Type I): Some of the panels had a ranch-style house attached.

VG-C6	EX-C7	LN-C8	Scarcity
5	10	15	4

26121 (Type II): Others came with a model of a Colonial house.

VG-C6	EX-C7	LN-C8	Scarcity
5	10	15	4

Values for each condition are in U.S. dollars. | **Scarcity** = Scale from 1-8 with 8 being the hardest to find.

215

26122 SCENIC STRAIGHT PANEL WITH REMOTE-CONTROL WHISTLE
Sold in 1965 and 1966, this straight scenic panel included a remote-control whistle and control.

VG-C6	EX-C7	LN-C8	Scarcity
10	20	30	4

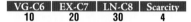
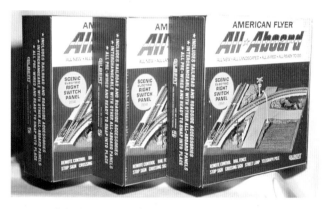

26141 SCENIC ELECTRIC RIGHT SWITCH PANEL
This 1965-66 scenic track panel included a right-hand Pike Master turnout.

VG-C6	EX-C7	LN-C8	Scarcity
7	15	25	4

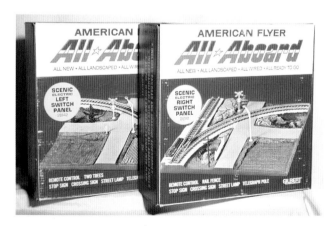

26142 SCENIC ELECTRIC LEFT SWITCH PANEL
This 1965-66 scenic track panel included a left-hand Pike Master turnout.

VG-C6	EX-C7	LN-C8	Scarcity
7	15	25	4

26151 SCENIC CROSSOVER PANEL
This 1965-66 track panel included a railroad bridge and 90-degree crossing.

VG-C6	EX-C7	LN-C8	Scarcity
5	10	15	4

26261: This snow-covered version of the 26101 was offered in 1966.

VG-C6	EX-C7	LN-C8	Scarcity
Too rarely traded to accurately establish pricing.			

26262: This snow-covered version of the 26121 was offered in 1966.

VG-C6	EX-C7	LN-C8	Scarcity
Too rarely traded to accurately establish pricing.			

26265: This snow-covered version of the 26151 was offered in 1966.

VG-C6	EX-C7	LN-C8	Scarcity
Too rarely traded to accurately establish pricing.			

26300 PIKE MASTER STRAIGHT TRACK
This 10-inch long section of straight track with 24 ties was sold from 1961 through 1964.

VG-C6	EX-C7	LN-C8	Scarcity
.10	.25	.50	1

26301 PIKE MASTER STRAIGHT TRACK
This short section of straight track with nine crossties was sold from 1961 through 1964.

VG-C6	EX-C7	LN-C8	Scarcity
.10	.25	.50	1

26302 PIKE MASTER STRAIGHT TERMINAL TRACK WITH UNCOUPLER
This 1961-64 section of track was both a terminal and manual uncoupler.

VG-C6	EX-C7	LN-C8	Scarcity
.50	1	2	1

26310 PIKE MASTER CURVE TRACK: This 12-inch long section of curved track with 26 ties was sold from 1961 through 1964.

VG-C6	EX-C7	LN-C8	Scarcity
.10	.20	.35	1

26320 PIKE MASTER RIGHT-HAND REMOTE SWITCH: This remote control turnout with controller was part of the 1961-64 Pike Master line.

VG-C6	EX-C7	LN-C8	Scarcity
6	9	12	1

26321 PIKE MASTER LEFT-HAND REMOTE SWITCH: This remote control turnout with controller was part of the 1961-64 Pike Master line.

VG-C6	EX-C7	LN-C8	Scarcity
6	9	12	1

26322 PIKE MASTER 90-DEGREE CROSSING: This was the 1961-64 Pike Master crossing.

VG-C6	EX-C7	LN-C8	Scarcity
1	2	3	1

26323 PIKE MASTER RIGHT-HAND MANUAL SWITCH: This manually operated turnout was part of the 1961-64 Pike Master line.

VG-C6	EX-C7	LN-C8	Scarcity
2	4	6	1

26324 PIKE MASTER LEFT-HAND MANUAL SWITCH: This manually operated turnout was part of the 1961-64 Pike Master line.

VG-C6	EX-C7	LN-C8	Scarcity
2	4	6	1

26340 PIKE MASTER STEEL TRACK PINS: From 1961-64, Gilbert sold these envelopes of steel pins for Pike Master track. Over time, quantities included in the package ranged from one to three dozen.

VG-C6	EX-C7	LN-C8	Scarcity
.40	.60	.80	1

26341 PIKE MASTER INSULATING TRACK PINS: From 1961-64, Gilbert sold these envelopes of insulating pins for Pike Master track. Included in the package were one dozen pins.

VG-C6	EX-C7	LN-C8	Scarcity
.40	.60	.80	1

26342 PIKE MASTER ADAPTER PINS: Four adapter pins were included in each of these 1961-64 packages.

VG-C6	EX-C7	LN-C8	Scarcity
.30	.45	.60	1

26343 PIKE MASTER TRACK LOCKS: This 1961-64 product was used to secure Pike Master track sections together when operating floor layouts. Originally packaged one dozen per package.

VG-C6	EX-C7	LN-C8	Scarcity
.30	.45	.60	1

26344 PIKE MASTER TRACK TERMINAL: Each of the two terminals in this 1961-64 package would attach to one rail.

VG-C6	EX-C7	LN-C8	Scarcity
.20	.30	.40	1

26415 TRACK ASSORTMENT PACK: This assortment of 72 various types of track sections were available to dealers in both 1960 and 1962.

VG-C6	EX-C7	LN-C8	Scarcity
Too rarely traded to accurately establish pricing.			

26419 ACCESSORY PACKAGE: This uncataloged retail counter display contained 12 straight and curved sections of track, lockons, a trestle set, uncoupler, and terminal track. All the contents are common; the value is in the packaging.

VG-C6	EX-C7	LN-C8	Scarcity
10	15	20	4

26425 TRACK ASSORTMENT PACK: This bulk pack of straight track was sold in 1960.

VG-C6	EX-C7	LN-C8	Scarcity
10	15	20	1

26428 ACCESSORY PACK: This uncataloged assortment was sold in 1958.

It included the 748 girder, trestle and tower bridge set, and eight sections of curved track.

VG-C6	EX-C7	LN-C8	Scarcity
Too rarely traded to accurately establish pricing.			

26520 KNUCKLE COUPLER KIT: From 1957 through 1964, Gilbert sold this envelope containing one pair of knuckle couplers with split shank, two rivets and a rivet-removing tool.

VG-C6	EX-C7	LN-C8	Scarcity
2	3	5	1

26521 KNUCKLE COUPLER KIT: This 1957-58 envelope contains 12 knuckle couplers, rivets and a rivet-removing tool.

VG-C6	EX-C7	LN-C8	Scarcity
5	10	15	7

26601 STRAIGHT FIBER ROADBED: This gray fiber roadbed for standard S-Gauge straight track was sold from 1959 through 1962.

VG-C6	EX-C7	LN-C8	Scarcity
.15	.50	.75	1

26602 CURVED FIBER ROADBED: Gray fiber roadbed was also sold for standard S-Gauge curved track in 1959, as well as 1961-62.

VG-C6	EX-C7	LN-C8	Scarcity
.15	.30	.50	1

Values for each condition are in U.S. dollars. | **Scarcity** = Scale from 1-8 with 8 being the hardest to find.

26670 TRACK TRIP: Offered in 1957 and 1958, the trip clipped to one rail and could be used to control block signals, turnouts, signals, etc.

VG-C6	EX-C7	LN-C8	Scarcity
5	10	20	1

26671 ELECTRIC TRACK TRIP: This 1959 device came with three 707 track terminals, two fiber track pins, and yellow and black wire. It acted as a relay to control accessories.

VG-C6	EX-C7	LN-C8	Scarcity
5	10	15	4

26672 ELECTRIC TRACK TRIP: In 1960, a revised relay was given a new number.

VG-C6	EX-C7	LN-C8	Scarcity
2	4	8	3

26673 ELECTRIC TRACK TRIP: This 1961-64 relay controlled two trains when operating on the same track.

VG-C6	EX-C7	LN-C8	Scarcity
2	4	8	3

26690 TRACK TERMINAL: This 1957-59 was identical to a 690 lockon but for the number printed on the envelope it originally came in.

VG-C6	EX-C7	LN-C8	Scarcity
.50	1.50	2	1

26691 STEEL TRACK PINS: This 12-pack of steel conventional track pins was sold from 1957 through 1960, and again in 1964.

VG-C6	EX-C7	LN-C8	Scarcity
.30	.50	.75	1

26692 FIBER TRACK PINS: This four pack of fiber conventional track pins was sold from 1957 through 1960, and again in 1964.

VG-C6	EX-C7	LN-C8	Scarcity
.20	.40	.60	1

26693 TRACK LOCKS: These locks, sold to secure conventional S-Gauge track sections when used in floor layouts, was offered from 1957 through 1960, then again in 1964. They were slightly thinner than the earlier, similar 693 locks. Originally packaged in one, two or three dozen lots. Priced by the dozen.

VG-C6	EX-C7	LN-C8	Scarcity
2	5	8	1

26700 STRAIGHT TRACK: When Gilbert adopted the five-digit number system in 1957, the 700 became the 26700, the number which the 10-inch long straight section was sold under through 1964.

VG-C6	EX-C7	LN-C8	Scarcity
.15	.25	1	1

26708 ELECTRONIC HORN CONTROL: This 1957-58 sound control was identical to the 1956 708, but for the number.

VG-C6	EX-C7	LN-C8	Scarcity
4	7	10	4

26710 STRAIGHT TRACK HALF SECTION: The five-inch section of conventional S track was given this number in 1957, and kept it through 1964.

VG-C6	EX-C7	LN-C8	Scarcity
.15	.25	.50	1

26718 LEFT-HAND REMOTE-CONTROL SWITCH: This remote-control left-hand illuminated turnout with controller was sold in 1957. The turnout included a switch allowing the selection of regular or two-train operation.

VG-C6	EX-C7	LN-C8	Scarcity
5	10	20	1

26719 RIGHT-HAND REMOTE-CONTROL SWITCH:

This remote-control right-hand illuminated turnout with controller was sold in 1957. The turnout included a switch allowing the selection of regular or two-train operation.

VG-C6	EX-C7	LN-C8	Scarcity
5	10	20	1

26720 CURVE TRACK:

When Gilbert adopted the five-digit number system in 1957, the 720 became the 26720, the number that the standard curved section was sold under through 1964. Twelve pieces formed a circle.

VG-C6	EX-C7	LN-C8	Scarcity
.15	.25	.55	1

26722 CURVE TRACK:

Twelve pieces of standard curve track were also packed in a plain brown box marked "26722."

VG-C6	EX-C7	LN-C8	Scarcity
5	10	20	2

26726 RUBBER ROADBED HALF STRAIGHT:

This number was assigned to half-lengths of a straight rubber roadbed in 1958.

VG-C6	EX-C7	LN-C8	Scarcity
.50	.75	2	2

26727 RUBBER ROADBED HALF CURVED:

This number was assigned to half-lengths of a curved rubber roadbed in 1958.

VG-C6	EX-C7	LN-C8	Scarcity
.50	.75	2	2

26730 CURVE TRACK HALF SECTION:

This number was assigned to a half section of standard curve track sold from 1957 through 1964.

VG-C6	EX-C7	LN-C8	Scarcity
.15	.25	.35	1

26739 ELECTRONIC WHISTLE CONTROL:

The good 739 whistle control of 1956 was continued with this five-digit number in 1957 and 1958. A slide lever was at the front of the base.

VG-C6	EX-C7	LN-C8	Scarcity
10	25	40	5

26742 REMOTE-CONTROL SWITCHES:

This pair of conventional S-Gauge illuminated turnouts was sold in 1957 and 1958. A single two-lever illuminated controller operated both turnouts. A sliding switch on the turnout had two positions, regular and two-train.

VG-C6	EX-C7	LN-C8	Scarcity
15	25	45	4

26744 MANUAL SWITCHES:

The manual turnouts were renumbered in 1957, and the new number was used through 1958. An electrical switch was provided to allow either regular or two-train operation.

VG-C6	EX-C7	LN-C8	Scarcity
10	15	20	2

26745 RAILROAD CROSSING:

The familiar 90-degree crossing was sold from 1957 through 1964. This unit can only be distinguished from the 725 by the number stamped on the original packaging.

VG-C6	EX-C7	LN-C8	Scarcity
2	5	10	1

26746 STRAIGHT RUBBER ROADBED:

The full-length straight rubber roadbed with 23 molded-in ties for standard track was sold under this number from 1957 through 1964.

VG-C6	EX-C7	LN-C8	Scarcity
.50	.75	2	2

26747 CURVED RUBBER ROADBED:

The full-length curved rubber roadbed with 23 molded-in ties for standard track was sold under this number from 1957 through 1964.

VG-C6	EX-C7	LN-C8	Scarcity
.50	.75	1.50	2

26748 AUTOMATIC RE-RAILER:

From 1957 through 1964, Gilbert sold this 10-inch section equipped with a plastic grade crossing molding, which served as a rerailer.

VG-C6	EX-C7	LN-C8	Scarcity
5	10	20	2

26749 BUMPER:

The unpainted green bumper with 10-inch straight track was offered with this number from 1957 through 1960.

VG-C6	EX-C7	LN-C8	Scarcity
3	9	15	1

26751 PIKE PLANNING KIT:

This 1957-59 tool set included a plastic template of Gilbert track components, sheets of Dietzgen graph paper, a M3127 Instruction book and "American Flyer MODEL RAILROAD HANDBOOK."

VG-C6	EX-C7	LN-C8	Scarcity
10	15	25	2

26752 REMOTE-CONTROL UNCOUPLER:

This was the remote-control uncoupler with small tool shed was sold by Gilbert in 1957 and 1958, then again in 1960 and 1961.

VG-C6	EX-C7	LN-C8	Scarcity
1	2	4	1

Values for each condition are in U.S. dollars. | **Scarcity** = Scale from 1-8 with 8 being the hardest to find.

219

26756 BUMPER: This 1961-64 illuminated bumper could be used with either standard S or Pike Master track.

VG-C6	EX-C7	LN-C8	Scarcity
5	10	20	1

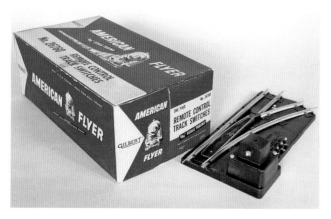

26760 REMOTE-CONTROL SWITCHES: This pair of conventional S-Gauge illuminated turnouts was sold from 1958 through 1964. A single two-lever non-illuminated controller operated the turnouts. A sliding switch on each turnout had two positions; regular and two-train.

VG-C6	EX-C7	LN-C8	Scarcity
15	20	35	1

26761 LEFT-HAND REMOTE-CONTROL SWITCH: This left-hand conventional S-Gauge illuminated turnout

was sold from 1958 through 1964. A single switch non-illuminated controller operated the turnout. A sliding switch on the turnout had two positions, regular and two-train.

VG-C6	EX-C7	LN-C8	Scarcity
7	12	17	1

26762 RIGHT-HAND REMOTE-CONTROL SWITCH: This right hand conventional S-Gauge illuminated turnout was sold from 1958 through 1964. A single switch non-illuminated controller operated the turnout. A sliding switch on the turnout had two positions, regular and two-train.

VG-C6	EX-C7	LN-C8	Scarcity
7	12	17	1

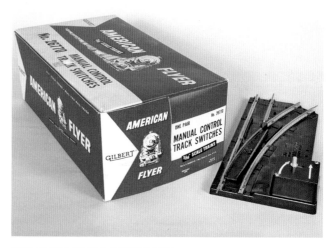

26770 MANUAL SWITCHES: This pair of conventional S-Gauge manual turnouts was sold from 1959 through 1964. Despite not have a sliding switch, the turnout had the regular and two-train markings.

VG-C6	EX-C7	LN-C8	Scarcity
5	10	15	1

26781 RAILROAD TRESTLE SET: In 1957, Gilbert sold this 24-piece orange trestle set. Track locks were included with the set.

VG-C6	EX-C7	LN-C8	Scarcity
10	15	25	1

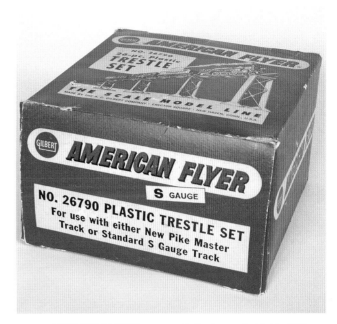

26782 RAILROAD TRESTLE SET: From 1958 through 1960, Gilbert sold this 26-piece black trestle set in a cylindrical container.

VG-C6	EX-C7	LN-C8	Scarcity
5	10	15	1

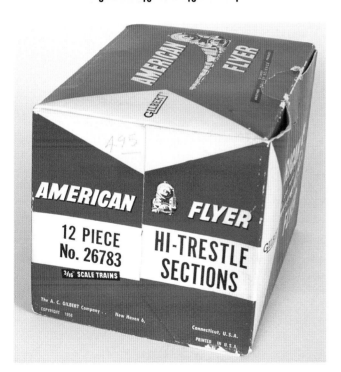

26783 HI-TRESTLES: Twelve orange plastic trestle piers were included in this 1957 accessory. Together with the included dozen of track locks, this could extend the 26781.

VG-C6	EX-C7	LN-C8	Scarcity
10	15	20	3

26790 TRESTLE SET: From 1961 through 1964, Gilbert sold this 26-piece graduated black trestle set. It was designed for use with either conventional S-Gauge track or Pike Master track.

VG-C6	EX-C7	LN-C8	Scarcity
10	15	20	4

26810 POW-R-CLIPS: These 1960-64 terminal clips allowed connection to the transformer.

VG-C6	EX-C7	LN-C8	Scarcity
.20	.30	.40	1

27443 LAMPS: This box of three 18-volt green lamps was sold from 1958 through 1964.

VG-C6	EX-C7	LN-C8	Scarcity
1	2	3	3

27460 LAMP ASSORTMENT KIT: This assortment of 54 lamps was sold from 1958 through 1964.

VG-C6	EX-C7	LN-C8	Scarcity
25	45	80	5

Values for each condition are in U.S. dollars. | **Scarcity** = Scale from 1-8 with 8 being the hardest to find.

221

One of the hottest areas of collecting today is boxed sets. While in most instances on Christmas morning the original packaging was discarded—rendering the former contents to be merely a "group of old trains today," some people kept the original packaging. Today, those packages continue to truly be "sets" and are highly prized collectors items. Much of the values assigned in the listings below are due to the presence of these boxes.

In addition to the locomotives and rolling stock shown in these listings, outfits typically came with instruction books and sheets, wire, contacts, brochures, smoke fluid (if applicable), and in many instances power packs. All of these items must be present to realize the full value shown.

Frequently, the track is not included when sets are sold among collectors, and the absence of standard straight and curved sections does not affect the value of the sets.

That is because such track is so common it is almost worthless, and most collectors feel that the damage caused to the boxes by the track rubbing on it exceeds the value of the track. Because the value of an outfit is so dependent on the presence and condition of the outfit and component boxes, values are listed for Excellent and Like New examples.

The listings are done in numeric order. The outfit number, year, catalog name and the catalog numbers of major components, beginning with locomotives, are shown.

Please note, American Flyer produced many uncataloged outfits as well; some were offered through the normal dealer network, others through mass merchandisers such as Sears and J.C. Penney. These uncataloged outfits, some quite collectable, are not listed here.

48T ROYAL BLUE FREIGHT TRAIN: 1948, 350 locomotive and tender, with handrails, no smoke or "Choo-Choo": 633R, 630, 631, twelve 702 curved track, two 700 straight track, 706, 690, No. 2 (75-Watt transformer).

EX-C7	LN-C8	Scarcity
300	450	6

490T THREE-CAR ATLANTIC FREIGHT SET: 1949, 300 locomotive and tender, no smoke or "Choo-Choo": 638, 639, 640, twelve 702 curved track, 704, 690, No. 1 (25-Watt transformer).

EX-C7	LN-C8	Scarcity
140	200	4

490T THREE-CAR ATLANTIC FREIGHT SET: 1950, 300AC locomotive and tender, no smoke or "Choo-Cho": 638, 639, 640, twelve 702 curved track, 704, 690, twelve 693 track lock, No. 1 (25-Watt transformer).

EX-C7	LN-C8	Scarcity
140	200	4

501T ATLANTIC THREE-CAR FREIGHT SET: 1951, 302 locomotive and sheet metal tender, smoke and "Choo-Choo": 638, 640, 642, twelve 702 curved track, 704, 690, No. 1 (25-Watt transformer), smoke capsule and funnel.

EX-C7	LN-C8	Scarcity
140	200	4

501T ATLANTIC THREE-CAR FREIGHT SET: 1952, 302 locomotive and tender, smoke and "Choo-Choo": 638, 640, 642, twelve 702 curved track, 704, 690, No. 1 (25-Watt transformer), smoke capsule and funnel.

EX-C7	LN-C8	Scarcity
140	200	4

521T AMERICAN FLYER 19-PIECE FREIGHT SET: 1952, 300 locomotive and tender, no smoke or "Choo-Choo": 631, 638, twelve 702 curved track, 704, 690, No. 1 (25-Watt transformer).

EX-C7	LN-C8	Scarcity
125	175	5

590T ATLANTIC THREE-CAR FREIGHT: 1951, 300 locomotive and sheet metal tender, no smoke or "Choo-Choo": 638, 641, 642, twelve 702 curved track, 704, 690, No. 1 (25-Watt transformer).

EX-C7	LN-C8	Scarcity
125	175	5

4601 ATLANTIC FREIGHT TRAIN: 1946-47, 300 locomotive and tender, no smoke or "Choo-Choo": 628, 630, 633, twelve 702 curved track, 700, 705, 690.

EX-C7	LN-C8	Scarcity
275	375	6

4602: It is not believed that this 1946-cataloged set was actually produced.

4603 ATLANTIC PASSENGER SET: 1946-47, 300 locomotive and tender, no smoke or "Choo-Choo": two 650G, 651G, twelve 702 curved track, 700, 705, 690.

EX-C7	LN-C8	Scarcity
375	450	6

4604: It is not believed that this 1946-cataloged set was actually produced.

4605 PENNSYLVANIA FREIGHT TRAIN: 1946, 310 locomotive and tender, no smoke or "Choo-Choo": orange 625, 630, 632, twelve 702 curved track, 700, 705, 690.

EX-C7	LN-C8	Scarcity
1,500	2,000	8

4605 PENNSYLVANIA FREIGHT TRAIN: 1947, 310 locomotive and tender, no smoke or "Choo-Choo": 625, 630, 632, twelve 702 curved track, 700, 705, 690.

EX-C7	LN-C8	Scarcity
400	500	5

4606: It is not believed that this 1946-cataloged set was actually produced.

4607 PENNSYLVANIA FREIGHT TRAIN: 1946, 312 locomotive and tender, smoke and "Choo-Choo": orange 625, 630, 632, twelve 702 curved track, 700, 705, 690.

EX-C7	LN-C8	Scarcity
1,500	2,000	8

4607 PENNSYLVANIA FREIGHT TRAIN: 1947, 312 locomotive and tender, smoke and "Choo-Choo": 625, 630, 632 twelve 702 curved track, 700, 705, 690.

EX-C7	LN-C8	Scarcity
400	500	5

4607A PENNSYLVANIA FREIGHT TRAIN: 1948, 312 or 312AC locomotive and tender, smoke and "Choo-Choo": 625, 630, 632 twelve 702 curved track, two 700 straight track, 706, 690.

EX-C7	LN-C8	Scarcity
275	350	5

4607A PENNSYLVANIA FREIGHT TRAIN: 1949, 312AC locomotive and tender, smoke and "Choo-Choo": 625, 630, 632 twelve 702 curved track, two 700 straight track, 706, 690, fourteen 693 track lock.

EX-C7	LN-C8	Scarcity
275	350	5

4608: It is not believed that this 1946-cataloged set was actually produced.

4609 PENNSYLVANIA PASSENGER TRAIN: 1946-47, 312 locomotive and tender, smoke and "Choo-Choo": two 650R, 651R, twelve 702 curved track, 700, 705, 690.

EX-C7	LN-C8	Scarcity
500	650	6

4609A PENNSYLVANIA PASSENGER TRAIN: 1948, 312AC locomotive and tender, smoke and "Choo-Choo": two 650R, 651R, twelve 702 curved track, two 700 straight track, 706, 690.

EX-C7	LN-C8	Scarcity
450	550	5

4609A PENNSYLVANIA PASSENGER TRAIN: 1949, 312AC locomotive and tender, smoke and "Choo-Choo": two 650R, 651R, twelve 702 curved track, two 700 straight track, 706, 690, fourteen 693 track lock.

EX-C7	LN-C8	Scarcity
450	550	5

4610 NYC FREIGHT SET: 1946-47, 321 locomotive and tender, smoke and "Choo-Choo": 629, 630, 634, 716, twelve 702 curved track, 705, 710, 690.

EX-C7	LN-C8	Scarcity
600	700	6

4611 NEW YORK CENTRAL FREIGHT TRAIN: 1946-47, 322 locomotive and tender, smoke and "Choo-Choo": 629, 630, 634, 716, twelve 702 curved track, 705, 710, 690.

EX-C7	LN-C8	Scarcity
550	650	6

4611A NYC FREIGHT TRAIN: 1948-49, (1949 catalog erroneously lists this outfit as 4611) 322AC locomotive and tender, smoke and "Choo-Choo": 629, 630, 634, 716, twelve 702 curved track, four 700 straight track, 706, 712, 690.

EX-C7	LN-C8	Scarcity
400	500	5

4612: It is not believed that this 1946-cataloged set was actually produced.

4613 NYC PASSENGER TRAIN: 1946-47, 322 locomotive and tender, smoke and "Choo-Choo": two 652R, 653R, 654R, twelve 702 curved track, three 700 straight track, 705, 690.

EX-C7	LN-C8	Scarcity
1,600	1,800	7

Values for each condition are in U.S. dollars. | **Scarcity** = Scale from 1-8 with 8 being the hardest to find.

223

4613A NYC PASSENGER TRAIN: 1948, 322AC locomotive and tender, smoke and "Choo-Choo": two 652R, 653R, 654R, twelve 702 curved track, four 700 straight track, 706, 690.

EX-C7	LN-C8	Scarcity
850	1,000	6

4615 UNION PACIFIC FREIGHT TRAIN: 1947, 332DC locomotive with smoke in tender and "Choo-Choo": 628, 630, 632, 633, 635, twelve 702 curved track, three 700 straight track, 705, 690.

EX-C7	LN-C8	Scarcity
5,000	5,500	8

4615 UNION PACIFIC FREIGHT TRAIN: 1948, 332DC locomotive and tender, smoke and "Choo-Choo": 628, 630, 632, 633, 635, twelve 702 curved track, four 700 straight track, 706, 690.

EX-C7	LN-C8	Scarcity
2,200	2,500	6

4615 UNION PACIFIC FREIGHT TRAIN: 1949, 332DC locomotive and tender, smoke and "Choo-Choo": 628, 630, 632, 633, 635, twelve 702 curved track, four 700 straight track, 706, 690, sixteen 693 track lock.

EX-C7	LN-C8	Scarcity
2,200	2,500	6

4617 UNION PACIFIC PASSENGER TRAIN: 1947, 332DC locomotive with smoke in tender, smoke and "Choo-Choo": two 652G, 653G, 654G, twelve 702 curved track, three 700 straight track, 705, 690.

EX-C7	LN-C8	Scarcity
6,000	6,750	8

4617 UNION PACIFIC PASSENGER TRAIN: 1948, 332DC locomotive and tender, smoke and "Choo-Choo": two 652G, 653G, 654G, twelve 702 curved track, four 700 straight track, 706, 690.

EX-C7	LN-C8	Scarcity
2,200	2,500	7

4617 UNION PACIFIC PASSENGER TRAIN: 1949, 332DC locomotive and tender, smoke and "Choo-Choo": two 652G, 653G, 654G, twelve 702 curved track, four 700 straight track, 706, 690, sixteen 693 track lock.

EX-C7	LN-C8	Scarcity
2,200	2,500	7

4618 NICKEL PLATE SWITCHER: 1947, 342DC locomotive with smoke in tender and "Choo-Choo": 630, 631, 634, 715 with armored car, twelve 702 curved track, three 700 straight track, 705, 712, 690.

EX-C7	LN-C8	Scarcity
1,250	1,450	7

4618 NICKEL PLATE SWITCHER: 1948, 342DC locomotive and tender, smoke and "Choo-Choo": 630, 631, 634, 715 with armored car, twelve 702 curved track, four 700 straight track, 706, 712, 690.

EX-C7	LN-C8	Scarcity
800	900	6

4618 NICKEL PLATE SWITCHER: 1949, 342DC locomotive and tender, smoke and "Choo-Choo": 630, 631, 634, 715 with Manoil coupe, twelve 702 curved track, four 700 straight track, 706, 712, 690, sixteen 693 track lock.

EX-C7	LN-C8	Scarcity
750	850	6

4619 PENNSYLVANIA FREIGHT TRAIN: 1946, 312 locomotive and tender, smoke and "Choo-Choo": 627, 630, 632, 717, 751, twelve 702 curved track, 705, 710, 690.

EX-C7	LN-C8	Scarcity
800	950	6

4619 PENNSYLVANIA FREIGHT TRAIN: 1947, 312 locomotive and tender, smoke and "Choo-Choo": 627, 630, 632, 717, 751, twelve 702 curved track, three 700 straight track, 705, 721, 690.

EX-C7	LN-C8	Scarcity
800	950	6

4619A PENNSYLVANIA FREIGHT TRAIN: 1948, 312AC locomotive and tender, smoke and "Choo-Choo": 627, 630, 632, 717, 751, twelve 702 curved track, four 700 straight track, 706, 712, 690.

EX-C7	LN-C8	Scarcity
775	900	6

4619A PENNSYLVANIA FREIGHT TRAIN: 1949, 312AC locomotive and tender, smoke and "Choo-Choo": 627, 630, 632, 717, 751, twelve 702 curved track, four 700 straight track, 706, 712, 690, sixteen 693 track lock.

EX-C7	LN-C8	Scarcity
775	900	6

4620 NYC FREIGHT TRAIN: 1946, 322 locomotive and tender, smoke and "Choo-Choo": 630, 633, 635, 716, 752, twelve 702 curved track, two 700 straight track, 705, 710, 690.

EX-C7	LN-C8	Scarcity
875	1,000	7

4620 NYC FREIGHT TRAIN: 1947, 322 locomotive and tender, smoke and "Choo-Choo": 630, 633, 635, 716, 752, twelve 702 curved track, three 700 straight track, 705, 712, 690.

EX-C7	LN-C8	Scarcity
875	1,000	7

4620A NEW YORK CENTRAL FREIGHT TRAIN: 1948, 322 locomotive and tender, smoke and "Choo-Choo": 630, 633, 635, 716, 752, twelve 702 curved track, four 700 straight track, 706, 712, 690.

EX-C7	LN-C8	Scarcity
775	900	7

4620A NEW YORK CENTRAL FREIGHT TRAIN: 1949, 322AC locomotive and tender, smoke and "Choo-Choo": 630, 633, 635, 716, 752, twelve 702 curved track, four 700 straight track, 706, 712, 690, sixteen 693 track lock.

EX-C7	LN-C8	Scarcity
775	900	7

4621 UNION PACIFIC PASSENGER TRAIN: 1947, 332 locomotive with smoke in tender and "Choo-Choo": two 650R, 652R, 654R, 718R, twelve 702 curved track, five 700 straight track, 705, 713, 690.

EX-C7	LN-C8	Scarcity
5,000	6,000	8

4621 UNION PACIFIC PASSENGER TRAIN: 1948, 332DC locomotive and tender, smoke and "Choo-Choo": two 650R, 652R, 654R, 718R, twelve 702 curved track, six 700 straight track, 706, 713, 690.

EX-C7	LN-C8	Scarcity
2,200	2,500	7

4622: Though cataloged in 1946, it is not believed that this set was produced until 1947.

4622A AMERICAN FLYER COMPLETE RAILROAD SYSTEM: 1947-48, 332DC locomotive and tender, smoke and "Choo-Choo," 650R, 652R, 654R, 718R; 342DC locomotive and tender, smoke and "Choo-Choo," 629, 630, 631, 633, 634, 715, sixteen 702 curved track, thirteen 700 straight track, two 705, 713, 712, pair of 720 turnouts, 690; 577, two 579, two 580, 589, 585, 750, 583, 581, 596, 586F, 578, 591, 14.

EX-C7	LN-C8	Scarcity
Too rarely traded to accurately establish pricing.		

4730 NICKEL PLATE SWITCHER: 1947, 342AC locomotive and tender, smoke and "Choo-Choo": 630, 631, 634, 715 with armored car twelve 702 curved track, four 700 straight track, 706, 712, 690.

EX-C7	LN-C8	Scarcity
775	900	6

4730A NICKEL PLATE SWITCHER: 1948, 342 locomotive and tender, smoke and "Choo-Choo": 630, 631, 634, 715 with armored car, twelve 702 curved track, four 700 straight track, 706, 712, 690.

EX-C7	LN-C8	Scarcity
725	800	6

4730A NICKEL PLATE SWITCHER: 1949, 342AC locomotive and tender, smoke and "Choo-Choo": 630, 631, 634, 715 with armored car, twelve 702 curved track, four 700 straight track, 706, 712, 690, sixteen 693 track lock.

EX-C7	LN-C8	Scarcity
725	800	6

4801A ATLANTIC FREIGHT SET: 1948, 302 locomotive and tender, smoke and "Choo-Choo": 628, 630, 633R, twelve 702 curved track, two 700 straight track, 706, 690.

EX-C7	LN-C8	Scarcity
150	200	3

4803A ATLANTIC PASSENGER SET: 1948, 302AC locomotive and tender, smoke and "Choo-Choo": two 650G, 651G, twelve 702 curved track, two 700 straight track, 706, 690.

EX-C7	LN-C8	Scarcity
300	350	4

4901T FOUR-CAR ATLANTIC FREIGHT SET: 1949, 300AC locomotive and tender, no smoke or "Choo-Choo": 638, 639, 640, 641, twelve 702 curved track, two 700 straight track, 704, 690, No. 1 (25-Watt transformer).

EX-C7	LN-C8	Scarcity
125	175	3

4904T PACIFIC FREIGHT TRAIN: 1949-51, 290 locomotive and tender, smoke and "Choo-Choo": 638, 639, 640, twelve 702 curved track, two 700 straight track, 706, 690, No. 2 (75-Watt transformer), smoke capsule and funnel.

EX-C7	LN-C8	Scarcity
225	275	2

4904T PACIFIC FREIGHT TRAIN: 1952, 282 locomotive and tender, smoke and "Choo-Choo": 638, 639, 640, twelve 702 curved track, two 700 straight track, 706, 690, No. 2 (75-Watt transformer), smoke capsule and funnel.

EX-C7	LN-C8	Scarcity
225	275	2

4907AW PENNSYLVANIA K-5 FREIGHT TRAIN: 1949, 314AW locomotive and tender, smoke, "Choo-Choo" and whistle; 625, 630, 632, twelve 702 curved track, two 700 straight track, 706, 690, fourteen 693 track lock, whistle control.

EX-C7	LN-C8	Scarcity
750	850	6

4914A NEW YORK CENTRAL FOUR-CAR PASSENGER TRAIN: 1949-50, 322AC locomotive and tender, smoke and "Choo-Choo": three 650R, 718R, twelve 702 curved track, four 700 straight track, 706, 712, 690, sixteen 693 track lock.

EX-C7	LN-C8	Scarcity
600	650	5

5001T AMERICAN FLYER RAILROAD SYSTEM: 1950, 300AC locomotive and tender, no smoke or "Choo-Choo": 638, 639, 640, 641, twelve 702 curved track, two 700 straight track, 704, 690, fourteen 693 track lock, farm scene inserts, No. 1 (25-Watt transformer).

EX-C7	LN-C8	Scarcity
2,300	2,800	7

5002T AMERICAN FLYER CIRCUS TRAIN: 1950-51, 353 locomotive and tender, no smoke or "Choo-Choo": two 643, 649, twelve 702 curved track, two 700 straight track, fourteen 693 track lock, 690, 704, circus scene kit, tickets, No. 1 (25-Watt transformer).

EX-C7	LN-C8	Scarcity
4,100	4,800	7

5003T PACIFIC FAST PASSENGER: 1950, 290 locomotive and tender, smoke and "Choo-Choo": 651G, two 650G, twelve 702 curved track, two 700 straight track, 706, 690, fourteen 693 track lock, No. 2 (75-Watt transformer).

EX-C7	LN-C8	Scarcity
450	650	5

Values for each condition are in U.S. dollars. | **Scarcity** = Scale from 1-8 with 8 being the hardest to find.

225

5004 NICKEL PLATE RAILROAD SWITCHER SET: 1950-51, 342AC locomotive and tender, smoke and "Choo-Choo": 630, 631, 646, 715 with Manoil coupe, twelve 702 curved track, four 700 straight track, 706, 690, sixteen 693 track lock, smoke capsule and funnel.

EX-C7	LN-C8	Scarcity
700	750	5

5004 NICKEL PLATE RAILROAD SWITCHER SET: 1952, 342 locomotive and tender, smoke and "Choo-Choo": 630, 631, 646, 715 with Manoil coupe, twelve 702 curved track, four 700 straight track, 706, 690, sixteen 693 track lock, smoke capsule and funnel.

EX-C7	LN-C8	Scarcity
750	800	5

5005WT PENNSYLVANIA K-5 FREIGHT TRAIN: 1950, 314AW locomotive and tender, smoke, "Choo-Choo" and whistle, 625, 630, 632, twelve 702 curved track, two 700 straight track, 706, 690, fourteen 693 track lock, No. 2 (75-Watt transformer).

EX-C7	LN-C8	Scarcity
750	825	6

5006WT HUDSON FREIGHT: 1950, 324AC locomotive and tender, smoke, "Choo-Choo" and whistle; 629, 630, 631, 717, twelve 702 curved track, four 700 straight track, 706, 690, sixteen 693 track lock, No. 2 (75-Watt transformer).

EX-C7	LN-C8	Scarcity
800	850	6

5007 SANTA FE DIESEL FREIGHT: 1950, 362 (360/361) PA/PB Diesel, air-chime horn: 627, 630, 636, 732, twelve 702 curved track, four 700 straight track, 706, 690, sixteen 693 track lock. (Values below include chrome-plated diesels. Deduct 25 percent for painted units.)

EX-C7	LN-C8	Scarcity
800	850	5

5008 DELUXE DIESEL STREAMLINED PASSENGER: 1950, 362 (360/361) PA/PB Diesel, air-chime horn; 660, 662, 663 aluminum passenger cars, twelve 702 curved track, six 700 straight track, 706, 690, eighteen 693 track lock. (Values below include chrome-plated diesels. Deduct 25 percent for painted units.)

EX-C7	LN-C8	Scarcity
850	900	6

5009 NICKEL PLATE ELECTRONIC SWITCHER FREIGHT SET: 1950, 342DC locomotive and tender, smoke and "Choo-Choo": 630, 631, 646, 715 with Manoil coupe, twelve 702 curved track, four 700 straight track, 706, 690, sixteen 693 track lock.

EX-C7	LN-C8	Scarcity
800	875	4

5010W UNION PACIFIC ELECTRONIC FREIGHT TRAIN: 1950, 334DC locomotive and tender, smoke, "Choo-Choo," and whistle; 627, 628, 644, 645, twelve 702 curved track, six 700 straight track, 706, 690, eighteen 693 track lock.

EX-C7	LN-C8	Scarcity
1,200	1,350	6

5011BBW UNION PACIFIC STREAMLINED PASSENGER TRAIN: 1950, 332DC locomotive and tender, smoke, "Choo-Choo," and whistle: 660, 661, 663 aluminum passenger cars, twelve 702 curved track, six 700 straight track, 706, eighteen 693 track lock. (Note: a 334DC replaced the 332DC in some outfits.)

EX-C7	LN-C8	Scarcity
1,250	1,450	6

5012T DIESEL SWITCHER FREIGHT: 1950, 370 GP-7 Diesel: 630, 633, 715 with Manoil coupe, twelve 702 curved track, four 700 straight track, 706, 690, sixteen 693, No. 2 (75-Watt transformer).

EX-C7	LN-C8	Scarcity
475	550	4

5103WT PACIFIC PASSENGER TRAIN: 1951, 295 locomotive and tender, smoke, "Choo-Choo," and whistle; two 650G, 651G, twelve 702 curved track, two 700 straight track, 706, 690, sixteen 693 track lock, No. 2 (75-Watt transformer), smoke capsule, and funnel.

EX-C7	LN-C8	Scarcity
650	725	4

5103WT PACIFIC PASSENGER TRAIN: 1952, 285 locomotive and tender, smoke, "Choo-Choo," and air-chime whistle; two 650G, 651G, twelve 702 curved track, two 700 straight track, 706, 690, sixteen 693 track lock, No. 2 (75-Watt transformer), smoke capsule, and funnel.

EX-C7	LN-C8	Scarcity
525	600	3

5106T HUDSON FREIGHT SET: 1951, 322 locomotive and tender, smoke and "Choo-Choo": 625, 629, 630, 631, twelve 702 curved track, four 700 straight track, 706, 690, sixteen 693 track lock, No. 2 (75-Watt transformer), smoke capsule, and funnel.

EX-C7	LN-C8	Scarcity
450	500	3

5106WT HUDSON FREIGHT SET: 1951, 325AC locomotive and tender, smoke, "Choo-Choo," and whistle; 625, 629, 630, 631, twelve 702 curved track, four 700 straight track, 706, 690, sixteen 693 track lock, No. 2 (75-Watt transformer), air-chime whistle control unit, smoke capsule, and funnel.

EX-C7	LN-C8	Scarcity
500	550	4

5107W DIESEL FREIGHT SET: 1951-52, 365 (360/364) PA/PB Diesel, air-chime whistle; 630, 631, 636, 734, twelve 702 curved track, four 700 straight track, 706, 690, sixteen 693 track lock, air-chime whistle control unit.

EX-C7	LN-C8	Scarcity
525	600	5

5108W DELUXE PASSENGER SET: 1951, 365 (360/364) PA/PB Diesel, air-chime whistle: 660, 662, 663 aluminum passenger cars, twelve 702 curved track, six 700 straight track, 706, 690, eighteen 693 track lock, air-chime whistle control unit.

EX-C7	LN-C8	Scarcity
600	650	5

5108W DELUXE PASSENGER SET: 1952, 365 (360/364 satin silver) PA/PB Diesel, air-chime whistle; 660, 662, 663 plastic passenger cars, twelve 702 curved track, six 700 straight track, 706, 690, eighteen 693 track lock, air-chime whistle control unit.

EX-C7	LN-C8	Scarcity
600	650	5

5110 AMERICAN FLYER UNION PACIFIC FREIGHT TRAIN: 1951, 332AC locomotive and tender, smoke and "Choo-Choo": 628, 631, 644, 645A, twelve 702 curved track, six 700 straight track, 706, 690, eighteen 693 track lock, smoke capsule and funnel.

EX-C7	LN-C8	Scarcity
700	800	5

5112T AMERICAN FLYER DIESEL SWITCHER FREIGHT: 1951-52, 370 GP-7 Diesel: 630, 633, 715, twelve 702 curved track, four 700 straight track, 706, 690, sixteen 693 track lock, No. 2 (75-Watt transformer).

EX-C7	LN-C8	Scarcity
425	500	3

5114 PENNSYLVANIA DELUXE PASSENGER SET: 1951-52, 312AC locomotive and tender, smoke and "Choo-Choo": two 650R, 718R or G, twelve 702 curved track, four 700 straight track, 712, 706, 690, sixteen 693 track lock, smoke capsule and funnel.

EX-C7	LN-C8	Scarcity
400	450	4

5204W AMERICAN FLYER FREIGHT SET: 1952, 315 locomotive and tender, smoke, "Choo-Choo," and air-chime whistle; 625, 630, 632, 633, twelve 702 curved track, two 700 straight track, 706, 690, fourteen 693 track lock, smoke capsule and funnel, remote control whistle unit.

EX-C7	LN-C8	Scarcity
650	750	6

5205W AMERICAN FLYER SILVER STREAK: 1952, 405 PA Diesel, air-chime whistle; 660, 661, 662 plastic passenger cars, twelve 702 curved track, two 700 straight track, 706, 690, fourteen 693 track lock, air-chime whistle control.

EX-C7	LN-C8	Scarcity
1,200	1,400	5

5300T MINERS WORK TRAIN: 1953-54, 740 handcar, red tipple, blue tipple, green tipple, twelve 702 curved track, 690, No. 1-1/2 (45- {1953} or 50- {1954} Watt transformer).

EX-C7	LN-C8	Scarcity
500	575	5

5301T CRUSADER: 1953, 301 locomotive and tender, "Choo-Choo" only: 605, 638, twelve 702 curved track, 704, 690, No. 1-1/2 (45-Watt transformer).

EX-C7	LN-C8	Scarcity
125	150	1

5306T THE SILVER BULLET: 1953, 356 locomotive and tender, smoke and "Choo-Choo": two 655 chrome-plated passenger cars, twelve 702 curved track, 704, 690, 40, No.

1-1/2 (45-Watt transformer). (A 50 percent premium above the values below should be allowed for sets containing a satin-silver painted 356.)

EX-C7	LN-C8	Scarcity
800	1,000	5

5311T THE BLACK DIAMOND: 1953, 302 locomotive and tender, smoke and "Choo-Choo": 651G, two 655G, twelve 702 curved track, 704, 690, 40, No. 1-1/2 (45-Watt transformer).

EX-C7	LN-C8	Scarcity
225	275	2

5312T THE BLACK DIAMOND: 1953, 302 locomotive and tender, smoke and "Choo-Choo": 623, 625, 638, 641, twelve 702 curved track, 704, 690, 40, No. 1-1/2 (45-Watt transformer).

EX-C7	LN-C8	Scarcity
125	175	1

5317T: 1953, 370 GP-7 Diesel: 606, 607, 609, twelve 702 curved track, 704, 690, No. 1-1/2 (45-Watt transformer).

EX-C7	LN-C8	Scarcity
400	500	4

5322T THE MOUNTAINEER: 1953, 282 locomotive and tender, smoke and "Choo-Choo": 651R, 652R, two 655R, twelve 702 curved track, two 700 straight track, 706, 690, fourteen 693 track lock, 40, No. 2 (75-Watt transformer).

EX-C7	LN-C8	Scarcity
850	1,000	5

5323T THE MOUNTAINEER: 1953, 282 locomotive and tender, smoke and "Choo-Choo": 623, 625, 631, 630, 640, 642, twelve 702 curved track, two 700 straight track, 706, 690, fourteen 693 track lock, 40, No. 2 (75-Watt transformer).

EX-C7	LN-C8	Scarcity
225	300	3

5500T THE NEW CRUSADER FREIGHT: 1955, 307 locomotive and tender, no smoke or "Choo-Choo": 923, 938, 940, twelve 702 curved track, 704, 690, No. 1-1/2 (50-Watt transformer).

EX-C7	LN-C8	Scarcity
100	150	2

5505T THE NEW BLACK DIAMOND FREIGHT: 1955, 303 locomotive and tender, smoke and "Choo-Choo": 911, 913, 938, twelve 702 curved track, 704, 690, 40, No. 1-1/2 (50-Watt transformer).

EX-C7	LN-C8	Scarcity
150	200	3

5510T THE NEW MOUNTAINEER FREIGHT: 1955, 283 locomotive and tender, smoke and "Choo-Choo": 921, 925, 931, 938, twelve 702 curved track, 706, 690, 40, No. 1-1/2 (50-Watt transformer).

EX-C7	LN-C8	Scarcity
300	350	3

Values for each condition are in U.S. dollars. | **Scarcity** = Scale from 1-8 with 8 being the hardest to find.

227

5515T THE NEW ARROW PASSENGER: 1955, 283 locomotive and tender, smoke and "Choo-Choo": 951R, two 955R, twelve 702 curved track, 706, 690, 40, No. 1-1/2 (50-Watt transformer).

EX-C7	LN-C8	Scarcity
800	925	4

5520T THE NEW G. M. UNION PACIFIC FREIGHT: 1955, 372 GP-7 Diesel: 911, 915 with Renewal gasoline tanker truck, 924, 930, twelve 702 curved track, four 700 straight track, 706, 690, No. 1-1/2 (50-Watt transformer). (Value listed here presumes locomotive marked "BUILT BY GILBERT," if instead the locomotive is marked "BUILT BY AMERICAN FLYER," the values should be increased 50 percent.)

EX-C7	LN-C8	Scarcity
800	900	4

5525TBW THE NEW METEOR FREIGHT: 1955, 293 locomotive and tender, smoke and "Choo-Choo": 912, 916, 930, 937, twelve 702 curved track, four 700 straight track, 706, 690, 40, No. 1-1/2 (50-Watt transformer), 566 billboard whistle.

EX-C7	LN-C8	Scarcity
400	500	5

5530TBH THE NEW SILVER FLASH FREIGHT: 1955, 479 PA Diesel: 921, 926, 920, 930, 947, twelve 702 curved track, four 700 straight track, 706, 690, sixteen 693 track lock, No 1-1/2 (50-Watt transformer), 561 billboard horn.

EX-C7	LN-C8	Scarcity
850	1,100	6

5535TBH THE NEW SILVER COMET PASSENGER: 1955, 466 PA Diesel: 960, 962, 963 blue-striped passenger cars twelve 702 curved track, four 700 straight track, 706, 690, sixteen 693 track lock, No. 1-1/2 (50-Watt transformer), 561 billboard horn.

EX-C7	LN-C8	Scarcity
800	900	4

5540TBW THE NEW TRAIL BLAZER FREIGHT: 313 locomotive and tender, smoke and "Choo-Choo": 913, 919, 926, 930, 940, twelve 702 curved track, four 700 straight track, 706, 690, sixteen 693 track lock, 40, No. 1 (50-Watt transformer), 566 billboard whistle.

EX-C7	LN-C8	Scarcity
750	900	5

5542H THE NEW SUNSHINE SPECIAL FREIGHT: 1955, 3745 (374/375) twin GP-7 Diesel, Diesel horn; 920, 921, 922, 926, 929, 930, twelve 702 curved track, four 700 straight track, 706, 690, sixteen 693 track lock, 708 Diesel horn control.

EX-C7	LN-C8	Scarcity
900	1,050	4

5545W THE NEW YARD KING: 1955, 346 locomotive and tender, smoke, "Choo-Choo," and steam whistle; 944, 945, 946, 953R twelve 702 curved track, four 700 straight track, 706, 690, sixteen 693 track lock, 40, 710 steam whistle control.

EX-C7	LN-C8	Scarcity
1,250	1,500	7

5550W THE NEW PACEMAKER FREIGHT: 1955, 326 locomotive and tender, smoke, "Choo-Choo," and steam whistle; 912, 913, 914, 921, 922, 977, twelve 702 curved track, six 700 straight track, 706, 690, eighteen 693 track lock, 40, 710 steam whistle control.

EX-C7	LN-C8	Scarcity
850	1,000	5

5555W THE NEW PACEMAKER PASSENGER: 1955, 326 locomotive and tender, smoke, "Choo-Choo," and steam whistle; 918, 952R, 953R, 954R, twelve 702 curved track, six 700 straight track, 913 mailbag hook, 706, 690, eighteen 693 track lock, 40, 710 steam whistle control.

EX-C7	LN-C8	Scarcity
3,000	3,500	7

5565W THE NEW FLYING FREIGHTER: 1955, 336 locomotive and tender, smoke, "Choo-Choo," and steam whistle; 916, 924, 926, 929, 947, 977, twelve 702 curved track, six 700 straight track, 706, 690, eighteen 693 track lock, 40, 710 steam whistle control.

EX-C7	LN-C8	Scarcity
850	1,000	5

5570H THE NEW SILVER ROCKET PASSENGER: 1955, 4745 (474/475) PA/PA Diesel, Diesel horn: 960, 961, 962, 963 passenger cars with green stripe, twelve 702 curved track, eight 700 straight track, 706, 690, twenty 693 track lock, 708 Diesel horn control.

EX-C7	LN-C8	Scarcity
1,500	1,700	5

5580H THE NEW CHIEF PASSENGER: 1955, 4713 (470/471/473) PA/PB/PA Diesel, with Diesel horn and Diesel Roar: 960, two 962, 963 passenger cars with red stripe, twelve 702 curved track, eight 700 straight track, 690, twenty 693 track lock, 708 Diesel horn control.

EX-C7	LN-C8	Scarcity
1,900	2,100	5

5585H THE NEW CHIEF FREIGHT: 1955, 4713 (470/471/473) PA/PB/PA Diesel, Diesel horn, Diesel Roar; 914, 916, 919, 940, 974, 977, twelve 702 curved track, eight 700 straight track, 706, 690, twenty 693 track lock, K775, 708 Diesel horn control.

EX-C7	LN-C8	Scarcity
2,500	3,000	7

5605T THE FLYING FREIGHTER: 1956, 355 Baldwin: 802, 804, 806, twelve 702 curved track, 704, 690, No. 1 (35-Watt transformer).

EX-C7	LN-C8	Scarcity
225	275	3

5610T THE NEW CRUSADER: 1956, 308 locomotive and tender, "Choo-Choo" only: 801, 803, 805, 806, twelve 702 curved track, two 700 straight track, 704, 690, No. 1 (35-Watt transformer).

EX-C7	LN-C8	Scarcity
150	200	3

5615T THE NEW BLACK DIAMOND FREIGHT: 1956, 303 locomotive and tender, smoke and "Choo-Choo": 801, 804, 806, 970, twelve 702 curved track, two 700 straight track, 704, 690, No. 1-1/2B (50-Watt transformer).

EX-C7	LN-C8	Scarcity
250	325	3

5620T THE NEW MOUNTAINEER: 1956, 283 locomotive and tender, smoke and "Choo-Choo": 925, 928, 937, 977, twelve 702 curved track, two 700 straight track, 706, 690, No. 1-1/2B (50-Watt transformer).

EX-C7	LN-C8	Scarcity
350	400	3

5625T THE NEW G. M. UNION PACIFIC: 1956, 372 GP-7 Diesel: 904, 911, 924, 941, 970, twelve 702 curved track, two 700 straight track, 706, 690, No. 1-1/2B (50-Watt transformer).

EX-C7	LN-C8	Scarcity
600	650	5

5630TBW THE NEW METEOR: 1956, 293 locomotive and tender, smoke and "Choo-Choo": 904, 916, 940, 984, twelve 702 curved track, four 700 straight track, 706, 690, No. 1-1/2B (50 Watt transformer), 568 billboard whistle.

EX-C7	LN-C8	Scarcity
500	575	4

5635 THE NEW YARD KING: 1956, 343 locomotive and tender, smoke and "Choo-Choo": 928, 944, 945, 946, twelve 702 curved track, two 700 straight track, 706, 690, fourteen 693 track lock.

EX-C7	LN-C8	Scarcity
750	850	5

5640TBH THE EL CAPITAN: 1956, 472 PA Diesel: 961, 962, 963, passenger cars with red stripe, twelve 702 curved track, four 700 straight track, 706, 690, sixteen 693 track lock, No. 1-1/2B (50-Watt transformer), 561 billboard horn.

EX-C7	LN-C8	Scarcity
750	850	5

5645TRH THE NEW SILVER FLASH: 1956, 481 PA Diesel, electronic horn and Diesel Roar; 904, 911, 920, 921, 926, 947, twelve 702 curved track, four 700 straight track, 706, 690, sixteen 693 track lock, No. WB (50-Watt transformer), 708 electronic Diesel horn control.

EX-C7	LN-C8	Scarcity
900	1,000	5

5650TBW THE NEW TRAIL BLAZER: 1956, 313 locomotive and tender, smoke and "Choo-Choo": 916, 928, 930, 973, 980, twelve 702 curved track, four 700 straight track, 706, 690, sixteen 693 track lock, No. 1-1/2B (50-Watt transformer), 568 billboard whistle.

EX-C7	LN-C8	Scarcity
900	1,000	5

5655RH THE NEW SUNSHINE SPECIAL: 1956, 3778 (378/377) Twin GP-7 Diesel, electronic horn and Diesel Roar: 920, 921, 924, 926, 977, 989, twelve 702 curved track, four 700 straight track, 706, 690, sixteen 693 track lock, 708 electronic Diesel horn control.

EX-C7	LN-C8	Scarcity
900	1,000	5

5660TW THE NEW PACEMAKER: 1956, 326 locomotive and tender, smoke, "Choo-Choo," and electronic whistle: 911, 912, 921, 922, 930, 971, twelve 702 curved track, six 700 straight track, 706, 690, eighteen 693 track lock, No. 4B (100-Watt transformer), 710 whistle control.

EX-C7	LN-C8	Scarcity
800	900	5

5665W THE NEW CHALLENGER: 1956, 336 locomotive and tender, smoke, "Choo-Choo," and electronic whistle: 916, 924, 926, 929, 940, 947, 977, 982, twelve 702 curved track, six 700 straight track, 706, 690, eighteen 693 track lock, 710 electronic steam whistle control.

EX-C7	LN-C8	Scarcity
1,100	1,350	6

5670TRH THE CLIPPER: 1956, 4945 (494/495) PA/PA Diesel, electronic horn and Diesel Roar: 960, 961, 962, 963 passenger cars with orange stripe, twelve 702 curved track, eight 700 straight track, 706, 690, twenty 693 track lock, No. 4B (100-Watt transformer), 708 electronic Diesel horn control.

EX-C7	LN-C8	Scarcity
2,400	2,700	7

5675TRH THE HOT SHOT: 1956, 4945 (494/495) PA/PA Diesel, electronic horn and Diesel Roar; 911, 914, 930, 936, 983, 984, twelve 702 curved track, eight 700 straight track, 706, 690, twenty 693 track lock, No. 4B (100-Watt transformer), 708 electronic horn control.

EX-C7	LN-C8	Scarcity
2,000	2,400	6

5680RH THE CHIEF: 1956, 4856 (484/485/486) PA/PB/PA Diesel, electronic horn and Diesel Roar; 916, 919, 928, 956, 977, 981, 982, 988, twelve 702 curved track, eight 700 straight track, 706, 690, twenty 693 track lock, 708 Diesel horn control.

EX-C7	LN-C8	Scarcity
2,600	2,900	7

5683RH THE CHIEF: 1956, 4713 (470/471/473) PA/PB/PA Diesel, electronic horn and Diesel Roar: 960, 961, two 962, 963 passenger cars with red stripe, twelve 702 curved track, eight 700 straight track, 706, 690, twenty 693 track lock, 708 electronic horn control.

EX-C7	LN-C8	Scarcity
1,800	2,100	7

5685RH THE VISTA DOME LIMITED: 1956, 4913 (490/491/493) PA/PB/PA Diesel, electronic horn and Diesel Roar; 900, 901, two 902, 903, twelve 702 curved track, eight 700 straight track, 706, 690, twenty 693 track lock, 708 electronic horn control.

EX-C7	LN-C8	Scarcity
5,000	6,000	7

20035 YARD KING: 1957, 343 locomotive and tender, smoke and "Choo-Choo": 928, 944, 945, 946, twelve 26720 curved track, two 26700 straight track, 26752, 26690.

EX-C7	LN-C8	Scarcity
700	825	5

Values for each condition are in U.S. dollars. | **Scarcity** = Scale from 1-8 with 8 being the hardest to find.

20083 SANTA FE CHIEF: 1957-58, 21902 (470/471/473) PA/PB/PA Diesel, electronic horn and Diesel Roar; 960, 961, two 962, 963 passenger cars with red stripe, twelve 26720 curved track, eight 26700 straight track, 26752, 26690, twenty 26693 track lock, 26708 electronic horn control.

EX-C7	LN-C8	Scarcity
2,700	3,100	6

20305 THE FLYING FREIGHTER: 1957, 355 Baldwin: 802, 804, 806, twelve 26720 curved track, 704, 26690, No. 22004 (40-Watt transformer).

EX-C7	LN-C8	Scarcity
250	300	3

20310 THE NEW CRUSADER: 1957, 303 locomotive and tender, smoke and "Choo-Choo": 801, 806, 807, twelve 26720 curved track, two 26700 straight track, 704, 26690, No. 22004 (40-Watt transformer).

EX-C7	LN-C8	Scarcity
225	275	3

20315 THE KEYSTONE ROCKET: 1957, 21004 locomotive and tender, smoke and "Choo-Choo": 805, 806, 969, twelve 26720 curved track, four 26700 straight track, 704, 26690, No. 22004 (40-Watt transformer).

EX-C7	LN-C8	Scarcity
750	875	5

20320 THE MOUNTAINEER FREIGHT: 1957, 283 or 21084 locomotive and tender, smoke and "Choo-Choo": 925, 928, 937, 979, twelve 26720 curved track, two 26700 straight track, 26752, 26690, No. 22020 (50-Watt transformer). (Increase values listed below by 10 percent when 21084 is included instead of 283.)

EX-C7	LN-C8	Scarcity
375	450	3

20325 UNION PACIFIC DIESEL FREIGHT: 1957, 372 GP-7 Diesel: 911, 924, 930, 941, 970, twelve 26720 curved track, two 26700 straight track, 26752, 26690, No. 22020 (50-Watt transformer).

EX-C7	LN-C8	Scarcity
650	750	5

20330 METEOR FREIGHT: 1957, 293 locomotive and tender, smoke and "Choo-Choo": 916, 930, 940, 984, twelve 26720 curved track, four 26700 straight track, 26752, 26690, No. 22020 (50-Watt transformer), 23568 billboard whistle.

EX-C7	LN-C8	Scarcity
550	650	5

20340 THE NEW CLIPPER: 1957, 497 PA Diesel: 960, 961, 963 passenger cars with orange stripe, twelve 26720 curved track, four 26700 straight track, 26752, 26690, sixteen 26693 track lock, No. 22020 (50-Watt transformer), 23561 billboard horn.

EX-C7	LN-C8	Scarcity
1,300	1,500	6

20345 NEW HAVEN MAINLINE ELECTRIC FREIGHT: 1957, 499 electric, electronic whistle; 911, 920, 921, 935, 958, 985, twelve 26720 curved track, four 26700 straight track, 26752, 26690, sixteen 26693 track lock, No. 22020 (50-Watt transformer), 26739 electronic whistle control.

EX-C7	LN-C8	Scarcity
1,400	1,600	5

20350 THE TRAIL BLAZER: 1957, 313 locomotive and tender, smoke and "Choo-Choo": 916, 928, 935, 973, 980, twelve 26720 curved track, four 26700 straight track, 26752, 26690, sixteen 26693 track lock, No. 22020 (50-Watt transformer), 23568 billboard whistle.

EX-C7	LN-C8	Scarcity
900	1,100	5

20355 SUNSHINE SPECIAL FREIGHT: 1957, 21908 (377/378) twin GP-7 Diesel, electronic horn and Diesel Roar; 920, 921, 924, 926, 979, 989, twelve 26720 curved track, four 26700 straight track, 26752, 26690, sixteen 26693 track lock, 26708 Diesel electronic horn control.

EX-C7	LN-C8	Scarcity
950	1,200	5

20360 THE PACEMAKER FREIGHT: 1957, 326 locomotive and tender, smoke, "Choo-Choo": and electronic whistle: 911, 912, 921, 922, 935, 971 twelve 26720 curved track, six 26700 straight track, 26752, 26690, eighteen 26693 track lock, No. 22030 (100-Watt transformer), 26739 electronic whistle control.

EX-C7	LN-C8	Scarcity
900	1,000	5

20365 THE CHALLENGER FREIGHT: 1957, 336 locomotive and tender, smoke, "Choo-Choo": and electronic whistle: 916, 924, 926, 940, 947, 979, 982, 994, twelve 26720 curved track, six 26700 straight track, 26752, 26690, eighteen 26693 track lock, 26739 electronic whistle control.

EX-C7	LN-C8	Scarcity
1,900	2,200	7

20370 VISTA DOME NORTH COAST LIMITED: 1957, 21916 (490/492) PA/PA Diesel, electronic horn and Diesel Roar: 900, 901, 902, 903, twelve 26720 curved track, eight 26700 straight track, 26752, 26690, twenty 26693 track lock, No. 22030 (100-Watt transformer), 26708 electronic Diesel horn control.

EX-C7	LN-C8	Scarcity
2,400	2,700	7

20375 THE HIGHBALLER FREIGHT: 1957, 21916 (490/492) PA/PA Diesel, electronic horn and Diesel Roar: 911, 914, 936, 984, 983, 935, twelve 26720 curved track, eight 26700 straight track, 26752, 26690, twenty 26693 track lock, No. 22030 (100-Watt transformer), 26708 electronic horn control.

EX-C7	LN-C8	Scarcity
2,200	2,600	7

20380 SANTA FE CHIEF FREIGHT: 1957, 21910 (484/485/486) PA/PB/PA Diesel, electronic horn and Diesel Roar; 916, 919, 928, 956, 979, 981, 982, 988, twelve 26720 curved track, eight 26700 straight track, 26752, 26690, twenty 26693 track lock, 26708 electronic horn control.

EX-C7	LN-C8	Scarcity
2,500	3,000	7

20405 DOCKSIDER: 1958, 21155 locomotive, smoke and "Choo-Choo": 24003, 24203, 24603, twelve 26720 curved track, 704, 26690, No. 22004 (40-Watt transformer).

EX-C7	LN-C8	Scarcity
700	800	5

20410 FLYING FREIGHTER: 1958, 21801 Baldwin: 24103, 24403, 24603, twelve 26720 curved track, 704, 26690, No. 22004 (40-Watt transformer).

EX-C7	LN-C8	Scarcity
275	325	3

20415 BLACK DIAMOND: 1958, 21105 locomotive and tender, smoke and "Choo-Choo": 24309, 24516, 24603, twelve 26720 curved track, 704, 26690, No. 22004 (40-Watt transformer).

EX-C7	LN-C8	Scarcity
300	350	5

20420 MOUNTAINEER: 1958, 21085 locomotive and tender, smoke and "Choo-Choo": 24219, 24543, 24546, twelve 26720 curved track, two 26700 straight track, 704, 26690, No. 22004 (40-Watt transformer).

EX-C7	LN-C8	Scarcity
350	400	4

20425 KEYSTONE: 1958, 21005 locomotive and tender, smoke and "Choo-Choo": 25045, 24549, 24626, twelve 26720 curved track, two 26700 straight track, 704, 26690, No. 22004 (40-Watt transformer).

EX-C7	LN-C8	Scarcity
1,750	2,000	7

20430 SUNSHINE SPECIAL: 1958, 21831 GP-7 Diesel: 24029, 24209, 24539, 24626, 25049, twelve 26720 curved track, four 26700 straight track, 704, 26690, No. 22004 (40-Watt transformer). Values listed below assume locomotive lettered "AMERICAN FLYER LINES" if locomotive lettered "TEXAS AND PACIFIC" values should be increased 30 percent.

EX-C7	LN-C8	Scarcity
1,600	1,900	6

20435 METEOR: 1958, 21099 locomotive and tender, smoke, "Choo-Choo" and True-Tone electronic steam whistle; 24216, 24316, 24419, 977 or 25031, twelve 26720 curved track, two 26700 straight track, 704, 26690, No. 22020 (50-Watt transformer).

EX-C7	LN-C8	Scarcity
1,300	1,500	6

20440 SEABOARD HOT SHOT: 1958, 21918 and 21918-1 Twin Baldwin Diesel: 24033, 24109, 24216, 24309, 24413, 24619, twelve 26720 curved track, four 26700 straight track, 26752, 26690, No. 22020 (50-Watt transformer).

EX-C7	LN-C8	Scarcity
2,000	2,250	7

20445 NORTH COAST LIMITED: 1958, 21551 PA Diesel: 24843, 24846, 24849, 24853, twelve 26720 curved track, four 26700 straight track, 26752, 26690, No. 22020 (50-Watt transformer), 23561 billboard horn.

EX-C7	LN-C8	Scarcity
1,600	1,900	7

20450 TRAIL BLAZER: 1958, 21115 locomotive and tender, smoke and "Choo-Choo": 24016 or 937, 24029, 24043, 24113, 24213, 24319, 24409 or 947, 24619, twelve 26720 curved track, six 26700 straight track, 26752, 26690, eighteen 26693 track lock.

EX-C7	LN-C8	Scarcity
4,000	4,500	8

20455 MAINLINER: 1958, 21573 Electric, 24006 or 913, 24023, 24026, 24036, 24076, 24116, 24206, 24313, 24619, twelve 26720 curved track, six 26700 straight track, 26752, 26690, eighteen 26693 track lock.

EX-C7	LN-C8	Scarcity
2,300	2,800	7

20460 YARD KING SPECIAL: 1958, 21145 locomotive and tender, smoke and "Choo-Choo": 24003, 24109, 24110, 24113, two 24216, two 24309, 24403, two 24516, 24539, 24603, eighteen 26720 curved track, four 26700 straight track, four 26710s, 26745 Crossing, 26690, twenty-four 26693 track lock.

EX-C7	LN-C8	Scarcity
2,500	3,000	7

20465 MISSOURI PACIFIC FAST FREIGHT: 1958, 21920 (21920 and 21920-1) PA/PA Diesel, electronic Diesel horn: 24016 or 937, 24033, 24206, 24209, 24313, 25003 or 914, 25052, twelve 26720 curved track, six 26700 straight track, 26752, 26690, eighteen 26693 track lock, No. 22030 (100-Watt transformer). (Reduce values listed

Values for each condition are in U.S. dollars. | **Scarcity** = Scale from 1-8 with 8 being the hardest to find.

231

below by 30 percent if 914 and 937 are present rather than five-digit number cars.)

EX-C7	LN-C8	Scarcity
5,000	6,000	7

20470 PACEMAKER: 1958, 21129 locomotive and tender, smoke, "Choo-Choo," and electronic whistle: 24109, 24043, 24413, 24519, 24536, 25016, 25052, twelve 26720 curved track, six 26700 straight track, 26752, 26690, eighteen 26693 track lock, No. 22030 (100-Watt transformer).

EX-C7	LN-C8	Scarcity
6,000	7,000	7

20475 EAGLE: 1958, 21920 (21920 and 21920-1) PA/PA Diesel, electronic Diesel horn: 24856, 24859, 24863, 24866, twelve 26720 curved track, six 26700 straight track, 26752, 26690, eighteen 26693 track lock, No. 22030 (100-Watt transformer).

EX-C7	LN-C8	Scarcity
5,400	6,200	7

20480 CHIEF: 1958, 21910 (21910 and 21910-1 and 21910-2) PA/PB/PA Diesel, electronic True-Tone horn and Diesel Roar; 24006 or 913, 24036, 24206, 24213, 24313, 24416, 25019, 25052, twelve 26720 curved track, eight 26700 straight track, 26752, 26690, twenty 26693 track lock.

EX-C7	LN-C8	Scarcity
3,500	4,500	7

20485 CHALLENGER: 1958, 21139 locomotive and tender, smoke, "Choo-Choo": and electronic whistle: 24023, 24036, 24076, 24209, 24316, 24529, 24553, 25042, 25052, twelve 26720 curved track, eight 26700 straight track, 26752, 26690, twenty 26693 track lock.

EX-C7	LN-C8	Scarcity
3,500	4,100	7

20505 HOTSHOT: 1959, 21156 docksider locomotive, no smoke or "Choo-Choo": 24219, 24039, 24321, 24627, twelve 26720 curved track, 704, 26690, No. 22004 (40-Watt transformer).

EX-C7	LN-C8	Scarcity
650	750	5

20510 RAMBLER: 1959, 21812 Baldwin: 24047, 24322, 24539, 24632, twelve 26720 curved track, 704, 26690, No. 22004 (40-Watt transformer).

EX-C7	LN-C8	Scarcity
900	1,100	5

20515 RELIABLE: 1959, 21085 locomotive and tender, smoke and "Choo-Choo": 24113 (with only three containers), 24546, 24556, 24561, twelve 26720 curved track, two 26700 straight track, 704, 26690, No. 22004 (40-Watt transformer).

EX-C7	LN-C8	Scarcity
350	450	4

20520 BANKERS: 1959, 21573 Electric: 24776, 24816, 24836 passenger cars with orange stripe, twelve 26720 curved track, two 26700 straight track, 704, 26690, No. 22020 (50-Watt transformer).

EX-C7	LN-C8	Scarcity
1,500	1,750	7

20525 THE DEFENDER: 1959, 21234 GP-7 locomotive with ringing bell, 24549, 24557, 24631, 25056, twelve 26720 curved track, four 26700 straight track, 26752, 26690, No. 22020 (50-Watt transformer).

EX-C7	LN-C8	Scarcity
2,100	2,500	7

20530 NIGHT HAWK: 1959-60, 21130 locomotive and tender, smoke and "Choo-Choo": 24043, 24109, 24316, 24413, 24558, 24633, twelve 26720 curved track, four 26700 straight track, 26752, 26690, No. 22020 (50-Watt transformer).

EX-C7	LN-C8	Scarcity
1,800	2,100	7

20535 PONY EXPRESS: 1959-60, 21925 (21925 and 21925-1) PA/PA Diesel, ringing bell: 24837, 24838, 24839, 24840, twelve 26720 curved track, six 26700 straight track, 26752, 26690, No. 22030 (100-Watt transformer).

EX-C7	LN-C8	Scarcity
3,400	4,000	7

20540 MERCHANDISER: 1959, 21922 (21922 and 21922-1) PA/PA Diesel, ringing bell: 24036, 24077, 24213, 24216, 24221, 24323, 24633, twelve 26720 curved track, eight 26700 straight track, 26752, 26690, No. 22030 (100-Watt transformer).

EX-C7	LN-C8	Scarcity
3,600	4,200	7

20540 THE MERCHANDISER: 1960, 21922 (21922 and 21922-1) PA/PA Diesel, ringing bell: 24036, 24077, 24213, 24216, 24221, 24323, 24633, twelve 26720 curved track, eight 26700 straight track, 26752, 26690, No. 22030 (100-Watt transformer).

EX-C7	LN-C8	Scarcity
3,500	4,100	7

20545 PATHFINDER: 1959-60, 21140 or 21139 locomotive and tender, smoke and "Choo-Choo": 24029, 24048, 24076, 24116, 24209, 24324, 24557, 24633, twelve 26720 curved track, eight 26700 straight track, 26752, 26690, No. 22030 (100-Watt transformer). (Values listed below assume 21139. If 21140 is substituted, increase values by 20 percent.)

EX-C7	LN-C8	Scarcity
3,200	3,800	6

20550 FRONTIERSMAN: 1959, 21088 locomotive and tender, smoke and "Choo-Choo": two 24720, twelve 26720 curved track, 26690, No. 22004 (40-Watt transformer).

EX-C7	LN-C8	Scarcity
250	300	3

20550 FRONTIERSMAN PASSENGER: 1960, 21088 locomotive and tender, smoke and "Choo-Choo": 24720, 24730, 24740, twelve 26720 curved track, 26690, No. 22004 (40-Watt transformer).

EX-C7	LN-C8	Scarcity
300	350	3

20605 THE ARROW: 1960, 21105 locomotive and tender, smoke and "Choo-Choo": 24066, 24225, 24627, twelve 26720 curved track, two 26700 straight track, 26752, two 26810s power clips, No. 22004 (40-Watt transformer).

EX-C7	LN-C8	Scarcity
400	500	5

20610 THE DISPATCHER: 1960, 21812 Baldwin: 24216, 24561, 24562, 24627, 26752, twelve 26720 curved track, two 26700 straight track, 704, two 26810s power clips, No. 22004 (40-Watt transformer).

EX-C7	LN-C8	Scarcity
550	625	6

20615 THE THUNDERBOLT: 1960, 21085 locomotive and tender, smoke and "Choo-Choo": 24065, 24125, 24575, 24631, twelve 26720 curved track, two 26700 straight track, 704, two 26810s power clips, No. 22004 (40-Watt transformer).

EX-C7	LN-C8	Scarcity
500	600	5

20620 THE CHIEF: 1960, 21927 PA Diesel: 24773, 24813, 24833 passenger cars with red stripe, twelve 26720 curved track, two 26700 straight track, 704, two 26810s power clips, No. 22020 (50-Watt transformer).

EX-C7	LN-C8	Scarcity
1,110	1,350	6

20625 THE DEFENDER: 1960, 21234 GP-7 locomotive, ringing bell: 24577, 25059, 25515, 24574, 24631, twelve 26720 curved track, two 26700 straight track, 704, two 26810s power clips, No. 22020 (50-Watt transformer).

EX-C7	LN-C8	Scarcity
2,000	2,300	6

20655 FRONTIERSMAN FREIGHT: 1960-61, 21089 locomotive and tender, smoke and "Choo-Choo": 24055, 24565, 24750, twelve 26720 curved track, two 26700 straight track, 26690, No. 22004 (40-Watt transformer).

EX-C7	LN-C8	Scarcity
1,200	1,500	5

20705 THE PIONEER FLYER: 1961, 21165 locomotive and tender, no smoke or "Choo-Choo": 24052, 24127 or C2009, 24636, eight 26310s, 26300, 26302, transformer.

EX-C7	LN-C8	Scarcity
125	175	1

20710 THE BULLET: 1961, 21205 F-9 Diesel: 24329, 24636, 25081, eight 26310s, 26300, 26302, transformer.

EX-C7	LN-C8	Scarcity
350	400	3

20711 THE ROCKET: 1962, L2004 F-9 Diesel: 24328, 24578, 24636, 25082, eight 26310s, three 26300s, 26302, transformer.

EX-C7	LN-C8	Scarcity
650	750	4

20715 THE ROCKET: 1961, 21210 F-9 Diesel: 25081, 24126, 24330, 24636, eight 26310s, 26300, 26302, transformer.

EX-C7	LN-C8	Scarcity
450	550	3

Values for each condition are in U.S. dollars. | Scarcity = Scale from 1-8 with 8 being the hardest to find.

233

20720 THE PRAIRIE MARKSMAN: 1961-62, 21168 locomotive and tender, smoke and "Choo-Choo": 24054 or 24056, 24230, 24636, 25071, eight 26310s, 26300, 26302, transformer. (If 24056 is included rather than 24054, increase values 50 percent.)

EX-C7	LN-C8	Scarcity
275	350	4

20725 THE TRAILBLAZER: 1961, 21215 (21215 and 21215-1) Twin F-9 A-units: 24230, 24561, 24572, 25071, eight 26310s, three 26300s, 26302, No. 22020 (50-Watt transformer).

EX-C7	LN-C8	Scarcity
550	675	5

20730 THE CHAMPION: 1961, 21085 locomotive and tender, smoke and "Choo-Choo": 24330, 24566 (if gray, double values listed below), 24633, 25071, 25082, eight 26310s, three 26300s, 26302, No. 22020 (50-Watt transformer).

EX-C7	LN-C8	Scarcity
600	700	4

20730 THE CHAMPION: 1962, 21085 locomotive and tender, smoke and "Choo-Choo": 24328, 24566, 24633, 25071, 25082, eight 26310s, three 26300s, 26302, No. 22020 (50-Watt transformer).

EX-C7	LN-C8	Scarcity
550	650	4

20735 THE CHIEF: 1961-62, 21927 PA Diesel: 24773, 24813, 24833, passenger cars with red stripe, eight 26310s, three 26300s, 26302, No. 22020 (50-Watt transformer).

EX-C7	LN-C8	Scarcity
1,100	1,350	6

20740 THE DEFENDER: 1961, 21234 GP-7 locomotive, ringing bell: 24574, 24577, 24631, 25059, 25515, eight 26310s, three 26300s, 26302, No. 22020 (50-Watt transformer).

EX-C7	LN-C8	Scarcity
2,000	2,500	7

20741 THE METEOR FREIGHT: 1962, 21130 locomotive and tender, smoke and "Choo-Choo": 24566, 24575, 24633, 25058, 25062, twelve 26310s, three 26300s, 26302, 26322 90-degree crossing, No. 22020 (50-Watt transformer).

EX-C7	LN-C8	Scarcity
1,600	1,900	7

20763 THE CASEY JONES: 1963-64, 21166 locomotive and tender, no smoke or "Choo-Choo": 24058, 24124, 24627 or 24636, eight 26310s, 26300, 25302, transformer.

EX-C7	LN-C8	Scarcity
125	175	1

20764 THE KLONDIKE: 1963-64, 21207 and 21207-1 Twin F-9 A-units: 24060, 24127, 24203, 24328, 24631, eight 26310s, 26300, 26302, transformer.

EX-C7	LN-C8	Scarcity
525	650	5

20765 THE HAWKEYE: 1963, 21168 locomotive and tender, smoke and "Choo-Choo": 24059, 24222, 24539, 24575, 24636, eight 26310s, 26300, 26302, transformer.

EX-C7	LN-C8	Scarcity
900	1,150	7

20766 THE MOHAWK: 1963-64, 21085 locomotive and tender, smoke and "Choo-Choo": 24103, 24230, 24329, 24422, 24566, 24634, eight 26310s, three 26300s, 26302, No. 22020 (50-Watt transformer).

EX-C7	LN-C8	Scarcity
550	675	5

20767 THE EAGLE: 1963-64, 21920 PA Diesel: 24856, 24859, 24863, 24866, eight 26310s, three 26300s, 26302, No. 22020 (50-Watt transformer).

EX-C7	LN-C8	Scarcity
2,600	3,500	7

20768 THE SMOKEY MOUNTAIN: 1963-64, 21130 locomotive and tender, smoke and "Choo-Choo": 24065, 24076, 24125, 24225, 24329, 24566, 24577, 24634, eight 23610s, five 26300s, 26302, No. 22020 (50-Watt transformer).

EX-C7	LN-C8	Scarcity
1,800	2,200	6

20773 THE ALLEGHENY: 1964, 21107 locomotive and tender, smoke and "Choo-Choo": C2009, 24566, 24575, 24633, eight 26310s, 26300, 26302, No. 22020 (50-Watt transformer).

EX-C7	LN-C8	Scarcity
450	550	3

20800 GAME TRAIN: 1963, L2001 "CASEY JONES" locomotive and tender, no smoke or "Choo-Choo": "Buffalo Hunt" gondola, "Freight Ahead" caboose, eight 26310s, 26300, 26302, No. 22006 (25-Watt transformer), game board and game accessories.

EX-C7	LN-C8	Scarcity
225	275	3

20811 THE PIONEER 600: 1965-66, 21166 locomotive and tender, no smoke or "Choo-Choo": 24125, 24422, 24636, four 26101 curved panels, two 26121 straight panels, transformer.

EX-C7	LN-C8	Scarcity
175	250	3

20812 THE CHAMPION 800: 1965-66, 21107 locomotive and tender, smoke and "Choo-Choo": 24127, 24225, 24324, 24636, four 26101 curved panels, two 26121 straight panels, 26141 right switch panel, 26142 left switch panel, transformer.

EX-C7	LN-C8	Scarcity
275	350	3

20813 THE WESTERNER 1200: 1965-66, 21085 locomotive and tender, smoke and "Choo-Choo": 24054, 24328, 24566, 24575, 24634, four 26101 curved panels, four 26121 straight panels, 26141 right switch panel, two 26142 left switch panel, 26151 crossover panel, transformer.

EX-C7	LN-C8	Scarcity
450	525	4

20814 WINTER WONDERLAND: 1966, 21107 locomotive and tender, smoke and "Choo-Choo": 24127, 24225, 24329, 24636, four 26101 curved snow panels, two 26121 straight snow panels, transformer.

EX-C7	LN-C8	Scarcity
850	1,000	7

23099 FRONTIERSMAN: 1959, 21088 locomotive and tender, smoke and "Choo-Choo": two 24720s.

EX-C7	LN-C8	Scarcity
250	300	3

23099 FRONTIERSMAN PASSENGER: 1960, 21088 locomotive and tender, smoke and "Choo-Choo": 24720, 24730, 24740.

EX-C7	LN-C8	Scarcity
300	350	4

K5206W AMERICAN FLYER FREIGHT: 1952, K325 locomotive and tender, smoke, "Choo-Choo," and air-chime whistle: 925, 929, 930, 931, twelve 702 curved track, four 700 straight track, 706, 690, sixteen 693 track lock, smoke capsule and funnel, air-chime whistle control.

EX-C7	LN-C8	Scarcity
650	800	5

K5210W AMERICAN FLYER FREIGHT: 1952, K335 locomotive and tender, smoke, "Choo-Choo," and air-chime whistle: 928, 931, 944, 945, twelve 702 curved track, six 700 straight track, 706, 690, eighteen 693 track lock, smoke capsule and funnel.

EX-C7	LN-C8	Scarcity
800	950	5

K5328 THE METEOR STEAM PASSENGER TRAIN: 1953, 293 locomotive and tender, smoke and "Choo-Choo": 951G, 952G, 953G, 954G, twelve 702 curved track, four 700 straight track, 706, 690, sixteen 693 track lock, 40.

EX-C7	LN-C8	Scarcity
1,200	1,500	6

K5329 THE METEOR STEAM FREIGHT TRAIN: 1953, 293 locomotive and tender, smoke and "Choo-Choo": 924, 925, 927, 929, 930, 933, twelve 702 curved track, four 700 straight track, 706, 690, sixteen 693 track lock, 40.

EX-C7	LN-C8	Scarcity
475	550	4

K5334T THE SILVER COMET: 1953, 466 PA Diesel: 960, 962, 963, twelve 702 curved track, two 700 straight track, 706, 690, fourteen 693 track lock, No. 2 (75-Watt transformer).

EX-C7	LN-C8	Scarcity
700	900	5

K5335T THE SILVER COMET: 1953, 466 (chrome) PA Diesel: 934, 936, 928, 945, twelve 702 curved track, two 700 straight track, 706, 690, fourteen 693 track lock, No. 2 (75-Watt transformer).

EX-C7	LN-C8	Scarcity
550	650	4

K5340T THE YARD KING: 1953, 343 locomotive and tender, smoke and "Choo-Choo": 934, 944, 945, 953R, twelve 702 curved track, four 700 straight track, 706, 690, sixteen 693 track lock, 40, No. 2 (75-Watt transformer).

EX-C7	LN-C8	Scarcity
800	1,050	5

K5345W THE TRAIL BLAZER: 1953-54, 316 locomotive and tender, smoke, "Choo-Choo," and air-chime whistle: 918R, 952R, 953R, 954R, twelve 702 curved track, four 700 straight track, 913, 706, 690, sixteen 693 track lock, 40, 708 air-chime whistle controller.

EX-C7	LN-C8	Scarcity
2,000	2,400	7

K5346W THE TRAIL BLAZER: 1953-54, 316 locomotive and tender, smoke, "Choo-Choo," and air-chime whistle: 915, 920, 928, 921, 922, 930, twelve 702 curved track, four 700 straight track, 706, 690, sixteen 693 track lock, 40, 708 air-chime whistle control unit.

EX-C7	LN-C8	Scarcity
700	900	5

K5351W THE PACEMAKER: 1953-54, 326 locomotive and tender, smoke, "Choo-Choo," and air-chime whistle: 960, 961, 962, 963 passenger cars with chrome finish, twelve 702 curved track, six 700 straight track, 706, 690, eighteen 693 track lock, 40, 708 air-chime whistle control unit.

EX-C7	LN-C8	Scarcity
1,000	1,300	6

K5352W THE PACEMAKER: 1953-54, 326 locomotive and tender, smoke, "Choo-Choo," and air-chime whistle: 926, 928, 930, 936, 937, 946, twelve 702 curved track, six 700 straight track, 706, eighteen 693 track lock, 40, 708 air-chime whistle control unit.

EX-C7	LN-C8	Scarcity
700	850	5

K5357W THE CHALLENGER: 1953-54, 336 locomotive and tender, smoke, "Choo-Choo," and air-chime whistle: 960, two 962s, 963 passenger cars with chrome finished, twelve 702 curved track, eight 700 straight track, 706, 690, twenty 693 track lock, 40, 708 air-chime whistle control unit.

EX-C7	LN-C8	Scarcity
1,500	1,800	6

K5358W THE CHALLENGER: 1953-54, 336 locomotive and tender, smoke, "Choo-Choo," and air-chime whistle: 921, 922, 924, 929, 930, 931, 947, twelve 702 curved track,

Values for each condition are in U.S. dollars. | Scarcity = Scale from 1-8 with 8 being the hardest to find.

235

eight 700 straight track, 706, 690, twenty 693 track lock, 40, 708 air-chime whistle control unit.

EX-C7	LN-C8	Scarcity
800	1,000	6

K5363W THE SILVER ROCKET: 1953-54, 4745 (474/475) (chrome-plated or silver-painted) PA/PA Diesel, air-chime whistle; 913, 925, 930, 936, 941, 946, twelve 702 curved track, six 700 straight track, 706, 690, eighteen 693 track lock, 708 air-chime whistle control.

EX-C7	LN-C8	Scarcity
900	1,200	6

K5364W THE SILVER ROCKET: 1953, 4745 (474/475) PA/PA Diesel, air-chime whistle; three chrome 962, and a 963, twelve 702 curved track, six 700 straight track, 706, 690, eighteen 693 track lock, 708 air-chime whistle control unit.

EX-C7	LN-C8	Scarcity
1,100	1,300	6

K5364W THE SILVER ROCKET: 1954, 4745 (474/475) PA/PA Diesel, air-chime whistle: three 962 and a 963 silver painted passenger cars with green stripes, twelve 702 curved track, six 700 straight track, 706, 690, eighteen 693 track lock, 708 air-chime whistle controller.

EX-C7	LN-C8	Scarcity
1,200	1,400	6

K5368WT THE SILVER FLASH: 1953, 4778 (477/478) (chrome) PA/PB Diesel, air-chime whistle; 928, 929, 940, 937, 930, twelve 702 curved track, four 700 straight track, 706, 690, No. 2 (75-Watt transformer), sixteen 693 track lock, 708 air-chime whistle control unit.

K5369WT THE SILVER FLASH: 1953, 4778 (477/478) PA/PB Diesel, air-chime whistle: 960, 961, 963, locomotives and cars chrome plated, twelve 702 curved track, four 700 straight track, 706, 690, No. 2 (75-Watt transformer), sixteen 693 track lock, 708 air-chime whistle control unit.

EX-C7	LN-C8	Scarcity
400	500	4

K5374W THE CHIEF DIESEL FREIGHT TRAIN: 1953-54, 4713 (470/471/473) (chrome or painted silver) PA/PB/PA Diesel, air-chime whistle; 924, 929, 947, 921, 925, 922, 930, twelve 702 curved track, eight 700 straight track, 706, 690, twenty 693 track lock, 708 air-chime whistle control unit.

EX-C7	LN-C8	Scarcity
1,400	1,600	4

K5375W THE CHIEF DIESEL PASSENGER TRAIN: 1953, 4713 (470/471/473) PA/PB/PA Diesel, air-chime whistle; 960, 961, 962, 963, locomotives and cars are chrome plated, twelve 702 curved track, eight 700 straight track, 706, 690, twenty 693 track lock, 708 air-chime whistle control unit.

EX-C7	LN-C8	Scarcity
1,600	2,000	6

K5375W THE CHIEF DIESEL PASSENGER TRAIN: 1954, 4713 (470/471/473) PA/PB/PA Diesel, air-chime whistle; 960, 961, 962, 963, cars and locomotives painted silver set, cars have red stripe, twelve 702 curved track, eight 700 straight track, 706, 690, twenty 693 track lock, 708 air-chime whistle controller.

EX-C7	LN-C8	Scarcity
1,700	2,100	6

K5401T THE CRUSADER: 1954, 307 locomotive and tender, no smoke or "Choo-Choo": 905, 938, twelve 702 curved track, 704, 690, No. 1-1/2 (50-Watt transformer).

EX-C7	LN-C8	Scarcity
125	175	1

K5406T THE SILVER BULLET PASSENGER SET: 354 satin silver painted locomotive and tender, smoke and "Choo-Choo": two 955, twelve 702 curved track, 704, 690, 40, No. 1-1/2 (50-Watt transformer).

EX-C7	LN-C8	Scarcity
1,000	1,200	4

K5407T THE SILVER BULLET STEAM FREIGHT TRAIN: 1954, 354 satin silver-painted locomotive and tender, smoke and "Choo-Choo": 906, 907, 40, twelve 702 curved track, 704, 690, No. 1-1/2 (50-Watt transformer).

EX-C7	LN-C8	Scarcity
650	850	5

K5411T THE ARROW STEAM PASSENGER TRAIN: 1954, 287 locomotive and tender, no smoke or "Choo-Choo": 951G, two 955G, twelve 702 curved track, 704, 690, No. 1-1/2 (50-Watt transformer).

EX-C7	LN-C8	Scarcity
500	600	4

K5412T THE ARROW STEAM FREIGHT TRAIN: 1954, 287 locomotive and tender, no smoke or "Choo-Choo": 923, 925, 938, 941, twelve 702 curved track, 704, 690, No. 1-1/2 (50-Watt transformer).

EX-C7	LN-C8	Scarcity
250	350	2

K5417T DIESEL SWITCHER WORK TRAIN: 1954, 371 GP-7 Diesel: 906, 907, 909, twelve 702 curved track, 704, 690, No. 1-1/2 (50-Watt transformer).

EX-C7	LN-C8	Scarcity
500	600	4

K5418T THE BLACK DIAMOND STEAM PASSENGER TRAIN: 1954, 303 locomotive and tender, smoke and "Choo-Choo": 960, 962, 963 silver-painted cars with chestnut stripe, twelve 702 curved track, 706, 690, 40, No. 1-1/2 (50-Watt transformer).

EX-C7	LN-C8	Scarcity
1,100	1,450	7

K5419T THE BLACK DIAMOND STEAM FREIGHT: 1954, 303 locomotive and tender, smoke and "Choo-Choo": 928, 934, 936, 945, twelve 702 curved track, 706, 690, 40, No. 1-1/2 (50-Watt transformer).

EX-C7	LN-C8	Scarcity
450	550	5

K5422T THE MOUNTAINEER STEAM PASSENGER TRAIN: 1954, 283 locomotive and tender, smoke and "Choo-Choo": 951R, 952R two 955R, twelve 702 curved track, two 700 straight track, 706, 690, fourteen 693 track lock, 40, No. 1-1/2 (50-Watt transformer).

EX-C7	LN-C8	Scarcity
750	900	6

K5423T THE MOUNTAINEER STEAM FREIGHT TRAIN: 1954, 283 locomotive and tender, smoke and "Choo-Choo": 923, 925, 930, 931, 930, 940, 942, twelve 702 curved track, two 700 straight track, 706, 690, fourteen 693 track lock, 40, No. 1-1/2 (50-Watt transformer).

EX-C7	LN-C8	Scarcity
350	450	4

K5434T THE SILVER COMET DIESEL PASSENGER TRAIN: 1954, 466 PA Diesel; 960, 962, and 963 satin silver-painted set, cars with blue stripe, twelve 702 curved track, two 700 straight track, 706, 690, fourteen 693 track lock, No. 1-1/2 (50-Watt transformer).

EX-C7	LN-C8	Scarcity
700	850	6

K5435T THE SILVER COMET DIESEL FREIGHT TRAIN: 1954, 466 PA Diesel; 934, 936, 928, 945, twelve 702 curved track, two 700 straight track, 706, 690, fourteen 693 track lock, No. 1-1/2 (50-Watt transformer).

EX-C7	LN-C8	Scarcity
550	650	5

K5436T THE METEOR STEAM PASSENGER TRAIN: 1954, 293 locomotive and tender, smoke and "Choo-Choo": 951G, 952G, 953G, 954G, twelve 702 curved track, four 700 straight track, 706, 690, sixteen 693 track lock, 40, No. 4B (100-Watt transformer).

EX-C7	LN-C8	Scarcity
1,100	1,350	7

K5437T THE METEOR: 1954, 293 locomotive and tender, smoke and "Choo-Choo": 924, 925, 929, 930, 933, 930, 947, twelve 702 curved track, four 700 straight track, 706, 690, sixteen 693 track lock, 40, No. 4B (100-Watt transformer).

EX-C7	LN-C8	Scarcity
550	700	5

K5440T THE YARD KING: 1954, 343 locomotive and tender, smoke and "Choo-Choo": 934, 944, 945, 953R, twelve 702 curved track, four 700 straight track, 706, 690, sixteen 693 track lock, 40, No. 4B (100-Watt transformer).

EX-C7	LN-C8	Scarcity
850	1,000	5

K5468WT THE SILVER FLASH: 1954, 4778 (477/478) PA/PB Diesel, air-chime whistle: 928, 929, 930, 937, 940, twelve 702 curved track, four 700 straight track, 706, 690, sixteen 693 track lock, No. 4B (100-Watt transformer), 708 air chime whistle controller.

EX-C7	LN-C8	Scarcity
1,400	1,700	6

K5469WT THE SILVER FLASH: 1954, 4778 (477/478) PA/PB Diesel, air-chime whistle: 960, 961, 963, silver-painted passenger cars with chestnut stripe, twelve 702 curved track, four 700 straight track, 706, 690, sixteen 693 track lock, No. 4B (100-Watt transformer), 708 air chime whistle controller.

EX-C7	LN-C8	Scarcity
4,200	4,600	7

Values for each condition are in U.S. dollars. | **Scarcity** = Scale from 1-8 with 8 being the hardest to find.

237

HO-Gauge

HO STEAM LOCOMOTIVES

There's insufficient information at this time to provide a scarcity grade for these products.

112 LOCOMOTIVE: NYC, J3a Hudson 4-6-4 steam, A-C Spur Drive, headlight, remote control, number on side of cab "5318," also available in kit form as HO-112.

112 LOCOMOTIVE (TYPE I): Bakelite wheels with brass rims.

VG-C6	EX-C7	LN-C8	Scarcity
60	100	130	N/A

112 LOCOMOTIVE (TYPE II): Die-cast drive wheels.

VG-C6	EX-C7	LN-C8	Scarcity
80	150	200	N/A

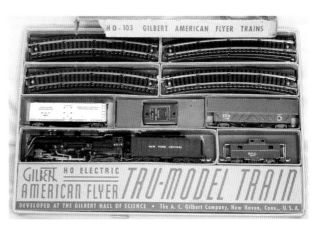

151 LOCOMOTIVE: NYC, J3a Hudson 4-6-4 steam, number on cab side "5318."

Values for each condition are in U.S. dollars. | **Scarcity =** Scale from 1-8 with 8 being the hardest to find.

239

155 SWITCHER

151 LOCOMOTIVE (TYPE I): D-C Worm Drive, smoke-in-boiler, no headlight, whitewall drive wheels.

VG-C6	EX-C7	LN-C8	Scarcity
125	170	200	N/A

151 LOCOMOTIVE (TYPE II): D-C Worm Drive, headlight, piston smoke unit in tender, whitewall drive wheels.

VG-C6	EX-C7	LN-C8	Scarcity
75	125	170	N/A

151 LOCOMOTIVE (TYPE III): 1947-49, D-C Worm Drive, headlight, bellows smoke unit in tender, whitewall drive wheels.

VG-C6	EX-C7	LN-C8	Scarcity
75	125	170	N/A

151 LOCOMOTIVE (TYPE IV): 1947-48, D-C Worm Drive, with headlight, piston smoke unit in tender, no cab number, whitewall drive wheels.

VG-C6	EX-C7	LN-C8	Scarcity
80	130	175	N/A

155 SWITCHER: PRR, B6sb 0-6-0 slant back steam, S/CC.

VG-C6	EX-C7	LN-C8	Scarcity
65	110	160	N/A

200 LOCOMOTIVE: NYC, J3a Hudson 4-6-4 steam.

200 LOCOMOTIVE (TYPE I): A-C Spur Drive, with headlight, remote control, Bakelite wheels with brass rims, number on cab "5318," also available in kit form as HO-1.

VG-C6	EX-C7	LN-C8	Scarcity
60	100	130	N/A

200 LOCOMOTIVE (TYPE II): A-C Spur Drive, no headlight, Bakelite wheels, single red window strut, number on cab "5318," also available in kit form as HO-1.

VG-C6	EX-C7	LN-C8	Scarcity
75	120	150	N/A

433 SWITCHER: PRR, B6sb 0-6-0 slantback steam, S/CC.

VG-C6	EX-C7	LN-C8	Scarcity
50	75	100	N/A

443 LOCOMOTIVE: NYC, J3a Hudson 4-6-4, whitewall drive wheels, S/CC.

VG-C6	EX-C7	LN-C8	Scarcity
60	90	125	N/A

446 LOCOMOTIVE: NYC, J3a Hudson 4-6-4, whitewall drive wheels, with whistle, S/CC.

VG-C6	EX-C7	LN-C8	Scarcity
70	100	150	N/A

5318 LOCOMOTIVE: See 112, 151 or 200.

31004 SWITCHER: PRR, B6sb 0-6-0 slantback S/CC.

VG-C6	EX-C7	LN-C8	Scarcity
40	65	85	N/A

31005 LOCOMOTIVE: NYC, J3a Hudson 4-6-4 steam S/CC.

VG-C6	EX-C7	LN-C8	Scarcity
55	80	110	N/A

31019 SWITCHER: B & O, B6sb 0-6-0 slantback S/CC.

VG-C6	EX-C7	LN-C8	Scarcity
95	155	210	N/A

200 LOCOMOTIVE

433 SWITCHER

446 LOCOMOTIVE

Values for each condition are in U.S. dollars. | **Scarcity** = Scale from 1-8 with 8 being the hardest to find.

241

31004 SWITCHER

31005 LOCOMOTIVE

31045 LOCOMOTIVE

433 SWITCHER

31031 LOCOMOTIVE: B & O, B6sb 0-6-0 slantback, no S/CC.

VG-C6	EX-C7	LN-C8	Scarcity
45	70	90	N/A

31036 LOCOMOTIVE: Erie, B6sb 0-6-0 slantback switcher, no S/CC.

VG-C6	EX-C7	LN-C8	Scarcity
40	65	80	N/A

31045 LOCOMOTIVE: Wabash, J3a Hudson 4-6-4 steam S/CC.

VG-C6	EX-C7	LN-C8	Scarcity
70	110	165	N/A

31088 LOCOMOTIVE: FY & P, Franklin 4-4-0 Old Time (Tyco), green and red.

VG-C6	EX-C7	LN-C8	Scarcity
150	250	325	N/A

HO DIESEL LOCOMOTIVES

420 LOCOMOTIVE: 📷 Lackawanna, F-3 A-unit EMD powered diesel, silver.

VG-C6	EX-C7	LN-C8	Scarcity
45	75	90	N/A

421 LOCOMOTIVE: B & O, F-3 A-unit EMD powered diesel, blue and gray.

VG-C6	EX-C7	LN-C8	Scarcity
50	75	100	N/A

422 LOCOMOTIVE: B & O, F-3 A-unit EMD dummy diesel, blue and gray.

VG-C6	EX-C7	LN-C8	Scarcity
80	150	175	N/A

423 LOCOMOTIVE: NP, F-3 A-unit EMD powered diesel, green.

VG-C6	EX-C7	LN-C8	Scarcity
85	120	140	N/A

424 LOCOMOTIVE: NP, F-3 A-unit EMD dummy diesel, green.

VG-C6	EX-C7	LN-C8	Scarcity
60	100	125	N/A

425 LOCOMOTIVE: Lackawanna F-3 B-unit EMD dummy diesel, no number, silver.

VG-C6	EX-C7	LN-C8	Scarcity
100	150	200	N/A

426 LOCOMOTIVE: B & O, F-3 B-unit EMD dummy diesel, blue and gray.

VG-C6	EX-C7	LN-C8	Scarcity
100	150	200	N/A

427 LOCOMOTIVE: NP, F-3 B-unit EMD dummy diesel, green.

VG-C6	EX-C7	LN-C8	Scarcity
100	150	200	N/A

Values for each condition are in U.S. dollars. | **Scarcity** = Scale from 1-8 with 8 being the hardest to find.

Gilbert HO Diesels

Modern Authentically Detailed Streamliners

$15.95

$4.95

No. HO-420 GENERAL MOTORS DIESEL "A" UNIT
WITH UNIVERSAL DRIVE

No HO layout is complete without a Diesel growler to take over the freight or passenger chores, and this one is a real beauty. From front to rear she's a perfect scale model of the prototype GM monsters that constitute the backbone of most locomotive fleets. With its Universal Drive all eight wheels on both trucks pull the load, thus creating top running performance. Exhausts, hatches, grillework, ladders, handrails and lucite headlight complete the detail. 7" long.

No. HO-425 GENERAL MOTORS DIESEL "B" UNIT

Add one, two or even more of these dummy "B" units to your powered "A" unit, and you've got a locomotive that looks more real than the real thing itself! For a long freight drag or a speedy varnish run, you'll want the realism one of these "B" units will provide. 7" long.

Here's what the head end of a long freight haul looks like when you attach a couple of "B" units behind your powered Diesel "A" locomotive. A three-unit job like this is just the ticket for your fast passenger runs, too.

18

420 LOCOMOTIVE

---

430 DL-600 DEMONSTRATOR: 📷 Alco, powered, maroon and gray.

VG-C6	EX-C7	LN-C8	Scarcity
50	70	100	N/A

L1001 LOCOMOTIVE: NP, F-3 A-unit Pikemaster, powered diesel, green.

VG-C6	EX-C7	LN-C8	Scarcity
125	150	200	N/A

L3003 LOCOMOTIVE: SF, F-3 A-unit Pikemaster, powered diesel, red.

VG-C6	EX-C7	LN-C8	Scarcity
25	40	55	N/A

31007 LOCOMOTIVE: 📷 B & O, F-3 A-unit EMD powered diesel, blue and gray.

VG-C6	EX-C7	LN-C8	Scarcity
95	140	180	N/A

31008 LOCOMOTIVE: B & O, F-3 B-unit EMD dummy diesel, blue and gray.

VG-C6	EX-C7	LN-C8	Scarcity
200	300	400	N/A

31009 LOCOMOTIVE: B & O, F-3 A-unit EMD dummy diesel, blue and gray.

VG-C6	EX-C7	LN-C8	Scarcity
90	140	160	N/A

430 DL-600 DEMONSTRATOR

GILBERT **HO** LOCOMOTIVES

No. 31007

No. 31010

NEW **No. 31007 B&O DIESEL (POWERED)** — This rugged growler holds the rails as though it were born to them and she's got power for those l-o-n-g hauls. Has headlight. 7″ long.

NEW **No. 31009 B&O DIESEL (NON-POWERED)** — Same as above, except without motor. Couples on behind your powered "A" unit for added train realism. 7″ long. (not illustrated)

NEW **No. 31010 NORTHERN PACIFIC DIESEL (POWERED)** — Husky GM diesel in colorful Northern Pacific finish. 7″ long.

NEW **No. 31012 NORTHERN PACIFIC DIESEL (NON-POWERED)** — Same as above, except without motor. 7″ long. (not illustrated)

No. 31011

No. 31008

NEW **No. 31011 NORTHERN PACIFIC "B" UNIT** — Use behind a powered "A" or between two "A's", one with and one without power, to create multi-unit locomotives. 7″ long.

NEW **No. 31008 B&O DIESEL "B" UNIT** — One of these between a powered "A" unit and a non-powered "A" makes the sweetest looking triple unit drag anywhere. 7″ long.

HO DIESEL LOCOMOTIVES

No. 31003

No. 31003 ALCO DIESEL

A handsome — and necessary — addition to any round-house! This slick Alco beauty is loaded with power and has new universal ball-and-socket drive: all 12 wheels pull the load! Includes multiple illuminated headlights (4 in front, 2 in rear) plus lighted number boards. An all-purpose loco to handle any freight or passenger assignment with ease. 8-7 16″ long.

No. 31004 PENNSYLVANIA SWITCHER

Sweetest coal-burning yard goat anywhere, bar none. With her worm-drive motor she's a real workhorse, too, with plenty of class to take yard abuse. Watch her bustle about on her chores, puffing Smoke and sounding off with Choo-Choos and you'll agree there's nothing finer in "HO." 9″ long.

No. 31004

No. 31006 HUDSON LOCOMOTIVE

One of the classic locomotives in the "HO" field is this magnificent N.Y. Central "Hudson", with puffing Smoke and a built-in Electronic Steam Whistle. Has powerful worm-drive motor and the most elaborate and authentic detail possible. A thoroughbred through-and-through. 14″ long.

No. 31005 HUDSON LOCOMOTIVE (Not illustrated)

Same as No. 31006 except without Whistle.

No. 31006

31007 LOCOMOTIVE

Values for each condition are in U.S. dollars. | **Scarcity =** Scale from 1-8 with 8 being the hardest to find.

245

31010 LOCOMOTIVE

31010 LOCOMOTIVE:  NP, F-3 A-unit EMD powered diesel, green.

VG-C6	EX-C7	LN-C8	Scarcity
100	150	170	N/A

31011 LOCOMOTIVE: NP, F-3 B-unit EMD dummy diesel, green.

VG-C6	EX-C7	LN-C8	Scarcity
100	125	150	N/A

31012 LOCOMOTIVE: NP, F-3 A-unit EMD dummy diesel, green.

VG-C6	EX-C7	LN-C8	Scarcity
100	125	150	N/A

31013 LOCOMOTIVE: Industrial, transfer diesel, black, with counterweight.

VG-C6	EX-C7	LN-C8	Scarcity
80	125	160	N/A

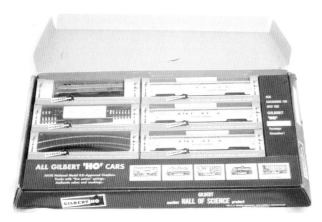

31014 LOCOMOTIVE: SP, F-3 A-unit EMD powered diesel, orange.

VG-C6	EX-C7	LN-C8	Scarcity
110	160	200	N/A

31017 LOCOMOTIVE: C & O, Alco DL-600, 600 on number boards, blue and yellow.

VG-C6	EX-C7	LN-C8	Scarcity
115	170	210	N/A

31021 LOCOMOTIVE: Industrial, transfer diesel, blue, no counterweight.

VG-C6	EX-C7	LN-C8	Scarcity
30	45	60	N/A

31022 LOCOMOTIVE: C & O, Alco DL-600 with ringing bell (see 31017), blue.

VG-C6	EX-C7	LN-C8	Scarcity
70	140	180	N/A

31025 LOCOMOTIVE: C & O, F-3 A-unit Pikemaster powered diesel, blue plastic.

VG-C6	EX-C7	LN-C8	Scarcity
25	50	75	N/A

31025 LOCOMOTIVE: C & O, F-3 A-unit Pikemaster, blue.

VG-C6	EX-C7	LN-C8	Scarcity
100	150	200	N/A

31022 LOCOMOTIVE

31032 LOCOMOTIVE: NP, F-3 A-unit Pikemaster powered diesel.

VG-C6	EX-C7	LN-C8	Scarcity
50	70	95	N/A

31037 LOCOMOTIVE: M & St. L, F-3 A-unit Pikemaster, without headlight, red/white.

VG-C6	EX-C7	LN-C8	Scarcity
95	145	175	N/A

31037 LOCOMOTIVE: M & St. L, F-3 A-unit Pikemaster powered diesel, red and white.

VG-C6	EX-C7	LN-C8	Scarcity
70	90	120	N/A

31038 LOCOMOTIVE: M & St. L, F-3 A-unit Pikemaster dummy diesel, red and white.

VG-C6	EX-C7	LN-C8	Scarcity
100	120	140	N/A

31039 LOCOMOTIVE: MP, F-3 A-unit EMD powered diesel, silver and blue.

VG-C6	EX-C7	LN-C8	Scarcity
150	225	300	N/A

35105 INSPECTION CAR: 📷 Marked "105," with a two-man crew.

VG-C6	EX-C7	LN-C8	Scarcity
35	65	95	N/A

Values for each condition are in U.S. dollars. | **Scarcity** = Scale from 1-8 with 8 being the hardest to find.

247

HO PASSENGER CARS

121K BAGGAGE CAR: NH, AF, kit, couplers on trucks, number on car side "2764."

VG-C6	EX-C7	LN-C8	Scarcity
28	48	85	N/A

122K COACH CAR: NH, AF, kit, couplers on trucks, number on car side "8302."

VG-C6	EX-C7	LN-C8	Scarcity
25	40	80	N/A

133 BAGGAGE CAR: NH, "American Flyer Style," green.

VG-C6	EX-C7	LN-C8	Scarcity
40	70	110	N/A

135 COACH, NH: "American Flyer Style," green.

VG-C6	EX-C7	LN-C8	Scarcity
25	65	100	N/A

208 COACH CAR: NH, AF, die-cast, couplers on trucks, number on car side "8301"; car also available in kit form as HO-9.

VG-C6	EX-C7	LN-C8	Scarcity
25	40	80	N/A

215 BAGGAGE CAR: NH, AF, couplers on body, number on car side "2764"; car also available in kit form as HO-14.

VG-C6	EX-C7	LN-C8	Scarcity
30	50	95	N/A

540 COMBINE CAR: NP, green, lighted.

VG-C6	EX-C7	LN-C8	Scarcity
25	35	50	N/A

541 COACH CAR: NP, green, lighted.

VG-C6	EX-C7	LN-C8	Scarcity
28	38	53	N/A

542 VISTA DOME: NP, green, lighted.

VG-C6	EX-C7	LN-C8	Scarcity
30	40	55	N/A

543 OBSERVATION CAR: NP, green, lighted.

VG-C6	EX-C7	LN-C8	Scarcity
28	38	53	N/A

C1002 COMBINE CAR: NP, Pikemaster, non-lighted, green.

VG-C6	EX-C7	LN-C8	Scarcity
100	150	200	N/A

C1003 VISTA DOME: NP, Pikemaster, non-lighted, green.

VG-C6	EX-C7	LN-C8	Scarcity
100	150	200	N/A

C1004 OBSERVATION CAR: NP, Pikemaster, non-lighted, green.

VG-C6	EX-C7	LN-C8	Scarcity
100	150	200	N/A

2764 BAGGAGE CAR: See 121 or 215.

8302 COACH CAR: See 122.

33530 COMBINE CAR: SP, lighted, silver and orange.

VG-C6	EX-C7	LN-C8	Scarcity
60	120	160	N/A

33531 COACH CAR: SP, lighted, silver and orange.

VG-C6	EX-C7	LN-C8	Scarcity
60	120	160	N/A

33540 COMBINE CAR: NP, lighted, green.

VG-C6	EX-C7	LN-C8	Scarcity
25	35	50	N/A

33541 COACH CAR: NP, lighted, green.

VG-C6	EX-C7	LN-C8	Scarcity
35	50	65	N/A

33542 VISTA DOME: NP, lighted, green.

VG-C6	EX-C7	LN-C8	Scarcity
30	45	60	N/A

33543 OBSERVATION CAR: NP, lighted, green.

VG-C6	EX-C7	LN-C8	Scarcity
32	45	62	N/A

33720 COACH: F Y & P, Old Time, by Mantua-Tyco, yellow.

VG-C6	EX-C7	LN-C8	Scarcity
95	150	210	N/A

33721 COMBINE CAR: MP, lighted, silver and blue.

VG-C6	EX-C7	LN-C8	Scarcity
75	125	150	N/A

33722 COACH CAR: MP, lighted (sold separately only), silver and blue.

VG-C6	EX-C7	LN-C8	Scarcity
120	180	200	N/A

33723 VISTA DOME: MP, lighted, silver and blue.

VG-C6	EX-C7	LN-C8	Scarcity
75	125	150	N/A

33724 OBSERVATION CAR: MP, lighted, silver/blue.

VG-C6	EX-C7	LN-C8	Scarcity
75	125	150	N/A

HO PASSENGER CARS

Values for each condition are in U.S. dollars. | **Scarcity** = Scale from 1-8 with 8 being the hardest to find.

HO FREIGHT CARS

113 REFRIGERATOR CAR: Prewar, PFE, die-cast, orange, couplers on body, number on car side "35901"; car also available in kit form as 113K.

VG-C6	EX-C7	LN-C8	Scarcity
20	40	60	N/A

114 REFRIGERATOR CAR: MDT, die-cast, white/brown, couplers on trucks, number on car side "49611," car also available in kit form as 114K.

VG-C6	EX-C7	LN-C8	Scarcity
20	40	60	N/A

115 TANK CAR: Prewar, Texaco, die-cast, black, couplers on body, car also available in kit form as 115K; number on car side "5802."

VG-C6	EX-C7	LN-C8	Scarcity
10	22	45	N/A

116 TANK CAR: Sinclair, gasoline, die-cast, black, couplers on trucks, car also available in kit form as 116K; number on car side "24712."

VG-C6	EX-C7	LN-C8	Scarcity
15	30	50	N/A

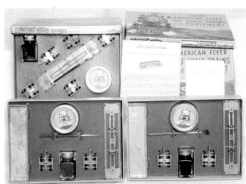

117 GONDOLA: LNE, die-cast, black, couplers on trucks, also available in kit form as item 117K, number on car side "15503."

VG-C6	EX-C7	LN-C8	Scarcity
10	22	45	N/A

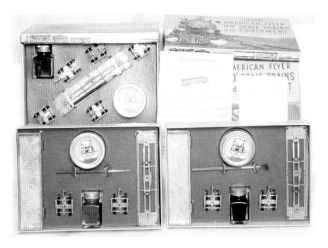

118 GONDOLA
118 GONDOLA: PRR, die-cast, brown, couplers on body, also available in kit form as item 118K; number on car side "147313."

VG-C6	EX-C7	LN-C8	Scarcity
12	28	50	N/A

119 FLATCAR: IC, with three-wheel sets, die-cast, gray, no number, couplers connected, also available in kit form as item 119K.

VG-C6	EX-C7	LN-C8	Scarcity
25	45	75	N/A

120 CABOOSE:  NYC, 1939, die-cast, red with center cupola, couplers on trucks, car also available in kit form as 120K, number on side of car "32404."

VG-C6	EX-C7	LN-C8	Scarcity
15	30	60	N/A

123 REFRIGERATOR CAR: PFE (Pacific Fruit Express) refrigerator.

123 REFRIGERATOR CAR (Type I): Encircled SP, orange and brown.

VG-C6	EX-C7	LN-C8	Scarcity
22	45	65	N/A

123 REFRIGERATOR CAR (Type II): PFE, encircled SP, all orange.

VG-C6	EX-C7	LN-C8	Scarcity
100	140	180	N/A

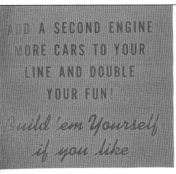

ADD A SECOND ENGINE MORE CARS TO YOUR LINE AND DOUBLE YOUR FUN!

Build 'em Yourself if you like

Build 'Em yourself — Miniature Tru-Model Locomotives and Rolling Stock in ready-to-assemble kits.

Building these realistic "HO" gauge Tru-Model locomotives, tenders and cars is nearly as much fun as running them afterwards. Actually to see a model of a true-to-life locomotive take shape in your own hands—as you add one part after another—gives you a glorious sense of achievement. And you don't have to be an expert craftsman to follow the easy instructions.

Kits are complete with die cast parts, automatic couplers, paints, brushes, decalcomanias — everything you'll need to build a model that will make you the envy of all your friends. Every section of every locomotive, tender and car is machined, drilled and tapped with flawless precision. No filing or scraping is necessary to make them fit perfectly. Get yourself an "extra bonus" in fun and enjoyment by making your own "HO" train — look over these splendid kits now and decide which ones you want first.

"HO" GAUGE THE HOBBYISTS' LINE

HO-120K CABOOSE . $1.75
This fascinating kit builds an authentic perfectly scaled caboose. Everything you need from start to finish is included along with easy-to-follow instructions.

HO-120 CABOOSE . $2.25
4½" long. Perfectly scaled. Cupola, end rails and ladders. Die-cast, 8 Bakelite wheels.

HO-117K "L.N.E." GONDOLA KIT and **HO-118K "PENN" GONDOLA KIT** . ea. $1.75
You'll want to build both these gondola cars. Each kit contains automatic couplers, paints and brushes.

HO-117 GONDOLA CAR $2.25
"Lehigh New England" 5⅜" Gondola. Metalcoat finish, white lettering.

HO-118 GONDOLA CAR $2.25
"Pennsylvania" 5⅜" Gondola, Tuscan red, white markings.

HO-113K "PAC. FRUIT EXP." HO-114K "MERCHANTS DES." REFRIG. CAR KITS . ea. $1.75
Die-cast sections, trucks, bake-lite wheels, automatic couplers, paint. Everything to build a fine refrigerator car.

HO-113 "PACIFIC FRUIT EXP." 5¾" LONG . . . $2.25
Tuscan Red finish, yellow sides.

HO-114 "M.D." REF. CAR 5¾" LONG $2.25
Ladders, catwalk, white sides.

HO-115 "TEXACO" TANK CAR KIT, HO-116 "SINCLAIR" CAR KIT . . . . ea. $1.75
Kits make Tank Cars which are exact replicas of those used by two of the major oil companies.

HO-115 "TEXACO" TANK CAR—5¾" LONG . $2.25
Silver finish, Black lettering on side of tank car.

HO-116 "SINCLAIR" TANK CAR—5¾" LONG . $2.25
Black, white letters.

HO-119K "ILLINOIS CENTRAL" FLAT CAR KIT . . . $1.75
This kit builds an "Ill. Cent." flat car that's right in every detail—with three trucks for load.

HO-119 "ILLINOIS CENTRAL" FLAT CAR—5¾" LONG . $2.25
Finished in black with white lettering, carrying three spare trucks for realism.

   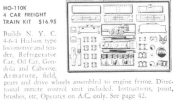

HO-112K N.Y.C. (4-6-4) LOCOMOTIVE AND TENDER KIT $11.95
Armature, field, gears and drive wheels assembled to engine frame. Directional remote control unit included. Instructions, paints, brushes, etc. Operates on A.C. only. See page 42.

HO-112 N.Y.C. (4-6-4) LOCOMOTIVE AND TENDER $14.95
Die-cast, directional remote control. Lucite headlight. 6 huge drive wheels. Motor has 50 to 1 gear reduction. Operates on A.C. only. See page 42.

HO-121K BAGGAGE AND MAIL CAR KIT $2.50
Builds authentic model of popular combination car. Automatic couplers and green enamel included.

HO-121 BAGGAGE AND MAIL CAR—9" LONG . . . $3.25
Die-cast, Tru-Model replica. Two 4 wheel trucks, automatic couplers, green enamel finish.

HO-122K PASSENGER COACH KIT $2.50
Loads of fun to put together. Die-cast, automatic couplers, double trucks, paints, decals, etc.

HO-122 PASSENGER COACH—9" LONG $3.25
Simulated glass windows, automatic couplers and finished in lustrous green enamel.

HO-110K 4 CAR FREIGHT TRAIN KIT $16.95
Builds N.Y.C. 4-6-4 Hudson type locomotive and tender, Refrigerator Car, Oil Car, Gondola and Caboose. Armature, field, gears and drive wheels assembled to engine frame. Directional remote control unit included. Instructions, paint, brushes, etc. Operates on A.C. only. See page 42.

HO-111K 3 CAR PASSENGER TRAIN KIT $16.95
Builds N.Y.C. 4-6-4 Hudson type, locomotive and tender, Baggage and Mail car and two Passenger cars. Armature, field, gears and drive wheels assembled to engine frame. Directional remote control unit included. Bulb for headlight. Instructions, paints, brushes, etc. Operates on A.C. only. See page 42.

 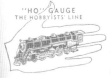    

120 CABOOSE

Values for each condition are in U.S. dollars. | Scarcity = Scale from 1-8 with 8 being the hardest to find.

251

AMERICAN FLYER HO ROLLING STOCK

HO-135 NEW HAVEN PASSENGER COACH Masterpiece of scaled realism! Body molded of New Haven Railroad green to include wealth of detail. Heavy die-cast chassis assures ruggedness and low center of gravity. Simulated glass windows. Interior illumination. 9" long.
Price, $4.50.   Denver and West, $4.75.

HO-133 NEW HAVEN BAGGAGE AND MAIL CAR Complete HO detail, including rivet heads, door chain, scale paneling, Mail Door bar latch and rod lock, truck springs, etc. Has heavy die-cast chassis. Couplers automatic. Low gravity center. 9" long.
Price, $4.50.   Denver and West, $4.75.

HO-129 TRANSFORMER CAR Minute molded detail — a real "must" for your HO Freight line! Depressed center Flat Car carries realistic Transformer. Note guy wires, insulators, planking, steps, truck springs, etc. Gray with white lettering. Couplers automatic. 5⅛" long.
Price, $2.95.   Denver and West, $3.10.

HO-131 CABOOSE Here's a realistic "shanty" for the tail end of your HO freights. Finish is authentic Caboose Red. Has cupola, stack, grab rails, rivet heads, windows, etc. Couplers automatic. Interior diffused illumination. 4-13/32" long.
Price, $2.95.   Denver and West, $3.10.

HO-119 FLAT CAR Patterned after Illinois Central Railroad type. Fully detailed, including simulated planking. Gray finish, white lettering. Loaded with three trucks. 5¾" long.
Price, $2.95.   Denver and West, $3.10.

HO-127 TEXAS & PACIFIC R.R. GONDOLA Load scrap iron, ore, slag, etc., into this scale Gondola. Die-cast truck frames, molded body. Green finish. 6" long.
HO-128 GONDOLA CAR Same as above except with "Lehigh New England" lettering and Gray body.
Price, each: $2.25.   Denver and West, $2.35.

HO-124 REFRIGERATOR CAR Accurately proportioned Reefer, with full body and chassis detail. Sides in white enamel; roof and dreadnaught ends in Tuscan red. Couplers automatic. 5-13/16" long.
HO-123 PACIFIC FRUIT EXPRESS CAR Same as above except body is orange with black lettering.
Price, each: $2.95.   Denver and West, $3.10.

HO-126 SINCLAIR TANK CAR Realistic black molded Tank with silver "Sinclair" lettering. Die-cast chassis. 5-9/16" long.
HO-125 SHELL TANK CAR Same as above except tank is silver finish with black "Shell" lettering.
Price, each: $2.95.   Denver and West, $3.10.

124 REFRIGERATOR CAR

124 REFRIGERATOR CAR: 📷 MDT, white and brown.

VG-C6	EX-C7	LN-C8	Scarcity
8	15	25	N/A

125 TANK CAR: Shell, plastic with die-cast frame, silver.

VG-C6	EX-C7	LN-C8	Scarcity
10	35	45	N/A

126 TANK CAR: Sinclair, plastic with die-cast frame, black.

VG-C6	EX-C7	LN-C8	Scarcity
15	40	50	N/A

127 GONDOLA (Type I): Gray, embossed "A.C. Gilbert Co."

VG-C6	EX-C7	LN-C8	Scarcity
12	28	40	N/A

127 GONDOLA (Type II): Green, embossed "A.C. Gilbert Co."

VG-C6	EX-C7	LN-C8	Scarcity
15	25	32	N/A

128 GONDOLA: LNE, embossed "A.C. Gilbert Co.," gray.

VG-C6	EX-C7	LN-C8	Scarcity
30	55	100	N/A

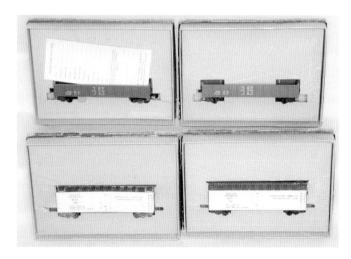

127 GONDOLA: T & P (Texas and Pacific).

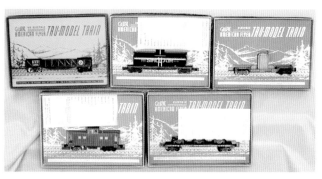

129 TRANSFORMER CAR: NYNH & H, depressed center flatcar with transformer, die-cast, black.

VG-C6	EX-C7	LN-C8	Scarcity
20	35	50	N/A

205 GONDOLA

131 CABOOSE: RDG, center cupola, illuminated, red.

VG-C6	EX-C7	LN-C8	Scarcity
12	20	35	N/A

201 REFRIGERATOR CAR: Prewar, PFE, die-cast, orange, couplers on body, number on car side "35901," also available in kit form as HO-2.

VG-C6	EX-C7	LN-C8	Scarcity
20	40	60	N/A

202 REFRIGERATOR CAR: Prewar, MDT, die-cast, white/brown, couplers on body, number on car side "49611," also available in kit form as HO-3.

VG-C6	EX-C7	LN-C8	Scarcity
20	40	60	N/A

203 TANK CAR: Prewar, Texaco, die-cast, black, couplers on body, car also available in kit form as HO-4; number on car side "5802."

VG-C6	EX-C7	LN-C8	Scarcity
10	22	45	N/A

204 TANK CAR: Prewar, Sinclair, die-cast, black, couplers on body, car also available in kit form as HO-5; number on car side "24712."

VG-C6	EX-C7	LN-C8	Scarcity
10	22	45	N/A

205 GONDOLA: Prewar, LNE (Lehigh and New England), die-cast, black or gray, couplers on body, number on car side "15503"; car also available in kit form as HO-6.

VG-C6	EX-C7	LN-C8	Scarcity
10	25	45	N/A

HO FREIGHT CARS

Values for each condition are in U.S. dollars. | **Scarcity** = Scale from 1-8 with 8 being the hardest to find.

253

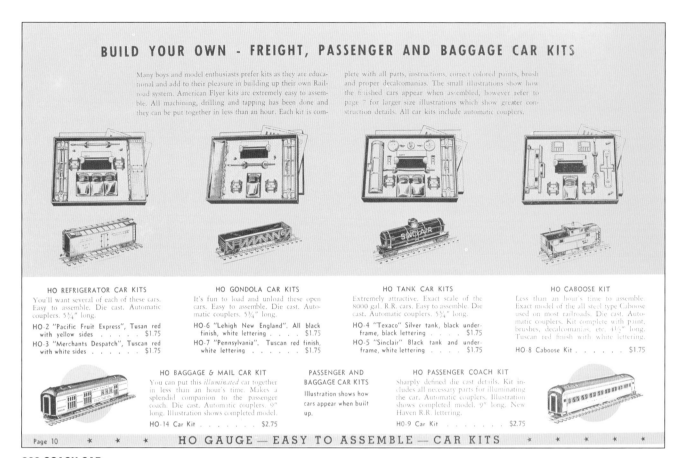

BUILD YOUR OWN - FREIGHT, PASSENGER AND BAGGAGE CAR KITS

Many boys and model enthusiasts prefer kits as they are educational and add to their pleasure in building up their own Railroad system. American Flyer kits are extremely easy to assemble. All machining, drilling and tapping has been done and they can be put together in less than an hour. Each kit is complete with all parts, instructions, correct colored paints, brush and proper decalcomanias. The small illustrations show how the finished cars appear when assembled, however refer to page 7 for larger size illustrations which show greater construction details. All car kits include automatic couplers.

HO REFRIGERATOR CAR KITS
You'll want several of each of these cars. Easy to assemble. Die cast. Automatic couplers. 5¾" long.
HO-2 "Pacific Fruit Express", Tusan red with yellow sides $1.75
HO-3 "Merchants Despatch", Tuscan red with white sides $1.75

HO GONDOLA CAR KITS
It's fun to load and unload these open cars. Easy to assemble. Die cast. Automatic couplers. 5¾" long.
HO-6 "Lehigh New England". All black finish, white lettering $1.75
HO-7 "Pennsylvania". Tuscan red finish, white lettering $1.75

HO TANK CAR KITS
Extremely attractive. Exact scale of the 8000 gal. R.R. cars. Easy to assemble. Die cast. Automatic couplers. 5¾" long.
HO-4 "Texaco" Silver tank, black underframe, black lettering $1.75
HO-5 "Sinclair" Black tank and underframe, white lettering $1.75

HO CABOOSE KIT
Less than an hour's time to assemble. Exact model of the all steel type Caboose used on most railroads. Die cast. Automatic couplers. Kit complete with paint, brushes, decalcomanias, etc. 4½" long. Tuscan red finish with white lettering.
HO-8 Caboose Kit $1.75

HO BAGGAGE & MAIL CAR KIT
You can put this *illuminated* car together in less than an hour's time. Makes a splendid companion to the passenger coach. Die cast. Automatic couplers. 9" long. Illustration shows completed model.
HO-14 Car Kit $2.75

PASSENGER AND BAGGAGE CAR KITS
Illustration shows how cars appear when built up.

HO PASSENGER COACH KIT
Sharply defined die cast details. Kit includes all necessary parts for illuminating the car. Automatic couplers. Illustration shows completed model. 9" long. New Haven R.R. lettering.
HO-9 Car Kit $2.75

Page 10 ★ ★ ★ **HO GAUGE — EASY TO ASSEMBLE — CAR KITS** ★ ★ ★

---

208 COACH CAR

206 GONDOLA: Prewar, PRR, die-cast, brown, couplers on body, number on car side "147313"; car also available in kit form as HO-7.

VG-C6	EX-C7	LN-C8	Scarcity
12	28	50	N/A

207 CABOOSE: 1938, NYC, die-cast, brown, couplers on body, with center cupola, number on car side "32404"; car also available in kit form as HO-8.

VG-C6	EX-C7	LN-C8	Scarcity
18	32	65	N/A

208 COACH CAR: 📷 NH, AF, die-cast, couplers on trucks, number on car side "8301"; car also available in kit form as HO-9.

VG-C6	EX-C7	LN-C8	Scarcity
25	40	80	N/A

215 BAGGAGE CAR: NH, AF, couplers on body, number on car side "2764"; car also available in kit form as HO-14.

VG-C6	EX-C7	LN-C8	Scarcity
30	50	95	N/A

216 FLATCAR: IC, die-cast, gray, with three-wheel sets, no number, couplers connected to body, car also available in kit form.

VG-C6	EX-C7	LN-C8	Scarcity
25	45	75	N/A

500 TANK CAR: Gulf, silver, single dome.
500 TANK CAR (Type I): Varney version.

VG-C6	EX-C7	LN-C8	Scarcity
7	12	18	N/A

500 TANK CAR (Type II): Gilbert version.

VG-C6	EX-C7	LN-C8	Scarcity
12	20	32	N/A

501 HOPPER: CB & Q, brown, with Coal Load.

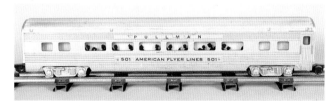

501 HOPPER (Type I): Varney version, panel sides.

VG-C6	EX-C7	LN-C8	Scarcity
4	8	12	N/A

501 HOPPER (Type II): Gilbert version, smooth sides.

VG-C6	EX-C7	LN-C8	Scarcity
8	15	20	N/A

502 STOCK CAR: MKT, yellow/brown.
502 STOCK CAR (Type I): Varney version.

VG-C6	EX-C7	LN-C8	Scarcity
5	8	12	N/A

502 STOCK CAR (Type II): Gilbert version.

VG-C6	EX-C7	LN-C8	Scarcity
7	12	20	N/A

503 FLATCAR: NYNH & H, black, with transformer load.

VG-C6	EX-C7	LN-C8	Scarcity
22	32	45	N/A

504 REFRIGERATOR CAR: Orange.

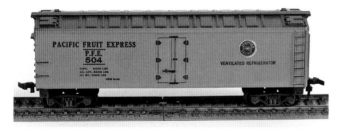

504 REFRIGERATOR CAR (Type I): PFE, encircled SP, one herald.

VG-C6	EX-C7	LN-C8	Scarcity
12	24	36	N/A

504 REFRIGERATOR CAR (Type II): PFE/UP, SP/UP Heralds, two heralds.

VG-C6	EX-C7	LN-C8	Scarcity
22	45	70	N/A

505 HOPPER: N & W, black, ink-stamped "Gilbert HO," early model.

VG-C6	EX-C7	LN-C8	Scarcity
5	12	20	N/A

506 CABOOSE: Red, with center cupola.

506 CABOOSE: Reading.

VG-C6	EX-C7	LN-C8	Scarcity
10	18	28	N/A

506 CABOOSE: Pennsylvania.

VG-C6	EX-C7	LN-C8	Scarcity
8	12	20	N/A

510 HOPPER: Covered, Monon, gray.

510 HOPPER (Type I): Varney version, with panel side.

VG-C6	EX-C7	LN-C8	Scarcity
4	8	12	N/A

510 HOPPER (Type II): Gilbert version, gray, with smooth side.

VG-C6	EX-C7	LN-C8	Scarcity
10	22	30	N/A

511 TANK CAR: Gulf, silver, with three domes.

VG-C6	EX-C7	LN-C8	Scarcity
22	35	48	N/A

HO FREIGHT CARS

512 BOXCAR: NH, orange.

VG-C6	EX-C7	LN-C8	Scarcity
10	15	20	N/A

513 BOXCAR: B & O, blue and orange.

VG-C6	EX-C7	LN-C8	Scarcity
18	30	55	N/A

514 BOXCAR: SBD, "Silver Meteor," brown.

VG-C6	EX-C7	LN-C8	Scarcity
15	30	45	N/A

516 CABOOSE: NYC, brown, lighted, with center cupola.

VG-C6	EX-C7	LN-C8	Scarcity
22	32	45	N/A

516 CABOOSE: RDG, red, lighted, center cupola.

VG-C6	EX-C7	LN-C8	Scarcity
22	32	45	N/A

517 TANK CAR: Mobilgas, red.

517 TANK CAR (Type I): Varney version.

VG-C6	EX-C7	LN-C8	Scarcity
3	10	15	N/A

517 TANK CAR (Type II): Gilbert version.

VG-C6	EX-C7	LN-C8	Scarcity
7	17	27	N/A

518 TANK CAR: Koppers, black.

NEW

Gilbert HO Scale

• LIVE SPRING TRUCKS • EQUALIZED WHEEL

GILBERT HO-512 BOX CAR

The "old reliable" of any freight fleet, the dependable box car — now all dressed up in striking orange New Haven R.R. colors with white and black lettering. Sliding doors, sprung trucks, complete detail. 5⅝" long.

HO-512 $2.95

GILBERT HO-513 BOX CAR

Add a couple of these beauties to your freight hauls and see how it sparks them up! New B. & O. blue-and-gold colors, with white lettering, are authentically reproduced. Sliding box car doors open to roomy interior. Sprung trucks provide equalizing action. Car is 5⅝" long.

HO-513 $3.50

HO-518 $3.50

HO-514 $3.25

GILBERT HO-518 CHEMICAL TANK CAR

Authentic model patterned after the kind used by Koppers to transport certain chemicals. Black tank with red lettering and red-white-gray emblem. Sprung trucks; N.M.R.A. couplers. 5" long.

GILBERT HO-514 BOX CAR

Rivet heads, dreadnaught ends, catwalk, ribs and other detail are all carefully reproduced on this model of the Silver Meteor *Seaboard R.R.* box car. Doors slide open to reveal interior. N.M.R.A. couplers; sprung trucks. 5⅝" long.

20

513 BOXCAR

518 TANK CAR (Type I): Varney version.

VG-C6	EX-C7	LN-C8	Scarcity
10	18	30	N/A

518 TANK CAR (Type II): Gilbert version.

VG-C6	EX-C7	LN-C8	Scarcity
20	30	45	N/A

520 REFRIGERATOR CAR: CNW, "Northwestern," green and yellow.

VG-C6	EX-C7	LN-C8	Scarcity
25	35	50	N/A

521 REFRIGERATOR CAR: NP, orange.

521 REFRIGERATOR CAR (Type I): Silver roof and ends.

VG-C6	EX-C7	LN-C8	Scarcity
60	75	110	N/A

521 REFRIGERATOR CAR (Type II): Brown roof and ends.

VG-C6	EX-C7	LN-C8	Scarcity
12	25	30	N/A

522 BOXCAR: B & M, blue and black.

VG-C6	EX-C7	LN-C8	Scarcity
15	25	45	N/A

523 BOXCAR: D & RGW, "Cookie Box," white.

VG-C6	EX-C7	LN-C8	Scarcity
18	22	30	N/A

524 REFRIGERATOR CAR: Morrell, orange and brown.

VG-C6	EX-C7	LN-C8	Scarcity
15	28	40	N/A

525 HOPPER CAR: 📷 B & O, black.

525 HOPPER CAR: Varney version, panel sides, with load.

VG-C6	EX-C7	LN-C8	Scarcity
6	12	20	N/A

525 HOPPER CAR: Gilbert version, smooth sides, no load.

VG-C6	EX-C7	LN-C8	Scarcity
10	18	28	N/A

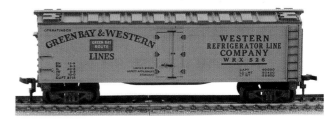

HO FREIGHT CARS

526 REFRIGERATOR CAR: G B & W, "Green Bay Route," gray and red.

VG-C6	EX-C7	LN-C8	Scarcity
22	35	55	N/A

C1006 HOPPER: C & O, covered, Pikemaster, yellow and white.

VG-C6	EX-C7	LN-C8	Scarcity
90	150	200	N/A

C1007 HOPPER: T & P, some are covered, Pikemaster, green and white.

VG-C6	EX-C7	LN-C8	Scarcity
90	150	200	N/A

C3008 CABOOSE: SF, bay window, Pikemaster, red.

VG-C6	EX-C7	LN-C8	Scarcity
8	15	25	N/A

5802 TANK CAR: See 115 or 203.
15503 GONDOLA: See 117 or 205.
24712 TANK CAR: See 116 or 204.
32404 CABOOSE: see 120 or 207.

Values for each condition are in U.S. dollars. | **Scarcity =** Scale from 1-8 with 8 being the hardest to find.

Model Rolling Stock NEW

ACTION • N.M.R.A. RATED "BEST" COUPLERS

GILBERT HO-517 TANK CAR

An everyday sight on real-life freight hauls is this vivid Mobilgas Tank Car with red body and white lettering. Loaded with detail throughout. Has sprung trucks. 5" long.

HO-517
$3.50

GILBERT HO-520 REEFER

You'll want at least one of these new Northwestern Refrigerator Line reefers, with its handsome green and yellow finish. Carries colorful Northwestern emblem. Trucks are sprung for equalizing action. 5⅝" long.

HO-520
$3.25

HO-525
$2.50

HO-521
$3.25

GILBERT HO-525 HOPPER CAR

Black body and large white Baltimore & Ohio lettering give this new hopper a just-like-real appearance. Has full detail: rivet heads, ribs, ladders, grab rails, brake wheel, etc. Trucks have "live spring" action; couplers are N.M.R.A. developed 4¼" long.

GILBERT HO-521 REEFER

Brand new Northern Pacific R.R. refrigerator car in orange body and black lettering. Roof, including hatches and catwalk, painted Tuscan red. Authentic detail. Sprung trucks and N.M.R.A. couplers. 5⅝" long.

21

525 HOPPER CAR

33002 BOXCAR: NYC, with large NYC oval sticker, green and white.

VG-C6	EX-C7	LN-C8	Scarcity
27	35	45	N/A

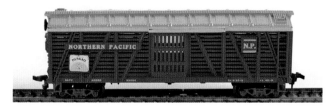

33004 STOCK CAR: NP, "Pig Palace," red with silver roof.

VG-C6	EX-C7	LN-C8	Scarcity
100	150	200	N/A

33006 STOCK CAR: GN, hay-jector eliminated, red.

VG-C6	EX-C7	LN-C8	Scarcity
80	110	150	N/A

33009 STOCK CAR: WAB, hay-jector eliminated, blue.

VG-C6	EX-C7	LN-C8	Scarcity
80	110	150	N/A

33010 STOCK CAR: UP, hay-jector eliminated, yellow.

VG-C6	EX-C7	LN-C8	Scarcity
90	140	190	N/A

33012 BOXCAR: SF, large Santa Fe cross, red and white.

VG-C6	EX-C7	LN-C8	Scarcity
80	140	180	N/A

33115 BALLAST CAR: MW, by TruScale, gray, Kleer-Pak or cardboard Gilbert box required.

33214 HOPPER: SF, covered, red and white.

VG-C6	EX-C7	LN-C8	Scarcity
10	22	35	N/A

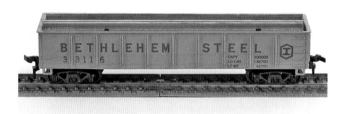

33116 GONDOLA: Bethlehem Steel.

VG-C6	EX-C7	LN-C8	Scarcity
40	80	110	N/A

33120 GONDOLA: T & P, Pikemaster, green and white.

VG-C6	EX-C7	LN-C8	Scarcity
60	100	130	N/A

33121 GONDOLA: NH, "Trap Rock," Pikemaster, tan and yellow.

VG-C6	EX-C7	LN-C8	Scarcity
80	150	200	N/A

33122 GONDOLA: N & W, Pikemaster, black.

VG-C6	EX-C7	LN-C8	Scarcity
50	95	125	N/A

33215 HOPPER: Peabody, no load, tan (tan color varies).

VG-C6	EX-C7	LN-C8	Scarcity
15	22	42	N/A

33217 HOPPER: NYC, covered, green/white.

VG-C6	EX-C7	LN-C8	Scarcity
10	20	30	N/A

33219 HOPPER: B & O, no load, black.

VG-C6	EX-C7	LN-C8	Scarcity
60	75	115	N/A

33220 HOPPER: CB & Q, with covered, red and white.

VG-C6	EX-C7	LN-C8	Scarcity
160	260	375	N/A

33312 TANK CAR: Karo, "Karo Syrup," white/red.

VG-C6	EX-C7	LN-C8	Scarcity
150	250	350	N/A

33313 TANK CAR: Hooker, chemical, orange/black.

VG-C6	EX-C7	LN-C8	Scarcity
75	110	140	N/A

33211 HOPPER: C & EI, no load, gray.

VG-C6	EX-C7	LN-C8	Scarcity
10	20	30	N/A

33212 HOPPER: SF, with gray stone load, red.

VG-C6	EX-C7	LN-C8	Scarcity
20	32	45	N/A

33314 TANK CAR: Cities, "Cities Service," green.

VG-C6	EX-C7	LN-C8	Scarcity
350	425	500	N/A

HO FREIGHT CARS

33315 TANK CAR: SOHIO, "Sohio," black.

VG-C6	EX-C7	LN-C8	Scarcity
375	450	550	N/A

33316 GONDOLA: Bethlehem Steel, gray and red.
33316 GONDOLA (Type I): With rail load.

VG-C6	EX-C7	LN-C8	Scarcity
45	85	125	N/A

33316 GONDOLA (Type II): Pikemaster, with rail load.

VG-C6	EX-C7	LN-C8	Scarcity
80	125	155	N/A

33317 GONDOLA: NH, Pikemaster, black and orange.

VG-C6	EX-C7	LN-C8	Scarcity
70	130	150	N/A

33403 REFRIGERATOR CAR: 📷 BAR, large BAR sticker, red.

VG-C6	EX-C7	LN-C8	Scarcity
70	100	150	N/A

33500 TANK CAR: Gulf, single dome, silver.

VG-C6	EX-C7	LN-C8	Scarcity
12	25	35	N/A

33501 HOPPER CAR: CB & Q, smooth side, brown, with coal load.

VG-C6	EX-C7	LN-C8	Scarcity
18	28	40	N/A

33502 STOCK CAR: 📷 MKT, yellow and brown.

VG-C6	EX-C7	LN-C8	Scarcity
55	75	95	N/A

33503 FLATCAR: NYNH & H, with transformer load, black.

VG-C6	EX-C7	LN-C8	Scarcity
50	75	125	N/A

33505 GONDOLA: N & W, black and white.

VG-C6	EX-C7	LN-C8	Scarcity
10	22	32	N/A

33506 CABOOSE: PRR, red, with center cupola.

VG-C6	EX-C7	LN-C8	Scarcity
5	12	20	N/A

33507 GONDOLA: D & H, brown.
33507 GONDOLA: With canister load.

VG-C6	EX-C7	LN-C8	Scarcity
30	60	75	N/A

33507 GONDOLA: Pikemaster version.

VG-C6	EX-C7	LN-C8	Scarcity
100	200	300	N/A

33508 GONDOLA: C & O, black and yellow, with pipe load.

VG-C6	EX-C7	LN-C8	Scarcity
20	35	55	N/A

33509 FLATCAR: WM, brown, with RISS trailer load.

VG-C6	EX-C7	LN-C8	Scarcity
42	55	80	N/A

33510 HOPPER: Monon, covered, gray and red.

VG-C6	EX-C7	LN-C8	Scarcity
80	130	170	N/A

33511 TANK CAR: Gulf, three domes, silver.

VG-C6	EX-C7	LN-C8	Scarcity
12	25	35	N/A

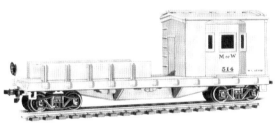

No. 33549 Boom & Work Car. Companion car for Crane; boom rests in forward area. Shanty for tools, equipment, etc. **$2.98**

No. 33548 Crane Car. Cab swivels, boom lifts, hook raises and lowers. Ideal for derailed cars or locomotives. Fully detailed. **$6.98**

No. 33005 L & N Box Car. Backbone of any freight drag are box cars like this one, a model of the kind seen on the Louisville & Nashville R.R. 5⅝". **$2.98**

No. 33403 Bangor & Aroostock Reefer. Colorful B & A refrigerator car, guaranteed to spice up any freight drag. **$2.98**

33403 REFRIGERATOR CAR

Values for each condition are in U.S. dollars. | **Scarcity** = Scale from 1-8 with 8 being the hardest to find.

261

N. M. R. A. Couplers · Freight Trucks with Real Springs

No. 33525 HOPPER
Big Baltimore & Ohio lettering plus minute detail make this car a perfect scale model of the McCoy. You'll want several. 4¼" long.

No. 33501 HOPPER CAR
The backbone of your freight fleet is the dependable hopper, and here's one that carries a load of anthracite. Fully detailed. 4¼" long.

No. 33500 TANK CAR
No freight drag is complete without an "old reliable" tanker . . . and this one is a beauty. 5" long.

No. 33502 CATTLE CAR
If you listen hard you can almost hear the steers bawling! Doors slide open. Katy markings. 5⅞".

No. 33505 GONDOLA CAR
Has large loading capacity for pipes, machinery or anything else too big for a box car. 5⅞" long.

No. 33510 CEMENT CAR
Complete with 8 simulated roof loading hatches, catwalk, rivets and other detail. 4¼" long.

No. 33513 BOX CAR
The drab freight train of yesteryear is fast disappearing . . . and this B&O job proves it. Doors slide open and shut. 5⅝" long.

No. 33514 BOX CAR
This Seaboard "Silver Meteor" really gets around, as freight hauls throughout the country will testify. Has sliding doors. 5⅝" long.

No. 33516 ILLUMINATED CABOOSE
A shanty to ride the tail ends of your freights in handsome style. Interior lighting. 4-3/16" long.

No. 33520 REFRIGERATOR CAR
Just as useful as it is handsome is this yellow-and-green reefer, seen from coast-to-coast. 5⅝" long.

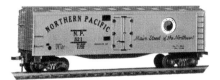

No. 33521 REFRIGERATOR CAR
Get your perishables to market fast — and fresh — in this colorful Northern Pacific R.R. reefer with elaborate detail. 5⅝" long.

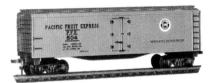

No. 33504 REFRIGERATOR CAR
A reefer to add color and realism to your HO layout. Fully detailed. 5⅝" long.

No. 33503 DEPRESSED CENTER
When you have a heavyweight load to carry (like the transformer here) this is the car for the job. 5" long.

5

33502 STOCK CAR

33512 BOXCAR: NH, orange.

VG-C6	EX-C7	LN-C8	Scarcity
12	24	36	N/A

33513 BOXCAR: B & O, blue and orange.

VG-C6	EX-C7	LN-C8	Scarcity
30	50	75	N/A

33514 BOXCAR: SBD, "Silver Meteor," brown.

VG-C6	EX-C7	LN-C8	Scarcity
20	45	65	N/A

33515 CABOOSE: C & O, lighted, yellow, with center cupola.

VG-C6	EX-C7	LN-C8	Scarcity
45	75	120	N/A

33516 CABOOSE: NYC, lighted, brown, with center cupola.

VG-C6	EX-C7	LN-C8	Scarcity
12	22	35	N/A

33517 TANK CAR: Mobil, "Mobilgas," red.

VG-C6	EX-C7	LN-C8	Scarcity
12	18	25	N/A

33518 TANK CAR: Koppers, chemical, black.

VG-C6	EX-C7	LN-C8	Scarcity
60	100	150	N/A

33519 CABOOSE: B & O, red, with center cupola.

VG-C6	EX-C7	LN-C8	Scarcity
10	22	35	N/A

33520 REFRIGERATOR CAR: CNW, green and yellow.

VG-C6	EX-C7	LN-C8	Scarcity
75	120	150	N/A

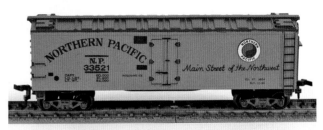

33521 REFRIGERATOR CAR: NP, orange and brown.

VG-C6	EX-C7	LN-C8	Scarcity
18	27	42	N/A

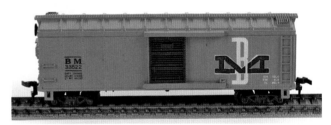

33522 BOXCAR: B & M, blue and black.

VG-C6	EX-C7	LN-C8	Scarcity
25	40	60	N/A

33523 BOXCAR: D & RGW, "Cookie Box," white and red.

VG-C6	EX-C7	LN-C8	Scarcity
20	30	45	N/A

33524 REFRIGERATOR CAR: Morrel, Orange and silver.

VG-C6	EX-C7	LN-C8	Scarcity
25	35	65	N/A

33525 HOPPER CAR: B & O, no load, smooth side, black.

VG-C6	EX-C7	LN-C8	Scarcity
45	90	120	N/A

33526 REFRIGERATOR CAR: GB & W, "Green Bay Route," gray and red.

VG-C6	EX-C7	LN-C8	Scarcity
30	42	55	N/A

33527 FLATCAR: NH, with lumber load and stakes, black.

VG-C6	EX-C7	LN-C8	Scarcity
20	32	45	N/A

33536 FLATCAR: PRR, with 10 stakes, brown.

VG-C6	EX-C7	LN-C8	Scarcity
60	95	135	N/A

Values for each condition are in U.S. dollars. | **Scarcity** = Scale from 1-8 with 8 being the hardest to find.

263

No. 33313 Hooker Chemical Car. On the big roads, this bright little number has created comment wherever it's seen. A must for your hauls. **$3.98**

No. 33537 Track Cleaning Car. Keep your track in tip top condition with this unique car that cleans and polishes the rails as it runs. Improves train performance. **$6.98**

No. 33517 Tank Car. Bright, colorful, authentic. That's the word for this Mobilgas tanker that deserves a home on any HO pike. 5" long. **$2.98**

No. 33516 Illuminated Caboose. A shanty to ride the tail ends of your freights in handsome style. Interior lighting. 4⅛" long. **$4.50**

No. 33540 Baggage & Club Car. Long, sleek, detailed. Has interior lighting, NMRA couplers and die-cast trucks. **$5.98**

No. 33541 Coach. Minutely detailed with authentic Northern Pacific finish. Illuminated. NMRA couplers, die-cast trucks. **$5.98**

36

No. 33542 Vista Dome. A real beauty and a car you'll want for your passenger division. Northern Pacific markings; interior lighting, die-cast trucks, NMRA couplers. **$6.98**

No. 33543 Observation. Coolest car on HO rails is this dreamliner observation, with Northern Pacific finish and lettering. Illuminated inside. Has NMRA couplers, die-cast trucks, equalized wheel action. **$6.98**

THE A.C. GILBERT COMPANY • ERECTOR SQUARE • NEW HAVEN, CONN.

D-2239   PRINTED IN U.S.A.

33516 CABOOSE

GILBERT HO CARS... Elaborate Detail

NEW No. 33541 COACH — Minutely detailed with authentic Northern Pacific finish. Illuminated. NMRA couplers, die-cast trucks.

NEW No. 33540 BAGGAGE & CLUB CAR — Long, sleek, detailed. Has interior lighting, NMRA couplers and die-cast trucks.

NEW No. 33542 VISTA DOME — A real beauty and a car you'll want for your passenger division. Northern Pacific markings; interior lighting, die-cast trucks, NMRA couplers.

NEW No. 33543 OBSERVATION — Coolest car on HO rails is this dreamliner observation, with Northern Pacific finish and lettering. Illuminated inside. Has NMRA couplers, die-cast trucks, equalized wheel action.

NEW No. 33524 REFRIGERATOR CAR — With reefers making up as many as half of some hauls, you'll need plenty of variety on your road. This Morrell number is a real dinger. 5⅝" long.

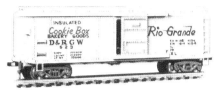

NEW No. 33523 BOX CAR — A car especially for bakery goods is the latest wrinkle on the Rio Grande — and this HO job is a perfect scale copy. Doors slide open. 5⅝" long.

NEW No. 33522 BOX CAR — Even seasoned railroad-men take a second look when this Boston & Maine beauty rolls by. Doors slide open. 5⅝" long.

NEW No. 33511 TANK CAR
Brand new tanker with 3 domes and famous GULF emblem. Loaded with detail. 5" long.

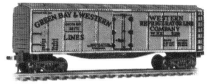

NEW No. 33526 REFRIGERATOR CAR — Spot a couple of these jazzy jobs in your drags and see how they give your freights new zip. Highly detailed; accurate 9/64" scale, 5⅝" long.

No. 33512 BOX CAR
Old trustworthy — all dressed up in the striking New Haven R.R. colors that are the talk of the railroad world. Sliding doors. 5⅝" long.

No. 33517 TANK CAR
Bright, colorful, authentic. That's the word for this Mobilgas tanker that deserves a home on any HO pike. 5" long.

No. 33518 CHEMICAL CAR
In this chemical age we live in, a Koppers car like this is a "must". Authentic from top to toe. 5" long.

HO FREIGHT CARS

33526 REFRIGERATOR CAR

Values for each condition are in U.S. dollars. | **Scarcity** = Scale from 1-8 with 8 being the hardest to find.

265

33537 TRACK CLEANING CAR: D & H, with D & H Canister, black.

VG-C6	EX-C7	LN-C8	Scarcity
22	40	65	N/A

33538 FLATCAR: US Air Force, with two Nike rockets, dark green.

VG-C6	EX-C7	LN-C8	Scarcity
60	125	155	N/A

33539 FLATCAR: RI, with two railcar trucks, gray and black.

VG-C6	EX-C7	LN-C8	Scarcity
38	65	100	N/A

33544 FLATCAR: CP, red, with Christmas tree load.

VG-C6	EX-C7	LN-C8	Scarcity
100	175	225	N/A

33545 FLATCAR: 📷 National, with Borden's Milk Tank, black and white.

VG-C6	EX-C7	LN-C8	Scarcity
20	40	80	N/A

33546 FLATCAR: 📷 IC, with jet engine case, black.

VG-C6	EX-C7	LN-C8	Scarcity
25	50	90	N/A

33548 CRANE: MW, X74 Brownhoist, by TruScale, red cab, Kleer-Pak or cardboard Gilbert.

VG-C6	EX-C7	LN-C8	Scarcity
90	150	200	N/A

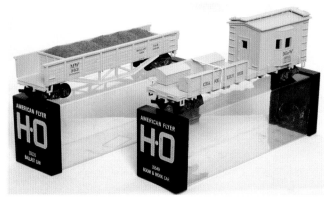

33549 CRANE TENDER: MW, by TruScale, typically 642, gray, Kleer-Pak or cardboard box.

VG-C6	EX-C7	LN-C8	Scarcity
40	70	100	N/A

33545 FLATCAR

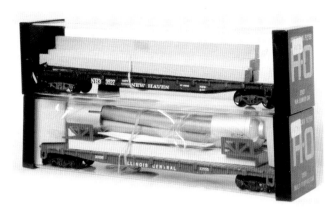

33555 FLATCAR: IC, with containers, lumber, pipes, brown.

VG-C6	EX-C7	LN-C8	Scarcity
45	70	90	N/A

33557 FLATCAR: WM, with Ross trailer van, brown.

VG-C6	EX-C7	LN-C8	Scarcity
42	55	80	N/A

33558 FLATCAR: IC, with load, similar to 33555, brown.

VG-C6	EX-C7	LN-C8	Scarcity
25	40	50	N/A

33615 CABOOSE: NYC, brown, with center cupola.

VG-C6	EX-C7	LN-C8	Scarcity
15	20	30	N/A

33616 CABOOSE: C & O, lighted, yellow, with center cupola.

VG-C6	EX-C7	LN-C8	Scarcity
33	55	80	N/A

33618 CABOOSE: Erie, bay window, Pikemaster, red.

VG-C6	EX-C7	LN-C8	Scarcity
8	15	25	N/A

33620 CABOOSE: WAB, bay window, Pikemaster, blue.

VG-C6	EX-C7	LN-C8	Scarcity
22	35	50	N/A

33621 CABOOSE: C & O, bay window, Pikemaster, yellow.

VG-C6	EX-C7	LN-C8	Scarcity
12	20	32	N/A

33623 CABOOSE: M & St. L, bay window, Pikemaster, red.

VG-C6	EX-C7	LN-C8	Scarcity
25	42	52	N/A

33625 CABOOSE: NYC, bay window, Pikemaster, red.

VG-C6	EX-C7	LN-C8	Scarcity
90	125	160	N/A

33626 CABOOSE: Work, Erie, no tie-jector, see 33820.

VG-C6	EX-C7	LN-C8	Scarcity
85	120	150	N/A

33627 CABOOSE: PRR, bay window, Pikemaster, red.

VG-C6	EX-C7	LN-C8	Scarcity
32	45	65	N/A

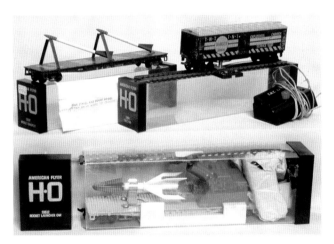

33804 BOXCAR: TNT, exploding "Boxcar," black/yellow.

VG-C6	EX-C7	LN-C8	Scarcity
40	55	90	N/A

33806 BOXCAR: MINE, Mine Carrying/Exploding "Boxcar," yellow.

VG-C6	EX-C7	LN-C8	Scarcity
30	45	70	N/A

Values for each condition are in U.S. dollars. | Scarcity = Scale from 1-8 with 8 being the hardest to find.

267

ALL AMERICAN FLYER HO CARS
AND LOCOMOTIVES HAVE SMOOTH-
WORKING N.M.R.A. COUPLERS

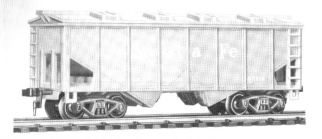

NEW! **No. 33214 Santa Fe Cement Car.** Authentic colors and markings — top, which is scale model of the real thing, can be removed, and Presto! you have a plain hopper car for hauling stone, coal, etc. **$2.98**

NEW! **No. 33215 Peabody Hopper Car.** Here's a new piece of rolling stock your Division Superintendent will find mighty versatile for hauling crushed stone, coal, etc. **$2.50**

NEW! **No. 33835 Automatic Hopper Car.** You'll need a string of these action cars to use as regular freight consist or with the No. 35785 Coal Unloader. **$2.98**

No. 33545 Borden's Milk Transport. Big tankers like this one haul milk from udder to you from Elsie and all her friends at Borden's. **$2.98**

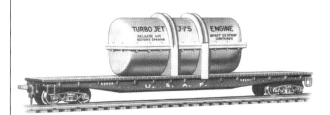

No. 33546 Jet Engine Transport. Giant power plants for today's bombers and fighters are carried to the airframe plants on flat cars like this authentic job. Fully detailed. **$2.98**

No. 33538 Missile Transport Car. Two "Nike" type missiles, carried in tandem aboard an Air Force flat car. **$2.98**

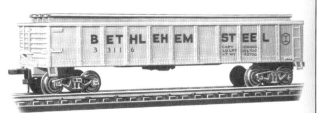

No. 33002 N. Y. Central Box Car. Brand new model from a famous old road. Painted authentic green, with Central lettering and emblems. Sliding doors. 5⅝". **$2.98**

No. 33116 Bethlehem Steel Car. Highly detailed Gondola with Bethlehem Steel lettering, carrying four rail lengths. **$2.98**

34

33546 FLATCAR

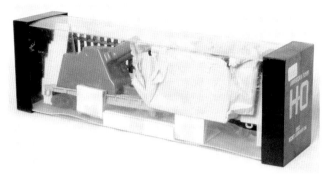

33812 ROCKET LAUNCHER CAR: USAF, with rocket, yellow/blue.

VG-C6	EX-C7	LN-C8	Scarcity
25	40	80	N/A

33820 CABOOSE: work, AF, Tie Car, ejects tie, orange and gray.

VG-C6	EX-C7	LN-C8	Scarcity
10	20 •	35	N/A

33835 HOPPER CAR: C & O, dumps coal load, black.

VG-C6	EX-C7	LN-C8	Scarcity
18	28	48	N/A

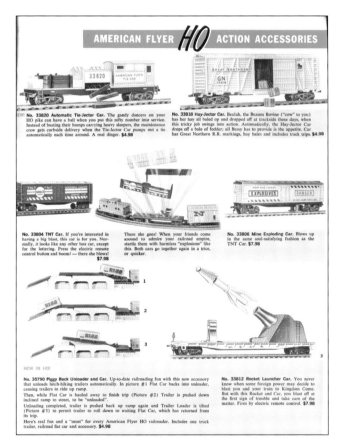

33818 CATTLE CAR: GN, ejects hay bale, red.

VG-C6	EX-C7	LN-C8	Scarcity
20	45	65	N/A

33819 CATTLE CAR: NYC, ejects hay bale, green.

VG-C6	EX-C7	LN-C8	Scarcity
25	50	70	N/A

35785 HOPPER CAR: C & O, dumps coal load, black.

VG-C6	EX-C7	LN-C8	Scarcity
18	28	48	N/A

35901 REFRIGERATOR CAR: See 201.
49611 REFRIGERATOR CAR: See 114 or 202.
147313 GONDOLA: See 118 and 206 .

Values for each condition are in U.S. dollars. | **Scarcity** = Scale from 1-8 with 8 being the hardest to find.

269

HO ACCESSORIES

HO-12 TUNNEL: 📷 Prewar.

VG-C6	EX-C7	LN-C8	Scarcity
Too rarely traded to accurately establish pricing.			

106K TRESTLE BRIDGE KIT:

VG-C6	EX-C7	LN-C8	Scarcity
Too rarely traded to accurately establish pricing.			

HO-250 TRACK TERMINAL: Prewar.

VG-C6	EX-C7	LN-C8	Scarcity
Too rarely traded to accurately establish pricing.			

HO-252 BLOCK SIGN: Prewar, black.

VG-C6	EX-C7	LN-C8	Scarcity
-	50	100	N/A

253 ROADSIDE DINER: Yellow, with sign and antenna.

VG-C6	EX-C7	LN-C8	Scarcity
-	45	95	N/A

HO-254 GIRDER BRIDGE: 📷 Prewar.

VG-C6	EX-C7	LN-C8	Scarcity
Too rarely traded to accurately establish pricing.			

HO-256 SIGNAL TOWER: Prewar.

VG-C6	EX-C7	LN-C8	Scarcity
Too rarely traded to accurately establish pricing.			

257 TALKING STATION: 1950.

VG-C6	EX-C7	LN-C8	Scarcity
-	150	300	N/A

HO-258 PASSENGER AND FREIGHT STATION: 📷
Prewar, metal, white/green/red.

VG-C6	EX-C7	LN-C8	Scarcity
-	70	100	N/A

259 WHISTLING STATION: Similar to 258, with whistle.

VG-C6	EX-C7	LN-C8	Scarcity
-	150	200	N/A

HO-261 CURVED TRACK: Prewar.

VG-C6	EX-C7	LN-C8	Scarcity
Too rarely traded to accurately establish pricing.			

HO-261 STRAIGHT TRACK: Prewar.

VG-C6	EX-C7	LN-C8	Scarcity
Too rarely traded to accurately establish pricing.			

HO-261 1/2 STRAIGHT TRACK: Prewar.

VG-C6	EX-C7	LN-C8	Scarcity
Too rarely traded to accurately establish pricing.			

HO-262 90-DEGREE CROSSOVER: Prewar.

VG-C6	EX-C7	LN-C8	Scarcity
Too rarely traded to accurately establish pricing.			

HO-264 1/2 CURVED TRACK: Prewar.

VG-C6	EX-C7	LN-C8	Scarcity
Too rarely traded to accurately establish pricing.			

HO-265 PAIR OF MANUAL TURNOUTS: 📷 Prewar.

VG-C6	EX-C7	LN-C8	Scarcity
Too rarely traded to accurately establish pricing.			

FOR THE FIRST TIME
AT POPULAR PRICES..

Because of the high degree of skill and workmanship employed in the creation of "HO" Tru-Model equipment, prices have previously been necessarily high. Today, thanks to improved production methods of the Gilbert Hall of Science, high quality miniature equipment is offered for the first time at popular prices. Vivid realism and exact authenticity is the keynote of each of the perfectly scaled models. When you select American Flyer Tru-Model equipment for your 'HO' train, you'll own a miniature railroad system that is unsurpassed in correctness of design and perfection of finish.

"HO" GAUGE
THE HOBBYISTS' LINE

HO-258 Passenger and Freight Station $2.95
Tru-Model illuminated station on raised platform with regulation bay window ticket office. Freight section has loading platform with sliding door.

HO-254 Girder Bridge $1.50
New—modern—girder type bridge authentically designed and built to correct scale dimensions. Beautifully finished in red and perfect in every detail.

HO-252 Block Signal $3.95
Exactly scaled to the line HO trains it controls, this ladder equipped signal is mounted on a rugged base. An electrically operated shutter turns light red or green.

HO-256 Signal Tower $2.95
Your HO roadway will have a new touch of realism when you add this brilliantly colored die-cast signal tower. Stairs lead up to lighted top floor.

HO-12 Tunnel $1.00
Realistically colored and solidly constructed this mountain-style 8" tunnel is a picturesque addition to your line. Like other HO equipment it's correctly scaled to trains.

HO-12 TUNNEL

HO-254 GIRDER BRIDGE

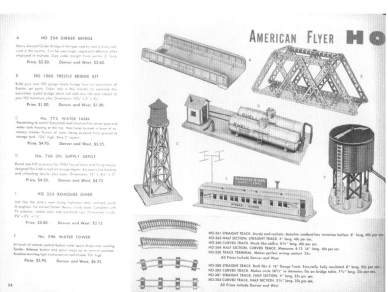

HO ACCESSORIES

HO-258 PASSENGER AND FREIGHT STATION

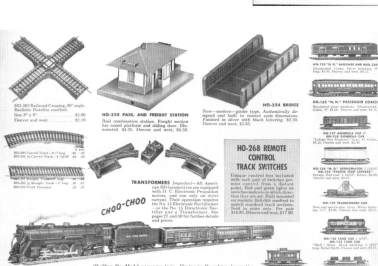

Values for each condition are in U.S. dollars. | **Scarcity** = Scale from 1-8 with 8 being the hardest to find.

271

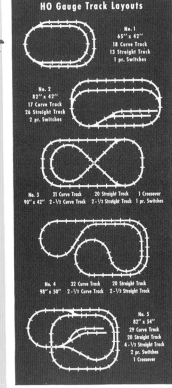

HO-265 PAIR OF MANUAL TURNOUTS

HO-268 PAIR OF REMOTE CONTROL TURNOUTS: Prewar.

VG-C6	EX-C7	LN-C8	Scarcity
Too rarely traded to accurately establish pricing.			

HO-277 TRACK TRIP: Prewar.

VG-C6	EX-C7	LN-C8	Scarcity
Too rarely traded to accurately establish pricing.			

700 GIRDER BRIDGE: Silver or red, "Lackawanna."

VG-C6	EX-C7	LN-C8	Scarcity
10	30	45	N/A

710 BLOCK SIGNAL WITH CONTROL:

VG-C6	EX-C7	LN-C8	Scarcity
Too rarely traded to accurately establish pricing.			

711 FLASHER SIGNAL:

VG-C6	EX-C7	LN-C8	Scarcity
15	40	60	N/A

35210 RADAR TOWER: Made for Ideal by Gilbert.

VG-C6	EX-C7	LN-C8	Scarcity
15	40	55	N/A

35212 CROSSING GATE: Made for Ideal by Gilbert.

VG-C6	EX-C7	LN-C8	Scarcity
10	35	50	N/A

35213 OIL STORAGE DEPOT:

VG-C6	EX-C7	LN-C8	Scarcity
40	75	110	N/A

35214 AUTOMATIC CROSSING WATCHMAN:

VG-C6	EX-C7	LN-C8	Scarcity
20	45	70	N/A

35759 DRUM LOADING CONVEYOR: "Oil Depot."

VG-C6	EX-C7	LN-C8	Scarcity
50	100	140	N/A

35780 COAL LOADER: "Elm City Coal Gravel & Sand Co."

VG-C6	EX-C7	LN-C8	Scarcity
50	70	100	N/A

35785 AUTOMATIC COAL UNLOADER: With 35785 hopper car

VG-C6	EX-C7	LN-C8	Scarcity
50	90	130	N/A

Catalogs

CATALOGS AND PAPER PRODUCTS

Through its history American Flyer distributed a wide array of catalogs, flyers, brochures and instruction books both for consumers and their dealer/distributor networks. Listed are some of the most widely collected, and in some cases reproduced, documents from the company's history.

Circa 1907 CATALOG: Eight-page 11-3/4 x 10-1/4-inch black and white from Edmonds-Metzel Mfg. Co. on 1088 Wilcox Ave., Chicago, Ill., U.S.A. Reproductions of this catalog were made in 1960, which are sometimes confused with originals.

VG-C6	EX-C7	LN-C8	Scarcity

Too rarely traded to accurately establish pricing.

1910 CATALOG: Eight-page 12 x 10-inch black and white catalog from the American Flyer Mfg. Co. at 1910-1920 Kinzie St., Chicago, Ill. An unmarked reproduction of this catalog was made in the 1970s.

VG-C6	EX-C7	LN-C8	Scarcity

Too rarely traded to accurately establish pricing.

1914 CATALOG: Though a black and white reproduction is shown here, the cover of the original 11 x 9-inch catalog was printed in color.

VG-C6	EX-C7	LN-C8	Scarcity

Too rarely traded to accurately establish pricing.

1915 CATALOG: Sixteen-page 7-7/8 x 9-1/4-inch catalog with gray, red, blue and white cover.

VG-C6	EX-C7	LN-C8	Scarcity

Too rarely traded to accurately establish pricing.

Circa 1916-1917 CATALOG: Twenty-page 11 x 7-3/4-inch catalog with color covers (inside and out) and black and white inner pages. The date is estimated because there is not a specific date given in the catalog, which lists the American Flyer address as 2219-39 South Halstead St., Chicago.

VG-C6	EX-C7	LN-C8	Scarcity

Too rarely traded to accurately establish pricing.

1918 CATALOG: Twenty-page catalog similar to the 1918 edition but with Toy Manufacturer's Association logo on upper right of front cover.

VG-C6	EX-C7	LN-C8	Scarcity
75	125	175	7

1919 CATALOG: Twenty-page 12 x 9-inch catalog similar to the 1918 edition but with red border on

CATALOGS AND PAPER PRODUCTS

cover. In the upper right corner of the cover is the Toy Manufacturer's Association logo. This catalog has been reproduced, with the reproduction notice appearing on the rear cover.

VG-C6	EX-C7	LN-C8	Scarcity
75	125	175	7

1920 CONSUMER CATALOG:

VG-C6	EX-C7	LN-C8	Scarcity
Too rarely traded to accurately establish pricing.			

1921 CONSUMER CATALOG: Unlike the 1922-24 catalogs, which use the same front cover illustration, the cover of this 13-3/4 x 10-1/4-inch catalog does not include any "New York Sales Office" information.

VG-C6	EX-C7	LN-C8	Scarcity
25	60	125	6

1922 CONSUMER CATALOG: This 16-page 13-3/4 x 10-1/4-inch used the same colored front cover illustration as the 1921 edition. On the rear cover is an elevation of the Halstead Street factory.

VG-C6	EX-C7	LN-C8	Scarcity
25	60	125	6

1923 CONSUMER CATALOG: This 16-page 13-3/4 x 10-1/4-inch used the same colored front cover as the 1921-22 editions. On the rear cover are eight photos of the Halstead Street factory with the message "THE HOME OF 3,500,000 AMERICAN FLYERS."

VG-C6	EX-C7	LN-C8	Scarcity
25	60	125	6

1924 CONSUMER CATALOG: This 16-page 13-3/4 x 10-1/4-inch used the same colored cover illustration as the 1921-23 editions. The rear cover is illustrated with a three-quarter view of the Halstead Street factory and includes the legend "THE HOME OF 4,000,000 AMERICAN FLYERS."

VG-C6	EX-C7	LN-C8	Scarcity
25	60	125	6

1925 CONSUMER CATALOG: This 24-page catalog, which had a colored front cover but black rear cover measured 12 x 9 inches. Reproductions exist, which are slightly smaller.

VG-C6	EX-C7	LN-C8	Scarcity
25	60	125	7

MINIATURE CATALOG: The same 1925 cover image, though not in full color, was used for this 16-page 6-1/16 x 4-1/2-inch duo-tone catalog. Reproductions have been made, which are somewhat larger than originals.

VG-C6	EX-C7	LN-C8	Scarcity
20	40	60	7

1926 CONSUMER CATALOG: This 12 x 9-inch horizontal format catalog featured the same full-color cover illustration as the 1925 catalog. However, the cover of this catalog has "1926 catalog" printed on it. The interior pages of the catalog are a mix of color and black and white pages. Reproductions of this catalog exist.

VG-C6	EX-C7	LN-C8	Scarcity
30	75	150	6

1927 CONSUMER CATALOG: Full-color catalog with dated front cover. Reproductions exist.

VG-C6	EX-C7	LN-C8	Scarcity
30	75	150	6

1928 CONSUMER CATALOG: Forty-eight 11-3/8 x 8-1/2-inch full-color pages. Reproductions have been made in both color and black and white.

VG-C6	EX-C7	LN-C8	Scarcity
30	75	150	6

1929 CONSUMER CATALOG: This full-color, 48-page 11-1/2 x 8-1/2-inch catalog had an illustration of the "The President's Special" on the cover, however the date is not on the cover of the originals. Reproductions in both black and white and color have been made.

VG-C6	EX-C7	LN-C8	Scarcity
30	75	150	6

1930 CONSUMER CATALOG: Full-size 48-page 11-5/8 x 8-9/16-inch consumer catalog. This catalog was reproduced in 1975 by Iron Horse Productions and these reproductions are marked inside.

VG-C6	EX-C7	LN-C8	Scarcity
40	70	100	5

1931 CONSUMER CATALOG: The 32-page catalog is 11-1/2 x 8-9/16 inches. There's no date on the cover, which is a duplicate of that on the front of the 1937 catalog. Back of the catalog is marked "JOB 414." This catalog has been reproduced by Greenberg and House of Heeg; some reproductions have a date on the cover.

VG-C6	EX-C7	LN-C8	Scarcity
25	75	100	5

Values for each condition are in U.S. dollars. | **Scarcity** = Scale from 1-8 with 8 being the hardest to find.

277

1932 CONSUMER CATALOG: Thirty-two full-color 11-5/8 x 8-1/2-inch pages. Rear of catalog marked "JOB 515." Original catalogs did not have a date on the front cover. Both House of Heeg and Greenberg have offered reproductions of this catalog.

VG-C6	EX-C7	LN-C8	Scarcity
20	45	85	4

1933 CONSUMER CATALOG: This 32-page catalog is 11-1/2 x 8-1/2 inches. Back of catalog marked "JOB 614." This catalog has been reproduced by Greenberg and House of Heeg; some reproductions have a date on the cover.

VG-C6	EX-C7	LN-C8	Scarcity
25	75	115	4

1934 CONSUMER CATALOG: This 11-1/2 x 8-1/2-inch catalog, marked "JOB 714," was a 32-page document. This catalog has been reproduced by both Greenberg

Publishing and House of Heeg. Original catalogs do not have dates on covers, but some reproductions do.

VG-C6	EX-C7	LN-C8	Scarcity
30	60	100	4

1935 CONSUMER CATALOG: Twenty-four 11-1/4 x 8-7/16-inch full-color pages. The catalog is marked "JOB 814." Reproductions have been made in both color and black and white by Greenberg as well as in full color by Iron Horse Productions.

VG-C6	EX-C7	LN-C8	Scarcity
25	60	90	4

1936 CONSUMER CATALOG: Twenty-four 11-7/16 x 8-1/2-inch full-color pages. The catalog is marked "JOB 914." This catalog has been reproduced in both color and in black and white. Unfortunately some of these reproductions are not well marked.

VG-C6	EX-C7	LN-C8	Scarcity
30	60	100	4

1937 CONSUMER CATALOG: Full-color 11-1/2 x 8-9/16-inch 24-page catalog marked "JOB 1014" on rear cover. The original catalog was not dated on the cover. Reproductions of this catalog have been made by a number of firms in both color and black and white, some of which have relatively obscure identification as reproductions.

VG-C6	EX-C7	LN-C8	Scarcity
25	50	75	4

1938 D1247 DEALER CATALOG:

VG-C6	EX-C7	LN-C8	Scarcity
80	120	150	7

D1259 CONSUMER CATALOG: This 32-page catalog is 10-5/16 x 6-1/2 inches. This catalog has been reproduced by Greenberg, and the reproductions have "1938" on the cover, while originals do not.

VG-C6	EX-C7	LN-C8	Scarcity
20	40	60	4

1939 D1311 CONSUMER CATALOG: Forty-eight 10-1/4 x 6-5/8-inch pages.

VG-C6	EX-C7	LN-C8	Scarcity
25	50	75	4

1940 D1333 CONSUMER CATALOG: This 48-page 10-3/4 x 8-1/4-inch catalog has four actual locomotives shown on the cover.

VG-C6	EX-C7	LN-C8	Scarcity
20	35	55	4

1941 D1389 ADVANCE CATALOG: 9 x 12-inch catalog printed in red, blue and black.

VG-C6	EX-C7	LN-C8	Scarcity
20	35	50	7

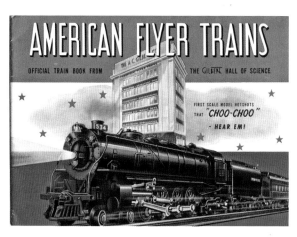

D1390 CONSUMER CATALOG: Red, white and blue covers were used on this 11-3/8 x 8-1/4-inch catalog, which had 48 pages.

VG-C6	EX-C7	LN-C8	Scarcity
30	50	75	4

1942 TRAIN PRICE LIST: Consumer Price List published Jan. 15, 1942 as Form 740. Reproductions are plentiful.

VG-C6	EX-C7	LN-C8	Scarcity
3	5	10	5

1946 D1451 CONSUMER CATALOG: Thirty-two-page full-color, 14-1/2 x 10-1/4-inch catalog titled "Railroading with AMERICAN FLYER."

Values for each condition are in U.S. dollars. | **Scarcity** = Scale from 1-8 with 8 being the hardest to find.

279

D1451 (TYPE I): Consumer catalog as described above

VG-C6	EX-C7	LN-C8	Scarcity
40	75	150	6

D1451 (TYPE II): Executive catalog with red plastic binding.

VG-C6	EX-C7	LN-C8	Scarcity
Too rarely traded to accurately establish pricing.			

D1455 DEALER: Pages are not marked.

VG-C6	EX-C7	LN-C8	Scarcity
40	75	150	8

D1457 POSTWAR GILBERT SCIENTIFIC TOYS: Eight-page black, white and yellow catalog.

VG-C6	EX-C7	LN-C8	Scarcity
15	20	30	6

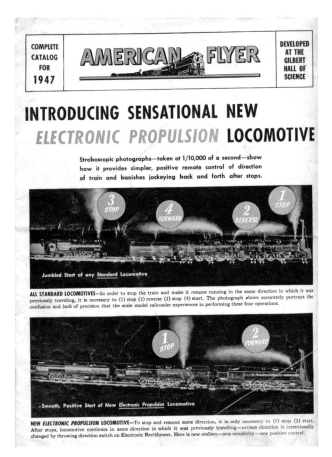

1947 D1472 CATALOG: Illustrating "Electronic Propulsion" locomotive on the cover, this 16-page black and blue catalog measures 9 x 12 inches.

VG-C6	EX-C7	LN-C8	Scarcity
25	50	75	7

D1473 CONSUMER CATALOG: Thirty-two-page full-color oversize catalog. Cover the same as in 1946 and 1948.

VG-C6	EX-C7	LN-C8	Scarcity
30	50	85	7

1948 D1505 ADVANCE CATALOG: Printed with red and black ink, this 15-page 9 x 12-inch catalog was prepared for distributors and dealers.

VG-C6	EX-C7	LN-C8	Scarcity
15	25	45	7

D1507 CONSUMER CATALOG: Full-color, oversized 32-page consumer catalog.

VG-C6	EX-C7	LN-C8	Scarcity
25	50	90	6

D1502 ADVANCE CATALOG: Sixteen-page full-size catalog printed in black and blue ink.

VG-C6	EX-C7	LN-C8	Scarcity
15	30	45	6

D1508: The headline of this full-color 32-page catalog reads "WITH SUPERMAN AT THE GILBERT HALL of SCIENCE."

VG-C6	EX-C7	LN-C8	Scarcity
25	50	100	7

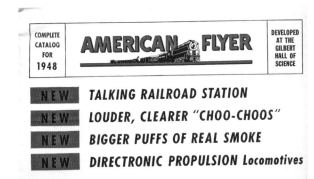

D1517: 16-page black and white HO catalog.

VG-C6	EX-C7	LN-C8	Scarcity
Too rarely traded to accurately establish pricing.			

1949 D1525 ADVANCE CATALOG: The cover of this 16-page catalog touts several sound-generating trains and accessories.

VG-C6	EX-C7	LN-C8	Scarcity
60	90	125	7

D1530 ADVANCE CATALOG: Sixteen-page full-size catalog printed in blue and black.

VG-C6	EX-C7	LN-C8	Scarcity
15	25	50	4

D1536 CONSUMER CATALOG: The cover of this 40-page full-cover catalog bore the legends "FUN & THRILLS," "AMERICAN FLYER" and "ERECTOR."

VG-C6	EX-C7	LN-C8	Scarcity
15	30	50	4

1950 D1578 DEALER CATALOG: The cover of this 32-page 12 x 9-inch dealer catalog is red and white with a black locomotive racing across it.

VG-C6	EX-C7	LN-C8	Scarcity
15	25	50	6

D1579 GILBERT TOYS: Sixteen-page catalog printed with green and black ink.

VG-C6	EX-C7	LN-C8	Scarcity
6	10	20	7

D1604 CONSUMER CATALOG: The cover of this 56-page catalog is marked "GILBERT TOYS American Flyer Trains."

VG-C6	EX-C7	LN-C8	Scarcity
20	35	60	4

D1631 DEALER TV: Four-page brochure about ad campaign for "American Flyer Boys Railroad Club" in 1950. Reproductions exist.

VG-C6	EX-C7	LN-C8	Scarcity
5	10	20	7

1951 D1637 DEALER CATALOG: Blue and black full-sized catalog.

VG-C6	EX-C7	LN-C8	Scarcity
10	15	25	7

D1640 CONSUMER CATALOG: The cover of this 48-page 11-1/16 x 8-inch full-color catalog reads "GILBERT TOYS American Flyer Trains." East and West region prices listed separately.

VG-C6	EX-C7	LN-C8	Scarcity
10	25	45	3

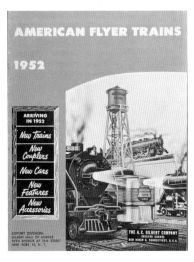

1952 D1667 ADVANCE CATALOG: The cover of this 40-page "Export Division" is orange and black.

VG-C6	EX-C7	LN-C8	Scarcity
15	25	35	7

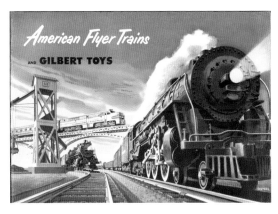

D1677 CONSUMER CATALOG: The cover of this 48-page full-color 11-1/2 x 8-inch catalog reads "American Flyer Trains and Gilbert Toys."

VG-C6	EX-C7	LN-C8	Scarcity
10	20	30	3

Values for each condition are in U.S. dollars. | Scarcity = Scale from 1-8 with 8 being the hardest to find.

283

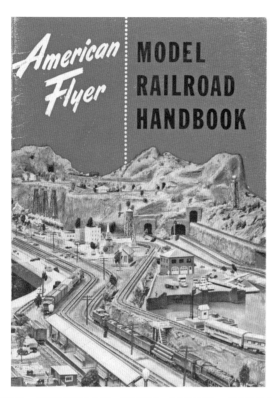

M2978 "AMERICAN FLYER MODEL RAILROAD HANDBOOK": Twenty-eight-page instruction book. Cover is made of blue heavy paper.

VG-C6	EX-C7	LN-C8	Scarcity
3	7	12	1

D1705: Twelve-page red and white brochure illustrating dealer displays.

VG-C6	EX-C7	LN-C8	Scarcity
Too rarely traded to accurately establish pricing.			

D1714 CONSUMER CATALOG: The cover of this 52-page Eastern region catalog is marked "American Flyer Trains ERECTOR AND OTHER GILBERT TOYS." This catalog came in two versions; one printed on pulp paper, the other on coated stock. There is no difference in value or desirability due to paper type.

VG-C6	EX-C7	LN-C8	Scarcity
10	15	25	3

1953 D1704 DEALER CATALOG: Thirty-six full-size black and orange pages of either coated or pulp paper, which does not affect value.

VG-C6	EX-C7	LN-C8	Scarcity
40	60	100	7

D1715 CONSUMER CATALOG: Identical to D1714, but with prices for Western distribution.

VG-C6	EX-C7	LN-C8	Scarcity
10	15	25	3

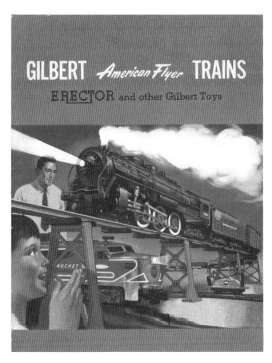

1954 D1748 ADVANCE CATALOG: This is a 32-page 8-1/2 x 11-inch catalog for the Eastern region.

VG-C6	EX-C7	LN-C8	Scarcity
7	15	25	5

D1749 ADVANCE CATALOG: Identical to D1748, but this catalog is for the Western region.

VG-C6	EX-C7	LN-C8	Scarcity
7	15	25	5

D1750 DEALER DISPLAYS: Twelve green and white pages of dealer display items. Beware, this item has been reproduced.

VG-C6	EX-C7	LN-C8	Scarcity
Too rarely traded to accurately establish pricing.			

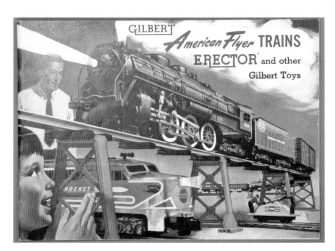

D1760 CONSUMER CATALOG: The cover of this consumer East 48-page 11-1/4 x 8-inch catalog is marked "GILBERT American Flyer TRAINS ERECTOR and other Gilbert Toys."

VG-C6	EX-C7	LN-C8	Scarcity
10	15	40	3

D1761 CONSUMER CATALOG: Identical to D1760, but consumer West.

VG-C6	EX-C7	LN-C8	Scarcity
10	15	40	3

1955 D1782 DEALER CATALOG: The interior of this 11-1/4 x 8-inch catalog was printed in black, yellow and white.

VG-C6	EX-C7	LN-C8	Scarcity
10	20	30	6

D1801 CONSUMER CATALOG: Eastern region 44-page full-color catalog. On cover is printed "AMERICAN FLYER Made by GILBERT."

VG-C6	EX-C7	LN-C8	Scarcity
5	10	20	3

D1802 CONSUMER CATALOG: Identical to D1801, but consumer West.

VG-C6	EX-C7	LN-C8	Scarcity
5	10	20	3

D1816 DEALER CATALOG: Yellow, black and white 36-page catalog.

VG-C6	EX-C7	LN-C8	Scarcity
12	20	30	6

Values for each condition are in U.S. dollars. | **Scarcity** = Scale from 1-8 with 8 being the hardest to find.

285

D1820 HO CONSUMER CATALOG: Twenty pages, two-color pocket-sized catalog.

VG-C6	EX-C7	LN-C8	Scarcity
5	10	20	3

D1840: Factory manila mailing envelope for large 11-1/4 x 8-inch catalogs.

D1840 (TYPE I): "Postpaid."

VG-C6	EX-C7	LN-C8	Scarcity
-	-	1	2

D1840 (TYPE II): "Not postpaid."

VG-C6	EX-C7	LN-C8	Scarcity
-	-	2	2

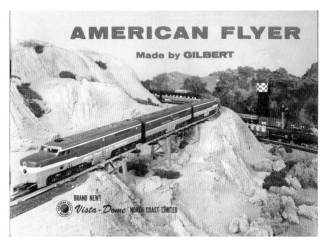

1956 D1866 CONSUMER CATALOG: This 52-page 11-1/4 x 8-inch full color catalog for the Eastern region is printed on pulp paper. The cover was slick and bore the message "AMERICAN FLYER Made by GILBERT."

VG-C6	EX-C7	LN-C8	Scarcity
10	15	25	3

D1867 CONSUMER CATALOG: Identical to D1866, except it's a Western edition.

VG-C6	EX-C7	LN-C8	Scarcity
10	15	25	3

D1874 DEALER CATALOG: Cover differs from that on D1866/1867 by not having "BRAND NEW Vista-Dome NORTH COAST LIMITED" printed on cover. Also, the inside pages are black, red and white rather than full color.

VG-C6	EX-C7	LN-C8	Scarcity
12	25	35	5

D1879 ERECTOR AND OTHER GILBERT "CAREER-BUILDING" TOYS: Twenty-four-page full-sized catalog with color cover and interior printed in blue and yellow.

VG-C6	EX-C7	LN-C8	Scarcity
2	5	10	6

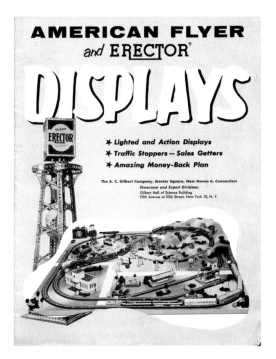

D1882 A. F. AND ERECTOR DISPLAYS: Twelve-page catalog illustrating displays available to dealers.

VG-C6	EX-C7	LN-C8	Scarcity
5	10	20	7

D1904 GILBERT HO TRAINS 1956 CATALOG: Full-color cover, with red and black interior pages.

VG-C6	EX-C7	LN-C8	Scarcity
5	10	20	4

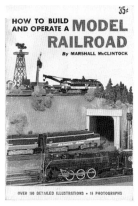

D1920 BOOK: Dell soft back 160-page book first published in 1955 titled "How to Build A Model Railroad" written by Marshall McClintock.

VG-C6	EX-C7	LN-C8	Scarcity
2	5	10	3

D1922 MINIATURE CATALOG: Fifty-two-page full-color 7-1/2 x 5-1/4-inch catalog titled "AMERICAN FLYER/Made by GILBERT."

VG-C6	EX-C7	LN-C8	Scarcity
5	10	20	3

1957 D1937 DEALER CATALOG: Full-color, full-size catalog with 48 pages.

VG-C6	EX-C7	LN-C8	Scarcity
20	30	40	6

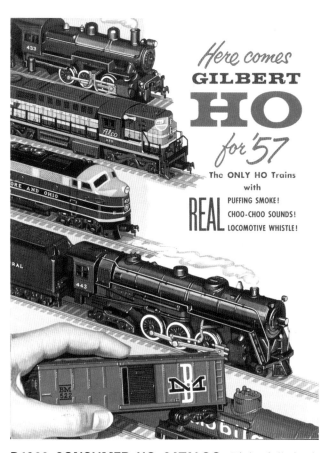

D1966 CONSUMER HO CATALOG: Eight full-sized, full-color pages.

VG-C6	EX-C7	LN-C8	Scarcity
2	4	8	3

D2006 CONSUMER CATALOG: Eastern edition of 48-page full-color catalog titled "GILBERT/AMERICAN FLYER TRAINS for 1957."

VG-C6	EX-C7	LN-C8	Scarcity
10	15	20	3

D2007 CONSUMER CATALOG: This Western edition 11-3/8 x 7-7/8-inch catalog is identical to D2006 except for the prices.

VG-C6	EX-C7	LN-C8	Scarcity
10	15	20	3

Values for each condition are in U.S. dollars. | **Scarcity** = Scale from 1-8 with 8 being the hardest to find.

287

D2031 CONSUMER CATALOG AND INSTRUCTION BOOK: Eight-page brochure of HO-Gauge trains.

VG-C6	EX-C7	LN-C8	Scarcity
7	10	15	3

D2086: Identical to D1980, except marked "Postpaid."

VG-C6	EX-C7	LN-C8	Scarcity
3	5	10	2

1958 D2047 CONSUMER CATALOG: Eastern edition of 48-page full-color catalog titled "AMERICAN FLYER by GILBERT."

VG-C6	EX-C7	LN-C8	Scarcity
25	55	100	3

D2048 CONSUMER CATALOG: Same as D2047 except Western edition with higher prices.

VG-C6	EX-C7	LN-C8	Scarcity
30	60	110	3

D2058 ERECTOR AND TOYS: Twelve-page catalog of Gilbert toys, no trains.

VG-C6	EX-C7	LN-C8	Scarcity
10	20	30	6

D2086 CONSUMER FOLDER: Eastern edition of full-color folder, which when folded is about the size of a #10 envelope, but opens to about 17 x 35 inches.

VG-C6	EX-C7	LN-C8	Scarcity
5	10	20	2

D2087 CONSUMER FOLDER: Western edition of D2086.

VG-C6	EX-C7	LN-C8	Scarcity
5	10	20	2

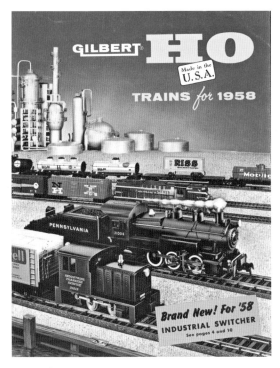

D4106 HO CONSUMER CATALOG: Twelve-page full-color full-size catalog, titled "Gilbert HO Trains for 1958."

VG-C6	EX-C7	LN-C8	Scarcity
10	15	20	3

1959 D2115 CATALOG: Twenty-four-page "AMERICAN FLYER for 1959" catalog. Full-color cover, black and red inner pages.

D2115 (TYPE I): Four Underwriters Laboratories ("UL") symbols shown with transformers.

VG-C6	EX-C7	LN-C8	Scarcity
8	16	35	4

D2115 (TYPE II): Two Underwriters Laboratories ("UL") symbols shown with transformers.

VG-C6	EX-C7	LN-C8	Scarcity
8	16	35	4

D2125 BROCHURE: Single-sheet promotion for Overland Express Baggage Car.

VG-C6	EX-C7	LN-C8	Scarcity
1	2	3	3

D2146 FOLDER: This Eastern region full-color folder, titled "AMERICAN FLYER 1959-60" folds to the size of a #10 envelope, yet opens to 17 x 34-5/8 inches.

VG-C6	EX-C7	LN-C8	Scarcity
2	5	10	2

D2148 FOLDER: Same as D2146 except Western region.

VG-C6	EX-C7	LN-C8	Scarcity
2	5	10	2

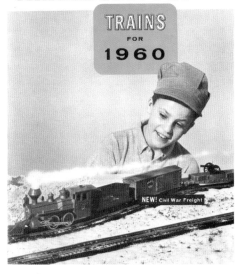

1960 D2192 (TYPE I) CONSUMER CATALOG: Twenty-page 8-1/2 x 11-inch green and black catalog titled "AMERICAN FLYER TRAINS FOR 1960."

VG-C6	EX-C7	LN-C8	Scarcity
10	20	30	2

D2192 (TYPE II): "ADVANCE catalog" printed in black block on upper cover.

VG-C6	EX-C7	LN-C8	Scarcity
Too rarely traded to accurately establish pricing.			

Values for each condition are in U.S. dollars. | **Scarcity** = Scale from 1-8 with 8 being the hardest to find.

289

D2192 (TYPE III): "ADVANCE catalog" printed on cover.

VG-C6	EX-C7	LN-C8	Scarcity
Too rarely traded to accurately establish pricing.			

D2192 (TYPE IV): "ADVANCE" printed on the cover.

VG-C6	EX-C7	LN-C8	Scarcity
Too rarely traded to accurately establish pricing.			

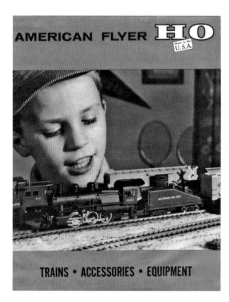

D2193 HO CONSUMER CATALOG: Blue and black catalog with 12 full-sized pages titled "American Flyer HO."

VG-C6	EX-C7	LN-C8	Scarcity
5	10	20	2

D2193REV: Same as D2193, but revised.

VG-C6	EX-C7	LN-C8	Scarcity
7	12	24	2

D2198 CATALOG: Four-page race car brochure printed in red and black titled "Action & fun for the entire family No. 19060 American Flyer Stock Car Race."

VG-C6	EX-C7	LN-C8	Scarcity
3	5	10	4

D2223 GILBERT SCIENCE TOYS: This red and black flyer, when folded, was about the size of a #10 envelope, yet opened to roughly 9 x 15 inches.

VG-C6	EX-C7	LN-C8	Scarcity
2	5	10	3

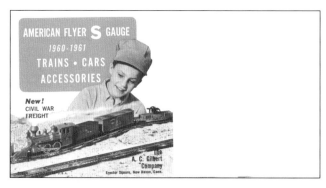

D2224 CONSUMER FOLDER: This gold and black folder opens from 4 x 9 inches to about 16 x 11 inches.

VG-C6	EX-C7	LN-C8	Scarcity
3	5	10	2

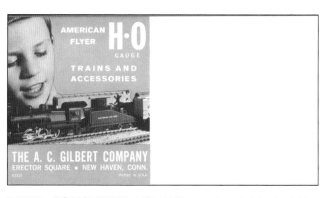

D2225 CONSUMER FOLDER: Red and black folder promoting American Flyer HO Trains; folded size of 4 x 9 inches, but opens to 12 x 8 inches.

VG-C6	EX-C7	LN-C8	Scarcity
3	5	10	2

D2230 CONSUMER CATALOG: Twenty-page full-sized catalog titled "AMERICAN FLYER TRAINS FOR 1960." Cover printed in orange and black.

VG-C6	EX-C7	LN-C8	Scarcity
15	30	50	2

D2231 HO CONSUMER CATALOG: Twelve-page full-sized catalog with red and black cover, titled "American Flyer HO."

VG-C6	EX-C7	LN-C8	Scarcity
5	10	20	2

1961 D2238 CAREER BUILDING SCIENCE TOYS: Twenty-four full-sized pages printed in red and black ink.

VG-C6	EX-C7	LN-C8	Scarcity
5	10	20	4

D2239 1961-62 CONSUMER CATALOG: Green and black 36-page 1961-62 catalog, printed on either glossy or pulp stock. No difference in value due to paper.

VG-C6	EX-C7	LN-C8	Scarcity
5	15	25	3

D2267 CONSUMER CATALOG: Twenty-four-page red and black full-sized catalog titled "AMERICAN FLYER TRAINS 1961-1962," "S/GAUGE" and "HO/GAUGE."

VG-C6	EX-C7	LN-C8	Scarcity
10	15	20	2

Values for each condition are in U.S. dollars. | **Scarcity =** Scale from 1-8 with 8 being the hardest to find.

291

CATALOGS AND PAPER PRODUCTS

D2268 FOLDER: Auto Rama.

VG-C6	EX-C7	LN-C8	Scarcity
2	5	10	4

1962 D2277 REV CONSUMER TOY CATALOG: Sixteen-page catalog with brown and tan cover titled "Career Building Science Toys."

VG-C6	EX-C7	LN-C8	Scarcity
15	25	40	4

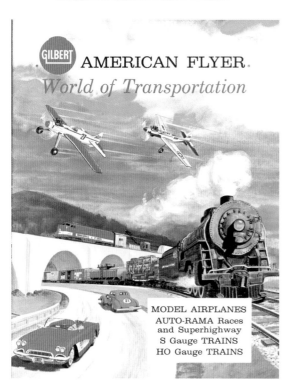

D2278 CATALOG: Thirty-six-page full-size catalog titled "GILBERT AMERICAN FLYER World of Transportation." The cover was printed in full-color, while the interior is black and green.

VG-C6	EX-C7	LN-C8	Scarcity
10	20	30	3

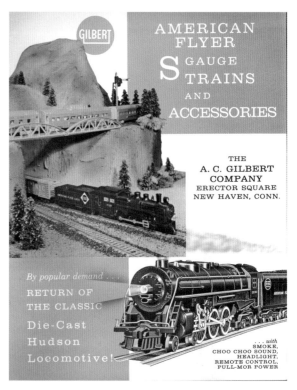

D2282 DEALER CATALOG: Seventy-six pages.

VG-C6	EX-C7	LN-C8	Scarcity
15	30	45	4

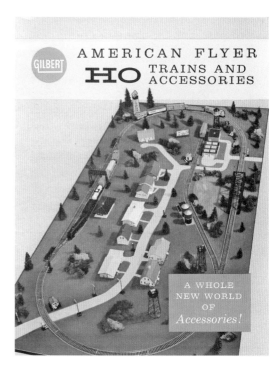

D2283 CONSUMER HO CATALOG: Twelve-page full-sized HO catalog.

VG-C6	EX-C7	LN-C8	Scarcity
5	10	15	3

D2310 CONSUMER CATALOG: Thirty-six-page full-size catalog with green and black interior pages and full-color cover.

VG-C6	EX-C7	LN-C8	Scarcity
5	10	20	4

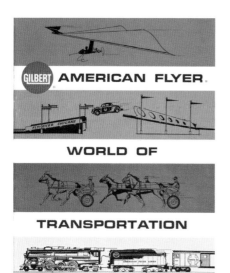

1963 D2321 CATALOG: Forty-eight-page full-color full-size catalog titled "GILBERT AMERICAN FLYER/ WORLD OF TRANSPORTATION."

VG-C6	EX-C7	LN-C8	Scarcity
10	15	30	3

X863-3 CONSUMER TOY CATALOG: Black-covered 32-page full-size full-color catalog titled "GILBERT TOYS 1963." No trains.

VG-C6	EX-C7	LN-C8	Scarcity
5	10	20	4

1964 X-264-6 CONSUMER CATALOG: Forty-page white-covered catalog titled "GILBERT TOYS AND TRANSPORTATION..1964."

VG-C6	EX-C7	LN-C8	Scarcity
5	10	20	4

1965 X165-12 DEALER CATALOG: Twenty-page full-color full-size catalog titled "65 THE YEAR TO GO GILBERT."

VG-C6	EX-C7	LN-C8	Scarcity
5	10	15	3

CATALOGS AND PAPER PRODUCTS

All Aboard

ALL LANDSCAPED · ALL WIRED · ALL READY TO GO

M6788: Titled "GILBERT AMERICAN FLYER All Aboard ALL LANDSCAPED—ALL WIRED—ALL READY TO GO," this 8-1/2 x 11-inch assembly and operating instructions pamphlet has a full-color cover.

VG-C6	EX-C7	LN-C8	Scarcity
10	15	20	1

1966 T-166-6 DEALER CATALOG: Sixteen-page full-color catalog titled "GILBERT TOYS 1966."

VG-C6	EX-C7	LN-C8	Scarcity
5	10	15	4

American Flyer

RACING SETS

All landscaped . . . all wired . . . all ready to race!

Each set includes six square panels that snap together to form a scenic racing layout — not just a stark oval or figure eight of roadway sections, but completely landscaped, completely wired! Rugged molded panels are hand-painted in the natural colors of lakes, hills, rocks, ravines, fields — even mountains. Roadway is built right into the scenery. No ordinary table-top racing set can offer so much fun, so much realism!

No. 19750 JAMES BOND 007 RACING SET — DELUXE. A dream layout that offers challenges to the skillful driver never before seen in table-top racing: Hill Climb, spectacular jump over "Bridge Out" gap, slippery oil slick, tight curves, alternate route-switching, narrow road that permits passage of only one car at a time. Includes: LeMans Start panel with switches that send cars alternately to mountain and valley routes; pit stop area with car lift and equipment; mountain-tunnel panel; power receive panel; power panel with hidden Power Pack (U.L.C.S.A. Approved); separate curved ramp, 2 curve panels; James Bond Aston-Martin and Mustang cars; 2 hand speed controls; flashing red warning lights; lap counters; over thirty signs, trees, fences and other scenic pieces. Layout size 33" x 50". Packed 1 per carton, shipping weight 17 lbs.

POWER STEERING
First time in miniature racing history, you steer your car to win! You're at the wheel exactly as if you were driving, steering right or left, or centering it on the straight-away. You must steer correctly all the time, or your car stops!

AUTO-RAMA SERIES 200 (19702)
With POWER STEERING and PIT STOP — A new, powerful Mustang and XKE Jaguar with new added detail are the competing cars on this stretched-out 8 that also includes Flip Flop Chicane (force your opponent to change lanes). You also get: 2 Power-Steering Speed Controls that put you "at the wheel" for real. Pit Stop, 30 Roadway sections, 14-piece plastic ramp set, plastic fence, plug-in Power Pack (U.L.C.S.A. Approved). Layout size: 6' 7" x 2' 6". Packed 2 per carton, shipping weight 21 lbs.

American Flyer INDUSTRIES
200 Fifth Avenue – 212 924-6300
New York, New York 10010

X-466-1 GILBERT TOYS CONSUMER CATALOG: Twenty-four-page, full-size, full-color toy catalog.

VG-C6	EX-C7	LN-C8	Scarcity
5	10	15	2

1967 AMERICAN FLYER INDUSTRIES: This four-page brochure contained two and a half pages of trains, the balance was slot cars.

VG-C6	EX-C7	LN-C8	Scarcity
Too rarely traded to accurately establish pricing.			

Wide and O Accessories

WIDE- AND O-GAUGE BRIDGES

Roar through dark tunnels — clatter over bridges and
operate your trains with resplendent realism...

The more stations, bridges, tunnels you have the more realistic your railroad system and the more fun you have. You've never been on regular train trip without going through a tunnel or over a bridge, so model your set after the real thing and have dark tunnels for your trains to whizz through and sturdy bridges for them to clatter over.

"O" GAUGE TUNNELS

No. 247 — 11" STRAIGHT............$1.00
No. 248 — 14" STRAIGHT............$2.00

Add extra thrills to model railroading when fast trains roar through at high speed. These tunnels are realistically designed and finished in brilliant colors.

"O" Gauge Scale

No. 581 GIRDER BRIDGE............$2.00

This modern girder type bridge is so carefully designed and scaled that it's a fitting companion to the perfectly executed locomotives and cars of the American Flyer "O" Gauge Line. As your train rushes over it, the side pieces echo and re-echo the clickety-clack of wheels pounding on rails. The finish is authentic railroad black. Size 10" x 1¾" x 4⅝".

No. 2 TRESTLE BRIDGE............$2.50

(Including Track Terminal)

Built of heavy steel and designed like the husky big ones, this trestle bridge is all ready for heavy duty work. Atop the bridge is an illuminated tender house to add another note of realism. The whole bridge is finished in a bright enamel finish. Size 25" x 5½" x 8½".

Page 49

---

2 Tresle Bridge

1 SINGLE SPAN BRIDGE: This 12-1/2-inch long, 5-1/2 x 3-3/4-inch red single-span metal bridge was offered in 1938 only.

VG-C6	EX-C7	LN-C8	Scarcity
5	10	15	5

2 TRESTLE BRIDGE: 📷 This 25-inch long red metal bridge was offered from 1938 through 1940. A bridge-tender's shack was mounted at the top of the 8-1/2-inch tall span.

VG-C6	EX-C7	LN-C8	Scarcity
15	25	35	4

95 FOOT BRIDGE: This German-produced pedestrian bridge was sold from 1909-1914.

VG-C6	EX-C7	LN-C8	Scarcity
20	50	75	8

M95 FOOT BRIDGE WITH SIGNAL: Similar to the 1909-1914 bridge, this 1914-16 version featured a manually operated signal at the center of the span.

VG-C6	EX-C7	LN-C8	Scarcity
20	50	75	8

112 STEEL BRIDGE or STEEL SPAN BRIDGE: This 30-inch long three-piece O-Gauge lithographed bridge was sold from 1925-1932.

VG-C6	EX-C7	LN-C8	Scarcity
20	35	50	6

123 STEEL BRIDGE: This windup-equipped 30-inch long three-piece O-Gauge lithographed bridge was sold from 1925-1927.

VG-C6	EX-C7	LN-C8	Scarcity
20	35	50	6

206 TURN BRIDGE: This German-made 35-1/2-inch long metal swing span is believed to date from the 1910-15 era. It was equipped with a windup-type track.

VG-C6	EX-C7	LN-C8	Scarcity
50	100	150	8

211 UNIVERSAL BRIDGE: This 28-inch long one-piece bridge, made of wood, could accommodate either O- or Wide-Gauge track, and was sold in 1931-1932.

VG-C6	EX-C7	LN-C8	Scarcity
15	30	50	5

212 TRESTLE BRIDGE: Measuring 51 inches long, this red wooden O-Gauge bridge was offered from 1925 through 1933.

VG-C6	EX-C7	LN-C8	Scarcity
20	40	60	6

213/M213 BRIDGE: This German-produced lithographed three-piece bridge, measuring 25 inches long, is believed to have been offered by American Flyer from 1910 through 1914.

VG-C6	EX-C7	LN-C8	Scarcity
25	50	75	8

213 CONSTRUCTION BRIDGE: This bridge was last shown in the 1924 catalog and is believed to have been first produced in 1917.

VG-C6	EX-C7	LN-C8	Scarcity
10	20	30	4

213 TRESTLE BRIDGE: This red 27-1/2-inch long single-span wooden bridge was cataloged in 1931-32. A lithographed bridge-tender's shack was mounted on top of the bridge.

M214 TURN BRIDGE: See 206.

581 GIRDER BRIDGE: This 10-inch long black girder bridge, stamped "LACKAWANNA" was cataloged 1938-1942.

VG-C6	EX-C7	LN-C8	Scarcity
5	10	15	3

611 TRESTLE BRIDGE: In 1941-1942, American Flyer offered this 17-3/4-inch long red metal bridge. A bridge-tender's house with a light was mounted at the top of the 8-1/4-inch tall span.

VG-C6	EX-C7	LN-C8	Scarcity
10	20	30	4

4218 TRESTLE BRIDGE: This 56-inch long red wood bridge for Wide-Gauge was offered from 1925 through 1927.

VG-C6	EX-C7	LN-C8	Scarcity
30	60	90	5

4219 TRESTLE BRIDGE: Brass nameplates were on each end of this 56-inch long red wooden Wide-Gauge span, which was offered from 1925 through 1933.

VG-C6	EX-C7	LN-C8	Scarcity
25	60	100	5

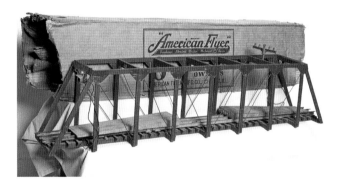

4220 LIGHTED TRESTLE BRIDGE: This impressive bridge was sold from 1928 through 1933. Three major components comprised this 70-1/2-inch long bridge: a 42-inch long red center span, plus two tapered approach pieces. On the top of the span was mounted two telegraph crossarms. On either end of the bridge was a die-cast light fixture and brass nameplates.

VG-C6	EX-C7	LN-C8	Scarcity
200	400	550	7

Values for each condition are in U.S. dollars. | Scarcity = Scale from 1-8 with 8 being the hardest to find.

WIDE- AND O-GAUGE BRIDGES

297

MINIATURE RAILROAD STATIONS

*J*UST look at these fine Passenger and Freight Stations and think of all the fun you can have, stopping your train at the stations and picking up and delivering both passengers and freight. These stations not only offer you a lot of fun but they add realism to your railroad system.

Built of heavy gauge steel and beautifully finished in a combination of colored enamels, with detailed lithographed sides, they are exact models of the real station you see in most every town. All lighted stations are illuminated with genuine Train lamps and are also equipped with our Universal Track Terminal Model 4455, adaptable to either narrow or wide gauge track. They differ in size, features and colors in order to meet your individual requirements.

CENTRAL STATION

A very attractive and also our largest station of the suburban type. It is illuminated with one interior and two exterior frosted Train lamps. The deeply embossed roof and the chimneys are enameled. The roof has a dormer window and all windows have frosted transparencies through which the interior light shines. Has four swinging brass doors. Size 13½″ long by 8″ wide by 7½″ high.
Model 102 Each..................$6.25—★$6.85

KENILWORTH

Equipped with an exterior frosted Train lamp. Has enameled roof and base with sides attractively reproduced in detail. Size 9¼″ long by 5¼″ wide by 5½″ high.
Model 104 Each $2.50 ★$2.75

Flossmoor
Same as station above Model 104 but without light.
Model 96
Each $1.25 ★$1.35

SWITCH TOWER HOUSE

This new Tower House has a large switch board with six knife switches for operating and controlling electrical lighting systems, automatic equipment, track layouts, etc. It will control six different circuits—an exclusive American Flyer feature. Has stairs leading up to the train observation platform, which is enclosed with a solid brass hand rail. The sixteen observation windows have solid brass frames and are equipped with imitation glass. It is electrically lighted with an interior Train lamp and is constructed of heavy gauge steel and finished in bright automobile enamels. Both the upper floor and the roof is removable so that it is easy to get at the wiring in back of the knife switches. Full instructions on the correct method of hooking up various electrical circuits are included. Size 12″ long by 7½″ wide by 9¼″ high.
Model 108 Each................................. $8.00—★$8.85

TERMINAL STATION

A very attractive station with two exterior frosted and one interior frosted Train lamps. All windows have frosted transparencies through which the light shines. The roof is embossed and enameled a beautiful orange. Has beautiful etched nameplate. Size: 12″ long by 7½″ wide by 7″ high.
Model 107 Each..................$4.75—★$5.25

FREIGHT STATION

A very realistic appearing freight station with two sliding doors one on each side at the head of the incline to the upper platform. The exterior is lighted with a frosted Train lamp. The roof has a lithographed tile effect while the lower platform is enameled gray. Size 12″ long by 7″ wide by 7″ high.
Model 97 Each $4.00—★$4.50

★ *Indicates Western Prices*

American Flyer

Page 21

Since the station was the point of contact between the public and trains, it is not surprising that American Flyer offered a myriad of such structures throughout the prewar era.

90/M90 PASSENGER STATION: Although stations with these numbers were sold by American Flyer from 1909 through 1933, the stations were by no means the same. In 1928, the 90 was assigned the name "HYDE PARK," which it retained through 1933.

90/M90 PASSENGER STATION (Type I): The earliest building assigned the numbers was made in Germany and were embossed to resemble brick.

VG-C6	EX-C7	LN-C8	Scarcity
15	25	50	6

90/M90 PASSENGER STATION (Type II): Around 1914, the building changed. Still made in Germany, the sides of the building are now lithographed, as is the simulated tile roof. This style of building is believed to have been used for about two years.

VG-C6	EX-C7	LN-C8	Scarcity
15	25	50	6

90/M90 PASSENGER STATION (Type III): Around 1916, the roof of the building was painted rather than lithographed. The walls were lithographed to resemble brick.

VG-C6	EX-C7	LN-C8	Scarcity
10	20	40	4

90/M90 PASSENGER STATION (Type IV): Beginning in 1925, the sides of the station were lithographed with one door and one window—rather than the two windows of previous editions. "WAITING ROOM" was printed above the doors. One window was on each end and the lithographed brick reached midway up the walls. The base of the structure was painted gray and the roof was red.

VG-C6	EX-C7	LN-C8	Scarcity
10	20	40	4

90/M90 PASSENGER STATION (Type V): Identical to Type IV, except for the green roof.

VG-C6	EX-C7	LN-C8	Scarcity
10	20	40	4

90/M90 PASSENGER STATION (Type VI): Identical to Type IV, but with "HYDE PARK STATION" markings below the clocks on the ends.

VG-C6	EX-C7	LN-C8	Scarcity
10	20	40	4

91 FAST FREIGHT STATION: The walls of this 1931-32 station are lithographed, with the lower portion of the walls simulating brick. The base for this station was painted gray. On the gable roof were signs reading "FLYER TOWN FREIGHT 91." The front and rear of the station were duplicates of each other and included "FLYER TOWN FREIGHT STATION" signs above the doors.

91 FAST FREIGHT STATION (Type I): Some of the stations came with roofs finished in an orange-red roof.

VG-C6	EX-C7	LN-C8	Scarcity
10	20	30	5

91 FAST FREIGHT STATION (Type II): Other stations had dark-red roofs.

VG-C6	EX-C7	LN-C8	Scarcity
10	20	30	5

91 STATION PLATFORM: Measuring just over 15 inches long, this gray platform with green and white striped roof was sold in the mid-1920s.

VG-C6	EX-C7	LN-C8	Scarcity
25	50	75	6

92 WOODEN BILLBOARD: This 9-1/2 x 5-1/4-inch high wooden billboard holding a paper printed sign reading "AMERICAN FLYER" was sold in the early 1920s.

VG-C6	EX-C7	LN-C8	Scarcity
25	50	75	6

92 WATCHMAN'S TOWER: This elevated structure consists of a lithographed shack mounted on top of a square post supported by a round base, which was green. A bell was mounted on the shack. This accessory was sold from 1929 through 1933.

VG-C6	EX-C7	LN-C8	Scarcity
10	20	30	4

93/M93 FREIGHT STATION: Much like the 90 Passenger station, the 93 freight station appeared in the American Flyer line for the biggest part of two decades—but in many different versions.

93/M93 FREIGHT STATION (Type I): From about 1909 into the early teens, the lithographed station had a sliding door.

VG-C6	EX-C7	LN-C8	Scarcity
12	25	40	7

93/M93 FREIGHT STATION (Type II): In the mid-teens, the station lost its sliding door, but gained a raised platform and its roof was lithographed to resemble shingles.

VG-C6	EX-C7	LN-C8	Scarcity
12	25	40	7

93/M93 FREIGHT STATION (Type III): Beginning in the late teens, and continuing through 1925, the ends of the station included a lithographed clock and a sign reading "FLYER TOWN DEPOT." The roof of the station was maroon and the base orange.

VG-C6	EX-C7	LN-C8	Scarcity
20	30	30	4

93/M93 FREIGHT STATION (Type IV): Almost identical to the Type III, this station differed by having its roof and base finished in black.

VG-C6	EX-C7	LN-C8	Scarcity
20	30	30	4

93 SUBURBAN STATION: The green roof of this 1928-31 station hung over a sign reading "American Flyer SUBURBAN WEST BOUNDTRAINS." The base of the illuminated station was painted gray and the sides finished in simulated brick, white and orange stucco.

VG-C6	EX-C7	LN-C8	Scarcity
15	25	50	5

95 FREIGHT STATION: This lithographed station was sold only in 1926-1927. The roof was red, with a brick chimney and the walls were two-tone red. On both sides a ramp led to a platform, onto which opened a sliding door. Two windows were on each end.

VG-C6	EX-C7	LN-C8	Scarcity
25	50	75	6

M96 DERRICK: This German produced 4-1/2-inch tall derrick was sold in the early teens.

VG-C6	EX-C7	LN-C8	Scarcity
Too rarely traded to accurately establish pricing.			

Values for each condition are in U.S. dollars. | **Scarcity** = Scale from 1-8 with 8 being the hardest to find.

299

WIDE- AND O-GAUGE BUILDINGS

96/104 STATIONS: But for the interior light, these two stations were twins. The 96 did not have an interior light, while the 104 did. Beginning in 1928, the 96 was known as the "Flossmoor" station.

96 FLOSSMOOR STATION: But for 1934, this station was cataloged continuously from 1923 through 1935. The walls of this station were lithographed brick. One end of the station had two small windows and above them a sign reading "FLYER TOWN-STATION NO. 96." Often, either the baggage or waiting room doors were formed in the open position.

96 FLOSSMOOR STATION (TYPE I): Green roof, gray base, multicolor brick walls and chimney.

VG-C6	EX-C7	LN-C8	Scarcity
15	30	50	5

96 FLOSSMOOR STATION (TYPE II): Green roof, dark gray base and brick of uniform color.

VG-C6	EX-C7	LN-C8	Scarcity
15	30	50	5

97 FREIGHT STATION: Even though the number lithographed on one end of this illuminated station was "95," this structure was cataloged as the 97 from 1928 through 1934. The station was marked "FLYER CITY/ FREIGHT STATION NO. 95" and "INBOUND/ FREIGHT STATION." The base of the station was 12 inches long.

VG-C6	EX-C7	LN-C8	Scarcity
35	75	110	6

97 FREIGHT STATION SET: This 19-inch long 1936-1939 accessory featured at one end a 97 freight station, and at the other end a crane. The crane consisted of the red cab of a 3025 wrecker crane mounted on a base. The oversized hook of the crane stands out.

97 FREIGHT STATION SET (Type I): The main base is finished in tan, while the crane sub base is green on this version. The decal on the crane reads "AMERICAN FLYER LINES."

VG-C6	EX-C7	LN-C8	Scarcity
50	100	150	6

97 FREIGHT STATION SET (Type II): Other sets were built on dark-red bases, with light-gray crane sub base. The decal on the crane reads "AMERICAN FLYER LINES."

VG-C6	EX-C7	LN-C8	Scarcity
50	100	150	6

97 FREIGHT STATION SET (Type III): The final version again used a red base, but the crane sub base was now medium-gray, and the lettering on the crane decal was shortened to read "AMERICAN FLYER."

VG-C6	EX-C7	LN-C8	Scarcity
50	100	150	6

97, 98 AND 99 PASSENGER STATIONS

The 97 passenger station was the basis for a whole series of stations offered during the 1920s. The 98 Passenger Station added interior illumination and isinglass windows, the 99 added two exterior lights to the 98, and the 105 was a 98 in a different paint scheme. A dormer window and simulated tile roof made this a 107 Terminal Station.

97 PASSENGER STATION: The walls of this unlighted 1923-26 station were lithographed white near the top and brown and orange brick at the bottom. The building was marked "FLYER TOWN STATION NO. 97." The building had a green hip roof and was mounted on a gray base. A chimney was mounted on the roof.

VG-C6	EX-C7	LN-C8	Scarcity
25	50	75	5

98 FREIGHT STATION WITH CRANE: Similar to the 97 freight station set, this 1940 accessory featured a 19-inch long red base supporting a yellow 514 crane cab and a station marked "FLYER CITY FREIGHT STATION NO. 95." The crane had a green die-cast boom and the station lithographed tile hip roof.

VG-C6	EX-C7	LN-C8	Scarcity
50	100	150	7

98 PASSENGER STATION: This 1923-1926 illuminated station had a red roof and gray base. Its windows were glazed and its walls lithographed multi-color brick. The end of the station is lettered "FLYER TOWN STATION NO. 98."

VG-C6	EX-C7	LN-C8	Scarcity
20	50	75	5

99 PASSENGER STATION: Almost identical to the 97, this 1925-26 station added window glazing, interior lights as well as two exterior lights at the front of the building.

VG-C6	EX-C7	LN-C8	Scarcity
40	80	125	7

100 PASSENGER STATION: Offered in the early 1920s was this small-lithographed station, the green base of which was 12-3/4 inches long. The roof of the station was painted maroon and there was no chimney. One side of the building had a protruding bay, while the other side was lithographed to look like it included a bay. Among the extensive lithography on this station is a Navy recruiting poster, a scale, a chalkboard headed "AMERICAN FLYER ON TIME" and numerous people visible through the windows.

VG-C6	EX-C7	LN-C8	Scarcity
75	150	225	7

101 PASSENGER STATION: In 1925-1927, this 13-1/2-inch long station was cataloged. It had a red hip roof and a gray base. The walls were lithographed brick with green doors, which were partially open on the trackside.

VG-C6	EX-C7	LN-C8	Scarcity
50	80	125	6

102 CENTRAL STATION: Offered for 10 years beginning in 1928, this 12-1/4 x 8-9/16-inch lithographed building sported a blackened brass plate marked "CENTRAL STATION American Flyer LINES," although the catalog number appeared nowhere on the accessory. Brass was also used for the hinged doors. The roof was green and the station not only had two interior lights, but two nickel lamps hung on the trackside of the station.

Values for each condition are in U.S. dollars. | **Scarcity =** Scale from 1-8 with 8 being the hardest to find.

301

102 CENTRAL STATION (Type I): Red base and red chimneys.

VG-C6	EX-C7	LN-C8	Scarcity
70	150	225	5

102 CENTRAL STATION (Type II): Orange base and orange chimneys.

VG-C6	EX-C7	LN-C8	Scarcity
70	150	225	5

104 KENELWORTH STATION: Two different structures were cataloged as the 104 station between 1925 and 1937. Until 1935, this was the same as the lithographed brick 96 Flossmoor station, but with the addition of a light. In some cases one or more of the doors of the station were punched and bent to look open. The latter station was slightly larger and had simulated clapboard and stucco walls.

104 KENELWORTH STATION (Type I): Dark-gray base, green roof, brick of uniform color.

VG-C6	EX-C7	LN-C8	Scarcity
20	40	60	4

104 KENELWORTH STATION (Type II): Gray base, green roof and multicolor brick.

VG-C6	EX-C7	LN-C8	Scarcity
20	40	60	4

104 KENELWORTH STATION (Type III): Gray base, red roof and multicolor brick.

VG-C6	EX-C7	LN-C8	Scarcity
20	40	60	4

104 KENELWORTH STATION (Type IV): Later-style station with crackle green roof and lithographed brick chimney.

VG-C6	EX-C7	LN-C8	Scarcity
25	50	70	4

104 KENELWORTH STATION (Type V): Later-style station with green roof and orange chimney.

VG-C6	EX-C7	LN-C8	Scarcity
25	50	70	4

104 KENELWORTH STATION (Type VI): Later-style station, with crackle salmon-colored roof, green chimney, dark green base.

VG-C6	EX-C7	LN-C8	Scarcity
25	50	70	4

104 KENELWORTH STATION (Type VII): Later-style station, with crackle orange roof, green chimney, gray base.

VG-C6	EX-C7	LN-C8	Scarcity
25	50	70	4

104 KENELWORTH STATION (Type VIII): Later-style station with red roof, gray base and yellow or green chimney.

VG-C6	EX-C7	LN-C8	Scarcity
25	50	70	4

104 KENELWORTH STATION (Type IX): Later-style station, with red crackle roof, gray base and yellow chimney.

VG-C6	EX-C7	LN-C8	Scarcity
25	50	70	4

105 PASSENGER STATION: This illuminated 1927 station had end lettering "FLYER TOWN STATION NO. 97," but had walls lithographed in colors of the later 107 station. The 9-1/2 x 4-3/8-inch structure was mounted on a gray base. Two lights were mounted on the corners of one side.

105 PASSENGER STATION (Type I): As described above with a green hip roof and punched out windows.

VG-C6	EX-C7	LN-C8	Scarcity
50	100	150	7

105 PASSENGER STATION (Type I): Other versions of the station had maroon roofs and unpunched windows.

VG-C6	EX-C7	LN-C8	Scarcity
20	40	60	5

107 TERMINAL STATION: Despite having end lettering reading "FLYER TOWN STATION NO. 97," this 1928 through 1932 station was cataloged as the 107, and is known among collectors as the "Terminal Station." This designation is of course taken from the roof-mounted brass plate reading "TERMINAL STATION American Flyer LINES." This sign was attached to a green dormer, in turn affixed to the orange roof.

VG-C6	EX-C7	LN-C8	Scarcity
50	100	150	6

108 SWITCH TOWER HOUSE: This impressive structure was cataloged from 1929 through 1934. On one side were six Fahnstock clips and two binding posts, on the other side were six knife switches.

108 SWITCH TOWER HOUSE (Type I): Some of the switch towers had red roofs, orange bases, green lower building and chimneys, and the handles on the knife switches were red.

VG-C6	EX-C7	LN-C8	Scarcity
200	500	700	7

108 SWITCH TOWER HOUSE (Type II): Other switch towers had green roofs with red chimneys, maroon bases, tan lower buildings and knife switches with black handles.

VG-C6	EX-C7	LN-C8	Scarcity
200	500	700	7

110 UNION STATION: This 1928 structure was the largest station offered by American Flyer and is unmistakable. The red composition board station with tower soared to a height of 17-1/2 inches. A blackened brass plate on the front read "UNION STATION AMERICAN FLYER LINES."

VG-C6	EX-C7	LN-C8	Scarcity
1,200	2,500	3,500	8

214 WATCHMAN'S TOWER: Two versions of this tower were produced. The first, which had a circular base in 1934-35, the second, with rectangular base, from 1936 through 1938.

214 WATCHMAN'S TOWER (Type I): Circular base.

VG-C6	EX-C7	LN-C8	Scarcity
5	10	20	3

214 WATCHMAN'S TOWER (Type II): Rectangular base.

VG-C6	EX-C7	LN-C8	Scarcity
5	10	20	3

234 SUBURBAN STATION: 1933-38, the 234 was earlier catalogued as a 93 starting in 1928, with a green roof. The station was cataloged only in the 210 Equipment Set for the last two years. While the picture in the 1937 catalog matches the 1936, a new picture was shown in 1938.

234 SUBURBAN STATION (Type I): Simulated orange stucco and brick walls, red roof. End of station lettered "American Flyer SUBURBAN WEST BOUND TRAINS."

VG-C6	EX-C7	LN-C8	Scarcity
10	20	30	3

234 SUBURBAN STATION (Type II): Yellow simulated stucco walls and red roof.

VG-C6	EX-C7	LN-C8	Scarcity
10	20	30	3

234 SUBURBAN STATION (Type III): Yellow simulated stucco walls and green roof.

VG-C6	EX-C7	LN-C8	Scarcity
10	20	30	3

234 SUBURBAN STATION (Type IV): Simulated clapboard walls with red roof.

VG-C6	EX-C7	LN-C8	Scarcity
10	20	30	3

236 CROSSING SET: See Signals and Crossing Gate section.

237 STATION SET: This 1933-1938 accessory, stretching just over 17 inches long, featured a passenger station, a freight station, a streetlight and a semaphore.

237 STATION SET (Type I): Red base with early 104 Kenelworth and 91 Fast Freight stations.

VG-C6	EX-C7	LN-C8	Scarcity
50	115	150	5

237 STATION SET (Type II): Green base, lamppost and semaphore, red roof on each station.

VG-C6	EX-C7	LN-C8	Scarcity
40	100	140	5

Values for each condition are in U.S. dollars. | **Scarcity** = Scale from 1-8 with 8 being the hardest to find.

303

237 STATION SET (Type III): Red base and 91 station roof, green semaphore, lamppost and 104 station roof. Station roof has crackle finish and matching chimney.

VG-C6	EX-C7	LN-C8	Scarcity
40	100	140	5

237 STATION SET (Type IV): Red base with late-style 104 Passenger station with green roof and orange chimney. The lamppost and semaphore are also green. The roof on the 91 is red, as is semaphore blade, which had two white stripes.

VG-C6	EX-C7	LN-C8	Scarcity
40	100	140	5

237 STATION SET (Type V): Similar to Type IV except semaphore and lampposts were blue.

VG-C6	EX-C7	LN-C8	Scarcity
40	100	140	5

237 STATION SET (Type VI): This version included a late-style 104 with a crackle-finished red roof. The semaphore and lampposts are green, and the roof of the small station was red.

VG-C6	EX-C7	LN-C8	Scarcity
40	100	140	5

M250 PASSENGER STATION: Sold in the early teens, this German-made two-story station was 14 inches long and 10 inches tall. A telegraph pole was mounted in the center of the simulated tile embossed roof.

VG-C6	EX-C7	LN-C8	Scarcity
100	200	300	8

251/M251 WATCHMAN'S HOUSE: Also sold in the early teens was this six-inch tall German-produced lithographed shanty with a single arm semaphore.

VG-C6	EX-C7	LN-C8	Scarcity
20	30	40	7

252/M252 CROSSING HOUSE/BELL STATION: Produced in Germany, Flyer offered this item in the early teens. When the train passed over the short integral track section a bell rang.

VG-C6	EX-C7	LN-C8	Scarcity
20	30	40	7

577 WHISTLING BILLBOARD: This classic accessory was offered from 1939 through 1942. A green sheet metal housing hid the whistle mechanism.

577 WHISTLING BILLBOARD (Type I): The advertisement on the 1939 version promoted Royal typewriters. It featured an illustration of a woman dressed as a magician, and bore the legend "ITS MAGIC The MAGIC* MARGIN ROYAL PORTABLE TYPEWRITER EASIER THAN WRITING BY HAND See Your Royal Portable Dealer."

VG-C6	EX-C7	LN-C8	Scarcity
25	50	75	6

577 WHISTLING BILLBOARD (Type II): From 1940 through 1942 the advertisement featured a clown and promoted the "RINGLING BROS. AND BARNUM & BAILEY," the "The GREATEST SHOW ON EARTH."

VG-C6	EX-C7	LN-C8	Scarcity
15	25	40	4

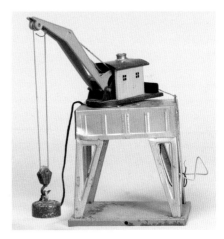

583 ELECTROMAGNETIC CRANE: This 1939-1942 accessory featured a gray base, yellow cab, green boom and red electromagnet.

VG-C6	EX-C7	LN-C8	Scarcity
50	75	100	6

585 TOOL SHED: This small white building with red roof and gray base was sold from 1939 through 1942. A red-outlined sign lettered "TOOL SHED" appeared on the building.

VG-C6	EX-C7	LN-C8	Scarcity
20	40	60	5

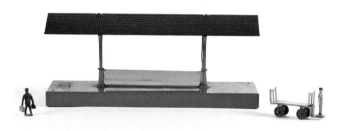

586 WAYSIDE STATION: From 1939 through 1942, Flyer sold this foot-long platform. Above its gray base was a red roof, supported by green posts. Between the die-cast posts was a yellow bench. Included were two figures and a cart. Several variations of the cart have been located, which do not seem to impact scarcity or value.

VG-C6	EX-C7	LN-C8	Scarcity
25	45	65	4

589 PASSENGER AND FREIGHT STATION: This version of the illuminated "MYSTIC" station was sold from 1939 through 1942. It had metal walls painted white and was mounted on a gray steel base. Its chimney was red. Without consequence to value or desirability, the roof could be either black or green.

VG-C6	EX-C7	LN-C8	Scarcity
25	50	75	3

593 SIGNAL TOWER: Also sold from 1939 through 1942 was this metal tower on gray base.

593 SIGNAL TOWER (Type I): White and red sides, along with a green roof were used on this version of the signal tower.

VG-C6	EX-C7	LN-C8	Scarcity
30	50	75	3

593 SIGNAL TOWER (Type II): Other versions had yellow and brown sides, but retained the green roof.

VG-C6	EX-C7	LN-C8	Scarcity
40	60	85	5

595 a-KOOSTIKIN TALKING TOOL SHED: Cataloged in 1939-1942, this white building on gray base housed a miniature record player. The mechanism of the unit would stop and start the train, as well as provide authentic sounds.

VG-C6	EX-C7	LN-C8	Scarcity
Too rarely traded to accurately establish pricing.			

598 a-KOOSTIKIN RECORD: This replacement record for the a-Koostikin was cataloged from 1940 through 1942.

VG-C6	EX-C7	LN-C8	Scarcity
10	20	30	6

599 a-KOOSTIKIN UNIT: Separate sale a-Koostikin mechanism cataloged in 1939.

VG-C6	EX-C7	LN-C8	Scarcity
Too rarely traded to accurately establish pricing.			

612 FREIGHT AND PASSENGER STATION WITH CRANE: In 1941-42, Flyer offered this combination unit featuring the 589 Mystic Station mounted on a single long base along with the yellow cab from a 514 crane.

VG-C6	EX-C7	LN-C8	Scarcity
40	70	90	4

2029 WHISTLE UNIT (BILLBOARD): Sold in 1937-1938, this 8-3/8 x 2-3/4-inch unit had identical advertising on each side of the green center section. The ad shows a 5200 NYC steam locomotive at speed.

VG-C6	EX-C7	LN-C8	Scarcity
10	20	30	4

Values for each condition are in U.S. dollars. | **Scarcity** = Scale from 1-8 with 8 being the hardest to find.

97, 98 AND 99 PASSENGER STATIONS

WIDE- AND O-GAUGE FIGURES, FLAG AND TELEGRAPH POLES

Prior to WWII, American Flyer offered a variety of figures, telegraph poles and even a patriotic flagpole to add life to miniature railroad empires.

122 MAILBAG SET: For most of the prewar era, American Flyer offered this O-Gauge sized Standard, Pickup Fork and Hook—to be used with the three mailbags included.

VG-C6	EX-C7	LN-C8	Scarcity
5	10	15	3

209 TELEGRAPH POLE: This simple sheet metal accessory was sold for a full decade, beginning in 1920.
209 TELEGRAPH POLE (Type I): Prior to 1927, only a single crossarm was installed.

VG-C6	EX-C7	LN-C8	Scarcity
1	2	3	1

209 TELEGRAPH POLE (Type II): After 1927, double crossarms were used.

VG-C6	EX-C7	LN-C8	Scarcity
1	2	3	1

210 TELEGRAPH POLE: From 1920 through 1923, this sheet metal telegraph pole with three crossarms was sold.

VG-C6	EX-C7	LN-C8	Scarcity
1	2	3	1

219 TELEGRAPH POLE: This sheet metal telegraph pole with two crossarms was sold in 1931-1932.

VG-C6	EX-C7	LN-C8	Scarcity
1	2	3	1

220 STATION CLOCK: This 1930-1932 item bore no maker name or part number and is sometimes thought to be Marx. It stood 6-3/4 inches tall.

VG-C6	EX-C7	LN-C8	Scarcity
5	10	15	3

240 EQUIPMENT SET: This 1933-34 package of line side accessories included six stamped sheet metal two-crossarm telegraph poles, a 218 Two-arm Semaphore, 220 Station Clock, 221 Crossing Gate, and 222 Banjo Signal.

VG-C6	EX-C7	LN-C8	Scarcity
20	30	40	5

578 STATION FIGURE SET: 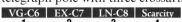 This set of six figures was cataloged from 1940 through 1942. Also included a baggage cart carrying goods. The original packaging is a significant part of the value of this item.

VG-C6	EX-C7	LN-C8	Scarcity
25	50	75	6

578 STATION FIGURE SET

594 TRACK GANG SET: One of the most desirable of all prewar Flyer items is this 1941-1942 animated accessory. On the green base was mounted a simulated yellow air compressor, a workman, a flagman and two workmen with air compressor. As a train neared, the flagman approached the track and the jack-hammer-wielding workman moved away from the track. Once the train passed, the workers all returned to their original positions.

VG-C6	EX-C7	LN-C8	Scarcity
500	1,500	2,500	8

2050 FLAGPOLE: From 1928 through 1934, this accessory was cataloged. Standing almost two feet tall, the white flagpole was supported by a blue base and capped by a gold-colored eagle. The miniature flag could actually be raised and lowered.

VG-C6	EX-C7	LN-C8	Scarcity
20	40	60	6

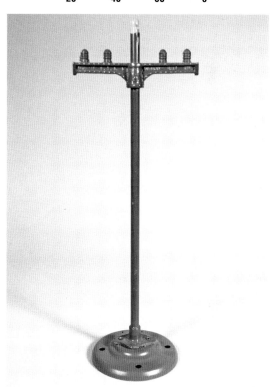

2290 TELEGRAPH POLE: From 1928 through 1933, this deluxe telegraph pole was sold. Its cast base measured 3-3/16 inches in diameter and supported a round green shaft, which in turn held a cast green crossarm with four insulators.

VG-C6	EX-C7	LN-C8	Scarcity
10	20	30	4

2294 TELEGRAPH POLE SET: In 1928, this set of four 2290 Telegraph Poles along with 30 feet of simulated telegraph cable was offered.

VG-C6	EX-C7	LN-C8	Scarcity
40	80	125	6

4122 MAILBAG SET: This was the Wide-Gauge version of the 122 and was offered throughout the Wide-Gauge era.

VG-C6	EX-C7	LN-C8	Scarcity
5	10	15	2

Values for each condition are in U.S. dollars. | **Scarcity** = Scale from 1-8 with 8 being the hardest to find.

307

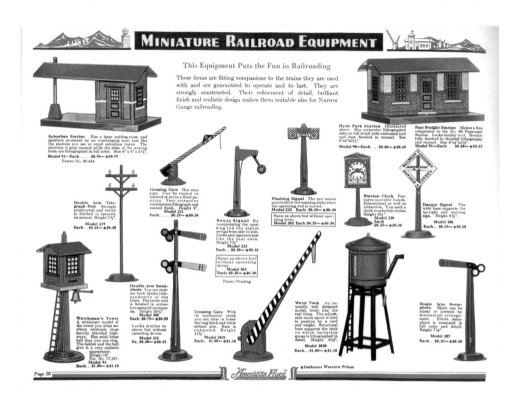

The number of signals and crossing gates offered by American Flyer during the prewar era is staggering. The initial items—which were O-Gauge—were made in Germany. These were replaced with American Flyer designed items in the mid-teens. When Flyer began producing Wide-Gauge trains, appropriate accessories were purchased from Lionel, remarked with American Flyer names and numbers and resold. With the passage of time Flyer replaced these Lionel items with their own. After the purchase of Flyer by A.C. Gilbert, a new line of signals was developed and sized to the new 3/16 size trains. Many of these signals remained in production after WWII—when they were included in the S-Gauge lines.

89/M89 SIGNAL BELL: Produced in Germany, Flyer offered this item in the early teens. When the train passed over the short integral track section a bell rang.

VG-C6	EX-C7	LN-C8	Scarcity
20	30	40	7

107 SINGLE-ARM SEMAPHORE: Offered in the mid-to-late teens, this stamped steel semaphore was mounted on a circular base. A rod actuated the arm.

VG-C6	EX-C7	LN-C8	Scarcity
2	5	10	6

201 SIGNAL SET: This 1936 combo pack included a 202 Banjo Signal, 206 Danger Signal, 218 Double-Arm Semaphore and 221 Crossing Gate.

VG-C6	EX-C7	LN-C8	Scarcity
10	20	30	6

202 BANJO SIGNAL: Produced from 1930 through 1938, this inexpensive signal was included in many sets. Made in red or green versions, this was basically a 222 sans operating mechanism.

VG-C6	EX-C7	LN-C8	Scarcity
1	2	3	2

203 FLASHING SIGNAL: This 1930-1932 item was essentially a 223 without an operating lever.

VG-C6	EX-C7	LN-C8	Scarcity
1	2	3	2

205 THREE-ARM SEMAPHORE: This early 15-inch tall signal was produced around 1910.

VG-C6	EX-C7	LN-C8	Scarcity
50	100	150	8

205 COMPLETE EQUIPMENT GROUP: This 1936 was comprised of a 201 Signal Set, 234 Suburban Station, 242 Tunnel, 253 Double Lamppost, and 2005 Triangle Light.

VG-C6	EX-C7	LN-C8	Scarcity
Too rarely traded to accurately establish pricing.			

206 DANGER SIGNAL: From about 1920 through 1932, this simple stamped steel sign was produced. Its white-painted diamond-shaped sign was lettered "RAILROAD CROSSING DANGER DANGER AMERICAN FLYER R.R."

206 DANGER SIGNAL (Type I): Black post and red base.

VG-C6	EX-C7	LN-C8	Scarcity
1	2	3	1

206 DANGER SIGNAL (Type II): Orange post and base.

VG-C6	EX-C7	LN-C8	Scarcity
1	2	3	1

206 DANGER SIGNAL (Type III): Green post and base.

VG-C6	EX-C7	LN-C8	Scarcity
1	2	3	1

206 DANGER SIGNAL (Type IV): Black post and base.

VG-C6	EX-C7	LN-C8	Scarcity
1	2	3	1

206 DANGER SIGNAL (Type V): Red post and base.

VG-C6	EX-C7	LN-C8	Scarcity
1	2	3	1

M207/207 SINGLE-ARM SEMAPHORE: This signal was produced in two major variations and numerous minor variations between 1910-1932.

M207/207 SINGLE-ARM SEMAPHORE (Type I): The earliest version of this signal was available in the early teens. It included a lever-operated semaphore blade.

VG-C6	EX-C7	LN-C8	Scarcity
10	20	30	5

M207/207 SINGLE-ARM SEMAPHORE (Type II): Beginning in the late teens and on through 1932, this signal was made of stamped sheet metal. A rod was used to move the semaphore blade. This item was made in a number of colors, which seem to be equally desirable and valuable.

VG-C6	EX-C7	LN-C8	Scarcity
2	4	6	2

208 SIGNAL: This 13-inch tall signal featured colored glass and is believed to date from about 1910.

VG-C6	EX-C7	LN-C8	Scarcity
10	20	40	7

208 SINGLE-ARM SEMAPHORE: In the mid teens this semaphore was sold. The 13-inch tall signal attaches to the track and a rod and lever was used to move the blade.

VG-C6	EX-C7	LN-C8	Scarcity
5	15	25	6

208 DOUBLE SEMAPHORE: From the mid-teens through 1931, this stamped steel signal was sold. Each blade had two lenses.

VG-C6	EX-C7	LN-C8	Scarcity
1	2	3	2

M209 DOUBLE SEMAPHORE: Made in Germany and sold by American Flyer in the mid-teens, this 15-1/2-inch tall signal supported two blades and oil lamps.

VG-C6	EX-C7	LN-C8	Scarcity
30	65	100	7

210 EQUIPMENT SET: This 1937-38 assortment contained a Banjo Signal, Crossing Gate, Danger Signal, a two-arm Semaphore, and a Suburban Station.

VG-C6	EX-C7	LN-C8	Scarcity
25	50	75	7

218 DOUBLE SEMAPHORE: This 1931-1932 signal was essentially a 208 without operating mechanism.

VG-C6	EX-C7	LN-C8	Scarcity
2	4	6	3

221 CROSSING: This manually operated sheet metal gate was produced from 1930 through 1938 and was included in many sets.

VG-C6	EX-C7	LN-C8	Scarcity
1	2	3	1

222 BANJO SIGNAL: This sheet metal accessory was sold from 1930 through 1932 and featured a rod to move the swinging "banjo."

VG-C6	EX-C7	LN-C8	Scarcity
1	2	3	1

Values for each condition are in U.S. dollars. | **Scarcity** = Scale from 1-8 with 8 being the hardest to find.

223 FLASHING SIGNAL: This sheet metal accessory was sold from 1930 through 1932 and featured a rod to move the red warning disks.

VG-C6	EX-C7	LN-C8	Scarcity
1	2	3	1

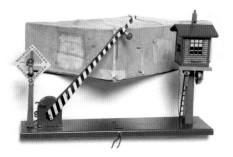

236 CROSSING SET: This 1933-1935 combination was mounted on a red sheet metal base and included a lighted 206 Danger Signal, 214 Watchman's Tower and a 2021 Crossing Gate.

VG-C6	EX-C7	LN-C8	Scarcity
25	50	75	5

240 EQUIPMENT SET: This assortment of line side accessories was sold in 1933-1934. Included in this set was a banjo signal, clock, crossing gate, semaphore, and six telegraph poles.

VG-C6	EX-C7	LN-C8	Scarcity
10	20	30	5

582 AUTOMATIC BLINKER SIGNAL: The yellow die-cast base of this 1940-42 signal supported a black die-cast light housing containing two red lights, which flashed when the train passed. The crossbuck read "RAILROAD CROSSING."

VG-C6	EX-C7	LN-C8	Scarcity
15	25	35	5

584 BELL DANGER SIGNAL: The die-cast base of this 1940-1942 accessory was primarily green and was painted to simulate a road and a walkway.

VG-C6	EX-C7	LN-C8	Scarcity

Too rarely traded to accurately establish pricing.

587 AUTOMATIC BLOCK SIGNAL: From 1939-1942, this signal with gray base and green signal head was offered. Its mechanism allowed for two trains to operate on the same track and in the same direction at the same time.

VG-C6	EX-C7	LN-C8	Scarcity
25	50	75	5

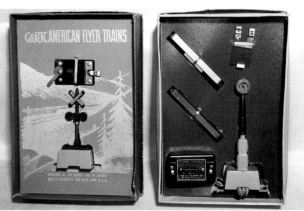

588 AUTOMATIC SEMAPHORE BLOCK SIGNAL: This signal with gray base and black signal head was cataloged in 1941-1942. Its mechanism allowed for two trains to operate on the same track and in the same direction at the same time.

VG-C6	EX-C7	LN-C8	Scarcity
Too rarely traded to accurately establish pricing.			

591 CROSSING GATE WITH WATCHMAN'S SHACK:
This 1939-42 die-cast accessory measured 10 x 5-1/4 inches. The sheet metal shanty was painted white and had a red trim and roof.

VG-C6	EX-C7	LN-C8	Scarcity
20	40	60	6

2004 CROSSING SET WITH AUTOMATIC BELL:
The gray base of this 1936-1938 accessory measured 9-1/2 x 5-1/2 inches. On it was mounted a 214 Watchman's Tower and a 2222 Crossing Gate.

VG-C6	EX-C7	LN-C8	Scarcity
20	40	60	5

2005 TRIANGLE LIGHT:
The head of this 1935-1939 block signal held three bulbs and on its rear was a selector switch.
2005 TRIANGLE LIGHT (Type I): Green.

VG-C6	EX-C7	LN-C8	Scarcity
5	10	15	3

2005 TRIANGLE LIGHT (Type II): Blue.

VG-C6	EX-C7	LN-C8	Scarcity
3	8	12	2

2011 SINGLE-ARM SEMAPHORE:
Signals with this catalog number were sold from the early 1920s through 1934 and was produced in two major variations. The mast and base were painted orange, and the blade was painted red with a white stripe.
2011 SINGLE-ARM SEMAPHORE (Type I): Signals produced in 1927 and earlier had a brass cap at the top of the mast.

VG-C6	EX-C7	LN-C8	Scarcity
5	15	25	4

2011 SINGLE-ARM SEMAPHORE (Type II): From 1928 onwards the mast was topped with a gold-painted finial.

VG-C6	EX-C7	LN-C8	Scarcity
5	15	25	4

2012 SEMAPHORE WITH LIGHT:
Similar to the 2011 and produced in like years, this manually operated semaphore was illuminated.
1922-1934: circular base with two screw posts, metal-finish square tapering post with girder-type construction. Red signal arm with light set in a square near top, manually controlled, red ladder from base to top.
2012 SEMAPHORE WITH LIGHT (Type I): Signals produced in 1927 and earlier had a brass cap at the top of the mast.

VG-C6	EX-C7	LN-C8	Scarcity
10	20	30	4

2012 SEMAPHORE WITH LIGHT (Type II): From 1928 onwards the mast was topped with a gold-painted finial.

VG-C6	EX-C7	LN-C8	Scarcity
10	20	30	4

2014 AUTOMATIC SEMAPHORE:
Offered in the early 1920s, a square tapered post rising from a circular base supported this semaphore.

VG-C6	EX-C7	LN-C8	Scarcity
10	20	30	6

Values for each condition are in U.S. dollars. | **Scarcity** = Scale from 1-8 with 8 being the hardest to find.

311

2015 AUTOMATIC SEMAPHORE WITH LIGHT: For most of the 1920s, American Flyer sold this cream-colored lighted signal with blue base.

2015 AUTOMATIC SEMAPHORE WITH LIGHT (Type I): Signals produced in 1927 and earlier had a brass cap at the top of the mast.

VG-C6	EX-C7	LN-C8	Scarcity
15	30	45	5

2015 AUTOMATIC SEMAPHORE WITH LIGHT (Type II): In 1928 and 1929, the mast was topped with a gold-painted finial.

VG-C6	EX-C7	LN-C8	Scarcity
15	30	45	5

2016 AUTOMATIC DANGER SIGNAL: This lighted signal, offered throughout the mid 1920s, included a nickel bell with an electric ringing mechanism mounted on a square tapered post. A diamond-shaped warning sign was included, which bore the markings "RAILROAD CROSSING," "AMERICAN FLYER R. R." and "LOOK OUT FOR CARS."

2016 AUTOMATIC DANGER SIGNAL (Type I): Green.

VG-C6	EX-C7	LN-C8	Scarcity
15	35	50	4

2016 AUTOMATIC DANGER SIGNAL (Type II): Orange.

VG-C6	EX-C7	LN-C8	Scarcity
15	35	50	4

2017 DANGER SIGNAL WITH LIGHT: Sold from 1925-1927, this green signal included a ladder reaching from top to bottom. A diamond-shaped warning signal was included, which bore the markings "RAILROAD CROSSING," "AMERICAN FLYER R. R." and "LOOK OUT FOR CARS." A brass cap topped the post.

VG-C6	EX-C7	LN-C8	Scarcity
10	20	30	4

2018 BLOCK SIGNAL LIGHTS: This 1925-1926 round-based signal featured a signal head on either side of its square tapered post. A ladder ran the length of the post, which was topped with a brass cap.

VG-C6	EX-C7	LN-C8	Scarcity
10	20	30	4

2021 CROSSING GATE: This manually operated gate was sold from 1925 through 1933.

VG-C6	EX-C7	LN-C8	Scarcity
5	10	15	2

2022 CROSSING GATE: This was a lighted counterpart to the 2021 and was also available from 1925 through 1927.

VG-C6	EX-C7	LN-C8	Scarcity
10	20	30	2

2032 CROSSING GATE: Sold from 1926 through 1929, this was merely a remarked Lionel No. 077 Crossing Gate. Versions were produced with either black or dark green, and maroon baseplate/housing combinations were sold. There is no difference in value or desirability today.

VG-C6	EX-C7	LN-C8	Scarcity
20	40	60	5

2033 AUTOMATIC TRAIN CONTROL: This 1926-1929 item was a repackaged Lionel No. 078.

VG-C6	EX-C7	LN-C8	Scarcity
40	70	110	6

2040 MANUAL CONTROL SEMAPHORE: This 1931-34 item was a manual version of the 2043 semaphore. When the semaphore blade is lowered, the train will stop. The accessory had a die-cast base and was illuminated.

VG-C6	EX-C7	LN-C8	Scarcity
100	200	300	7

Shown here are two of the best of American Flyer's prewar signals. At top, the 2043 Train Control Semaphore and at bottom the 2042 Automatic Crossing Gate.

2042 AUTOMATIC CROSSING GATE: This solenoid-operated illuminated crossing gate was sold from 1930 through 1939. The lamp was housed inside the green-painted base. A lighter shade of green was used in later years.

VG-C6	EX-C7	LN-C8	Scarcity
15	30	45	6

2043 TRAIN CONTROL SEMAPHORE: This 1930-1939 could be used with either O- or Wide-Gauge track. When the semaphore blade was moved to the lowered position, the train would stop. A remote control switch controlled the semaphore blade position.

VG-C6	EX-C7	LN-C8	Scarcity
100	200	300	7

2116 AUTOMATIC DANGER SIGNAL: This signal was cataloged from 1928 through 1939 and was produced in two major variations.

2116 AUTOMATIC DANGER SIGNAL (Type I): Up until 1935 the signal was mounted on a circular base.

VG-C6	EX-C7	LN-C8	Scarcity
15	25	40	5

2116 AUTOMATIC DANGER SIGNAL (Type II): Beginning in 1936 and through the end of production in 1939, the signal was mounted on a rectangular base.

VG-C6	EX-C7	LN-C8	Scarcity
10	20	30	4

2206 HIGHWAY FLASHING SIGNAL: This signal was offered in two major variations, the first in 1928-1934 and the second from 1936 through 1939.

2206 HIGHWAY FLASHING SIGNAL (Type I): The early version of the 2206 was supported by a diamond-shape base. A sign on the mast read "CROSS CROSSINGS CAUTIOUSLY."

VG-C6	EX-C7	LN-C8	Scarcity
20	35	50	5

2206 HIGHWAY FLASHING SIGNAL (Type II): The later version of the signal utilized a rectangular base. The signs on this version read "RAILROAD CROSSING" and "STOP on SIGNAL."

VG-C6	EX-C7	LN-C8	Scarcity
10	20	30	3

2216 CROSSING WARNING: Sold from 1928 through 1934, the diamond-shaped base of this accessory supported a diamond-shaped sign with the legend "RAILROAD CROSSING," "AMERICAN FLYER R. R." and "LOOK OUT FOR CARS."

VG-C6	EX-C7	LN-C8	Scarcity
10	20	30	4

2218 BLOCK SIGNAL: Two versions of this signal were produced, the first from 1928-1931 and the second from 1936-1939. When offered as Wide-Gauge, this was assigned catalog number "4218."

2218 BLOCK SIGNAL (Type I): From 1928 through 1931, the block signal was mounted on a diamond-shaped base casting.

VG-C6	EX-C7	LN-C8	Scarcity
15	25	40	5

2218 BLOCK SIGNAL (Type II): A rectangular base was used from 1936 through 1939.

VG-C6	EX-C7	LN-C8	Scarcity
15	25	40	5

Values for each condition are in U.S. dollars. | Scarcity = Scale from 1-8 with 8 being the hardest to find.

313

2222 CROSSING GATE: Two versions of this signal were produced, the first from 1928-1934 and the second from 1936-1939.

2222 CROSSING GATE (Type I): The early version was mounted on a red circular base.

VG-C6	EX-C7	LN-C8	Scarcity
10	15	20	4

2222 CROSSING GATE (Type II): Later version had a green rectangular base.

VG-C6	EX-C7	LN-C8	Scarcity
10	15	20	4

2230 ROADSIDE FLASHING SIGNAL: The base of this 1928-1935 accessory was lettered "YOU ARE APPROACHING American Flyer LINES ELECTRICAL MINIATURE RAILROAD."

VG-C6	EX-C7	LN-C8	Scarcity
15	30	45	4

The 4000 series accessories were Wide-Gauge versions of the O-Gauge products.

4004 CROSSING SET WITH AUTOMATIC BELL: This 1936 Wide-Gauge item combined the 214 Watchman's Tower and the 2222 Crossing Gate mounted on a 9-1/2 x 5-1/2-inch base.

VG-C6	EX-C7	LN-C8	Scarcity
40	60	80	7

4015 AUTOMATIC SEMAPHORE WITH LIGHT: This 1927-1929 illuminated semaphore included a ladder from the base to the semaphore blade.

4015 AUTOMATIC SEMAPHORE WITH LIGHT: In 1927, the mast was topped with a brass cap.

VG-C6	EX-C7	LN-C8	Scarcity
10	20	35	6

4015 AUTOMATIC SEMAPHORE WITH LIGHT: Later versions were capped with a gold-painted finial.

VG-C6	EX-C7	LN-C8	Scarcity
10	20	30	4

4016 AUTOMATIC DANGER SIGNAL: Painted green, this 1927 lighted signal included a nickel bell, with electric ringing mechanism mounted on a square tapered post. A diamond-shaped warning sign was included, which bore the markings "RAILROAD CROSSING," "AMERICAN FLYER R. R." and "LOOK OUT FOR CARS."

VG-C6	EX-C7	LN-C8	Scarcity
15	30	45	6

4032 CROSSING GATE: Sold from 1926 through 1929, this was merely a remarked Lionel No. 77 Crossing Gate. Versions were produced with either black or dark green, and maroon baseplate/housing combinations were sold. There is no difference in value or desirability today.

VG-C6	EX-C7	LN-C8	Scarcity
20	40	60	5

4033 AUTOMATIC TRAIN CONTROL: This 1926-1929 item was a repackaged Lionel No. 78.

VG-C6	EX-C7	LN-C8	Scarcity
Too rarely traded to accurately establish pricing.			

At left is a 4116 (Type I) Automatic Danger Signal and at right the 4042 Automatic Crossing Gate.

4042 AUTOMATIC CROSSING GATE: This solenoid-operated illuminated crossing gate was sold from 1930 through 1936. The lamp was housed inside the green-painted base.

VG-C6	EX-C7	LN-C8	Scarcity
15	30	45	6

4116 AUTOMATIC DANGER SIGNAL: This signal was cataloged from 1928 through 1936 and was produced in two major variations.

4116 AUTOMATIC DANGER SIGNAL (Type I): Up until 1935, the signal was mounted on a circular base.

VG-C6	EX-C7	LN-C8	Scarcity
15	25	40	5

4116 AUTOMATIC DANGER SIGNAL (Type II): In 1936, the signal was mounted on a rectangular base.

VG-C6	EX-C7	LN-C8	Scarcity
10	20	30	4

4206 HIGHWAY FLASHING SIGNAL: This signal was offered in two major variations, the first from 1928-1934 and the second in 1936 only.

4206 HIGHWAY FLASHING SIGNAL (Type I): The early version of the 4206 was supported by a diamond-shape base. A sign on the mast read "CROSS CROSSINGS CAUTIOUSLY."

VG-C6	EX-C7	LN-C8	Scarcity
20	30	40	4

4206 HIGHWAY FLASHING SIGNAL (Type II): The final version of the signal utilized a rectangular base. The signs on this version read "RAILROAD CROSSING" and "STOP on SIGNAL."

VG-C6	EX-C7	LN-C8	Scarcity
20	35	50	5

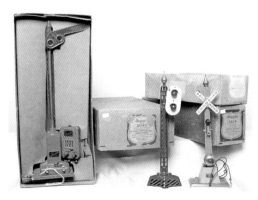

Shown left to right here are the 2043 Semaphore, 4218 Block Signal (Type I) and the 2116 (Type II) Danger Signal.

4218 BLOCK SIGNAL: This is the Wide-Gauge version of the 2218. Two versions of this signal were produced, the first from 1928-1931 and the later in 1936.

4218 BLOCK SIGNAL (Type I): From 1928 through 1931, the block signal was mounted on a diamond-shaped base casting.

VG-C6	EX-C7	LN-C8	Scarcity
15	25	40	5

4218 BLOCK SIGNAL (Type II): A rectangular base was used in 1936.

VG-C6	EX-C7	LN-C8	Scarcity
20	35	50	5

4230 ROADSIDE FLASHING SIGNAL: The base of this 1928-1935 accessory was lettered "YOU ARE APPROACHING American Flyer LINES ELECTRICAL MINIATURE RAILROAD."

VG-C6	EX-C7	LN-C8	Scarcity
15	30	45	4

Values for each condition are in U.S. dollars. | **Scarcity** = Scale from 1-8 with 8 being the hardest to find.

WIDE- AND O-GAUGE STREETLIGHTS

American Flyer offered a wide range of streetlights in the prewar era. The earliest of these were O-Gauge size and imported from Germany. The final versions were engineered to be compatible with the Gilbert-designed 3/16-inch scale line. In between were a host of items built by American Flyer, and others bought from Lionel.

M206 ARC LIGHT: This 13-inch tall German-made lamp was sold in the mid teens. It was fitted with a mechanism that could raise and lower the lamp.

VG-C6	EX-C7	LN-C8	Scarcity
Too rarely traded to accurately establish pricing.			

233 ARC LIGHT DOUBLE LAMPPOST: Two versions of this item were sold between 1933 and 1939. The first, which was sold through 1935, had a circular base, while the later version used a square base.

233 ARC LIGHT DOUBLE LAMPPOST (Type I): Blue-painted 7-3/8-inch tall stamped-steel post.

VG-C6	EX-C7	LN-C8	Scarcity
5	10	15	3

233 ARC LIGHT DOUBLE LAMPPOST (Type II): The later version could be blue or green and stood 8-1/8 inches tall.

VG-C6	EX-C7	LN-C8	Scarcity
5	10	15	3

579 STREETLIGHT: This green die-cast streetlight was sold from 1939 through 1942. It had a square base and an eight-sided post.

VG-C6	EX-C7	LN-C8	Scarcity
5	10	15	2

580 DOUBLE-ARC LIGHT: This silver-painted die-cast double light post was sold from 1939 through 1942.

VG-C6	EX-C7	LN-C8	Scarcity
10	15	20	3

2009 SINGLE-ARC LIGHT: Sold in the early 1920s, this green 10-7/8-inch tall lamp featured a cast-iron circular base and a post made of brass tubing.

2009 SINGLE-ARC LIGHT (Type I): The earliest version of the 2009 stood 10-3/8 inches tall.

VG-C6	EX-C7	LN-C8	Scarcity
15	30	45	4

2009 SINGLE-ARC LIGHT (Type II): Later lights were almost 10-7/8 inches tall.

VG-C6	EX-C7	LN-C8	Scarcity
15	30	45	4

2010 DOUBLE ARC LIGHT: Sold in the early 1920s, this green 10-7/8-inch tall lamp featured a cast-iron circular base and a post made of brass tubing and a double gooseneck. It was painted dark green.

VG-C6	EX-C7	LN-C8	Scarcity
30	50	75	5

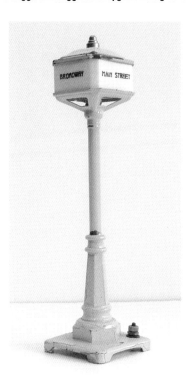

2013 STREETLIGHT: In 1927-1928, American Flyer sold a yellow version of the Lionel 57 lamp. Two sides of the lamp housing were labeled "BROADWAY" and the other two "MAIN STREET."

VG-C6	EX-C7	LN-C8	Scarcity
25	50	75	5

2109 SINGLE-ARM ARC LIGHT: Sold from 1926-1927, this maroon sheet metal lamp stood 9-5/8 inches tall.

VG-C6	EX-C7	LN-C8	Scarcity
10	20	30	4

2110 DOUBLE-ARM LAMPPOST: Sold from 1926-1927, this maroon sheet metal lamp stood 9-5/8 inches tall and held two lamps.

VG-C6	EX-C7	LN-C8	Scarcity
15	30	45	5

2209 SINGLE-ARM LAMPPOST: This 10-1/8-inch tall stamped-steel lamppost was sold from 1928 through 1935. It featured a tapered square post attached to a 3-3/16-inch diameter sheet metal base. The lamp housing was painted brass color and the finial on the post top painted gold.

2209 SINGLE-ARM LAMPPOST (Type I): Overall maroon.

VG-C6	EX-C7	LN-C8	Scarcity
10	20	30	4

2209 SINGLE-ARM LAMPPOST (Type II): Overall red.

VG-C6	EX-C7	LN-C8	Scarcity
10	20	30	4

2209 SINGLE-ARM LAMPPOST (Type III): Medium blue base, bracket and lamp shield mounted on turquoise shaft.

VG-C6	EX-C7	LN-C8	Scarcity
10	20	30	4

Values for each condition are in U.S. dollars. | **Scarcity** = Scale from 1-8 with 8 being the hardest to find.

317

2209 SINGLE-ARM LAMPPOST (Type IV): Turquoise base, bracket and lamp shield mounted on blue shaft.

VG-C6	EX-C7	LN-C8	Scarcity
10	20	30	4

2210 DOUBLE-ARM LAMPPOST: This stamped-steel lamppost was sold from 1928 through 1935. It featured a four-sided tapered square post attached to a 3-3/16-inch diameter sheet metal base. The double lamp housing was painted brass color and the finial on the post top gold.

2210 DOUBLE-ARM LAMPPOST (Type I): Green base, sub base and lamp shields with orange post and lamp support brackets.

VG-C6	EX-C7	LN-C8	Scarcity
15	30	45	4

2210 DOUBLE-ARM LAMPPOST (Type II): Red base and sub base with green post and lamp support brackets.

VG-C6	EX-C7	LN-C8	Scarcity
15	30	45	4

2210 DOUBLE-ARM LAMPPOST (Type III): Gray base with green sub base and orange post and arms.

VG-C6	EX-C7	LN-C8	Scarcity
15	30	45	4

2210 DOUBLE-ARM LAMPPOST (Type IV): Gray base and sub base with orange post, lamp support brackets and shields.

VG-C6	EX-C7	LN-C8	Scarcity
15	30	45	4

WIDE- AND O-GAUGE TRACK AND TRANSFORMERS

Track and transformers from Flyer's prewar era are of limited interest to collectors. Therefore, to allow greater space for photos and descriptions of items of greater interest, this section has been abbreviated.

There can be a few generalized statements made regarding products of this era and category. Transformers of this era tend to be viewed as novelties of limited appeal. Few individuals actually use them, and even fewer collect them.

Track of this—or any—era, tends to be near worthless unless in pristine condition. Tracks were produced in such huge quantities that none of it can be considered collectible. Straight track is of moderate interest for use of building shelf displays or large layouts, but all collectors have far more curved track then they could ever use.

Turnouts, or switches, have some value. Lionel made American Flyer's initial offerings of Wide-Gauge turnouts. In 1930, Flyer introduced their own Wide-Gauge turnouts, which not surprisingly work better with Flyer's trains. Even then, only the remote control units raise any collector interest.

91/M91 BUMPER: This square upright bumper was made in Germany in the 1910-1917 era.

VG-C6	EX-C7	LN-C8	Scarcity
10	20	30	6

92/M92 TURNTABLE: Also made in Germany during the 1910-1917 era was this turntable.

VG-C6	EX-C7	LN-C8	Scarcity
10	20	30	6

94 TURNTABLE: At least two versions of this U.S. made turntable exists.

94 TURNTABLE (Type I): The 1919 edition was rectangular.

VG-C6	EX-C7	LN-C8	Scarcity
5	10	20	6

94 TURNTABLE (Type II): In 1920, the accessory became circular.

VG-C6	EX-C7	LN-C8	Scarcity
5	10	20	6

95 BUMPER: This bumper, mounted on a short section of track, was offered in the late teens and early '20s.

VG-C6	EX-C7	LN-C8	Scarcity
5	10	20	6

450 TRACK TERMINAL: This track terminal was designed for use with O-Gauge track.

VG-C6	EX-C7	LN-C8	Scarcity
2	3	5	1

621 THREE-RAIL STRAIGHT TRACK, HALF-SECTION: Sold for many years prior to WWII, this half-section of three-rail O-Gauge straight track was again offered from 1946 through 1948.

VG-C6	EX-C7	LN-C8	Scarcity
.20	.30	.50	1

622 THREE-RAIL CURVE TRACK, HALF-SECTION: Sold for many years prior to WWII, this half-section of three-rail O-Gauge curved track was again offered from 1946 through 1948.

VG-C6	EX-C7	LN-C8	Scarcity
.20	.30	.50	1

680 THREE-RAIL CURVE TRACK: Sold for many years prior to WWII, this section of three-rail O-Gauge curved track was again offered from 1946 through 1948.

VG-C6	EX-C7	LN-C8	Scarcity
.20	.30	.50	1

681 THREE-RAIL STRAIGHT TRACK: Sold for many years prior to WWII, this section of three-rail O-Gauge straight track was again offered from 1946 through 1948.

VG-C6	EX-C7	LN-C8	Scarcity
.20	.30	.50	1

688 THREE-RAIL REMOTE-CONTROL SWITCHES: Introduced prior to WWII, this O-Gauge turnout was also sold from 1946 through 1948.

VG-C6	EX-C7	LN-C8	Scarcity
.20	.30	.50	1

Values for each condition are in U.S. dollars. | **Scarcity** = Scale from 1-8 with 8 being the hardest to find.

319

WIDE- AND O-GAUGE TUNNELS

American Flyer offered a myriad of tunnels throughout the prewar era. Sadly, few carried any American Flyer or model number markings — and on those that were marked it was merely a pasted on label. With papier-mâché being the primary construction material, few of these bulky accessories survive in collectible condition — with many being discarded as homemade or unknown origin items.

80 TUNNEL: In the mid to late teens a 6-1/2-inch long tunnel was offered.

VG-C6	EX-C7	LN-C8	Scarcity
10	20	30	7

81 TUNNEL: Catalogs from the mid teens into the mid-20s listed an O-Gauge tunnel with this number; during this time the length was variously listed as 8-1/2, eight and seven inches.

VG-C6	EX-C7	LN-C8	Scarcity
10	20	30	7

82 TUNNEL: Catalogs from the mid teens into the mid-20s listed an O-Gauge tunnel with this number, during this time the length was listed as either 10 or 11 inches.

VG-C6	EX-C7	LN-C8	Scarcity
10	20	30	7

83 TUNNEL: Catalogs from the mid teens into the mid-20s listed an O-Gauge tunnel with this number, during this time the length was variously listed as 14, 14-1/2, 15 and 14-3/4 inches.

VG-C6	EX-C7	LN-C8	Scarcity
15	25	35	7

84 TUNNEL: Catalogs from the mid teens into the mid-20s listed an O-Gauge tunnel with this number, during this time the length was listed as 16 or 18 inches.

VG-C6	EX-C7	LN-C8	Scarcity
15	25	35	7

86 TUNNEL: This 16-1/2-inch long, nine-inch tall O-Gauge tunnel was cataloged in 1925-26. The scene on the side of the tunnel depicts a road angling upward.

VG-C6	EX-C7	LN-C8	Scarcity
15	25	25	6

M88/M88A/M88B TUNNELS: Cataloged in the early teens was this series of tunnels of various lengths.
M88 TUNNEL: Eight inches long.

VG-C6	EX-C7	LN-C8	Scarcity
10	15	20	7

M88A TUNNEL: Nine inches long.

VG-C6	EX-C7	LN-C8	Scarcity
10	15	20	7

M88B TUNNEL: 14 inches long.

VG-C6	EX-C7	LN-C8	Scarcity
15	20	25	7

241 TUNNEL: This 1927 O-Gauge tunnel was eight inches long, six inches wide and 6-1/4 inches tall.

VG-C6	EX-C7	LN-C8	Scarcity
10	15	20	6

242 TUNNEL: American Flyer cataloged two O-Gauge tunnels with this number at various times, and they were different dimensions as well.
242 TUNNEL (Type I): In 1927, the tunnel was listed as 10 inches long, eight inches wide and 7-1/4 inches tall.

VG-C6	EX-C7	LN-C8	Scarcity
10	15	20	6

242 TUNNEL (Type II): In 1936-1938, only the length was listed, now at 10-1/2 inches.

VG-C6	EX-C7	LN-C8	Scarcity
10	15	20	6

243 TUNNEL: Cataloged in 1927, this O-Gauge tunnel was listed as 14 inches long, 8-3/4 inches wide and eight inches tall.

VG-C6	EX-C7	LN-C8	Scarcity
15	20	25	6

244 TUNNEL: Cataloged in 1927, the O-Gauge tunnel was listed as 16 inches long, 10-3/4 inches wide and nine inches tall.

VG-C6	EX-C7	LN-C8	Scarcity
15	20	25	6

245 LIGHTED TUNNEL: Cataloged in 1934, this 16-inch long tunnel features two lights.

VG-C6	EX-C7	LN-C8	Scarcity
20	30	40	7

246 LIGHTED TUNNEL: Cataloged in 1935, this 15-1/2-inch long tunnel features two lights.

VG-C6	EX-C7	LN-C8	Scarcity
20	30	40	7

247 TUNNEL: This 11-inch long O-Gauge tunnel was cataloged from 1935 through 1941.

VG-C6	EX-C7	LN-C8	Scarcity
10	15	20	6

248 TUNNEL: Two versions of this O-Gauge were cataloged between 1936 and 1941.

248 TUNNEL (Type I): In 1936-1938, the tunnel was listed as 15 inches long.

VG-C6	EX-C7	LN-C8	Scarcity
10	15	20	6

248 TUNNEL (Type II): From 1939 through 1941, the length was shown as 14 inches.

VG-C6	EX-C7	LN-C8	Scarcity
10	15	20	6

251 TUNNEL: Two different size O-Gauge tunnels with this number were cataloged between 1925 and 1928.

251 TUNNEL (Type I): The 1925-26 edition of the tunnel was cataloged with the dimensions of 8-1/2 inches long and 7-1/2 inches tall.

VG-C6	EX-C7	LN-C8	Scarcity
10	15	20	6

251 TUNNEL (Type II): In 1928, in the catalog, the 251 is listed as the "HUDSON TUNNEL" and its length was given as eight inches.

VG-C6	EX-C7	LN-C8	Scarcity
10	15	20	6

252 TUNNEL: Two different size O-Gauge tunnels with this number were cataloged between 1925 and 1928.

252 TUNNEL (Type I): The 1925-26 edition of the tunnel was cataloged with the dimensions of 10 inches long and 8-1/2 inches tall.

VG-C6	EX-C7	LN-C8	Scarcity
10	15	20	6

252 TUNNEL (Type II): In 1928, in the catalog, the 251 is listed as the "HUDSON TUNNEL" and its length was given as 11 inches.

VG-C6	EX-C7	LN-C8	Scarcity
10	15	20	6

253 TUNNEL: Two different size O-Gauge tunnels with this number were cataloged between 1925 and 1928.

253 TUNNEL (Type I): The 1925-26 edition of the tunnel was cataloged with the dimensions of 14-1/2 inches long and eight inches tall.

VG-C6	EX-C7	LN-C8	Scarcity
15	20	25	6

253 TUNNEL (Type II): In 1928, in the catalog, the 251 is listed as the "MOFFAT TUNNEL" and its length was given as 15 inches.

VG-C6	EX-C7	LN-C8	Scarcity
15	20	25	6

254 TUNNEL: The 1925 and 1926 catalogs list this as a 17-inch long, 8-3/4-inch tall O-Gauge tunnel.

VG-C6	EX-C7	LN-C8	Scarcity
15	20	25	6

260 WASHINGTON TUNNEL: This O-Gauge tunnel is listed with differing sizes in the 1930 and 1931 American Flyer catalogs.

260 WASHINGTON TUNNEL (Type I): Listed in the 1930 catalog as 6-1/2 inches long.

VG-C6	EX-C7	LN-C8	Scarcity
10	15	20	6

260 WASHINGTON TUNNEL (Type II): Listed in the 1931 catalog as seven inches long.

VG-C6	EX-C7	LN-C8	Scarcity
10	15	20	6

261 TUNNEL: Two different size O-Gauge tunnels with this number were cataloged between 1929 and 1935.

261 TUNNEL (Type I): In 1929, this eight-inch tunnel was known as the "HUDSON TUNNEL."

VG-C6	EX-C7	LN-C8	Scarcity
10	15	20	6

261 TUNNEL (Type II): From 1932 through 1935, the tunnel was 8-1/2 inches long and from 1932 until 1934 this was known as the "JEFFERSON TUNNEL."

VG-C6	EX-C7	LN-C8	Scarcity
10	15	20	6

262 TUNNEL: Cataloged from 1929-1934, this 10-inch long O-Gauge tunnel was known as the "BLUE RIDGE" through 1933.

VG-C6	EX-C7	LN-C8	Scarcity
10	15	20	6

263 TUNNEL: Cataloged from 1929-1934, this 12-inch long O-Gauge tunnel was known as the "HOOSAC" through 1933.

VG-C6	EX-C7	LN-C8	Scarcity
10	15	20	6

264 MOFFAT TUNNEL: This 16-inch long O-Gauge tunnel was offered from 1929 through 1933.

VG-C6	EX-C7	LN-C8	Scarcity
15	20	25	6

4254 ALLEGHENY TUNNEL: Offered in 1928, this Wide-Gauge papier-mâché tunnel was 19-1/2 inches long.

VG-C6	EX-C7	LN-C8	Scarcity
25	50	75	7

4255 TUNNEL: Catalogs from 1925 through 1927 listed a Wide-Gauge tunnel with this number. During this time various sizes were given.

4255 TUNNEL (Type I): In 1925-1926, the tunnel measured 17-5/8 inches long, 15 inches wide and 10-5/8 inches tall.

VG-C6	EX-C7	LN-C8	Scarcity
25	50	75	7

4255 TUNNEL (Type II): The 1927 catalog listed the dimensions as 18 inches long, 13-1/2 inches wide and 10-1/2 inches tall.

VG-C6	EX-C7	LN-C8	Scarcity
25	50	75	7

4256 TUNNEL: Catalogs from 1925 through 1927 listed a Wide-Gauge tunnel with this number. During this time various sizes were given.

Values for each condition are in U.S. dollars. | **Scarcity** = Scale from 1-8 with 8 being the hardest to find.

321

4256 TUNNEL (Type I): In 1925-1926, the tunnel measured 22 inches long.

VG-C6	EX-C7	LN-C8	Scarcity
25	50	75	7

4256 TUNNEL (Type II): The 1927 catalog listed the dimensions as 22 inches long, 16 inches wide and 12 inches tall.

VG-C6	EX-C7	LN-C8	Scarcity
25	50	75	7

4257 CASCADE TUNNEL: This 23-inch long Wide-Gauge tunnel was offered in 1928. Near the summit were two telegraph poles utilizing 2290 crossbars.

VG-C6	EX-C7	LN-C8	Scarcity
50	75	100	7

4266 ALLEGHANY TUNNEL: Cataloged from 1929 through 1933, but with two different lengths. Note the spelling of the tunnel name differed from that of the 4254.

4266 ALLEGHANY TUNNEL (Type I): In 1929, the tunnel was listed as 16 inches long.

VG-C6	EX-C7	LN-C8	Scarcity
50	75	100	7

4266 ALLEGHANY TUNNEL (Type II): The 1930 through 1933 catalogs list the length as 19 inches.

VG-C6	EX-C7	LN-C8	Scarcity
50	100	150	7

4267 CASCADE TUNNEL: The largest of American Flyer's tunnels was this 1929-1934 Wide-Gauge offering. Measuring 23 inches long and 19 inches tall, this tunnel featured two telegraph poles near the summit. The crossbars used on these were taken from the 2290 telegraph pole.

VG-C6	EX-C7	LN-C8	Scarcity
75	150	300	8

4268 LIGHTED TUNNEL: This illuminated 18-inch long Wide-Gauge tunnel was cataloged in 1934.

VG-C6	EX-C7	LN-C8	Scarcity
50	100	150	7

WIDE- AND O-GAUGE WATER TOWERS

From the early 1920s onward American Flyer sold water towers. Such towers were a common sight alongside railroads at the time, as steam locomotives consume far more water than fuel.

While one basic tower was sold through 1940, it was joined in 1939 by a far more realistic tower, which would remain in the American Flyer product line into the S-Gauge era.

215 WATER TANK: This 9-1/2-inch tall red tank was sold from 1934 through 1940. Its spout and support structure was black, and a light was mounted on the roof.

215 WATER TANK (Type I): Some towers had a green ladder and brass light housing.

VG-C6	EX-C7	LN-C8	Scarcity
10	20	30	4

215 WATER TANK (Type II): Other towers had a red ladder and brass light housing.

VG-C6	EX-C7	LN-C8	Scarcity
10	20	30	4

215 WATER TANK (Type III): Yellow ladders and a black light housing were used on some towers.

VG-C6	EX-C7	LN-C8	Scarcity
10	20	30	4

235 WATER TANK SET: 📷 This 15-1/4-inch long accessory set was sold from 1933 through 1935. Mounted on a red sheet metal base were a lighted lithographed shanty, a manually operated semaphore and a red water tank with a black support structure and spout and a red ladder. A brass lamp housing capped the tower.

VG-C6	EX-C7	LN-C8	Scarcity
25	50	75	5

Values for each condition are in U.S. dollars. | **Scarcity** = Scale from 1-8 with 8 being the hardest to find.

323

235 WATER TANK SET

596 WATER TANK: In 1940-1942, and again during the postwar era, American Flyer sold this large tank with a

remote-control lowered spout. Many color combinations are known to exist, which seem to be equally valued. The roof could be black or gray, but always came with a yellow arrow decal. The legs too came in black or gray, while the tank itself is found in Tuscan or burnt orange.

VG-C6	EX-C7	LN-C8	Scarcity
25	50	75	4

2020 WATER TANK: From the early 1920s until 1933, this four-legged water tank was sold. The front of the tank featured a decal reading "American Flyer Lines." A black spout with a counterweight was installed.

2020 WATER TANK (Type I): As initially produced the tower had a red tank with a maroon roof and black supporting structure and a ladder.

VG-C6	EX-C7	LN-C8	Scarcity
10	20	30	4

2020 WATER TANK (Type II): Later towers used a red roof, but were otherwise identical.

VG-C6	EX-C7	LN-C8	Scarcity
10	20	30	4

2020 WATER TANK (Type III): Some towers were equipped with a red roof and a green ladder.

VG-C6	EX-C7	LN-C8	Scarcity
10	20	30	4

Wide-Gauge

WIDE-GAUGE ELECTRIC LOCOMOTIVES

During the Wide-Gauge era, American Flyer produced an assortment of electric locomotives in three major styles and range of colors. Most of these had brass nameplates with the American Flyer name, but there were some uncataloged versions produced with the nation wide name instead.

In North America, steam locomotives are typically described using the Whyte classification system. An example of this would be 2-8-4, which describes a locomotive with a two-wheel pilot or leading truck, eight coupled driving wheels (four on each side) and a four-wheel trailing truck. An articulated locomotive, which essentially had two engines under one boiler, had an extra digit added for each set of coupled driving wheels. Union Pacific's famed Big Boy was a 4-8-8-4.

Electric locomotives are not classified by the Whyte system. Instead, a system of letters, numbers and signs was used to describe the *axle* arrangement, rather than the *wheel* arrangement used by Whyte. Letters represent the number of powered axles. B is two, C is three, etc. A plus sign (+) is used to represent multiple powered axle sets on separate articulated frames. Numerals are used to represent the number of non-powered axles on leading and trailing trucks. Therefore, in electric locomotive terms the two engines described in the paragraph above would be a 1-D-2 and a 2-D+D-2 respectively. The two wheel arrangements used by American Flyer for their Wide-Gauge line were 0-B-0 and 2-B-2, representative of 0-4-0 and 4-4-4.

4000 LOCOMOTIVE: The first Wide-Gauge locomotive offered by American Flyer was this 0-B-0, which was sold from 1925 through 1927. The 14-1/2-inch long locomotive came in various shades of dark green. These locomotives were not equipped with reversing units.

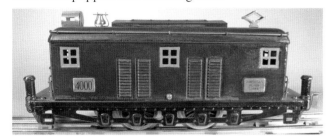

4000 LOCOMOTIVE (Type I): The very first locomotives were painted dark-green. The windows were painted yellow-orange, the 3-1/2-inch wide pilots were painted red, and the frame painted black—it had one male coupler. On each side of the locomotive were two brass nameplates. One read "AMERICAN FLYER LINES," and the other "4000."

VG-C6	EX-C7	LN-C8	Scarcity
125	250	350	4

4000 LOCOMOTIVE (Type II): In 1926 and 1927, the locomotive's base color changed to medium green and the windows were painted yellow. The frame remained black and the pilot was widened to 3-3/4 inches. The brass nameplates were the same as those on the Type I.

VG-C6	EX-C7	LN-C8	Scarcity
125	250	350	3

4000 LOCOMOTIVE (Type III): Versions of this locomotive have been reported to be painted orange, with blue window frames, but such a combination was not listed in the American Flyer catalog.

VG-C6	EX-C7	LN-C8	Scarcity
175	325	500	5

4000 LOCOMOTIVE (Type IV): Another variation, also uncataloged, was finished in maroon.

VG-C6	EX-C7	LN-C8	Scarcity
175	325	500	5

4019 LOCOMOTIVE: A second 0-B-0 was issued from 1925 to 1927. The cab of this 14-1/2-inch long locomotive was painted maroon-brown with yellow windows and doors, and mounted on a black frame. On each side of the locomotive were two brass plates. One bore the number "4019" and the other carried the name "AMERICAN FLYER LINES." These locomotives were equipped with electric reversing units.

4019 LOCOMOTIVE (Type I): The 1925 edition had a maroon cab. Inserts were used for the yellow-orange windows and doors. The red-painted cast-iron pilot of this locomotive is 3-1/2 inches wide.

VG-C6	EX-C7	LN-C8	Scarcity
275	600	850	5

4019 LOCOMOTIVE (Type II): Later production dispensed with the inserts. Instead, the stamped windows were painted yellow.

VG-C6	EX-C7	LN-C8	Scarcity
150	300	500	5

4019 LOCOMOTIVE (Type III): On what was believed to be the final version of the locomotive, the body was painted maroon with yellow-painted windows. The cast-iron pilot, which was painted red, was 3-3/4 inches wide. Two small bosses are adjacent to the two cast sand barrels. These bosses are absent from the other versions of this locomotive.

VG-C6	EX-C7	LN-C8	Scarcity
125	225	350	4

4039 LOCOMOTIVE: This buff-colored 0-B-0 locomotive was produced in 1926. It had yellow windows and a black

Values for each condition are in U.S. dollars. | **Scarcity** = Scale from 1-8 with 8 being the hardest to find.

327

frame, with red-painted cast-iron pilots on each end. There were two brass plates on each side of the body, one read "4039" and the other "AMERICAN FLYER LINES." The locomotive was trimmed with two green flags, nickel-plated bell, small nickel pantograph and two nickel headlamps.

VG-C6	EX-C7	LN-C8	Scarcity
150	300	425	4

4633 LOCOMOTIVE: This 13-1/4-inch long 0-B-0 was offered from 1930-1931. The body was red and the frame gray with red cast-iron pilots. One of the two brass plates on each side bore the locomotive's catalog number and the other the legend "BUILT BY 'American Flyer' Lines." The locomotive featured a ringing bell, die-cast headlight housings on each end, a brass bell and a brass pantograph. On each end of the locomotive was a brass door and above that a brass plate stamped "AMERICAN FLYER LINES."

VG-C6	EX-C7	LN-C8	Scarcity
200	400	800	4

4635 LOCOMOTIVE: This 1929 to 1930 0-B-0 featured a red cab mounted on a gray frame with red cast-iron pilots. Two brass flag holders were mounted at each end of the 13-1/4-inch long locomotive. A "BUILT BY 'American Flyer' Lines" and "4635" plate, made of brass, adorned each side. Two die-cast headlights, a brass bell and a brass pantograph were mounted on the roof. On each end was a brass door, and above it, a brass plate reading "AMERICAN FLYER LINES."

VG-C6	EX-C7	LN-C8	Scarcity
125	225	350	4

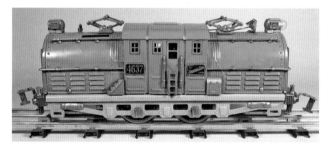

4637 LOCOMOTIVE: This massive, 15-inch long green and Rookie Tan locomotive was sold from 1929 through 1933. Like most Flyer electrics, it had a 0-B-0 wheel arrangement. Inside was a ringing bell and remote control reverse. Two brass-lettering plates were attached to each side, one with the catalog number "4637," the other with the legend "BUILT BY 'American Flyer' Lines." Gold-painted trim adorned the sides and on the roof were two large brass pantographs, two die-cast headlight housings and a brass

bell. On each end of the locomotive was a brass door and above the door a brass plate reading "SHASTA."

VG-C6	EX-C7	LN-C8	Scarcity
200	450	650	5

4643 LOCOMOTIVE: This little 12-inch long 0-B-0 was only available in 1927. A green cab was mounted on a black frame and trimmed with yellow windows. There was a number and nameplate on each side, in this case one reading "4643" and the other "AMERICAN FLYER LINES." The sand barrels at each end can be either black or maroon.

VG-C6	EX-C7	LN-C8	Scarcity
100	200	400	5

4644 LOCOMOTIVE: This popular 12-inch long 0-B-0 locomotive was available from 1928 through 1933. During this time it was produced in at least nine versions.

4644 LOCOMOTIVE (Type I): The initial production of the locomotive is believed to be this version with a red cab and red sand barrels. The windows were painted gold and a black one-piece frame was used. Brass plates were mounted on each side. The two plates read "4644" and "BUILT BY 'American Flyer' LINES." On the roof was a brass bell, brass pantograph and gold-painted die-cast headlight housing.

VG-C6	EX-C7	LN-C8	Scarcity
100	200	325	5

4644 LOCOMOTIVE (Type II): Later production retained the red cab and gold-painted windows, but brass flag holders replaced the red sand barrels at the ends. The brass nameplates and other trim were unchanged from the Type I.

VG-C6	EX-C7	LN-C8	Scarcity
100	175	275	5

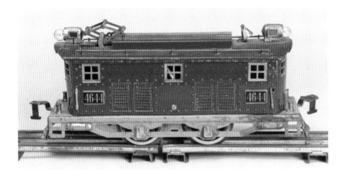

4644 LOCOMOTIVE (Type III): But for its gray frame, this locomotive was identical to the Type II.

VG-C6	EX-C7	LN-C8	Scarcity
75	160	250	4

4644 LOCOMOTIVE (Type IV): This locomotive is identical to the Type II except for one very apparent difference—its cab was painted green. Brass "4644" and "BUILT BY 'American Flyer' LINES" continued to be installed.

VG-C6	EX-C7	LN-C8	Scarcity
75	160	250	3

4644 LOCOMOTIVE (Type V): Later green locomotives were fitted with a body that had a small oval hole punched in the cab side to allow the motor to be lubricated without dismantling the unit.

VG-C6	EX-C7	LN-C8	Scarcity
75	175	275	4

4644 LOCOMOTIVE (Type VI): Green cabs with oval lubrication holes were also sometimes mounted on gray frames, producing this variation.

VG-C6	EX-C7	LN-C8	Scarcity
75	175	275	4

4644 LOCOMOTIVE (Type VII): Otherwise identical to the Type VI, this locomotive had a second "BUILT BY 'American Flyer' LINES" plate replacing the normal "4644" plate on each side.

VG-C6	EX-C7	LN-C8	Scarcity
75	175	275	3

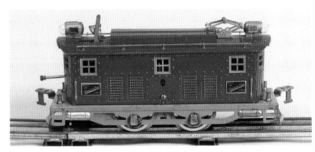

4644 LOCOMOTIVE (Type VIII): But for its red cab, this locomotive was a duplicate of the Type VII.

VG-C6	EX-C7	LN-C8	Scarcity
75	175	275	3

4644 LOCOMOTIVE (Type IX): An uncataloged version of the locomotive was nearly identical to the Type III, but for its brass plates. A plate reading "NATION WIDE LINES" replaced the normal "BUILT BY 'American Flyer' LINES" plate. The second plate on each side continued to be numbered "4644."

VG-C6	EX-C7	LN-C8	Scarcity
200	450	650	6

4644R/C LOCOMOTIVE: This 1931-1933 locomotive was essentially identical to 4644 Type III, except it featured a remote-control reverse motor. "R/C" did not appear on the brass number plate, which instead read the conventional "4644."

VG-C6	EX-C7	LN-C8	Scarcity
100	225	325	4

Values for each condition are in U.S. dollars. | **Scarcity** = Scale from 1-8 with 8 being the hardest to find.

329

4653 LOCOMOTIVE: This 1927 only 0-B-0 was 12 inches long and featured an orange cab and black frame. The cab was trimmed with dark orange painted windows, a nickel headlight, nickel bell, and nickel pantograph. One brass plate was attached to each side. One side read "AMERICAN FLYER LINES" while the plate on the other side bore the number "4653."

VG-C6	EX-C7	LN-C8	Scarcity
130	275	600	6

4654 LOCOMOTIVE: Introduced in 1928, this orange-cabbed 0-B-0 remained in the product line through 1931. The 12-inch long locomotive had blue-green painted doors and pale blue green windows. The cab was mounted on a one-piece frame, which was painted gray and had two brass flag holders mounted on each end.

The cab had two brass plates attached to each side, one numbered "4654," while the other carried the legend "BUILT BY 'American Flyer' LINES." On top of the locomotive were a brass bell, brass pantograph and two die-cast headlight housings painted gold.

VG-C6	EX-C7	LN-C8	Scarcity
100	200	300	4

4667 LOCOMOTIVE: The 15-inch long, red-cabbed 0-B-0 was only available in 1927. It had windows painted yellow and was built on a black frame. A red-painted cast-iron pilot was mounted at each end of the frame. There was a pair of brass plates mounted on each side of the locomotive. One of these was lettered "AMERICAN FLYER LINES" and the other was numbered "4667." A bell, pantograph and a pair of headlamp brackets, all nickel plated, were mounted on the roof.

4667 LOCOMOTIVE (Type I): As described above, with an overall red finish.

VG-C6	EX-C7	LN-C8	Scarcity
200	400	600	6

4667 LOCOMOTIVE (Type II): Identical to Type I, but raised portion of roof painted black.

VG-C6	EX-C7	LN-C8	Scarcity
Too rarely traded to establish accurate pricing.			

4677 LOCOMOTIVE: This buff-colored locomotive was only available in 1927. Like most Flyer electrics, it had a 0-B-0 wheel arrangement. The 15-inch long locomotive had a black frame casting and yellow windows. On the roof was mounted a railing, two green flags, nickel-plated bell and pantograph, and two nickel headlamp housings. Two brass plates were attached to each side of the locomotive. These plates were marked "AMERICAN FLYER LINES" and "4677."

VG-C6	EX-C7	LN-C8	Scarcity
150	300	450	5

4678 LOCOMOTIVE: This two-tone red 1928-1929 0-B-0 measured 15 inches long. The locomotive featured a gray frame and a brass railing. There's also a pantograph and bell on the roof.

4678 LOCOMOTIVE (Type I): The earliest locomotives had the four ventilator openings on each side painted gold. Two brass lettering plates were found on each side—one bore the number "4678," the other was lettered "BUILT BY 'American Flyer' LINES."

VG-C6	EX-C7	LN-C8	Scarcity
175	375	500	5

4678 LOCOMOTIVE (Type II): During later production the ventilators became brass. Perhaps even more notable was the presence of three brass plates per side. The central plate read "4678" and the plates toward each end were lettered "BUILT BY 'American Flyer' LINES."

VG-C6	EX-C7	LN-C8	Scarcity
150	350	475	4

4683 LOCOMOTIVE: This 0-B-0 locomotive was cataloged from 1930 through 1934, with the exception of 1932. The red locomotive with gray frame was 13-1/4 inches long and had hard red cast-iron pilots. The locomotive had a ringing bell and a remote control reverse motor. A brass bell, pantograph and two gold-painted headlight housings were mounted on the roof. Two brass flag holders were mounted on each end of the frame and on each end of the cab was a brass door and above it a brass plate lettered "AMERICAN FLYER LINES."

4683 LOCOMOTIVE (Type I): One version of the locomotive had two brass plates on each side. One of these plates bore the number "4683" and the other was lettered "BUILT BY 'American Flyer' Lines."

VG-C6	EX-C7	LN-C8	Scarcity
125	325	450	4

4683 LOCOMOTIVE (Type II): Other locomotives had two matching plates on each side, both lettered "BUILT BY 'American Flyer' Lines."

VG-C6	EX-C7	LN-C8	Scarcity
125	325	450	4

4683 LOCOMOTIVE (Type III): Rubber-stamped white lettering on the underside of the locomotive distinguished this locomotive from the Type II. The white rubber-stamped lettering read "4683 R/C."

VG-C6	EX-C7	LN-C8	Scarcity
150	350	475	4

4684 LOCOMOTIVE: This 12-inch long 1928-1931 0-B-0 was a near duplicate of the 4644 and 4654, but featured a remote-control reverse motor. On the roof were a brass bell, brass pantograph and a gold-painted die-cast headlight housing. Typically for one of Flyer's larger locomotives, two brass plates were on each side of the cab. One with the number "4684" and the other with the familiar legend "BUILT BY 'American Flyer' LINES."

4684 LOCOMOTIVE (Type I): As described above, with green cab and gold-painted windows and doors, and a black frame.

VG-C6	EX-C7	LN-C8	Scarcity
80	175	275	3

4684 LOCOMOTIVE (Type II): Identical to Type I, but cab painted red.

VG-C6	EX-C7	LN-C8	Scarcity
80	175	275	3

4684 LOCOMOTIVE (Type III): Some of the red-cabbed locomotives had gray frames. Otherwise they're identical to the Type I.

VG-C6	EX-C7	LN-C8	Scarcity
80	175	275	3

4684 LOCOMOTIVE (Type IV): Some locomotives had an orange-painted cab mounted on a gray frame. The windows were painted green.

VG-C6	EX-C7	LN-C8	Scarcity
100	200	300	4

4684 LOCOMOTIVE (Type V): Some of the red cabs included an oval hole in the side to permit lubricating the mechanism without dismantling the locomotive. These cabs were mounted on gray frames.

VG-C6	EX-C7	LN-C8	Scarcity
100	200	300	4

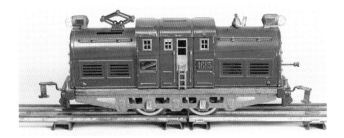

4685 LOCOMOTIVE: In 1929 and 1930, this red 13-1/4-inch long 0-B-0 was sold. The locomotive had a gray frame and cast-iron pilots painted red. Two brass flag holders were mounted on each end of the frame and a brass door on each end of the body. Above each end door was attached a brass plate lettered "AMERICAN FLYER LINES." On both sides of the locomotive there were two additional brass plates, one with the number "4685" and the other lettered "BUILT BY 'American Flyer' Lines."

VG-C6	EX-C7	LN-C8	Scarcity
250	400	700	5

4686 LOCOMOTIVE: This impressive 2-B-2 locomotive debuted in 1928 and remained in the line into 1929. The

Values for each condition are in U.S. dollars. | **Scarcity** = Scale from 1-8 with 8 being the hardest to find.

331

massive blue locomotive measured 18-1/2 inches long. The locomotive was built on a black frame, and attached to the black pilot trucks were red cast-iron pilots. On the roof were nickel headlamps, two white flags, a brass bell and a brass pantograph.

4686 LOCOMOTIVE (Type I): The earliest locomotives had four gold-painted ventilator grilles and two brass plates on each side. The lettering on the plates read "4686" and "BUILT BY 'American Flyer' LINES."

VG-C6	EX-C7	LN-C8	Scarcity
400	1,000	1,400	5

4686 LOCOMOTIVE (Type II): Later units had four brass ventilators on each side and now three brass plates were installed on each side. The center plate bore the name "The Ace," while the other two read "4686" and "BUILT BY 'American Flyer' LINES."

VG-C6	EX-C7	LN-C8	Scarcity
400	1,000	1,400	5

4687 LOCOMOTIVE: Sold only in 1927, this giant 18-1/2-inch long 2-B-2 locomotive brought a new level of detail and realism to American Flyer's Wide-Gauge locomotive line. Its blue cab had gold-painted window trim and was mounted on a black frame. At each end of the frame were attached black four-wheel pilot trucks, themselves having red-painted cast-iron pilots affixed. Two brass lettering plates were attached on each side, one reading "AMERICAN/FLYER/LINES," the other stamped "4687." Extensive nickel trim was installed, including ladders, headlamps, bell, eagle, and two pantographs.

VG-C6	EX-C7	LN-C8	Scarcity
400	1,000	1,800	6

4689 LOCOMOTIVE: Sold from 1928 through 1934, this 18-1/2-inch long 2-B-2 replaced the 4687 of 1927.

4689 LOCOMOTIVE (Type I): The most common version of this spectacular locomotive was painted two-tone blue. It had a black frame and on each end of the frame was a pilot truck, also black, to which were attached red-painted cast-iron pilots. Above one of these pilot trucks was a brass eagle. Brass was also used for the four ventilators on each side, and the three plates on each side. The middle plate was lettered "The Commander," while the ones flanking it read "4689" and "BUILT BY 'American Flyer' LINES" respectively. On the roof were a brass perimeter railing, two white flags, a pair of brass pantographs and a brass bell, as well as a pair of nickel-plated headlamp housings.

VG-C6	EX-C7	LN-C8	Scarcity
550	1,500	2,100	4

4689 LOCOMOTIVE (Type II): A scarce version of the 4689 had a chrome-plated body rather than blue-painted. These locomotives had extensive brass trim. Reproduction, re-plated and outright fraudulent examples of this locomotive far outnumber authentic pieces—so buyer caution cannot be more emphasized.

VG-C6	EX-C7	LN-C8	Scarcity
5,000	10,000	15,000	8

4743 LOCOMOTIVE: This uncataloged 12-inch long 0-B-0 was painted red. It had a black frame and yellow windows. One brass plate is installed in each side, one reading "4743."

VG-C6	EX-C7	LN-C8	Scarcity
Too rarely traded to establish accurate pricing.			

4753 LOCOMOTIVE: An uncataloged red 12-inch long 0-B-0 has been reported wearing this number. It is reported with a black frame and yellow windows. One brass plate is installed in each side, one reading "4753."

VG-C6	EX-C7	LN-C8	Scarcity
Too rarely traded to establish accurate pricing.			

4664 4-4-2 LOCOMOTIVE AND TENDER: This locomotive was similar to the 4694, which was equipped with only a manual control reverse. The 4664 utilized an Ives-designed boiler shell—taken from the Ives 1134—and were cataloged only in 1929. The locomotive was paired with a 4693 Vanderbilt tender riding on gray flex trucks and equipped with brass plates reading "4694" and "AMERICAN FLYER LINES"—the print set against a red background. The combined length of the locomotive and tender was 25 inches.

VG-C6	EX-C7	LN-C8	Scarcity
600	2,500	3,000	7

4672 LOCOMOTIVE AND TENDER: From 1931 through 1932, American Flyer offered this 23-inch long cast-iron locomotive. The boiler and cab casting, baring the number "4670," was formed in two pieces that were then riveted together. The pilot and steam chest were separate castings. A green stripe along the edge of the running board and beneath the cab window highlighted the otherwise glossy black locomotive. A brass plate below the cab window read "AMERICAN FLYER" and inside the cab was a ballast weight for improved traction.

Values for each condition are in U.S. dollars. | **Scarcity** = Scale from 1-8 with 8 being the hardest to find.

333

4672 LOCOMOTIVE AND TENDER (Type I): For 1931 and 1932, the locomotive had a 2-4-2 wheel arrangement. The boiler casting included an integral headlight visor. Rubber stamped beneath the pilot was the number "4670 R/C." Valve motion was virtually non-existent, with little more than main rod and piston rods installed. Brass air tanks were mounted above the cylinders and brass flag holders on the pilot. A brass whistle was mounted atop the boiler near the cab; while at the other end was a brass stack and bell. A brass handrail ran the length of the boiler. The locomotive was paired with a 4671 rectangular tender equipped with gray set trucks and "AMERICAN FLYER LINES" brass plates on its flanks.

VG-C6	EX-C7	LN-C8	Scarcity
350	550	750	4

4672 LOCOMOTIVE AND TENDER (Type II): Locomotives were also produced in 1932 which were identical to the Type I, except having more elaborate valve gear.

VG-C6	EX-C7	LN-C8	Scarcity
350	550	750	4

4672 LOCOMOTIVE AND TENDER (Type III): Reportedly a 4-4-2 variation produced in 1932 exists with a lighted firebox in addition to the more elaborate valve motion found on the Type II. It is reported as being devoid of the brass air tanks, but having one of the cast-in domes painted gold.

VG-C6	EX-C7	LN-C8	Scarcity
Too rarely traded to report accurate values.			

4672 LOCOMOTIVE AND TENDER (Type IV): An uncataloged 4-4-2 version of the locomotive was one of the most elaborately decorated variations of the 4672. This unit had the lighted firebox and elaborate valve gear, although it did lack the brass air tanks. However the headlight visor was removed and replaced by a brass ring, and a brass turning replaced the cast dome. This locomotive had green running board stripes and cab window frames.

VG-C6	EX-C7	LN-C8	Scarcity
400	600	1,000	4

4672 LOCOMOTIVE AND TENDER (Type V): An uncataloged 4-4-2 version of the locomotive was one of the most elaborately decorated variations of the 4672. Like certain of the locos above, this unit had the lighted firebox and elaborate valve gear, although it did lack the brass air tanks. However, the headlight visor was removed and replaced by a brass ring, and a brass turning replaced the cast dome. This locomotive had turquoise running board stripes and cab window frames.

VG-C6	EX-C7	LN-C8	Scarcity
400	600	1,000	5

4675 LOCOMOTIVE AND TENDER: This die-cast 24-1/2-inch long 4-4-2 locomotive and tender combination was offered in 1931-1932. The firebox sides, steam chest and pilot were separate from the boiler casting. The cab was decorated with brass window frames and brass plates beneath both windows reading "AMERICAN FLYER." A green stripe was painted on the running board edge, which today is often worn off. A chain secured the removable drawbar pin to the cab side. The number "4692" was cast into the boiler front beneath the headlight visor.

4675 LOCOMOTIVE AND TENDER (Type I): Locomotive as described above, with remote-control reverse and 4671 Tender.

VG-C6	EX-C7	LN-C8	Scarcity
500	800	1,200	5

4675 LOCOMOTIVE AND TENDER (Type II): Identical to Type I, except manual-reverse locomotive with 4671 tender.

VG-C6	EX-C7	LN-C8	Scarcity
300	500	700	4

4675 LOCOMOTIVE AND TENDER (Type III): Identical to Type I, but with brass "ANNAPOLIS" plate replacing "American Flyer" under cab window.

VG-C6	EX-C7	LN-C8	Scarcity
500	800	1,200	5

4675 LOCOMOTIVE AND TENDER (Type IV): Identical to Type I, but with brass "ADAMS" plate under cab window rather than "American Flyer" and cataloged from 1931-1933.

VG-C6	EX-C7	LN-C8	Scarcity
500	800	1,200	5

4681 LOCOMOTIVE AND TENDER: This 1934-1936 4-4-2 locomotive and tender was one of the most elaborate sold by American Flyer. Measuring 24-1/2 inches long, this die-cast locomotive had extensive bright metal trim representing sand and steam lines. The handrails along the boiler sides, as well as a representative coupler lift bar on the pilot beam were also brass, as was a ring on the headlight. Walschaert valve motion was installed.

On top of the boiler there was a brass bell, copper lines, a brass knob for the bell, a brass dome, and a brass whistle.

Green was the color used for both the marker lights and for the stripe along the running board edge. The cab window frame was painted gold, as were the steps leading from the pilot to the running boards. Beneath the cab window could be found either a brass plate or gold-colored decal reading "AMERICAN FLYER."

Internally, a remote control motor with ringing bell and black drive wheels powered the locomotive. A ballast weight was mounted in the cab, as was a chain to secure the drawbar pin. In many cases "4695" was rubber stamped underneath near the trailing truck.

The tender was the 4671 square-type riding on gray set trucks. It was marked with decal or brass plates with the lettering "AMERICAN FLYER LINES."

VG-C6	EX-C7	LN-C8	Scarcity
500	800	1,000	4

4682 LOCOMOTIVE AND TENDER: This 1933 4-4-2 steamer measured 24-1/2 inches long. Its die-cast boiler housed a remote-control motor with black drive wheels, as well as a ballast weight in the cab. The cab windows were painted gold and beneath them were brass plates reading "AMERICAN FLYER." A green stripe was painted along the edge of the running board. The headlight visor was painted gold and both marker lights were green. The number "4680" was rubber stamped under the trailing truck.

4682 LOCOMOTIVE AND TENDER (Type I): Locomotive as described above and paired with a 4671 tender equipped with gray set trucks.

VG-C6	EX-C7	LN-C8	Scarcity
400	800	1,200	5

4682 LOCOMOTIVE AND TENDER (Type II): As described and illustrated above, except with additional copper line between dome and whistle.

VG-C6	EX-C7	LN-C8	Scarcity
400	800	1,200	5

4694 LOCOMOTIVE AND TENDER: This 4-4-2 locomotive was produced in seven major variations and numerous sub varieties. In 1929 and 1930, the locomotive was based on the Ives 1134, sharing the Bridgeport product's body die-casting. The red wheels also readily distinguish these locomotives.

From 1931 through 1934, a new body casting of American Flyer origin was the basis for the 4-4-2. Black wheels and repositioned headlights are two easily notable ways to distinguish these locomotives from their predecessors.

Values for each condition are in U.S. dollars. | **Scarcity =** Scale from 1-8 with 8 being the hardest to find.

335

4694 LOCOMOTIVE AND TENDER (Type I): Both the locomotive and tender in this 26-inch long combination utilized Ives castings, though the tender rode on American Flyer black flex trucks. On the flanks of the tender was brass plates lettered "GOLDEN STATE." This locomotive had a manual reverse.

VG-C6	EX-C7	LN-C8	Scarcity
800	1,200	3,000	6

4694 LOCOMOTIVE AND TENDER (Type II): Otherwise identical locomotives were produces with automatic reverse.

VG-C6	EX-C7	LN-C8	Scarcity
800	1,200	3,000	6

4694 LOCOMOTIVE AND TENDER (Type III): Some of the Ives-based locomotives were paired with American Flyer-designed 4693 Vanderbilt tenders, rendering a pair 25 inches long. The tender was decorated with a red "4694" and "AMERICAN FLYER LINES" brass plates, and rode on gray flex trucks. This version was cataloged in 1930-31.

VG-C6	EX-C7	LN-C8	Scarcity
600	1,200	2,600	6

4694 LOCOMOTIVE AND TENDER (Type IV): This 1931-34 American Flyer-designed locomotive was rubber stamped "4692XR/C" on the underside of the pilot. The headlight had a cast-in visor. It had black wheels, brass dome, brass whistle and brass exhaust stack. The edge of the running board was painted turquoise and the window frame gold. A brass plate below the cab window bore the legend "AMERICAN FLYER." A pin, secured by a chain to the interior cab side, was used to couple the engine to the tender.

It was accompanied by a 4693 Vanderbilt tender riding on gray flex trucks. The tender featured brass plates marked "4693" and "AMERICAN FLYER LINES."

VG-C6	EX-C7	LN-C8	Scarcity
400	650	950	4

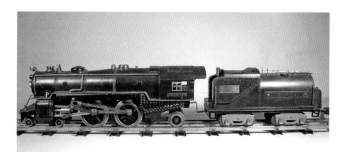

4694 LOCOMOTIVE AND TENDER (Type V): Some locomotives had an illuminated firebox and the headlight was equipped with a brass rim. The tender furnished with this loco was the 4693, now riding on set trucks, and sometimes having a data plate rather than number plate. This version was cataloged from 1931 through 1934.

VG-C6	EX-C7	LN-C8	Scarcity
400	650	950	4

4694 LOCOMOTIVE AND TENDER (Type VI): Similar to the Type VI, the tender furnished with this 1930-31 loco had a data plate rather than number plate.

VG-C6	EX-C7	LN-C8	Scarcity
425	675	1,000	5

4696 LOCOMOTIVE AND TENDER: This 27-inch long monster rode the pages of the American Flyer catalog from 1931 through 1936: The 4-4-2 had a die-cast body and ringing bell. Its cab windows and the steps from the pilot to running board were painted gold. A green stripe was painted on the edge of the running board. A brass "AMERICAN FLYER" plate was under the cab window.

4694 LOCOMOTIVE AND TENDER (Type III)

4696 LOCOMOTIVE AND TENDER (Type I): Locomotive as described above rubber stamped "4695R/C" beneath pilot. At the front of the locomotive was a black headlight with integral visor. The locomotive was combined with a 4693 Vanderbilt tender. The tender was equipped with "4693" and "AMERICAN FLYER LINES" brass plates and rode on gray flex trucks.

VG-C6	EX-C7	LN-C8	Scarcity
500	850	1,250	4

4696 LOCOMOTIVE AND TENDER (Type II): Identical to the Type I, except the tender was equipped with gray set trucks.

VG-C6	EX-C7	LN-C8	Scarcity
500	850	1,250	4

4696 LOCOMOTIVE AND TENDER (Type III): Other locomotives came with tenders with red "4694" and "AMERICAN FLYER LINES" plates. The balance of the loco-tender combination duplicated the Type I.

VG-C6	EX-C7	LN-C8	Scarcity
500	850	1,250	4

4696 LOCOMOTIVE AND TENDER (Type IV): 📷 Other locomotives featured a brass headlight rim and green marker lights. The underside of these locomotives were rubber stamped "4695" above the trailing truck frame. The tender, which was a 4693 Vanderbilt-type, was equipped with gray set trucks. Brass plates with capacity data were affixed to the tender sides.

VG-C6	EX-C7	LN-C8	Scarcity
500	850	1,250	4

4696 LOCOMOTIVE AND TENDER (Type VI): This locomotive is similar to the Type V but with nickel trim and brass pilot wheels.

VG-C6	EX-C7	LN-C8	Scarcity
2,500	4,000	5,000	7

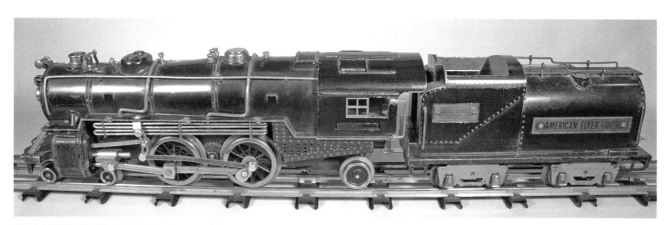

4696 LOCOMOTIVE AND TENDER (Type IV)

Values for each condition are in U.S. dollars. | **Scarcity** = Scale from 1-8 with 8 being the hardest to find.

4040 MAIL AND BAGGAGE: These lithographed 14-inch long cars were offered from 1925 through 1927. Five windows and two lithographed sliding doors decorated each side, and underneath the car were black air tanks. The cars were equipped with black four-wheel flex trucks and interior illumination. The actual car ends bore the lettering "AMERICAN FLYER LINES" at the top and "MADE IN U.S.A." along the bottom. The sides of the cars were marked in white with "AMERICAN FLYER LINES" centered near the roof and "UNITED STATES MAIL/RAILWAY POST OFFICE" centered between the baggage doors. The upper corners of each side were lettered "A.F.L." and the lower corners "4040."

The smooth stamped roof of the car was held in place by a cam-locking device. Cars furnished in sets are known to have come with a 4122 mailbag catcher.

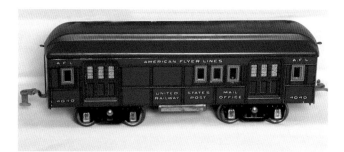

4040 MAIL AND BAGGAGE (Type I): Some cars had maroon sides and doors and dark maroon roofs. The lithographed trim was presented in yellow, black and white. The car was further trimmed with brass air tanks and journal boxes.

VG-C6	EX-C7	LN-C8	Scarcity
35	100	150	4

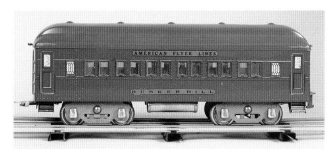

4040 MAIL AND BAGGAGE (Type II): Other cars were near duplicates of the Type I except the air tanks were black rather than brass, and the flex trucks did not come with journal boxes.

VG-C6	EX-C7	LN-C8	Scarcity
35	100	150	4

4040 MAIL AND BAGGAGE (Type III): This car differed from the Type I by having red sides and roof rather than maroon.

VG-C6	EX-C7	LN-C8	Scarcity
35	100	150	4

4040 MAIL AND BAGGAGE (Type IV): Notably different was this car with dark-green sides and roof. Yellow, black and white lithographed detail decorated the car, which rode on black trucks without journal boxes.

VG-C6	EX-C7	LN-C8	Scarcity
35	100	150	4

4040 MAIL AND BAGGAGE (Type V): Identical to the Type IV, but with medium green replacing the dark green.

VG-C6	EX-C7	LN-C8	Scarcity
35	100	150	4

4041 PULLMAN: These lithographed 14-inch long cars were offered from 1925 through 1927. Twelve open windows, two lithographed restroom windows and two spring-loaded doors decorated each side. Underneath the car were black air tanks. The cars were equipped with black four-wheel flex trucks and interior illumination. The actual car ends bore the white lettering "AMERICAN FLYER LINES" at the top and "MADE IN U.S.A." along the bottom. The sides of the cars were marked in white with "AMERICAN FLYER LINES" centered near the roof and "AMERICA" centered on each side beneath the windows. The smooth stamped roof of the car was held in place by a cam-locking device.

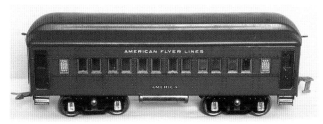

4041 PULLMAN (Type I): Some cars had maroon sides and doors and dark maroon roofs. The lithographed trim was presented in yellow, black and white. The car was further trimmed with brass steps, air tanks and journal boxes.

VG-C6	EX-C7	LN-C8	Scarcity
35	100	150	4

4041 PULLMAN (Type II): Other cars were near duplicates of the Type I except the air tanks and steps were black rather than brass, and the flex trucks did not come with journal boxes. The catalog number "4041" was rubber stamped on the underside of the car.

VG-C6	EX-C7	LN-C8	Scarcity
35	100	150	4

4041 PULLMAN (Type III): This car differed from the Type I by having red sides and roof rather than maroon.

VG-C6	EX-C7	LN-C8	Scarcity
35	100	150	4

4041 PULLMAN (Type IV): Notably different was this car with dark-green sides and roof. Yellow, black and white lithographed detail decorated the car, which rode on black trucks without journal boxes. The air tanks and corner steps were painted black. Beneath the windows was the name "PLEASANT VIEW" rather than "America."

VG-C6	EX-C7	LN-C8	Scarcity
35	100	150	4

4041 PULLMAN (Type V): The car was a near duplicate of the Type IV, except for the medium-green sides, which carried the name "AMERICA."

VG-C6	EX-C7	LN-C8	Scarcity
35	100	150	4

4042 OBSERVATION: These lithographed 14-inch long cars were offered from 1925 through 1927. Twelve open windows, two lithographed restroom windows and a spring-loaded door decorated each side. The brass-railed observation platform carried a plate marked "FLYER LIMITED." A spring-loaded door connected the observation platform to the car interior, and like the interior the observation platform was lighted. Underneath the car were black air tanks. The cars were equipped with black four-wheel flex trucks and interior illumination. The end of the car opposite the platform was marked "AMERICAN FLYER LINES" at the top and "MADE IN U.S.A." along the bottom in white. The sides of the cars were marked in white with "AMERICAN FLYER LINES" centered near the roof and "PLEASANT VIEW" centered on each side beneath the windows. The smooth stamped roof of the car was held in place by a cam-locking device.

Values for each condition are in U.S. dollars. | **Scarcity** = Scale from 1-8 with 8 being the hardest to find.

339

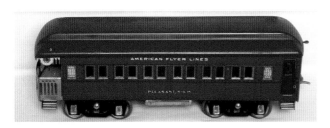

4042 OBSERVATION (Type I): Some cars had maroon sides and doors and dark maroon roofs. The lithographed trim was presented in yellow, black and white. The car was further trimmed with brass steps, air tanks and journal boxes.

VG-C6	EX-C7	LN-C8	Scarcity
35	100	150	4

4042 OBSERVATION (Type II): Other cars were near duplicates of the Type I except the air tanks and steps were black rather than brass, and the flex trucks did not come with journal boxes. The catalog number "4042" was rubber stamped on the underside of the car.

VG-C6	EX-C7	LN-C8	Scarcity
35	100	150	4

4042 OBSERVATION (Type III): This car differed from the Type I by having red sides and roof rather than maroon.

VG-C6	EX-C7	LN-C8	Scarcity
35	100	150	4

4042 OBSERVATION (Type IV): Notably different was this car with dark-green sides and roof. Yellow, black and white lithographed detail decorated the car, which rode on black trucks without journal boxes. The air tanks and corner steps were painted black.

VG-C6	EX-C7	LN-C8	Scarcity
35	100	150	4

4042 OBSERVATION (Type V): Identical to the Type IV, but with medium green replacing the dark green.

VG-C6	EX-C7	LN-C8	Scarcity
35	100	150	4

4042 Observation (Type VI): Other cars were identical to the Type I, except they were lettered "AMERICA" rather than "PLEASANT VIEW," and their tanks were black.

VG-C6	EX-C7	LN-C8	Scarcity
35	100	150	4

4080 MAIL AND BAGGAGE: These light brown-lithographed 19-inch long cars were offered in 1926 and 1927. Eight windows and two lithographed sliding doors decorated each side. The cars were equipped with black four-wheel flex trucks and interior illumination. The sides of the cars were marked in white with "AMERICAN FLYER LIMITED" centered near the roof and "UNITED STATES MAIL/ RAILWAY POST OFFICE" centered between the baggage doors. The upper corners of each side were lettered "A.F.L."

The smooth stamped roof of the car was held in place by a cam-locking device. Cars furnished in sets are known to have come with a 4122 mailbag catcher.

4080 MAIL AND BAGGAGE (Type I): As produced in 1926, the car had no journal boxes and the air tanks and battery box were painted black.

VG-C6	EX-C7	LN-C8	Scarcity
75	50	225	6

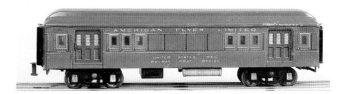

4080 MAIL AND BAGGAGE (Type II): The 1927 version of the car sported brass journal boxes and air tanks.

VG-C6	EX-C7	LN-C8	Scarcity
75	150	225	6

4081 PULLMAN: These light brown lithographed 19-inch long cars were offered in 1926 and 1927. Sixteen window openings, two lithographed restroom windows and two spring-loaded doors decorated each side. The cars were equipped with black four-wheel flex trucks and three-lamp interior illumination. The sides of the cars were marked in white with "AMERICAN FLYER LIMITED" centered near the roof and "WASHINGTON" centered below the windows. The smooth stamped roof of the car was held in place by a cam-locking device.

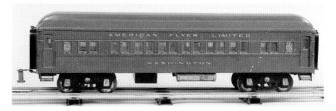

4081 PULLMAN (Type I): The 1926 version of the car had black air tanks and battery boxes, and there were no journal boxes on the trucks.

VG-C6	EX-C7	LN-C8	Scarcity
75	150	225	6

4081 PULLMAN (Type II): The 1927 version featured brass journal boxes and air tanks.

VG-C6	EX-C7	LN-C8	Scarcity
75	150	225	6

4081 PULLMAN (Type III): Identical to Type II except lettered "VALLEY FORGE" rather than Washington.

VG-C6	EX-C7	LN-C8	Scarcity
100	175	250	6

4082 OBSERVATION: These light brown lithographed 19-inch long cars were offered in 1926 and 1927. Sixteen window openings, two lithographed restroom windows and a spring-loaded door decorated each side. The brass-railed observation platform carried a lighted sign marked "AMERICAN FLYER LIMITED." A spring-loaded door connected the observation platform to the car interior, and like the interior the observation platform was lighted. The cars were equipped with black four-wheel flex trucks and two-lamp interior illumination. The sides of the cars were marked in white with "AMERICAN FLYER LIMITED" centered near the roof and "VALLEY FORGE" centered below the windows. The smooth stamped roof of the car was held in place by a cam-locking device.

4082 OBSERVATION (Type I): As produced in 1926, the car had no journal boxes and the air tanks and battery box were painted black.

VG-C6	EX-C7	LN-C8	Scarcity
75	150	225	6

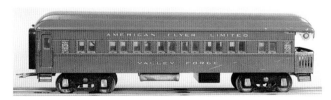

4082 OBSERVATION (Type II): The 1927 version of the car featured brass journal boxes and air tanks.

VG-C6	EX-C7	LN-C8	Scarcity
75	150	225	6

4090 MAIL AND BAGGAGE: In 1927, American Flyer produced this attractive 19-inch long illuminated car. Its sides were blue and the lithographed trim was in yellow, black and white. The sides of the cars were marked in white with "AMERICAN FLYER LIMITED" centered near the roof and "UNITED STATES MAIL/RAILWAY

POST OFFICE" centered between the baggage doors. The upper corners of each side were lettered "A.F.L." in yellow. The car rode on six-wheel flex trucks with brass journal boxes. Cars in sets were equipped with a 4122 automatic mailbag catcher.

4090 MAIL AND BAGGAGE (Type I): As described above, and with yellow window trim.

VG-C6	EX-C7	LN-C8	Scarcity
125	275	400	7

4090 MAIL AND BAGGAGE (Type II): Identical to Type I, but with red window trim.

VG-C6	EX-C7	LN-C8	Scarcity
125	275	400	7

4091 PULLMAN: Constructed in 1927, this 19-inch long Pullman matched the 4090 Mail and Baggage car. The lithographed trim was yellow, black and white. The sides of the cars were marked in white with "AMERICAN FLYER LIMITED" centered near the roof and "WEST POINT" centered below the 16 punched-open windows. There were also two lithographed restroom windows and two spring-loaded doors on each side. Brass steps were mounted beneath the doors. The car rode on six-wheel flex trucks with brass journal boxes.

4091 PULLMAN (Type I): As described above, and with yellow window trim.

VG-C6	EX-C7	LN-C8	Scarcity
125	275	400	7

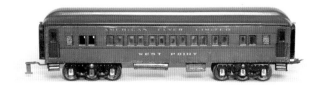

4091 PULLMAN (Type II): Identical to Type I, but with red window trim.

VG-C6	EX-C7	LN-C8	Scarcity
125	275	400	7

Values for each condition are in U.S. dollars. | **Scarcity** = Scale from 1-8 with 8 being the hardest to find.

341

4092 OBSERVATION: Constructed in 1927, this 19-inch long Pullman matched the 4090 Mail and Baggage car and 4091 Pullman. The lithographed trim was yellow, black and white. The sides of the cars were marked in white with "AMERICAN FLYER LIMITED" centered near the roof and "ANNAPOLIS" centered below the 16 punched-open windows. There were also two lithographed restroom windows and a spring-loaded door on each side. Brass steps were mounted beneath the doors. The car rode on six-wheel flex trucks with brass journal boxes. At the rear of the car was an illuminated observation platform with brass railing. On the railing was a sign reading "AMERICAN FLYER LIMITED," and a spring-loaded door lead from the observation platform to the interior of the car.

4092 OBSERVATION (Type I): As described above, and with yellow window trim.

VG-C6	EX-C7	LN-C8	Scarcity
125	275	400	7

4092 OBSERVATION (Type II): Identical to Type I, but with red window trim.

VG-C6	EX-C7	LN-C8	Scarcity
125	275	400	7

4141 PULLMAN: This 14-inch long lithographed car debuted in 1927. Riding on four-wheel flex trucks, these cars featured interior lighting and a removable roof, secured by a cam-locking device. Twelve window openings were located on each side, along with two non-functioning restroom windows and doors. Beneath the doors were steps. The ends of the cars were marked "AMERICAN FLYER LINES" near the top and "MADE IN U.S.A." at the bottom.

4141 PULLMAN (Type I): Some of these cars were orange, with red, white and black lithographed detail.

Above the windows the car was lettered "AMERICAN FLYER LINES" and centered beneath the windows was the car name "BUNKER HILL." These markings were applied in black. The car did not have brass journal boxes, but it did have black air tanks.

VG-C6	EX-C7	LN-C8	Scarcity
45	100	150	4

4141 PULLMAN (Type II): Other cars were green with yellow, white and black lithographed detail and green roof. "AMERICAN FLYER LINES" markings were centered above the windows and "AMERICA" below the windows. These cars were equipped with gray flex trucks without journal boxes.

VG-C6	EX-C7	LN-C8	Scarcity
40	80	125	3

4141 PULLMAN (Type III): Some of the green cars were equipped with brass steps, air tanks and journal boxes.

VG-C6	EX-C7	LN-C8	Scarcity
40	100	135	3

4141 PULLMAN (Type IV): A scarce version of the car was red with yellow, black and white lithographed detail. Above the windows the car was lettered "EMPIRE EXPRESS" and centered beneath the windows was the car name "KNICKERBOCKER." The car rode on black flex trucks without journal boxes.

VG-C6	EX-C7	LN-C8	Scarcity
Too rarely traded to establish accurate pricing.			

4142 OBSERVATION: This 14-inch long lithographed car debuted in 1927. Riding on four-wheel flex trucks, these cars featured interior lighting and a removable roof, secured by a cam-locking device. Twelve window openings were located on each side, along with two non-functioning restroom windows and a lithographed door. At the rear of the car was a brass observation platform, on its railing mounted a sign reading "FLYER LIMITED." A spring-loaded door connected the platform with the interior of the car. At each corner of the car were mounted four black steps. The ends of the cars were marked "AMERICAN FLYER LINES" near the top and "MADE IN U.S.A." at the bottom.

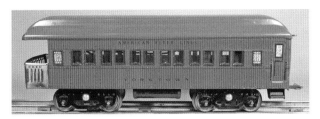

4142 OBSERVATION (Type I): Orange sides with red, black and white detail and orange roof. Door to platform is orange. "AMERICAN FLYER LINES" centered across top of car and "YORKTOWN" below the windows, both in black. Black air tanks and black flex trucks with no journal boxes.

VG-C6	EX-C7	LN-C8	Scarcity
50	100	150	4

4142 OBSERVATION (Type II): Green sides with yellow, black and white detail and green roof. Door to platform is lithographed in wood grain. "AMERICAN FLYER LINES" centered across top of car and "PLEASANT VIEW" below the windows, both in white. Black flex trucks with no journal boxes.

VG-C6	EX-C7	LN-C8	Scarcity
35	80	125	3

4142 OBSERVATION (Type III): Some of the green cars were equipped with brass steps, air tanks and journal boxes.

VG-C6	EX-C7	LN-C8	Scarcity
40	100	135	3

4142 OBSERVATION (Type IV): A scarce version of the car was red with yellow, black and white lithographed detail. Above the windows the car was lettered "EMPIRE EXPRESS" and centered beneath the windows was the car name "KNICKERBOCKER." The car rode on black flex trucks without journal boxes.

VG-C6	EX-C7	LN-C8	Scarcity
Too rarely traded to establish accurate pricing.			

4142 OBSERVATION (Type V): This orange car was a duplicate of the Type I car, but was lettered "AMERICA" rather than "Yorktown" below the windows.

VG-C6	EX-C7	LN-C8	Scarcity
35	80	125	3

4150 CLUB CAR: Club car for use with Eagle set.

4150 CLUB CAR (Type I): Red.

VG-C6	EX-C7	LN-C8	Scarcity
100	300	600	7

4150 CLUB CAR (Type II): Other cars had orange lithographed sides and maroon roofs..

VG-C6	EX-C7	LN-C8	Scarcity
100	300	600	7

4151 PULLMAN: From 1928 through 1931, this 14-inch long illuminated passenger car was offered. The car was equipped with gray four-wheel flex trucks and brass steps beneath each door. These doors were either lithographed or spring loaded. Two lithographed restroom windows as well as 12 open windows were found on each side of the car. The ends of the cars were marked "AMERICAN FLYER LINES" near the top and "MADE IN U.S.A." at the bottom. The roof had five raised embossed "ventilators" dotting it.

4151 PULLMAN (Type I): Some cars had green sides and roofs, and were decorated with yellow, black and white lithographed detail. A cam-locking device retained the roof. Above the windows was the legend "AMERICAN FLYER LINES" while below the windows was "AMERICA," both printed in white inside a black surround.

VG-C6	EX-C7	LN-C8	Scarcity
35	80	120	3

4151 PULLMAN (Type II): Other cars were orange with red, black and white lithographed detail. Cam-locking devices held the orange roof in place. Black "AMERICAN FLYER LINES" lettering was centered above the windows and "BUNKER HILL" below.

VG-C6	EX-C7	LN-C8	Scarcity
40	100	135	3

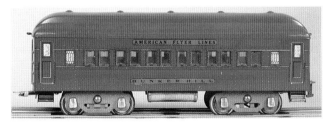

4151 PULLMAN (Type III): Orange sides with red, gold, green, black, and white detail and orange roof. Black lettering in green letter board with red border; "AMERICAN FLYER LINES" centered across the top of car and "BUNKER HILL" below the windows.

VG-C6	EX-C7	LN-C8	Scarcity
40	100	135	3

4151 PULLMAN (Type IV): But for the car name "YORKTOWN," this car was identical to the Type III.

VG-C6	EX-C7	LN-C8	Scarcity
40	100	135	3

Values for each condition are in U.S. dollars. | **Scarcity** = Scale from 1-8 with 8 being the hardest to find.

343

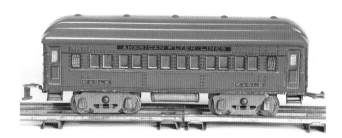

4151 PULLMAN (Type V): Some cars were finished in green with gold, orange, black and white lithographed detail. Rather than the brass air tanks found on most 4151 cars, this version had instead gray truss rods. The upper "AMERICAN FLYER LINES" and lower "EAGLE" lettering was gold and emblazoned on black letter boards with gold borders.

VG-C6	EX-C7	LN-C8	Scarcity
40	100	135	3

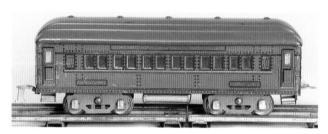

4151 PULLMAN (Type VI): Other cars had orange sides and green roofs. The lithographed detail on these cars was red, gold, black and white. The lettering was gold and applied to a red-bordered green letter board. Above the windows was "AMERICAN FLYER LINES" and below the windows "STATESMAN."

VG-C6	EX-C7	LN-C8	Scarcity
50	110	150	4

4151 PULLMAN (Type VII): Cars with red sides and roofs were also produced. These cars had green, gold, black and white lithographed detail. Gold lettering was applied to black letter boards with gold borders. The lettering centered above the windows read "AMERICAN FLYER LINES" and centered below the windows was "EAGLE."

VG-C6	EX-C7	LN-C8	Scarcity
40	100	135	3

4152 OBSERVATION: From 1928 through 1931, this 14-inch long illuminated observation car was offered. The car was equipped with gray four-wheel flex trucks and brass steps beneath each door. These doors were either lithographed or spring loaded. Two lithographed restroom windows as well as 12 open windows were found on each side of the car. At one end of the car was an observation platform with a brass railing. The ends of the cars were marked "AMERICAN FLYER LINES" near the top and "MADE IN U.S.A." at the bottom. The roof had five raised embossed "ventilators" dotting it.

4152 OBSERVATION (Type I): Some cars had green sides and roofs and were decorated with yellow, black and white lithographed detail. A cam-locking device retained the roof. Above the windows was the legend "AMERICAN FLYER LINES" with "PLEASANT VIEW" printed in white inside a black surround below the windows.

VG-C6	EX-C7	LN-C8	Scarcity
35	80	120	3

4152 OBSERVATION (Type II): Other cars were orange with red, black and white lithographed detail. Cam-locking devices held the orange roof in place. Black "AMERICAN FLYER LINES" lettering was centered above the windows and "BUNKER HILL" below.

VG-C6	EX-C7	LN-C8	Scarcity
40	100	135	3

4152 OBSERVATION (Type III): This car was a duplicate of the Type II, except "YORKTOWN" was printed below the windows.

VG-C6	EX-C7	LN-C8	Scarcity
40	100	135	3

4152 OBSERVATION (Type IV): Another orange car featured gold, red, green, black, and white lithographed detail. The black lettering of this car was applied to green letter boards with red borders. The upper letter board was marked "AMERICAN FLYER LINES" and the lower one "YORKTOWN."

VG-C6	EX-C7	LN-C8	Scarcity
40	100	135	3

4152 OBSERVATION (Type V): Some cars were finished in green with gold, orange, black and white lithographed detail. Rather than the brass air tanks found on most 4152 cars, this version had gray truss rods instead. The upper

"AMERICAN FLYER LINES" and lower "EAGLE" lettering was gold and emblazoned on black letter boards with gold borders. Stock number is rubber stamped on underside of car.

VG-C6	EX-C7	LN-C8	Scarcity
40	100	135	3

4152 OBSERVATION (Type VI): Other cars had orange sides and green roofs. The lithographed detail on these cars was red, gold, black and white. The lettering was gold and applied to a red-bordered green letter board. Above the windows was "AMERICAN FLYER LINES" and below the windows "STATESMAN."

VG-C6	EX-C7	LN-C8	Scarcity
50	110	150	4

4152 OBSERVATION (Type VII): Cars with red sides and roofs were also produced. These cars had green, gold, black and white lithographed detail. Gold lettering was applied to black letter boards with gold borders. The lettering centered above the windows read "AMERICAN FLYER LINES" and centered below the windows was "EAGLE."

VG-C6	EX-C7	LN-C8	Scarcity
40	100	135	3

4250 CLUB: This 14-inch long illuminated car was offered from 1929 through 1931. Its bluish-green body was lithographed with red, gold and black details, and the roofs were painted red. Five raised humps, representing ventilators, were pressed into the roof. Ten windows were punched from each side, and each side also had one lithographed restroom window and one solid brass door, as well as one red sliding door. The ends of the cars were marked "AMERICAN FLYER LINES" near the top and "MADE IN U.S.A." at the bottom. Above the side windows was a brass plate reading "LONE SCOUT," while beneath the windows were two small brass plates. One of these bore the name "AMERICAN FLYER," the other "CLUB 4250."

The car rode on gray set trucks. When included in sets, the car came with the 4122 automatic mailbag catcher.

4250 CLUB (TYPE I): Some cars had brass air tanks mounted under the body.

VG-C6	EX-C7	LN-C8	Scarcity
50	125	150	4

4250 CLUB (TYPE II): Other cars had gray truss rods with integral air tanks in lieu of the brass air tanks.

VG-C6	EX-C7	LN-C8	Scarcity
50	125	150	4

4251 PULLMAN: This 14-inch long illuminated car was offered from 1929 through 1931. Its bluish-green body was lithographed with red, gold and black details, and the roofs were painted red. Five raised humps, representing ventilators, were pressed into the roof. Twelve windows were punched from each side, and each side also had a pair of lithographed restroom windows and two solid brass doors. The ends of the cars were marked "AMERICAN FLYER LINES" near the top and "MADE IN U.S.A." at the bottom. Above the side windows was a brass plate reading "LONE SCOUT," while beneath the windows were two small brass plates. One of these bore the name "AMERICAN FLYER," the other "PULLMAN 4251." The car rode on gray set trucks.

4251 PULLMAN (TYPE I): Some cars had brass air tanks mounted under the body.

VG-C6	EX-C7	LN-C8	Scarcity
50	125	150	4

4251 PULLMAN (TYPE II): Other cars had gray truss rods with integral air tanks in lieu of the brass air tanks.

VG-C6	EX-C7	LN-C8	Scarcity
50	125	150	4

4252 OBSERVATION: This 14-inch long illuminated car was offered from 1929 through 1931. Its bluish-green body was lithographed with red, gold and black details, and the roofs were painted red. Five raised humps, representing ventilators, were pressed into the roof. Twelve windows were punched from each side, and each side also had a pair of lithographed restroom windows and a solid brass door. A brass railing surrounded the observation platform. An "AMERICAN FLYER LINES" plate hung from the railing, and a spring-loaded door connected the observation platform with the interior car. The ends of the cars were marked "AMERICAN FLYER LINES" near the top and "MADE IN U.S.A." at the bottom. Above the side

Values for each condition are in U.S. dollars. | **Scarcity** = Scale from 1-8 with 8 being the hardest to find.

345

windows was a brass plate reading "LONE SCOUT," while beneath the windows were two small brass plates. One of these bore the name "AMERICAN FLYER," the other "OBSERVATION 4252." The car rode on gray set trucks.

4252 OBSERVATION (Type I): Some cars had brass air tanks mounted under the body.

VG-C6	EX-C7	LN-C8	Scarcity
50	125	150	4

4252 OBSERVATION (Type II): Other cars had gray truss rods with integral air tanks in lieu of the brass air tanks.

VG-C6	EX-C7	LN-C8	Scarcity
50	125	150	4

4331 PULLMAN: From 1931 through 1936 this 14-inch long illuminated passenger car was offered. Six double and two single windows, with brass trim, were punched in each enamel side. Atop the car was a roof with five stamped ventilator bumps, and beneath the car were gray set trucks and gray trusses. The stock number "4331" was rubber stamped on the underside of the car. Decals were used for the gold-bordered black letter board with gold "AMERICAN FLYER LINES" lettering, and the smaller "PULLMAN" lettering below the windows.

4331 PULLMAN (Type I): Some cars had matching red bodies and roofs. On each side two decals represent doors.

VG-C6	EX-C7	LN-C8	Scarcity
40	100	125	3

4331 PULLMAN (Type II): Other cars had a darker red roof combined with the red body. These cars had two solid brass doors on each side.

VG-C6	EX-C7	LN-C8	Scarcity
50	125	150	4

4332 OBSERVATION: From 1931 through 1936, this 14-inch long illuminated passenger car was offered. Six double and two single windows, with brass trim, were punched in each enamel side. Atop the car was a roof with five stamped ventilator bumps, and beneath the car were gray set trucks and gray trusses. The stock number "4332" was rubber stamped on the underside of the car. Decals were used for the gold-bordered black letter board with gold "AMERICAN FLYER LINES" lettering, and the smaller "PULLMAN" lettering below the windows.

4332 OBSERVATION (Type I): Some cars had matching red bodies and roofs. On each side two decals represent doors.

VG-C6	EX-C7	LN-C8	Scarcity
40	100	125	3

4332 OBSERVATION (Type II): Other cars had a darker red roof combined with the red body. These cars had two solid brass doors on each side.

VG-C6	EX-C7	LN-C8	Scarcity
50	125	150	4

4340 CLUB: This enameled 1928-1932 passenger car measured 14 inches long. Ten windows were formed from each side, and brass trim decorated them. A sliding baggage door with brass knob and a brass passenger door were installed in each side as well. A brass step hung beneath the passenger door. The car was equipped with interior illumination and when included in a set was fitted with a 4122 automatic mailbag catcher.

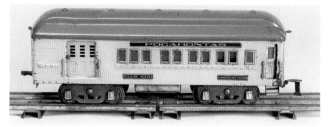

4340 CLUB (Type I): Some cars had Rookie Tan bodies and matching baggage doors. Green was the color of the roof and flex trucks—the latter which were fitted with brass journal boxes. Centered on the sides near the car roof was a brass plate reading "POCAHONTAS," while smaller "CLUB 4340" and "AMERICAN FLYER" plates were mounted below the windows.

VG-C6	EX-C7	LN-C8	Scarcity
60	175	250	5

4340 CLUB (Type II): Some cars are reported to exist with brass plates reading "AMERICAN LEGION" rather than "POCAHONTAS."

VG-C6	EX-C7	LN-C8	Scarcity
Too rarely traded to establish accurate pricing.			

4340 CLUB (Type III): Red bodies and darker red roofs were used on other versions of this car. The sliding baggage door of these cars matched the roof. Centered on the sides near the car roof was a brass plate reading "HAMILTONIAN," while smaller "CLUB 4340" and "AMERICAN FLYER" plates were mounted below the windows. The car rode on gray flex trucks with brass journal boxes.

VG-C6	EX-C7	LN-C8	Scarcity
50	150	225	5

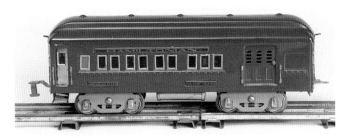

4340 CLUB (Type IV): This car was a near duplicate of the Type III, except the baggage doors were painted the same color as the body.

VG-C6	EX-C7	LN-C8	Scarcity
50	150	225	5

4341 PULLMAN: This enameled 1928-1932 passenger car measured 14 inches long. Fourteen windows were formed from each side and brass trim decorated them. Two brass spring-loaded passenger doors were installed in each side as well. A brass step hung beneath each passenger door. The car was equipped with interior illumination.

4341 PULLMAN (Type I): Some cars had Rookie Tan bodies with green roofs and flex trucks—the latter were fitted with brass journal boxes. Centered on the sides near the car roof was a brass plate reading "POCAHONTAS," while smaller "PULLMAN 4341" and "AMERICAN FLYER" plates were mounted below the windows.

VG-C6	EX-C7	LN-C8	Scarcity
60	175	250	5

4341 PULLMAN (Type II): Some cars are reported to exist with brass plates reading "AMERICAN LEGION" rather than "POCAHONTAS."

VG-C6	EX-C7	LN-C8	Scarcity
Too rarely traded to establish accurate pricing.			

4341 PULLMAN (Type III): Cars have been reported that nearly duplicate the Type I, except for the nameplates. On these cars the upper plate reads "AMERICAN FLYER," while each of the lower plates is marked "PULLMAN 4341." This car has gray set trucks and gray truss rods.

VG-C6	EX-C7	LN-C8	Scarcity
60	175	250	5

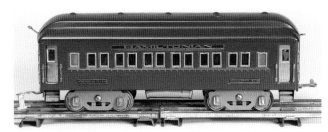

4341 PULLMAN (Type IV): Red bodies and darker red roofs were used on other versions of this car. Centered on the sides near the car roof was a brass plate reading "HAMILTONIAN," while smaller "PULLMAN 4341" and "AMERICAN FLYER" plates were mounted below the windows. The car rode on gray flex trucks with brass journal boxes.

VG-C6	EX-C7	LN-C8	Scarcity
50	150	225	5

4342 OBSERVATION: This enameled 1928-1932 passenger car measured 14 inches long. Eight windows were formed from each side and brass trim decorated them. A brass passenger door was installed in each side as well. A brass step hung beneath each passenger door. On the opposite end from the passenger doors was a brass railed observation platform. The railing was decorated with a plate reading "AMERICAN FLYER LIMITED." A spring-loaded brass door led from the platform, which was illuminated, to the interior of the car that was also lighted.

4342 OBSERVATION (Type I): Some cars had Rookie Tan bodies with green roofs and flex trucks—the latter were fitted with brass journal boxes. Centered on the sides near the car roof was a brass plate reading "POCAHONTAS," while smaller "OBSERVATION 4342" and "AMERICAN FLYER" plates were mounted below the windows.

VG-C6	EX-C7	LN-C8	Scarcity
60	175	250	5

Values for each condition are in U.S. dollars. | **Scarcity** = Scale from 1-8 with 8 being the hardest to find.

347

4342 OBSERVATION (Type II): Some cars are reported to exist with brass plates reading "AMERICAN LEGION" rather than "POCAHONTAS."

VG-C6	EX-C7	LN-C8	Scarcity
Too rarely traded to establish accurate pricing.			

4342 OBSERVATION (Type III): Cars have been reported that nearly duplicate the Type I, except for the nameplates. On these cars the upper plate reads "AMERICAN FLYER," while each of the lower plates is marked "OBSERVATION 4342." This car has gray set trucks and gray truss rods.

VG-C6	EX-C7	LN-C8	Scarcity
60	175	250	5

4342 OBSERVATION (Type IV): Red bodies and darker red roofs were used on other versions of this car. Centered on the sides near the car roof was a brass plate reading "HAMILTONIAN," while smaller "OBSERVATION 4342" and "AMERICAN FLYER" plates were mounted below the windows. The car rode on gray flex trucks with brass journal boxes.

VG-C6	EX-C7	LN-C8	Scarcity
50	150	225	5

4343 DINING: This enameled 1928-1932 dining car measured 14 inches long. Six large and two small windows were formed from each side and brass trim decorated them. Two brass spring-loaded passenger doors were installed in each side as well. A brass step hung beneath each passenger door. The car was equipped with interior illumination.

4343 DINING (Type I): Some cars had Rookie Tan bodies with green roofs and flex trucks—the latter were fitted with brass journal boxes. Centered on the sides near the car roof was a brass plate reading "POCAHONTAS," while smaller "OBSERVATION 4343" and "AMERICAN FLYER" plates were mounted below the windows.

VG-C6	EX-C7	LN-C8	Scarcity
100	200	300	6

4343 DINING (Type II): Some cars are reported to exist with brass plates reading "AMERICAN LEGION" rather than "POCAHONTAS."

VG-C6	EX-C7	LN-C8	Scarcity
Too rarely traded to establish accurate pricing.			

4343 DINING (Type III): Similar to Type I except "AMERICAN FLYER LINES" plates rather than "POCAHONTAS." Gray set trucks and truss rods were used on this car.

VG-C6	EX-C7	LN-C8	Scarcity
100	200	300	6

4343 DINING (Type IV): Matches 4342 Type IV.

VG-C6	EX-C7	LN-C8	Scarcity
Too rarely traded to establish accurate pricing.			

4350 CLUB: This 14-inch long illuminated car was offered in 1931. Its bluish-green enameled body was capped with a red roof. Five raised humps, representing ventilators, were pressed into the roof. A baggage door, painted to match the roof, and a solid-brass door with matching step was installed on each side. Ten full windows and one restroom window were punched from either side of the car. Above the windows was an "AMERICAN FLYER LINES" decal, and below the windows a pair of "PULLMAN" decals. Beneath each car were red-painted truss rods and the rubber-stamped number "4350."

VG-C6	EX-C7	LN-C8	Scarcity
50	125	175	5

4351 PULLMAN: This 1931 Pullman matches the 4350 listed above, and 4352 listed below.

VG-C6	EX-C7	LN-C8	Scarcity
50	125	175	5

4352 OBSERVATION: This 1931 Observation car matches the 4350 and 4351 listed above.

VG-C6	EX-C7	LN-C8	Scarcity
50	125	175	5

4380 CLUB: This massive 19-inch long passenger car was cataloged from 1928 through 1932, except for 1930. Three lamps illuminated the interior, the light pouring from the 14 brass trimmed windows on each side. Two sliding doors, matching the flanks, and two spring-loaded brass doors were installed in each side. Beneath the car were brass battery boxes and air tanks. Brass was also used for the simulated diaphragms on each end as well as the handrails adjacent to each door.

4380 CLUB (Type I): This car was dark blue and rode on gray flex trucks. Centered above the windows was a brass plate marked "FLYING COLONEL," while below the windows were three smaller plates reading "AMERICAN FLYER," "MADISON" and "CLUB 4380."

VG-C6	EX-C7	LN-C8	Scarcity
175	425	600	7

4380 CLUB (Type II): Similar to Type I, but with Rookie Tan sides and baggage door, green roof and black trucks.

VG-C6	EX-C7	LN-C8	Scarcity
175	425	600	7

4380 CLUB (Type III): Similar to Type I, but with Rookie Tan sides, green baggage door and roof. Upper plate reads "POCAHONTAS." Center lower plate reads "ANNAPOLIS," while small plates at either end are marked "AMERICAN FLYER" and "CLUB 4380." Under the car were brass truss rods and gray flex trucks.

VG-C6	EX-C7	LN-C8	Scarcity
175	425	600	7

4381 PULLMAN: Matching the 4380 and 4382, this massive 19-inch long passenger car was also cataloged from 1928 through 1932, except for 1930. Three lamps illuminated the interior. Eighteen brass-trimmed windows and two spring-loaded brass doors were installed in each side. Beneath the car were brass battery boxes and air tanks. Brass was also used for the simulated diaphragms on each end as well as the handrails on either side of every door.

4381 PULLMAN (Type I): This car was dark blue and rode on gray flex trucks. Centered above the windows was a large brass plate marked "FLYING COLONEL," while below the windows were three smaller plates reading "AMERICAN FLYER," "HANCOCK" and "PULLMAN 4381."

VG-C6	EX-C7	LN-C8	Scarcity
175	425	600	7

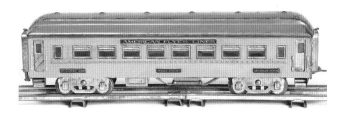

4381 PULLMAN (Type II): Similar to Type I, but with Rookie Tan sides and green roof. Large upper nameplate reads "AMERICAN FLYER LINES," while a center lower plate carries the name "WEST POINT." The car was equipped with gray flex trucks.

VG-C6	EX-C7	LN-C8	Scarcity
175	425	600	7

4381 PULLMAN (Type III): Same as Type II, but with a "HANCOCK" nameplate centered below the windows.

VG-C6	EX-C7	LN-C8	Scarcity
175	425	600	7

4381 PULLMAN (Type IV): This car had the coloration of the Type II, but the markings of the Type I. It rode on black flex trucks.

VG-C6	EX-C7	LN-C8	Scarcity
175	425	600	7

4382 OBSERVATION: Matching the 4380 and 4381, this impressive 19-inch long passenger car was also cataloged from 1928 through 1932, except for 1930. Two lamps illuminated the interior and two more the observation platform. Four large and nine small brass-trimmed windows and a spring-loaded brass door were installed in each side. Beneath the car were brass battery boxes and air tanks. Brass was also used for the simulated diaphragms on each end as well as the handrails on either side of every door. Brass was used as well to form the observation platform railing.

4382 OBSERVATION (Type I): This car was dark blue and rode on gray flex trucks. Centered above the windows was a large brass plate marked "FLYING COLONEL," while below the windows were three smaller plates reading "AMERICAN FLYER," "ADAMS" and "OBSERVATION 4382."

VG-C6	EX-C7	LN-C8	Scarcity
175	425	600	7

Values for each condition are in U.S. dollars. | Scarcity = Scale from 1-8 with 8 being the hardest to find.

349

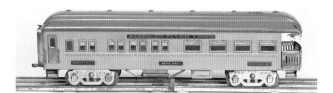

4382 OBSERVATION (Type II): Similar to Type I, but with Rookie Tan sides and green roof. Rather than "ADAMS," the lower center plate reads "ARMY-NAVY."

VG-C6	EX-C7	LN-C8	Scarcity
175	425	600	7

4382 OBSERVATION (Type III): This car also had Rookie Tan sides and a green roof. The large upper plate was marked "AMERICAN FLYER LINES" while the center lower plate read "HANCOCK."

VG-C6	EX-C7	LN-C8	Scarcity
175	425	600	7

4390 CLUB: This car and its companions were the top of the line for American Flyer passenger cars. Between 1928 and 1934, these 19-inch cars were offered in two major variations—enameled and plated. The former termed the "Presidents Special," while the latter was part of the coveted Mayflower set. Spring-loaded brass doors, brass simulated diaphragms, brass handrails and air tanks or truss rods, even a brass battery box which held an on-off switch for the interior lights were all part of the trim of these cars.

The club car featured 14 brass-trimmed windows, a brass passenger door and a baggage door on each side. Nameplates sometimes vary from those listed below, with no effect on value.

4390 CLUB (Type I): The body of this car was Rolls Royce Blue, while the roof and sliding baggage door were a dark blue. Centered above the windows was a large brass plate reading "PRESIDENT'S SPECIAL." Centered beneath the windows was a small plate reading "WEST POINT," flanked by smaller plates bearing "AMERICAN FLYER" and "CLUB 4390" legends. Beneath the car hung brass air tanks. The car rode on chromed six-wheel flex trucks with red wheels and brass journal boxes.

VG-C6	EX-C7	LN-C8	Scarcity
275	550	800	7

4390 CLUB (Type II): Similar to Type I, but the large upper nameplate emblazoned "AMERICAN FLYER LINES" while each of the smaller plates read "PULLMAN." Rather than brass air tanks the car was equipped with brass truss rods. The sides of the wheels of this car were not painted red.

VG-C6	EX-C7	LN-C8	Scarcity
275	550	800	7

4390 CLUB (Type III): This spectacular car was similar to the Type I, but rather than being painted, it was chrome plated. Beware of forgeries.

VG-C6	EX-C7	LN-C8	Scarcity
550	1,100	2,000	8

4390 CLUB (Type IV): This car was virtually a duplicate of the Type III, except rather than air tanks it had truss rods. Beware of forgeries.

VG-C6	EX-C7	LN-C8	Scarcity
550	1,100	2,000	7

4391 PULLMAN: This 1928-1934 was a matching companion to the 4390 described above. It had 18 brass-trimmed windows and two spring-loaded brass doors per side. Nameplates sometimes vary from those listed below.

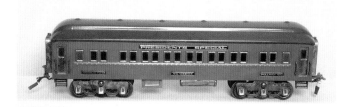

4391 PULLMAN (Type I): The body of this car was Rolls Royce Blue, while the roof and sliding baggage door were a dark blue. Centered above the windows was a large brass plate reading "PRESIDENT'S SPECIAL." Centered beneath the windows was a small plate reading "ACADEMY," flanked by smaller plates bearing "AMERICAN FLYER" and "PULLMAN 4391" legends. Beneath the car hung brass air tanks. The car rode on chromed six-wheel flex trucks with red wheels and brass journal boxes.

VG-C6	EX-C7	LN-C8	Scarcity
275	550	800	7

4391 PULLMAN (Type II): The upper nameplate of this car was marked "AMERICAN FLYER LINES" rather than "President's Special," and beneath the car were truss rods rather than air tanks.

VG-C6	EX-C7	LN-C8	Scarcity
275	550	800	7

4391 PULLMAN (Type III): Same as Type I except the small center plate read "ANNAPOLIS" rather than "Academy."

VG-C6	EX-C7	LN-C8	Scarcity
275	550	800	7

4391 PULLMAN (Type IV): This spectacular car was similar to the Type I, but rather than being painted, it was chrome plated. Beware of forgeries.

VG-C6	EX-C7	LN-C8	Scarcity
550	1,100	2,000	8

4391 PULLMAN (Type V): This car was virtually a duplicate of the Type III, except rather than air tanks it had truss rods. Beware of forgeries.

VG-C6	EX-C7	LN-C8	Scarcity
550	1,100	2,000	8

4392 OBSERVATION: This 1928-1934 was a matching companion to the 4390 and 4391 described above. It had 13 brass-trimmed windows and spring-loaded brass doors on each side. At the rear of the car was an illuminated observation platform with a brass railing. To this railing was attached a sign reading "AMERICAN FLYER LIMITED." Nameplates sometimes vary from those listed below.

4392 OBSERVATION (Type I): The body of this car was Rolls Royce Blue, while the roof and sliding baggage door were a dark blue. Centered above the windows was a large brass plate reading "PRESIDENT'S SPECIAL." Centered beneath the windows was a small plate reading "ARMY-NAVY" flanked by smaller plates bearing "AMERICAN FLYER" and "OBSERVATION 4392" legends. Beneath the car hung brass air tanks. The car rode on chromed six-wheel flex trucks with red wheels and brass journal boxes.

VG-C6	EX-C7	LN-C8	Scarcity
275	550	800	7

4392 OBSERVATION (Type II): Similar to Type I, but the large upper nameplate emblazoned "AMERICAN FLYER LINES" while each of the smaller plates read "PULLMAN." Rather than brass air tanks the car was equipped with brass truss rods. The sides of the wheels of this car were not painted red.

VG-C6	EX-C7	LN-C8	Scarcity
275	550	800	7

4392 OBSERVATION (Type III): This spectacular car was similar to the Type I, but rather than being painted, it was chrome plated. Beware of forgeries.

VG-C6	EX-C7	LN-C8	Scarcity
550	1,100	2,000	8

4392 OBSERVATION (Type IV): This car was virtually a duplicate of the Type III, except rather than air tanks it had truss rods. Beware of forgeries.

VG-C6	EX-C7	LN-C8	Scarcity
550	1,100	2,000	8

4393 DINER: This 1928-1934 was a companion to the 4390, 4391 and 4392 described above. It had 10 brass-trimmed windows and two spring-loaded brass doors on each side. Nameplates sometimes vary from those listed below.

4393 DINER (Type I): The body of this car was Rolls Royce Blue, while the roof and sliding baggage door were a dark blue. Centered above the windows was a large brass plate reading "PRESIDENT'S SPECIAL." Centered beneath the windows was a small plate reading "ANNAPOLIS" flanked by smaller plates bearing "AMERICAN FLYER" and "DINER 4393" legends. Beneath the car hung brass air tanks. The car rode on chromed six-wheel flex trucks with red wheels and brass journal boxes.

VG-C6	EX-C7	LN-C8	Scarcity
275	550	800	7

4393 DINER (Type II): Same as Type I, but center lower nameplate reads "ACADEMY."

VG-C6	EX-C7	LN-C8	Scarcity
275	550	800	7

4393 DINER (Type III): Identical to Type I, but with "WEST POINT" nameplate centered beneath windows.

VG-C6	EX-C7	LN-C8	Scarcity
275	550	800	7

4393 DINER (Type IV): The upper nameplate of this car was marked "AMERICAN FLYER LINES" rather than "President's Special," and beneath the car were truss rods rather than air tanks. The wheels were not painted red.

VG-C6	EX-C7	LN-C8	Scarcity
275	550	800	7

4393 DINER (Type V): This spectacular car was similar to the Type I, but rather than being painted, it was chrome plated. Beware of forgeries.

VG-C6	EX-C7	LN-C8	Scarcity
550	1,100	2,000	8

4393 DINER (Type VI): This car was virtually a duplicate of the Type V, except rather than air tanks it had truss rods. Beware of forgeries.

VG-C6	EX-C7	LN-C8	Scarcity
550	1,100	2,000	8

Values for each condition are in U.S. dollars. | **Scarcity** = Scale from 1-8 with 8 being the hardest to find.

Ives Cars with American Flyer Bodies

In 1928 and 1929, Ives sold passenger cars that were built using American Flyer bodies combined with Ives trucks and couplers. These 19-inch long, 12-wheel illuminated cars came in three styles: Club, Parlor and Observation. All had brass air tanks, battery boxes, steps and simulated diaphragms. They are listed below for reference. Beware; excellent reproductions of these cars have been produced.

241 CLUB CAR: This car had 14 brass-framed windows, a sliding baggage door and a spring-loaded passenger door on each side. Above the windows was centered a brass nameplate reading "THE IVES RAILWAY LINES." Below the windows were three smaller plates, the legends on which read, left to right "MADE IN THE IVES SHOPS," "CLUB CAR" and "241."

241 CLUB CAR (Type I): Black, with red roof and trucks.

VG-C6	EX-C7	LN-C8	Scarcity
600	1,500	2,000	8

241 CLUB CAR (Type II): Green, with green roof and black trucks.

VG-C6	EX-C7	LN-C8	Scarcity
1,200	2,000	2,600	8

241 CLUB CAR (Type III): Orange, with black roof and trucks.

VG-C6	EX-C7	LN-C8	Scarcity
1,200	2,000	2,600	8

241 CLUB CAR (Type IV): Copper-plated body. Nickel roof, trim and trucks.

VG-C6	EX-C7	LN-C8	Scarcity
1,200	2,000	2,600	8

242 PARLOR CAR: This car had 10 brass-framed windows and two spring-loaded passenger doors on each side. Above the windows was centered a brass nameplate reading "THE IVES RAILWAY LINES." Below the windows were three smaller plates, the legends on which read, left to right "MADE IN THE IVES SHOPS," "PARLOR CAR" and "242."

242 PARLOR CAR (Type I): Black, with red roof and trucks.

VG-C6	EX-C7	LN-C8	Scarcity
600	1,500	2,000	8

242 PARLOR CAR (Type II): Green, with green roof and black trucks.

VG-C6	EX-C7	LN-C8	Scarcity
1,200	2,000	2,600	8

242 PARLOR CAR (Type III): Orange, with black roof and trucks.

VG-C6	EX-C7	LN-C8	Scarcity
1,200	2,000	2,600	8

242 PARLOR CAR (Type IV): Copper-plated body. Nickel roof, trim and trucks.

VG-C6	EX-C7	LN-C8	Scarcity
1,200	2,000	2,600	8

243 OBSERVATION: This car had 13 brass-framed windows and a spring-loaded passenger door on each side. Above the windows was centered a brass nameplate reading "THE IVES RAILWAY LINES." Below the windows were three smaller plates, the legends on which read, left to right "MADE IN THE IVES SHOPS," "PARLOR CAR" and "242." A brass-railed observation platform was at the rear of the car.

243 OBSERVATION (Type I): Black, with red roof and trucks.

VG-C6	EX-C7	LN-C8	Scarcity
600	1,500	2,000	8

243 OBSERVATION (Type II): Green, with green roof and black trucks.

VG-C6	EX-C7	LN-C8	Scarcity
1,200	2,000	2,600	8

243 OBSERVATION (Type III): Orange, with black roof and trucks.

VG-C6	EX-C7	LN-C8	Scarcity
1,200	2,000	2,600	8

243 OBSERVATION (Type IV): Copper-plated body. Nickel roof, trim and trucks.

VG-C6	EX-C7	LN-C8	Scarcity
1,200	2,000	2,600	8

WIDE-GAUGE FREIGHT CARS

American Flyer entered the Wide-Gauge market in 1925. The initial rolling stock offerings were passenger cars, but these were joined in 1926 by four freight cars: a caboose, a boxcar, a gondola car and a stock car. However, though they had American Flyer trucks, these cars actually all utilized bodies made—and apparently decorated—by Lionel. In 1927 that changed, and Flyer began producing their own cars. In addition to the four car types previously offered, a flatcar joined the lineup.

Freight cars remained separate sale only items until 1928, when they were offered in sets as well. Also new in 1928 was the first Wide-Gauge tank car to be offered by Flyer, the 4010.

In 1931, the final new body style was introduced—the hopper car. Because of its late debut, the hopper tends to be harder to find today than the other freight cars.

It's believed that W.O. Coleman chose to exit the Wide-Gauge market as early as 1933—and that only existing inventory was sold in the following years.

Values for each condition are in U.S. dollars. | **Scarcity** = Scale from 1-8 with 8 being the hardest to find.

353

Box, Stock and Automobile Cars

4005 STOCK CAR: American Flyer first offered a Wide-Gauge stock car in 1926. This car was in fact an unlettered green Lionel 13 stock car. The car rode on black flex trucks and lacked brakewheels and journal boxes. The underside of the car was rubber stamped "AMERICAN FLYER LINES No. 4005."

VG-C6	EX-C7	LN-C8	Scarcity
75	175	325	5

4008 BOXCAR: Another 1926 Flyer offering of Lionel origin was this Wide-Gauge boxcar. The orange car was a Lionel 14, and even included the Lionel "CM & ST P" and "98237" rubber stamping on the sides. Underneath, between the two black flex trucks, was rubber stamped "AMERICAN FLYER LINES No. 4008." The car did not have brakewheels or journal boxes.

VG-C6	EX-C7	LN-C8	Scarcity
75	175	325	5

4008 BOXCAR: In 1927, American Flyer developed their own 14-inch boxcar. The car body was painted yellowish orange—roofs in a variety of colors were used.

4008 BOXCAR (Type I): One of the initial offerings of the car had doors painted to match the body—its roof was painted orange and its frame black. Both sides of the car were decorated with three brass plates. The three plates read: "OVER 6 MILLION HAPPY OWNERS," "LENGTH 46 FT/WIDTH 10 FT/HEIGHT 8 FT/CAPACITY-140,000 LBS./CAPACITY-3680 CU. FT." and "4008 American Flyer LINES."

The car rode on black flex trucks with brass journal boxes.

VG-C6	EX-C7	LN-C8	Scarcity
100	225	425	4

4008 BOXCAR (Type II): Other cars had red roofs and lacked the "6 MILLION" plate, instead having a "BUILT BY 'American Flyer' LINES" plate.

VG-C6	EX-C7	LN-C8	Scarcity
100	250	450	4

4008 BOXCAR (Type III): Other cars were near duplicates of the Type II except they were equipped with turquoise rather than red roofs.

VG-C6	EX-C7	LN-C8	Scarcity
100	250	400	4

4018 AUTOMOBILE CAR: This 14-inch long boxcar, dubbed an automobile car in Flyer literature, was offered from 1928 through 1936. The sides of the car were painted Rookie Tan and the roof and doors were turquoise blue top or blue green. The doors and roofs don't always match, but the door guides were normally black. There was one brass ladder on the right end of each side and on each end.

4018 AUTOMOBILE CAR (Type I): The early cars were adorned with three brass plates on each side. One of these plates bore the inscription "OVER 6 MILLION HAPPY OWNERS," another the legend "LENGTH 46 FT/WIDTH 10 FT/HEIGHT 8 FT/CAPACITY— 140,000 LBS./CAPACITY—3680 CU. FT." and the third was marked "4018 American Flyer Lines." This car had a blue-green roof and rode on gray flex trucks. The journal boxes of the trucks, as well as the U-shaped steps, were brass, as was the brakewheel on each end of the car.

VG-C6	EX-C7	LN-C8	Scarcity
150	280	400	4

4018 AUTOMOBILE CAR (Type II): Virtually identical cars were made with but one brakewheel and topped with a turquoise blue roof.

VG-C6	EX-C7	LN-C8	Scarcity
150	280	400	4

4018 AUTOMOBILE CAR (Type III): Some of the blue-roofed cars lacked the "6 Million" plate, having in its place a plate reading "BUILT BY 'American Flyer' LINES."

VG-C6	EX-C7	LN-C8	Scarcity
150	280	400	4

4018 AUTOMOBILE CAR (Type IV): Later cars were near-duplicates of the Type I, but for the single brakewheel—and the replacement of the "6 Million plate" with one reading "OVER 7 MILLION HAPPY OWNERS."

VG-C6	EX-C7	LN-C8	Scarcity
150	280	400	4

4018 AUTOMOBILE CAR (Type V): Turquoise blue roofs were also used on cars with "7 MILLION" plates. These cars had blue-green doors.

4018 AUTOMOBILE CAR (Type VI): Near the end of production of the 4018, the roof and door guides were painted blue-green. The cars continued to have one brass brakewheel

Values for each condition are in U.S. dollars. | Scarcity = Scale from 1-8 with 8 being the hardest to find.

355

and on each side were three plates. However, the lettering on the plates now read as follows: "OVER 8 MILLION HAPPY OWNERS," "LENGTH 46 FT/WIDTH 10 FT/HEIGHT 8 FT/CAPACITY-140,000 LBS./CAPACITY-3680 CU. FT." in five lines, and "BUILT BY 'American Flyer' LINES." Since the model number designation was now absent from the car sides, on the bottom was rubber stamped "4018."

VG-C6	EX-C7	LN-C8	Scarcity
150	280	400	4

4020 STOCK CAR: This attractive 14-inch long two-tone blue stock car was offered from 1928 through 1936.

4020 STOCK CAR (Type I): The cars that are believed to be the earliest of this series were painted two-tone Rolls Royce blue. The roof was dark blue, while the sides and doors were a lighter shade. The car was fitted with gray flex trucks and trimmed with brass journal boxes, U-shaped steps, and on each end was a brass brakewheel. Two brass plates on each side reading "OVER 6 MILLION HAPPY OWNERS" and "4020 American Flyer Lines" provided further decoration.

VG-C6	EX-C7	LN-C8	Scarcity
150	280	400	4

4020 STOCK CAR (Type II): Some of the cars had their doors painted the same dark blue as the roof. These cars also had only one brakewheel. They used the same "OVER 6 MILLION HAPPY OWNERS" plate and "4020 American Flyer Lines" plates as the Type I cars.

VG-C6	EX-C7	LN-C8	Scarcity
150	280	400	4

4020 STOCK CAR (Type III): The doors on this car were painted the same dark blue as the roof. The two brass plates on each side were marked "LENGTH 46 FT/WIDTH 10 FT/HEIGHT 8 FT/CAPACITY-140,000 LBS./CAPACITY-3680 CU. FT." and "4020 American Flyer Lines." The car had one brass brakewheel and gray U-shaped steps. It rode on gray flex trucks with brass journal boxes.

VG-C6	EX-C7	LN-C8	Scarcity
150	280	400	4

4020 STOCK CAR (Type IV): Rather than having an "OVER 6 MILLION HAPPY OWNERS" plate, this car instead had a "LENGTH 46 FT/WIDTH 10 FT/HEIGHT 8 FT/CAPACITY-140,000 LBS./CAPACITY-3680 CU. FT." plate. The "4020" was accordingly rubber stamped on the bottom between the two set trucks. The doors on this car were painted the same color as the roof.

VG-C6	EX-C7	LN-C8	Scarcity
150	280	400	4

4677 AUTOMOBILE CAR: This uncataloged car was identical to the 4018, except for its brass nameplates. The plates on this car were marked "NATION/WIDE/LINES," "LENGTH 46 FT/WIDTH 10 FT/HEIGHT 8 FT/CAPACITY-140,000 LBS./CAPACITY-3680 CU. FT.," and "4677."

VG-C6	EX-C7	LN-C8	Scarcity
Too rarely traded to establish values.			

20-192 MERCHANDISE CAR: In 1928-1929, Ives, as their Merchandise car, sold the 14-inch American Flyer automobile car. Naturally, these cars were equipped with Ives trucks and had Ives nameplates. The three brass plates included an upper left nameplate reading "THE IVES RAILWAY LINES," a lower right plate numbered

"20-192" and a lower left plate reading "LENGTH 46 FT/ WIDTH 10 FT/HEIGHT 8 FT/CAPACITY-140,000 LBS./ CAPACITY-3680 CU. FT." These cars were equipped with short versions of the Snake Track Pull coupler.

20-192 MERCHANDISE CAR (Type I): The uncataloged 1928 version of the car had a pea-green body and dark-red roof.

VG-C6	EX-C7	LN-C8	Scarcity
150	350	450	6

20-192 MERCHANDISE CAR (Type II): In 1929, the car was shown in the Ives catalog and now had a yellow body and blue-green roof.

VG-C6	EX-C7	LN-C8	Scarcity
125	250	350	6

20-192-C CIRCUS EQUIPMENT CAR (Type I): Another version of the yellow 1929 car came with a red roof and was rubber stamped "The Ives R.R. Circus."

VG-C6	EX-C7	LN-C8	Scarcity
650	1,200	2,000	8

20-192-C CIRCUS EQUIPMENT CAR (TYPE II): Perhaps even more difficult to locate is a second version of the yellow and red 1929 Circus Equipment Car, which was completely devoid of the rubber-stamped circus markings.

VG-C6	EX-C7	LN-C8	Scarcity
			Too scarcely traded to establish accurate values.

20-193 STOCK CAR: The 14-inch American Flyer stock car was also incorporated into the Ives product line. Two brass plates were installed on each side of these cars, the left plate bearing the legend "THE IVES/RAILWAY LINES" while the right plate bore the number "20-193." The cars had Ives trucks and Snake Track Pull couplers. Brass ladders and journals were used.

20-193 STOCK CAR (Type I): The 1928 version of the car had a pea-green body and a red roof. Two brakewheels were installed.

VG-C6	EX-C7	LN-C8	Scarcity
150	300	400	6

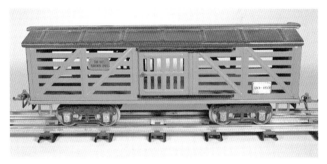

20-193 STOCK CAR (Type II): In 1929, the color of the body changed to orange and the roof to a darker maroon-red. Only one brakewheel was mounted.

VG-C6	EX-C7	LN-C8	Scarcity
125	225	325	6

20-193-C CIRCUS ANIMAL CAR: Also offered in 1929 was this circus animal car. Essentially the same as the 20-193, these yellow cars with maroon-red roofs were rubber stamped "THE IVES RAILWAY LINES" low on each side of the doors. The brass plates affixed to each side were identical to those on the other 20-193 cars.

VG-C6	EX-C7	LN-C8	Scarcity
650	1,200	1,600	8

WIDE-GAUGE FREIGHT CARS

Cabooses

4000 CABOOSE: This uncataloged caboose is identical to the yellow and brown 4011 except it has two number plates reading "4000" rather than 4011 and "Built by American Flyer Lines."

4011 CABOOSE (Type I): As with all 1926 American Flyer freight cars, the caboose offered in that year had a body built by Lionel. The Lionel 17 body was painted red with a black roof. Like 17, the car was stamped on each side with "NYC & HRRRR" and "4351." While modified Lionel hook couplers were used, the car rode on black American Flyer flex trucks, without journal boxes. The trucks were mounted with solid rivets. The underside of the car is rubber stamped "AMERICAN FLYER LINES No. 4011."

VG-C6	EX-C7	LN-C8	Scarcity
75	175	325	7

4011 CABOOSE: Beginning in 1927 and continuing through 1932, the 4011 was produced with an American Flyer-built body, measuring 14 inches long. Like the 1926 edition, the later 4011 versions lacked illumination.

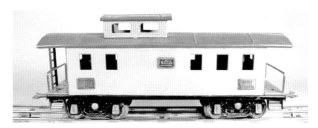

4011 CABOOSE (Type II): As first offered, the Flyer-designed caboose had pale yellow sides and the roof of both the car and cupola was brown. The body was mounted to a black-painted frame. Six window openings were punched in each side of the body. At either end of the body were brass end railings and beneath their platforms brass steps. A brass ladder adorned one end.

On each side of the car were three brass plates: Etched on each plate was a distinctive legend: "BUILT BY 'American Flyer' LINES," "OVER 6 MILLION HAPPY OWNERS" and "4011 American Flyer Lines." The flex trucks the car rode on had black sideframes with brass journal boxes.

VG-C6	EX-C7	LN-C8	Scarcity
150	325	600	6

4011 CABOOSE (Type III): Another version of the car was almost identical to the Type II listed above, except it had only five rather than six windows on each side.

VG-C6	EX-C7	LN-C8	Scarcity
Too rarely traded to establish accurate pricing.			

4011 CABOOSE (Type IV):  Some of the yellow-sided, six-window cabooses had brass trim inserts installed in their window openings. The cars also had brass handrails on each corner and a brass smokejack on the roof.

VG-C6	EX-C7	LN-C8	Scarcity
Too rarely traded to establish accurate pricing.			

4011 CABOOSE (Type V): Some of the cars were produced with red rather than yellow bodies and cupola.

4011 CABOOSE (Type IV)

Values for each condition are in U.S. dollars. | **Scarcity** = Scale from 1-8 with 8 being the hardest to find.

359

These cars had six windows on each side and were decorated with three etched-brass nameplates: "BUILT BY 'American Flyer' LINES," "OVER 7 MILLION HAPPY OWNERS" and "4011 American Flyer Lines." The roof of both the body and cupola were painted a darker red. The car did not have a smokejack, but the hole continued to be stamped for it in the roof. The car had brass passenger-car style steps, roof ladder and end railings. It rode on gray flex trucks with brass journal boxes.

VG-C6	EX-C7	LN-C8	Scarcity
100	150	250	4

4011 CABOOSE (Type VI): Some of the red cars had brass window trim and were equipped with a brass smokejack.

VG-C6	EX-C7	LN-C8	Scarcity
100	150	250	4

4011 CABOOSE (Type VII): Other red cabooses were equipped with simple U-shaped steps and rode on gray set-type trucks. These cars had brass window trim and had only two etched brass nameplates. The legends on the plates read: "BUILT BY 'American Flyer' LINES" and "4011 American Flyer Lines." The underside of the car was rubber stamped with "4011." The end railings of the car were painted red.

VG-C6	EX-C7	LN-C8	Scarcity
40	90	175	4

4011 CABOOSE (Type VIII): Black roofs were installed on both the car body and cupola of some of the red cabooses. These cars were fitted with brass journal-equipped black flex trucks. These cars had three etched-brass plates that read: "BUILT BY 'American Flyer' LINES," "OVER 6 MILLION HAPPY OWNERS" and "4011 American Flyer Lines."

VG-C6	EX-C7	LN-C8	Scarcity
Too rarely traded to establish accurate pricing.			

4021 CABOOSE: Introduced in 1928, this 14-inch long illuminated caboose remained in the American Flyer line through 1936. Most variations of this car are two-tone red with brass trim.

The sides are red with a darker red roof on both car body and cupola. Color of base matches roof on some cars, while on others it matches the sides. Also, the shade of red on the roof varies in darkness for those cabooses that are two-tone. Brass handrails on each corner, brass platform rail and base plated, and brass ladder on each end. Two-piece brass railing on cupola, brass smokejack and brass window trim.

4021 CABOOSE (Type I): Brass passenger car-style steps and grey flex trucks are found on many of these cars. Brass platform rails, smokejack, window trim, ladders, and journal boxes decorated the car. The three etched-brass plates installed on the car bore the

legends "BUILT BY 'American Flyer' LINES," "OVER 6 MILLION HAPPY OWNERS" and "4021 American Flyer Lines."

VG-C6	EX-C7	LN-C8	Scarcity
75	150	300	3

4021 CABOOSE (Type II): Also common is an identical caboose, but for its red-painted steps.

VG-C6	EX-C7	LN-C8	Scarcity
75	150	300	3

4021 CABOOSE (Type III): Some of the cars with brass steps had only two nameplates. They read "BUILT BY 'American Flyer' LINES" and "4021 American Flyer Lines."

VG-C6	EX-C7	LN-C8	Scarcity
75	150	300	3

4021 CABOOSE (Type IV): Gray U-shaped steps were installed on some of the illuminated cars. These cars had "4021" rubber stamped in white on their underside and were fitted with two etched-brass nameplates. The plates read "BUILT BY 'American Flyer' LINES" and "4021 American Flyer Lines."

VG-C6	EX-C7	LN-C8	Scarcity
75	150	300	3

4021 CABOOSE (Type V): Nearly identical to the Type I car was this caboose, differing by having two "BUILT BY 'American Flyer' LINES" plates and an "OVER 6 MILLION HAPPY OWNERS" plate.

VG-C6	EX-C7	LN-C8	Scarcity
75	150	300	3

4021 CABOOSE (Type VI): Also similar to a Type I caboose was this car, whose decoration omitted the brass window trim.

VG-C6	EX-C7	LN-C8	Scarcity
75	150	300	3

4021 CABOOSE (Type VII): Gray, rather than brass, steps distinguish this car from the Type V car listed above.

VG-C6	EX-C7	LN-C8	Scarcity
75	150	300	3

4021 CABOOSE (Type VIII): This variation was painted a uniform overall red color rather than the two-tone versions listed above. Three etched brass plates were installed on each side of the car—two "BUILT BY 'American Flyer' LINES" and a single "OVER 8 MILLION HAPPY OWNERS." The car rode on gray set trucks and was equipped with U-shaped steps. Lacking a smokejack, this car can be further identified by a differing style of ladder and by the installation of four brass handrails on the cupola roof.

VG-C6	EX-C7	LN-C8	Scarcity
75	150	300	4

4677 CABOOSE: Essentially identical to the 4021 Type I caboose, the roofs of this uncataloged car were painted a darker shade of red. The three etched-brass plates on each side were unique as well. Two were marked "4677" and the third with "NATION/WIDE/LINES." The car notably had a ladder on only one end.

VG-C6	EX-C7	LN-C8	Scarcity
Too rarely traded to establish accurate pricing.			

20-195 CABOOSE: In 1928, Ives marketed the 14-inch American Flyer 4021 caboose as their product. The cars rode on Ives trucks and were equipped with shortened versions of the Snake Track Pull coupler.

Three brass name and number plates and six narrow brass windows adorned each side of the car. Lettering on the plates bore the markings "THE IVES RAILWAY LINES," "MADE IN THE IVES SHOPS" and "20-195." The illuminated caboose was decorated with a brass smokejack, as well as brass ladders and steps. Several color combinations were produced.

20-195 CABOOSE (Type I): Some cars had dark-red bodies with maroon roofs on both the cupola and main body.

VG-C6	EX-C7	LN-C8	Scarcity
100	200	400	5

20-195 CABOOSE (Type II): Other cars were virtually identical, but for their blue-green cupola roof.

VG-C6	EX-C7	LN-C8	Scarcity
100	200	400	5

20-195 CABOOSE (Type III): The most desirable version of this car was painted overall light green.

VG-C6	EX-C7	LN-C8	Scarcity
200	500	950	6

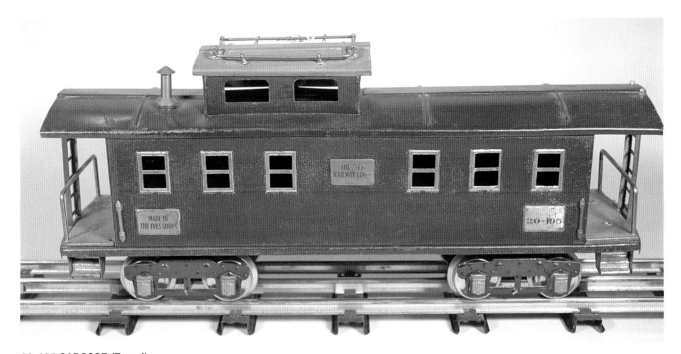

20-195 CABOOSE (Type I)

Values for each condition are in U.S. dollars. | **Scarcity** = Scale from 1-8 with 8 being the hardest to find.

361

Flatcars

4000 FLATCAR: This uncataloged car is believed to have been issued around 1927. The car is identical to the 4012, however the number plates installed on the car read "4000," rather than "4012."

VG-C6	EX-C7	LN-C8	Scarcity
Too rarely traded to establish accurate pricing.			

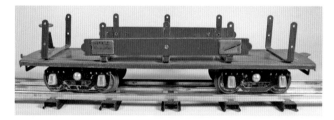

4012 FLATCAR: This 14-inch long American Flyer-designed car was offered in 1927. All known versions of the car are painted blue with blue sidebars. The cars rode on black flex trucks with brass journal boxes. Two brass name and number plates are mounted on each side of the car. These plates read "4012" and "BUILT BY 'American Flyer' LINES." Each car came with a brass brakewheel, but no steps were fitted.

VG-C6	EX-C7	LN-C8	Scarcity
150	300	450	5

4022 MACHINERY CAR: From 1928 through 1933, American Flyer billed their 14-inch long flatcar as a machinery car. The car was painted orange and most had turquoise-blue sidebars. Various shades of turquoise were used throughout the production run. Five stakes were installed on each side. A strengthener plate was installed on the bottom of the car.

4022 MACHINERY CAR (Type I): Some of the cars were adorned with a pair of etched-brass nameplates attached to the turquoise-blue sidebars. The legends on these plates bore "BUILT BY 'American Flyer' LINES" and "4022 American Flyer Lines." Further brass trim on these cars was the U-shaped steps as well as the journal boxes on the gray flex trucks. A brakewheel was installed on either end with black stanchions.

VG-C6	EX-C7	LN-C8	Scarcity
30	70	100	3

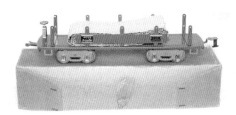

4022 MACHINERY CAR (Type II): Other cars came with gray trucks and gray U-shaped steps. The two brass nameplates on each side of these cars were stamped "4022 American Flyer Lines" and "OVER 6 MILLION HAPPY OWNERS." These cars each had a single brakewheel secured with an orange stanchion. Rather than turquoise, the car had orange sidebars. Brass journal boxes were installed on the trucks.

VG-C6	EX-C7	LN-C8	Scarcity
30	70	100	3

4022 MACHINERY CAR (Type III): This car differed by having "8 MILLION" plates rather than "6 MILLION" plates found on the Type II car.

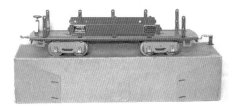

4022 MACHINERY CAR (Type IV): Similar to the Type I was this car, which had a long decal reading "AMERICAN FLYER LINES" applied to the turquoise sidebar in lieu of the brass nameplates. Gray trucks with brass journal boxes, as well as brass steps were installed on the car. Orange stanchions supported the brass brakewheel mounted at either end. The number "4022" was rubber stamped on the underside of the car.

VG-C6	EX-C7	LN-C8	Scarcity
30	70	100	2

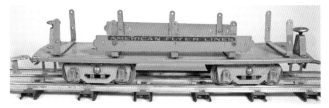

4022 MACHINERY CAR (Type V): Nearly identical to the Type IV car was this car—the most notable difference being the sidebars finished in the same color as the car body rather than turquoise. A long decal with "AMERICAN

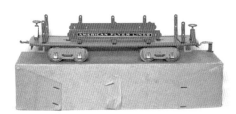

FLYER LINES" appeared on each sidebar. Orange stanchions supported the brass brakewheel mounted on each end; "4022" was rubber stamped on bottom.

VG-C6	EX-C7	LN-C8	Scarcity
30	70	100	2

4023 LOG CAR: In 1934, the name the flatcar was cataloged under was changed again. Now known as a "log car"—the name the 14-inch car would bare through 1936—the car now fittingly was burdened with a rectangular wood load. A strengthener plate could be found on the bottom.

4023 LOG CAR (Type I): The "log car" was painted orange, as were the sidebars. On each of those sidebars were two etched-brass plates, both reading "BUILT BY 'American Flyer' LINES." The car had one brakewheel and rode on gray set trucks. Gray was also the color of the U-shaped steps on each end. The bottom of the car was rubber stamped "4023."

VG-C6	EX-C7	LN-C8	Scarcity
45	90	125	3

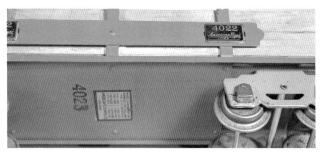

4023 LOG CAR (Type II): Some of the cars had two "4022" brass plates on each side, rather than the "BUILT BY" plates found on the Type I.

VG-C6	EX-C7	LN-C8	Scarcity
45	90	125	3

Hopper Cars

4006 HOPPER: American Flyer offered a 14-inch hopper car of their own design from 1931 through 1936. All known variations of this car are painted red and have two manually operated hopper doors on the bottom. Most have "4006" rubber stamped on the bottom of the car.

4006 HOPPER (Type I): Many of the cars have gray set trucks and U-shaped steps. Two lettering plates were mounted on each side, one reading "BUILT BY 'American Flyer' LINES" and the other "OVER 6 MILLION HAPPY OWNERS." One brass brakewheel was mounted on the car.

VG-C6	EX-C7	LN-C8	Scarcity
150	350	600	5

4006 HOPPER (Type II): Other cars were fitted with gray flex trucks with brass journal boxes. These cars also had U-

shaped steps, but now these steps were brass. Also brass were the two brakewheels, one mounted on each end. Once again, two nameplates were mounted on each side, but the lettering differed slightly from that of the Type I. Now, in addition to the "BUILT BY 'American Flyer' LINES" plates, there was a plate reading "OVER 7 MILLION HAPPY OWNERS."

VG-C6	EX-C7	LN-C8	Scarcity
200	400	700	6

4006 HOPPER (Type III): Virtually identical to the Type I car was this hopper with an "8 Million" number plate in addition to the "BUILT BY 'American Flyer' LINES."

VG-C6	EX-C7	LN-C8	Scarcity
150	350	600	5

Gondola and Sand Cars

gray and rubber stamped "ROCK ISLAND LINES" in the center of each side. Near each end was additional stamping "65784," "CAPACITY 20000 LBS" and "WEIGHT 10000." The bottom of the car was rubber stamped "AMERICAN FLYER LINES No. 4007." The car was equipped with brakewheels on each end and rode on black flex trucks without journal boxes.

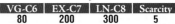

VG-C6	EX-C7	LN-C8	Scarcity
80	200	300	5

4007 SAND CAR (Type I): The first gondola car offered in Wide-Gauge by American Flyer utilized a body made—and lettered—by Lionel. The car, which Flyer termed a "sand car" when it was released in 1926 was like the number 12 Lionel on which it was based, painted

4007 SAND CAR (Type II): When the 1927 line was shipped, the sand car (gondola) was now a purely American

Values for each condition are in U.S. dollars. | Scarcity = Scale from 1-8 with 8 being the hardest to find.

365

Flyer product. The 14-inch long maroon car had a black frame—which matched its flex trucks—and a brakewheel was attached to each end. Trim consisted of brass journal boxes and three brass nameplates on each side, but it lacked steps. Two of the plates read "BUILT BY 'American Flyer' LINES" and the third was embossed "4007 American Flyer LINES." Some cars were equipped with an internal brace.

VG-C6	EX-C7	LN-C8	Scarcity
100	250	400	6

4007 SAND CAR (Type III): Otherwise identical to the Type II, some cars were also finished in black enamel.

VG-C6	EX-C7	LN-C8	Scarcity
Too rarely traded to establish accurate pricing.			

4017 SAND CAR (Gondola): The sand car was renumbered in 1928. It would wear its new number, "4017," through 1936. The 14-inch car frequently, but not always, included a center reinforcing rib at the center of its body. The rib was sometimes black, other times green. The presence or absence of this feature is not distinguished in the listings below. Many of these cars were painted green, in a host of shades, which are not distinguished below.

4017 SAND CAR (Type I): Presumably one of the earliest of the 4017 gondolas was this green car with green frame. Three etched-brass plates were attached to each side. These plates bore the legends "4017 American Flyer Lines," "BUILT BY 'American Flyer' LINES" and "OVER 6 MILLION HAPPY OWNERS." Other brass fittings included the U-steps and brakewheels on each end, a brass ladder on each side, the journal boxes on the black flex trucks.

VG-C6	EX-C7	LN-C8	Scarcity
30	60	100	3

4017 SAND CAR (Type II): Other cars were identical to the Type I cars except for the frame, which was black.

VG-C6	EX-C7	LN-C8	Scarcity
30	60	100	2

4017 SAND CAR (Type III): Other green cars had gray flex trucks, but were otherwise duplicates of the Type I cars.

VG-C6	EX-C7	LN-C8	Scarcity
30	60	100	2

4017 SAND CAR (Type IV): A fourth version of the car omitted the numberplate, replacing it with a second "BUILT BY 'American Flyer' LINES." The remaining plate continued to be an "OVER 6 MILLION HAPPY OWNERS" plate. The U-shaped steps, as well as the flex trucks, were gray. The car was equipped with two brakewheels.

VG-C6	EX-C7	LN-C8	Scarcity
30	60	100	2

4017 SAND CAR (Type V): But for the gray set trucks and single brakewheel, this car was identical to the Type IV.

VG-C6	EX-C7	LN-C8	Scarcity
30	60	100	2

4017 SAND CAR (Type VI): Later production cars duplicated the Type I except the "6 MILLION" plate was replaced with one reading "OVER 7 MILLION HAPPY OWNERS."

VG-C6	EX-C7	LN-C8	Scarcity
30	60	100	2

4017 SAND CAR (Type VII): Still later, the plates were changed again. Now two "OVER 8 MILLION HAPPY OWNERS" number plates, along with one "BUILT BY 'American Flyer' LINES" plate were attached to each side. These cars had green frames and rode on gray set trucks. The steps were also gray and one brass brakewheel was installed.

VG-C6	EX-C7	LN-C8	Scarcity
30	60	100	2

4017 SAND CAR (Type VIII): Other cars were the inverse of the Type VII in terms of plates. These cars had two "BUILT BY 'American Flyer' LINES" and one "OVER 8 MILLION HAPPY OWNERS," but the remainder of the car was a duplicate of the car above.

VG-C6	EX-C7	LN-C8	Scarcity
35	65	120	3

4017 SAND CAR (Type IX): Same as (A), except with a green frame with gray set trucks and steps, and one brakewheel. Two "BUILT BY 'American Flyer' LINES" and one "OVER 8 MILLION HAPPY OWNERS" number plate and rubber stamped "4017" on bottom.

VG-C6	EX-C7	LN-C8	Scarcity
35	65	120	3

4017 SAND CAR (Type X): Some cars featured plates reading "The Commander" in place of the numberplates. On this scarce variation, the stock number "4017" was rubber stamped on the bottom of the car. The other two plates on each side read "OVER 8 MILLION HAPPY OWNERS" and "MADE BY/AMERICAN FLYER/ MFG. CO./CHICAGO ILLINOIS/PATENTED." These cars rode on gray set trucks and had only one brakewheel.

VG-C6	EX-C7	LN-C8	Scarcity
Too rarely traded to establish accurate pricing.			

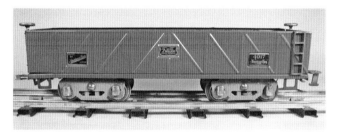

4017 SAND CAR (Type XI): The gondola was also produced in orange rather than green. These cars, which were equipped with gray flex trucks, used "OVER 7 MILLION HAPPY OWNERS" number plates.

VG-C6	EX-C7	LN-C8	Scarcity
50	100	200	4

4677 SAND: This uncataloged gondola was actually a green 4017 which was factory assembled with two "4677"

number plates and a "NATION/WIDE/LINES" plate. The car was equipped with gray flex trucks and brass U-shaped steps. A brakewheel was mounted on each end.

VG-C6	EX-C7	LN-C8	Scarcity
Too rarely traded to establish accurate pricing.			

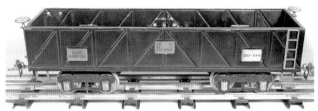

20-194 GRAVEL CAR: This car is in fact a 20-198, discussed below. However, some of these cars were fitted with number plates reading "20-194." These plates had been intended for a hopper car, which was not produced. Some cars reportedly have a mix of 20-194 and 20-198 plates installed on them.

VG-C6	EX-C7	LN-C8	Scarcity
Too rarely traded to establish accurate pricing.			

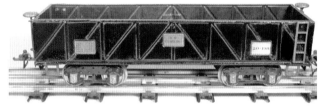

20-198 GRAVEL CAR (GONDOLA): In 1929, the 14-inch long American Flyer-designed gondola car was sold by Ives. These cars were equipped with Ives trucks and Snake Track Pull couplers. Like their Flyer brothers, each side of the car sported three brass plates; the center plate proclaiming "THE IVES RAILWAY LINES," while the left-hand plate provided dimensional data and the right-hand plate bore the number "20-198." These cars had brass journals, ladders and steps, and could have one or two brakewheels. It was produced in both glossy and matte black, the latter being slightly more desirable and valuable than the glossy version priced below.

VG-C6	EX-C7	LN-C8	Scarcity
100	200	350	5

Values for each condition are in U.S. dollars. | **Scarcity** = Scale from 1-8 with 8 being the hardest to find.

367

Tank Cars

4010 TANK CAR: Introduced in 1928 and remaining in the line through 1936, this American Flyer-designed 14-inch long car came in two colors and numerous variations.

Details that changed through production, but are not noted below, are the number of grab irons and the use of bolts or rivets in construction.

4010 TANK CAR (Type I): The car that is believed to be the first of the Flyer Wide-Gauge tank car had a dark-blue frame, upon which was placed a cream-colored tank. The tank was secured by brass bands and a brass ladder on each side ran from the frame to the dome, and brass railings were attached to the tank. The platform near the dome was painted the same dark blue as the frame. Brass U-shaped steps and two brakewheels were used, as were gray flex trucks with brass journal boxes. Two etched brass plates were attached to the side; the left-hand plate bore the legend "AMERICAN FLYER TANK LINES" while the right-hand plate was emblazoned with the number "4010."

VG-C6	EX-C7	LN-C8	Scarcity
150	300	450	5

4010 TANK CAR (Type II): A few of the cars were produced with the number plate on the left end of the car rather than the right. These cars were otherwise identical to the Type I cars.

VG-C6	EX-C7	LN-C8	Scarcity
150	300	450	5

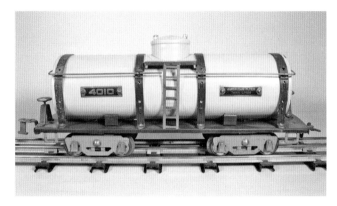

4010 TANK CAR (Type III): Similar cars were produced with blue rather than brass bands securing the tank. These cars also had gray-painted U-shaped steps.

VG-C6	EX-C7	LN-C8	Scarcity
100	225	350	4

4010 TANK CAR (Type IV): Some of the cars with blue bands and gray steps lacked the "4010" plate, instead having two "AMERICAN FLYER TANK LINES." These cars also rode on set trucks and had only one brakewheel.

VG-C6	EX-C7	LN-C8	Scarcity
100	225	350	4

4010 TANK CAR (Type V): Very desirable versions of the tank car were decorated with a large "A.F. LINES AIR SERVICE" decal. To prevent the circular decal from being obscured, these cars did not have ladders or platforms. The bands securing the tank on this car could be unpainted brass, or painted silver color, and the U-shaped steps were painted gray, as were the flex trucks the car rode on.

VG-C6	EX-C7	LN-C8	Scarcity
225	450	700	7

4010 TANK CAR (Type V)

Values for each condition are in U.S. dollars. | **Scarcity** = Scale from 1-8 with 8 being the hardest to find.

369

4010 TANK CAR (Type VI): Some of the cars with the "Air Service" decals were equipped with gray set trucks.

VG-C6	EX-C7	LN-C8	Scarcity
225	450	700	7

4010 TANK CAR (Type VII): Similar to the Type I, this car was devoid of both brass plates and railings. In fact, the body of the car was not even punched to accept the plate. It is believed to be originally paper labels promoting the Tillamook Cheese Co.

VG-C6	EX-C7	LN-C8	Scarcity
Too rarely traded to accurately establish pricing.			

4010 TANK CAR (Type VIII): This car is a near duplicate of the Type VII, except both the dome and the bands securing the tank were painted gold.

VG-C6	EX-C7	LN-C8	Scarcity
Too rarely traded to accurately establish pricing.			

4010 TANK CAR (Type IX): Ultimately, the tank bodies were painted blue. The ladders and traps were brass. The car rode on gray flex trucks.

VG-C6	EX-C7	LN-C8	Scarcity
200	400	600	6

4010 TANK CAR (Type X): Another version of the all-blue car had two "4010" numberplates on each side.

VG-C6	EX-C7	LN-C8	Scarcity
200	400	600	6

20-190 TANK CAR: In 1928, Ives sold the American Flyer 4010 as its own. Painted orange, the tank was fitted with two riveted-on brass nameplates, the left reading "THE IVES LINES" and right "20-190." The frame of the car was blue and the car rode on Ives trucks.

VG-C6	EX-C7	LN-C8	Scarcity
300	750	1,100	7

190 TANK CAR: This 1929-30 Ives car is listed in this volume as a curiosity. The only parts of this car produced by American Flyer are the black frame, brakewheel and brakewheel support. The yellow tank was produced by Lionel—and from the 215—and the trucks belonged to Ives.

VG-C6	EX-C7	LN-C8	Scarcity
275	500	750	6

4010 TANK CAR (Type VII)

O-Gauge

There's insufficient information at this time to provide a scarcity grade for these products.

1 LOCOMOTIVE: 1907-16, wind-up.

VG-C6	EX-C7	LN-C8	Scarcity
50	100	150	N/A

1 TRANSFORMER: 25-Watt.

VG-C6	EX-C7	LN-C8	Scarcity
15	20	30	N/A

1 TRANSFORMER: 35-Watt.

VG-C6	EX-C7	LN-C8	Scarcity
19	25	35	N/A

2 LOCOMOTIVE: 1908-16, cast-iron, wind-up.

VG-C6	EX-C7	LN-C8	Scarcity
70	140	200	N/A

1-1/2 TRANSFORMER: 45-Watt.

VG-C6	EX-C7	LN-C8	Scarcity
23	30	40	N/A

1-1/2B TRANSFORMER: 50-Watt.

VG-C6	EX-C7	LN-C8	Scarcity
30	40	60	N/A

2 TRANSFORMER: 75-Watt.

VG-C6	EX-C7	LN-C8	Scarcity
38	50	75	N/A

1-1/2 TRANSFORMER: 50-Watt.

VG-C6	EX-C7	LN-C8	Scarcity
30	40	60	N/A

3 LOCOMOTIVE: Wind-up.

VG-C6	EX-C7	LN-C8	Scarcity
45	90	125	N/A

4 LOCOMOTIVE: 0-4-0, wind-up.

VG-C6	EX-C7	LN-C8	Scarcity
60	125	175	N/A

4A LOCOMOTIVE: Wind-up.

VG-C6	EX-C7	LN-C8	Scarcity
70	140	200	N/A

8B TRANSFORMER:

VG-C6	EX-C7	LN-C8	Scarcity
42	55	75	N/A

8B TRANSFORMER: 100-Watt, with bulb covers.

VG-C6	EX-C7	LN-C8	Scarcity
53	70	100	N/A

8B TRANSFORMER: 100-Watt, without bulb covers.

VG-C6	EX-C7	LN-C8	Scarcity
45	60	95	N/A

8B TRANSFORMER: With uncoupler, track, manual and buttons.

VG-C6	EX-C7	LN-C8	Scarcity
53	70	100	N/A

9 LOCOMOTIVE: 1926-27, 1929-32, 0-4-0, wind-up.

VG-C6	EX-C7	LN-C8	Scarcity
60	120	175	N/A

10 LOCOMOTIVE: 0-4-0, cast-iron, wind-up.

VG-C6	EX-C7	LN-C8	Scarcity
50	100	150	N/A

10 LOCOMOTIVE: 1925, electric.

VG-C6	EX-C7	LN-C8	Scarcity
120	240	350	N/A

11 LOCOMOTIVE: 1927-32, 0-4-0, wind-up.

VG-C6	EX-C7	LN-C8	Scarcity
90	180	275	N/A

12 LOCOMOTIVE: 1910-17, cast-iron.

VG-C6	EX-C7	LN-C8	Scarcity
50	100	150	N/A

12 SMOKE CARTRIDGES:

VG-C6	EX-C7	LN-C8	Scarcity
—	4	10	N/A

13 LOCOMOTIVE AND TENDER: 1917-22, 0-4-0, wind-up, black, orange and green.

VG-C6	EX-C7	LN-C8	Scarcity
75	150	225	N/A

14 LOCOMOTIVE: 1925-32, 0-4-0, wind-up.

VG-C6	EX-C7	LN-C8	Scarcity
45	90	150	N/A

15 LOCOMOTIVE: 1920-22, wind-up.

VG-C6	EX-C7	LN-C8	Scarcity
35	70	100	N/A

16 LOCOMOTIVE: 1923-26, 0-4-0, electric.

VG-C6	EX-C7	LN-C8	Scarcity
55	110	150	N/A

18B TRANSFORMER:

VG-C6	EX-C7	LN-C8	Scarcity
90	120	175	N/A

19B TRANSFORMER: 300-Watt with volt and amp.

VG-C6	EX-C7	LN-C8	Scarcity
75	100	150	N/A

28 LOCOMOTIVE: 0-4-0, wind-up.

VG-C6	EX-C7	LN-C8	Scarcity
40	85	115	N/A

29 LOCOMOTIVE: Cast-iron, first electric, wind-up.

VG-C6	EX-C7	LN-C8	Scarcity
75	150	225	N/A

34 LOCOMOTIVE: 1930-31, 0-4-0, wind-up.

VG-C6	EX-C7	LN-C8	Scarcity
70	140	225	N/A

40 LOCOMOTIVE: 0-4-0, wind-up.

VG-C6	EX-C7	LN-C8	Scarcity
70	140	225	N/A

92 SWITCH TOWER:

VG-C6	EX-C7	LN-C8	Scarcity
60	80	125	N/A

96 STATION: c. 1931.

VG-C6	EX-C7	LN-C8	Scarcity
30	40	60	N/A

104 KENILWORTH STATION:

VG-C6	EX-C7	LN-C8	Scarcity
18	25	40	N/A

105 PULLMAN:

VG-C6	EX-C7	LN-C8	Scarcity
30	60	100	N/A

119 HIAWATHA LOCOMOTIVE: Tin-plate, wind-up, with tender.

VG-C6	EX-C7	LN-C8	Scarcity
60	120	175	N/A

119 HIAWATHA LOCOMOTIVE: Tin-plate, electric.

VG-C6	EX-C7	LN-C8	Scarcity
90	180	225	N/A

119 TENDER: 1930-32.

VG-C6	EX-C7	LN-C8	Scarcity
30	60	100	N/A

120 TENDER:

VG-C6	EX-C7	LN-C8	Scarcity
40	80	120	N/A

121 TENDER: Black and white, marked "No. 121."

VG-C6	EX-C7	LN-C8	Scarcity
30	60	100	N/A

228 LOG CAR: 1939.

VG-C6	EX-C7	LN-C8	Scarcity
20	40	65	N/A

229 BOXCAR: 1939.

VG-C6	EX-C7	LN-C8	Scarcity
20	40	65	N/A

230 DUMP CAR: 1939.

VG-C6	EX-C7	LN-C8	Scarcity
20	40	65	N/A

231 TANK CAR: 1939.

VG-C6	EX-C7	LN-C8	Scarcity
20	40	65	N/A

O-GAUGE

Values for each condition are in U.S. dollars. | **Scarcity** = Scale from 1-8 with 8 being the hardest to find.

373

328 TENDER: 1907-26.

VG-C6	EX-C7	LN-C8	Scarcity
30	60	100	N/A

356 TENDER: Comet.

VG-C6	EX-C7	LN-C8	Scarcity
40	80	125	N/A

401 LOCOMOTIVE: See 403.

VG-C6	EX-C7	LN-C8	Scarcity
88	175	250	N/A

403 LOCOMOTIVE: 1939-40, 2-4-4.

VG-C6	EX-C7	LN-C8	Scarcity
65	125	200	N/A

404 PULLMAN: 1939.

VG-C6	EX-C7	LN-C8	Scarcity
30	60	100	N/A

405 OBSERVATION CAR: 1939.

VG-C6	EX-C7	LN-C8	Scarcity
30	60	100	N/A

406 LOG CAR: 1939, green or orange.

VG-C6	EX-C7	LN-C8	Scarcity
18	35	50	N/A

407 SAND CAR: 1939, green.

VG-C6	EX-C7	LN-C8	Scarcity
20	40	60	N/A

408 BOXCAR: 1939-40, orange.

VG-C6	EX-C7	LN-C8	Scarcity
20	45	70	N/A

409 DUMP CAR: 1939.

VG-C6	EX-C7	LN-C8	Scarcity
30	65	100	N/A

410 LOCOMOTIVE:

VG-C6	EX-C7	LN-C8	Scarcity
55	110	170	N/A

410 TANK CAR: 1939-40, silver tank, greenframe; or green on blue frame

VG-C6	EX-C7	LN-C8	Scarcity
25	55	80	N/A

411 CABOOSE: 1939-40, similar to 3211, red.

VG-C6	EX-C7	LN-C8	Scarcity
20	40	60	N/A

412 MILK CAR: 1939-40.

VG-C6	EX-C7	LN-C8	Scarcity
	95	150	N/A

415 FLOODLIGHT CAR: 1939.

VG-C6	EX-C7	LN-C8	Scarcity
45	90	150	N/A

416 WRECKER CAR: 1939.

VG-C6	EX-C7	LN-C8	Scarcity
100	200	300	N/A

419 LOCOMOTIVE: 1939, streamliner.

VG-C6	EX-C7	LN-C8	Scarcity
135	275	400	N/A

420 LOCOMOTIVE: See 422.

VG-C6	EX-C7	LN-C8	Scarcity
100	200	300	N/A

421 TENDER:

VG-C6	EX-C7	LN-C8	Scarcity
35	70	100	N/A

422 LOCOMOTIVE: 1939, 2-4-2.

VG-C6	EX-C7	LN-C8	Scarcity
125	250	375	N/A

423 LOCOMOTIVE:

VG-C6	EX-C7	LN-C8	Scarcity
90	175	250	N/A

424 LOCOMOTIVE: 1939, 2-4-4.

VG-C6	EX-C7	LN-C8	Scarcity
60	125	185	N/A

425 LOCOMOTIVE: see 427.

VG-C6	EX-C7	LN-C8	Scarcity
100	200	300	N/A

427 LOCOMOTIVE: 1939-40, 2-6-4.

VG-C6	EX-C7	LN-C8	Scarcity
200	400	600	N/A

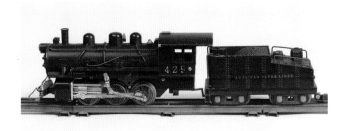

429: See 431.

431 LOCOMOTIVE: 1939-40, 0-6-0.

VG-C6	EX-C7	LN-C8	Scarcity
425	850	1,275	N/A

432 LOCOMOTIVE: See 434.

VG-C6	EX-C7	LN-C8	Scarcity
300	600	900	N/A

434 LOCOMOTIVE: 1939, 4-4-2.

VG-C6	EX-C7	LN-C8	Scarcity
350	700	1,050	N/A

436 LOCOMOTIVE: 1939-40, 4-6-2.

VG-C6	EX-C7	LN-C8	Scarcity
550	1,100	1,650	N/A

437 LOCOMOTIVE: 1939, 2-4-2.

VG-C6	EX-C7	LN-C8	Scarcity
560	850	NA	N/A

449 LOCOMOTIVE: 1939, 2-6-4.

VG-C6	EX-C7	LN-C8	Scarcity
840	1,680	2,520	N/A

436 LOCOMOTIVE

Values for each condition are in U.S. dollars. | **Scarcity** = Scale from 1-8 with 8 being the hardest to find.

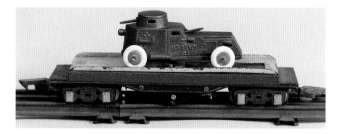

472 UNLOADING CAR: 1940-41, Army, with Tootsietoy armored car.

VG-C6	EX-C7	LN-C8	Scarcity
60	115	175	N/A

474 DUMP CAR: 1941, automatic.

VG-C6	EX-C7	LN-C8	Scarcity
100	200	300	N/A

476 GONDOLA: 1940-41, green.

VG-C6	EX-C7	LN-C8	Scarcity
25	50	75	N/A

478 BOXCAR: 1940-41, 1946 white with red roof.

VG-C6	EX-C7	LN-C8	Scarcity
20	40	60	N/A

480 TANK CAR: 1940, yellow, Shell, or silver and blue.

VG-C6	EX-C7	LN-C8	Scarcity
25	50	75	N/A

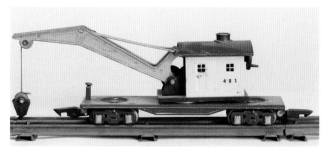

481 WRECKER CAR: 1941, black or red frame.

VG-C6	EX-C7	LN-C8	Scarcity
40	80	120	N/A

482 LUMBER CAR: 1940-41, green or black.

VG-C6	EX-C7	LN-C8	Scarcity
30	65	95	N/A

483 GIRDER CAR: 1941, black with orange girder.

VG-C6	EX-C7	LN-C8	Scarcity
25	50	75	N/A

484 CABOOSE: 1940-46, red.

VG-C6	EX-C7	LN-C8	Scarcity
15	35	50	N/A

486 HOPPER: 1940-41, yellow.

VG-C6	EX-C7	LN-C8	Scarcity
40	80	120	N/A

488 FLOODLIGHT CAR: 1940-41.

VG-C6	EX-C7	LN-C8	Scarcity
50	100	150	N/A

490 WHISTLE CAR: 1940-41, gray.

VG-C6	EX-C7	LN-C8	Scarcity
40	75	115	N/A

490B WHISTLE CAR: 1940, blue.

VG-C6	EX-C7	LN-C8	Scarcity
40	75	115	N/A

492R MAIL PICKUP CAR: 1941, red.

VG-C6	EX-C7	LN-C8	Scarcity
30	60	90	N/A

492G MAIL PICKUP CAR: 1941, green.

VG-C6	EX-C7	LN-C8	Scarcity
30	60	90	N/A

492T MAIL PICKUP CAR: 1941, Tuscan.

VG-C6	EX-C7	LN-C8	Scarcity
30	60	90	N/A

494R BAGGAGE CAR: 1940-41, red.

VG-C6	EX-C7	LN-C8	Scarcity
30	60	90	N/A

494G BAGGAGE CAR: 1940, green.

VG-C6	EX-C7	LN-C8	Scarcity
30	60	90	N/A

494B BAGGAGE CAR: 1940-41, blue.

VG-C6	EX-C7	LN-C8	Scarcity
30	60	90	N/A

494T BAGGAGE CAR: 1941, tuscan.

VG-C6	EX-C7	LN-C8	Scarcity
30	60	90	N/A

495R COACH CAR: 1940-41, red.

VG-C6	EX-C7	LN-C8	Scarcity
35	70	100	N/A

495RL COACH CAR: 1940-41, red, illuminated.

VG-C6	EX-C7	LN-C8	Scarcity
35	70	100	N/A

495G COACH CAR: 1940-41, green.

VG-C6	EX-C7	LN-C8	Scarcity
35	70	100	N/A

495GL COACH CAR: 1940-41, green, illuminated.

VG-C6	EX-C7	LN-C8	Scarcity
35	70	100	N/A

495B COACH CAR: 1940-41, blue.

VG-C6	EX-C7	LN-C8	Scarcity
35	70	100	N/A

495BL COACH CAR: 1940-41, blue, illuminated.

VG-C6	EX-C7	LN-C8	Scarcity
35	70	100	N/A

495T COACH CAR: 1941, Tuscan.

VG-C6	EX-C7	LN-C8	Scarcity
35	70	100	N/A

495TL COACH CAR: 1941, Tuscan, illuminated.

VG-C6	EX-C7	LN-C8	Scarcity
35	70	100	N/A

496RL PULLMAN: 1941, red, illuminated.

VG-C6	EX-C7	LN-C8	Scarcity
90	175	275	N/A

O-GAUGE

Values for each condition are in U.S. dollars. | **Scarcity** = Scale from 1-8 with 8 being the hardest to find.

377

496GL PULLMAN: 1941, green, illuminated.

VG-C6	EX-C7	LN-C8	Scarcity
90	175	275	N/A

496T PULLMAN: 1941, Tuscan.

VG-C6	EX-C7	LN-C8	Scarcity
90	175	275	N/A

496TL PULLMAN: 1941, Tuscan, illuminated.

VG-C6	EX-C7	LN-C8	Scarcity
90	175	275	N/A

497R OBSERVATION CAR: 1941, red.

VG-C6	EX-C7	LN-C8	Scarcity
50	95	150	N/A

497RL OBSERVATION CAR: 1941, red, illuminated.

VG-C6	EX-C7	LN-C8	Scarcity
50	95	150	N/A

497GL OBSERVATION CAR: 1941, green, illuminated.

VG-C6	EX-C7	LN-C8	Scarcity
50	95	150	N/A

497T OBSERVATION CAR: 1941, Tuscan.

VG-C6	EX-C7	LN-C8	Scarcity
50	95	150	N/A

497TL OBSERVATION CAR: 1941, Tuscan, illuminated.

VG-C6	EX-C7	LN-C8	Scarcity
50	95	150	N/A

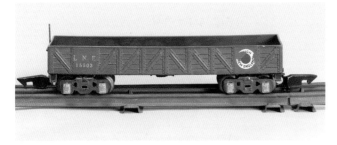

504 GONDOLA: 1939-41, diecast gray or Tuscan.

VG-C6	EX-C7	LN-C8	Scarcity
100	200	300	N/A

506 BOXCAR: 1939-41, Baltimore and Ohio, white.

VG-C6	EX-C7	LN-C8	Scarcity
50	100	150	N/A

508 HOPPER: 1939-41, Virginian.

VG-C6	EX-C7	LN-C8	Scarcity
65	130	200	N/A

510 CATTLE CAR: 1939-41, Missouri Pacific, brown.

VG-C6	EX-C7	LN-C8	Scarcity
40	75	115	N/A

512 TANK CAR: 1939-41, Texaco, silver or gray.

VG-C6	EX-C7	LN-C8	Scarcity
40	75	115	N/A

513 OBSERVATION CAR: 1932-35.

VG-C6	EX-C7	LN-C8	Scarcity
15	25	40	N/A

514 WRECKER CAR: 1939-41.

VG-C6	EX-C7	LN-C8	Scarcity
100	200	300	N/A

515 COACH CAR: Tin-plate, lithographed, yellow, red, black and orange, early.

VG-C6	EX-C7	LN-C8	Scarcity
15	25	40	N/A

516 CABOOSE: 1939-41, illuminated, UP or NYC.

VG-C6	EX-C7	LN-C8	Scarcity
45	85	125	N/A

518 BAGGAGE CAR: 1931-32.

VG-C6	EX-C7	LN-C8	Scarcity
25	50	75	N/A

519 PULLMAN: 1931-32.

VG-C6	EX-C7	LN-C8	Scarcity
25	50	75	N/A

521 BAGGAGE CLUB CAR: 1939-41, Tuscan.

VG-C6	EX-C7	LN-C8	Scarcity
100	200	300	N/A

524 PULLMAN: 1939-41, Tuscan.

VG-C6	EX-C7	LN-C8	Scarcity
300	600	900	N/A

531 LOCOMOTIVE: 1940-41, 4-6-4.

VG-C6	EX-C7	LN-C8	Scarcity
450	900	1,350	N/A

534 LOCOMOTIVE: 1940-41, 4-8-4.

VG-C6	EX-C7	LN-C8	Scarcity
1,400	2,800	4,250	N/A

545 LOCOMOTIVE: 1940, 4-4-2.

VG-C6	EX-C7	LN-C8	Scarcity
50	100	150	N/A

553 LOCOMOTIVE: 1940, steam.

VG-C6	EX-C7	LN-C8	Scarcity
55	110	175	N/A

555C TENDER: 1941.

VG-C6	EX-C7	LN-C8	Scarcity
30	60	90	N/A

556 LOCOMOTIVE: Royal Blue, 1940-41, 4-6-2.

VG-C6	EX-C7	LN-C8	Scarcity
55	115	175	N/A

558C TENDER: 1941, with chugger.

VG-C6	EX-C7	LN-C8	Scarcity
35	65	100	N/A

559 LOCOMOTIVE: 1940-41, 4-6-2, Pennsylvania K5.

VG-C6	EX-C7	LN-C8	Scarcity
175	350	525	N/A

561 STEAM LOCOMOTIVE: 1940-41, 4-6-2, Pennsylvania K5.

VG-C6	EX-C7	LN-C8	Scarcity
105	210	325	N/A

564 LOCOMOTIVE: 1939, 4-6-4.

VG-C6	EX-C7	LN-C8	Scarcity
1,250	2,500	2,750	N/A

564C TENDER: 1941.

VG-C6	EX-C7	LN-C8	Scarcity
25	50	75	N/A

565 LOCOMOTIVE: 4-4-2, 1941, 1945-46.

VG-C6	EX-C7	LN-C8	Scarcity
75	150	225	N/A

568 LOCOMOTIVE: 1939, 4-8-4.

VG-C6	EX-C7	LN-C8	Scarcity
1,500	3,000	4,500	N/A

570 STEAM LOCOMOTIVE: 1940-41, 4-6-4, New York Central J3, 3/16.

VG-C6	EX-C7	LN-C8	Scarcity
150	300	450	N/A

571 STEAM LOCOMOTIVE: 3/16 scale, 4-8-4.

VG-C6	EX-C7	LN-C8	Scarcity
200	400	600	N/A

O-GAUGE

574 LOCOMOTIVE: 1941, 0-8-0, switcher.

VG-C6	EX-C7	LN-C8	Scarcity
700	1,400	2,100	N/A

574B LOCOMOTIVE: 0-8-0.

VG-C6	EX-C7	LN-C8	Scarcity
1,000	2,000	3,000	N/A

597 PASSENGER AND FREIGHT STATION:

VG-C6	EX-C7	LN-C8	Scarcity
35	70	100	N/A

616 LOCOMOTIVE: Wind-up.

VG-C6	EX-C7	LN-C8	Scarcity
75	150	225	N/A

617 LOCOMOTIVE: 1933-35, 2-4-2.

VG-C6	EX-C7	LN-C8	Scarcity
50	100	150	N/A

622 LOCOMOTIVE: 1934.

VG-C6	EX-C7	LN-C8	Scarcity
40	80	125	N/A

640 STEAM LOCOMOTIVE: 1936, 0-4-2, black.

VG-C6	EX-C7	LN-C8	Scarcity
100	150	225	N/A

641 LOCOMOTIVE: 1936, 2-4-2.

VG-C6	EX-C7	LN-C8	Scarcity
350	700	1,050	N/A

816 LOCOMOTIVE: Wind-up, three cars.

VG-C6	EX-C7	LN-C8	Scarcity
300	600	900	N/A

830 LOCOMOTIVE: Wind-up, two cars.

VG-C6	EX-C7	LN-C8	Scarcity
140	275	425	N/A

832 LOCOMOTIVE: Wind-up, three cars.

VG-C6	EX-C7	LN-C8	Scarcity
140	275	425	N/A

960T LOCOMOTIVE: Two cars.

VG-C6	EX-C7	LN-C8	Scarcity
175	350	525	N/A

961T LOCOMOTIVE: 0-4-0, three cars.

VG-C6	EX-C7	LN-C8	Scarcity
140	275	425	N/A

964T LOCOMOTIVE: Three cars.

VG-C6	EX-C7	LN-C8	Scarcity
200	400	600	N/A

970T HIAWATHA SET: Includes locomotive tender, two coaches and observation car.

VG-C6	EX-C7	LN-C8	Scarcity
335	670	1,000	N/A

1025 RAILWAY EXPRESS MAIL CAR:

VG-C6	EX-C7	LN-C8	Scarcity
30	60	90	N/A

1026 PASSENGER CAR:

VG-C6	EX-C7	LN-C8	Scarcity
15	25	40	N/A

1045 TRANSFORMER: 25-Watt.

VG-C6	EX-C7	LN-C8	Scarcity
15	20	35	N/A

1093 LOCOMOTIVE: 1930-31.

VG-C6	EX-C7	LN-C8	Scarcity
220	440	675	N/A

1094 LOCOMOTIVE:

VG-C6	EX-C7	LN-C8	Scarcity
350	700	1,100	N/A

1096 BOX CAB LOCOMOTIVE: 1925-27, 0-4-0, with square headlight, rubber stamped.

VG-C6	EX-C7	LN-C8	Scarcity
75	150	225	N/A

1097 ENGINE: 0-4-0, lithographed, orange, green and red, with nickel trim.

VG-C6	EX-C7	LN-C8	Scarcity
75	150	225	N/A

1103 PASSENGER CAR:

VG-C6	EX-C7	LN-C8	Scarcity
30	60	100	N/A

1104 BAGGAGE CAR:

VG-C6	EX-C7	LN-C8	Scarcity
30	60	100	N/A

1105 BAGGAGE CAR: Marked "American Express."

VG-C6	EX-C7	LN-C8	Scarcity
60	120	175	N/A

1105 CANADIAN NATIONAL RAILWAYS DOMINION
FLYER: Lithographed, red and black, with nickel trim.

VG-C6	EX-C7	LN-C8	Scarcity
30	60	100	N/A

1106 COACH: Lithographed, brown and black, marked "Dominion Flyer."

VG-C6	EX-C7	LN-C8	Scarcity
40	80	125	N/A

1106 LUMBER CAR: 1930, black.

VG-C6	EX-C7	LN-C8	Scarcity
20	35	60	N/A

1106 PARLOR CAR: Lithographed, yellow, black and green.

VG-C6	EX-C7	LN-C8	Scarcity
30	60	100	N/A

1106 PARLOR CAR: Lithographed, green with black roof, four wheels.

VG-C6	EX-C7	LN-C8	Scarcity
30	60	100	N/A

1107 COACH CAR: Lithographed.

VG-C6	EX-C7	LN-C8	Scarcity
20	35	60	N/A

1108 BAGGAGE CAR: Lithographed.

VG-C6	EX-C7	LN-C8	Scarcity
25	45	75	N/A

1109 SAND CAR: Lithographed, red.

VG-C6	EX-C7	LN-C8	Scarcity
20	35	60	N/A

1110 BOXCAR:

VG-C6	EX-C7	LN-C8	Scarcity
25	50	75	N/A

1111 CABOOSE: 1919-35.

VG-C6	EX-C7	LN-C8	Scarcity
25	50	75	N/A

1112 BOXCAR: 1919-35, NYC Reefer, lithographed 1115 on side.

VG-C6	EX-C7	LN-C8	Scarcity
30	60	100	N/A

1112 BOXCAR: 1930, lithographed, yellow.

VG-C6	EX-C7	LN-C8	Scarcity
35	70	110	N/A

1113 GONDOLA: 1925, lithographed, green.

VG-C6	EX-C7	LN-C8	Scarcity
20	35	60	N/A

1114 CABOOSE: Lithographed, red, green and white, with brass trim.

VG-C6	EX-C7	LN-C8	Scarcity
25	50	75	N/A

1115 AUTOMOBILE BOXCAR:

VG-C6	EX-C7	LN-C8	Scarcity
40	80	125	N/A

1115 BOXCAR: See 1112.
1116 GONDOLA:

VG-C6	EX-C7	LN-C8	Scarcity
25	50	75	N/A

1116 SAND CAR:

VG-C6	EX-C7	LN-C8	Scarcity
60	120	200	N/A

1117 CABOOSE:

VG-C6	EX-C7	LN-C8	Scarcity
35	70	110	N/A

1118 TANK CAR: Lithographed, gray-white and black.

VG-C6	EX-C7	LN-C8	Scarcity
45	90	150	N/A

O-GAUGE

Values for each condition are in U.S. dollars. | **Scarcity** = Scale from 1-8 with 8 being the hardest to find.

1119 STOCK CAR:

VG-C6	EX-C7	LN-C8	Scarcity
40	80	125	N/A

1120 CABOOSE:

VG-C6	EX-C7	LN-C8	Scarcity
25	50	75	N/A

1120 OBSERVATION CAR: 1923-29.

VG-C6	EX-C7	LN-C8	Scarcity
25	50	75	N/A

1120 PASSENGER CAR: 1923-29.

VG-C6	EX-C7	LN-C8	Scarcity
25	50	75	N/A

1121 LOCOMOTIVE: With whistle and tender, 2-4-0.

VG-C6	EX-C7	LN-C8	Scarcity
30	60	100	N/A

1122 BLUESTREAK PASSENGER CAR:

VG-C6	EX-C7	LN-C8	Scarcity
25	50	75	N/A

1123 PASSENGER CAR: Tuscan.

VG-C6	EX-C7	LN-C8	Scarcity
20	40	60	N/A

1123 PASSENGER CAR:

VG-C6	EX-C7	LN-C8	Scarcity
20	40	60	N/A

1124 PULLMAN:

VG-C6	EX-C7	LN-C8	Scarcity
60	120	200	N/A

1127 CABOOSE:

VG-C6	EX-C7	LN-C8	Scarcity
15	30	50	N/A

1128 TANK CAR:

VG-C6	EX-C7	LN-C8	Scarcity
15	30	50	N/A

1141 LOG CAR:

VG-C6	EX-C7	LN-C8	Scarcity
40	80	125	N/A

1146 LOG CAR:

VG-C6	EX-C7	LN-C8	Scarcity
40	80	125	N/A

1147 OBSERVATION CAR:

VG-C6	EX-C7	LN-C8	Scarcity
50	100	150	N/A

1157 OBSERVATION CAR:

VG-C6	EX-C7	LN-C8	Scarcity
50	100	150	N/A

1200 BAGGAGE CAR: Lithographed, four-wheel.

VG-C6	EX-C7	LN-C8	Scarcity
30	60	100	N/A

1200 BAGGAGE CAR: Lithographed, eight-wheel.

VG-C6	EX-C7	LN-C8	Scarcity
30	60	100	N/A

1201 LOCOMOTIVE: 1920-24, steeple cab, black or dark green.

VG-C6	EX-C7	LN-C8	Scarcity
45	90	140	N/A

1201 PASSENGER CAR: Lithographed, red with black roof.

VG-C6	EX-C7	LN-C8	Scarcity
30	60	100	N/A

1202 BAGGAGE CAR: Express.

VG-C6	EX-C7	LN-C8	Scarcity
35	65	100	N/A

1202 BAGGAGE CAR: Electric Service.

VG-C6	EX-C7	LN-C8	Scarcity
40	80	125	N/A

1203 COACH CAR: Lithographed, eight-wheel, early.

VG-C6	EX-C7	LN-C8	Scarcity
35	65	100	N/A

1203 PASSENGER CAR: 1933, lithographed, blue with black roof.

VG-C6	EX-C7	LN-C8	Scarcity
35	65	100	N/A

1204 BAGGAGE CAR: 1933-34.

VG-C6	EX-C7	LN-C8	Scarcity
60	120	200	N/A

1205 BAGGAGE CAR: American Railway Express.

VG-C6	EX-C7	LN-C8	Scarcity
30	60	100	N/A

1205 MAIL CAR: 1924-26.

VG-C6	EX-C7	LN-C8	Scarcity
30	60	100	N/A

1206 PASSENGER CAR: 1922-26, red or orange.

VG-C6	EX-C7	LN-C8	Scarcity
40	75	125	N/A

1206 PULLMAN:

VG-C6	EX-C7	LN-C8	Scarcity
40	75	125	N/A

1207 OBSERVATION CAR: 1926.

VG-C6	EX-C7	LN-C8	Scarcity
40	75	125	N/A

1208 LOCOMOTIVE:

VG-C6	EX-C7	LN-C8	Scarcity
80	160	250	N/A

1209 OBSERVATION CAR:

VG-C6	EX-C7	LN-C8	Scarcity
60	120	200	N/A

1211 LOCOMOTIVE: 1920-24, steeple cab, black or dark green.

VG-C6	EX-C7	LN-C8	Scarcity
45	90	150	N/A

1211 PASSENGER COACH: 1934.

VG-C6	EX-C7	LN-C8	Scarcity
30	60	100	N/A

1212 OBSERVATION CAR: 1934.

VG-C6	EX-C7	LN-C8	Scarcity
100	200	300	N/A

1213 PULLMAN: 1934.

VG-C6	EX-C7	LN-C8	Scarcity
60	120	200	N/A

1214 BAGGAGE: 1934.

VG-C6	EX-C7	LN-C8	Scarcity
60	120	200	N/A

1217 LOCOMOTIVE: 0-4-0, electric.

VG-C6	EX-C7	LN-C8	Scarcity
60	120	200	N/A

O-GAUGE

Values for each condition are in U.S. dollars. | **Scarcity** = Scale from 1-8 with 8 being the hardest to find.

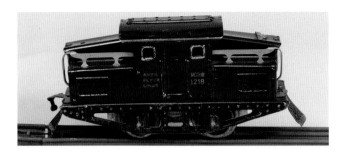

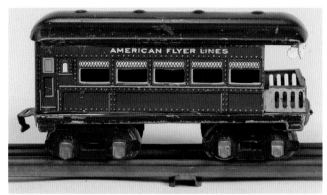

1218 LOCOMOTIVE: 1920-25, 0-4-0, black, red and yellow, electric.

VG-C6	EX-C7	LN-C8	Scarcity
75	150	225	N/A

1219 COACH CAR:

VG-C6	EX-C7	LN-C8	Scarcity
20	40	60	N/A

1223 COACH CAR:

VG-C6	EX-C7	LN-C8	Scarcity
20	40	60	N/A

1225 LOCOMOTIVE: 1919, 0-4-0, cast-iron.

VG-C6	EX-C7	LN-C8	Scarcity
100	200	300	N/A

1257 OBSERVATION CAR: 1933.

VG-C6	EX-C7	LN-C8	Scarcity
120	240	375	N/A

1270 LOCOMOTIVE:

VG-C6	EX-C7	LN-C8	Scarcity
100	200	300	N/A

1287 OBSERVATION CAR: 1925, Chicago.

VG-C6	EX-C7	LN-C8	Scarcity
45	90	150	N/A

1290 TRANSFORMER:

VG-C6	EX-C7	LN-C8	Scarcity
30	40	100	N/A

1306 PASSENGER CAR: 1922-26, four- or eight-wheel, blue, green, red or brown.

VG-C6	EX-C7	LN-C8	Scarcity
25	50	75	N/A

1322RT LOCOMOTIVE: Four cars.

VG-C6	EX-C7	LN-C8	Scarcity
550	1,100	1,700	N/A

1621 PULLMAN: 1936-39.

VG-C6	EX-C7	LN-C8	Scarcity
65	135	200	N/A

1622 OBSERVATION CAR: 1936-39.

VG-C6	EX-C7	LN-C8	Scarcity
65	135	200	N/A

1286 PULLMAN: 1925.

VG-C6	EX-C7	LN-C8	Scarcity
45	90	150	N/A

1641 HIAWATHA COACH: 1936-37.

VG-C6	EX-C7	LN-C8	Scarcity
50	150	250	N/A

1642 HIAWATHA OBSERVATION: 1936-37.

VG-C6	EX-C7	LN-C8	Scarcity
50	150	250	N/A

1681 LOCOMOTIVE: 1936-38, 2-6-4.

VG-C6	EX-C7	LN-C8	Scarcity
250	500	750	N/A

1683 LOCOMOTIVE: 1936-37.

VG-C6	EX-C7	LN-C8	Scarcity
700	1,400	2,100	N/A

1684 LOCOMOTIVE: 1936-39.

VG-C6	EX-C7	LN-C8	Scarcity
60	120	180	N/A

1686 STEAM LOCOMOTIVE: 1937, 4-4-2, streamlined.

VG-C6	EX-C7	LN-C8	Scarcity
110	220	350	N/A

1687 LOCOMOTIVE: 1937, 2-4-2.

VG-C6	EX-C7	LN-C8	Scarcity
350	700	1,100	N/A

1688 LOCOMOTIVE: 1937, 2-4-2.

VG-C6	EX-C7	LN-C8	Scarcity
150	275	425	N/A

1710 LOCOMOTIVE:

VG-C6	EX-C7	LN-C8	Scarcity
75	150	225	N/A

1730RW STREAMLINER: 1935, Union Pacific, 51 inches long.

VG-C6	EX-C7	LN-C8	Scarcity
200	425	625	N/A

1835TW TENDER:

VG-C6	EX-C7	LN-C8	Scarcity
75	150	225	N/A

2005 TRIANGLE LIGHT:

VG-C6	EX-C7	LN-C8	Scarcity
45	70	120	N/A

2010 DOUBLE ARC LAMPPOST: 12-1/2 inches high.

VG-C6	EX-C7	LN-C8	Scarcity
35	70	110	N/A

2020 WATER TANK:

VG-C6	EX-C7	LN-C8	Scarcity
50	100	150	N/A

2029 WHISTLE UNIT: Remote control.

VG-C6	EX-C7	LN-C8	Scarcity
30	60	100	N/A

2043 SEMAPHORE:

VG-C6	EX-C7	LN-C8	Scarcity
175	225	400	N/A

3000 BAGGAGE: Lithographed, black and two-tone green.

VG-C6	EX-C7	LN-C8	Scarcity
50	100	150	N/A

3001 PULLMAN: 1922-24, Illini.

VG-C6	EX-C7	LN-C8	Scarcity
50	100	150	N/A

3004 CABOOSE: Illuminated.

VG-C6	EX-C7	LN-C8	Scarcity
60	120	200	N/A

3005 OBSERVATION CAR: Illini.

VG-C6	EX-C7	LN-C8	Scarcity
30	60	100	N/A

3006 FLATCAR: 1924-27.

VG-C6	EX-C7	LN-C8	Scarcity
10	20	30	N/A

O-GAUGE

Values for each condition are in U.S. dollars. | **Scarcity** = Scale from 1-8 with 8 being the hardest to find.

385

3007 SAND CAR: 1925-27.

VG-C6	EX-C7	LN-C8	Scarcity
250	500	750	N/A

3008 BOXCAR: 1925-27, lithographed, GN, ART, B & O, or Nickel Plate.

VG-C6	EX-C7	LN-C8	Scarcity
250	500	750	N/A

3009 DUMP CAR: 1934-35, decaled.

VG-C6	EX-C7	LN-C8	Scarcity
5	10	15	N/A

3010 TANK CAR: 1925-27, gray with black nickel trim.

VG-C6	EX-C7	LN-C8	Scarcity
50	100	150	N/A

3011 LOCOMOTIVE: 1926-27.

VG-C6	EX-C7	LN-C8	Scarcity
100	175	275	N/A

3012 BOXCAR: 1930-35, rubber stamped.

VG-C6	EX-C7	LN-C8	Scarcity
15	30	45	N/A

3012 LOCOMOTIVE: 1925-27, 0-4-0, lithographed, headlight in cab, electric.

VG-C6	EX-C7	LN-C8	Scarcity
100	200	300	N/A

3013 GONDOLA: 1930-35.

VG-C6	EX-C7	LN-C8	Scarcity
25	50	75	N/A

3013 LOCOMOTIVE:

VG-C6	EX-C7	LN-C8	Scarcity
400	800	1,250	N/A

3014 CABOOSE: Decaled set.

VG-C6	EX-C7	LN-C8	Scarcity
25	50	75	N/A

3014 LOCOMOTIVE:

VG-C6	EX-C7	LN-C8	Scarcity
550	1,100	1,700	N/A

3015 BOXCAR: 1930-32, 1934-35.

VG-C6	EX-C7	LN-C8	Scarcity
20	40	60	N/A

3015 LOCOMOTIVE: 1927, green.

VG-C6	EX-C7	LN-C8	Scarcity
150	275	425	N/A

3016 SAND CAR:

VG-C6	EX-C7	LN-C8	Scarcity
25	50	75	N/A

3017 CABOOSE: Eight-wheel.

VG-C6	EX-C7	LN-C8	Scarcity
15	25	40	N/A

3018 TANK CAR: 1930-32, yellow and black, with copper trim.

VG-C6	EX-C7	LN-C8	Scarcity
30	65	100	N/A

3018 TANK CAR: 1934-35, eight-wheel.

VG-C6	EX-C7	LN-C8	Scarcity
75	175	250	N/A

3019 DUMP CAR: 1934, 1935, 1938, eight-wheel.

VG-C6	EX-C7	LN-C8	Scarcity
15	35	50	N/A

3019 ELECTRIC LOCO: 1923-24, dark green, black frame and maroon windows, rubber stamped, headlight.

VG-C6	EX-C7	LN-C8	Scarcity
200	400	600	N/A

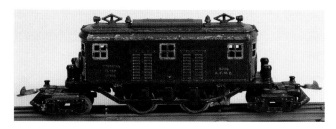

3020 ENGINE: 1922-25, 4-4-4, maroon and black, with nickel trim.

VG-C6	EX-C7	LN-C8	Scarcity
250	500	750	N/A

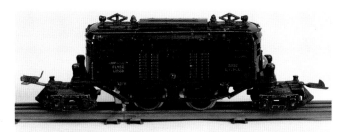

3020 ENGINE: 1922-25, 4-4-4, black and yellow, with nickel trim.

VG-C6	EX-C7	LN-C8	Scarcity
200	400	600	N/A

3025 CRANE CAR: 1936-38.

VG-C6	EX-C7	LN-C8	Scarcity
50	100	150	N/A

3045 WRECKER CAR: 1930-31.

VG-C6	EX-C7	LN-C8	Scarcity
70	140	210	N/A

3046 LUMBER CAR: 1930-32, 1934, 1935, eight-wheel.

VG-C6	EX-C7	LN-C8	Scarcity
20	40	60	N/A

3080 MAIL CAR:

VG-C6	EX-C7	LN-C8	Scarcity
40	80	125	N/A

3081 PULLMAN: Illini.

VG-C6	EX-C7	LN-C8	Scarcity
40	80	125	N/A

3085 OBSERVATION CAR: Columbia.

VG-C6	EX-C7	LN-C8	Scarcity
40	80	125	N/A

3100 LOCOMOTIVE: 1930-33, 0-4-0 red, black, gold, with brass trim and plates.

VG-C6	EX-C7	LN-C8	Scarcity
60	120	200	N/A

3102 LOCOMOTIVE: 1926, lithographed.

VG-C6	EX-C7	LN-C8	Scarcity
50	100	150	N/A

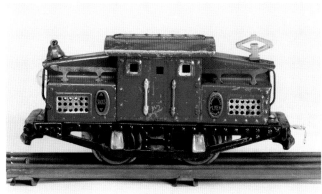

3103 LOCOMOTIVE: 1930.

VG-C6	EX-C7	LN-C8	Scarcity
225	450	700	N/A

3105 LOCOMOTIVE: Blue.

VG-C6	EX-C7	LN-C8	Scarcity
140	240	400	N/A

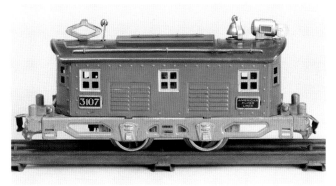

3107 LOCOMOTIVE: 1930-32, 0-4-0.

VG-C6	EX-C7	LN-C8	Scarcity
75	150	225	N/A

3107RC LOCOMOTIVE: 1930-32.

VG-C6	EX-C7	LN-C8	Scarcity
250	500	750	N/A

O-GAUGE

Values for each condition are in U.S. dollars. | **Scarcity** = Scale from 1-8 with 8 being the hardest to find.

387

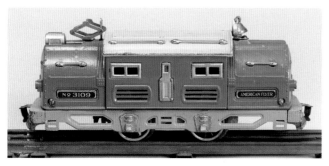

3109 ENGINE: 1930-31, 0-4-0, green, brown, with brass trim.

VG-C6	EX-C7	LN-C8	Scarcity
100	200	300	N/A

3110 LOCOMOTIVE: 1928-29, 0-4-0, with headlight.

VG-C6	EX-C7	LN-C8	Scarcity
125	250	375	N/A

3112 LOCOMOTIVE: 1928-29, orange, brown or maroon litho body.

VG-C6	EX-C7	LN-C8	Scarcity
75	125	200	N/A

3113 LOCOMOTIVE: 1928-29.

VG-C6	EX-C7	LN-C8	Scarcity
110	220	330	N/A

3113 LOCOMOTIVE: 0-4-0, two-tone blue with two-tone blue coaches marked "Nationwide Lines" made for J.C. Penney Co., extremely rare; set complete in original boxes.

VG-C6	EX-C7	LN-C8	Scarcity
500	1,000	1,400	N/A

3113 LOCOMOTIVE: 0-4-0, two-tone blue with two-tone blue coaches marked, American Flyer Bluebird, American Flyer Lines lettering.

VG-C6	EX-C7	LN-C8	Scarcity
150	350	600	N/A

3115 ENGINE: 1928-30, 0-4-0, peacock blue, with brass trim.

VG-C6	EX-C7	LN-C8	Scarcity
60	120	190	N/A

3116 ENGINE: 1928-29, 0-4-0, turquoise and black, with brass trim.

VG-C6	EX-C7	LN-C8	Scarcity
200	400	600	N/A

3117 ENGINE: 1928-29, 0-4-0, red with brass trim.

VG-C6	EX-C7	LN-C8	Scarcity
150	300	450	N/A

3140 BAGGAGE CAR: 1932-33.

VG-C6	EX-C7	LN-C8	Scarcity
70	140	225	N/A

3141 PULLMAN: 1930-32, red and black, with brass trim.

VG-C6	EX-C7	LN-C8	Scarcity
50	90	150	N/A

3142 OBSERVATION CAR: 1930-32, red, black and gold, with brass trim.

VG-C6	EX-C7	LN-C8	Scarcity
50	90	150	N/A

3150 BAGGAGE CAR: 1930-33.

VG-C6	EX-C7	LN-C8	Scarcity
50	90	150	N/A

3151 PASSENGER CAR: 1930-33.

VG-C6	EX-C7	LN-C8	Scarcity
30	55	90	N/A

3152 OBSERVATION CAR: 1930-33, two-tone orange, with brass trim.

VG-C6	EX-C7	LN-C8	Scarcity
50	100	150	N/A

3161 PASSENGER CAR: 1930-33.

VG-C6	EX-C7	LN-C8	Scarcity
75	150	225	N/A

3162 OBSERVATION CAR: 1930-33, with brass trim.

VG-C6	EX-C7	LN-C8	Scarcity
30	60	100	N/A

3171 PULLMAN: 1930-33, 1934, 1936-38, with brass trim.

VG-C6	EX-C7	LN-C8	Scarcity
20	40	60	N/A

O-GAUGE

Values for each condition are in U.S. dollars. | Scarcity = Scale from 1-8 with 8 being the hardest to find.

389

3172 OBSERVATION CAR: 1930-33, 1934, 1936-38, O ga., with brass trim.

VG-C6	EX-C7	LN-C8	Scarcity
20	40	60	N/A

3176 PULLMAN: 1931, 1937.

VG-C6	EX-C7	LN-C8	Scarcity
25	50	75	N/A

3177 OBSERVATION CAR: 1931, 1937.

VG-C6	EX-C7	LN-C8	Scarcity
30	60	90	N/A

3178 COACH: 1935.

VG-C6	EX-C7	LN-C8	Scarcity
200	400	600	N/A

3179 OBSERVATION: 1935.

VG-C6	EX-C7	LN-C8	Scarcity
40	75	150	N/A

3180 CLUB CAR: Beige and green, with brass trim, marked "Potomac."

VG-C6	EX-C7	LN-C8	Scarcity
40	75	120	N/A

3180 CLUB CAR: Two-tone red, green, with brass trim.

VG-C6	EX-C7	LN-C8	Scarcity
25	50	75	N/A

3181 PULLMAN: 1928-30, beige and green, with brass trim, marked "Potomac."

VG-C6	EX-C7	LN-C8	Scarcity
40	75	120	N/A

3182 LOCOMOTIVE: 1931, 0-4-0.

VG-C6	EX-C7	LN-C8	Scarcity
200	400	600	N/A

3182 OBSERVATION CAR: 1928-30, beige and green, with brass trim, marked "Potomac."

VG-C6	EX-C7	LN-C8	Scarcity
40	75	120	N/A

3184 LOCOMOTIVE: 1931, 0-4-0.

VG-C6	EX-C7	LN-C8	Scarcity
250	500	750	N/A

3185 LOCOMOTIVE: 1928-30, turquoise/teal blue.

VG-C6	EX-C7	LN-C8	Scarcity
225	450	700	N/A

3186 LOCOMOTIVE: 1928-29.

VG-C6	EX-C7	LN-C8	Scarcity
400	800	1,250	N/A

3187 LOCOMOTIVE: 1928-32, red.

VG-C6	EX-C7	LN-C8	Scarcity
300	600	900	N/A

3188 LOCOMOTIVE: 1931, 0-4-0.

VG-C6	EX-C7	LN-C8	Scarcity
250	500	750	N/A

3191 LOCOMOTIVE: 1931, 2-4-0, remote control reverse.

VG-C6	EX-C7	LN-C8	Scarcity
160	320	500	N/A

3192 LOCOMOTIVE: 1930-31.

VG-C6	EX-C7	LN-C8	Scarcity
40	80	125	N/A

3197 LOCOMOTIVE: 1930, 0-4-0.

VG-C6	EX-C7	LN-C8	Scarcity
250	500	750	N/A

3198 LOCOMOTIVE: 1931, cast-iron.

VG-C6	EX-C7	LN-C8	Scarcity
90	180	275	N/A

3201 CABOOSE: 1932.

VG-C6	EX-C7	LN-C8	Scarcity
25	50	75	N/A

3206 FLATCAR: 1928-35, orange, with lumber.

VG-C6	EX-C7	LN-C8	Scarcity
45	90	150	N/A

3207 GONDOLA: 1928-38.

VG-C6	EX-C7	LN-C8	Scarcity
20	35	60	N/A

3208 BOXCAR: 1928-38, orange and blue.

VG-C6	EX-C7	LN-C8	Scarcity
55	110	175	N/A

3210 TANK CAR: 1928-38.

VG-C6	EX-C7	LN-C8	Scarcity
45	90	150	N/A

3211 CABOOSE: 1928-38.

VG-C6	EX-C7	LN-C8	Scarcity
40	75	120	N/A

3212 MILK CAR: 1938.

VG-C6	EX-C7	LN-C8	Scarcity
40	80	125	N/A

3213 FLOODLIGHT CAR: 1938.

VG-C6	EX-C7	LN-C8	Scarcity
75	150	225	N/A

3216 LOG CAR: 1937.

VG-C6	EX-C7	LN-C8	Scarcity
30	65	100	N/A

3219 DUMP CAR: 1934-38.

VG-C6	EX-C7	LN-C8	Scarcity
40	80	125	N/A

3280 CLUB CAR: 1928-31, 1934, two-tone blue, with brass trim, marked "Golden State" or "Jeffersonian."

VG-C6	EX-C7	LN-C8	Scarcity
180	360	550	N/A

3281 PULLMAN: Turquoise/teal blue, 1928-31, 1933-34.

VG-C6	EX-C7	LN-C8	Scarcity
90	180	275	N/A

3281 PULLMAN: Two-tone blue, with brass trim, marked "Golden State" or "Jeffersonian."

VG-C6	EX-C7	LN-C8	Scarcity
180	360	550	N/A

3282 OBSERVATION CAR: 1928-31, 1933-34, two-tone blue, with brass trim, marked "Golden State."

VG-C6	EX-C7	LN-C8	Scarcity
180	360	550	N/A

Values for each condition are in U.S. dollars. | **Scarcity** = Scale from 1-8 with 8 being the hardest to find.

391

3282 OBSERVATION CAR: 1928-31, 1933-34, turquoise/teal blue.

VG-C6	EX-C7	LN-C8	Scarcity
90	180	275	N/A

3302 LOCOMOTIVE: 1931, 2-4-2.

VG-C6	EX-C7	LN-C8	Scarcity
250	500	750	N/A

3304 LOCOMOTIVE: 1934, 2-4-2.

VG-C6	EX-C7	LN-C8	Scarcity
150	300	450	N/A

3307 LOCOMOTIVE: 1932-33, bell in cab.

VG-C6	EX-C7	LN-C8	Scarcity
100	200	300	N/A

3308 LOCOMOTIVE: 1932-33, 2-4-2.

VG-C6	EX-C7	LN-C8	Scarcity
150	300	450	N/A

3309 LOCOMOTIVE: 1934, 2-4-2.

VG-C6	EX-C7	LN-C8	Scarcity
200	400	600	N/A

3310 LOCOMOTIVE: 📷 1934, 2-4-2.

VG-C6	EX-C7	LN-C8	Scarcity
100	200	300	N/A

3313 LOCOMOTIVE: 1935, 2-4-2.

VG-C6	EX-C7	LN-C8	Scarcity
200	400	600	N/A

3315 LOCOMOTIVE: 1932-35.

VG-C6	EX-C7	LN-C8	Scarcity
350	700	1,100	N/A

3316 LOCOMOTIVE: 1932-35, 2-4-2.

VG-C6	EX-C7	LN-C8	Scarcity
30	60	100	N/A

3322 LOCOMOTIVE: 1936.

VG-C6	EX-C7	LN-C8	Scarcity
150	300	400	N/A

3323 LOCOMOTIVE: 1934, 2-4-2.

VG-C6	EX-C7	LN-C8	Scarcity
250	500	750	N/A

3324 LOCOMOTIVE: 1935, 2-4-2.

VG-C6	EX-C7	LN-C8	Scarcity
250	500	750	N/A

3326 LOCOMOTIVE: 1932-35, 2-4-2.

VG-C6	EX-C7	LN-C8	Scarcity
65	135	200	N/A

3380 BAGGAGE CAR: Red with dark red roof and brass window inserts and decals, eight-wheel, lighted.

VG-C6	EX-C7	LN-C8	Scarcity
60	120	190	N/A

3381 COACH CAR: Red with dark red roof and brass window insert and decal, eight-wheel, lighted.

VG-C6	EX-C7	LN-C8	Scarcity
60	120	190	N/A

3382 OBSERVATION CAR: Red with dark red roof and brass window insert and decal, eight-wheel, lighted.

VG-C6	EX-C7	LN-C8	Scarcity
60	120	190	N/A

3541 PULLMAN:

VG-C6	EX-C7	LN-C8	Scarcity
70	140	225	N/A

3542 OBSERVATION CAR:

VG-C6	EX-C7	LN-C8	Scarcity
70	140	225	N/A

4321 LOCOMOTIVE: 0-6-0 black and white, with nickel trim, with tender.

VG-C6	EX-C7	LN-C8	Scarcity
115	225	350	N/A

4603 LOCOMOTIVE: 1938, 2-4-4.

VG-C6	EX-C7	LN-C8	Scarcity
150	300	450	N/A

4615 LOCOMOTIVE: 1938, 2-4-2 or 4-4-2.

VG-C6	EX-C7	LN-C8	Scarcity
350	700	1,100	N/A

4629 LOCOMOTIVE: 1938.

VG-C6	EX-C7	LN-C8	Scarcity
150	300	450	N/A

4677 LOCOMOTIVE: 1938.

VG-C6	EX-C7	LN-C8	Scarcity
300	600	950	N/A

3310 LOCOMOTIVE AND CARS

5160 CABOOSE: 1939-41, Union Pacific.

VG-C6	EX-C7	LN-C8	Scarcity
25	50	75	N/A

5640 HUDSON: 1939, 4-6-4, with tender.

VG-C6	EX-C7	LN-C8	Scarcity
350	700	1,100	N/A

9217 STREET LAMP: Green metal.

VG-C6	EX-C7	LN-C8	Scarcity
15	30	45	N/A

9910 LOCOMOTIVE: Cast aluminum, electric, Burlington Zephyr.

VG-C6	EX-C7	LN-C8	Scarcity
265	525	800	N/A

9910 LOCOMOTIVE: Wind-up, Burlington Zephyr.

VG-C6	EX-C7	LN-C8	Scarcity
85	175	275	N/A

9910 LOCOMOTIVE: Tinplate, electric, Burlington Zephyr.

VG-C6	EX-C7	LN-C8	Scarcity
125	275	400	N/A

9911 BAGGAGE CAR:

VG-C6	EX-C7	LN-C8	Scarcity
150	300	450	N/A

9912 OBSERVATION CAR:

VG-C6	EX-C7	LN-C8	Scarcity
150	300	450	N/A

9913 PULLMAN:

VG-C6	EX-C7	LN-C8	Scarcity
150	300	450	N/A

9914 LOCOMOTIVE:

VG-C6	EX-C7	LN-C8	Scarcity
400	800	1,200	N/A

9915 LOCOMOTIVE:

VG-C6	EX-C7	LN-C8	Scarcity
600	1,200	1,800	N/A

Unnumbered Baggage: 1927, American Flyer Lines, blue, from Bluebird set.

Unnumbered Pullman: 1927, American Flyer Lines, blue, from Bluebird set.

Unnumbered Observation: 1927, American Flyer Lines, blue, from Bluebird set.

Unnumbered Baggage: 1927, Pennsylvania, red, from Broadway Limited set.

Unnumbered Pullman: 1927, Pennsylvania, red, from Broadway Limited set.

Unnumbered Observation: 1927, Pennsylvania, red, from Broadway Limited set.

O-GAUGE

Values for each condition are in U.S. dollars. | **Scarcity** = Scale from 1-8 with 8 being the hardest to find.

393

GLOSSARY

AAR: Association of American Railroads, an industry standards and lobbying group.

Archbar truck: Trucks constructed with side frames consisting of two strips of bar iron or steel, called Arch Bars. These bars are bent so that placed mirrored to each other they roughly form a diamond shape with extended ends. Between these ends are the axle journal boxes. These trucks were banned from interchange service in 1939.

Bakelite: A brand of hard, brittle thermoset plastic. Heating Bakelite does not soften it, making it popular for electrical components. Lionel also used Bakelite occasionally for car bodies.

Commutator: An insulated segmented copper plate connected to the coils of direct-current and universal electric motors. Current flows from the carbon brushes to the commutator segments. This allows for the reversal of current into the coils of the motor

Cupola: The raised structure on the roof of a caboose that allowed a clear view of the sides of the train, making dragging equipment and "hot boxes" easily spotted regardless of the height of the remainder of the train.

Coupler: The device for mechanically interconnecting the individual cars of a train and transmitting the draft forces. Modern railroad couplers are of the "knuckle" type, but previously link and pin as well as other types were used.

Die-casting: Manufacturing process that involves forcing molten metal, usually a zinc alloy, into a mold, called a die, under high pressure. Rugged, detailed, precisely made parts can be mass-produced in this manner.

E unit: Two meanings. A) In Lionel trains, the electromechanical switch that selects motor contacts, and thus the motor's direction of rotation, is called an "E-unit." They are usually cycled by interrupting the current flow to the track. These come in two position (forward-reverse) or three-position versions, as well as a manual version which is two position, but requires hands-on operation by the operator. Three-position E-

units are the most common, and their sequence of operation is forward-neutral-reverse-neutral-forward, and so on. B) In real railroading, E-unit is slang for a General Motors Electro-Motive Division E-series twin-engine diesel that rode on two A-1-A trucks. The two terms are not generally confused as Lionel did not build a miniature E-unit during the postwar era.

Gauge: The distance between the tops of the rails. On most real U.S. railroads this is 4 feet 8 1/2 inches. For Lionel's most popular size of trains this width is 1 1/4 inches.

Heat-stamping: A decorating process whereby a heated die is used to transfer and adhere a colored decoration to the subject piece. When used on plastics, heat stamping often leaves an impression, the depth of which varies with the temperature of the tool and the duration of contact.

Hot box: Early railroad wheel bearings were lubricated with oil-soaked cotton called "waste." If the lubrication ran dry, the bearing would overheat, setting fire to the waste. If the train continued to operate, the bearing would fail, derailing the train.

House car: A term used for enclosed freight cars such as box, stock, refrigerator, and poultry cars. These cars are used for lading requiring protection from weather.

Magnetraction: This feature was intended to better keep the locomotive on the track and increase its pulling power by using powerful Alnico magnets to magnetize the wheel, "sticking" the train to Lionel's tin-plated steel track

Rubber stamping: A decorating process which uses an engraved rubber block that is inked and then pressed to the subject. Rubber stamping tends to not be as bold, or as permanent, as heat-stamping. However, rubber stamping can be used on irregular surfaces, which heat-stamping cannot, and the set up cost is considerably less.

Scale: A numeric ratio describing the relative size of a miniature to an original.

Siderail: Handrail extending alongside a locomotive or railcar.

Silk screening: A labor-intensive decorating process. A piece of sheer fabric (originally silk, now polyester) is stretched tight. A thin sheet of plastic with holes cut out to reveal where ink is to appear on the work piece is placed over the screen. The screen is pressed to the work piece ink, then forced through the openings in the plastic, and through the screen onto the work surface. Multi-color designs require multiple screens, and the inks are applied sequentially starting with the lightest color and moving up to the darkest.

Sintered iron: Sintering is a metallurgical process whereby powdered metal is poured into a mold and subjected to heat and pressure, forming it into a single piece.

Smokejack: The railroad term for the smokestack found on cabooses and other freight and passenger cars.

Tack board: Wooden panels on an otherwise steel door that provide a place to attach notes.

Tender: The tender of a real steam locomotive is semi-permanently linked to the locomotive by means of a drawbar. The tender carries the water supply for the steam locomotive as well as the fuel, be it coal, oil or wood.

Truck: The structure consisting of paired wheels with axles, side frame, bolster, and suspension system beneath railroad cars. Referred to as a "bogie" in Europe.

INDEX

760: 198
761: 198
762: 199
764: 199
766: 199-200
767: 200
768: 200
768G: 200
769: 201
769A: 201
770: 201
771: 201-202
772: 202-203
773: 203
774: 203-204
775: 204
778: 204
779: 204
780: 205
781: 205
782: 205
783: 205
784: 205
785: 205
787: 205
788: 206
789: 206
790: 206
792: 206
793: 206
794: 207
795: 207
799: 207
801: 95
802: 111
803: 111
804: 95
806: 62
807: 111-112
812: 45
816: 380
830: 380
832: 380
900: 148
901: 148
902: 148
903: 148
904: 62
905: 80
906: 71
907: 62, 80
909: 80-81
910: 131
911: 95
912: 132
913: 112
914: 81
915: 81
916: 95-96
918: 148
919: 96
920: 96
921: 102
922: 112
923: 112
924: 102
925: 132
926: 132
928: 81-82
929: 112-113
930: 63
931: 96
933: 113
934: 63, 82
935: 63
936: 82
937: 113
938: 64
940: 102
941: 96
942: 113
944: 71
945: 64, 82-83
946: 83
947: 114
948: 83
951: 149
952: 149
953: 149-150
954: 150
955: 150-151
956: 83
957: 114
958: 132-133
960: 151-152
960T: 380
961: 152
961T: 380
962: 152-153
963: 153-154

964T: 380
969: 84
970: 114
970T: 380
971: 84
973: 114
974: 115
975: 154
976: 115
977: 64
978: 154-155
979: 64
980: 115
981: 115-116
982: 116
983: 116
984: 116
985: 116
988: 116
989: 117
994: 117
1001: 117, 244
1002: 249
1003: 249
1004: 249
1006: 257
1007: 257
1025: 380
1026: 380
1045: 380
1093: 380
1094: 380
1096: 380
1097: 380
1103: 380
1104: 380
1105: 380, 381
1106: 381
1107: 381
1108: 381
1109: 381
1110: 381
1111: 381
1112: 381
1113: 381
1114: 381
1115: 381
1116: 381
1117: 381
1118: 381
1119: 382
1120: 382
1121: 382
1122: 382
1123: 382
1124: 382
1127: 382
1128: 382
1141: 382
1146: 382
1147: 382
1157: 382
1200: 382
1201: 382
1202: 382
1203: 383
1204: 383
1205: 383
1206: 383
1207: 383
1208: 383
1209: 383
1211: 383
1212: 383
1213: 383
1214: 383
1217: 383
1218: 384
1219: 384
1223: 384
1225: 384
1257: 384
1270: 384
1286: 384
1287: 384
1290: 384
1306: 384
1322RT: 384
1621: 384
1622: 384
1641: 385
1642: 385
1681: 385
1683: 385
1684: 385
1686: 385
1687: 385
1688: 385
1710: 385
1730RW: 385

1835TW: 385
2001: 31, 117-118
2002: 32
2004: 45, 311
2005: 311, 385
2009: 96, 316
2010: 317, 385
2011: 311
2012: 311
2013: 317
2014: 311
2015: 312
2016: 312
2017: 312
2018: 312
2020: 324, 385
2021: 312
2022: 312
2029: 385
2032: 312
2033: 312
2040: 313
2042: 313
2043: 313, 385
2050: 307
2109: 317
2110: 317
2116: 313
2206: 313
2209: 317-318
2210: 318
2216: 313
2218: 313
2222: 314
2230: 314
2290: 307
2294: 307
2764: 249
3000: 385
3001: 385
3003: 244
3004: 385
3005: 385
3006: 385
3007: 385
3008: 257, 386
3009: 386
3010: 386
3011: 386
3012: 386
3013: 386
3014: 386
3015: 386
3016: 386
3017: 386
3018: 386
3019: 386
3020: 386-387
3025: 387
3045: 387
3046: 387
3080: 387
3081: 387
3085: 387
3100: 387
3102: 387
3103: 387
3105: 387
3107: 387
3107RC: 387
3109: 388
3110: 388
3112: 388
3113: 388
3115: 388
3116: 388
3117: 388
3140: 389
3141: 389
3142: 389
3150: 389
3151: 389
3152: 389
3161: 389
3162: 389
3171: 389
3172: 390
3176: 390
3177: 390
3178: 390
3179: 390
3180: 390
3181: 390
3182: 390
3184: 390
3185: 390
3186: 390
3187: 390
3188: 390
3191: 391

3192: 391
3197: 391
3198: 391
3201: 391
3206: 391
3207: 391
3208: 391
3210: 391
3211: 391
3212: 391
3213: 391
3216: 391
3219: 391
3280: 391
3281: 391
3282: 391-392
3302: 392
3304: 392
3307: 392
3308: 392
3309: 392
3310: 392
3313: 392
3315: 392
3316: 392
3322: 392
3323: 392
3324: 392
3326: 392
3380: 392
3381: 392
3382: 392
3541: 392
3542: 392
3745: 45-46
3778: 46
4000: 327, 358, 362
4004: 314
4005: 354
4006: 364
4007: 365-366
4008: 354-355
4010: 368-370
4011: 358-360
4012: 362
4015: 314
4016: 314
4017: 366-367
4018: 355
4019: 327
4020: 356
4021: 360-361
4022: 362-363
4023: 363
4032: 314
4033: 314
4039: 328
4040: 338-339
4041: 339
4042: 315, 339-340
4080: 340
4081: 340
4082: 341
4090: 341
4091: 341
4092: 341-342
4116: 315
4122: 307
4141: 342
4142: 342-343
4150: 343
4151: 343-344
4152: 344-345
4206: 315
4218: 297, 315
4219: 297
4220: 297
4230: 315
4250: 345
4251: 345
4252: 345-346
4254: 321
4255: 321
4256: 321-322
4257: 322
4266: 322
4267: 322
4268: 322
4321: 392
4331: 346
4332: 346
4340: 346-347
4341: 347
4342: 347-348
4343: 348
4350: 348
4351: 348
4352: 348
4380: 349
4381: 349

4382: 349-350
4390: 350
4391: 350-351
4392: 351
4393: 351
4601: 223
4602: 223
4603: 223, 392
4604: 223
4605: 223
4606: 223
4607: 223
4607A: 223
4608: 223
4609: 223
4609A: 223
4610: 223
4611: 223
4611A: 223
4612: 223
4613: 223
4613A: 224
4615: 224, 392
4617: 224
4618: 224
4619: 224
4619A: 224
4620: 224
4620A: 224
4621: 225
4622: 225
4622A: 225
4629: 392
4633: 328
4635: 328
4637: 328
4637: 328
4643: 328
4644: 328-329
4644R/C: 330
4653: 330
4654: 330
4664: 333
4667: 330
4672: 333-334
4675: 335
4677: 330, 356, 361, 367, 392
4678: 330-331
4681: 335
4682: 335-336
4683: 331
4684: 331
4685: 331
4686: 332
4687: 332
4689: 332
4694: 336
4696: 336-337
4713: 46-47
4730: 225
4730A: 225
4743: 332
4745: 47
4753: 332
4778: 47
4801A: 225
4856: 47-48
4901T: 225
4904T: 225
4907AW: 225
4913: 48
4914A: 225
4945: 48
5001T: 225
5002T: 225
5003T: 225
5004: 226
5005WT: 226
5006WT: 226
5007: 226
5008: 226
5009: 226
5010W: 226
5012T: 226
5103WT: 226
5106T: 226
5106WT: 226
5107W: 226
5108W: 226-227
5110: 227
5112T: 227
5114: 227
5160: 393
5204W: 227
5205W: 227
5206W: 235
5210W: 235
5011BBW:226
5300T: 227

5301T: 227
5306T: 227
5311T: 227
5312T: 227
5317T: 227
5318: 240
5322T: 227
5323T: 227
5328: 235
5329: 235
5334T: 235
5335T: 235
5340T: 235
5345W: 235
5346W: 235
5351W: 235
5352W: 235
5357W: 235
5358W: 235
5363W: 235
5364W: 236
5368WT: 236
5369WT: 236
5374W: 236
5375W: 236
5401T: 236
5406T: 236
5407T: 236
5411T: 236
5412T: 236
5417T: 236
5418T: 236
5419T: 236
5422T: 236
5423T: 237
5434T: 237
5435T: 237
5436T: 237
5437T: 237
5440T: 237
5468WT: 237
5469WT: 237
5500T: 227
5505T: 227
5510T: 227
5515T: 228
5520T: 228
5525T: 228
5530TBH: 228
5535TBH: 228
5540TBW: 228
5542H: 228
5545W: 228
5550W: 228
5555W: 228
5565W: 228
5570H: 228
5580H: 228
5585H: 228
5605T: 228
5610T: 228
5615T: 229
5620T: 229
5625T: 229
5630TBW: 229
5635: 229
5640: 393
5640TBH: 229
5645TRH: 229
5650TBW: 229
5655RH: 229
5660TW: 229
5665W: 229
5670RH: 229
5675TRH: 229
5680RH: 229
5683RH: 229
5685RH: 229
5802: 257
7210: 84
8302: 249
9910: 393
9911: 393
9912: 393
9913: 393
9914: 393
9915: 393
15503: 257
20035: 229
20083: 230
20305: 230
20310: 230
20315: 230
20320: 230
20325: 230
20330: 230
20340: 230
20345: 230
20350: 230
20355: 230

20360: 230
20365: 230
20370: 230
20375: 230
20380: 231
20405: 231
20410: 231
20415: 231
20420: 231
20425: 231
20430: 231
20435: 231
20440: 231
20445: 231
20450: 231
20455: 231
20460: 231
20465: 231
20470: 232
20475: 232
20480: 232
20485: 232
20505: 232
20510: 232
20515: 232
20520: 232
20525: 232
20530: 232
20535: 232
20540: 232-233
20545: 233
20550: 233
20605: 233
20610: 233
20615: 233
20620: 233
20625: 233
20655: 233
20705: 233
20710: 233
20711: 233
20715: 233
20720: 233
20725: 234
20730: 234
20735: 234
20740: 234
20741: 234
20763: 234
20764: 234
20765: 234
20766: 234
20767: 234
20768: 234
20773: 234
20800: 234
20811: 234
20812: 234
20813: 234
20814: 234
21004: 32
21005: 32
21030: 32
21034: 32
21044: 32
21058: 33
21084: 33
21085: 33
21088: 33-34
21089: 34
21095: 34
21099: 34-35
21100: 35
21105: 35
21106: 35-36
21107: 36
21115: 36
21129: 36-37
21130: 37
21139: 37
21140: 37
21145: 37
21155: 38
21156: 38
21158: 38
21160: 38
21161: 38-39
21165: 39
21166: 39
21168: 39
21205-1: 48
21205: 48
21210: 49
21216: 50
21234: 50
21551: 50
21552/21556: 51
21560: 51
21561: 51

21570: 56
21571: 56
21573: 56
21720: 51
21800: 51
21801-1: 51-52
21801: 51
21808: 52
21812: 52
21813: 52
21820: 52
21821: 53
21831: 53
21910/21910-1/21910-2, 53
21916: 53-54
21206/21206-1: 48-49
21207/21207-1: 49
21215/21215-1: 50
21918/21918-1: 54
21920/21920-1: 54
21922/21922-1: 54
21925/21925-1: 54
21927: 54
22004: 207
22006: 207
22020: 207
22030: 207
22033: 207
22034: 207-208
22035: 208
22040: 208
22050: 208
22060: 208
22080: 208
22090: 208
23021: 208
23022: 208
23023: 208
23024: 208
23025: 208
23026: 208
23027: 209
23028: 209
23032: 209
23036: 209
23040: 209
23099: 235
23249: 209
23561: 209
23568: 209
23571: 210
23581: 210
23586: 210
23589: 210
23590: 210
23596: 210
23598: 210
23599: 210
23600: 211
23601: 211
23602: 211
23743: 58
23750: 211
23758: 211
23759: 211
23760: 211
23761: 212
23763: 212
23764: 212
23769: 212
23771: 212
23772: 212
23774: 212
23778: 213
23779: 213
23780: 214
23785: 214
23786: 214
23787: 214
23788: 214
23789: 214
23791: 214-215
23796: 215
23830: 215
24003: 118
24006: 118
24016: 118
24019: 118
24022: 118
24023: 118
24025: 118
24026: 119
24029: 119
24030: 119
24033: 119
24035: 119
24036: 119-120
24039: 120

24042: 120
24043: 120
24045: 120
24047: 120
24048: 120
24052: 121
24054: 121
24055: 121-122
24056: 122
24057: 122
24058: 122
24059: 122
24060: 123
24065: 123
24066: 123
24067: 123
24068: 123
24072: 124
24075: 124
24076: 124
24077: 124
24103: 97
24106: 97
24108: 97
24109: 97
24110: 97
24112: 97
24113: 97
24115: 98
24116: 98
24120: 98
24122: 98
24124: 98
24125: 98
24126: 98
24127: 99
24130: 99
24203: 102-103
24205: 103
24206: 103
24208: 103
24209: 103
24213: 103
24216: 103
24219: 103
24221: 103
24222: 104
24225: 104
24230: 104
24305: 133
24309: 133
24310: 133
24312: 133
24313: 133
24315: 133
24316: 134
24319: 134
24320: 134-135
24321: 135
24322: 135
24323: 135-136
24324: 136
24325: 136-137
24328: 137
24329: 137-138
24330: 138
24403: 124
24409: 124
24413: 124-125
24416: 125
24419: 125
24420: 125
24422: 125-126
24425: 126
24426: 126
24515: 84
24516: 84
24518: 84
24519: 84
24523: 72
24525: 84
24529: 84
24533: 85
24535: 85
24536: 85
24537: 85
24539: 85-86
24540: 86
24543: 72
24546: 65, 86
24547: 86
24549: 87
24550: 87
24553: 87
24556: 87-88
24557: 88
24558: 88
24559: 88
24561: 72

24562: 88
24564: 88
24565: 88-89
24566: 89
24569: 72
24572: 89
24574: 89
24575: 89-90
24577: 90
24578: 90
24579: 90
24603: 65
24608: 65
24610: 66
24618: 66
24619: 66
24626: 66
24627: 66
24630: 66-67
24631: 67
24632: 67
24633: 67
24634: 67-68
24636: 68
24638: 68
24702: 155
24705: 155
24708: 155
24712: 155, 257
24720: 155
24730: 155
24733: 155
24739: 155
24740: 155
24750: 156
24772: 156
24773: 156
24775: 156
24776: 156
24792: 156
24793: 156
24794: 156
24795: 156
24796: 156
24812: 156
24813: 156
24816: 157
24832: 157
24833: 157
24835: 157
24836: 157
24837: 157
24838: 158
24839: 158
24840: 158
24843: 158
24846: 158
24849: 158
24853: 158
24856: 158-159
24859: 159
24863: 159
24866: 159
24867: 159
24868: 160
24869: 160
24963: 160
25003: 91
25005: 160
25006: 160
25008: 99
25012: 126
25015: 91
25016: 91
25018: 126
25019: 126
25025: 99
25031: 68
25032: 91
25033: 91
25035: 68
25036: 68
25042: 127
25044: 91
25045: 91
25046: 91
25049: 127
25052: 68
25056: 91-92, 127
25057: 127
25058: 92
25059: 92
25060: 99
25061: 128
25062: 128
25071: 92
25081: 128
25082: 128
25515: 92

25516: 58
26101: 215
26121: 215
26122: 216
26141: 216
26142: 216
26151: 216
26261: 216
26262: 216
26265: 216
26300: 216
26301: 216
26302: 216
26310: 217
26320: 217
26321: 217
26322: 217
26323: 217
26324: 217
26340: 217
26341: 217
26342: 217
26343: 217
26344: 217
26415: 217
26419: 217
26425: 217
26428: 217
26520: 217
26521: 217
26601: 217
26602: 217
26670: 218
26671: 218
26672: 218
26673: 218
26690: 218
26691: 218
26692: 218
26693: 218
26700: 218
26708: 218
26710: 218
26718: 218
26719: 219
26720: 219
26722: 219
26726: 219
26727: 219
26730: 219
26739: 219
26742: 219
26744: 219
26745: 219
26746: 219
26747: 219
26748: 219
26749: 219
26751: 219
26752: 219
26756: 220
26760: 220
26761: 220
26762: 220
26770: 220
26781: 220
26782: 221
26783: 221
26790: 221
26810: 221
27443: 221
27460: 221
31004: 240
31005: 240
31007: 244
31008: 244
31009: 244
31010: 246
31011: 246
31012: 246
31013: 246
31014: 246
31017: 246
31019: 240
31021: 246
31022: 246
31025: 246
31031: 242
31032: 247
31036: 242
31037: 247
31038: 247
31039: 247
31045: 242
31088: 242
32404: 257
33002: 258
33004: 258
33006: 258

33009: 258
33010: 258
33012: 258
33115: 259
33116: 259
33120: 259
33121: 259
33122: 259
33211: 259
33212: 259
33214: 259
33215: 259
33217: 259
33219: 259
33220: 259
33312: 259
33313: 259
33314: 259
33315: 260
33316: 260
33317: 260
33403: 260
33500: 260
33501: 260
33502: 260
33503: 260
33505: 260
33506: 260
33507: 260
33508: 260
33509: 260
33510: 260
33511: 260
33512: 263
33513: 263
33514: 263
33515: 263
33516: 263
33517: 263
33518: 263
33519: 263
33520: 263
33521: 263
33522: 263
33523: 263
33524: 263
33525: 263
33526: 263
33527: 263
33530: 249
33531: 249
33536: 263
33537: 266
33538: 266
33539: 266
33540: 249
33541: 249
33542: 249
33543: 249
33544: 266
33545: 266
33546: 266
33548: 266
33549: 266
33555: 267
33557: 267
33558: 267
33615: 267
33616: 267
33618: 267
33620: 267
33621: 267
33623: 267
33625: 267
33626: 267
33627: 267
33720: 249
33721: 249
33722: 249
33723: 249
33724: 249
33804: 267
33806: 267
33812: 269
33818: 269
33819: 269
33820: 269
33835: 269
35105: 247
35210: 272
35212: 272
35213: 272
35214: 272
35759: 272
35780: 272
35785: 269, 272
35901: 269
49611: 269
147313: 269

Many of the photos in this volume were provided by Stout Auctions, one of the nation's premier toy train auctioneers. Located in both Williamsport, Indiana and West Middlesex, Pennsylvania, Stout specializes in liquidating collections of premium quality trains, including the previous owner of Lionel and other high profile individuals. Stout currently has many record auction items including one of the most important toy trains ever sold- the brass Lionel 700E scale Hudson that sat in Joshua Lionel Cowen's office. Consigned items are offered for both on-site and internet bidding. For more information call 765-764-6901, or visit www.stoutauctions.com

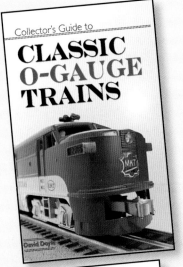
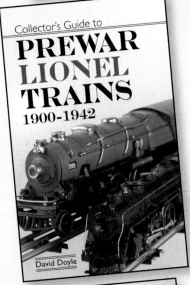